MOON

YOSEMITE, SEQUOIA & KINGS CANYON

ANN MARIE BROWN

Contents

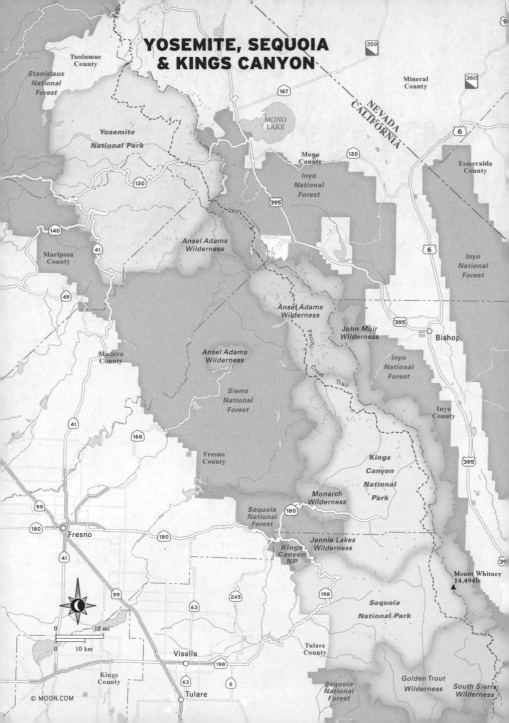

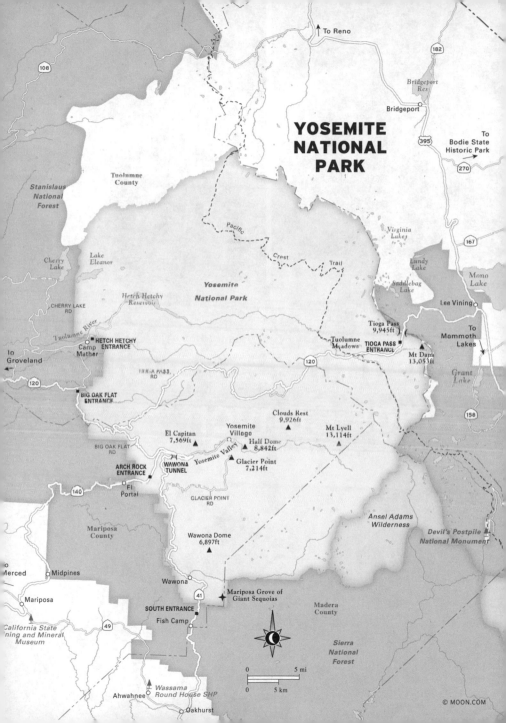

DISCOVER

Yosemite, Sequoia & Kings Canyon

Plunging waterfalls, stark granite, alpine lakes, pristine meadows, giant sequoia trees, and raging rivers—you'll find them all in the national parks of Yosemite, Sequoia, and Kings Canyon.

From Yosemite Valley's famous waterfalls, which are among the tallest in the world, to the towering granite domes and glistening meadows of Tioga Pass, Yosemite is a place that can only be described in superlatives. At 1,169 square miles (3,028 sq km), the park is nearly the size of Rhode Island and is one of the most popular national parks in the United States, visited by about four million people each year.

Set aside as a national park in 1890, Yosemite is a place that is synonymous with scenery. The 7-mile-long (11.3-km) Yosemite Valley, with its 3,000-foot (900-m) granite walls and leaping waterfalls, is known the world over as an incomparable natural wonder. It is estimated that more than half of the park's visitors see only the valley when they travel to Yosemite, even though it comprises less than 1 percent of the park.

Beyond the Valley lies the pristine high country of Tioga Pass Road and Tuolumne Meadows' subalpine expanse, bordered by precipitous mountain

---

Clockwise from top left: yellow-bellied marmot; purple shooting stars; Lower Yosemite Fall; winter at Glacier Point; Sierra juniper near Monarch Lake; photographers in Yosemite Valley.

summits and granite domes. To the northwest lies Hetch Hetchy, a reservoir in a valley considered a twin of Yosemite Valley. To the south are Glacier Point, with its picture-postcard vistas, and the marvels of the Mariposa Grove of Giant Sequoias—the largest living trees on earth.

Just 75 miles (121 km) south of Yosemite are two national parks that hold the greatest concentration of these botanical wonders—but with about half the visitors of Yosemite. Sequoia and Kings Canyon National Parks harbor more than 50 of the world's 75 remaining groves of giant sequoias. Adjacent to the national parks are the lands of Giant Sequoia National Monument, which are managed by the U.S. Forest Service. This distinction is inconsequential to most visitors: Park roads such as the winding Kings Canyon Scenic Byway and the epic Generals Highway cross park and forest boundaries, and the lovely Sierra scenery knows no limits.

Clockwise from top left: the Congress Trail in Sequoia; Hetch Hetchy; black bear; Vernal Fall.

10 TOP
EXPERIENCES

1 **See the Park's Greatest Hits from Glacier Point:** The commanding vista from Glacier Point, a 7,214-foot (2,200-m) granite precipice, takes in the park's most famous landmarks—Half Dome, Clouds Rest, Liberty Cap, Vernal and Nevada Falls, and the surrounding High Sierra (page 116).

2 **Admire Yosemite Falls:** The tallest free-leaping waterfall in North America, Yosemite Falls drops in a foaming torrent of three tiers that total nearly a half-mile of vertical whitewater. Climb to the top of **Upper Yosemite Fall** (page 51) or take in its magnificence from the base of **Lower Yosemite Fall** (page 53).

3 **Scale Half Dome:** Climbing this granite dome is a once-in-a-lifetime hike, where you're in for a 16-mile (25.8-km) round-trip journey with a 4,800-foot (1,463-m) elevation gain (page 57).

4 **Visit in Winter:** Highlights of a winter visit include ice-skating in the shadow of Half Dome, snowshoeing, skiing, or just cozying up with a warm drink at a park lodge (page 38).

5 **Behold Yosemite's Best Waterfalls:** Increase your chances of seeing the park's many waterfalls by timing your visit for April through June, when the falls are at their most powerful (page 35).

6 **Sip a Drink at the Majestic Yosemite Hotel:** This historic building boasts timber beams, stained-glass windows, and Native American tapestries—the perfect setting for a drink (page 49).

<<<

7 **Explore Tuolumne Meadows:** In this pristine subalpine meadow, you can hike Lembert and Pothole Domes, fish on the Tuolumne River, or visit Parsons Memorial Lodge and Soda Springs (page 154).

>>>

8 **Climb Mist Trail's Famous Stairs:** Every park visitor should climb this popular granite stairway whose namesake mist cools you as you approach Vernal Fall (page 54).

<<<

9 **Stand at the Feet of Giants:** In Sequoia National Park's Giant Forest, 8,000 giant sequoia trees grow, including the General Sherman, a 2,100-year-old tree (page 282).

10 **Summit Moro Rock:** Ascend 390 stairsteps carved into stone, then take in the view of the saw-toothed Great Western Divide from this bald granite dome. Even young children can conquer this peak (page 284).

Planning Your Trip

Where to Go

Yosemite Valley

The majority of park visitors spend their time in Yosemite Valley. This is where most of the park's **lodgings** and **restaurants** are located, where most **guided tours** take place, and where a wealth of **organized activities** happen daily: ranger walks, biking, art classes, photography seminars, and more. The Valley is also a geologic marvel: Yosemite's world-famous **waterfalls** drop from the valley rim, and **El Capitan,** the largest single piece of granite rock on earth, and **Half Dome,** one of the most photographed landmarks in the West, are both located here.

Wawona and Glacier Point

In southern Yosemite, near the hamlet of Wawona, are two of the park's premier attractions: the **Mariposa Grove of Giant Sequoias** and **Glacier Point.** The Mariposa Grove boasts several hundred giant trees, while Glacier Point is a drive-to overlook that offers one of the best views in the West, encompassing all the major granite landmarks of Yosemite Valley and the surrounding high country. History lovers will enjoy **Wawona,** with its historic buildings at the **Pioneer Yosemite History Center** and 19th-century **Big Trees Lodge,** formerly known as the Wawona Hotel.

Tioga Pass and Tuolumne Meadows

The Tuolumne Meadows region is ideal for **hikers** and **backpackers.** At an elevation of 8,600 feet (2,600 m), **Tuolumne Meadows** is one of the park's most photographed areas. Its wide, grassy expanse is bound by high granite domes and peaks. Trails lead to **alpine lakes** set below the spires of Cathedral Peak and Unicorn

Peak, to roaring waterfalls on the Tuolumne River, and to the summits of lofty granite domes with commanding vistas of the high country. **Visitor services are few** and far between here, but hikers, campers, and nature lovers will be in their element.

Hetch Hetchy

Hetch Hetchy, a granite-walled valley similar in appearance to Yosemite Valley, was flooded in 1923 to create a water supply for San Francisco. Today it is the **least visited region** of the park and offers **no visitor services.** In the spring, Hetch Hetchy's **waterfalls** spill over its massive cliffs. Wildflowers bloom April-June. Visitors make day trips here to admire the enormous **O'Shaughnessy Dam** or hike along the edges of its reservoir. **Backpackers** come to Hetch Hetchy for its access to Yosemite's backcountry and its solitude.

The Eastern Sierra

The Eastern Sierra is an outdoors lover's playground: **Skiers** and **snowboarders** swoosh down mountain slopes, **hikers** and **mountain bikers** explore miles of trails, anglers cast into crystal-clear streams and rivers, and scenery enthusiasts and photographers enjoy alpine lakes backed by granite cliffs. The region hosts two good-sized mountain towns, **Mammoth Lakes** and **June Lake,** and worthwhile destinations such as **Bodie State Historic Park,** a gold rush-era ghost town, and **Mono Lake,** a 700,000-year-old saline lake.

Sequoia and Kings Canyon

South of Yosemite lie two less visited national parks: Sequoia and Kings Canyon. Peppered with the greatest number of the world's remaining

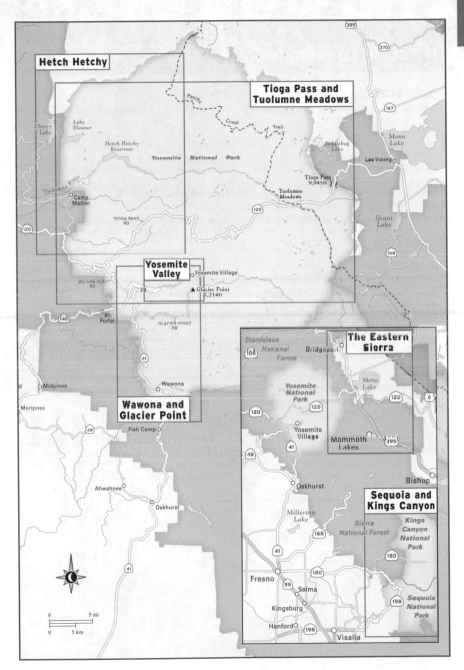

Hetch Hetchy

Tioga Pass and
Tuolumne Meadows

Yosemite
Valley

Wawona and
Glacier Point

The Eastern
Sierra

Sequoia and
Kings Canyon

Cherry
Lake

Lake
Eleanor

Hetch Hetchy
Reservoir

Yosemite National Park

Tuolumne River

Camp
Mather

TIOGA PASS
RD

Pacific

Crest

Trail

Saddlebag
Lake

Mono
Lake

Lee Vining

Tioga Pass
9,945ft

Tuolumne
Meadows

BIG OAK FLAT
RD

Yosemite Village

Glacier Point
7,214ft

Grant
Lake

El
Portal

GLACIER POINT
RD

Midpines

Mariposa

Wawona

Fish Camp

Ahwahnee

Oakhurst

Stanislaus
National
Forest

Bridgeport

Yosemite
National
Park

Mono
Lake

Yosemite
Village

Mammoth
Lakes

Oakhurst

Bishop

Millerton
Lake

Sierra
National Forest

Kings
Canyon
National
Park

Fresno

Selma

Kingsburg

Hanford

Visalia

Sequoia
National
Park

0   5 mi

0   5 km

If You're Looking for...

ALPINE LAKES

Yosemite's Tioga Pass Road offers hiking access to Cathedral, Gaylor, Sunrise, May, Elizabeth Lakes. In the Eastern Sierra, drive the June Lake Loop. In Kings Canyon, the 40-mile Rae Lakes Loop visits a half-dozen lakes above 10,000 feet.

BICYCLING

Ride the Yosemite Valley bike paths. In the Eastern Sierra, mountain bike the Panorama Mountain Trail near June Lake or head to Mammoth Mountain Bike Park.

BACKPACKING

From Yosemite's Tuolumne Meadows, hike to Ten Lakes and Grant Lakes or follow the Vogelsang Loop. In Wawona, hike the Chiquito Pass Trail into the Ansel Adams Wilderness. In Sequoia, the High Sierra Trail starts at Giant Forest and travels 60 miles to Mount Whitney.

FISHING

Try the South Fork Merced River in Wawona or the South Fork Tuolumne River along Tioga Pass Road. In the Eastern Sierra, fish at Saddlebag Lake.

GIANT SEQUOIAS

In Yosemite, Wawona's Mariposa Grove of Giant Sequoias is a great introduction to the largest living trees on earth. To see the biggest of the leviathans, head for Sequoia's Giant Forest to see the General Sherman Tree.

HIKING

Yosemite Valley's Yosemite Falls, Mist, and Half Dome Trails are crowded and popular. In summer, hike Tuolumne Meadows' Lembert Dome Trail or Cathedral Lakes Trail. The Lakes Trail in Sequoia shows off a stark granite landscape studded with glacially formed lakes.

HORSEBACK RIDING

In Yosemite, Wawona's Big Trees Stable offers guided horse and mule rides. In Kings Canyon, trail rides are available at Grant Grove and Cedar Grove.

ROCK CLIMBING

Take a lesson from Yosemite Mountaineering School and Guide Service.

SCENIC DRIVE-TO OVERLOOKS

In Yosemite, Glacier Point (at the east end of Glacier Point Road), Inspiration Point (at Wawona Tunnel), and Olmsted Point (on Tioga Pass Road) offer jaw-dropping views. In Kings Canyon, drive the Kings Canyon Scenic Byway and stop at Junction View to look deep into the canyons of the Kings River's Middle and South Forks.

WATERFALLS

In Yosemite, Bridalveil Fall and Lower Yosemite Fall are easily accessible via short walks, or take a longer hike to Vernal and Nevada Falls. In Kings Canyon National Park, an easy saunter leads to Roaring River Falls, or a more ambitious trek travels to Mist Falls.

giant sequoias—including the must-see **General Grant** and **General Sherman**—these parks offer **fewer crowds,** more **backcountry** **wilderness,** and granite peaks and deep canyons similar to their more famous neighbor to the north.

When to Go

High Season (May-Sept.)

Be prepared for **crowds** if you visit in the high season (May-Sept.). Summer weekends are the busiest days and are best avoided, especially in Yosemite Valley. But summer (June-Oct.) is when Yosemite's high country—**Glacier Point, Tuolumne Meadows,** and **Tioga Pass**—is open and accessible, so you have the most options for hiking and sightseeing. In most years, **all park roads and services are open** by early June.

In **Sequoia and Kings Canyon,** summer temps have melted the High Sierra snows, and all park facilities—including **Crystal Cave**—and roads are open.

Mid-Season (Apr.-May, Sept.-Oct.)

Spring is a wonderful time for visiting **Yosemite Valley,** when its famous **waterfalls are at their peak flow.** First-time visitors would do well to time their initial Yosemite trip for April or May, when the Valley is at its most photogenic and the waterfalls are shimmering white-water cascades.

Autumn is also a fine time to visit Yosemite, even though most of the waterfalls will have run dry. The show of **fall colors** on the valley floor and the chance for **solitude** in this well-loved park are worthy reasons to visit. Popular sites such as the **Mariposa Grove** are easy to visit without crowds.

a giant sequoia in the snow

Summer weekends can mean long lines at Yosemite's entrance stations.

Yosemite In-Park Lodging

	Location	Price	Season	Amenities
Camp 4	Yosemite Valley	$6	year-round	tent sites
Upper, North, and Lower Pines	Yosemite Valley	$26	Mar.-Oct.; Upper Pines open year-round	tent and RV sites
Half Dome Village	Yosemite Valley	$83-195	year-round	motel rooms, wooden cabins, tent cabins, restaurants
Housekeeping Camp	Yosemite Valley	$108-133	Apr.-Oct.	duplex camp units, showers, laundry
Yosemite Valley Lodge	Yosemite Valley	$162-270	year-round	hotel rooms, restaurants
Majestic Yosemite Hotel	Yosemite Valley	$425-590	year-round	hotel rooms, cottages, suites, fine dining
Bridalveil Creek	Wawona	$18	July-Sept.	tent and RV sites
Wawona	Wawona	$26	year-round	tent and RV sites
Big Trees Lodge	Wawona	$145-295	Apr.-Dec.	hotel rooms, restaurant
The Redwoods	Wawona	$249-980	year-round	vacation homes

Tioga Road usually closes on November 1 and doesn't reopen until June. The road may also close for a day or two during late September and early October when brief, early-winter storms roll through.

The high country of Sequoia and Kings Canyon may still be snow-covered in April and May, though the **Foothills** region is warmer and more accessible. In fall, most park services begin to shorten their hours, though **crowds are fewer.**

Low Season (Nov.-Mar.)

Winter is the **quietest season** in Yosemite. The lowest visitation levels are recorded November-March, except for the holidays. Many Yosemite fans think these months are the best time of the year. Visitors can see **Yosemite Valley** or **Wawona**'s giant sequoias crowned in snow, ice-skate on an outdoor rink with Half Dome as a backdrop, and ski and snowboard at **Yosemite Ski & Snowboard Area** near Glacier Point. In winter, always carry **chains** for your car tires, even if you have a four-wheel-drive vehicle. Chains can be required on any park road at any time, and that's federal law.

Glacier Point Road, Tioga Pass Road, and the **Mariposa Grove Road may close** as early as November 1.

In Kings Canyon, the **Kings Canyon Scenic Byway closes** in winter, and services in Cedar Grove close for the season. Sections of **Generals Highway may close** for plowing; chains are required for all vehicles.

	Location	Price	Season	Amenities
Yosemite West	Wawona	$375-750	year-round	vacation homes
Tamarack Flat	Tuolumne Meadows	$12	late June-mid-Oct.	tent sites
Yosemite Creek	Tuolumne Meadows	$12	late June-early Sept.	tent sites
Porcupine Flat	Tuolumne Meadows	$12	July-mid-Oct.	tent and RV sites
White Wolf	Tuolumne Meadows	$18	late June-mid-Sept.	tent and RV sites
Hodgdon Meadow	Tuolumne Meadows	$26	year-round	tent and RV sites
Crane Flat	Tuolumne Meadows	$26	July-mid-Oct.	tent and RV sites
Tuolumne Meadows	Tuolumne Meadows	$26	late June-late Sept.	tent and RV sites
White Wolf Lodge	Tuolumne Meadows	$137-156	mid-June-early Sept	wooden cabins, tent cabins, restaurant
Tuolumne Meadows Lodge	Tuolumne Meadows	$137-157	mid-June-mid-Sept.	tent cabins, restaurant

Before You Go

Park Fees and Passes

The entrance fee at Yosemite is **$35 per vehicle** (car, RV, truck, etc.) and $30 per motorcycle. The entrance fee at Sequoia and Kings Canyon National Parks is **$35 per vehicle** (car, RV, truck, etc.) and $30 per motorcycle. The fee is good for seven days, and you must show your receipt any time you pass through one of the park entrance stations. Other fee options include:

- **Yosemite Annual Pass ($70):** Provides entrance to Yosemite for one year.
- **Sequoia and Kings Canyon Annual Pass ($60):** Provides entrance to both parks for one year.

- **America the Beautiful Interagency Annual Pass ($80):** Provides entrance to all national parks and federal recreation sites in the United States for one year.

- **Senior Pass ($80):** Lifetime version of the Interagency Pass for seniors 62 and older. An annual senior pass is also available for $20 per year.

If you have your heart set on climbing Half Dome, you'll need to secure a **Half Dome permit** up to one year in advance. Backpackers should also secure **wilderness permits** far in advance.

Sequoia and Kings Canyon In-Park Lodging

	Location	Price	Season	Amenities
Sunset Camp	Grant Grove, Kings Canyon	$22	mid-May–mid-Sept.	tent and RV sites
Azalea Camp	Grant Grove, Kings Canyon	$18	year-round	tent and RV sites
Crystal Springs	Grant Grove, Kings Canyon	$18	mid-May–mid-Sept.	tent and RV sites
Grant Grove Cabins	Grant Grove, Kings Canyon	$70-129	year-round; tent cabins May-Nov.	wooden and tent cabins, restaurant
John Muir Lodge	Grant Grove, Kings Canyon	$200-250	year-round	hotel rooms, restaurant
Sheep Creek	Cedar Grove, Kings Canyon	$18	May–mid-Oct.	tent and RV sites
Sentinel	Cedar Grove, Kings Canyon	$18	May-Sept.	tent and RV sites
Moraine	Cedar Grove, Kings Canyon	$18	May-Sept.	tent and RV sites
Canyon View	Cedar Grove, Kings Canyon	$35-50	May–mid-Oct.	group tent sites
Cedar Grove Lodge	Cedar Grove, Kings Canyon	$120-165	late May–mid-Oct.	hotel rooms, restaurant
Wuksachi Lodge	Lodgepole, Sequoia National Park	$225-365	year-round	hotel rooms, restaurant
Lodgepole	Lodgepole, Sequoia National Park	$22	mid-Apr.–mid-Oct.	tent and RV sites, restaurants
Dorst Creek	Lodgepole, Sequoia National Park	$22	mid-May–early Sept.	tent and RV sites
Potwisha	Foothills, Sequoia National Park	$22	year-round	tent and RV sites, flush toilets
Buckeye Flat	Foothills, Sequoia National Park	$22	Apr.-Oct.	tent sites
South Fork	Foothills, Sequoia National Park	$12	year-round	tent sites
Cold Springs	Mineral King, Sequoia National Park	$12	late May–mid-Oct.	tent sites
Atwell Mill	Mineral King, Sequoia National Park	$12	late May–mid-Oct.	tent sites
Silver City Mountain Resort	Mineral King, Sequoia National Park	$170-495	late May–late Oct.	cabins, chalets, restaurant

Entrance Stations

Yosemite National Park has five entrance stations:

- **Arch Rock** (Hwy. 140): the main entrance to the park; provides access to Yosemite Valley from the west (San Francisco, Sacramento)

- **Big Oak Flat** (Hwy. 120): provides access to Yosemite Valley and Tuolumne Meadows (summer only) from the north (San Francisco, Sacramento)

- **South** (Hwy. 41): provides access to Wawona from the south (Fresno, Los Angeles)

- **Tioga Pass** (Hwy. 120): provides access to Tuolumne Meadows and the Eastern Sierra in summer only

- **Hetch Hetchy**: the only access to the Hetch Hetchy region of the park

Sequoia and Kings Canyon have two main entrance stations:

- **Big Stump** (Hwy. 180): provides access to Kings Canyon from the north

- **Ash Mountain/Foothills** (Hwy. 198): provides access to Sequoia National Park from the south

Reservations

Show up without a lodging or camping reservation during the busy season (May-Sept.) or during the winter holidays, and you could face an ordeal.

- For Yosemite accommodations and organized activities: **Aramark's Yosemite Hospitality** (888/413-8869, www.travelyosemite.com)

- For Yosemite campground reservations: **reservations office** (877/444-6777, www.recreation.gov)

- For Sequoia and Kings Canyon accommodations: **DNC Parks and Resorts at Sequoia** (866/807-3598, www.visitsequoia.com)

- For Sequoia and Kings Canyon campground reservations: **reservations office** (877/444-6777, www.recreation.gov)

In the Park

Visitors Centers

The largest of Yosemite's visitors centers is the **Valley Visitor Center** (shuttle stop 5, 209/372-0298, 9am-5pm daily in summer, bookstore open until 7pm year-round), located in Yosemite Valley. Park in the main day-use lot in Yosemite Village.

Campgrounds

The following **first-come, first-served** Yosemite campgrounds are your best bets for snagging a last-minute site. Try to arrive before noon on weekdays and by midmorning on weekends, especially in summer.

- Camp 4 (Yosemite Valley): 35 sites; open year-round

- Tamarack Flat (Tioga Rd.): 52 sites; late May-mid-Oct.

- Yosemite Creek (Tioga Rd.): 74 sites; late June-mid-Sept.

- Tuolumne Meadows (Tioga Rd.): 304 sites; June-late Sept.

- Bridalveil Creek (Glacier Point Rd.): 110 sites; July-early Sept.

- Porcupine Flat (Tioga Rd.): 52 sites; July-Oct.

- Hodgdon Meadows (Big Oak Flat entrance): 105 sites; first come, first served Oct.-Apr. only

- Wawona Campground (Wawona): 93 sites; first come, first served Oct.-Apr. only

Many of the campgrounds in **Sequoia and Kings Canyon National Parks** and their surrounding parklands are first come, first served.

Getting Around

The free **Yosemite Valley Shuttle** (7am-10pm daily in summer, shorter hours in winter)

The Yosemite shuttle is a great way to get around the park.

transports visitors around the valley floor year-round. Other free, seasonal park shuttles include:

- Wawona-Mariposa Grove Shuttle (spring-fall)
- Wawona-Yosemite Valley Shuttle (Memorial Day-Labor Day)
- Yosemite Ski & Snowboard Area (twice daily from Yosemite Valley, mid-Dec.-Mar.)
- Tuolumne Meadows Shuttle (between Tioga Pass and Olmsted Point, mid-July-early Sept.)

Sequoia National Park operates a **free shuttle bus system** (9am-6pm daily) from late May through September 1.

Weather, rockfalls, fire, and other natural occurrences can affect driving routes and lodging options. No matter when you go, it's unwise to travel without checking the current conditions: **Yosemite** (209/372-0200), **Sequoia and Kings Canyon** (559/565-334).

The Best of Yosemite

Day 1

Take a ride on an **open-air tram** through **Yosemite Valley.** The two-hour **Valley Floor Tour** is educational, interesting, and fun, and you can feel good about not destroying the ozone layer by driving your own car. Buy tickets and start the tour at **Yosemite Valley Lodge.** In the busy summer months, it is best to show up right after breakfast to see if you can get tickets for that day.

Afterward, **rent bikes** at Yosemite Valley Lodge or Half Dome Village and cruise around Yosemite Valley on its 12 miles (19.3 km) of paved bike paths. The Valley's bike paths are so flat that the rental bikes don't even have gears—you spend much of your time coasting. Make reservations in advance to spend the evening at the park's **Glacier Point stargazing tour.** The tour bus leaves Yosemite Valley Lodge around 7pm and arrives at Glacier Point before darkness falls, so you have a chance to take in the spectacular view.

After dark, enjoy a one-hour astronomy program before being chauffeured back down to the Valley.

Day 2

No visit to Yosemite is complete without hitting at least one trail. Shuttle stop 6 drops you at the short, 0.25-mile (0.4-km) trail to **Lower Yosemite Fall;** the falls roar in spring but are nonexistent by midsummer. The **Mist Trail to Vernal Fall** won't disappoint, though. The 3-mile (4.8-km) round-trip hike ascends a granite staircase to the top of Vernal Fall. If you want more, keep going to the top of **Nevada Fall** for a 6.8-mile (10.9-km) round-trip hike.

In the heat of summer, head for one of Yosemite's great **swimming holes.** Relax in the soft sand alongside the Merced River at **Sentinel Beach** and gaze at Yosemite Valley's spectacular scenery. At day's end, head over to the **Majestic Yosemite Hotel Bar**—unlike the restaurant, there's no dress code here.

Open-air trams make it easy to see the sights in Yosemite Valley.

National parks are famous for summer crowds and Yosemite is no exception. But with a little fore-thought, you can visit the park without subjecting yourself to packed parking lots and long lines of cars and people.

First, whenever possible, **visit in the off-season.** Any day from **mid-September until mid-April** (except major holidays like Christmas, New Year's, Easter, and Presidents' Day) is going to be less crowded than a summer day. Also, at any time of the year, choose **weekdays over weekends.** Tuesday through Thursday are always the quietest days of the week in Yosemite.

Second, **get up early.** Even in the summer months, Yosemite Valley is relatively serene until 9am or so. If you go for a hike at 7am, you will see almost no one. And if you can't get up early, **stay out late.** When the days are long in summer, you can go for a hike at 5pm and still enjoy three hours of daylight while everyone else is having dinner. Just remember that if you head out late in the day, carry a flashlight with you just in case it gets dark sooner than you expected.

As you explore the park, keep in mind that the vast majority of Yosemite visitors visit only Yosemite Valley and perhaps Glacier Point. Any time you head to **Tuolumne Meadows, Hetch Hetchy,** or **Wawona,** you avoid Yosemite's most crowd-im-

Off-season hiking provides the best chance of solitude.

pacted area. And lastly, if you are a hiker, you already know that there is one sure way to get away from the masses, and that's to point your feet uphill. Most people avoid steep trails, so any time you gain elevation you have a better chance at solitude.

Day 3

Take a drive or ride the tour bus to **Glacier Point.** This is world-class Sierra scenery that you'd expect to have to backpack for several days to find, but it's completely accessible by car. Order an ice cream at the Glacier Point snack stand while you gaze at the view of Half Dome, Vernal and Nevada Falls, and the crest of Yosemite's high country. If you start in the morning, you can ride the bus to Glacier Point and then hike back to the Valley via the **Panorama Trail.** Shorter hikes from Glacier Point Road lead to spectacular viewpoints at **Sentinel Dome** and **Taft Point.**

At the end of the day, head back to Yosemite Valley and attend the evening program at the **Yosemite Theater** or **Yosemite Valley Lodge Amphitheater.**

If You Have More Time

Drive your own car or get tickets for the tour bus to the **Mariposa Grove of Giant Sequoias** in **Wawona,** the south part of the park. Afterward, stop by the historic **Big Trees Lodge** for refreshing libations.

From Mariposa Grove, you're in an ideal location to continue southward to **Kings Canyon National Park.** You'll need about 2.5 hours to travel the 120 miles (193 km) to Kings Canyon's **Grant Grove Village.** The **Big Trees/ Wuksachi Lodge** area of **Sequoia National Park** is 45 minutes beyond Grant Grove.

The Best of Sequoia and Kings Canyon

It's common to assume it's a quick drive from Yosemite to Kings Canyon (and neighboring Sequoia). After all, the parks are in the same mountain range, right? True, but driving from one to the next is more time-consuming than it looks, mostly due to winding mountain roads. Even though you're covering a distance of only 155 miles (250 km) from Yosemite Valley to Grant Grove, you'll need nearly four hours to accomplish it.

Depending on park traffic, it takes 65-75 minutes to drive from Yosemite Valley to Wawona, the southernmost region of Yosemite National Park. After exiting the park, Highway 41 takes you to the city of Fresno in about 1.5 hours. (If evening is falling, this large city is a good bet for hotels, motels, and restaurants.) From Fresno, you'll head east on Highway 180 for a little more than an hour to reach Grant Grove Village in Kings Canyon.

Kings River and admire what geology has created in this magnificent canyon. Shortly past the Cedar Grove turnoff, stop and take a brief walk to **Roaring River Falls,** a snowmelt-fed cataract that drops through a narrow gorge into the South Fork Kings River.

Continue to the trailhead for **Zumwalt Meadow.** Walk this scenic 1.8-mile (2.9-km) loop alongside the Kings River, enjoying views of the Grand Sentinel and North Dome towering more than 3,500 feet (1,100 m) above the valley floor.

At **Road's End,** take the short walk to **Muir Rock,** where you can sit by the river and watch the water roll by, or go for a quick dip.

Grab an early dinner at **Cedar Grove Lodge** and spend the night here or in one of the Cedar Grove campgrounds. Otherwise head back to Grant Grove before dark so you can enjoy this spectacular scenery all over again.

Day 1
KINGS CANYON

Spend the night prior at one of the campgrounds or cabins near **Grant Grove.** In the morning, wake up and walk the short trail to **Panoramic Point** to watch the sunrise. After breakfast at the **Grant Grove Restaurant,** stop in at the **Kings Canyon Visitor Center** for maps and information.

From Grant Grove Village, drive 1 mile (1.6 km) northwest on Highway 180 to the left turnoff for the **General Grant Tree.** Walk the 0.6-mile (1-km) loop around the world's second-largest tree and pay homage to the General and its many neighboring behemoths.

Return to Highway 180 and cruise east on the **Kings Canyon Scenic Byway** (road open May-Oct.), stopping at the roadside overlook at **Junction View.** Here you can peer down at the confluence of the Middle and South Forks of the

Day 2
SEQUOIA NATIONAL PARK

From Grant Grove, drive 1.5 miles (2.4 km) west on Highway 180 and turn left onto the **Generals Highway,** heading south for Sequoia National Park. It's a winding and scenic 26 miles (42 km)—plan 45 minutes—to **Lodgepole,** where you can pick up maps and information. Along the way, stop off at **Wuksachi Lodge,** just north of Lodgepole, for breakfast or lunch in the forest-view dining room.

Once at **Lodgepole Visitor Center,** buy Crystal Cave tour tickets and grab some picnic supplies at the Lodgepole Market Center. Stretch your legs with a 3.6-mile (5.8-km) round-trip hike to **Tokopah Falls.** You'll have plenty of marmots for company on this forested trail through a U-shaped glacial valley.

Back on Generals Highway, continue south and park your car across the road from the **Giant**

Forest Museum. Take a peek at the fascinating exhibits inside, then ride the shuttle bus to the **General Sherman Tree.** Get your picture taken at the largest tree on earth, then leave the crowds behind on the 2.1-mile (3.4-km) **Congress Trail,** which travels among hundreds of cinnamon-colored giant sequoias. Or if the shuttle bus is running along Crescent Meadow Road, ride it to the **Moro Rock** parking lot and climb the 390 stairs to the top of this 6,725-foot (2,050-m) granite precipice.

The twisting, 6.5 miles (10.5 km) road to **Crystal Cave** lies just south of Giant Forest off Generals Highway (look for the turnoff on the right). Plan to arrive prior to your scheduled tour time to make the 0.5-mile (0.8-km) walk to the cave entrance. Formed of limestone that metamorphosed into marble, fascinating Crystal Cave lies hidden behind an impressive spider-web gate. Beyond it, you can explore the secret underground world of Sequoia.

After the cave tour, return to Generals Highway and drive south for 8.5 miles (13.7 km) along the road's multiple twists and turns. Stop at **Hospital Rock** to picnic among the Native American pictographs. The Ash Mountain entrance lies a mere 6 miles (9.7 km) west. Six more miles (9.7 km) west of the Ash Mountain entrance on Highway 198 is the gateway town of **Three Rivers,** which offers overnight accommodations.

Alternatively, you could start your tour from the south, beginning at the Ash Mountain entrance. Continue north all the way to Kings Canyon, or simply stop at Lodgepole and explore from there.

Kings Canyon's sequoia groves are filled with gargantuan trees.

Best Hikes

Easy Hikes

These hikes require only a couple of hours to complete and are suitable for families with children or visitors who don't hike frequently.

LOWER YOSEMITE FALL, YOSEMITE

Get soaked to the skin by North America's **tallest freefalling waterfall.** As **Yosemite Falls** roars with snowmelt from March to June, its icy spray drenches and delights onlookers who follow the easy, 1-mile (1.6-km), **wheelchair-accessible trail** to its base. This crowd-pleasing walk is a must-do in the spring, but it's also amazing on winter mornings, when Yosemite Falls' lower drop is framed by a crystallized "ice cone"—but it only lasts until the sun rises high enough to melt it.

SENTINEL DOME AND TAFT POINT, YOSEMITE

Glacier Point offers one of Yosemite's **most** enticing vistas, and nearby **Sentinel Dome** and **Taft Point,** both 2.2-mile round-trips, provide jazzy riffs on that same view. Sentinel Dome, a **granite dome** at 8,122 feet (2,476 m), offers a breathtaking perspective on Yosemite Falls, and that's only one small piece of its 360-degree panorama. Taft Point's view is completely different—a head-on look at El Capitan and a stomach-churning view of the Yosemite Valley floor, 3,500 feet (1,100 m) below. Access both destinations from the same trailhead, 1 mile (1.6 km) west of Glacier Point.

LEMBERT DOME, YOSEMITE

The glacially polished **Lembert Dome** is an example of a **roche moutonnée,** a dome with one gently sloping side and one side that drops off steeply. Rock climbers tackle Lembert Dome's south escarpment, but hikers can follow the 2.8-mile (4.5-km) round-trip trail around its east side and up to the bald dome's 9,430-foot (2,000 m)

Yosemite Falls

summit. The reward is an **astonishing view** of Tuolumne Meadows and surrounding peaks, plus the chance to walk on Yosemite's surprisingly "grippy" granite.

ZUMWALT MEADOW, KINGS CANYON

There's no better introduction to the beauty of Kings Canyon than the **Zumwalt Meadow Loop,** which starts near Road's End. This 1.8-mile (2.9-km) **self-guided loop** meanders along the banks of the South Fork Kings River and offers views of two imposing granite cliffs that were carved by glacial action, the Grand Sentinel and North Dome. At the edge of fern-filled Zumwalt Meadow lie **crystal-clear pools** and a fragrant forest of incense cedars and pines.

TOKOPAH FALLS, SEQUOIA

Tokopah Falls is a **waterfall** that even small children will enjoy hiking to. The easy 3.6-mile (5.8-km) round-trip trail crosses footbridges and winds past meadows overflowing with wildflowers. Cute **yellow-bellied marmots** sun themselves on boulders and whistle as you walk by. The path offers views of the **Watchtower,** a glacially carved cliff guarding the east end of Tokopah Valley. At trail's end, 1,200-foot-high (365-m) Tokopah Falls pours down a granite wall.

CONGRESS TRAIL, SEQUOIA

Giant Forest boasts the Sierra Nevada's most impressive collection of **giant sequoias,** including the chart-topping **General Sherman,** the largest living thing on earth by volume. Next to this behemoth lies the **Congress Trail,** a 2.1-mile (3.4-km) loop that travels through dozens of sequoias with diameters the size of your living room. The **House and Senate Groves,** two massive sequoia clusters near the trail's end, are guaranteed to blow your mind.

Moderate Hikes

These hikes are moderate to strenuous in difficulty and can be accomplished by most physically fit hikers. Plan on 5-6 hours to complete the round-trip, including time for taking photographs and enjoying the destination.

MIST TRAIL TO VERNAL AND NEVADA FALLS, YOSEMITE

Of all the **watery splendors** that Yosemite Valley offers, a hike on the **Mist Trail** may be the most exciting. The trail ascends **granite stair steps** to the brink of **Vernal Fall,** before continuing on to **Nevada Fall.** The biggest thrill is hiking so close to the waterfalls that you can get thoroughly soaked by their spray. It's easy to turn this into a loop by returning via the John Muir Trail, making for a 6.8-mile (10.9-km) round-trip hike.

UPPER YOSEMITE FALL, YOSEMITE

Yosemite Falls holds the undisputed title of the **tallest waterfall** in North America. The upper, lower, and middle falls combined top out at a prodigious 2,425 feet (739 m). It's a **strenuous** 7.4-mile (11.9-km) round-trip hike to reach the top of the upper fall, but the base of the lower fall can be visited via an easy, level stroll of a few hundred yards. Bring your rain gear between April and June; the fall's overspray drenches all who come near.

PANORAMA TRAIL, YOSEMITE

The **Panorama Trail** traces a spectacular 8.5-mile (13.7-km) route from Glacier Point to Yosemite Valley, heading downhill most of the way and delivering nonstop views of a banquet of peaks, domes, and precipices. Take the morning tour bus from Yosemite Valley Lodge to the trailhead at Glacier Point, then lace up your boots. Follow Panorama Trail as it switchbacks downhill, providing ever-changing perspectives on Half Dome, Basket Dome, North Dome, and Liberty Cap. You'll also hike past **three major waterfalls**—Illilouette, Nevada, and Vernal—and miles of **postcard-quality Sierra scenery.** Finish out the trip at Happy Isles, where you can catch a free shuttle bus back to Yosemite Valley Lodge.

One Day in Yosemite

There is a famous story about a Yosemite visitor who goes up to a park ranger and asks, "I'm only visiting the park for one day. How should I spend my time?"

And the ranger replies, "If I only had one day in Yosemite, I would sit right down and have myself a good cry."

Certainly it's not ideal to spend only one day in Yosemite, but if that's the way your vacation is scheduled, you'd better dry your tears and get busy.

First, you'll need to limit your travels to one small portion of the park. For most visitors, the portion of choice is **Yosemite Valley.** During the busy season, it's smart to park your car in the Valley as soon as possible after your arrival and choose from these transportation options: (1) Pay for a guided tour on the open-air tram that leaves from Yosemite Valley Lodge. (2) Rent a bicycle at **Yosemite Valley Lodge** or **Half Dome Village** and ride the paved bike paths in the Valley. (3) Design your own tour of the Valley by walking and riding the free Valley shuttle bus. The option you choose will determine your itinerary.

The **open-air tram tours** travel all over the Valley and are narrated by an interpreter. You're not stuck in an enclosed bus; you're out in the open, smelling the Valley air and getting a much better view than you'd have from your car windshield. Tours last about two hours and are highly informative.

On a **bicycle**, you can easily visit **Lower Yosemite Fall** and **Mirror Lake** (you'll park your bike at the trailheads for both destinations and walk a short distance). You can also tour a large expanse of the Valley, including stops at the visitors center and Yosemite Village or Half Dome Village for water and snacks.

On foot, and by taking short hops on the free Yosemite Valley **shuttle bus,** you can see all of the Valley's famous sights. However, this requires a little more map reading and planning than other options.

bike riding in Yosemite Valley

If possible, leave enough time in your one Yosemite day to take a drive to **Glacier Point.** You can do so in your own car or ride the tour bus that leaves from Yosemite Valley Lodge. The ideal time to be at Glacier Point is at sunset, when Half Dome turns pink from the bottom up, but the view from the point will knock your socks off at any time of day.

To capture the essence of Yosemite, try to squeeze in at least one **hike** during your stay. A few easy-to-moderate hikes recommended for short-stay visitors are the trails to **May Lake** and **Lembert Dome** on Tioga Pass Road and the trails to **Sentinel Dome** and **Taft Point** on Glacier Point Road. In Yosemite Valley, make sure you take the short walks to **Lower Yosemite Fall** and **Bridalveil Fall** (each walk is less than a half mile). If you have a little more time in the Valley and don't mind hiking with a crowd, take the spectacular **Mist Trail** to the top of Vernal Fall.

CATHEDRAL LAKES, YOSEMITE

Don't forget your camera to capture the beauty of Yosemite's high country on this classic hike to **Cathedral Lakes,** two **glacial cirque lakes** that are set below the iconic granite of 10,840-foot (3,304-m) Cathedral Peak. Starting from the edge of Tuolumne Meadows, this 7.4-mile (11.9-km) round-trip has only a 1,000-foot (300-m) elevation gain, making it ideal for a day hike or a short backpacking trip.

NORTH DOME, YOSEMITE

Situated right across Tenaya Canyon, **North Dome** offers the best possible perspective on famous Half Dome. A 9-mile (14.5-km) round-trip leads to **sublime views** from North Dome's smooth granite summit, plus a chance to visit **Indian Rock,** the only granite arch in Yosemite.

MIDDLE AND UPPER GAYLOR LAKES, YOSEMITE

In Yosemite's high country at 10,000 feet (3,000 m) and above, the summer months bring an explosive display of **alpine wildflowers.** Catch some of the color at **Gaylor Lakes,** a steep 4-mile (6.4-km) round-trip hike from the Tioga Pass entrance station. At Middle Gaylor Lake, look for fire-red Indian paintbrush and tiny blue lupines, then continue northward to reach smaller Upper Gaylor Lake, a shallow tarn nestled in a flower-filled meadow below 11,004-foot (3,354-m) Gaylor Peak.

Butt-Kicker Hikes

These hikes will challenge you almost every step of the way. You'll burn lots of calories on these treks, so make sure your day pack is full of water and snacks. Make sure you're in great physical condition before tackling these trails.

HALF DOME, YOSEMITE

You will need to have secured a **permit** in advance for this hike. Start as early in the morning as you can because you have **16 miles** (26 km) and a whopping 4,800 feet (1,465 m) of elevation gain ahead of you. Start at Happy Isles and proceed up the **Mist Trail** past **Vernal and**

Half Dome in the clouds

Nevada Falls. Above Nevada Fall, take the left fork for **Half Dome**. The trail is relatively easy from here (you've completed about half of the ascent already) until you reach the infamous **steel cables** that run up the back of the dome. It takes two hands and two feet to haul yourself up the cables, ascending 440 feet (134 m) of nearly vertical granite. On top, you can bask in your accomplishment while taking in the commanding view.

MOUNT DANA, YOSEMITE

The 13,053-foot (3,979-m) summit of **Mount Dana** can be reached with a rather **brutal ascent** that gains 3,100 feet (950 m) over a mere 3 miles (4.8 km). Start at the Tioga Pass entrance station and hike southeast on the trail. You'll climb all the way to the Dana Plateau at 11,600 feet (3,535 m), a good rest stop. Another mile and 1,500 feet (455 m) of elevation gain await, but the hard work is completely worth it. Your reward is one of the **finest views** in the Sierra, encompassing Mono Lake, Ellery and Saddlebag Lakes, Tuolumne Meadows, and an untold wealth of high peaks.

CLOUDS REST, YOSEMITE

The summit of **Clouds Rest** beckons vista lovers. It's 1,000 feet (300 m) higher than Half Dome, with an even better view looking down into Yosemite Valley. The hike is **14 miles (22.5 km) round-trip** from the Sunrise Lakes Trailhead on Tioga Pass Road. Good news—the total elevation gain is only 2,300 feet (700 m), so it's much easier than Half Dome. The final summit ascent travels along a series of **granite "pancakes."** Be sure to stop at **Sunrise Lakes** for a swim on your way back to the trailhead.

ALTA PEAK, SEQUOIA

Mount Whitney is the Sierra's highest and most famous peak, but it's plagued by popularity. An equally **breathtaking vista** and much less company are found on the trail to 11,204-foot (3,415-m) **Alta Peak**. A thigh-burning, 4,000-foot (1,200-m) climb rewards you with views of the Great Western Divide's countless crags, plus a dizzying 6,000-foot (1,800 m) drop to the Kaweah River canyon. From the Wolverton trailhead, the round-trip is 13 miles (20.9 km)—and worth every step.

Best Waterfalls

People come from all over the world to get a negative-ion fix from the plentiful waterfalls in Yosemite National Park. But there's a catch: Show up in mid- to late summer and your waterfall fantasies may be all dried up. Waterfall aficionados should time their Yosemite visit for April, May, or June, the months during which 75 percent of the high country's snowmelt occurs, producing powerful cascades of water. Start with Yosemite Valley's waterfalls, which are easily seen by walking, driving your car, riding the free Yosemite Valley shuttle bus, riding a bike, or any combination of the above.

Bridalveil Fall

Bridalveil Fall in its 620 feet (189 m) of cascading glory is an obvious must-see, but don't miss some of the lesser-known falls nearby. At the overlook for Bridalveil Fall, turn directly around and you'll see **Ribbon Fall** pouring off the north rim of the Valley. Also look for **Sentinel Fall** on the south canyon wall, roughly across from Yosemite Falls, just west of Sentinel Rock.

Yosemite Falls

Lower Yosemite Fall is an easy walk, but waterfall lovers can't leave Yosemite without a trip to the top of **Upper Yosemite Fall**. Start hiking at the trailhead behind Camp 4, and after

3.7 miles (6 km) and 2,700 feet (825 m) of elevation gain, you're at a railed overlook that is perched alongside the brink of this behemoth. Yosemite Falls is the highest waterfall in North America, at 2,425 feet (739 m).

Vernal and Nevada Falls

Hike the **Panorama Trail** from Glacier Point down to Yosemite Valley. It's an 8.5-mile (13.7-km) one-way trek; you'll need to catch the tour bus at Yosemite Valley Lodge in the morning to deliver you to the trail's start. Just 2 miles (3.2 km) downhill from Glacier Point you'll come to the lip of 370-foot (115-m) **Illilouette Fall.** Keep going and an hour or so later you'll reach the brink of **Nevada Fall,** then finally **Vernal Fall.** It is a dizzying experience to stand at the railing-lined overlooks on top of these two falls and stare down into the powerful plunge of white water below.

Tuolumne Falls

For waterfall fans who are unlucky enough to miss the prime falling-water season in Yosemite, there's still hope. July and August park visitors can enjoy a waterfall-laden hike along the Tuolumne River that leads past four falls: **Tuolumne, California, LeConte,** and **Waterwheel.** The trailhead is on Tioga Pass Road near Lembert Dome and Soda Springs, and the trail is not usually accessible until July each year due to snow and wet conditions. This epic hike is a whopping 16 miles (26 km) round-trip, but with only 1,900 feet (580 m) of elevation change. The good news is that you don't have to hike the entire distance to enjoy some of the falls. The first one, Tuolumne Falls, is only 4.5 miles (7.2 km) from the trailhead.

Chilnualna Falls

Drive to the south part of the park to see a lesser-known waterfall. Hike the 8.2-mile (13.2-km) round-trip trail to **Chilnualna Falls,** located near **Wawona.**

Tueeulala Fall and Wapama Fall

Head to Hetch Hetchy Valley to see its spectacular free-leaping falls. **Tueeulala Fall** and

people at the overlook on top of Vernal Fall

A family cools off in the Tuolumne River.

You may be enthralled by Yosemite's scenery, but your kids are a bit harder to impress. Let's face it, children like different stuff than adults. Fortunately, there are plenty of family-friendly activities in Yosemite:

- Rent bikes at the **Half Dome Village** or **Yosemite Valley Lodge** recreation centers and ride around Yosemite Valley.

- Go for a hike on the quieter trails off Glacier Point Road. The easy trails to **Taft Point** and **Sentinel Dome** make good family hikes; each is only 2.2 miles (3.5 km) round-trip.

- Sign up for rock climbing lessons at the **Yosemite Mountaineering School and Guide Service.**

- Go see a live show at the **Yosemite Theater** (kids' tickets are discounted).

- Drive to Wawona to see the giant sequoias in the **Mariposa Grove.**

- Take a trip through history and go for a horse-drawn wagon ride at the **Pioneer Yosemite History Center** in Wawona.

- In early summer, float in a raft on the **Merced River.** In late summer, enjoy a swim at **Sentinel Beach.**

- Sign up for a two-hour morning mule ride at **Big Trees Stable.**

- Go for a **Junior Ranger walk.**

- Stop in at the **Happy Isles Art and Nature Center** in Yosemite Valley to take part in children's art classes.

Wapama Fall can be seen via an easy-to-moderate 4.8-mile (7.7-km) round-trip hike along the edge of Hetch Hetchy Reservoir. Park near the dam, walk across it, and then follow the trail through a tunnel and along the north edge of the reservoir. You'll cross over the flow of both falls on a series of sturdy bridges.

Many seasoned Yosemite visitors insist that the best time to see the park is in winter. Rates drop considerably at park lodgings. Crowds are nonexistent. Think you'll miss out on Yosemite's scenic beauty by visiting in the colder months of the year? Just take a look at some of Ansel Adams's photographs and you'll see that Yosemite in winter is incredibly beautiful. Here are a few of the highlights of a winter visit.

SNOWSHOEING

No experience is required; snowshoeing is as easy as walking, and rentals cost only a few bucks an hour. Rent a pair of snowshoes at Half Dome Village or Yosemite Ski & Snowboard Area. Beginners can snowshoe amid the giant sequoia trees at the **Merced Grove, Tuolumne Grove,** or **Mariposa Grove.** More experienced snowshoers can head out from **Yosemite Ski & Snowboard Area** to Dewey Point, a 7-mile (11.3-km) round-trip, or follow one of several other marked snowshoe/cross-country ski trails from Yosemite Ski & Snowboard Area or Crane Flat. If you don't want to set out on your own, join a ranger-guided snowshoe walk.

snowman in Yosemite Valley

off completely by 9am or 10am, so an early start is critical.

SLEDDING AND ICE-SKATING

Sled in the morning and ice-skate in the afternoon. Snow-play areas are located near **Crane Flat** (Highway 120/Big Oak Flat entrance). Bring along a garbage can lid or a cheap plastic saucer and for a few brief moments you'll feel like a kid again. Then head to **Half Dome Village** for an afternoon skate session, where you can practice your figure eights with a head-on view of Half Dome. Can't skate? Then sit by the warming hut's fire pit and treat yourself to a cup of hot chocolate while you watch other skaters perform triple camels (or just fall down).

WINTER WALK

During most of the winter, the Valley is often snow-free. The Valley's paved bike trails make easy walking paths even when they are covered with a few inches of snow. Get out and about before the sun gets too high and you may get to see the ice cone that forms around **Yosemite Falls** on cold winter nights. On most sunny days, the cone melts

SKIING AND SNOWBOARDING

Yosemite Ski & Snowboard Area is one of the mellowest ski resorts in the entire Sierra. Lift lines? High-priced lift tickets? No such thing here. If you don't feel like driving on snow-covered roads, you can take the shuttle bus to **Yosemite Ski & Snowboard Area** from Yosemite Valley Lodge. If you don't know how to ski or snowboard, Badger's 85 acres (34 hectares) of slopes are the perfect place to learn. Lessons are offered daily. Or, keep it simple—go "snow tubing" on the Yosemite Ski & Snowboard Area hills. It's just like sledding, only safer, because you are cushioned by a big, billowy inner tube.

COCKTAILS BY THE FIRE

After a day playing in the white stuff, head to the **Majestic Yosemite Hotel Bar** for appetizers and a warming cocktail, then choose a comfy seat in one of the Majestic Yosemite's public rooms and read a book by a blazing fire. Or, head to the bar at **Yosemite Valley Lodge** in Yosemite Valley for drinks, snacks, and a seat around the fire.

Yosemite Valley

Seven miles (11.3 km) long and 1 mile (1.6 km)

across at its widest point, Yosemite Valley is a mélange of landscapes. It is verdant meadows bisected by the clear Merced River. It is powerful waterfalls plunging thousands of feet over sheer granite walls. It is the forested home of a rich tapestry of wildlife, including black bears, mule deer, and chipmunks.

It is also the home of several hundred people who are employed in the park (or married to someone who is), and the destination of many thousands more who visit each day. It is a small city with sewage lines, garbage collection, a dentist's office, jail, courtroom, auto garage, and church.

The Valley is the centerpiece of Yosemite and the place where the

Highlights

Look for ★ to find recommended sights, activities, dining, and lodging.

Map labels:

Lower Yosemite Fall ★
Yosemite Theater ★
Yosemite Village
Half Dome ★
★ The Majestic Yosemite/ Ahwahnee Hotel
★ El Capitan
NORTHSIDE DR
SOUTHSIDE DR
★ Bridalveil Fall
GLACIER POINT RD
Merced River
★ Mist Trail to Vernal Fall
0   1 mi
0   1 km
© MOON.COM

★ **El Capitan:** Towering 3,593 feet (1,095 m), El Cap is the undisputed king of the granite monoliths and a mecca for daredevil rock climbers. Get a good look at "The Chief" from the meadow at its base (page 47).

★ **The Majestic Yosemite Hotel:** It costs a bundle to spend the night here, but it is completely free of charge to wander amid the "public rooms" of this splendid 1920s-era hotel, formerly known as the **Ahwahnee Hotel.** Check out the stained-glass windows, historical Yosemite paintings and drawings, and Native American baskets (page 49).

★ **Half Dome:** Your first look at this sheared-off granite dome always comes as a surprise, even though you've undoubtedly seen its image on postcards, calendars, and Ansel Adams prints. Hard-core hikers who secure a permit in advance can trek to its summit; everybody else can admire it from below (page 49).

★ **Lower Yosemite Fall:** Upper, Lower, and Middle Yosemite Falls combined make up the highest waterfall in North America, topping out at a prodigious 2,425 feet (739 m). It's a strenuous hike to reach the top of the upper fall, but the base of the lower fall can be visited via an easy, level stroll (page 53).

★ **Mist Trail to Vernal Fall:** If you're only going to do one hike from Yosemite Valley, this should be it. The 3-mile (4.8-km) round-trip is strenuous, with plenty of rock stairsteps to climb and descend, but it's short enough to be doable by most everyone. The big thrill is hiking so close to Vernal Fall that you will feel like you're a part of it (page 54).

★ **Bridalveil Fall:** The most dependable waterfall in Yosemite Valley, 620-foot (189-m) Bridalveil flows year-round, even in the dry late summer and fall. A short walk will take you to an overlook point below the falls (page 60).

★ **Yosemite Theater:** For only a few bucks, you can take in some live theater in a small, intimate auditorium. Entertaining and informative plays depict slices of Yosemite and California history (page 70).

vast majority of visitors spend most of their time. It offers the greatest number of organized activities of any region of the park, ranging from nature walks to evening theater, from ice-skating to photography seminars, from Indian basketmaking to rock climbing. The daily array of scheduled events and activities runs the gamut from highly athletic to nearly sedentary and can keep even the most ambitious visitor busy.

PLANNING YOUR TIME

Yosemite Valley is open **year-round,** and its weather is dependably mild. Summer days and nights are usually warm and dry, with temperatures reaching 80-90°F (27-32°C) during the day and 50-60°F (10-15°C) at night. Autumn and spring are generally 10-20 degrees cooler. Winter daytime temperatures average 30-55°F (–1-13°C), and nights often drop below freezing. Snow falls in Yosemite Valley typically a few times each winter, but it usually does not cover the ground for more than a few weeks. Rain is more common in winter than snow.

Exploring Yosemite Valley

VISITORS CENTERS
Valley Visitor Center
The largest of the park's visitors centers is located in Yosemite Valley. The **Valley Visitor Center** (shuttle stop 5 or 9, 209/372-0299, 9am-5pm daily) has natural history displays, including a glass-enclosed stuffed black bear standing on its hind legs, audiovisual programs, a well-stocked **bookstore** (9am-5pm daily, until 7pm in summer), and staff on hand to answer questions. Free day-hiking brochures are available. An exhibit hall interprets the geologic history of Yosemite Valley and explains park wildlife and how it adapts to the Sierra Nevada's seasonal changes. Charts are posted with current road closures and openings and the status of campsite availability throughout the park.

A National Park Service-sanctioned 23-minute film, *The Spirit of Yosemite,* is shown in the **Valley Visitor Center Theater** on the half hour starting at 9:30am except on Sunday, when the first showing is at 12:30pm. The film explains some of the basics about Yosemite's geology and history but mostly consists of a lot of beautiful videography. *Ken Burns' Yosemite: A Gathering of Spirit* plays on

the hour (10am, 11am, etc.). The Burns film documents the park's creation through the Yosemite Grant, the act that brought to life the conservation vision of Abraham Lincoln, Theodore Roosevelt, John Muir, Galen Clark, and others.

First-time visitors sometimes have a difficult time finding the visitors center when driving their own cars. It's not along a main road or next to a day-use parking lot. If you're riding the free Valley shuttle bus, get off at stop 5 or 9 (the bus driver will point you in the right direction). If driving, leave your car at the main day-use parking lot south of the Yosemite Village Store and then walk northwest about 750 feet (230 m). The visitors center is just west of the post office. Next door to the visitors center is the Wilderness Center, where visitors can pick up backpacking permits, buy maps and guidebooks, and rent bear canisters.

Happy Isles Art and Nature Center
A lesser-known visitors center is the **Happy Isles Art and Nature Center** (shuttle stop 16, 9am-4pm daily Apr.-Oct.). This small

Previous: Upper Yosemite Fall; Half Dome summit; rafting on the Merced River.

Yosemite Valley

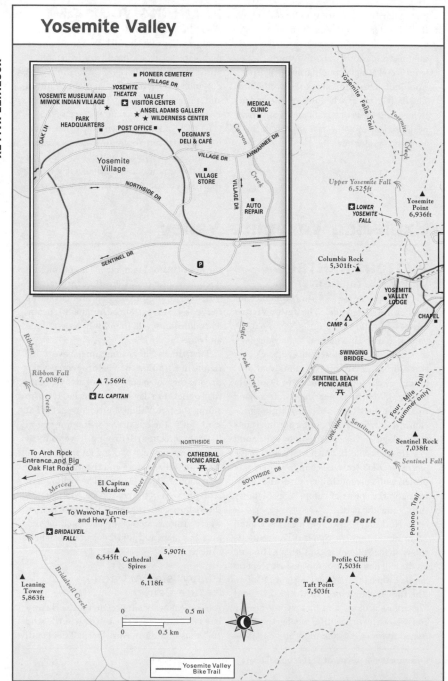

PIONEER CEMETERY

VILLAGE DR

YOSEMITE MUSEUM AND
MIWOK INDIAN VILLAGE

YOSEMITE
THEATER

VALLEY
VISITOR CENTER

ANSEL ADAMS GALLERY

WILDERNESS CENTER

PARK
HEADQUARTERS

POST OFFICE

DEGNAN'S
DELI & CAFÉ

MEDICAL
CLINIC

AHWAHNEE DR

Canyon

Creek

VILLAGE DR

Yosemite
Village

VILLAGE
STORE

VILLAGE DR

NORTHSIDE DR

AUTO
REPAIR

SENTINEL DR

P

OAK LN

Yosemite Falls Trail

Yosemite Creek

Upper Yosemite Fall
6,525ft

LOWER
YOSEMITE
FALL

Yosemite
Point
6,936ft

Columbia Rock
5,301ft

YOSEMITE
VALLEY
LODGE

CAMP 4

CHAPEL

SWINGING
BRIDGE

Ribbon Creek

Ribbon Fall
7,008ft

7,569ft

EL CAPITAN

Eagle Peak Creek

SENTINEL BEACH
PICNIC AREA

ONE-WAY

Sentinel Creek

Four Mile Trail
(summer only)

Sentinel Rock
7,038ft

Sentinel Fall

To Arch Rock
Entrance and Big
Oak Flat Road

Merced River

El Capitan
Meadow

NORTHSIDE DR

CATHEDRAL
PICNIC AREA

SOUTHSIDE DR

To Wawona Tunnel
and Hwy 41

BRIDALVEIL
FALL

Yosemite National Park

Pohono Trail

6,545ft

Cathedral
Spires

5,907ft

Profile Cliff
7,503ft

Leaning
Tower
5,863ft

Bridalveil Creek

6,118ft

Taft Point
7,503ft

0   0.5 mi

0   0.5 km

Yosemite Valley
Bike Trail

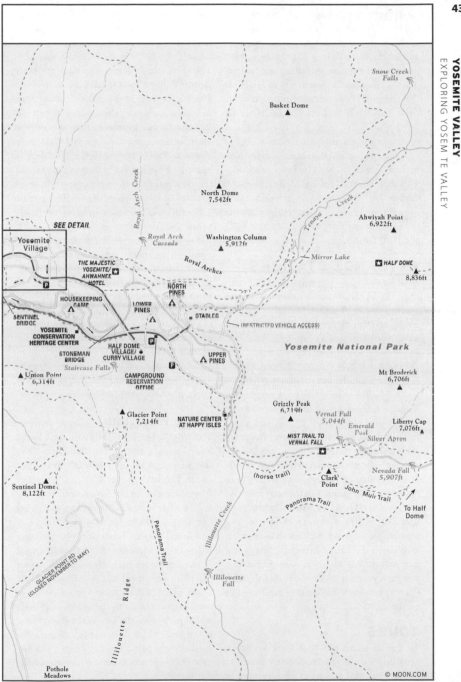

interpretive center has family-oriented exhibits on the natural history and geology of the Valley, including wildlife dioramas and interactive displays. Short nature trails lead from the center, including one that explores evidence of a massive 1996 landslide that completely devastated this region of the park. Art classes for kids and adults are offered Monday through Saturday. Register online (www.yosemiteconservancy.org) to secure a spot, or show up at 9:30am for last-minute openings. They also host open studio workshop hours (11am-3pm daily Apr.-Oct.). Classes are held outside when weather permits. Happy Isles is also the trailhead for the famous hikes to **Vernal** and **Nevada Falls** and **Half Dome.**

ENTRANCE STATIONS

Arch Rock (Hwy. 140), only a 15- to 20-minute drive, is the closest entrance station to Yosemite Valley. **Big Oak Flat** (Hwy. 120) offers access from the north; it's about a 45-minute drive to Yosemite Valley.

SHUTTLES

Free hybrid shuttle buses transport visitors around the Yosemite Valley floor year-round. To get a seat on one of these buses, simply stand at one of the shuttle stops and wait a few minutes until one shows up. The main **Valley shuttle** runs 7am-10pm daily in summer, with shorter hours in winter (the shuttle visits each stop every 10 minutes during peak hours, every 30 minutes in the early morning and evening). The **El Capitan shuttle** (9am-3pm daily mid-June-early Oct.) operates on a separate loop around the Valley's west end. If arriving in the Valley during the busy summer season, it is highly recommended that you park your car and use the free shuttles. All of the Valley's major sights are accessible via the shuttle.

TOURS

Several different bus **tours** are available, ranging in duration from a few hours to all day. Bus tour tickets can be reserved in advance (888/413-8869, www.travelyosemite.com). If you're already in the park, stop by the **Yosemite Valley Lodge Tour Desk** (shuttle stop 8, Yosemite Valley Lodge lobby, 209/372-1240, 7:30am-7pm daily), the **Half Dome Village Tour Desk** (next to the Half Dome Village registration desk, 7:30am-3pm daily in summer), or the outdoor **Yosemite Village ticket kiosk** (next to the Village Store, summer only). All tours depart from Yosemite Valley Lodge, and its tour desk is open the longest; stop in during the evening to make plans for the next day, or show up first thing in the morning when it opens. Tours fill up in the summer, so reserve in advance when possible.

Because of traffic congestion, driving your own car around the Valley is not recommended, especially in summer. Instead, ride the **free Valley shuttle bus,** or take an organized tour in an open-air tram. Energetic visitors can tour Yosemite Valley on the seat of a bike—either your own two-wheeled steed or a rental bike from Yosemite Valley Lodge or Half Dome Village. If you must drive in Yosemite, your best bet is to drive *out* of the Valley, heading either to Glacier Point or Tuolumne Meadows/Tioga Pass.

Valley Floor Tour

The 26-mile (42-km) **Valley Floor Tour** (2 hours, departures hourly 10am-3pm daily summer, 10am and 2pm daily fall-spring, $37 adults, $27 children ages 5-12, children under 5 free) offers an interpretive tour through the Valley with easy viewing of famous sights like Yosemite Falls, Half Dome, El Capitan, and Bridalveil Fall. From late spring to early fall, tour participants are comfortably seated in an open-air tram; in winter, the tour takes place in an enclosed bus. Most Valley Floor Tours include a drive up to Tunnel View, just before the entrance to the Wawona Tunnel, which many consider one of the finest vistas in the park. Along the way, the tour guide remarks on the park's unique geology and history. Evening tours are offered on select dates during summer.

Yosemite Valley Shuttle Bus Stops

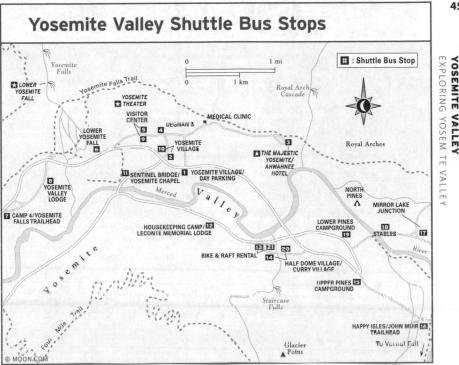

Moonlight Valley Floor Tour

A nighttime **Moonlight Valley Floor Tour** (2 hours, June-Sept., $37 adults, $27 children ages 5-12, children under 5 free) is offered on full-moon nights (usually over 4-5 nights per month). The tour takes place in an open-air tram, and hot chocolate is provided. Departure times vary depending on the time of the moonrise but are typically around 8:30pm.

Glacier Point Tour

A half-day excursion on a large enclosed bus leads to **Glacier Point** (late May-early Nov., snow conditions permitting, $52 adults, $32 children ages 5-12, children under 5 free). Buses depart from Yosemite Valley Lodge at 8:30am, 10:30am, and 1:30pm daily from late May to Labor Day, and at 8:30am and 1:30pm daily from Labor Day to early November.

Some hikers ride this bus one-way ($26 adults, $16.50 children ages 5-12) to Glacier Point and then hike back down to the Valley via either the Four-Mile Trail or the Panorama Trail.

Glacier Point Stargazing Tour

The **Glacier Point Starry Night Skies Over Yosemite Tour** (Sun.-Thurs. June-Sept., $64 adults, $55 children ages 5-12) departs Yosemite Valley Lodge at 7pm and arrives at Glacier Point just in time to take in the spectacular sunset view. After dark, a naturalist presents a one-hour astronomy program. If you prefer, you can drive your own car to Glacier Point and take part in the astronomy program ($10). Stargazing tours are occasionally canceled due to cloudy skies; ticket holders should call 209/372-1240 or 209/372-8243 the day of the tour to ensure the tour will take place (refunds are given if the tour is canceled).

Where Can I Find...?

- **Banks and ATMs:** There are no banks in Yosemite Valley, but several ATMs are available. In Yosemite Village, there is a Bank of America ATM south of the **Village Store** and an ATM inside the Village Store. In **Yosemite Valley Lodge,** there is an ATM near the main registration area. In **Half Dome Village,** there is an ATM inside the grocery store.

- **Gas and Garage Service:** There is **no gas station** in Yosemite Valley. The closest gas stations are in El Portal (12 mi/19.3 km) or at Crane Flat (15 mi/24 km); at both spots you can pay at the pump 24 hours a day with a credit card. Gas is also available in Wawona. If your car needs emergency gas or service, find the **Village Garage** (9002 Village Dr., 209/372-8320, 8am-5pm daily, 24-hour towing service available).

- **Internet/Wi-Fi: Degnan's Kitchen** (7am-6pm daily) has free Wi-Fi.

- **Laundry: Housekeeping Camp** (shuttle stop 12, Southside Dr.) has laundry service.

- **Post Office: Yosemite Village** (209/372-4475, 8:30am-5pm Mon.-Fri., 10am-noon Sat.) and **Yosemite Valley Lodge** (209/372-4853, 12:30pm-2:45pm Mon.-Fri.) have USPS outposts.

- **Religious Services:** Nondenominational services are held Sunday (9:15am, 11am, and 6:30pm) and Thursday (7pm) at **Yosemite Valley Chapel** on Southside Drive.

- **Showers: Half Dome Village** (24 hours daily year-round, $5) or **Housekeeping Camp** (7am-10pm daily Apr.-Oct., $5) have shower facilities. Outside of the park, you can get a shower at **Indian Flat RV Park** (9988 Hwy. 140, El Portal, 209/379-2339, $3 for noncampers).

Big Trees Tour

The **Big Trees Tour** ($52 adults, $32 children ages 5-12, children under 5 free) travels from Yosemite Valley to the **Mariposa Grove of Giant Sequoias,** the largest sequoia grove in Yosemite and home to over 500 mature giant sequoias. Visitors can take a self-guided hike around the grove. This five-hour tour runs from May through September, departing from Yosemite Valley Lodge at 8:30am daily.

Tuolumne Meadows

A bus from Yosemite Valley to **Tuolumne Meadows** (mid-June to mid-Sept.) leaves once a day at 8:30am, stopping at Crane Flat, White Wolf, Olmsted Point, and Tuolumne Meadows. The return bus departs Tuolumne Meadows at approximately 2pm daily. Visitors can take an all-day round-trip excursion ($28 adults, $14 children) or ride one-way and then hike back down to the Valley. One-way hikes can be accomplished en route; the ticket fare is adjusted according to which stop you take. The bus can be flagged for pickup or drop-off at any major trailhead on Tioga Road. In Yosemite Valley, the bus leaves from Half Dome Village, Yosemite Village, and Yosemite Valley Lodge.

Grand Tour

The **Yosemite Grand Tour** ($104 adults, $64 children ages 5-12, children under 5 free, late May-Sept.) is a full-day tour that travels from Yosemite Valley to Glacier Point and then on to the Mariposa Grove of Giant Sequoias. The Grand Tour departs from Yosemite Valley Lodge at 8:45am and returns at 5:30pm; prices include a picnic lunch.

Sights

The following Yosemite Valley sights are listed from west to east along the Valley floor starting on Southside Drive.

BRIDALVEIL FALL

This 620-foot (189-m) waterfall is easily reached by a 0.25-mile (0.4-km) walk from the well-signed parking lot just east of the Highway 41 turnoff from the Valley. The stunning view of **Bridalveil Fall** from the west end of the parking area will inspire you to take the short, paved walk to an overlook near the fall's base. In spring and early summer, you will feel the sprinkles of Bridalveil's billowing spray.

★ EL CAPITAN

The largest single piece of granite rock on earth, **El Capitan** (The Chief) towers 3,593 feet (1,095 m) above the Valley floor. It is arguably the most famous rock-climbing site in the world. Get a good look at this granite behemoth from El Capitan Meadow along Northside Drive. Many park visitors sit for hours in this meadow, binoculars in hand, watching the daring climbers inch their way up El Cap's sheer face.

YOSEMITE VALLEY CHAPEL

The **Yosemite Valley Chapel** (shuttle stop 11, 209/372-4831, www.yosemitevalleychapel.org) is the oldest of all the public structures still in use in Yosemite. Built under the sponsorship of the California State Sunday School Association, the small New England-style chapel held its first service on June 7, 1879. It was built near the base of the Four-Mile Trail but was moved here in 1901. All Yosemite visitors are invited to attend services at the chapel. Nondenominational services are held Sunday morning at 9:15am and 11am, Sunday evening at 6:30pm, and Thursday evening at 7pm. (Winter services are held only on Sundays.) The chapel is on Southside Drive, right before Sentinel Bridge.

YOSEMITE VILLAGE

Yosemite Museum

Next door to the Valley Visitor Center is the **Yosemite Museum** (Yosemite Village, 209/372-0200, 9am-4pm daily, free), where the Indian Cultural Exhibit interprets the life of the Miwok and Paiute Indians from 1850 to the present. On display are Indian deerskin dresses and dance regalia, as well as natural fiber and beaded baskets. Rotating works of local artists are on display in the **Museum Gallery** (9am-4pm daily June-Sept., 10am-noon and 1pm-4pm daily Oct.-May), and the **Yosemite Museum Store** features local American Indian arts and crafts. Behind the museum is the **Miwok Indian Village**, a year-round outdoor exhibit of local Native American culture. This exhibit is an excellent way to teach children about the Indians who once lived in Yosemite Valley. Visitors can walk among traditional Indian dwellings and watch live demonstrations of basket weaving and beadwork. A self-guided loop trail called "The Miwok in Yosemite" leads through the village. Interpretive brochures are available at the trailhead and in the museum.

Yosemite Valley Cemetery

Across the street from the Yosemite Museum is the **Yosemite Valley Cemetery** (Yosemite Village), the final resting place of many notable people from the Valley's history. Among the gravestones you'll find the names of Galen Clark, Yosemite's first guardian; George Anderson, the man who first climbed Half Dome; and three members of the Hutchings family, including Florence Hutchings, the first Caucasian child born in Yosemite. Purchase a guide to the cemetery at the Valley Visitor Center.

Waterfall Wonders

Yosemite is a park well known for superlatives. Among its many bragging rights, the park's waterfalls are perhaps the most famous and revered. Most geographers agree that Yosemite Valley contains 2 of the world's 10 tallest waterfalls: 2,425-foot (739-m) **Yosemite Falls** at number 5 and 2,000-foot (610-m) **Sentinel Fall** at number 7. Yosemite Falls also holds the undisputed title of the tallest waterfall in North America.

Other, less famous Valley falls boast their own impressive statistics: **Ribbon Fall** at 1,612 feet (491 m) holds the title of tallest free-leaping waterfall in Yosemite Valley. Unlike Yosemite Falls, Ribbon's cascade never touches the granite wall behind it; its fall is unbroken or "free-leaping." Ribbon Fall ranks among the world's 20 tallest waterfalls.

If you want to see Yosemite Valley when its granite walls are graced by the white plumes of gushing waterfalls, you must time your trip carefully. Many a first-time Yosemite visitor has shown up in August or September

Vernal Fall

and questioned why the Park Service has "turned off" the waterfalls. Unlike at New York's famous Niagara Falls, the bureaucrats are not in charge of the water flow in Yosemite—Mother Nature is. Because the Valley's waterfalls are mostly fed by snowmelt in the high country above the Valley rim, the waterfalls are at their fullest flow in spring and early summer.

Approximately 75 percent of the high country's snowmelt occurs in **April, May,** and **June,** making these the prime months for waterfall viewing. By late July, Yosemite Falls may be only a dribble—or it may be completely dry. Water flows year-round in only a few of the Valley's famous falls—**Bridalveil Fall, Vernal Fall,** and **Nevada Fall**—but their flow in late summer can be as little as 5 percent of what it is from April to June.

Perhaps to compensate for its ephemeral nature, Yosemite Falls has a few tricks up its sleeve that may be seen by lucky Valley visitors. In winter, a giant ice cone forms at the base of **Upper Yosemite Fall.** Composed of frozen spray and fallen chunks of ice, the ice cone can sometimes grow to a height of 300 feet (90 m). And on full-moon nights in spring, a "moonbow" will sometimes appear around the base of **Lower Yosemite Fall.**

Another waterfall delight that can only be seen in the winter months is the "firefall" of **Horsetail Fall,** which can be witnessed along the edge of El Capitan. For approximately two weeks each February, the orbit of the earth around the sun creates a dramatic gold-to-red display as the setting sun illuminates the wispy spray of Horsetail Fall. For this flame-colored sunset magic to occur, the light has to be just right (not too much cloud cover), and there has to be sufficient flow in the falls.

Although the Valley is the best place in the park for waterfall viewing, other regions of the park have their own worthy cataracts. On the park's south side, be sure to visit **Chilnualna Falls** (best in early spring, usually April-May). From Tuolumne Meadows, hike downriver to **Tuolumne Falls** and **Waterwheel Falls** (best flow in summer, typically July).

Lower Yosemite Fall

No visit to Yosemite Valley would be complete without a walk to the base of **Lower Yosemite Fall** (shuttle stop 6, Northside Dr.), the bottom section of the highest waterfall in North America. The entire waterfall is 2,425 feet (739 m) high; the lower section is 320 feet (98 m). It's an easy stroll of only 0.25 mile (0.4 km) to one of the most thrilling sights in Yosemite, but you might as well walk the entire 1-mile (1.6-km) loop. The trail starts right across the park road from Yosemite Valley Lodge.

TOP EXPERIENCE

★ THE MAJESTIC YOSEMITE HOTEL

(FORMERLY AHWAHNEE HOTEL)

This National Historic Landmark is an attraction even for people who aren't sleeping or eating here. The **Majestic Yosemite Hotel** (shuttle stop 3, Ahwahnee Dr., 209/372-1426 or 888/413-8869) has several "public rooms" in which you can wander and marvel at the hotel's 1927 architecture, designed by Gilbert Stanley Underwood, plus its colorful stained-glass windows, Native American tapestries and baskets, Turkish kilim rugs, and paintings and artifacts from Yosemite's history. Take a walk around the **Great Lounge,** peek into the grand **Dining Room,** and buy a drink at the bar or a souvenir in one of the gift shops. Free **one-hour guided hotel tours,** designed for adults and mature children, are offered frequently throughout the year; check with the hotel's concierge desk for a current schedule. A small parking lot is at the end of Ahwahnee Drive, or ride the shuttle from the Yosemite Village parking lot.

YOSEMITE CONSERVATION HERITAGE CENTER

Built by the Sierra Club in 1904, this beautiful Tudor-revival-style building (previously known as **LeConte Memorial Lodge**) served as the Valley's first public visitors center and is now a National Historic Landmark (shuttle stop 12, 209/372-4542, 10am-4pm Wed.-Sun. May-Sept.). The structure's granite masonry and steep-pitched roof were designed to replicate the color, texture, and vertical nature of Yosemite Valley's walls. In 1919, the lodge was moved from its original location in Yosemite's Camp Curry to its present site east of the Yosemite Chapel on Southside Drive. Managed by a Sierra Club curator and more than 100 volunteers, the space hosts free **summer evening programs** (8pm Fri.-Sat., free) presented by historians, writers, and photographers. Originally named for Joseph LeConte, a geologist and Sierra explorer, the structure was renamed the **Yosemite Conservation Heritage Center** in 2017.

MIRROR LAKE

It is not hard to imagine how **Mirror Lake** (shuttle stop 17) got its name. When the lake is at its fullest in late spring, it reflects a lovely mirror image of Mount Watkins, a granite summit named for one of Yosemite's earliest photographers. A brief interpretive **loop trail** gives you a look into Yosemite's natural history and also its history as a world-famous park. The lake is actually not a lake at all, but a pool on Tenaya Creek that is slowly filling with sediment. By late summer each year, it looks more like a meadow than a lake, although the first winter rains fill it to the brim once more. In the 1880s the lake was dammed and a bathhouse was built on its edges; park visitors floated around its surface in small rowboats.

★ HALF DOME

Probably the most famous icon of Yosemite is the sheared-off granite dome known as **Half Dome.** Several spots on the Valley floor offer great views of this odd-looking rock formation. One is at Mirror Lake, or on the trail just beyond it, where you can stand at the base of the famous stone monolith. Other good viewing spots are at Stoneman Meadow, across the road from Half Dome Village, or at Tunnel View, just above the Valley on Highway 41.

Yosemite Valley Hikes

Trail	Effort	Distance	Duration
Bridalveil Fall	Easy	0.5 mi/0.8 km rt	30 min
Lower Yosemite Fall	Easy	1 mi/1.6 km rt	30 min
Mirror Lake Loop	Easy	4.6 mi/7.4 km rt	2 hr
Mist Trail to Vernal Fall	Moderate	3 mi/4.8 km rt	1.5-2 hr
Mist and John Muir Loop to Nevada Fall	Strenuous	6.8 mi/10.9 km rt	3-4 hr
Upper Yosemite Fall	Strenuous	7.4 mi/11.9 km rt	4-5 hr
Inspiration and Stanford Points	Strenuous	7.6 mi/12.2 km rt	4 hr
Four-Mile Trail	Strenuous	9.6 mi/15.5 km rt	5-6 hr
Eagle Peak	Very strenuous	13.4 mi/21.6 km rt	6-8 hr
Half Dome	Very strenuous	16 mi/26 km rt	8-10 hr

The undisputed best "drive-to" views of Half Dome are from Washburn Point and Glacier Point on Glacier Point Road. If you want to hike to the top of Half Dome (page 57), you will need to reserve a permit far in advance.

Recreation

DAY HIKES

From the floor of Yosemite Valley, it's hard to fathom that hikers can scale its massive granite walls and ascend to the top of Glacier Point or the brink of Yosemite Falls. It's difficult to comprehend that a trail could take you within a few feet of Vernal or Nevada Fall without sending you tumbling into its spray, or to the polished summit of Half Dome without careening you off the edge. But the well-built trails of Yosemite Valley make these destinations accessible, despite how daunting they may look. Hiking in and around the Valley reveals so many geological and natural wonders that it can often be more of an exercise in suspending disbelief than in physical exertion.

1: Bridalveil Fall 2: El Capitan 3: Yosemite Falls
4: the Yosemite Museum

You just have to experience it for yourself to believe it.

Upper Yosemite Fall

Distance: 7.4 miles (11.9 km) round-trip
Duration: 4-5 hours
Elevation Change: 2,700 feet (825 m)
Effort: Strenuous
Shuttle Stop: 7
Trailhead: Camp 4 (see map p. 52)
Directions: From Yosemite Village, drive west on Northside Drive 0.75 mile (1.2 km) to the Yosemite Valley Lodge parking lot on the left. Park on the far west side of the lot and walk across the road to Camp 4 (do not park in spaces marked Permit Parking Only). The Upper Yosemite Fall Trailhead is between the parking lot for Camp 4 and the camp itself.

Yosemite Falls

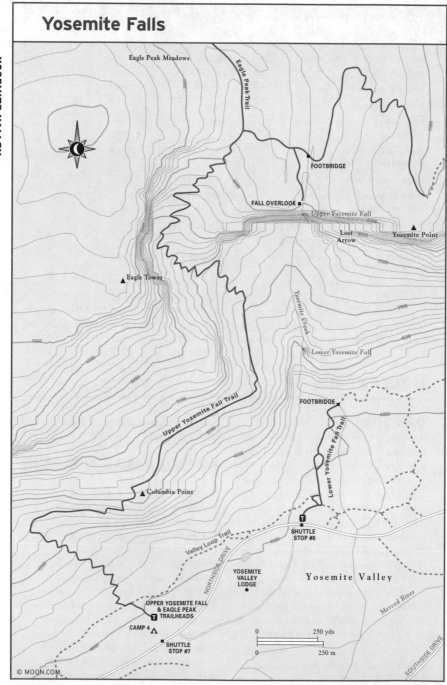

Eagle Peak Meadows

Eagle Peak Trail

FOOTBRIDGE

FALL OVERLOOK

Upper Yosemite Fall

Lost Arrow

▲ Yosemite Point

▲ Eagle Tower

Yosemite Creek

Lower Yosemite Fall

FOOTBRIDGE

Lower Yosemite Fall Trail

Upper Yosemite Fall Trail

▲ Columbia Point

Valley Loop Trail

SHUTTLE STOP #6

NORTHSIDE DRIVE

YOSEMITE VALLEY LODGE

Yosemite Valley

Merced River

UPPER YOSEMITE FALL & EAGLE PEAK TRAILHEADS

CAMP 4

SHUTTLE STOP #7

0   250 yds

0   250 m

SOUTHSIDE DRIVE

© MOON.COM

At 2,425 feet (739 m), Yosemite Falls is the highest waterfall in North America and the fifth highest in the world. That's why hundreds of park visitors hike this strenuous trail every day in the spring and summer. There's no feeling quite like standing at the waterfall's brink and realizing you've conquered a landmark of this magnitude.

Still, if you tucker out on this demanding climb to Upper Yosemite Fall, just remember that you always have a fallback option: You can hike only 1.2 miles (1.9 km) one-way to the **Columbia Point viewpoint** (also called Columbia Rock), ascending more than **100 switchbacks** for a total gain of 1,200 feet (365 m), and then turn around and call it a day. The view of Yosemite Valley from Columbia Point is a stunner, and plenty of people who planned on hiking to Upper Yosemite Fall turn around here and still leave satisfied.

Those who push on are also rewarded. After a level section and then a short descent, the trail switchbacks up and up until at 3.7 miles (6 km), and after a total 2,700-foot (823-m) climb, you reach the brink of **Upper Yosemite Fall.** Make sure you take the cutoff trail on your right to reach the **fall overlook;** the main trail doesn't go there. From the lip of the fall you have an amazing perspective on the waterfall's plunge to the Valley floor far below.

If this trip hasn't provided you with enough exertion, continue another 0.75 mile (1.2 km), crossing the **bridge** above the falls to reach **Yosemite Point** (6,936 ft/2,114 m in elevation), where you get a stunning view of the south rim of the Valley, Half Dome, and North Dome, and a look at the top of Lost Arrow Spire, a single shaft of granite jutting into the sky.

Eagle Peak

Distance: 13.4 miles (21.6 km) round-trip
Duration: 6-8 hours
Elevation Change: 3,800 feet (1,160 m)
Effort: Very strenuous
Shuttle Stop: 7
Trailhead: Camp 4 (see map p. 52)

Directions: From Yosemite Village, drive west on Northside Drive 0.75 mile (1.2 km) to the Yosemite Valley Lodge parking lot on the left. Park on the far west side of the lot and walk across the road to Camp 4 (do not park in spaces marked Permit Parking Only). The Upper Yosemite Fall Trailhead is located between the parking lot for Camp 4 and the camp itself. Or, take the free Valley shuttle bus to stop 7 for Camp 4.

If you seek more of a challenge than the day hike to Upper Yosemite Fall, the trail to Eagle Peak delivers the same stunning destinations as the shorter trip—Columbia Point and Upper Yosemite Fall—plus an **additional 3 miles (4.8 km) one-way** to a lookout atop the highest rock of the Three Brothers formation. Not only can you see all of Yosemite from Eagle Peak, but on rare, extremely clear days you can also see the mountains and foothills of the Coast Range, 100 miles (160 km) to the west.

Follow the trail notes for the hike to Upper Yosemite Fall; then, after taking the spur trail to the brink of the fall, backtrack 0.25 mile (0.4 km) to the trail junction for the **Eagle Peak Trail.** Follow the Eagle Peak Trail northwest for 1.5 miles (2.4 km) and then hike south for 1 mile (1.6 km) through **Eagle Peak Meadows.** At a trail junction with the **El Capitan Trail,** bear left for a 0.5-mile (0.8-km) ascent to your final destination—the summit of Eagle Peak, elevation 7,779 feet (2,371 m). After completing this trip, you'll never view the Three Brothers the same way again.

★ Lower Yosemite Fall

Distance: 1 mile (1.6 km) round-trip
Duration: 30 minutes
Elevation Change: 50 feet (15 m)
Effort: Easy
Shuttle Stop: 6
Trailhead: Lower Yosemite Fall or Yosemite Valley Lodge (see map p. 52)
Directions: From Yosemite Village, drive west on Northside Drive 0.75 mile (1.2 km) to Yosemite Valley Lodge. Unless you are staying at the lodge, parking

is difficult in this area, so riding the shuttle bus is recommended. The shuttle bus will drop you off at the official Lower Yosemite Fall trailhead along Northside Drive. If you must drive your car, there is limited parking on both sides of the road (east of Yosemite Valley Lodge on Northside Drive).

It's so short you can hardly call it a hike, and the route is perpetually crawling with people. Still, the trail to Lower Yosemite Fall is an absolute must for visitors to Yosemite Valley. When the falls are roaring with snowmelt in the spring and early summer, they never fail to please even the most seasoned hikers.

About 10 minutes of walking from the Yosemite Fall trailhead brings you to the **footbridge** below the falls, where in the spring you can get soaking wet from the incredible mist and spray. By late summer, on the other hand, the fall often dries up completely. Be sure to walk the entire loop instead of just heading out and back to the fall; there is much to see along the way. And most important of all: If you really want to view the waterfall at its most magnificent stage, plan your trip for some time between **April and June,** during peak snowmelt. Seasoned waterfall lovers should also plan to visit on full-moon nights in April and May, when if conditions are just right, they are treated to the appearance of a "moonbow" surrounding the lower fall.

TOP EXPERIENCE

★ Mist Trail to Vernal Fall

Distance: 3 miles (4.8 km) round-trip
Duration: 1.5-2 hours
Elevation Change: 1,050 feet (320 m)
Effort: Moderate
Shuttle Stop: 16
Trailhead: Happy Isles (see map p. 55)
Directions: From the Arch Rock entrance station on Highway 140, drive 11.6 miles (18.7 km) east to the day-use parking lot at Half Dome Village. Board the free Yosemite Valley shuttle bus to Happy Isles, stop number 16. In winter when the shuttle does not run, you must hike from Half Dome Village, adding 2 miles (3.2 km) to your round-trip. Trails may be closed in

winter; call to check weather conditions.

This is a hike that every visitor to the Valley should take, even if it's the only trail they walk all year. Despite how crowded the trail inevitably is, this is a world-class hike to one of the most photographed waterfalls in the world. Make your trip more enjoyable by starting as early in the morning as possible, before the hordes are out in full force.

Start by taking the free Yosemite shuttle bus to the trailhead at **Happy Isles.** (Or you can add an extra mile each way by hiking from the day-use parking area in Half Dome Village to Happy Isles.) The partially paved route is a moderate 500-foot (150-m) climb to the Vernal Fall **footbridge,** then a very steep tromp up the seemingly endless granite staircase to the top of the fall. Although many people hike only to the footbridge, 0.8 mile (1.3 km) from Happy Isles, it's definitely worth the extra effort to push on another 0.5 mile (0.8 km) to reach the top of Vernal Fall.

Doing so means ascending another 500 feet (150 m) on the Mist Trail's famous **granite stairway,** which frames the edge of Vernal Fall. You will come so close to the plunging spray that you may feel as if you are part of it. Sometimes you are—during peak snowmelt in spring, hikers are frequently drenched in spray and mist. Remember to bring a rain poncho if you don't like getting wet. When you reach the 317-foot-high (97-m) fall's brink, you can stand at the railing and watch the dizzying flow of rushing white water as it tumbles downward. This is a trip you have to do at least once in your life.

Mist and John Muir Loop to Nevada Fall

Distance: 6.8 miles (10.9 km) round-trip
Duration: 3-4 hours
Elevation Change: 2,600 feet (790 m)
Effort: Strenuous
Shuttle Stop: 16
Trailhead: Happy Isles (see map p. 55)
Directions: From the Arch Rock entrance station on Highway 140, drive 11.6 miles (18.7 km) east to the day-use parking lot at Half Dome Village. Board the

Mist Trail

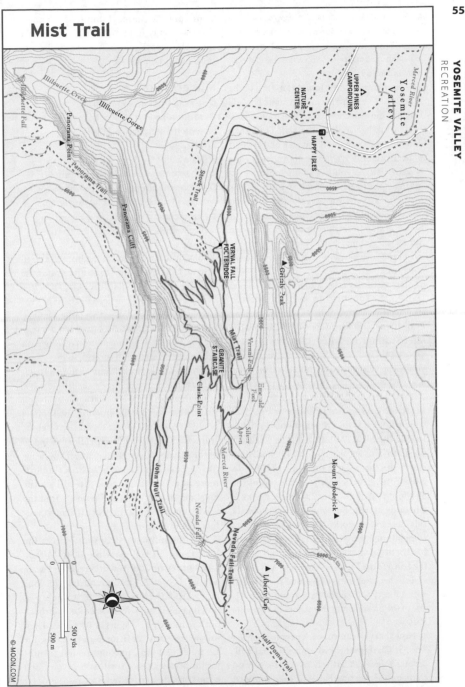

Illilouette Fall

Illilouette Creek

Illilouette Gorge

Merced River

Yosemite Valley

UPPER PINES CAMPGROUND

NATURE CENTER

HAPPY ISLES

Panorama Point

Panorama Trail

Panorama Cliff

Stork Trail

VERNAL FALL FOOTBRIDGE

Grizzly Peak

Mist Trail

Vernal Fall

GRANITE STAIRCASE

Emerald Pool

Clark Point

Silver Apron

Merced River

John Muir Trail

Nevada Fall

Nevada Fall Trail

Mount Broderick

Liberty Cap

Half Dome Trail

0
500 yds
0
500 m

© MOON.COM

free Yosemite Valley shuttle bus to Happy Isles. In winter when the shuttle does not run, you must hike from Half Dome Village, adding 2 miles (3.2 km) to your round-trip. Trails may be closed in winter; call to check weather conditions.

You can hike either the John Muir Trail or the Mist Trail to reach Yosemite's classic Nevada Fall, but the best choice is to make a loop out of it by hiking uphill on the Mist Trail, then downhill partway or all the way on the John Muir Trail. Both trails join above and below Nevada Fall, so you have some options. By hiking uphill rather than downhill on the Mist Trail's treacherous granite staircase, you can look around at the gorgeous scenery every time you stop to catch your breath. The John Muir Trail is somewhat less scenic, especially in its lower reaches, so save it for the way back downhill.

Start at **Happy Isles** and follow the signed trail to the **footbridge** over the Merced River, below Vernal Fall. After crossing the bridge, stay close along the river's edge on the **Mist Trail** for 1.2 miles (1.9 km) to the top of **Vernal Fall.** If it's springtime, make sure you bring your rain gear for this stretch, or you will be drenched in spray. After a brief rest at the waterfall **overlook,** continue along the river's edge, passing a gorgeous stretch of stream known as the **Emerald Pool,** still following the Mist Trail. In 0.5 mile (0.8 km), the path crosses the river again and then climbs another mile to the brink of **Nevada Fall.** Total elevation gain to the top of the 594-foot (191-m) falls is 2,600 feet (790 m), a healthy ascent. But when you get to walk this close to two world-class waterfalls, who's complaining? For your return trip, cross the **footbridge** above Nevada Fall and follow the **John Muir Trail** to loop back. As you descend, check out the great view of Nevada Fall with Liberty Cap in the background. This is one of the most memorable scenes in Yosemite Valley.

Note that you can cut back over to the Mist Trail at Clark Point, just above Vernal Fall, if you so desire. That way, you get a second chance to see Vernal Fall and hike the Mist

Trail's granite staircase. But let your knees decide—plenty of hikers don't want to face those stairsteps a second time, especially in the downhill direction.

Mirror Lake Loop

Distance: 4.6 miles (7.4 km) round-trip
Duration: 2 hours
Elevation Change: 80 feet (24 m)
Effort: Easy
Shuttle Stop: 17
Trailhead: Mirror Lake Junction (see map p. 57)
Directions: From the Arch Rock entrance station on Highway 140, drive 11.6 miles (18.7 km) east to the day-use parking lot at Half Dome Village. Board the free Yosemite Valley shuttle bus to Mirror Lake Junction.

Thousands of Yosemite visitors walk to Mirror Lake every day in summer, but the vast majority of them miss the best part of this hike. The first thing you need to know: Mirror Lake is not really a lake; it's a large, shallow pool in Tenaya Creek. The pool is undergoing the process of sedimentation (filling with sand and gravel from the creek), so every year it shrinks a little more. Many visitors walk up and down this canyon, shake their heads, and ask each other, "Where's Mirror Lake?" If you know what you are looking for, the shallow pool is interesting to see, especially when its still waters produce a lovely reflective image of the granite domes above. But if you leave Mirror Lake behind and head back a mile or more into Tenaya Canyon, you will get the most out of this hike, and perhaps find the kind of quiet nature experience that most visitors seek in Yosemite.

Start by riding the free shuttle from the Half Dome Village parking lot to **Mirror Lake Junction.** (Or walk there, if you wish, adding 1.5 mi/2.4 km round-trip to your hike.) From the bus stop, walk 0.5 mile (0.8 km) on pavement to **Mirror Lake** and check out the interpretive signs at its edges. Then follow the **foot trail** up Tenaya Creek for 1.5 miles (2.4 km), passing the left turnoff for the **Snow Creek Trail.** When you reach a **footbridge** across Tenaya Creek, cross it

Mirror Lake Loop

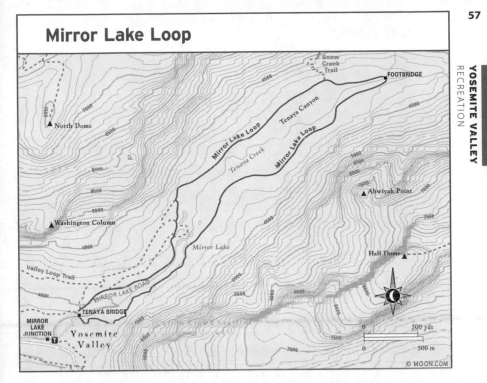

© MOON.COM

and loop back on the other side. Views of Half Dome, Mount Watkins, and their neighboring granite walls are spectacular, and the forested creek canyon presents an intimate amphitheater in which to view them. Find a boulder somewhere, have a seat, and take in the show. This loop trail is nearly level the whole way, and once you go beyond Mirror Lake and into the lower Tenaya Creek Canyon, you are likely to find a little solitude.

TOP EXPERIENCE

Half Dome

Distance: 16 miles (26 km) round-trip
Duration: 8-10 hours
Elevation Change: 4,800 feet (1,465 m)
Effort: Very strenuous
Shuttle Stop: 16
Trailhead: Happy Isles (see map p. 58)
Directions: From the Arch Rock entrance station on Highway 140, drive 11.6 miles (18.7 km) east to the

day-use parking lot at Half Dome Village. Board the free Yosemite Valley shuttle bus to Happy Isles, stop number 16.

No argument about it, Half Dome is one of those once-in-your-life-you-gotta-do-it hikes. Just be sure you know what you're in for before you set out on this epic trail. You're in for 16 miles (26 km) round-trip, a 4,800-foot (1,465-m) elevation gain, and a staggering amount of company.

When to Go: Half Dome's cables are usually in place only from **late May to mid-October,** so that's the only time to attempt the trip.

Permits: During the summer, about 300 people a day make the trek to Half Dome's summit, a number that is strictly regulated by a permit system. The permits are designed to limit the amount of hiker traffic on Half Dome's famous cables. Most hikers make the trek as a day hike, but whether you do it in one day or opt for an overnight backpacking

Half Dome

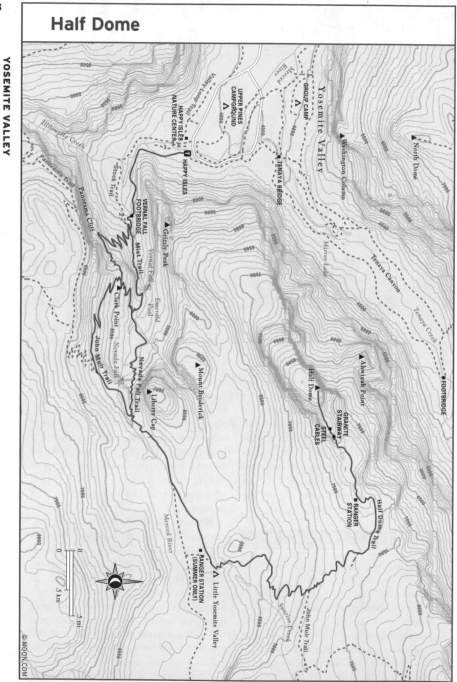

trip, you need to have a permit. Permits are acquired via two lottery processes. The pre-season lottery takes place throughout the month of March, with results announced in mid-April (apply online at www.recreation. gov or by calling 877/444-6777). If you don't succeed in scoring a permit in March, you can try for the daily lottery, which takes place every day the cables are in place. Only 50 permits per day are given out in the daily lottery, and you must apply for a hiking permit two days in advance of your hike.

Planning: Plan on an early-morning start to beat the heat and the possibility of afternoon clouds and/or thundershowers (**5am** is a common start time). Plan on not seeing your car again for about 10-12 hours, during which time you must have everything you need in your day pack. Bring plenty of **water** and **food.** You'll be handing it out to others who are not so well prepared as well as gulping it down yourself. And consider carrying along a pair of **gloves** to keep your hands from slipping or chafing on the cables. (If you forget, you can often find a discarded pair at the base of the cables, left by previous hikers.)

The Hike: Follow either the **John Muir Trail** or the **Mist Trail** from **Happy Isles** to the top of **Nevada Fall** (the Mist Trail is 0.6 mi/1 km) shorter); then turn left and enter **Little Yosemite Valley,** where backpackers make camp. At 6.2 miles (10 km) the John Muir Trail splits off from the **Half Dome Trail;** head left for Half Dome. Just under 2 miles (3.2 km) later you approach Half Dome's shoulder, which is a massive hump affectionately called **Sub Dome.** Here, during almost every single daylight hour, a **ranger** is stationed to make sure that hikers have a permit (hikers without permits are not allowed beyond Sub Dome's base). From this point, a **granite stairway** consisting of about 600 steps leads up the dauntingly steep face of Sub Dome. The views are outstanding, though, so there is plenty of reason to stop and catch your breath. Then the trail descends a bit before reaching the **steel cables** that run 440 feet (134 m) up the back of Half Dome.

This is where many hikers start praying and wishing there weren't so many other hikers on the cables at the same time. Do some soul-searching before you begin the cable ascent—turning around is not a good option once you're halfway up, since you'll create a logjam. Pull on your gloves; you'll need them to protect your hands as you pull yourself up the cables. Arm strength as well as leg strength is required to haul yourself up 440 feet (134 m) of nearly vertical granite.

When you reach the top, the views are so incredible that you forget all about your exertion. There's plenty of room for everyone on top of Half Dome; its vast, mostly flat surface covers about 13 acres (5 hectares).

Backpack option: To make the trip easier, you can camp at **Little Yosemite Valley,** 4.7 miles (7.6 km) in (overnight wilderness permit required), and save the final ascent for the next day. The best part of an overnight trip is that you can access the cables and the summit long before the day hikers arrive. Figure on a little over two hours of hiking from your Little Yosemite Valley campsite to the summit. Then just get up early and go. You'll enjoy a much more peaceful experience.

Inspiration and Stanford Points

Distance: 7.6 miles (12.2 km) round-trip
Duration: 4 hours
Elevation Change: 2,250 feet (685 m)
Effort: Strenuous
Trailhead: Wawona Tunnel (see map p. 60)
Directions: From the Arch Rock entrance station on Highway 140, drive 6.3 miles (10.1 km) east and turn right at the fork for Highway 41/Wawona/Fresno. Continue 1.5 miles (2.4 km) to the parking lots on either side of the road just before the Wawona Tunnel. The trailhead is on the left (south) side of the road.

Many consider the view from Inspiration Point at the entrance to the Wawona Tunnel to be one of the finest scenes in Yosemite—a wide panorama of Yosemite Valley, El Capitan, Half Dome, and Bridalveil Fall. If you like this view, you might want to see more of it by taking this hike from the trailhead at

Inspiration and Stanford Points

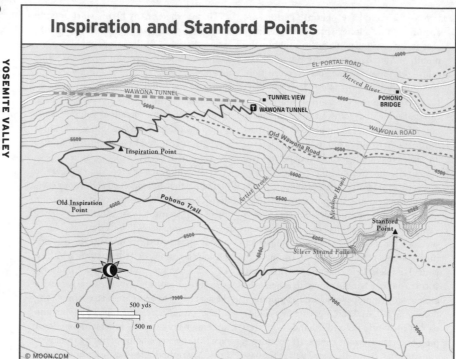

the **vista point parking lot.** The Pohono Trail leads uphill on a moderately steep grade until at 1.3 miles (2.1 km) it reaches the "old" **Inspiration Point.** This is where the road to Yosemite Valley passed through in the days before the Wawona Tunnel, and the view is now largely obscured by trees. Keep climbing, however, because with another 1,000 feet (300 m) of elevation gain, you will cross **Meadow Brook** and reach the left cutoff trail for **Stanford Point.** You're 3.8 miles (6.1 km) from the trailhead and you've climbed 2,200 feet (670 m), but your reward is an eagle's-eye view of the valley floor, 3,000 feet (900 m) below, and a vista to the east of Half Dome and all its granite cousins. This stretch of the Pohono Trail is a dependable workout and the trail is never crowded with hikers.

★ Bridalveil Fall

Distance: 0.5 mile (0.8 km) round-trip
Duration: 30 minutes

Elevation Change: None
Effort: Easy
Trailhead: Bridalveil Fall
Directions: From the Arch Rock entrance station on Highway 140, drive 6.3 miles (10.1 km) east and turn right at the fork for Highway 41/Wawona/Fresno. Turn left almost immediately into the Bridalveil Fall parking lot. The trail begins at the far end of the parking lot. If you are driving into Yosemite Valley on Highway 41 from the south, watch for the Bridalveil Fall turnoff on your right about 1 mile (1.6 km) after you exit the Wawona Tunnel.

Bridalveil Fall is right up there with Lower Yosemite Fall as a must-do walk for visitors (including non-hikers) to Yosemite Valley. Like that other famous waterfall walk, the path to Bridalveil Fall is paved with people. But the best thing about this waterfall is that, unlike other falls in Yosemite Valley, Bridalveil runs year-round. It never dries up and disappoints visitors. The walk to its **overlook** is short and nearly level; the trail

Four-Mile Trail

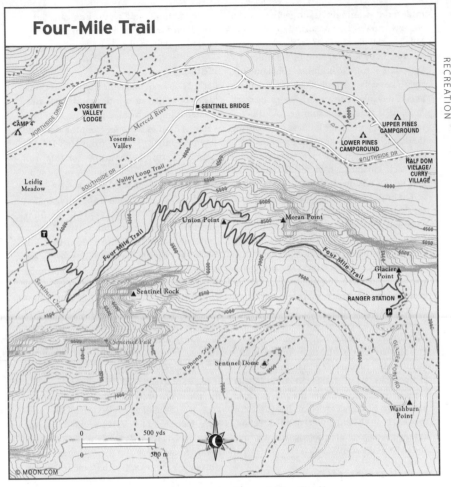

delivers you to a small **viewing area** about 150 feet (45 m) from the fall. You can look straight up and see Bridalveil Creek plunging 620 feet (189 m) off the edge of the south canyon wall. In high wind the fall billows and sways; if you are lucky you might see rainbows dancing in its mist. Another bonus is that your position at the Bridalveil overlook is such that if you do an about-face, you have an excellent view of Ribbon Fall flowing off the north rim of Yosemite Valley. At 1,612 feet (491 m), Ribbon Fall is the highest single drop in the park, but it only flows during the peak snowmelt months of spring.

Four-Mile Trail

Distance: 9.6 miles (15.5 km) round-trip
Duration: 5-6 hours
Elevation Change: 3,200 feet (975 m)
Effort: Strenuous
Trailhead: Four-Mile (see map p. 61)
Directions: From the Arch Rock entrance station on Highway 140, drive 9.5 miles (15.3 km) east to the Four-Mile Trailhead, next to mile marker V18 on the right side of Southside Drive. Park in the pullouts along the road.

Although the vast majority of Yosemite visitors get to Glacier Point by driving there, your arrival at this dramatic overlook is somehow made more meaningful if you get there under your own power. That means hiking the Four-Mile Trail all the way up from the valley floor, gaining 3,200 feet (975 m) in 4.8 miles (7.7 km)—not 4 miles (6.4 km), as the name implies. The trail is partially shaded and makes a terrific day hike with an early-morning start. A bonus is that in the summer months the snack stand on Glacier Point is open during the day, so you can hike to the top with a light day pack and then order whatever you want for lunch. Go ahead, have the chili dog—the hike back is all downhill.

The trail is remarkably well graded, and surprisingly, sections of it are paved, or partially paved. After the first mile or so, the trail breaks out from the trees and delivers nonstop views every step of the way. The big reward comes when you reach **Glacier Point,** where you have unobstructed views of just about every major landmark in Yosemite Valley, most notably Half Dome, Basket Dome, Yosemite Falls, Vernal and Nevada Falls, and the valley floor far, far below you.

Note that you'll see many more people hiking downhill on this trail than uphill; that's because they've ridden the tour bus to Glacier Point so that they can make the one-way hike back down to the valley floor. But honestly, this trail is much better in the uphill direction, as the amazing views unfold with every turn and twist in the trail.

BACKPACKING

Although the hiking trails in Yosemite Valley are most heavily used by day hikers, several trails begin in the Valley and lead out of it to overnight camping destinations. Far and away the most popular of these is the busy trail from Happy Isles. Every day in summer, day hikers swarm the trail to Vernal and Nevada Falls, and many continue on for the long trek to Half Dome.

No matter where you decide to go, remember that if you want to strap on a backpack and spend the night in Yosemite's wilderness, you must have a **permit** (209/372-0740, www.nps.gov/yose/planyourvisit/wildpermits.htm).

Backpackers must always use bear canisters to store their food for overnight trips. Hanging food from trees is illegal in Yosemite.

Half Dome

Backpackers can make the trip to Half Dome easier by splitting it into two days. A designated camp is located at Little Yosemite Valley, 4.7 miles (7.6 km) from the start and about 3.5 miles (5.6 km) from Half Dome's summit. Permit reservations for this trail are nearly impossible to come by in the summer months, so you need to plan early. A less crowded and perhaps more appealing option for Half Dome backpackers is to continue past this camp on the John Muir Trail—heading toward **Tuolumne Meadows**—or follow the other fork toward **Merced Lake.** Backpackers are permitted to set up camp as long as they are at least 2 miles (3.2 km) from Little Yosemite Valley. Either one of these options offers lovely scenery, although of course they add time and distance to the next day's summit ascent.

Snow Creek Trail

If you want to get away from the crowds, take the **Snow Creek Trail** from the Mirror Lake area up and out of the Valley. Of all the pathways that ascend the Valley's high walls, this one is the steepest. It heads up switchbacks toward Snow Creek and then gains the north rim of the Valley near North Dome and Basket Dome. You must travel at least 4 miles (6.4 km) beyond the Yosemite Valley floor before camping.

Yosemite Falls

Although you can't camp at the top of Yosemite Falls, you can take a backpack trip up the **Upper Yosemite Fall Trail,** visit the waterfall's exhilarating brink, and then continue on to **Eagle Peak, El Capitan,** or **North Dome.** As long as you are 4 miles (6.4 km) from the Yosemite Valley floor and 1 mile (1.6 km) from the top of Yosemite Falls, you can make camp.

BIKING

The **Yosemite Valley bike path** is the best way to escape the car trap in the Valley. With 12 miles (19.3 km) of smooth, paved bike paths to ride, you can see the entire Valley without once having to worry about where to park.

You can start your bike tour of Yosemite Valley from just about anywhere. The bike path runs right past Yosemite Valley Lodge and Half Dome Village and parallels the stretch of Northside and Southside Drives that runs between the two lodging facilities. If you wish, you can make stops at the trailheads for Lower Yosemite Fall and Mirror Lake. If you are on a rental bike, you are not permitted to ride your bike down the hill from Mirror Lake; there are too many pedestrians in this area, and their safety is a concern. Go ahead and ride your bike up this hill, then park it in the bike rack and take a stroll around Mirror Lake. Then walk your bike back down. When you reach the flat stretch at the bottom, go ahead and start pedaling.

One of the best lengths of the looping bike path is on the western end, where it crosses the picturesque Swinging Bridge over the Merced River and provides a straight-on view of billowing Yosemite Falls. Now isn't this better than driving a car?

Bike Rentals

Didn't bring your bike? No problem—you can rent one at **Yosemite Valley Lodge** or **Half Dome Village Recreation Center** (209/372-1208 or 209/372-8323, 9am-6pm daily spring and fall, 8am-8pm daily summer) for $12.50 per hour or $30.50 per day. They have bikes for men, women, and children, plus bikes with trailers for the little ones ($19 per hour), as well as baby strollers. The rental bikes are cruiser models that anyone can ride, even if you haven't been on a bike in years. They have no gears to fiddle with, and they are equipped with coaster brakes (you simply pedal backward to stop). Helmets come with all rentals. Remember that bikes are not allowed on any dirt trails in Yosemite Valley;

keep your bike on the paved paths and roads and you won't risk getting a ticket.

FISHING

Planning on going trout fishing in Yosemite Valley? Don't waste your time. Oh, sure, plenty of people drop a line in the Merced River and then sit down and admire the scenery. But if you want to actually catch fish, head just outside the park boundaries and you'll have a greater chance at success.

The Merced River in Yosemite Valley has been hit with a ton of fishing pressure over the course of many decades, and the few trout that live here are wary and smart. These waters are home to some of California's most challenging brown trout, plus a small population of native rainbows (the remaining native rainbow trout are protected by catch-and-release-only regulations). Although the planting of brown trout was suspended throughout the entire park in 1948, brown trout still thrive in the Merced and are occasionally caught, but only by the wiliest of anglers. Generally, the best luck is had very early in the morning or just before nightfall.

Trout season runs from the last Saturday in April until November 15 in all park rivers and streams. (Yosemite's lakes may be fished year-round, but it isn't easy to get to them through 10 feet/3 meters of snow.) A valid California **fishing license** is required for all anglers 16 and older and must be visibly displayed on an outer layer of clothing above the angler's waist. Licenses can be purchased at the Yosemite Village Store, the Wawona Store, and the Tuolumne Meadows Store. One-day ($15), two-day ($24), and 10-day licenses ($47) are available for California residents and nonresidents, in addition to annual licenses ($47-126).

From Happy Isles downstream to the Foresta Bridge in El Portal, no bait fishing is allowed—it's **catch-and-release** only using artificial flies and lures with barbless hooks. All rainbow trout must be released; a limit of five brown trout may be taken per day. No fishing is permitted from park bridges.

Half Dome Permits

Permits to hike to the top of Half Dome are **required seven days per week.** A maximum of 300 hikers are allowed per day on the Half Dome Trail beyond the granite formation known as Sub Dome. Of those 300 hikers, approximately 225 are day hikers and 75 are backpackers. Permits are distributed by lottery via the website www.recreation.gov. A preseason lottery, held in March, is supplemented by daily lotteries during the hiking season.

COSTS

A nonrefundable fee of $6 is charged when you submit an application. A second fee of $10 per person is charged only if you win the lottery and will receive a permit. Call for more information about daily Half Dome permits (209/372-0826, 9am-4:30pm Mon.-Fri. May-Sept.).

PRESEASON LOTTERY (MAR.)

Half Dome day hikers can apply for up to **six permits** (six people maximum). Each lottery application allows for a choice of up to **seven dates.** Hikers who choose dates that fall from **Monday through Thursday** have a much better chance of winning than hikers who choose Friday, Saturday, and Sunday dates, when demand is much higher. Applications are taken **online March 1-31** (www.recreation.gov). Lottery results are announced by email in **mid-April.**

How to Apply

On each application, a **trip leader** and **alternate trip leader** must be designated. Each person may apply as a trip leader only once per lottery. (People applying multiple times as trip leader will have all their lottery applications canceled.) Preseason applications are successful if the number of permits requested are available on at least one of the requested dates. If permits are available for more than one of the requested dates, they are automatically awarded to the **highest priority date,** as specified by the applicant. Permits are valid only if the trip leader and/or alternate leader is accompanying the group using the permits. The trip leader must carry a photo ID and show up together with his or her entire group at the base of Sub Dome, where **rangers check for permits.** Permits are not transferable. Any resale or auction of permits will make the permit/contract null and void.

West of the Park: Highway 140

Fishing opportunities abound if you're willing to drive a few miles out of the park on Highway 140. The Merced River below Yosemite, from **El Portal** to the **Briceburg** area, is filled with beautiful wild rainbow trout. Much of the river is a designated native trout area, which means only barbless hooks are permitted, and fishing is catch-and-release only. Tim Hutchins of **Yosemite Fly Fishing** offers guided half- and full-day fishing trips and fly-fishing instruction on the Merced River (209/379-2746 or 209/769-5534, www.yosemiteflyfishing.net). Trips include lessons, equipment, and lunch. For a half-day trip, the first person pays $405 and each additional person pays $50.

If you would rather fish the Merced on your own, the El Portal area just outside the Arch Rock entrance is best in the autumn. Flies with barbless hooks are required. Anglers can also head farther west on the river to the Briceburg Visitor Center. Cross over the river on the old bridge; leave your car near one of the primitive campgrounds. Hike along the dirt road (the old bed of the Yosemite Railroad) as far as you wish and drop your line in any inviting pool. Brown and rainbow trout are found in these waters, but since this is a designated wild trout area, all the usual rules apply.

RAFTING

On any warm early-summer day in Yosemite you can take a drive up to Glacier Point, look down over its mighty edge, and see a flotilla

DAILY LOTTERY (MAY-OCT.)

Hikers who didn't enter or succeed in the preseason lottery can try their luck at the daily lottery. Approximately 50 day-hiking permits are available each day by lottery during the hiking season. The lottery is open for 13 hours each day (midnight-1pm PST). If you are trying for the daily lottery, you have a much better chance (56 percent) of winning the lottery on a weekday. Only 31 percent of hikers who try for a weekend day will get a permit.

How to Apply

To apply for a daily lottery permit, go to www.recreation.gov or call 877/444-6777. For the daily lottery you must apply online two days prior to your desired hiking date, and you will be notified of the lottery results late the same night. (So, to hike on Saturday, you would apply on Thursday and receive an email notification of results late Thursday night.) Results are also available online or by phone the next morning.

hikers ascending the Half Dome cables

BACKPACKING

Hikers who want to climb Half Dome as part of an overnight trip need to follow a completely different process, they must obtain a wilderness permit (www.nps.gov/yose/planyourvisit/wpres.htm) for backpacking and request a Half Dome permit for hiking to the summit. Permits for overnight trips can be obtained up to 24 weeks in advance by filling out the online wilderness permit request form at www.yosemiteconservancy.org.

of rafters drifting lazily downstream on the Merced River. Lazily? Yes, indeed. This is not river rafting as most people think of it. "River meandering" would be a better term.

Still, rafting is one of the greatest ways to see Yosemite Valley in early summer, with no traffic jams and no need for constant vigilance over oblivious pedestrians. Rafting is a matter of simply lying on your back, trailing a few fingers in the water, and gazing up at the granite walls as you float by. Sadly, the rafting season in Yosemite Valley is painfully short. The water level isn't usually low enough to be safe until late May or early June, and the season ends when the river gets too low and the rafts start scraping the river bottom, which is usually in late July.

Inflatable rafts can be rented at Half Dome Village Recreation Center (209/372-4386 or 209/372-8323, www.travelyosemite.com, 10am-4pm daily, $30 per person, rafts hold 2-4 people); the put-in point is nearby. Rental rafts come complete with mandatory life jackets and paddles, although you are unlikely to need the former and you will only make minimal use of the latter. You float 3 miles (4.8 km) downstream and then ride a shuttle bus back to your starting point. The whole adventure takes 3-4 hours. Children under 50 pounds (23 kg) are not permitted on rafts.

If you have your own inflatable raft or inner tube, you can bring it to the park and float on your own from 10am to 6pm. For $5.50, you can catch the shuttle back to your starting point. Life jackets are mandatory;

if you didn't bring one, you can rent one for $5.50 per person.

While you're out on the water, remember to protect the beautiful Merced River. If you choose to disembark, do so only on sandy beaches or gravel bars. Stay away from vegetated stream banks to protect the delicate riparian habitat.

West of the Park: Highway 140

If you'd like to try true, shoot-the-rapids, adrenaline-pumping, thrills-and-chills river rafting, you need only drive a few miles outside of Yosemite Valley to the section of the **Wild and Scenic Merced River** below El Portal. This is one of the most popular river rafting runs in the Sierra, mostly because it packs a whole lot of excitement into a one-day trip. The 16 miles (26 km) of river below El Portal include several rollercoaster-like Class III and IV rapids, interspersed with calm sections where rafters can catch their breath (or hold a water fight with their friends). For one-day trips, the put-in is near **Redbud Picnic Area** and the take-out is at Railroad Flat, below Briceburg Visitor Center. A few outfitters also offer half-day trips on the Merced, covering 11 river miles (18 km). Adventurous beginners and intermediates can easily handle the one-day and half-day trips; the minimum age is usually 9-12 years, depending on water levels. Two-day trips are popular for more experienced rafters; these trips run from Redbud to Lake McClure.

The rafting season on the Merced usually begins in **mid-April,** depending on snow runoff. Several private companies offer rafting trips daily from mid-April through July, when the water level usually drops too low. Trips include lunch, parking, wetsuits when the water is cold, and a round-trip bus shuttle to and from the river. Typical rates for one-day trips are $149-189 per person. For more information, contact **All-Outdoors California Whitewater Rafting** (800/247-2387, www. aorafting.com), **Zephyr Whitewater** (800/431-3636, www.zrafting.com), or **OARS Inc.** (800/346-6277, www.oars.com).

ROCK CLIMBING

Yosemite is well known as a mecca for rock climbers. But even experienced climbers who have tackled high walls in parks and public lands near their homes are sometimes daunted when they get their first look at Yosemite Valley's massive vertical walls. If you don't have experience with granite crack climbing or traditional climbing, you might want to consider utilizing **Yosemite Mountaineering School and Guide Service** (Half Dome Village, 209/372-8344, www.travelyosemite.com, classes 8:30am daily mid-Apr.-Oct., $145-170), which conducts seminars and classes for beginning, intermediate, and advanced climbers; equipment rentals are available. Private guided climbs lasting up to six hours are also available ($283 per person for individuals or $163 per person for groups of three). The school is in the Mountain Shop at Half Dome Village.

If you decide to set out on your own, be aware that the few "easier grade" climbs in Yosemite are quite popular. If you don't start early in the morning, you may be forced to wait in line. The greatest numbers of climbers hit the Valley in May and then again in September and October. The walls are less crowded in the summer when the temperatures are high.

Experienced climbers visiting the Valley for the first time should head for the **Royal Arches** (just east of the Majestic Yosemite Hotel), the southeast face of **Half Dome,** and a climb known as **Munginella** near Yosemite Falls. These climbs are mostly rated 5.6 and 5.7, but many find them more difficult than their ratings indicate. El Capitan is *definitely* not recommended for first-timers, or even many "experienced" intermediate climbers, although El Cap has a few routes that are much easier than others.

1: rafting the Merced River **2:** the tour and rental desk at Yosemite Valley Lodge **3:** view of Half Dome

Half Dome's First Mountaineers

Anyone making the epic trek to the bald summit of 8,836-foot (2,693-m) Half Dome will at some point in the journey begin to wonder about those who have gone before. Perhaps the most interesting of the Half Dome mountaineers is the man who did it first—despite Josiah Whitney's claim that the summit would never be conquered. "Never has been, and never will be trodden by human foot," said the famous geologist in 1868.

The man who proved Whitney wrong was **George Anderson,** a Scot who worked in Yosemite Valley as a laborer from 1870 until his death in 1884. In October 1875 he drilled holes and inserted a series of bolts and pegs into the hard granite on the dome's back side. Upward he worked, standing on each new bolt as he drilled in the next, a few feet higher. At 3pm on October 12, he made it to the top and then carefully made his way back down. A few days later he ascended Half Dome again, this time with a huge coil of rope on his back. He knotted one end to a bolt on the summit, then started downward and secured the remainder of the rope to each of the bolt "stairsteps." This rope ladder was the predecessor of today's steel cables.

Within a few weeks, several other brave souls made the ascent to the summit of Half Dome, using Anderson's rope ladder to pull themselves up. **Galen Clark** and **John Muir** were two of the first dozen people, as was pioneer **Sally Dutcher,** who goes down in history as the first woman to climb Half Dome.

Those who enjoy **bouldering** will find plenty of it on the rocks around Camp 4. Other popular bouldering areas are found near Cathedral Rocks (directly across from El Capitan, on the south side of the Valley and just east of Bridalveil Fall) and the Majestic Yosemite Hotel.

If you'd rather **watch rock climbers** than be a rock climber, congratulate yourself on your levelheadedness and head to El Capitan Meadow, where with a pair of binoculars you can watch the slow progress of climbers heading up the face of **El Capitan.** Ever since this 3,593-foot (1,095-m) rock face was conquered in the 1950s, bold successors have inched their way to the top. Most take anywhere between three and five days to do so; they spend their nights sleeping on ledges or tethered into hammocks. However, brazen new "speed climbers" have completed the ascent of "The Nose" at El Cap in a couple of hours. A record of 1 hour, 58 minutes, and 7 seconds was set by Tommy Caldwell and Alex Honnold in June 2018.

Swan Slab across from Yosemite Valley Lodge (between the Lower Yosemite Fall parking lot and Camp 4) is another good place to watch climbers strut their stuff.

If you'd like to learn more about Yosemite climbing, head over to the El Capitan Bridge and have a chat with one of the **Yosemite Climbing Rangers.** The "Ask a Climber" program (11am-3pm daily in summer) is a gathering for rangers, climbers, curious onlookers, and anyone who has questions about Yosemite's rocks.

SWIMMING

From **mid-July to late September,** plenty of swimming holes can be found along the Merced River's sandy beaches on the Valley's east end, especially near Housekeeping Camp and the Pines campgrounds in an area called **Sentinel Beach.** The sandy bars found here are ideal for lounging along the river and are also the most ecologically sound spots for entering and exiting the water. In the interest of protecting the Merced's fragile shoreline, always stay off grassy meadow areas.

Avoid spring and early summer, when swimming anywhere in the Merced River is a very bad idea—the current can be much stronger than it looks. The same is true for the pools above Vernal and Nevada Falls, Illilouette Fall, and Upper Yosemite Fall. Although the water looks tempting after a hot and sweaty hike, even in late summer the current above these waterfalls can be deceptively swift—even deadly.

Guests staying at Yosemite Valley Lodge and Half Dome Village can enjoy the use of the facilities' **swimming pools** (Memorial Day to Labor Day, $5 adults, $4 children for nonguests) at no charge. The Majestic Yosemite Hotel has a swimming pool, but it is off-limits to nonguests.

WINTER SPORTS

At Half Dome Village, you can practice your figure eights on an **outdoor ice-skating rink** daily from approximately late November to March (209/372-8319, weather permitting, $11 adults, $10 children). The original Curry Village skating rink had a long history in Yosemite Valley; it was started in 1928 by the Yosemite Park and Curry Company. The current rink, which first opened in winter 2016, is modular and can be easily removed when the season is over. Sessions are held in the afternoons and evenings on weekdays and from morning until evening on weekends. Ice skate rentals ($5) are available and helmets are free upon request. If you find yourself falling down more often than performing graceful pirouettes, head for the warming hut's fire pit and snack stand and treat yourself to a cup of hot chocolate.

If you prefer winter footwear that's more stable than the thin blades on ice skates, **snowshoe rentals** ($21 half day, $24 full day) are available at the **Mountain Shop at Half Dome Village** (9am-5pm daily). However, the Valley rarely has enough snow for snowshoeing, except in the canyon beyond Mirror Lake. You may have to carry your snowshoes as you walk up the paved road to the lake and then strap them on when you hit the trail. A 4-mile (6.4-km) loop can be made from Mirror Lake up Tenaya Canyon. It's a delightful surprise to see this area when it's peaceful, serene, and snow-covered (compared to the summer when it's packed with sightseers).

Alternatively, you can take your rental snowshoes up to the giant sequoias in **Tuolumne Grove** or **Merced Grove** and meander among the trees. If you don't want to snowshoe by yourself, check the free Yosemite newspaper for guided events. In the winter months, park rangers and/or naturalists often lead **snowshoe walks** in the Valley, in the sequoia groves, or at Yosemite's ski area. The most popular of these are the full-moon walks offered 3-4 nights each month.

If you are staying in Yosemite Valley and would like to take advantage of the **downhill skiing** and **snowboarding** opportunities at **Yosemite Ski & Snowboard Area** on Glacier Point Road, you don't have to drive your car and risk icy conditions on the roads. Buses for Glacier Point leave from Yosemite Valley Lodge (209/372-1240 or 209/372-8323) every morning and return in the afternoon; check with the lodge tour desk for exact times.

Entertainment and Shopping

RANGER TALKS AND WALKS

Ranger walks take place daily in Yosemite Valley. Typical subjects include Yosemite's indigenous people, bears, waterfalls, rock climbing, birds, and geology. Walks leave from various locations—the campgrounds, visitors center, Happy Isles, and other Valley trailheads—throughout the day. Ranger walks are free; no reservations are necessary. The park concessionaire and the Yosemite Mountaineering School also lead fee-based **group hikes** ($20-75 per person, depending on the length of the trip). Ranger-led sit-down programs are held year-round at the **Lower Pines Campground Amphitheater** every summer morning at 8am ("Coffee with a Ranger") and every evening at 8:30pm. Visit or phone the Yosemite Valley visitors center (209/372-8615) to confirm the schedule.

Evening Programs

Often led by people other than park rangers, evening programs include films and presentations on subjects ranging from Ansel Adams to rock climbing to the building of the Majestic Yosemite Hotel. Evening programs are usually conducted simultaneously at the **Half Dome Village Amphitheater** and **Yosemite Valley Lodge Amphitheater.** Most programs start at 7:30pm or 8:30pm. Information, times, and locations for these talks are published in the Valley newspaper and posted at the visitors center. During the winter, programs are held indoors at Yosemite Valley Lodge and the Majestic Yosemite Hotel.

Run by the Sierra Club, the **Yosemite Conservation Heritage Center** (previously LeConte Memorial Lodge, shuttle stop 12, 209/372-4542) offers programs on summer evenings. Typical offerings include presentations and talks on John Muir, Hetch Hetchy Valley, Yosemite's indigenous people, Frederick Olmsted, wildflower identification, and general programs on Yosemite and other national parks. The center also runs a series of programs geared toward children and families.

Evening Walking Tours

For people interested in learning about the night sky, the **Starry Skies** program is offered every summer night in Yosemite Valley (209/372-1153, $10 per person, 9pm in summer, 8:30pm in winter) and on weekend nights in winter. During the one-hour walking tour, a naturalist explains the constellations visible over Yosemite Valley. Space is limited and reservations are required. **Night Prowl** guided one-hour evening hikes are also available (209/372-1153, $10 per person, 9pm in summer, 8pm in winter). This family-oriented tour is led by a naturalist who talks about the nightlife of Yosemite's animals.

★ YOSEMITE THEATER

Various programs are scheduled at the **Yosemite Theater** (Yosemite Village, www.yosemiteconservancy.org, 7pm nightly May-Oct., less often in winter, $10 adults, children 12 and under free), but actor **Lee Stetson** (Wed.-Thurs.) always steals the show. Stetson has been portraying naturalist John Muir at the Yosemite Theater since 1983. He acts out a handful of rotating programs, during which

Yosemite visitors can take advantage of free ranger talks offered every summer day.

he puts on a convincing Scottish brogue and becomes the voice of Muir for an hour or so. The theater sets the scene perfectly: It is small, intimate, and casual enough for hiking boots.

Other performances include shows on Yosemite's search-and-rescue program, *Return to Balance: A Climber's Journey,* and *Yosemite Through the Eyes of a Buffalo Soldier,* which details the history of African American soldiers who protected Yosemite in the early 1900s. Tickets are available at any tour desk in Yosemite, or you can buy them outside the theater (behind the Valley Visitor Center) before the show if seats are still available.

ANSEL ADAMS GALLERY

The **Ansel Adams Gallery** (Yosemite Village, 209/372-4413, www.anseladams.com or www.travelyosemite.com, 9am-5pm daily) sponsors four-hour **photography classes** ($95 per person, 10 people max) a few days each week. "In the Footsteps of Ansel Adams" is a guided tour with an experienced photographer-teacher. Students carry their cameras with them and learn how to take Yosemite landscape and nature photos. "Using Your Digital Camera" is an instructional class focused on proper exposure, depth of field, shutter speed, and more. Multiday workshops and private photography tours are also available. Make reservations in person at the gallery or by phone.

HAPPY ISLES ART AND NATURE CENTER

Yosemite's **art center,** previously in Yosemite Village, has been moved to the **Happy Isles visitors center** (209/372-0631, www.yosemiteconservancy.org, adult classes April-Oct., children's classes June-Aug., 9:30am-4:30pm Mon.-Sat.). This wonderful facility offers low-cost art workshops that focus on nature sketching, watercolors, plein air painting, and silk-screening. The adult classes focus on a different medium each week—acrylics, pastels, watercolors, and more. Kids' classes are offered Mon.-Thurs. in summer; classes are different each day but often feature craft-making from natural objects like pinecones, journaling, or watercolor painting. Classes typically last four hours and cost $10-20 per person per day. Art supplies are sold at the center, so you don't need to bring your brushes with you.

EVENTS

Bracebridge Dinner

Heading the bill each winter at **The Majestic Yosemite Hotel** is the annual **Bracebridge Dinner** (www.bracebridgedinners.com, reservations at 888/413-8869 or www.travelyosemite.com, $430 adult, $236 children under 12, select evenings in Dec.), a lavish 18th-century English Christmas celebration featuring more than 100 performers and a seven-course feast. The pricy but spectacular event, a loose adaptation of an episode from Washington Irving's *Sketch Book,* has been held every year at the Ahwahnee/Majestic Yosemite Hotel since 1927. The four-hour dinner show features Middle Ages music, Renaissance rituals, traditional yuletide decorations, and plentiful food, song, and mirth. The event takes place on only about a dozen nights in mid- to late December, so tickets often sell out fast. Many Bracebridge guests purchase a package that includes dinner tickets and one night's lodging at Yosemite Valley Lodge or the Majestic Yosemite Hotel (rates with lodging start at $645 per person, double occupancy). Is it worth the hefty price tag? Absolutely yes.

Grand Grape Celebration and A Taste of Yosemite (FORMERLY VINTNERS' AND CHEFS' HOLIDAYS)

Although the annual Bracebridge Dinner is the most famous winter event in Yosemite Valley, two other popular events are the Grand Grape Celebration and A Taste of Yosemite, in which California's finest winemakers and chefs showcase their creations.

The Grand Grape Celebration, a toast to winemakers' fall harvests, takes place on select days in November. Offerings include

Ansel Adams: Yosemite Visionary

One of Yosemite Valley's most famous residents was Ansel Adams, the great photographer who captured Yosemite and many other national parks and beautiful landscapes in complex and delicate shades of black and white. Although most people are familiar with Adams's famous photographs, fewer realize that the man had another well-developed talent: He was a concert-quality pianist. He met his wife, Virginia Best, because her father, painter Harry Best, owned one of only two pianos in Yosemite Valley and allowed Adams to practice there. Virginia and Adams were married in 1928 at Best's Studio, which is now the Ansel Adams Gallery. When Harry Best died, his daughter and son-in-law took over the studio.

Adams made his first trip to Yosemite when he was only 14 years old. It was 1916, and his parents gave him a Box Brownie camera that he used to take his first pictures of Yosemite. A few years later he moved to the Valley to run the Sierra Club's LeConte Memorial Lodge (now the Yosemite Conservation Heritage Center). He led hikes throughout the Valley and into the backcountry; in doing so, he developed a deep understanding of the nuances of light and shadow in the Sierra. Later he worked as a commercial photographer, shooting pictures for the Curry Company. Many of Adams's images of skiers and toboggan riders are on display at the Majestic Yosemite Hotel.

Adams's love of the camera won out over his musical ability, and over the years he started to shoot and sell more of his own artistic work. He was also a great conservationist and used his talent to photograph places that needed the attention of the federal government for protection and preservation. In 1934, he was elected to the Sierra Club Board of Directors, a position he held for 37 years. Soon after, the National Park Service hired him to photograph several national parks.

Adams and his wife continued to live in Yosemite Valley until the 1960s, when they moved to Carmel, California. The great photographer died in April 1984, but visitors can still find his spirit, and his photographs, at the **Ansel Adams Gallery** in Yosemite Village.

three-day sessions of wine-tasting seminars, chitchat with the vintners, and a gala five-course dinner with carefully paired wines ($208 per person for a three-day session; lodging is additional).

Also in November is **A Taste of Yosemite,** when California's finest chefs strut their stuff in a three-day epicurean event. Sessions include a meet-and-mingle reception, a cooking skills demonstration, and a five-course dinner ($208 per person for a three-day session; lodging is additional). Attendees are usually allowed insider access to the Majestic Yosemite Hotel's kitchen. Beneath its 35-foot (11-m) ceilings are culinary antiques like the hotel's original 1927 walk-in refrigerators, which were kept cool with 500-pound (225-kg) blocks of ice from nearby Mirror Lake.

Ticket and lodging packages are available for both events (888/413-8869, www.travelyosemite.com, starting at $325 per night, double occupancy).

New Year's Eve

Every year, guests ring in the New Year in classic style with a lavish six-course dinner, live music, and dancing at the **Majestic Yosemite Hotel** (888/413-8869, www.travelyosemite.com, $225 per person). Reservations for this black-tie event sell out early.

SHOPPING

No matter where they happen to be, some people just have to go shopping. If you fall into that category, you'll find some excellent browsing and buying opportunities at these Valley establishments. The shops in the Valley have shorter hours in winter.

Yosemite Village

The **Village Store** (209/372-1253, 8am-10pm daily in summer) is a huge general merchandise store that has an amazing selection of groceries and just about everything else you can think of, from camping supplies and hiking socks to clothing, magazines, and souvenirs. Plus, the store has a convenient parking lot right out front.

Over at Yosemite Valley Lodge, the **Yosemite Valley Lodge Gift and Grocery Store** (no phone, 8am-10pm daily in summer) is a convenient choice if you need an extra sweatshirt or some shaving cream. It also carries enough snacks, beverages, and picnic supplies to hold you over until dinner. The store sells plenty of souvenir trinkets here, too—key chains, mugs, and stuffed animals—but for more interesting take-home gifts, head over to the **Yosemite Museum Store** (Yosemite Village, no phone, 9am-5pm daily). The museum sells Native American arts and crafts, plus an extensive collection of books. Or take home a beautiful photograph from the **Ansel Adams Gallery** (209/372-4413, www.anseladams.com, 9am-6pm daily summer). The gallery also offers an expansive selection of film, digital photography supplies, and camera and tripod rentals. Photography workshops are offered daily in summer.

The Majestic Yosemite Hotel
(FORMERLY AHWAHNEE HOTEL)

At the **Majestic Yosemite Hotel Gift Shop** (no phone, 8am-10pm daily in summer), you can purchase the Majestic Yosemite Hotel's very own china (a fresh set, not the one they used for last night's dinner). In addition, the shop has a large and varied selection of Native American art and jewelry and Yosemite art and photographs. In the winter months, this is a great place to purchase unique Christmas ornaments and decorations. The neighboring **Sweet Shop** (no phone, 7am-10pm daily in summer) has more than just sweets; it's also a good bet for wines, picnic foods, and greeting cards.

Half Dome Village
(FORMERLY CURRY VILLAGE)

The **Mountain Shop at Half Dome Village** (no phone, 8am-8pm daily in summer) is a miniature version of REI, with everything an outdoor adventurer could need. If you are considering buying the newest kind of water purifier or the latest high-tech sleeping bag, this store probably carries it, and the employees will know each product's pros and cons. Prices are about the same as you'd find at any high-quality outdoor store.

Half Dome Village also has a small grocery store, but for serious groceries, it's best to head to the Village Store. If you are looking for just the basics, there's always the **Housekeeping Camp Store** (shuttle stop 12, Southside Dr., no phone, 8am-7pm daily Apr.-Oct.). If your cooler is out of ice or you need a few postcards, you'll find them here.

Food

Without fail, the busiest locations in Yosemite Valley are the places that serve food. Judging from the lines out the door of most of the Valley's dining establishments, you might think that people came to this national park just to grab a meal. Or perhaps the lines are due to Yosemite's sweet mountain air making visitors hungry.

The Valley offers a wide range of food choices, and most are several steps up from blackened hot dogs and marshmallows at a Camp 4 campsite. Four central areas of the Valley serve food in either sit-down or carryout form: Yosemite Valley Lodge, Yosemite Village, Half Dome Village, and the Majestic Yosemite Hotel. If you're visiting in the summer season, you'll find that most food establishments are open only until 9pm. This means if you're up at Glacier Point for sunset during the long days of summer, you may have trouble getting back down to the Valley in time for dinner. Plan carefully. Thankfully, the Half Dome Village Pizza Patio stays open until 10pm. For current hours of operation for all the in-park restaurants, call 209/372-1001 (hours change seasonally).

INSIDE THE PARK
Yosemite Village

Yosemite Village (shuttle stops 2 and 10) has a few options. **Degnan's Kitchen** (888/413-8869, 7am-6pm daily in summer, 7am-5pm daily in winter, $7-9) is a busy place at lunchtime. Since the new park concessionaire Aramark took over in 2016, what was once a simple sandwich-and-potato-chip shop is now a somewhat more refined dining experience. Sandwiches are still the main event, but they're made with lots of creative and locally grown ingredients. The kitchen also offers freshly baked breads (including gluten-free choices), fruit smoothies, espresso, and wine and beer. Upstairs, **The Loft at Degnan's** is open from noon to 9pm daily, serving artisan pizza, Mexican food, Asian rice bowls, craft beer, and wine. If you need to find out how your favorite Major League Baseball team is doing, this is the place—the televisions show sports channels all day.

The Village Grill (11am-8pm daily Apr.-Oct., $8-12) serves hamburgers (including a grass-fed option), veggie burgers, fish sandwiches, and other fast-food items. There are no tables inside, so patrons eat out on the deck. There's nothing quite like a Village Grill milk shake on a hot summer day.

Half Dome Village
(FORMERLY CURRY VILLAGE)

Half Dome Village (shuttle stops 14 and 20) offers a variety of food options, although it would be a stretch to call any of it "dining." In the cheap-and-easy category, you can always get a veggie burger or grass-fed beef burger at the **Meadow Grill** (11am-8pm daily Apr.-Sept.) or a pizza at the **Pizza Patio** (noon-10pm daily in summer). Beer is served next door at the **Half Dome Village Bar** (11am-10pm daily Apr.-Oct.).

If you'd prefer to eat indoors, try the cafeteria-style buffet at **Half Dome Village Pavilion** for breakfast (7am-10am daily in summer, $12) and dinner (5:30pm-8pm daily in summer, $16). The food is nothing to write home about, but there's ample variety. Come hungry if you want to get your money's worth.

For caffeine and sugar addicts, there's the **Coffee Corner** (6:30am-10pm daily in summer) right next to the Pavilion. Lattes, mochas, ice cream, and assorted pastries and snacks are available all day. All of the coffee served in Yosemite Valley is Starbucks.

Note that before Memorial Day and after Labor Day the restaurants' hours usually decrease, and some of the restaurants close. For example, the Pavilion's breakfast buffet is not usually served in the winter; instead, limited breakfast items are available at the Coffee Corner. The free Yosemite newspaper has all the latest details on opening and closing times for the park's food establishments.

Yosemite Valley Lodge
MOUNTAIN ROOM

The ★ **Mountain Room** (shuttle stop 8, 209/372-1274 or 209/372-1403, 5pm-10pm daily, $20-40) is the fanciest of a handful of dining choices at Yosemite Valley Lodge; it's a real sit-down dining room with classic entrées like steaks, seafood, and pasta dishes. Try to get a table near the windows so you can enjoy the spectacular view. If you have dinner before dark, you can gaze up at Lower Yosemite Fall while you eat. Diners show up wearing everything from high heels to hiking boots, so come as you are. Steaks are a popular item, but several kinds of pasta, fish, and chicken are available also (try the mountain trout, ahi tuna, or tequila shrimp). Vegetarians can always find a pasta dish to suit their tastes. Everything on the menu is à la carte, so if you order an appetizer, an entrée, and dessert, you can easily spend more than $100 for two people without even opening the wine list. The food is good and the servers are pleasant; the only real downer at the Mountain Room is that they **don't take reservations** unless your party is larger than eight people. Everybody else just puts their name on the list, gets handed a buzzer, and is told to wait—a process that

Finding Espresso in Yosemite

I'm hooked, you're hooked, we're all hooked. It used to be that only visiting Europeans yearned for a morning sip of espresso or a flavorful cappuccino, but now almost every Yosemite visitor is a card-carrying Starbucks devotee. Let's face it, a couple of shots of the strong stuff first thing in the morning can certainly help you climb those 100 switchbacks to Upper Yosemite Fall.

Where can you find a decent latte in the park?

- The Coffee Corner at Half Dome Village
- Starbucks at Yosemite Valley Lodge
- Degnan's Kitchen at Yosemite Village
- The Majestic Hotel Dining Room
- The Mountain Room at Yosemite Valley Lodge
- The Big Trees Lodge Dining Room in Wawona

What about outside of the park?

- Pony Expresso in Mariposa (page 81)
- Mountain Sage in Groveland (page 83)
- Firefall Coffee Roasting Company In Groveland (page 83)
- The Cool Bean Cafe In Oakhurst (page 141)
- Starbucks in Oakhurst
- Tioga Gas Mart/Whoa Nellie Deli in Lee Vining (page 228)
- Latte Da Coffee Café in Lee Vining (page 230)

is made fairly painless by the presence of the neighboring Mountain Room Lounge.

MOUNTAIN ROOM LOUNGE

If you just want a quick, casual meal, and maybe a libation to go with it, try the **Mountain Room Lounge** (shuttle stop 8, 4:30pm-10pm Mon.-Fri., noon-10pm Sat.-Sun., $10-18), which has a comfortable cocktail lounge with good seating, sports on TV, an open-sided fireplace, and a spacious bar. Housed in a separate building about 50 feet (15 m) from the Mountain Room Restaurant, it's a great place to while away the waiting period until your name is called (or your buzzer goes off) for a table. Those who are starving for dinner can order from the Lounge's short but adequate menu, which includes a few sandwiches, chili, chef's salad, and soup.

BASE CAMP EATERY

If you have a lot of mouths to feed and some of those mouths are of the age where they'll eat only macaroni and cheese, you might do well at Yosemite Valley Lodge's **Base Camp Eatery** (shuttle stop 8, 6:30am-10pm daily, $6-13), a glorified cafeteria. Patrons work their way through the lines and fill their trays with their food choices, then pay the cashier and find a seat in the large dining room. Because almost everything is à la carte, you may get a small shock when you find out the combined total of the items on your tray. Dinner entrées like Asian chicken and rice bowls, or spaghetti with meatballs, cost about $13. A slice of pizza will set you back $6. Dessert is another $6. Still, this place has a large selection—including lots of vegetarian choices—and it's open for three meals a day year-round.

STARBUCKS

In 2018, the park concessionaire opened Yosemite's first official **Starbucks** location at Yosemite Valley Lodge, so it's now possible to sip a Frappuccino by the falls—for better or worse. The shop offers a decent selection of food—sandwiches, salads, and breakfast items. The only thing that sets this location apart from the 27,000 others around the world is a lack of exterior signage. But it's easy to find—it's right next to Base Camp Eatery in the courtyard behind the lobby at Yosemite Valley Lodge.

The Majestic Yosemite Hotel

THE MAJESTIC YOSEMITE HOTEL DINING ROOM

If you like formality and have money to blow, don't hesitate for even a moment: Get a reservation for dinner at ★ **The Majestic Yosemite Hotel Dining Room** (shuttle stop 3, 209/372-1489, 7am-10am, 11:30am-3pm, and 5:30pm-9pm daily, $25-50). Ties and jackets are certainly apropos for this elegant restaurant, but in recent years the hotel has slackened its dress code to "resort casual," meaning that men should wear collared shirts and long pants, and women should wear dresses, skirts, or slacks and blouses. No jeans, tennis shoes, or T-shirts are permitted. Considering the quality of the food and the accompanying astronomical prices, formal attire seems fitting here. If you're dying to eat at the Majestic Yosemite Hotel but you're not the dress-up type, show up for breakfast or lunch, when even shorts and hiking boots will gain you entrance to the grand dining room.

Just how grand is it? The dining room fills a space 130 feet (40 m) long and has towering 37-foot-high (11-m) ceilings. It contains dozens of wrought-iron chandeliers and enormous picture windows that look out on classic Valley scenery. Four hundred people can eat dinner under its open-beamed roof all at once, with plenty of room to spare. Bounded by massive timbered walls, the place looks downright medieval.

Best of all, the food tastes as good as the dining room looks. The menu changes constantly, but certain well-loved items show up frequently, like salmon stuffed with Dungeness crab. In recent years the chef has placed a greater emphasis on organic and sustainably harvested ingredients, creating signature dishes such as pan-roasted, line-caught halibut and grilled wild king salmon. A children's menu is available.

The hotel's lavish Sunday **brunch** (7am-3pm Sun., $49 adults, $15 children) is legendary. **Breakfast** (7am-10am Mon.-Sat.) and **lunch** (11:30am-3pm Mon.-Sat.) are not only the most casual meals of the day, they are also the most affordable ($16-22). Keep in mind that if you want to eat any meal other than breakfast at the Majestic Yosemite Hotel, **reservations are a must.**

MAJESTIC YOSEMITE HOTEL BAR

You can still eat at the Majestic Yosemite Hotel even if your budget won't stretch far enough for the dining room. The **bar and lounge** (11:30am-11pm daily, $10-25) serves light lunch and dinner fare, cocktails, and a sampling of fine liquors year-round. "Light fare" here includes items like house-made paté, smoked fish, and Basque-inspired sandwiches. In the drink category, martinis are a specialty. During the evenings, a pianist tickles the black-and-whites with graceful melodies while you and your loved one sip a glass of port and share a dessert. On summer days, the bar opens up to an outside deck near the hotel swimming pool. Put on your best sunglasses, order a salad and a tonic water, sit out on the deck, and pretend you're a movie star.

WEST OF THE PARK: HIGHWAY 140

Although there is plenty of good food to be found outside of the park, many restaurants keep capricious hours, which change not just seasonally but also sometimes daily—at the whim of the owner or chef. The establishments listed here are generally open for dinner seven days a week in the **high season** (Memorial Day-Labor Day), but much less or

Dining West of the Park: Highway 140

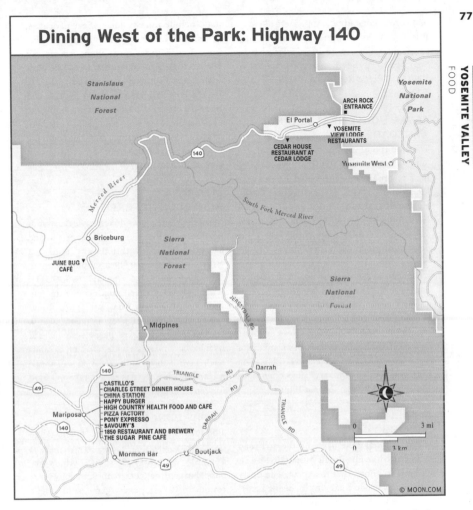

© MOON.COM

not at all during the off-season. Typical dinner hours are 5pm-9pm, but then again, if business is slow, it's not uncommon for the doors to close earlier. If you have your heart set on eating somewhere, make a reservation, or at least call in advance to obtain current operating hours.

El Portal
YOSEMITE VIEW LODGE RESTAURANTS
This place can save you from going to bed without supper if you come back late after a

hike in Yosemite Valley. Whereas the Valley's restaurants stop serving food at 9pm or thereabouts, the two restaurants at **Yosemite View Lodge** (11136 Hwy. 140, El Portal, 209/379-2681, www.stayyosemiteviewlodge. com, breakfast 7am-11am, dinner 5:30pm-10pm, shorter winter hours, $13-25), only 2 miles (3.2 km) from the Arch Rock entrance, stay open until 10pm in summer. The main dining room, called the River Restaurant, serves up a lovely river view and fairly standard American dinners: chicken marsala, New York steak, broiled salmon, burgers, and vegetarian entrées. Appetizers like calamari strips, potato skins, and buffalo wings are popular. For a more affordable way to fill your belly, try the pizza at the neighboring **Parkside Pizza Restaurant** (209/379-2183, 5:30pm-9:30pm daily).

CEDAR HOUSE RESTAURANT AT CEDAR LODGE

The food is nothing to get excited about. The hours, on the other hand, are worth singing a few praises over. Located 8 miles (12.9 km) from the Arch Rock entrance, **Cedar House Restaurant at Cedar Lodge** (9968 Hwy. 140, El Portal, 209/379-2316, www.stayyosemitecedarlodge.com, 7am-11pm daily in summer, winter hours vary, $12-28) is a traditional American dining room that serves pork ribs, chicken marsala, salmon, and ravioli. The pastas are more budget-minded (around $14), and a children's menu is offered. But the really good news is that the restaurant opens at 7am and closes at 10pm, so you can get food whenever you want it. For night owls, the Canyon Bar and Grill (also on the Cedar Lodge property) stays open until 1am, but the kitchen closes at 10pm.

Midpines
JUNE BUG CAFÉ

When you make the drive up the dirt road to the Yosemite Bug Rustic Mountain Resort, it's hard to know what to expect. The dusty path brings you to a parking lot below a cluster of buildings, and a short walk leads you to the registration building and the **June Bug Café** (6979 Hwy. 140, Midpines, 209/966-6666, www.yosemitebug.com, 7am-9:30pm daily, $6-23). Walk up to the kitchen counter, order your food, and then settle in on the glassed-in deck to enjoy your meal, or have a seat in the college dorm-style lounge and read a book or surf the Internet while you eat. The café is as casual as it gets, but the food is surprisingly gourmet. The menu is a mix of American and Mediterranean, and many of the greens served here come straight from the lodge's organic garden. Breakfast (7am-10am)

may include muesli, buckwheat pancakes, or omelets; lunch sandwiches are available until 3pm. Dinner (6pm-9pm) features an ever-changing menu with entrées like pan-seared salmon and chicken tandoori ($12-23). Vegetarians will have plenty of choices, and there is a variety of beers on tap (including the ever-popular Guinness) along with a selection of good wines. Christmas and Thanksgiving feasts are big events; reserve far in advance if you want to be a part of the fun.

Mariposa
HIGH COUNTRY CAFÉ

Mariposa is such an Old West-style meat-and-potatoes town that you wouldn't expect to find a health food store within the city limits. But **High Country Cafe** (49er Shopping Center, 5186 Hwy. 49 N., Mariposa, 209/966-5111, www.highcountryhealthfoods.com, 8am-7pm Mon.-Sat., 9am-5pm Sun., $6-11) has always done a solid business in town. Its café, next to the health food store, prepares fresh juices at its juice bar and has a wide selection of sandwiches (with and without meat) as well as salads and quiches. This is perfect take-out food for your trip into Yosemite.

HAPPY BURGER

The local high school sports teams come to **Happy Burger** (5120 Hwy. 140 at 12th St., Mariposa, 209/966-2719, www.happyburgerdiner.com, 6am-9pm daily year-round, $5-10) after every game, so that tells you what kind of place this is. This burger joint and soda fountain boasts having "the Sierra's largest menu," and when you peruse its eight pages, you may agree. Breakfast items include that Mariposa favorite, biscuits and gravy. Order a burger, fries, and an all-you-can-drink soda, and two can eat for $20. Check out the ceiling while you dine: It's lined with record albums, most of which date back to the groovy 1970s. You can bring your laptop if you wish; the Wi-Fi is fast and reliable.

1: the deck of the Priest Station Café 2: The Village Grill 3: Iron Door Saloon in Groveland

SAVOURY'S

Most Mariposa locals will tell you that a sure bet for a well-prepared meal is **Savoury's** (5034 Hwy. 140, Mariposa, 209/966-7677, 5pm-9:30pm daily in summer, Thurs.-Tues. in winter, $16-31). The restaurant serves dinner in a sparse bistro-style setting—black lacquer tables and chairs, concrete floors, and brick walls—that evokes downtown San Francisco far more than Yosemite. Entrées include several pastas and vegetarian selections in addition to grilled New York steak, rack of lamb, chicken marsala, and lamb chops. Despite the chic look of the place, Savoury's is still kid-friendly, and you won't be ostracized for wearing hiking clothes.

1850 RESTAURANT AND BREWERY

Ever since the **1850 Restaurant and Brewery** (5114 Hwy. 140, Mariposa, 209/966-2229, www.1850restaurant.com, 11am-9:30pm daily, $12-24) started brewing its own craft beers in 2017, the place has been packing in a crowd. The brewery serves all its beers on tap—coffee stout, red IPA, honey blond ale, and wheat ale—and you can take home a growler if you like. Meals comprise dependable comfort food served in huge portions (plan to share whatever you order). Popular entrées include rib-eye and porterhouse steaks, salmon, smoked venison, and an unusual twist on fried chicken. Even salad and soup lovers will find plenty of choices. On summer evenings, you can sit outside on the patio.

SUGAR PINE CAFÉ

For a classic diner-style breakfast, nab a red counter stool at the **Sugar Pine Café** (5038 Hwy. 140, Mariposa, 209/742-7793, www.sugarpinecafe.com, 7am-3pm daily, $8-18) and watch your bacon and eggs be prepared by the short-order cooks in the open kitchen. Probably the first thing you'll notice is how many patrons have ordered the biscuits and gravy. That's because biscuits—and an array of other baked goods—are the Sugar Pine's pride and joy. But all the breakfast bases

are covered well here—bacon, sausage, hash browns, scrambled eggs, omelets, and pancakes. The restaurant's decor is new but with a retro 1950s look, including a checkered linoleum floor and red Naugahyde booths. The lunch menu is lined with classic American sandwiches like tuna melts, grilled ham and cheese, and hamburgers.

CHARLES STREET DINNER HOUSE

If you are a big eater who likes a classic Western steak house-style meal, it's worth setting aside a couple hours to make a trip into or out of Yosemite for dinner at the **Charles Street Dinner House** (5043 Hwy. 140, Mariposa, 209/966-2366, www.charlesstreetdinnerhouse.net, lunch 11am-2pm Mon.-Fri., dinner 5pm-9:30pm daily, $18-38). This restaurant serves a baked potato that's so big, you will want to split it with a friend. It comes alongside a delicious range of hearty entrées, like filet mignon, bone-in pork chop, New Zealand lamb chops, and bacon-wrapped sirloin steak. The cozy dining room is filled with antiques and mining relics. Eating here feels a lot like having dinner at a friend's house (if your friend happened to live in the Old West). Charles Street has received many accolades over the years, and if you're a fan of traditional, hearty meals, you'll see why.

CHINA STATION

A little to-go Mandarin or Cantonese food could be just the thing to tide you over for the ride into or out of Yosemite. **China Station** (5004 Hwy. 140, Mariposa, 209/966-3889, 10:30am-9pm daily, $7-15) serves Mariposa's only Asian food, featuring a big menu filled with chow meins, fried rice, chop suey, hot soups, and stir-fried meats and vegetables. The sizzling beef or chicken and the mu shu vegetables are good bets. Unlike so many restaurants that come and go, China Station has been alive and well in Mariposa since 1985.

PIZZA FACTORY

With all the tourist activity in Mariposa in the summer months, **Pizza Factory** (5005 5th St.,

Mariposa, 209/966-3112, www.pizzafactory. com, 11am-11pm daily in summer, shorter winter hours winter, $7-20) is always hopping at dinnertime. Expect to find good budget-minded food on the menu: pizza, calzones, pasta, a salad bar, and deli sandwiches.

PONY EXPRESSO

Mariposa's beloved little espresso joint, **Pony Expresso** (5182 Hwy. 49 N., Mariposa, 209/966-5053, www.ponyexpressomariposa. com, 6:30am-4:30pm Mon.-Fri., 7am-3pm Sat.-Sun.), offers caffeine-craving Yosemite travelers coffee drinks, chai, smoothies, and flavored ices, plus soups and sandwiches. Do yourself a favor and try the carrot cake.

CASTILLO'S

Popular Mexican restaurant **Castillo's** (4995 5th St., Mariposa, 209/742-4413, www. castillosmexicanrestaurant.com, 11am-9pm daily, $7-17) is one block off the main drag and is open for lunch and dinner only. Castillo's is designed for lingering, with a cheerful, comfortable dining room that has been open since 1955. The carne asada is revered throughout the foothills. Vegetarians will like the wide variety of veggie burritos, tostadas, and tacos. Service is speedy and friendly, and two can eat a big dinner here for about $30.

WEST OF THE PARK: HIGHWAY 120

Groveland and Vicinity

BUCK MEADOWS RESTAURANT

One of the best things about the **Buck Meadows Restaurant** (7647 Hwy. 120, Buck Meadows, 209/962-5181, www.buckmeadowsrestaurant.com, 7am-10pm daily, dinner $15-24) is its dependability: It's open seven days a week May-September. The rest of the year, the doors are often locked. Located right next door to the Yosemite Westgate Lodge in the tiny hamlet of Buck Meadows, the restaurant serves good old-fashioned American roadhouse food: three-egg omelets, several types of steaks, hamburgers with all the trimmings, hot dogs, French fries,

spaghetti and meatballs, liver and onions, and so on. Portions are big and the servers are friendly. Just one caveat: Don't check your cholesterol level after you eat here.

TANGLED HEARTS BAKERY

If you're driving from Groveland to Yosemite or back again, the **Tangled Hearts Bakery** (2400 Casa Loma Rd., Buck Meadows, 209/962-0907, www.tangledheartsbakery. com, 6:30am-4pm Tues.-Sun., $5-8) is a must-stop. Long-time Yosemite visitors know this spot as La Casa Loma Store, or the place where the river rafters meet up to head down the dirt road to the Tuolumne River. Now the rafters make it a point to arrive early so they can nosh on the hearty breakfasts and yummy baked goods served here (corned beef hash, breakfast burrito, waffles). Owners Amy and Bubba are both terrific chefs who have given Buck Meadows a great eatery.

TWO GUYS PIZZA PIES

Just a short distance off Highway 120, **Two Guys Pizza Pies** (18955 Ferretti Rd., Groveland, 209/962-4897, 11am-10pm daily, $11-30) serves pizzas and calzones, oven-baked subs, and appetizers like buffalo wings and salads. Locals love this place, but tourists often miss it because it's off of Groveland's main drag (turn north on Ferretti Road and drive about 600 ft/185 m).

PROVISIONS AT THE GROVELAND HOTEL

Gone is the formal dining room at the Groveland Hotel, and in its place is a more casual eatery that fits the bill for tired and hungry Yosemite travelers. **Provisions** (18767 Hwy. 120, Groveland, 209/962-4000, www.groveland.com, 7am-9pm daily, $7-20) is open for three meals a day, and its varied menu ensures you'll find something that appeals. If you're lingering at dinnertime, sit on the back patio and dine on honey-glazed pork shank or house-made gnocchi. Grab-and-go items like deli sandwiches, salads, and yogurt

Dining West of the Park: Highway 120

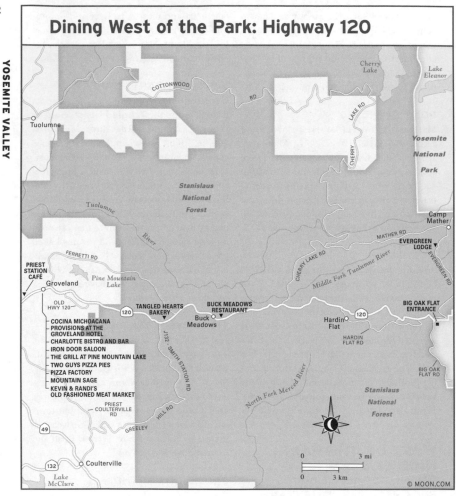

parfaits make good sense when you're hitting the road.

IRON DOOR SALOON

Next door to the Groveland Hotel is the infamous **Iron Door Saloon** (18761 Main St., Groveland, 209/962-6244, www.iron-door-saloon.com, grill 7am-10pm daily, bar until 2am, $12-25), reputed to be the oldest saloon in California. (It opened its doors in 1852, but a bar in Bolinas, California, claims to have opened for business a year earlier. The debate rages on.) In addition to the hard stuff, the saloon offers up a long list of microbrews and selections from California foothill wineries. Adjacent to the saloon is the **Iron Door Grill**, where you'll find delicious casual food, from eggs and omelets to meal-size salads to buffalo burgers to pastas and steaks. A burger and some sweet potato fries will set you back about $19, so this isn't the cheapest place in town to eat (plenty of tour buses stop here for the Old West ambience, and the prices reflect that). Sit in the bar so you can stare at all the animal heads on the walls and the hundreds of dollar bills plastered to the ceiling. Or, if the bar is too noisy, a separate dining room is also available, lined with old black-and-white photographs of Groveland and the Hetch Hetchy area. In summer, take the kids along and enjoy a hot fudge sundae or old-fashioned malt from the soda fountain next door. Coffee lovers can find caffeine next door at the **Firefall Coffee Roasting Company** (18749 Main St., Groveland, 209/962-7704, www.firefallcoffee. net, 6am-3pm Mon.-Fri., 8am-3pm Sat.-Sun.).

CHARLOTTE BISTRO & BAR

The Hotel Charlotte's in-house restaurant, **Charlotte Bistro & Bar** (Hotel Charlotte, 18736 Hwy. 120, Groveland, 209/962-6455, www.hotelcharlotte.com, 5pm-9:30pm Wed.-Sun., $9-25), is casual and classy, befitting the historic building it occupies. New chef and general manager Doug Edwards combines local and seasonal ingredients to make tapas-style small plates, including plenty of vegetarian choices. Be sure to try one of the local Gold Country wines.

KEVIN AND RANDI'S OLD-FASHIONED MEAT MARKET

Finally Groveland has a great spot where Yosemite visitors can score sandwiches and other easy-to-carry foods to take along on their Yosemite excursions. Run by a husband and wife team, **Kevin and Randi's Old-Fashioned Meat Market** (18687 Main St., Groveland, 209/962-5500, 10am-6pm Mon.-Sat., $6-12) makes big, fresh, meaty sandwiches on high-quality breads (including some gluten-free options). Choose from corned beef, tri-tip, cashew chicken, Virginia ham, chipotle roast beef, and lots more, and make sure you save room for potato salad. If you feel like doing some cooking on your Yosemite vacation, take home a lamb roast or grass-fed beef burgers.

MOUNTAIN SAGE

The coffee is great at **Mountain Sage** (18653 Main St., Groveland, 209/962-4686, www. mtsage.com, 7am-3pm daily, $3-8), but really,

it's the ambience that draws in the crowds. Set amid the grounds and historic buildings of a plant nursery, this coffeehouse serves coffee, smoothies, and a few pastries and snacks. More importantly, it provides a big helping of Groveland-style serenity. Have a seat in the outdoor or indoor lounge areas, and you'll be tempted to pick up a book and start reading. An array of comfy seating makes it hard to get up and leave. Check your blood pressure when you leave—it just dropped a few points.

COCINA MICHOACANA

If you're craving a little salsa on your way into or out of Yosemite, **Cocina Michoacana** (18730 Hwy. 120, Groveland, 209/962-6651, 10am-10pm daily) will graciously provide it. The kitchen cooks up huevos rancheros, chorizo, and other specialties for breakfast ($8) and a wide array of tamales, enchiladas, tacos, taquitos, and sopes for lunch and dinner ($9-16). The dining room is windowless and a bit dark, but the food is tasty and authentic. Chips and salsa are delivered to your table as soon as you sit down. This is about the only place in Groveland where you might be able to find food after 9pm; if the restaurant is busy enough, the owners keep serving until 10pm.

THE GRILL AT PINE MOUNTAIN LAKE

Pine Mountain Lake, about a mile outside of Groveland, is a resort community with a golf course, a lake, and a lot of friendly retired people. Residents enjoy all the amenities of a resort combined with proximity to Yosemite. **The Grill at Pine Mountain Lake** (12765 Mueller Dr., 209/962-8638, www. pinemountainlake.com, 11am-9pm Mon.-Fri., 8am-9pm Sat.-Sun., $20-38) is a safe bet for a typical golf club dinner, with entrées like prime rib, rib-eye steak, and salmon. Weekend breakfasts consist of hearty portions of eggs Benedict, frittatas, and steak and eggs. The dining room has a sweeping view of the pastoral golf course, and you can sit outside on the deck if the weather is nice.

PIZZA FACTORY

The tiny town of Groveland has not one, but two great pizza parlors—the independently owned Two Guys Pizza Pies and the **Pizza Factory** (18583 Hwy. 120, Groveland, 209/962-7757, www.pizzafactory.com, 10am-10pm Sun.-Thurs., 10am-11pm Fri.-Sat., $20-26). The restaurants are a mere 0.25 mile (0.4 km) apart, but Pizza Factory is larger and has more tables. Expect delicious pizza, calzones, pasta, deli sandwiches, and a surprisingly good salad bar. Pizza Factory is a bonanza for hungry bargain hunters; the extra-large four-topping pizza is only $26. Play checkers on the glass tabletops while you wait for your food. During the busy summer season, Pizza Factory often stays open until midnight, but if you are coming into town late and hungry, call ahead to be sure.

PRIEST STATION CAFÉ

This historic stagecoach stop at the top of Old Priest Grade, one of the most precipitous roads in California, had fallen into ruins over the years. Then in 2009, the **Priest Station Café** (16756 Old Priest Grade, Big Oak Flat, 209/962-1888, www.prieststation.com, 8am-8pm daily in summer, shorter winter hours, $12-20) was blessed with ambitious new owners. Denise and Steve Anker are descendants of the original owners from the 1850s and also brother and sister of the famous rock climber Conrad Anker. The pair have turned a ramshackle building into an adorable café with an unforgettable view from its outdoor deck, which overlooks the treacherous Priest Grade and Yosemite Valley far below. On clear days, you can see all the way to the Coast Range. If your body is weary from the ride to Yosemite from the Bay Area or Sacramento, stop here for a grass-fed Angus beef or veggie burger and leave your road cares behind. On this high promontory, you have officially left the valley behind and are now entering mountain country. Celebrate the moment with homemade lemonade and some sweet potato fries. Memorable touches include a nod to Conrad Anker—the bathroom keys are attached to ice climbing anchors—and a to-die-for German cheesecake. The Ankers also rent two cabins on the property, so if you're too weary to travel any farther, you can spend the night here.

Accommodations

Of the seven lodgings available inside the park boundaries, four are in Yosemite Valley—the marvelous but pricey Majestic Yosemite Hotel, the midpriced Yosemite Valley Lodge, and the budget-priced but bare-bones Half Dome Village and Housekeeping Camp.

INSIDE THE PARK
Reservations

Reservations for park lodgings inside Yosemite are made through Aramark's **Yosemite Hospitality** by phone (888/413-8869, 7am-8pm Mon.-Fri., 7am-7pm Sat.-Sun. summer, shorter winter hours) or online (www.travelyosemite.com).

APRIL-OCTOBER

For stays from late April to mid-October and during winter holidays, it is wise to make reservations **up to a year in advance.** Cancellations happen frequently, so if you strike out, keep calling back.

NOVEMBER-MARCH

During the off-season it is not terribly difficult to get a room, even in Yosemite Valley, particularly **midweek.** A few days' notice should be all you need, except during holiday periods.

To save money, visit Yosemite during **"value season"** (Nov.-Mar., excluding major holidays). Value-season rates (as much as 40 percent lower than regular rates) can be obtained at Half Dome Village, Yosemite Valley Lodge, and the Majestic Yosemite Hotel. However, note that the "major holiday" exclusion knocks out a fair number of winter days. Higher-priced dates include the four-day Thanksgiving weekend, the last two weeks of December, the three-day weekend surrounding Martin Luther King Jr. Day (Jan.), and the week surrounding Presidents' Day (Feb.).

Housekeeping Camp

From the outside, **Housekeeping Camp** (shuttle stop 12, Southside Dr., 888/413-8869, www.travelyosemite.com, Apr.-Oct., $108-133) looks a lot like a crowded inner-city slum in a developing country. Nonetheless, many repeat visitors to Yosemite Valley are devotees of Housekeeping Camp, for two main reasons: location (it's situated right on the Merced River) and value. The **266 duplex units** are all the same—a strange hybrid between a cabin and a campsite. Each unit consists of one room that will sleep up to four people in one double bed ("cot" is a more accurate description) and one set of twin bunk beds. Two additional cots may be added to increase the total sleeping capacity to six people who don't mind being packed in like sardines. A table, chairs, a mirror, and electric lights are provided. Each unit has a concrete floor, three concrete walls, and a curtain for a fourth wall. A canvas awning covers the roof and extends over a patio, which also serves as the cooking and dining area. The patio has a small table with a light and electrical outlet where you can set up your camp stove and electric coffeemaker. A fire grill is provided, so with a small stack of chopped wood, you can blacken all the hot dogs and marshmallows you can eat.

Unlike at nearby Half Dome Village, you can park your car right beside your Housekeeping Camp unit. All units are near a popular sandy beach on the Merced River, so many people spend their afternoons playing in the water. Some of the units have first-rate views of Yosemite Falls or Half Dome. Unfortunately, they are also located on the busy road to Half Dome Village and the Pines campgrounds. Earplugs are a wise investment, especially for sleeping. And don't count on much privacy.

The overall experience at Housekeeping Camp is only a very small step up from camping. An advantage is that you don't need any equipment to stay here; you can rent everything you need ("bedpacks" consisting of two sheets, two blankets, and two pillows are $2.50 per night). Or save a few bucks and bring this stuff from home.

Showers and restrooms are in communal buildings nearby. A **laundry** center and small **grocery** store are on the premises. Food-storage rules are in effect: To keep the bears away, stow everything after you finish cooking. Bear boxes are provided.

Half Dome Village
(FORMERLY CURRY VILLAGE)

Many visitors have a love-hate relationship with **Half Dome Village** (shuttle stops 14 and 20, Southside Dr., 888/413-8869, www.travelyosemite.com, year-round, $83-195). On one hand, they love Half Dome Village because it's centrally located and it comes with all the amenities. On the other hand, they hate Half Dome Village because it embodies the worst of Yosemite Valley on its most hectic summer days: too many people, too crowded, too noisy. Not only that, but Half Dome Village is below an unstable cliff that is prone to rockslides: In 2008, a big slide forced the National Park Service to permanently close more than 200 of the cabins.

Families with kids tend to be pretty happy here. Half Dome Village is relatively inexpensive and it also has many "extras" on the grounds: a cafeteria, pizza and beer joint, coffee and ice cream place, grocery store, camping and outdoor equipment shop, an outdoor swimming pool with lifeguards, amphitheater with nightly programs, a post office, and bicycle and raft rentals. You can walk to Mirror Lake, Happy Isles, and Vernal and Nevada Falls from your cabin door. There's even an ice-skating rink in the winter months.

First, make sure you know what you are signing up for when you book a stay here.

MOTEL ROOMS

There are 18 standard motel rooms, each with a private bath, located in a building called the **Stoneman Cottage** ($196-296). These rooms will save you a hike to the restroom in the middle of the night.

WOODEN CABINS

In the off-season (or even in summer if you plan way in advance), you could be fortunate enough to rent one of Half Dome Village's 60 private, cozy, **wooden cabins** ($230-300). If you were born under a lucky star, you might even score one of the cabins with a private bath (46 of the wooden cabins are so equipped; the other 14 have access to a communal bathhouse). There are also three "specialty cabins" with baths; these historic buildings have one or two bedrooms, a sitting area, and a television. Two cabins have fireplaces. They're pricey but worth it ($280-380 in summer).

TENT CABINS

The vast majority of the time (and for the vast majority of visitors), the only cabins available at Half Dome Village are the 403 **canvas tent cabins** ($140-170 in summer, $130-160 in winter). What you need to know about these cabins is that they are made of canvas and they are placed about 9 inches (23 cm) apart. This is convenient if you want to stay up late and learn a new language from the bevy of international visitors. It's terribly inconvenient if you enjoy sleeping. Seasoned Half Dome Village veterans travel with earplugs.

The tent cabins have electric lights, and some are **heated** (but the heaters only operate Sept.-Apr.; the heated cabins are priced about $30 higher). Other than that, don't expect much more than a couple of beds with sheets, wool blankets, and pillows; a small dresser; and a bedside lantern. Bedspreads made to look and feel like sleeping bags give the cabins a cozy feel. Bathrooms and showers are a short walk away; soap and towels are provided. There are no phones or televisions in the tent cabins, and there are no electrical outlets. (But you can plug in your hair dryer in the bathhouse.) No cooking is permitted in or near the cabins, so guests must eat at Half Dome Village restaurants or other Valley food establishments.

If you stay in the tent cabins, you have to put up with a few inconveniences: First, you won't be able to drive right up to your lodging. You'll park in a central lot and then carry your suitcases a few hundred feet. Also, bears are a major problem in and around Half Dome Village, so you won't be able to keep anything scented (food, toothpaste, sunscreen, cosmetics) in either your cabin or your car. Bear-proof storage lockers are provided alongside each tent cabin and must be used. Rangers strictly enforce the bear-proofing rules.

Yosemite Valley Lodge

Yosemite Valley Lodge (shuttle stop 8, www.travelyosemite.com, 888/413-8869, $162-270) has undergone a face-lift in an effort to make it more ecofriendly. The lodge's rooms have been remodeled with carpets made from recycled materials, energy-saving lighting, Energy Star-rated televisions, and quartz countertops.

Yosemite Valley Lodge's 245 rooms are arranged in several small buildings, with interior hallways that look rather like college dorm halls, but the rooms themselves are nice. All rooms have private bathrooms, telephones, and televisions. You do get to choose between room types:

The 199 **deluxe rooms** ($230-270) are larger and airier. They come with either a patio or a balcony and have either one king bed or two double beds.

The 15 **standard rooms** ($200-225) are smaller and, well, standard, with either one king or queen bed.

The 27 **deluxe bunk rooms** ($240-260) have one queen bed and one set of bunk beds.

The four **family rooms** are the largest rooms available and are priced according to the size of your party. Rooms have one king bed, a set of bunk beds, one sleeper sofa with a double-sized mattress, and a dining table.

The lodge is comfortable, clean, and nothing fancy—think of it as the Best Western of Yosemite Valley. Its major selling point is its ideal location, directly across from Yosemite Falls. In fact, a couple of rooms have a first-rate view of the falls. You can sit outside on your balcony, drink your coffee, and study the incredible flow of white water pouring down. Unfortunately, you can't make a reservation for any particular room. Your place is assigned when you arrive, so you only get the waterfall-view rooms by sheer good fortune. Still, most of the rooms have decent views of woods or meadows.

Besides its location, guests at Yosemite Valley Lodge appreciate its amenities. Three restaurants and a cocktail lounge, a swimming pool, bike rentals, and a grocery store are all part of the deal. Many of the park's most popular tours depart from the lodge. The trailhead for Yosemite Falls is right across the street.

If you need to stay connected to the Internet, wireless hot spots are found throughout the lodge. Even if you left your laptop at home, you can still check your email via public **Internet kiosks** ($0.25 per minute) available in six different languages.

The Majestic Yosemite Hotel
(FORMERLY AHWAHNEE HOTEL)

If a wad of bills is burning a hole in your pocket, book a stay at ★ **The Majestic Yosemite Hotel** (shuttle stop 3, 888/413-8869, www.travelyosemite.com, $425-590 in summer, less in winter). If your budget runs more to cheeseburgers than to caviar, at least pay a visit to the hotel's public rooms. The old stone lodge is a classic, with fireplaces so large you could hold a tea party inside them.

Built in 1927, the Majestic Yosemite Hotel is a National Historic Landmark. Stained glass and wrought-iron chandeliers are a given. The public areas of the hotel are decorated with Native American motifs and Miwok basketry. Turkish kilim rugs serve as wall hangings. Six historic paintings, created when the hotel opened, depict Yosemite's waterfalls and sequoias. The elegant dining room is a perfect setting for the hotel's annual Bracebridge Dinner, a re-creation of an 18th-century English Christmas feast.

Some say the rooms at the Majestic Yosemite Hotel are overrated and overpriced. True, they are small, in typical 1920s fashion.

interior of The Majestic Yosemite Hotel

But the views from the windows of the rooms often override any shortcomings in square footage or decor. One side of the hotel faces Glacier Point and Half Dome. The other side faces Yosemite Falls. The higher the room, the better the view, so be sure to request a spot on the 4th, 5th, or 6th floor. If you have an unlimited budget, reserve one of the handful of ultrapricy **two-room suites** on the top floor ($1,225). The Mary Tresidder Curry Suite, where Queen Elizabeth II stayed in 1983, has a four-poster bed and a Craftsman-inspired bathroom with bidet.

If that's not an option, go for one of the 24 **cottages** in the forest behind the hotel. The suites have the best views, but the cottages offer the most privacy. Two of the most coveted cottages have fireplaces. All of the Majestic Yosemite Hotel's rooms cost a bundle, but you will feel pampered. Even in the hotel's 99 "ordinary" rooms, expect plenty of small luxuries: terry cloth bathrobes, plush towels, valet parking, bell service, turndown service, mini refrigerators, and televisions. If a TV insults your national park sensibilities, ask the management to remove it and they will do so graciously. Wireless Internet is available in all of the rooms.

On warm summer days, you'll want to hang out by the hotel's small heated swimming pool or have lunch on the terrace and enjoy the Yosemite Valley scenery. In winter, relax with a book in the **Great Lounge,** where afternoon tea is served at 5pm daily. Watch the flames flicker in the hotel's many fireplaces, or gaze at snowflakes falling or deer grazing on the meadow outside.

Knowing that Queen Elizabeth slept here, as well as John F. Kennedy, Ronald Reagan, and Winston Churchill, it probably won't surprise you that the hotel is full-service. In addition to its world-class **restaurant,** the Majestic Yosemite also has gift shops, a cocktail lounge, a tennis court, and a tour desk. Anything you might need or want that you can't find here is available nearby at Yosemite Village.

Make sure you book early. Even with its sky-high prices, the Majestic Yosemite is often full.

WEST OF THE PARK: HIGHWAY 140

Visitors approaching Yosemite from San Jose, the Central Coast, or the San Joaquin Valley frequently use the Highway 140 approach through Merced and **Mariposa,** especially if they are heading for the **Arch Rock entrance** to Yosemite. Keep in mind that Highway 140 is a mountain road, not a superhighway, so you won't drive much faster than 45 miles (72 km) per hour. Mariposa is the last chance for supplies before driving the final stretch along the flowing Merced River to the Arch Rock entrance.

A devastating landslide in May 2006 forced a section of Highway 140 between Mariposa and the Arch Rock entrance to be rerouted along a **one-lane bypass** that crosses and recrosses the river on two temporary bridges. Stoplights are in place on either end of the bypass, which may cause backups in the summer months, especially on weekends. The state highway department has spent years trying to build a more permanent fix, which involves clearing away all the debris and building a "rock shed"—a tunnel-like structure made with Roman arches designed to withstand the weight of future rockslides. The project is expected to be finished in 2019. From Arch Rock, plan on an **hour drive to Yosemite Valley**—or longer if you get stuck at the bypass—but what a scenic drive it is.

For information on local bed-and-breakfasts, contact the **Yosemite-Mariposa Bed and Breakfast Association** (209/742-7666, www.yosemitebnbs.com). Lodgings are listed according to their proximity to the Arch Rock entrance.

El Portal

If you can reserve a place to stay in El Portal, you are only a handful of miles from the Arch Rock entrance, or **14 miles (22.5 km) from Yosemite Valley** (and you will not have to deal with the Highway 140 rockslide bypass).

An Abbreviated History of the Majestic Yosemite Hotel

In the early 1900s the first director of the National Park Service, Stephen Mather, decided that Yosemite needed a first-class hotel. A clever politician, Mather understood that persuading wealthy and powerful people to visit the park was critical to its preservation. Experiencing Yosemite's beauty firsthand would surely lead them to support the efforts of the new National Park Service. At that time, park appropriations were directly related to the number of visitors, and certainly some visitors were more important than others.

Mather provided $200,000 of his own money for Yosemite's two concessionaires to merge into one company: the Yosemite Park and Curry Company. The contract that the new company signed with the National Park Service required the construction of a hotel that would be fireproof and be capable of operating year-round.

Architect Gilbert Stanley Underwood was chosen to design the hotel; he was already well known for the buildings he had designed for Zion and Bryce Canyon National Parks. Later he would also design the Grand Canyon Lodge, the San Francisco Mint, and Timberline Lodge in Oregon. Contractor James McLaughlin was to build the structure at a cost of $525,000. The cornerstone was laid on August 1, 1925, and the plan was to work seven days a week in order to be able to open the hotel four months later. Of course, work progressed much slower than that, resulting in huge cost overruns. The budget nearly doubled during construction, and the workers wound up seven months behind schedule. At last the Ahwahnee Hotel's grand opening was held on July 16, 1927.

Over the years the hotel has seen many famous and important guests. It also served as a Navy hospital during World War II. After the war, the hotel was returned to civilian use, and once again it became a playground for the rich and famous. The 6th-floor apartment underwent extensive remodeling in the early 1980s in preparation for a visit by Queen Elizabeth II. Other notables who have graced the guest list include Dwight D. Eisenhower, the Shah of Iran, Herbert Hoover, Eleanor Roosevelt, Gertrude Stein, Charlie Chaplin, Will Rogers, Lucille Ball, Ronald Reagan, Walt Disney, Greta Garbo, John F. Kennedy, and Prince Phillip.

In 2016, in a bizarre twist of politics, the Ahwahnee received a sudden and surprising name change—along with many other famous places in Yosemite, including Curry Village and the Wawona Hotel (now Half Dome Village and the Big Trees Lodge, respectively). When the National Park Service selected a new concessionaire to run the park's hotels and visitor services, a messy trademark spat ensued with the previous concessionaire. The outgoing concessionaire, Delaware North Corporation (DNC), sued the National Park Service, stating that the park could not use the business names that DNC had trademarked, including "Ahwahnee," "Wawona Hotel," "Badger Pass," and "Curry Village." These place-names were commonly used in Yosemite long before DNC trademarked them, but nonetheless, during its 24 years managing the park's operations, DNC obtained the trademarks. Like it or not, the law is on their side.

By whatever name you choose, it's a worthwhile splurge to stay in one of the Majestic Yosemite Hotel's (or Ahwahnee's) 123 rooms, suites, or cottages, but even if you don't, you can still book a table for the sumptuous Sunday brunch at the Majestic Yosemite Dining Room, or simply sit by the fireplace in the Great Lounge, peek at the wrought-iron chandeliers dropping from the dining room's 34-foot (10-m) ceilings, or enjoy a cocktail at the bar. Free one-hour guided tours of the Majestic Yosemite are offered throughout the year; check with the hotel's concierge desk for a current schedule.

YOSEMITE BLUE BUTTERFLY INN

Short of staying inside the park, you can't get any closer to Yosemite Valley than the ★ Yosemite Blue Butterfly Inn (11132 Hwy. 140, El Portal, 209/379-2100, www. yosemitebluebutterflyinn.com, $200-345 including breakfast, lower winter rates). A mere 2 miles (3.2 km) from Yosemite's Arch Rock entrance, this B&B could easily succeed on its proximity alone, but the Blue Butterfly doesn't

Lodging West of the Park: Highway 140

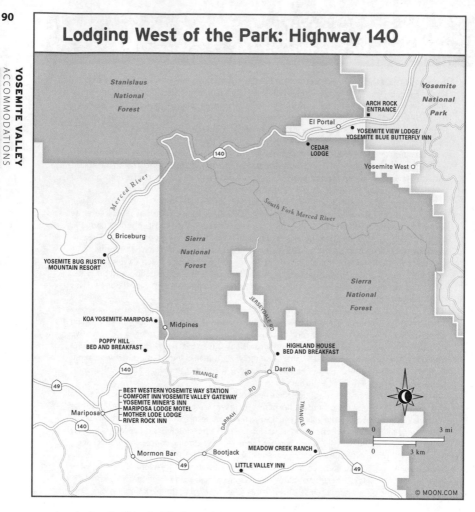

Stanislaus National Forest

Yosemite National Park

ARCH ROCK ENTRANCE

El Portal

YOSEMITE VIEW LODGE/ YOSEMITE BLUE BUTTERFLY INN

CEDAR LODGE

Yosemite West

Merced River

South Fork Merced River

Briceburg

Sierra National Forest

YOSEMITE BUG RUSTIC MOUNTAIN RESORT

JERSEYDALE RD

Sierra National Forest

KOA YOSEMITE-MARIPOSA

Midpines

POPPY HILL BED AND BREAKFAST

HIGHLAND HOUSE BED AND BREAKFAST

TRIANGLE RD

Darrah

BEST WESTERN YOSEMITE WAY STATION
COMFORT INN YOSEMITE VALLEY GATEWAY
YOSEMITE MINER'S INN
MARIPOSA LODGE MOTEL
MOTHER LODE LODGE
RIVER ROCK INN

Mariposa

DARRAH RD

TRIANGLE RD

MEADOW CREEK RANCH

Mormon Bar

Bootjack

LITTLE VALLEY INN

0   3 mi
0   3 km

© MOON.COM

rest on its location laurels. The beautiful inn is inside the Yosemite View Lodge complex, behind the restaurant and pizza parlor and overlooking the Merced River. It seems a bit strange when you first drive onto the property, but once you're inside, you'll be very happy. Five guest rooms offer king- or queen-size beds and decks overlooking the river. You'll enjoy a gourmet breakfast (and British-style tea in the afternoons) as you gaze at Yosemite's granite cliffs. Leave the kids at home—the Blue Butterfly is for adults only. Owners Ron and Liz Skelton have lived in the area for 35

years and will gladly help you plan your time in the park.

YOSEMITE VIEW LODGE

In the same location as the Yosemite Blue Butterfly Inn, this huge lodge complex is as close as you can get to Yosemite National Park's west side and Yosemite Valley without being in the park. The lodge is set right on the Merced River, only 2 miles (3.2 km) from Yosemite's Arch Rock entrance and about 20 minutes from Yosemite Valley. Managed by the same company that handles nearby Cedar

Lodge and several other local accommodations, ★ **Yosemite View Lodge** (11136 Hwy. 140, El Portal, 209/379-2681, www.stayyosemiteviewlodge.com, $179-469 including breakfast) has 335 rooms, including some family units with kitchenettes, all with cable TV and HBO. Many of the rooms have fireplaces and spa tubs; the most desirable ones have balconies or patios with riverfront views (two-bedroom suites run as high as $469). Get a riverfront room in the spring or early summer and you'll be able to listen to the music of the Merced all night. The huge complex has one indoor and three outdoor pools, five spas, a cocktail lounge, and two **restaurants**—a pizza parlor and a more formal dining room. Leave your car here during the day and ride the YARTS bus into Yosemite.

CEDAR LODGE

Only 8 miles (12.9 km) from the Arch Rock entrance, **Cedar Lodge** (9966 Hwy. 140, El Portal, 209/379-2612, www.stayyosemitecedarlodge.com, $179-489 in summer, lower winter rates) offers a choice of room types, including a master suite that sleeps 14 and has its own private outdoor pool, family units with kitchenettes, honeymoon suites, and regular rooms sized for 1-2 people. The best bet here is one of the deluxe rooms with a king-size four-poster bed. With 211 rooms, the lodge is large enough to have all the amenities of a major hotel: phone, cable TV, HBO, indoor and outdoor swimming pools, cocktail lounge, conference room, two **restaurants,** and a gift shop. It doesn't offer much in the way of personality, but it is convenient.

Cedar Lodge's best selling point, at least in summer, is private beach access to the Merced River. The beach is a haven for swimmers and bathers on warm days, and a great place to watch river rafters in the early summer.

Midpines

An overnight stay in the smaller hamlet of Midpines will put you **26 miles (42 km) from the Arch Rock entrance** to Yosemite.

YOSEMITE BUG RUSTIC MOUNTAIN RESORT

The quirky name of this establishment tells you something about its fun-loving feel. For the young and young at heart, the **Yosemite Bug** (6979 Hwy. 140, Midpines, 209/966-6666 or 866/826-7108, www.yosemitebug.com, $65-135 w/shared bath, $85-175 w/private bath) is an inexpensive, rustic lodging that provides the antithesis of the impersonal chain-motel experience. This complex was once a dorm camp that catered to youth and work project groups before it opened in its present incarnation in 1996. The Bug's atmosphere is very social and friendly, both for the staff and guests.

The range of available accommodations runs the gamut: modern cabins with private baths, lodge rooms with shared baths, tent cabins, hostel-style dormitories, and even campsites. **Tent cabins** ($40-75) with shared baths sleep up to four people. In the **hostel rooms** ($23-34 per person) you'll share a large bunk-style room with 6-12 people. Large groups can rent the **Starlite House** ($260-380), which sleeps up to nine people.

In keeping with the "young at heart" theme, the Yosemite Bug is all about outdoor recreation. Staff members can fill you in on everything you want to know about the area's hiking, mountain biking, rafting, and rock-climbing opportunities. And if you'd rather relax than exercise, Yosemite Bug's spa has redwood hot tubs and a massage room.

You won't have to go far to find food if you stay at the Bug. Its on-site **June Bug Café** serves breakfast, lunch, and dinner and is well known locally for its delicious food. It's also the central hangout spot at the resort, with a wood-burning stove, comfortable couches, games, books, and musical instruments.

The Bug is 22 miles (35 km) from the Arch Rock entrance to Yosemite, or 9.5 miles (15.3 km) east of Mariposa on Highway 140.

Mariposa

A stay in Mariposa puts you **30 miles (48 km) from the Arch Rock entrance** to Yosemite, or 44 miles (71 km) from Yosemite

Valley. Mariposa, the county seat for the county of the same name, is a small town at the junction of Highway 140 and Highway 49, comprising a six-block-long main street lined with small shops and restaurants. A side street leads up the hill to the county courthouse, the oldest one still in use west of the Rocky Mountains. Many other historic buildings are found in the downtown area. The town has several bed-and-breakfasts, inns, and motels, some on the main drag and others spread around the surrounding countryside.

RIVER ROCK INN

A great alternative to the half dozen chain motels in Mariposa, the **River Rock Inn** (4993 7th St., Mariposa, 209/966-5793 or 209/259-6803, www.riverrockmariposa.com, $149-189 in summer, $79 in winter) provides a creative and charming place to spend the night, with eight simply but tastefully decorated rooms and a garden patio. Rates include a continental breakfast, and the friendly innkeeper will leave freshly baked cookies in your room.

YOSEMITE MINER'S INN

Located at the junction of Highway 140 and Highway 49, the **Yosemite Miner's Inn** (5181 Hwy. 49 N., Mariposa, 209/742-7777 or 888/646-2244, www.yosemiteminersinn. com, $199-249 in summer, $79-209 in winter) is best described as a low-budget chain motel with a Western theme, but if you need a place to sleep in Mariposa, it serves that purpose just fine. The priciest of the 78 rooms have king beds, spa tubs, balconies, and propane fireplaces. Televisions, air-conditioning, and a free continental breakfast come standard. The inn complex has a **restaurant,** lounge, swimming pool, and on-site gift and wine shop. A decent-sized shopping center is right next door.

MARIPOSA LODGE MOTEL

The 45 rooms at the **Mariposa Lodge Motel** (5052 Hwy. 140, Mariposa, 209/966-3607 or 800/966-8819, www.mariposalodge.com, $159-189 in summer, $69-129 in winter), a member of the Best Value Inn chain, are a safe bet for lodging in downtown Mariposa. The motel is AAA-approved and comes with everything that all the neighboring chain motels offer: HBO, refrigerators, phones, wireless Internet, in-room coffee, outdoor pool, and spa. Strategically placed gazebos and patios, secluded from the highway, provide benches and seating areas from which you can enjoy Mariposa's warm summer evenings. Rooms are clean, modern, and comfortable. Pets are allowed for an additional $20 per night.

MOTHER LODE LODGE

In the budget category, the **Mother Lode Lodge** (5051 Hwy. 140, Mariposa, 209/966-2521 or 800/398-9770, www.mariposamotel. com, $109-189 in summer, lower winter rates) does the trick. The 14 no-frills rooms have one or two queen-size beds, a small desk, cable TV, refrigerator, microwave, and coffeemaker. On hot summer evenings in Mariposa, you can swim in the outdoor pool. The lodge is downtown, so you can walk to restaurants and shops.

COMFORT INN YOSEMITE VALLEY GATEWAY

Mariposa's **Comfort Inn** (4994 Bullion St., Mariposa, 209/966-4344 or 800/691-5838, www.comfortinn.com, $199-299 in summer, $109-169 in winter) offers all the standard chain amenities: phone, cable TV, HBO, outdoor pool and spa, family suites, free wireless Internet access, coffee and continental breakfast every morning in the lobby, and wheelchair-accessible rooms. Personality? No. A place to sleep within an hour of Yosemite? Yes. The Comfort Inn is a short distance off the highway, so its 59 rooms are a little quieter than many of Mariposa's motels on the main drag. Pets are not permitted.

1: The Majestic Yosemite Hotel 2: wooden cabins in Half Dome Village

BEST WESTERN YOSEMITE WAY STATION

What you get at the **Best Western Yosemite Way Station** (4999 Hwy. 140, Mariposa, 209/966-7545 or 800/564-2515, www. bestwesterncalifornia.com, $199-289 in summer, $119 in winter) is the typical Best Western experience—clean and predictable. You can count on certain classic BW elements: a coffeemaker in each of the 78 rooms, plus phone, cable TV, HBO, and a complimentary continental breakfast that will spike your blood sugar. Still, you are only one block from downtown Mariposa, so you can wander around, explore the local shops, and dine at the local restaurants. After a day in the park, you can come back to the Best Western and relax in its outdoor pool and spa.

POPPY HILL BED AND BREAKFAST

Time it right and you'll stay here in springtime, when the poppies are in full bloom along the hillsides surrounding this bed-and-breakfast. **Poppy Hill** (5218 Crystal Aire Dr., Mariposa, 209/742-6273 or 800/587-6779, www.poppyhill.com, $160 including breakfast) is a lovingly restored country home decorated with impeccable taste, inside and out. Four guest rooms have queen-size beds and private baths. All the rooms are lovely, but a favorite is the antique-filled Poppy Room, with its old spinning wheel and a private sitting room overlooking the garden. Innkeeper Mary Ellen Kirn keeps a refrigerator stocked with complimentary soft drinks, and guests can use the hot tub on the patio. You will remember the taste of Mary Ellen's puffed apple pancakes long after your visit.

HIGHLAND HOUSE BED AND BREAKFAST

Imagine a charming cottage in the English countryside and you might envision something like the **Highland House** (3125 Wild Dove Ln., Mariposa, 559/696-3341, www. highlandhouseinn.com, $140-170, May-Nov. only). Set on 10 acres (4 hectares) of incense-cedars, pines, and black oaks backing up to

Sierra National Forest, this delightful bed-and-breakfast offers three guest rooms. The Forest Retreat room has a mahogany four-poster bed and fireplace, plus a private bath with a two-person shower and soaking tub. Spring Creek has two rocking chairs and a king bed or two twin beds. Morning Dove is a smaller, dormer-style room. All three rooms have down comforters and pillows, fine linens, and soft robes. Breakfast is a highlight here and usually includes freshly baked breads and/or gourmet pancakes. The inn is about 6 miles (9.7 km) off Highway 140, so this will add some time to your drive to Yosemite, but guests say it's worth it.

MEADOW CREEK RANCH

The most popular accommodation at **Meadow Creek Ranch** (2669 Triangle Rd., Mariposa, 209/966-3843, www. meadowcreekranchinn.com, $180 including breakfast) is, believe it or not, the chicken coop. The owners of this 1858 stagecoach stop converted the coop into a charming guest cottage, complete with an Austrian carved wood canopy bed, a claw-foot tub, wicker furniture, and a gas fireplace. Guests can also stay in the Garden Gate Room, furnished with antiques and accessed via a private garden patio entrance. The Garden Gate has a carved oak queen-size bed, plus a twin bed tucked into an alcove, which works well if you are traveling with a child. The ranch is situated on 7 acres (2.8 hectares) of peaceful countryside, so there is plenty of room to roam. Guests look forward to the inn's bountiful homemade breakfast served each morning, which includes treats like blueberry walnut pancakes made with nuts from the ranch's trees.

LITTLE VALLEY INN

If you've ever wanted to try panning for gold, you can do so at **Little Valley Inn** (3483 Brooks Rd., Mariposa, 209/742-6204, www. littlevalley.com, $149-249). This six-room inn has a creek running right alongside it, and every year numerous guests search its streambed for those elusive shiny nuggets.

Each cabin-style room has its own private entrance and private deck, and is equipped with a private bath, satellite television, free wireless Internet, air-conditioning, and a small refrigerator. One larger suite has a fully equipped kitchen.

The inn is about 8 miles (13 km) south of the town of Mariposa, so you'll have to drive a bit to get into town, but plenty of repeat guests are perfectly happy with that arrangement.

WEST OF THE PARK: HIGHWAY 120

Visitors approaching from Sacramento, San Francisco, and Northern California often use the Highway 120 approach through the **Big Oak Flat entrance** to Yosemite. From the gateway town of **Groveland**, it's a 45-minute drive to the Big Oak Flat entrance and another 30 minutes (20 mi/32 km) to Yosemite Valley along Big Oak Flat Road. A few lodgings are closer to the park. Plan on a **75- to 90-minute drive to Yosemite Valley**, depending on traffic and road conditions.

For information on local lodgings, visit the **Stay Near Yosemite** lodging association website (www.staynearyosemite.com). You'll be able to check availability at multiple Groveland-area hotels, cabins, and bed-and-breakfasts simultaneously, which can save you some phone calls.

Lodgings are listed according to their proximity to Yosemite's Big Oak Flat entrance.

Hardin Flat

Hardin Flat lies only **5 miles (8 km) from the Big Oak Flat entrance,** along Hardin Flat Road off Highway 120.

RUSH CREEK LODGE

A sister property to nearby Evergreen Lodge (see the *Hetch Hetchy* chapter), the newly constructed **Rush Creek Lodge** (34001 Hwy. 120, 209/379-2373, www.rushcreeklodge.com, $210-390) opened to rave reviews in 2016. Located within 0.5 mile (0.8 km) of Big Oak Flat entrance, Rush Creek sits on 20 acres (8 hectares) of wooded private property.

This is the closest lodging to the Merced and Tuolumne groves of giant sequoias, and it provides relatively easy access to Yosemite Valley (about a 30-minute drive) and Tuolumne Meadows (about an hour). Even if you don't go to Yosemite, there are plenty of activities right on the property, including table tennis, shuffleboard, board games, a huge saltwater pool, fire pits with evening s'mores, and so on. The 143 beautifully designed rooms are comfortable and quiet, the on-site restaurant and tavern serve up pricey but good meals, and the overall experience is fairly luxurious. But by far the biggest selling point here is location, location, location—you can't get closer to the Big Oak Flat entrance without being inside the gates.

SUNSET INN

For a sweet and secluded stay in a mountain setting nearly a stone's throw from Yosemite, book one of the three Craftsman-style cabins at **Sunset Inn** (33569 Hardin Flat Rd., Groveland, 888/962-4360 or 209/962-4360, www.sunsetinn-yosemitecabins.com, $230-345). Located off the main highway a mere 2 miles (3.2 km) from the Big Flat Oak entrance, the cabins are set on a lush meadow surrounded by huge pine trees. One cabin is perfectly sized for two and has a fully equipped kitchen, private bathroom, and wood-burning stove. The "family cabin" has two separate bedrooms and can accommodate up to five people. A big bonus to staying here is that if it's a hot summer day in Groveland, it will be much more comfortable here at 4,500 feet (1,370 m) elevation. Owners Lauren and Bill Nickell are wonderful people and longtime Yosemite locals who love to provide their guests with helpful information for trip planning. They also manage some nearby vacation homes ($295-425), so if you have a larger group, they can accommodate you.

YOSEMITE LAKES

Run by the Thousand Trails/NACO camping organization, **Yosemite Lakes** (31191 Hardin Flat Rd., Groveland, 209/962-0121 or

Lodging West of the Park: Highway 120

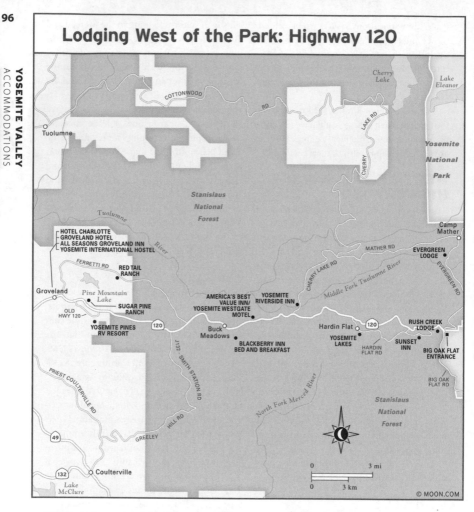

© MOON.COM

877/570-2267, www.stayatyosemite.com, $169-209) rents cabins, yurts, and hostel rooms that work well for families and are situated only 5 miles (8 km) from the entrance to Yosemite. This isn't the place for couples to go for a romantic retreat, but kids will be very happy here. The 2013 Rim Fire burned miles of forest in every direction around this resort, but the fire spared the property itself, and the region is slowly turning green again.

The 10 bunkhouse **cabins** ($100) are rustic wood-frame units with beds that sleep four; a shared bathroom is a short walk from the cabins. The 26 **yurts** ($160-200), which can accommodate four to five people, are the most luxurious. These circular, tentlike structures have a skylight and windows and are equipped with kitchens and bathrooms. They even have air-conditioning, heating, and satellite TV. Fourteen yurts are clustered on a hillside in "Yurt Village," each one surrounded by a fair-sized lawn. Eight yurts are down by the river. Propane barbecue grills and picnic tables are set outside each yurt.

Mobile homes and trailers are also for rent, and an on-site hostel offers nine rooms with

1-3 double beds in a room for $39-89. The hostel rooms share common showers and restrooms.

A café, grocery store, and gas station are part of the Yosemite Lakes complex, as is a huge RV and tent campground, so it's a bit like a small city here. Thousand Trails/NACO members receive a 10 percent discount on the regular lodging prices.

Most people who stay at Yosemite Lakes are there because it's only a 5-mile (8-km) drive into Yosemite National Park. But if you choose to hang around your lodging for the day, you'll find that recreation opportunities abound even closer. The South Fork Tuolumne River runs right through Yosemite Lakes' property. Kayaks, inner tubes, fishing poles, and gold pans are available for rent.

Buck Meadows

A stay in Buck Meadows puts you 13 miles (20.9 km) from the Big Oak Flat entrance.

YOSEMITE RIVERSIDE INN

Less than 1 mile (1.6 km) off Highway 120 and only a 10-mile (16.1-km) drive to the Big Oak Flat entrance, **Yosemite Riverside Inn** (11399 Cherry Lake Rd., Groveland, 209/962-7408 or 800/626-7408, www.yosemiteriversideinn.com) enjoys a park-like setting overlooking the Tuolumne River. The word "inn" is misleading here—the place is much more like a rustic fishing camp than an inn—but for many Yosemite travelers, it is sufficient. The surrounding forest was devastated by the 2013 Rim Fire, but fortunately the property itself was spared.

Yosemite Riverside has 20 **motel rooms** with and without river views ($199-249); one-bedroom river-view **log cabins** ($125-190); and **suites** with balconies overlooking the Middle Fork of the Tuolumne River ($275-345 summer, less in winter). Rates are for two people; add $20 for each additional adult and $10 for each additional child. The cabins have fully equipped kitchens, private baths, and satellite TV; the motel rooms have coffeemakers, private baths, and satellite TV.

A free continental breakfast is served each morning April-September. The place is popular with trout anglers because you can catch pan-size planted rainbow trout in the Middle Fork of the Tuolumne River a few steps from your door. If you seek more of a challenge, the main branch of the Tuolumne is only minutes away, where seasoned anglers catch trophy-size native trout. The inn also sees its share of rafters in the late spring and summer months; several commercial rafting outfitters operate on a nearby stretch of the Tuolumne.

AMERICA'S BEST VALUE INN/ YOSEMITE WESTGATE MOTEL

It's surprising how many visitors pass over this motel—it's clean, serviceable, affordable, quiet, and within 30 minutes of the Big Oak Flat entrance to Yosemite. The **Yosemite Westgate** (7633 Hwy. 120, Buck Meadows, 209/962-5281 or 800/253-9673, www.yosemitewestgate.com, $179-239 summer, from $99 winter) is a standard two-story motel that's a dependable bet. All the usual chain-motel amenities are available: cable TV, phone, in-room coffee, and an outdoor swimming pool and spa. Its 48 rooms come equipped with microwaves and mini-fridges. If you're hungry, the Buck Meadows Restaurant is next door, serving up big portions of classic American food.

BLACKBERRY INN BED AND BREAKFAST

This casually elegant bed-and-breakfast offers the perfect respite for nature lovers. Set on 5 acres (2 hectares) of oaks, pines, cedars, and meadows, the **Blackberry Inn** (7567 Hamilton Station Loop, Buck Meadows, 209/962-4663 or 888/867-5001, www.blackberry-inn.com, $205-305 including breakfast Apr.-Oct., lower winter rates) is home to hummingbirds, goldfinches, horses, deer, rabbits, and quail, as well as weary Yosemite travelers. The inn consists of two buildings; the original building is an inviting, two-story farmhouse with high ceilings, big windows, and a wraparound porch lined with multiple bird feeders. The Ahwahnee Suites building (built in 2013) has similar features. A total of 10 rooms are available with king- or queen-size beds and private baths. Bathrooms have either a whirlpool tub or an extra-long soaking tub. Gracious hosts Steve and Alexandra serve a huge home-cooked breakfast and chocolate chip cookies baked fresh daily, and they will gladly introduce you to their beautiful horses and other pets.

RED TAIL RANCH

Although this lovely B&B has a Groveland address, it's far enough east that it's closer to Buck Meadows, which shaves about 10 minutes off the drive to Yosemite. The **Red Tail Ranch** (22307 Ferretti Rd., Groveland, 209/962-0863, www.red-tail-ranch.com, $159-229) is at the end of a gravel road; if you like quiet and privacy, you'll love this place. The word "ranch" is not a euphemism—the property is home to 46 chickens, a handful of horses, and three friendly dogs, as well as owners Deborah and Kevin. With two new rooms added in spring 2017, the ranch now has four rooms for rent; the Ansel Suite is a popular choice thanks to its deck and hot tub. Guests rave about the breakfasts, which include eggs Benedict and orange brioche French toast.

Groveland

A stay in Groveland puts you **22 miles (35 km) from the Big Oak Flat entrance,** a distance that will take about 40 minutes to drive. It's then a **90-minute drive to Yosemite Valley**—still very doable for a day trip by typical Yosemite driving standards. The town also provides a convenient place to stay if you are visiting Tioga Pass Road, Tuolumne Meadows, or the Hetch Hetchy area of Yosemite.

Founded in 1849, Groveland was a rough-and-ready gold mining town. Until 1875 it was known as Garrote, which translates loosely from Spanish as "hanging place." The town was infamous for its swift and gruesome manner of carrying out Wild West justice, although whether this was more in reputation than in fact remains unknown. Groveland experienced a major boom beginning in 1914 with the building of the nearby Hetch Hetchy dam, when the town served as headquarters for more than a decade's worth of construction efforts. Today Groveland offers the convenience of shops, gas stations, and restaurants for Yosemite travelers.

YOSEMITE PINES RV RESORT

Despite its name, this is more of a campground than a resort. Still, **Yosemite Pines RV Resort** (20450 Old Hwy. 120, Groveland, 209/962-7690, www.yosemitepinesrv.com, $99-259 in summer, $59 in winter) rents a variety of **cabins** and **yurts,** which will appeal to the non-camping crowd. Some cabins have fully furnished kitchens and bathrooms; others are one-room units with a couple of beds, a countertop refrigerator, a microwave, a coffee pot, and cable television. For a small family on a budget, it's hard to beat the rate of the basic cabins and yurts; the trade-off is a short walk to the communal bathroom/shower house. If you want more creature comforts, the resort also rents standard, premium, deluxe, and luxury **cabins** ($209-409), which sleep five people and have private bathrooms and larger kitchens. Free wireless Internet access is available throughout the premises. Families will find plenty to keep the kiddies occupied: There's a petting zoo, gold panning, a swimming pool, sand volleyball, tetherball, and campfire storytelling. The resort's deli provides an easy option for meals.

YOSEMITE INTERNATIONAL HOSTEL

This budget-friendly lodging option in Groveland is just right for single travelers and works well for couples, too. The colorful **Yosemite International Hostel** (18605 Hwy. 120, Groveland, 209/962-0365, www.yosemitehostels.com) is a hostel in the truest sense, with **dorm beds** (shared bath and kitchen, $28-38 per person) and more **private rooms** ($36-53 per person) for couples or families. You'll hear snippets of languages from all over the world, especially in the summer months. The overall vibe is fun and welcoming, with travelers enjoying good fellowship and freebies like wireless Internet and coffee and tea.

HOTEL CHARLOTTE

The 13 rooms at the **Hotel Charlotte** (18736 Main St./Hwy. 120, Groveland, 209/962-6455 or 800/961-7799, www.hotelcharlotte.com, $179-299, lower winter rates) provide all the basics for a good night's sleep without a lot of unneeded frills. Located upstairs above the hotel's lobby and restaurant, most rooms have queen-size beds; a few have twin beds or double beds. Small groups and families will appreciate the adjoining rooms connected by a shared bathroom. Room rates are a bargain by Yosemite standards and include a continental breakfast. Guests appreciate the convenience of being right in the middle of Groveland and having a hotel with a good restaurant to return to after a day in Yosemite.

The hotel was built in 1918 by Charlotte DeFerreri, an ambitious young immigrant from Italy. Her inn provided a home for the workers who were building the Hetch Hetchy dam. Charlotte was well known as a gracious hostess and an excellent cook, and it is rumored that her ghost still roams the hotel's halls today. But even though this is a historic building in a historic town, the Hotel Charlotte is thoroughly modern—wireless Internet access is available throughout the building, the entire hotel is air-conditioned, and all rooms have satellite televisions. Owners Doug and Jenn Edwards run this iconic spot with cheerful efficiency (and they also own the Groveland Hotel across the street).

GROVELAND HOTEL

This charming hotel is one of the grande dames of the Gold Country. Built during the gold rush era, the **Groveland Hotel** (18767 Main St./Hwy. 120, Groveland, 209/962-4000 or 800/273-3314, www.groveland.com, rooms $179-299, suites $229-349, including

breakfast) was revered in those days as "The Best House on the Hill." The original 1849 adobe was reconstructed and added on to in 1914, when it was needed to house the big shots in charge of building Hetch Hetchy dam. Some of the original gold rush-era features remain, like the central staircase, casement windows, and wraparound veranda. They sit side by side with Queen Anne architecture of the early 20th century, plus even more modern additions.

The historic hotel was headed for demolition in the late 1980s until it was rescued by entrepreneur Peggy Mosley. She treated it to a multimillion-dollar face-lift, turning it into a place that *Country Inns* magazine rated as one of the top 10 inns in the United States; *Sunset* magazine ranked it one of the West's best inns. Peggy passed away in 2016, and today the inn is owned by the same couple who run the Charlotte Hotel across the street. Its 14 rooms and four suites (with spa tubs and fireplaces) were renovated and updated in 2017, and the Victorian wallpapers and floral frilliness were replaced by a much cleaner, more modern look. The old formal dining room was replaced by the chic Provisions café, which serves casual food to go as well as sit-down meals. If you've visited the Groveland Hotel in the past, you'll be amazed at the changes. But one thing that hasn't changed is the reputed presence of Lyle, the hotel's friendly resident ghost. Don't be surprised if you hear a few strange noises in the night.

ALL SEASONS GROVELAND INN

At the **All Seasons Groveland Inn** (18656 Main St./Hwy. 120, Groveland, 209/962-0232, www.allseasonsgrovelandinn.com, $139-259), you can choose from five themed rooms with murals painted on the walls, each with a private bath. Some have a whirlpool tub and fireplace. The Clouds Rest room has a mural of rainbows bursting out of clouds behind the headboard of the bed. A door opens to a private deck with a telescope. Emerald Pool features a mural of the famous wide, colorful stretch of the Merced River above Vernal

Fall; a steam room enhances the bathroom. Eagles Tower has a private deck and telescope, a mural of seven eagles and Half Dome, and a skylight over the whirlpool tub. The best of the lot may be Yosemite Falls, which has a slate waterfall and a wall-length mural of the tallest waterfall in North America. The inn is in the center of downtown Groveland, so shops and restaurants are a short walk away.

SUGAR PINE RANCH

Just 4 miles (6.4 km) east of the town of Groveland, the historic **Sugar Pine Ranch** (21250 Hwy. 120, Groveland, 209/962-7823, www.sugarpineranch.com, $140-220 summer, $99-180 winter) offers an out-of-town getaway on 62 pine-studded acres (25 hectares). In the 1860s, the property was used for lumber extraction and supplied an on-site sawmill. Later, a water ditch was constructed, and the property became a demonstration orchard planted with fruit trees. In the 1940s, the ranch became a stopover for Yosemite travelers, and the owners built the five one- and two-bedroom cottages that still exist today. The cottages have private baths, heating, and air-conditioning, but no kitchens. Three of the cabins feature Vermont cast-iron fireplaces and whirlpool tubs. Also for rent are three motel-style rooms in the "Uptown Cottage" (essentially a motor court). A swimming pool is on the property. Pets and children under the age of three are not permitted at Sugar Pine Ranch.

Camping

If you have your heart set on camping in Yosemite Valley, you'd better be one of those people who can plan far in advance. Either that or you should be one of those people who relishes camping in the middle of winter, which is the only time you can get away with not having an advance reservation for a Valley campsite. Simply put, these sites are at a premium. For the summer vacation season, every reservable site in Yosemite Valley is usually taken as soon as it shows up in the reservation system (five months in advance).

With all these hoops to jump through, you'd think that the campgrounds in Yosemite Valley would be fabulous. The truth is, they're not. Sure, they have all the amenities we've come to expect from campgrounds: picnic tables, drinking water, fire rings, and even that great unheralded luxury, flush toilets. But if you think camping should feel like a real "nature experience," you've come to the wrong place. The Valley's campsites are so close together that you'll feel like your neighbors are sharing your vacation with you. You'll hear the sound of cars driving around the campgrounds and nearby roads all night.

You'll also spend a fair portion of your camping time engaged in the business of "taking bear precautions." This means, first and foremost, that you do not store any food, or any item with a scent (including cosmetics, sunscreen, lip balm, toothpaste, and insect repellent) in your car or tent. Everything with a scent gets placed in your campsite's "bear box," including your cooler filled with food and ice. Most bear boxes are 33 inches (84 cm) deep, 45 inches (114 cm) wide, and 18 inches (46 cm) high, so make sure you don't have more stuff than will cram into that space. When you pull out food from the bear box to cook it, you must keep it within sight at all times. You shouldn't turn your back for a moment on a frozen chicken or some raw corn on the cob.

Thus, the preparation of every meal involves numerous trips back and forth to the bear box. While this may seem amusing at first, it quickly becomes a bit tiresome. If you slack in your duties, you risk having a bear steal all of your food faster than you can say, "Look, a bear is stealing our food." You also risk receiving a citation from a ranger.

Yosemite Valley Campground Rules

With all the people who want to camp in Yosemite, there have to be a few rules to keep things orderly. If you follow the guidelines listed here, you *and* your neighbors will be happy campers.

- May 1-September 15, you may camp for only seven days in Yosemite Valley. The rest of the year, there is a 14-day-stay limit.

- Only six people and two vehicles are allowed at each campsite, but parking for extra vehicles is available near the campground for a fee.

- You must keep your food properly stored from bears 24 hours a day. Store all food in the bear-proof container provided at your campsite. Do not store food, or anything with a scent, in your car.

- You may sleep in your vehicle only in designated campsites. Visitors caught sleeping in their cars outside of a campground will be asked to move, regardless of time of night, and may also be cited.

- Quiet hours are 10pm-6am.

- RV generators may be used sparingly 7am-7pm.

- Check-in and checkout are at 10am.

- April-October, campground fires are allowed 5pm-10pm only. Gas stoves may be used at any time.

- Firewood and kindling (including pinecones and needles) may not be collected in the Valley. You can purchase campfire wood from the stores in Yosemite Village and Half Dome Village. Please do not bring firewood into Yosemite that is purchased or cut from more than 50 miles (81 km) away; it can carry bugs and diseases that may spread to the park.

- The backpackers' campsites at the Valley's North Pines Campground ($6) are designated for those beginning or ending a wilderness trip. Campers who wish to stay in these sites may do so for only one night before or after their backpacking trip, and they must have their wilderness permit in hand. The sites are walk-in only, and only backpacking equipment may be brought in.

With all that said, there is still a big reason why Yosemite Valley's campsites are booked all summer long. This is Yosemite Valley—one of the most scenic places on earth. If you can put up with some inconveniences and you don't mind the crowds and lack of privacy, you will find yourself in an ideal location for exploring the Valley. In fact, there's a good chance you won't need your car at all once you're here. Most everything is within walking distance of Valley campgrounds, and free shuttle buses are available.

INSIDE THE PARK

Many visitors consider camping out an integral part of the national park experience. If you come to a national park for nature,

they reason, why spend the night walled off from it? One look at some of the park's campgrounds on a Saturday night may tell you why: because camping in Yosemite can sometimes be more like waging battle than communing with nature. But with some careful forethought and planning, you can secure a spot in or near the park and have the camping vacation of your dreams.

Reservations

Having reservations for a campsite in Yosemite Valley is imperative March through October. Contact **Recreation.gov** (877/444-6777 or 518/885-3639 from outside the U.S. and Canada, www.recreation.gov) up to **five months in advance** in order to reserve a site at one of three reservable campgrounds (Upper Pines, North Pines, and Lower Pines) in Yosemite Valley. Reservations are available in blocks of one month at a time, on the **15th of each month starting at 7am** (Pacific Standard Time). Both the telephone and the online reservation systems are open 7am-7pm (PST) November-February, and 7am-9pm (PST) March-October.

Nearly all reservations for the months of **May through September** are filled on the first morning they become available. In other words, you need to act early the morning of January 15 if you want a reservation for May 15-June 14. If you wait until the 16th of any month to make reservations, you'll probably be out of luck, although cancellations do occasionally create some vacancies.

Even with a reservation, it's wise to show up right around checkout time (10am or earlier) so that you can have your pick of available sites as campers vacate their spots. With your reservation, you are guaranteed a site, but you are not guaranteed a *good* site. Campers without reservations have an excellent chance of camping somewhere in the park (as long as they don't wait to look for a site until 6pm on Saturday evening); try the campgrounds along Big Oak Flat Road or the private campgrounds west of the park.

Upper Pines, North Pines, and Lower Pines

Of the three central Yosemite Valley camps collectively known as **"The Pines"** (shuttle stop 15, 877/444-6777 or 518/885-3639 from outside the U.S. and Canada, www.recreation.gov, $26), only Upper Pines is open year-round; the other two are open from the end of March until mid-October or early November. Upper Pines has 238 sites, North Pines has 81 sites, and Lower Pines has 60 sites. Which camp is best? All three are pretty similar, although North Pines has a slightly nicer setting with some sites right alongside the Merced River. All Pines camps offer easy access for hiking to Mirror Lake, Vernal and Nevada Falls, Half Dome, and the

Valley's other highlights. Pine trees keep most of the packed-together sites shaded, which is a real bonus in summer but a major negative in the winter, when you can freeze your buns off if you're in a tent instead of a heated RV. Even if there isn't snow, Upper Pines is often covered in ice November-February. The sun never hits it.

In summer, there is no guarantee of sleep in the three Pines campgrounds. It seems that during every hour of the night, someone is driving around, your neighbor is snoring like a locomotive, a bear is wreaking havoc somewhere in the campground, or a car alarm is going off. Asthmatics should be forewarned that during dinner hours, Yosemite Valley can become quite smoky from the campfires of nearly 400 campers at the combined Pines campgrounds (in summer, campfires are permitted only in the evening hours 5pm-10pm, not at any other time of day).

The camps have drinking water, flush toilets, picnic tables, and fire grills. All sites will accommodate tents or RVs up to 40 feet (12 m) long, except at North Pines where the limit is 35 feet (10.7 m) long. Upper Pines is the only Valley campground with an RV dump station.

The Pines camps are midway between Yosemite Village and Half Dome Village in Yosemite Valley.

Camp 4

Quite different in ambience from the three other Valley campgrounds, **Camp 4** (shuttle stop 7, first come, first served, $6 per person per night) was set aside to provide an inexpensive place for the Valley's rock climbers to stay (climbers are notorious for having empty wallets). If you think the three Pines campgrounds are crowded, wait till you see Camp 4. The 35 sites are packed in so tightly that each site is virtually indistinguishable from the next. Unlike for the three Pines campgrounds, **no reservations** are taken for Camp 4. Show up at 8:30am and you'll be assigned a site if one is available. If you don't have six people in your group, you will share your site with another group. The result is a

Camping West of the Park: Highway 140

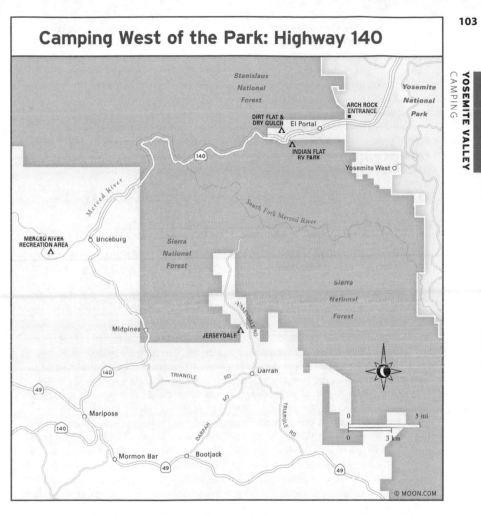

Stanislaus National Forest

Yosemite National Park

ARCH ROCK ENTRANCE

DIRT FLAT & DRY GULCH El Portal

140

INDIAN FLAT RV PARK

Yosemite West

Merced River

South Fork Merced River

MERCED RIVER RECREATION AREA

Briceburg

Sierra National Forest

Sierra National Forest

Midpines

JERSEYDALE

JERSEYDALE RD

Darrah

140

TRIANGLE RD

49

TRIANGLE RD

Mariposa

140

DARPAH RD

49

Mormon Bar

Bootjack

49

0   3 mi
0   3 km

© MOON.COM

very communal environment that appeals to some campers but not to others. (You know who you are.) It's worth noting that Camp 4 is listed in the National Register of Historic Places because of its significant role in the development of the sport of rock climbing. Don't plan on sleeping much. This is a party place, but you'll be hanging out with the cool kids (and in Yosemite, the cool kids are always the rock climbers).

Campers must walk in to Camp 4; all cars are left 100-200 feet (30-60 m) away in a large parking lot. You won't have an SUV fender parked next to your tent, and you won't have to listen to anybody's RV generator. The camp is equipped with drinking water, flush toilets, picnic tables, and fire grills. If you want to hike to the top of Upper Yosemite Fall, you couldn't be better situated: The trail begins right at Camp 4.

WEST OF THE PARK: HIGHWAY 140

Public campground pickings are slim along the 30-mile (48-km) stretch of Highway 140 leading to the park entrance: There are a couple of Forest Service camps and a small cluster of Bureau of Land Management camps located on the Merced River. Fortunately, free enterprise comes to the rescue with a handful of privately operated camps and RV parks that can save the weary traveler from a long night in the car.

These campgrounds are listed according to their proximity to Yosemite's **Arch Rock entrance** on Highway 140. The first listing is the closest to the park.

El Portal
DIRT FLAT AND DRY GULCH
Dirt Flat and Dry Gulch Campgrounds (877/444-6777 or 518/885-3639 from outside the U.S. and Canada, www.recreation. gov, $26 plus $7 for extra vehicles) have only a handful of sites—two at Dirt Flat and four at Dry Gulch—but what sweet sites they are (and for tent campers only; no RVs). Both are alongside the north bank of the Merced River just a few miles from the Arch Rock entrance to Yosemite. Many Yosemite-bound drivers cruising down Highway 140 see the campsites on the far side of the river but have no idea how to get to them. The only way is to cross over the river on the Foresta Bridge, then backtrack (head west) on Incline Road. The two separate camps are just off an old stretch of the Yosemite Railroad Grade. You park your car in a central parking lot and then walk a few hundred feet to your chosen site. The camps have picnic tables, fire grills, drinking water, and vault toilets. To reach the camps, turn left (north) on Foresta Road off Highway 140 in El Portal, near Redbud Picnic Area. Cross the river bridge, then turn left (west) and drive 1.4 miles (2.3 km) to the camps, which are 0.2 mile (0.3 km) apart.

INDIAN FLAT RV PARK
Location is everything, and **Indian Flat RV Park** (9988 Hwy. 140, El Portal, 300 ft/90 m east of Cedar Lodge, 209/379-2339, www. indianflatrvpark.com, $20-30 tents, $37-48 RVs) has it. Located 8 miles (12.9 km) from the Arch Rock entrance to Yosemite, this is

the closest private campground to Yosemite Valley. You can pull out of Indian Flat in the morning and be gazing at Half Dome 30 minutes later. The park has 25 RV sites with full water and electrical hookups (these are the closest hookups to Yosemite Valley), 25 tent sites, group sites for large groups, and even a few low-budget tent cabins and cottages ($59-169) if you forgot to bring your tent. It would be wise to make a reservation if you plan to stay here in the busy summer months.

Midpines and Vicinity
MERCED RIVER
RECREATION AREA
Yosemite travelers either know about these three Bureau of Land Management-run campgrounds (209/966-3192) along the Merced River, or they don't. Most don't because they aren't right along Highway 140; they are on the north side of the river and can only be accessed by a side road and an old suspension bridge. (Large RVs and trailers are not recommended.) The bridge is behind the Briceburg Visitor Center, a fairly prominent structure on a mostly desolate stretch of the highway. Although these campgrounds are largely unknown to Yosemite travelers, they are extremely well known to river rafters, many of whom use Railroad Flat as a take-out point. If you are visiting during the main part of the Merced rafting season (May-July), your chance of getting one of the 31 sites is slim. As soon as the river level drops, usually by late July, your chances improve greatly.

This is a lovely area along the river, with plentiful opportunities for hiking and fishing, but it gets terribly hot in summer. Also, if you are driving in late at night and are unfamiliar with the camp access road, exercise great caution; the dirt road is narrow and drops off steeply into the Merced River. Fortunately, it's an old railroad grade, so it's pretty smooth and fairly level. The three camps, **McCabe Flat, Willow Placer,** and **Railroad Flat** (first come, first served, $10), are each about 1 mile (1.6 km) apart (the first camp is 2.5 mi/4 km from the Briceburg Visitor Center; the last camp is almost 5 mi/8 km from it). Each camp has picnic tables, fire grills, and vault toilets. Bring your own drinking water. Most sites are walk-ins; a few will accommodate small RVs or trailers. The campgrounds are 12 miles (19.3 km) east of Mariposa off Highway 140. Turn left at the visitors center and cross the suspension bridge, then turn left and drive 2.5 miles (4 km) to the first camp. For more information, contact the Briceburg Visitor Center (209/379-9414, May-early Sept.) or the Bureau of Land Management Mother Lode Field Office (916/941-3101).

JERSEYDALE

If there is a "secret" campground in the Mariposa area and within an hour of Yosemite Valley, Jerseydale (off Jerseydale Road in Midpines, 559/877-2218 for the Sierra National Forest, May-Nov., free) is it. The camp is 9 miles (14.5 km) off Highway 140, and if you didn't know it was here, you'd never go looking for it. For people driving to Yosemite on Highway 140 late at night, this camp can be a lifesaver. You can almost always find a spot, even on holiday weekends. The camp is small and pleasant, with 10 sites tucked into a tall pine forest. It has everything a camper needs: drinking water, picnic tables, fire grills, and vault toilets. And it has one thing a camper can really appreciate: no fee.

The camp is on Jerseydale Road near its junction with Triangle Road. From Mariposa, drive 5 miles (8 km) northeast on Highway 140 to Triangle Road. Turn right and drive 6 miles (9.7 km) to Darrah and Jerseydale Road. Turn left and drive 3 miles (4.8 km) to the camp on the left.

WEST OF THE PARK: HIGHWAY 120

On Highway 120 east of Groveland you'll find several camps operated by the Groveland Ranger District of Stanislaus National Forest (209/962-7825, www.fs.usda.gov/stanislaus). In addition, several privately operated campgrounds are found here, including a few good camps for RVs.

One bugaboo for site-seekers to watch out for: Many guidebooks mention a series of three camps along the Tuolumne River called Lumsden, Lumsden Bridge, and South Fork. Although on maps it appears that these camps are 5-7 miles (8-11.3 km) off Highway 120 on Lumsden Road, those miles are dirt and gravel, extremely steep and narrow, and very dangerous to drive, especially at night. One wrong move and your car plunges hundreds of feet into the Tuolumne River canyon. Do not attempt this road unless you have a high-clearance vehicle and you're in the mood for adventure. If you want to drive into Yosemite in the morning, you'll spend at least 20 minutes crawling back out on Lumsden Road, then another 30 minutes on the highway. This area was also the starting point for the 2013 Rim Fire, so the forest has been torched. Your best bet is to camp somewhere else.

These campgrounds are listed according to their proximity to Yosemite's Big Oak Flat entrance on Highway 120.

Groveland and Vicinity
YOSEMITE LAKES

You don't have to be a member of the Thousand Trails/NACO club to camp at Yosemite Lakes (3119 Hardin Flat Rd., Groveland, 209/962-0103 or 877/570-2267, www.stayatyosemite.com, $47-72 tents or RVs), although that is a rarity in this nationwide chain of campgrounds. The camp is blessed with an unbelievably good location just 5 miles (8 km) from the Big Oak Flat entrance. Not surprisingly, it gets a lot of overflow traffic when the park's campgrounds are full.

But be forewarned: The campground is really a small city, with 254 full-hookup RV sites and 130 tent sites, plus rental trailers, cabins, and yurts. The South Fork Tuolumne River runs through the property and is ideal for swimming, fishing, and even trying your luck at gold panning. You can participate in all kinds of organized activities if you are so inclined: kids' games, kayak rentals, miniature golf, volleyball, and so forth. The best aspect

Camping West of the Park: Highway 120

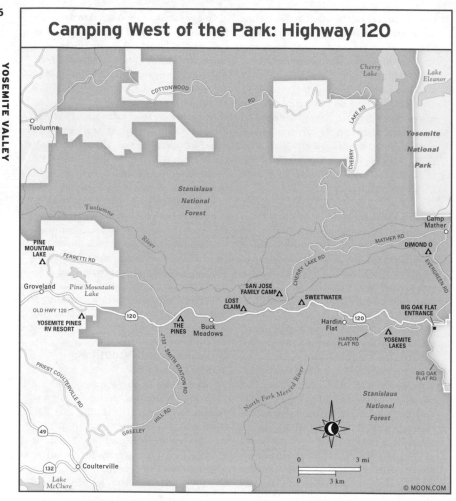

of all this development is that the camp store is reasonably well stocked with groceries and the like, but don't think of buying gasoline here: It's always priced at least 50 cents higher than it is in either Yosemite (Crane Flat) or Groveland. If you are a member of Thousand Trails/NACO, you get a discount on your overnight fees.

This camp is 18 miles (29 km) east of Groveland or 5 miles (8 km) west of the Big Oak Flat entrance; turn south off Highway 120 at Hardin Flat Road.

SWEETWATER

The Groveland Ranger District's **Sweetwater Campground** (209/962-7825, May-Sept., first come, first served, $22) sits in the midst of the 2013 Rim Fire devastation area, and it's closed until late 2019 due to a massive tree removal project. When it reopens, it will once again offer a clean and pleasant place to sleep that's less than 10 miles (16.1 km) from the Big Oak Flat entrance and directly on Highway 120. The camp has 12 sites with drinking water, picnic tables, fire grills, and vault toilets. It's on the north side of Highway 120, 15 miles (24 km) east of Groveland or 9 miles (14.5 km) west of the Big Oak Flat entrance.

SAN JOSE FAMILY CAMP AT YOSEMITE

Right next to the Yosemite Riverside Inn, the **San Jose Family Camp at Yosemite** (11401 Cherry Lake Rd., Groveland, 209/962-7277 or 408/794-6208, www.familycampreservations. com, $60-80 per person 16 and over, $50-70 children 4-15, including all meals) is a good choice for you guessed it—families. The surprising part is that you don't have to live or work in San Jose, California, to be able to camp here, even though the camp is run by San Jose Parks and Recreation. (San Jose residents get a discount on the fees, however.) This is an organized camp that provides tent cabins for all guests; you aren't allowed to set up your own gear. The 64 tent cabins have steel bed frames with mattresses, a wooden bookcase, and a small table with two benches. Rates at the camp are per person and include lodging, cafeteria-style meals, and a variety of organized activities. The camp is typically open from mid-June to late August for individual campers (before and after that period, it is only available to large groups). You must make reservations in advance.

LOST CLAIM

Lost Claim Camp (info at 209/379-2258, reserve at 877/444-6777 or www.recreation.gov, May-Sept., $22) is quite similar in appearance to nearby Sweetwater Camp, although a bit smaller and more protected from the sights and sounds of Highway 120, and a few bucks cheaper. Like everything else in this region east of Groveland, the surrounding forest was badly burned in the 2013 Rim Fire, but the vegetation is coming back. Nonetheless, with this camp's proximity to Yosemite and the fact that it has only 10 sites, you'll be quite lucky if you get a spot here on summer weekends. Tall pine trees and manzanitas provide some shade and screening for the sites. Trailers and large RVs are not recommended here because of the steep access road.

Unfortunately, like the other Forest Service camps in this area, Lost Claim is shut down soon after Labor Day each year, even though Yosemite's high country is open for another month. The camp has drinking water, picnic tables, fire grills, and vault toilets. It's on the north side of Highway 120, 12 miles (19.3 km) east of Groveland or 12 miles (19.3 km) west of the Big Oak Flat entrance. (It's less than a mile west of the Rim of the World Vista Point.)

PINES CAMPGROUND

This Stanislaus National Forest campground is just off Highway 120, only 15 miles (24 km) from the Big Oak Flat entrance to Yosemite. The **Pines Campground** (info at 209/379-2258, reserve at 877/444-6777 or www.recreation.gov, year round, $22) is behind the Forest Service ranger station, where you can get all the information you need for exploring the surrounding area. Its 11 sites are level and roomy enough; even small RVs can find a spot in here. But the Pines is less favorable than other camps for a few reasons: The sites are spaced much too close together and don't have enough foliage around them to provide privacy. Most are open and fully exposed to the sun, so don't expect the ice in your cooler to hold up in summer. Don't plan on sleeping late in your tent, either—you'll get baked at this 3,200-foot (975-m) elevation, where summer temperatures are often in the 90s.

Still, if you are driving into the park late at night and you just need a spot to lay your head, this camp will do the trick. The camp has drinking water, picnic tables, fire grills, and vault toilets. A 50-person **group site** (877/444-6777 or 518/885-3639 from outside the U.S. and Canada, www.recreation. gov, $90) is a short distance from the individual sites. This camp is on the south side of Highway 120, 7.5 miles (12.1 km) east of Groveland. Turn right at the Ranger Station sign and drive 0.5 mile (0.8 km) to the campground. (Another road enters this camp 1 mi/1.6 km farther east on Highway 120.)

YOSEMITE PINES RV RESORT

RVers like the fact that **Yosemite Pines RV Resort** (20450 Old Hwy. 120, 209/962-7690 or 877/962-7690, www.yosemitepinesrv.com, $18-46 tents, $32-69 RVs) has hookups—something you won't find in the park itself. Dusty hikers like the fact that this resort has showers. With 216 sites, this place feels more like a small city than a campground. It comes complete with a mini-mart, pool, laundry, clubhouse, and cabin and RV rentals. Kids will have plenty of fun with a petting zoo, pony rides, hay rides, gold panning, a gold mine tour, and campfire storytelling. The only downer: It's a 22-mile (35-km) drive to the Big Oak Flat entrance. You'll find "old" Highway 120 2 miles (3.2 km) east of Groveland off "new" Highway 120.

PINE MOUNTAIN LAKE CAMPGROUND

The **Pine Mountain Lake Campground** (13500 Rocky Point Dr., off Ferretti Rd., Groveland, 209/962-8615, www.pinemountainlake.com, $26 tents, $39 RVs, reduced rates for Pine Mountain Lake property owners) is little known except by those who know someone who lives in the Pine Mountain Lake development. It's only a couple miles from Highway 120 in Groveland and makes an easy, dependable layover on the way into the park. The camp is open all year, and you can even get a reservation in advance, if you wish, by phone or online. The 55 sites are spaced far enough apart in a pleasant pine, oak, cedar, and manzanita forest. It's clean and safe, and, most important, you can almost always find a site. Hookups and a dump station are available for RVs.

The camp has drinking water, picnic tables, fire grills, hot showers, flush toilets, horseshoe pits, and a volleyball court. From Highway 120, turn left on Ferretti Road, drive 2.5 miles (4 km) to Rocky Point Drive, turn left, and enter the camp.

Wawona and Glacier Point

To the Native Americans who traveled between the foothills and Yosemite Valley, Wawona was the halfway point on their journey. They called it Pallachun, meaning "a good place to stay." This popular encampment later became the site of a wayside inn built by Galen Clark. Today it is home to the historic Big Trees Lodge and a private community of homes, many of which can be rented by park visitors. Now, as then, Wawona is a good place to stay.

It's also a good place to visit, with fishing and swimming holes in the South Fork Merced River, an excellent hiking trail to Chilnualna Falls, the natural spectacle of the Mariposa Grove of Giant Sequoias, and an opportunity to "step back in time" at the Pioneer Yosemite History Center. Plus, Wawona offers convenient access to Glacier Point, one

Highlights

Look for ★ to find recommended sights, activities, dining, and lodging.

★ **Tunnel View and Inspiration Point:** The breathtaking vista of Yosemite Valley from Inspiration Point was made famous by an Ansel Adams photograph. See it via an easy 10-minute drive from the valley floor (page 116).

★ **Glacier Point:** This spectacular 7,214-foot (2,200-m granite precipice overlooks Yosemite Valley, Half Dome, and the High Sierra. If you can time it right, don't miss watching the sunset from here (page 116).

★ **Sentinel Dome and Taft Point:** Two short hikes to these two overlook points start at the same trailhead, just 1 mile (1.6 km) west of Glacier Point. Both hikes are short and easy enough for families to handle; each is 2.2 miles (3.5 km) round-trip (page 116).

★ **Yosemite Ski & Snowboard Area:** Only winter visitors to Yosemite will get to experience the joys of Yosemite Ski & Snowboard Area, formerly **Badger Pass,** which include short or nonexistent lift lines, relatively inexpensive lift tickets, and plenty of recreation options for non-skiers (page 118).

★ **Mariposa Grove of Giant Sequoias:** Yosemite's largest grove of giant sequoia trees, the largest living trees on earth by volume, is found near the southern entrance to the park. Casual visitors can wander through the lower grove to see the most famous trees; more serious hikers can trek to the upper grove as well (page 118).

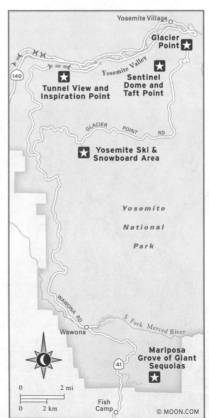

of the grandest viewpoints in the West. The commanding vista from Glacier Point takes in all the major granite landmarks of Yosemite Valley and the surrounding high country. For many park visitors, it is Yosemite's single most memorable spot.

PLANNING YOUR TIME

Glacier Point, at 7,214 feet (2,199 m) in elevation, is covered with deep snow **late October to late May,** and its access roads are closed. The snowpack is cause for celebration at Yosemite Ski & Snowboard Area, 6 miles (9.7 km) east on Glacier Point Road. Temperatures at Glacier Point during the summer and fall months are generally mild, ranging 60-80°F (15-26°C) during the day and 40-60°F (4-15°C) at night. Thunderstorms occur occasionally, most often on July and August afternoons.

Wawona and the Mariposa Grove of Giant Sequoias share approximately the same elevation (5,000 ft/1,500 m) and the same weather: warm, mild days and cooler nights. Summer temperatures typically reach the mid-80s or low 90s (29-34°C) during the day and drop into the 50s (10-15°C) at night. Both areas receive a few feet of snow over the course of the winter. Highway 41 stays open year-round, but drivers must carry chains in their vehicles at all times in winter.

Exploring Wawona and Glacier Point

VISITORS CENTER

The **Wawona Visitor Center at Hill's Studio** (209/375-9531, 8:30am-5pm daily May-Nov.) is the main visitors center for the southern part of Yosemite and is located at the Big Trees Lodge. Hill's Studio was where the famous 19th-century landscape painter Thomas Hill once worked. Today the center provides information on interpretive activities and programs in Wawona, Glacier Point, and the Mariposa Grove. Books, maps, and wilderness permits are available.

The Pioneer Yosemite History Center in Wawona is sometimes staffed with volunteers; if not, interpretive signs and brochures are available.

ENTRANCE STATION

The **South entrance** station is on Highway 41 and provides access to Wawona and the southern part of Yosemite National Park. Just inside the entrance station is a parking lot for the Mariposa Grove of Giant Sequoias. Visitors must park their cars and ride a free shuttle bus into the grove. To get to Glacier Point from the entrance station, continue 3 miles (4.8 km) north on Highway 41 to Wawona, then another 15 miles (24 km) to Chinquapin. Turn right here and drive 16 miles (26 km) to Glacier Point.

SHUTTLES AND TOURS

Mariposa Grove Shuttle

From mid-March to late November, free shuttle buses run from the Mariposa Grove parking lot near the Highway 41 entrance station and also from the Big Trees Lodge to the Mariposa Grove. As of 2017, you can no longer drive your own car to the grove unless you are arriving before or after the shuttles' operating times (8am-8pm daily May 15-Oct. 15, 8am-5pm daily Mar. 15-May 15 and Oct. 15-Nov.).

Wawona-Yosemite Valley Shuttle

During the summer months, a **free shuttle bus** (Memorial Day-Labor Day) is available from Wawona to Yosemite Valley. The bus

Previous: Ostrander Ski Hut; California Tunnel Tree in the Mariposa Grove; backpacker on the Panorama Trail.

Wawona and Glacier Point

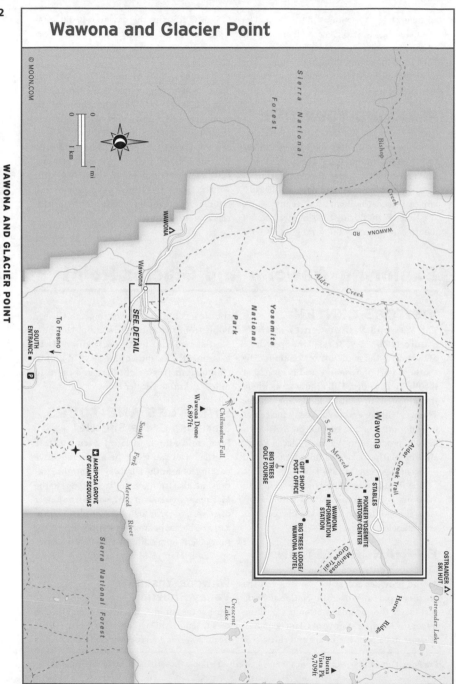

© MOON.COM

0 1 mi
0 1 km

Sierra National Forest

Bishop Creek

WAWONA RD

WAWONA

Wawona

SEE DETAIL

Alder Creek

Yosemite National Park

To Fresno

SOUTH ENTRANCE

Wawona Dome 6,897ft

Chilnualna Fall

South Fork Merced River

MARIPOSA GROVE OF GIANT SEQUOIAS

Sierra National Forest

Crescent Lake

Horse Ridge

Ostrander Lake

OSTRANDER SKI HUT

Buena Vista Pk 9,709ft

Wawona (detail)

Wawona

S Fork Merced R.

Alder Creek Trail

BIG TREES GOLF COURSE

GIFT SHOP/ POST OFFICE

STABLES

PIONEER YOSEMITE HISTORY CENTER

WAWONA INFORMATION STATION

BIG TREES LODGE/ WAWONA HOTEL

Mariposa Grove Trail

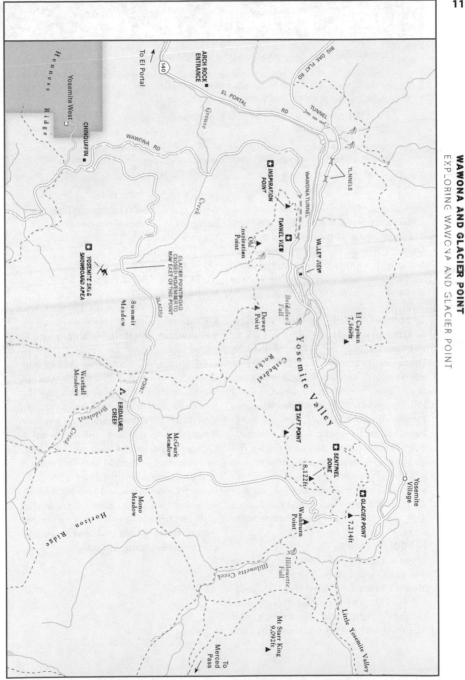

Where Can I Find...?

- **Banks and ATMs:** Wawona Store & Pioneer Gift Shop.

- **Gas:** Wawona has a **gas station** (near the Wawona Store) where you can pay at the pump 24 hours a day with a credit card. You can also buy gas a few miles outside the park in Fish Camp. There is no gas anywhere near Glacier Point.

- **Post Office:** Next door to the Wawona Store & Pioneer Gift Shop is a post office (9am-5pm Mon.-Fri., 9am-1pm Sat.).

- **Showers:** The **High Sierra RV Park** (559/683-7662, Oakhurst, www.highsierrarv.com, 8am-11am and 1pm-6pm daily) offers hot showers for $5 per person. Call to confirm hours.

departs daily from the Big Trees Lodge at 8:30am and from the Wawona Store at 8:35am. The return trip departs from Yosemite Valley Lodge at 3:30pm. For park visitors staying in the Wawona area, this free shuttle bus is a great way to visit Yosemite Valley without the hassles and expenses of driving.

Discover Yosemite

A private company outside the park in Oakhurst also provides bus tours of Yosemite. **Discover Yosemite** (559/642-4400 or 800/585-0565, www.discoveryosemite.com) takes visitors from Oakhurst, Bass Lake, and Fish Camp to the Mariposa Grove, Wawona's Pioneer Yosemite History Center, Glacier Point, and even Yosemite Valley. Guides provide a running commentary on the sights; frequent photo stops are made. Tours of various lengths (half day, full day, sunset, full moon) are available; typical rates for a full-day tour are $152 adults, $146 seniors, and $76 children ages 3-16, including lunch and beverages.

Model T Tours

If you're a history buff, considering driving into Yosemite in a Model T or Model A Ford. **Model T Tours** (7730 Laurel Way, Fish Camp, 559/641-7731, www.driveamodelt.com, $400-450 per day) rents antique Ford vehicles that date from 1915 to 1929 (both roadsters and

touring cars). After taking a short driving lesson, you can put the top down and cruise into the park.

Driving Tours
YOSEMITE VALLEY TO GLACIER POINT

From Yosemite Valley, it is a 14-mile (22.5-km) drive south on Wawona Road to **Chinquapin junction.** With a left turn at Chinquapin (restrooms available), it's 16 miles (26 km) east on **Glacier Point Road** through some lovely forested terrain to Washburn Point and Glacier Point. Visit the scenic Glacier Point overlook (snacks and restrooms available), then retrace your way back down Glacier Point Road. Turn left (south) at Chinquapin junction on Highway 41 and head for Wawona, 15 miles (24 km) distant. Stop in **Wawona** and visit the Pioneer Yosemite History Center (store and restrooms available), then continue 3 miles (4.8 km) farther south on Highway 41 to the parking area for the **Mariposa Grove of Giant Sequoias** near Yosemite's South entrance.

Yosemite Mountain Sugar Pine Railroad

Yosemite Mountain Sugar Pine Railroad

Although most visitors to Yosemite take tours on foot, or by bus or open-air tram, a more unusual tour can be taken on a vintage narrow-gauge steam train.

Just 3 miles (4.8 km) south of the park in Fish Camp is the **Yosemite Mountain Sugar Pine Railroad** (56001 Hwy. 41, Fish Camp, 559/683-7273, www.yosemitesteamtrains.com), an attraction that brings to life memories of long-gone logging camps. Using the same route on which sturdy flumes once transported lumber from Fish Camp to Madera, visitors today can ride the authentic narrow-gauge Logger Steam Train through scenic woodlands. One steam locomotive was built in 1913, another in 1928, and they can still pull a train of cars today.

Along the 4-mile (6.4-km) stretch of track, the beautifully restored and maintained engines pull cars with benches carved from giant trees through a wooded stretch of Sierra National Forest. In days gone by, this was the train that carried massive sugar pine logs to the mills, where they were sawed into timbers and boards to build the growing local communities. The narrated ride lasts about one hour and often includes a stop in the forest where riders can enjoy a picnic and a stroll. You might want to keep an eye on your wallet, though: on warm summer evenings you have to watch out for masked bandits who stage holdups on horseback—complete with blazing six-shooters.

The **Logger Steam Train** (1 hour, $24 adults, $12 children 3-12) departs daily at 11am, 12:30pm, and 2pm June through August (11am and 12:30pm Sat.-Sun. Apr.-May and Sept.-Oct.).

The **Moonlight Special** train ride (3 hours, 6pm Wed. and Sat. May-Sept., $58 adults, $29 children 3-12) comes complete with a New York steak, chicken, or vegetarian barbecue dinner and music and singing around a campfire.

Tours on **Jenny Railcars** (30 minutes, $19 adults, $9.50 children 3-12) are powered by antique Model A Ford gas engines. The railcars were once used to provide transportation for logging and track repair crews. Trains usually depart daily 9:30am-3pm (Mar.-Oct.), but the schedule varies. Call ahead to make a reservation, or book online.

Sights

★ TUNNEL VIEW AND INSPIRATION POINT

Don't miss this **viewpoint** as you drive out of the Valley on your way to Wawona or Glacier Point. The vista of Yosemite Valley here is a standout; you may recognize it from a famous Ansel Adams photograph. The view of Bridalveil Fall, El Capitan, and Half Dome is sublime. From Yosemite Valley, take Highway 41/Wawona Road; the turnout for the viewpoint is at the east end of the Wawona Tunnel, along Highway 41.

GLACIER POINT REGION

TOP EXPERIENCE

★ Glacier Point

Often referred to as "the grandest view in all the West," **Glacier Point** is a 7,214-foot (2,199-m) overlook with a vista of Yosemite Valley, Half Dome and all its granite neighbors, and the High Sierra. The overlook area features a beautiful amphitheater for evening ranger talks, an imposing log cabin housing a snack stand and gift shop (summer only), and a large and clean restroom, plus all the historical highlights of the point: the stone-constructed **Geology Hut** that faces Half Dome, and the rock railings that look out over Vernal and Nevada Falls and the Merced River canyon. A big hotel once stood on top of Glacier Point, but it burned to the ground in 1969 and was never rebuilt.

To reach Glacier Point from Wawona, drive 12 miles (19.3 km) north on Highway 41 and turn east onto Glacier Point Road. Continue 15 miles (24 km) east on Glacier Point Road to the parking lot; it's about a 400-foot (120-m)

walk to the overlook. From Yosemite Valley, drive 9 miles (14.5 km) south on Wawona Road to reach the Glacier Point turnoff.

Washburn Point

Many visitors bypass this overlook in their hurry to get to Glacier Point, but **Washburn Point** is worth a stop in its own right. Washburn Point offers a dizzying perspective of Half Dome and the granite country of the High Sierra. Although you won't see much of Yosemite Valley, it has the best possible view of Vernal and Nevada Falls. The overlook was named for the Washburn brothers, who owned the original Wawona Hotel and drove visitors by stagecoach to this spot in the 1870s.

Washburn Point is on Glacier Point Road, 0.75 mile (1.2 km) south of Glacier Point; look for a parking area on the left.

★ Sentinel Dome and Taft Point

These two spectacular overlooks cannot be seen from the car, but if you have the time and energy either destination will round out your trip to Glacier Point. **Sentinel Dome,** a granite dome topping out at 8,122 feet (2,476 m), offers a breathtaking view of Yosemite Falls and a 360-degree panorama of granite peaks and domes. The view from **Taft Point** is completely different: a head-on look at El Capitan and a stomach-churning view of the Yosemite Valley floor, 3,500 feet (1,100 m) below. Hold on to the railing while you peer over it.

The trailhead is on Glacier Point Road, about 2 miles (3.2 km) south of Glacier Point. Both trails lead from the same parking lot but head in opposite directions; each requires a hike of 1.1 miles (1.8 km) one-way.

1: Yosemite Falls from Glacier Point **2:** a tree in the Mariposa Grove **3:** Half Dome, as seen from Glacier Point **4:** Taft Point

★ Yosemite Ski & Snowboard Area

(FORMERLY BADGER PASS)

In the winter, **Yosemite Ski & Snowboard Area** (Dec.-Mar.) is the only destination you can drive to on Glacier Point Road. The road is plowed for 6 miles (9.7 km) to the ski area's entrance; just a few feet beyond, the ground is piled several feet high with snow. If you want to travel farther on Glacier Point Road, the ski area is your trailhead, and your mode of travel will be cross-country skis or snowshoes. But downhillers might want to carve a few turns on Yosemite's ski hill, which boasts of being the oldest ski resort in California. The resort offers downhill skiing, cross-country skiing, snowshoeing, snowboarding, and "snow tubing," or sledding on inner tubes. Even if you don't feel like playing in the snow, Yosemite Ski & Snowboard Area is a fine place to go for lunch on a sunny winter's day—buy a hamburger and a soda, sit outside on the deck, and watch the skiers carve S turns through the white stuff.

Yosemite Ski & Snowboard Area is on Glacier Point Road, 5 miles (8 km) from the turnoff from Wawona Road and 10 miles (16.1 km) south of Glacier Point.

WAWONA

Big Trees Lodge

(FORMERLY WAWONA HOTEL)

The historic Victorian-style **Big Trees Lodge** (8308 Wawona Rd., Wawona, 888/413-8869 or 209/375-6556, www.travelyosemite.com) makes a lovely sight alongside Highway 41 just south of Wawona. Have a seat inside the hotel **dining room** for breakfast, lunch, or dinner, or just drop by for a look at the old photographs in the lobby area. A gift shop, bookstore, and visitors center are across from the hotel.

Pioneer Yosemite History Center

The **Pioneer Yosemite History Center** in Wawona brings Yosemite's history to life. These historic buildings, many of which were relocated from other places in the park to this collection, are from different periods of Yosemite's history—a **U.S. Cavalry office,** the **bakery** the Degnan family used to bake bread in the Valley, a **Wells Fargo station** that served stagecoach passengers, a **jail,** and a few homesteads. Live demonstrations are often held at the **blacksmith shop** and other buildings (check the Yosemite newspaper for dates and times). **Horse-drawn carriage rides** (10 minutes, $5 adults, $4 children 3-12) are offered daily. You can walk around the buildings' exteriors on your own (an interpretive brochure is available); in the summer months, docents sometimes dress in period costumes and lead visitors on free tours inside the buildings.

To reach the Pioneer Yosemite History Center, cross Forest Drive and walk through a **covered bridge** across the South Fork Merced River. The bridge was built in 1857 by the Washburn brothers, who established a tourist facility in what later became Wawona. Although the elaborate bridge served a practical purpose—the covered deck and truss portion protected the bridge from winter weather—it may have been built more to satisfy the Washburns' longing for the familiar sights of their East Coast family home. The Washburn brothers owned the Wawona Hotel (now the Big Trees Lodge) and most of the land in this area until 1932, when the National Park Service purchased it.

★ MARIPOSA GROVE OF GIANT SEQUOIAS

The **Mariposa Grove** is the largest grove of sequoias in the park. Its 250 acres (100 hectares) contain more than 500 mature trees, each more than 10 feet (3 m) in diameter, as well as hundreds of smaller trees. The grove is divided into two areas—upper and lower. Most casual visitors stroll through the lower grove to see the most famous "named" trees, like the Grizzly Giant. Adventurous hikers will want to wander around both the upper and lower groves, a 6.6-mile (10.6-km)

Understanding Giant Sequoias

Sierra redwoods, or *Sequoiadendron giganteum,* are the largest living things on earth by volume—not by height alone, but by a combination of height and girth. Whereas coast redwoods can grow 365 feet (111 m) tall and up to 18 feet (5.5 m) across, giant sequoias grow "only" 310 feet tall (94 m), but up to 30 feet (9 m) in diameter. Remarkably, a tree this large grows from a seed the size of a single flake of oatmeal.

The sequoia's immense girth is often what makes the strongest impression on Yosemite visitors. Walking around the base of one of these giants is a slow task. If your hiking partner heads in one direction and you head in the opposite, a few long seconds will pass until you meet on the far side.

The giant sequoias of the Mariposa Grove are astounding.

The oldest sequoias are around 3,000 years old, but despite their advanced age, they are not the oldest trees on Earth. That honor goes to the ancient bristlecone pines that are found east of Yosemite in the White Mountains, Death Valley National Park, and Nevada. (The oldest known bristlecone pine is 4,600 years old; the oldest known giant sequoia is a mere 3,200 years old.)

Giant sequoias once ranged across the globe, but now they are found only in a narrow strip of the western Sierra Nevada, 250 miles (405 km) long and 15 miles (24 km) wide, at elevations ranging 4,000-7,000 feet (1,200-2,100 m). A total of only 75 scattered groves are found in this belt. By all appearances, the sequoia seems to be slowly disappearing from the earth. Some of the Sierra's existing groves are quite healthy and will continue to reproduce, most likely for many more centuries. Other groves have only a few older trees and not enough young ones to replace the ancients when they die. The northernmost groves of sequoias, such as a small grove in Placer County near Foresthill, California, seem to be in the greatest danger of extinction. The largest, healthiest groves of sequoias are south of Yosemite in Sequoia and Kings Canyon National Parks and Giant Sequoia National Monument.

Giant sequoias have many interesting characteristics, but one of their most unusual features is that their bark can grow up to 2 feet (60 cm) thick. This makes the sequoia extremely insect- and fire-resistant. In fact, rather than harming the trees, fire is essential to the sequoia life cycle: It takes extreme heat to open up the sequoia cone and spread its tiny seeds along the forest floor. Sequoia seedlings survive best in a forest that experiences frequent, small fires, which thin out competing trees and distribute more sunlight and other resources to the young sequoias. Animals also aid in the sequoia life cycle: The chickaree (Douglas squirrel) fells green sequoia cones, sends them plummeting to the ground, and then eats the fleshy part, leaving the cones' seeds to germinate on the forest floor.

round-trip with a substantial amount of climbing (about 1,200 ft/365 m).

The Mariposa Grove reopened in June 2018 after being closed three years for restoration. The massive project improved habitat for the sequoias by removing parking lots and roads and restoring the natural flow of water to the giant trees. A raised boardwalk trail now travels through the lower grove, minimizing visitor impact on the sequoias' fragile roots and providing better access for wheelchairs and strollers. The main parking lot was relocated 2 miles (3.2 km) away from the grove near the park's South entrance. Now, for most of the year, visitors can visit the grove only via shuttle bus. To access the Mariposa Grove from March to November, take one of the free **shuttle buses** from the huge, 300-car parking lot near the park's South entrance. Buses run every 10-15 minutes 8am-8pm daily mid-May to mid-October and 8am-5pm in early spring and late fall. If you arrive very early in the morning before the shuttle buses are running, you may be able to drive your own car into the grove (about two dozen parking spots remain after the renovation). From December to mid-March, shuttles do not run, but visitors can park in the lot and snowshoe or walk along the road into the grove. The Park Service is constructing a hiking trail that will lead from the parking lot to the grove so that hikers have an alternative to riding the bus or walking on the road. It's expected to open in late summer 2019.

Lower Grove

Many visitors choose to visit only some of the more "famous" trees by walking a shorter loop (about 0.5 mi/0.8 km) that passes the Fallen Monarch, the Grizzly Giant, and the California Tunnel Tree. Interpretive signs on the trail to the Grizzly Giant provide an informative, self-guided tour.

The **Fallen Monarch,** which fell more than 300 years ago, was made famous by an 1899 photograph of U.S. Cavalry troopers and their horses standing on top of it. A short walk east from the parking lot is the **Grizzly Giant,** the largest tree in this grove at 210 feet (64 m) tall and 31 feet (9.4 m) across at its base. The most photographed sequoia in Yosemite, this

behemoth is about 1,800 years old. Its massive, gnarled branches appear to be sculpted by some unseen hand. One particularly impressive branch measures almost 7 feet (2 m) in diameter—larger than the trunks of most trees.

Slightly north, the **California Tunnel Tree** was tunneled in 1895 so that stagecoaches could drive through. In the early 1900s it was used as a "substitute" for the more famous Wawona Tunnel Tree, located in the upper portion of the Mariposa Grove, which was frequently inaccessible due to winter storms. Today you can walk through the California Tunnel Tree. The Wawona Tunnel Tree collapsed in 1969 at the ripe age of 2,200 years. Most likely it died prematurely; the 26-foot-long (8-m), 10-foot-high (3-m) tunnel carved into its base weakened its ability to withstand that year's heavy winter snowfall.

Upper Grove

The upper grove contains the interesting **Mariposa Grove Museum** (10am-4pm daily in summer), housed in a log cabin, with exhibits on the history of this region and humanity's long fascination with the giant sequoia. The museum sits on the spot where Galen Clark, the first official guardian of Yosemite, once had his home. Nearby is an unusual sequoia known as the **Telescope Tree,** whose hollowed-out trunk creates a telescoping effect if you stand inside it and look upward. It's a 2-mile (3.2-km) hike from the shuttle stop to the museum.

Wawona and Glacier Point Hikes

Trail Name	Effort	Distance	Duration
Sentinel Dome	Easy	2.2 mi/3.5 km rt	1 hr
Taft Point and the Fissures	Easy	2.2 mi/3.5 km rt	1 hr
Bridalveil Creek	Easy	3.2 mi/5.2 km rt	1.5 hr
Wawona Meadow Loop	Easy	3.2 mi/5.2 km rt	1.5 hr
Mariposa Grove	Easy/moderate	2-6.4 mi/3.2-10.3 km rt	1-3 hr
McGurk Meadow and Dewey Point	Easy/moderate	2-7 mi/3.2-11.3 km rt	1-4 hr
Illilouette Fall	Easy/moderate	4 mi/6.4 km rt	2 hr
Panorama Trail	Moderate/strenuous	8.5 mi/13.7 km one-way	4-5 hr
Chilnualna Falls	Strenuous	8.2 mi/13.2 km rt	4-5 hr
Ostrander Lake	Strenuous	12.5 mi/20.1 km rt	6-7 hr
Pohono Trail	Very strenuous	13 mi/20.9 km one-way	6-8 hr

Recreation

DAY HIKES

The trails in the Wawona area, with the exception of the busy paths through the Mariposa Grove of Giant Sequoias, are relatively crowd-free. Although the trails on Glacier Point Road are popular, hiking here sets you free from the masses in Yosemite Valley.

Glacier Point

These eight hikes on Glacier Point Road are listed in the order their trailheads appear along the road, traveling from west to east (Chinquapin junction to Glacier Point).

MCGURK MEADOW AND DEWEY POINT

Distance: 2-7 miles (3.2-11.3 km) round-trip
Duration: 1-4 hours
Elevation Change: 300-500 feet (90-150 m)
Effort: Easy to moderate
Trailhead: McGurk Meadow

Directions: From Highway 41, turn east on Glacier Point Road and drive 7.5 miles (12.1 km) to the McGurk Meadow Trailhead on the left. Park in the pullout about 225 feet (70 m) farther up the road.

Some trails seem to capture the essence of Yosemite, and the McGurk Meadow Trail is one of those. The trailhead is the first one you reach as you wind along Glacier Point Road to spectacular Glacier Point. It's worth a stop to take the short walk through a fir-and-pine forest to pristine **McGurk Meadow,** a mile-long meadow crossed by a footbridge over a small feeder creek. A few hundred feet before the meadow, the trail passes by an old pioneer cabin, still standing in half-decent repair.

You can turn around at the meadow for a short and easy trip, or you can cross the meadow and continue along the trail until it connects to the **Pohono Trail,** which traverses Yosemite's south rim. An ideal destination is **Dewey Point,** a spectacular promontory with an unforgettable view of Yosemite Valley, located just off the Pohono Trail. That option turns this hike into a 7-mile (11.3-km) round-trip with only 200 feet (60 m) of additional elevation gain.

BRIDALVEIL CREEK

Distance: 3.2 miles (5.2 km) round-trip
Duration: 1.5 hours
Elevation Change: 70 feet (21 m)
Effort: Easy
Trailhead: Ostrander Lake (see map p. 123)
Directions: From Highway 41, turn east on Glacier Point Road and drive 8.9 miles (14.3 km) to the Ostrander Lake Trailhead on the right.

Maybe the best time to hike to Bridalveil Creek is immediately after visiting Bridalveil Fall. After a short walk from the trailhead on Glacier Point Road through a regenerated forest fire area, you wind up at the edge of Bridalveil Creek, a babbling brook that seems far too tame to produce the giant waterfall downstream. It's a great lesson for children, as is the abundance of new growth in the burned areas of the forest. To make the trip, follow the **Ostrander Lake Trail** for 1.4 miles (2.3 km). This stretch is almost completely level and framed by colorful bunches of lupine in midsummer. Where the trail splits, take the right fork toward **Bridalveil Creek.** You reach it in less than 0.25 mile (0.4 km). The stream is so peaceful here that there is no bridge to cross—it's just an easy rock-hop by midsummer. Pick a spot along its banks and spend some time counting the wildflowers, or watch the small darting trout.

OSTRANDER LAKE

Distance: 12.5 miles (20.1 km) round-trip
Duration: 6-7 hours
Elevation Change: 1,600 feet (500 m)
Effort: Strenuous
Trailhead: Ostrander Lake (see map p. 123)
Directions: From Highway 41, turn east on Glacier Point Road and drive 8.9 miles (14.3 km) to the Ostrander Lake Trailhead on the right.

Many people take short day hikes from Glacier Point Road, but a longer 12.5-mile

(20-km) trip to Ostrander Lake will better suit the avid hiker. Although many backpackers set up camp near Ostrander Lake's shores, it also makes a fine day-hiking destination. The wide blue lake, set at 8,580 feet (2,615 m), is the site of the stone-built **Ostrander Ski Hut,** used by cross-country skiers in the winter. The trail is surprisingly easy considering the number of miles; the first half is quite level. Although the trail (really an old road) travels through a regenerated forest fire area, it ends up in a high country landscape of firs, pines, and, as you ascend, granite. You gain 1,600 feet (500 m) along the way, most of it in the final 3 miles (4.8 km) to the lake. The culmination of the climb occurs nearly 6 miles (9.7 km) out as you reach the trail's highest point, a saddle on top of 8,700-foot (2,650-m) **Horizon Ridge.** Here you are rewarded with excellent views of Half Dome, North Dome, Basket Dome, and Liberty Cap—a fine place to catch your breath. From here, **Ostrander Lake** is less than 0.5 mile (0.8 km) farther. On summer days, bring your swimsuit and a book and plan to spend a few hours on Ostrander's sandy, boulder-lined shore.

SENTINEL DOME

Distance: 2.2 miles (3.5 km) round-trip
Duration: 1 hour
Elevation Change: 400 feet (120 m)
Effort: Easy
Trailhead: Taft Point/Sentinel Dome
Directions: From Highway 41, turn east on Glacier Point Road and drive 13.2 miles (21.3 km) to the Taft Point/Sentinel Dome Trailhead on the left.

It's hard to believe you can get so much for so little, but on the Sentinel Dome Trail you can. The granite dome is about a mile west of Glacier Point, and its elevation is 1,000 feet (300 m) higher than the point's. Views from the dome's summit extend a full 360 degrees. A short and nearly level walk leads you to the base of the dome, and a 300-foot (90-m) climb up its smooth granite backside brings you to its summit. There you are greeted by stunning vistas in all directions, including an unusual perspective on Upper and Lower Yosemite

Ostrander Lake

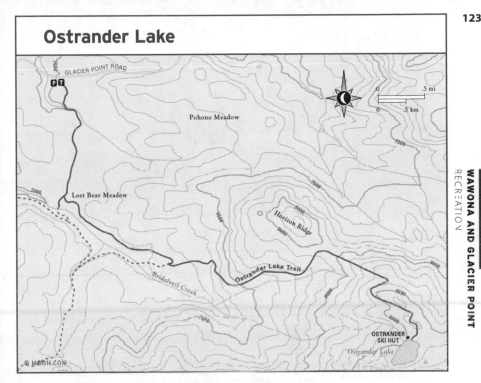

Falls. This is one of the best places in Yosemite to watch the sun set. To make a longer excursion, you can easily combine this hike with the hike to **Taft Point and the Fissures,** which starts from the same trailhead but heads in the opposite direction.

TAFT POINT AND THE FISSURES

Distance: 2.2 miles (3.5 km) round-trip
Duration: 1 hour
Elevation Change: 250 feet (75 m)
Effort: Easy
Trailhead: Taft Point/Sentinel Dome
Directions: From Highway 41, turn east on Glacier Point Road and drive 13.2 miles (21.3 km) to the Taft Point/Sentinel Dome Trailhead on the left.

It's not so much the sweeping vista from Taft Point that you remember, although certainly you could say that the views of El Capitan, Yosemite's north rim, and the Yosemite Valley floor are stunning. What you remember is the incredible sense of awe that you feel, perhaps mixed with a little fear and a lot of respect, as you peer down into the fissures in Taft Point's granite—huge cracks in the rock that plunge hundreds of feet down toward the Valley. One of the fissures has a couple of large boulders captured in its jaws; they're stuck there waiting for the next big earthquake or ice age to set them free. After a brief and mostly forested walk, you come out to the metal railing at the edge of **Taft Point's** cliff, where you can hold on tight and peer down at the Valley far, far below. If you have kids with you or anyone who is afraid of heights, be sure to keep a tight handhold on them.

POHONO TRAIL

Distance: 13 miles (20.9 km) one-way
Duration: 6-8 hours
Elevation Change: 2,800 feet (850 m)
Effort: Very strenuous
Trailhead: Glacier Point (see map p. 124)
Directions: From Highway 41, turn east on Glacier

Pohono Trail

© MOON.COM

Point Road and drive 15.7 miles (25.2 km) to Glacier Point. Park and walk toward the main viewing area across from the café and gift shop. Look for the Pohono Trail sign about 150 feet (45 m) southeast of the café, on your right.

If you can arrange a shuttle trip, the Pohono Trail from Glacier Point downhill to its end at Wawona Tunnel is worth every step of its 13 miles (20.9 km). The two ends of the trail have the best drive-to viewing points in all of Yosemite, and in between you are treated to dozens of other scenic spots, including Sentinel Dome at 1.5 miles (2.4 km), Taft Point at 3.8 miles (6.1 km), and four bird's-eye lookouts over the valley floor: Inspiration, Stanford, Dewey, and Crocker Points. Starting at **Glacier Point** and ending at **Wawona Tunnel,** you'll cover a 2,800-foot (855-m) descent, but there are some "ups" along the way, too, such as the stretch from Glacier Point to **Sentinel Dome,** and between Bridalveil Creek and Dewey Point. The trail stays on or near Yosemite Valley's south rim the entire way except for one major detour into the woods to reach the bridge across **Bridalveil Creek.**

Bring along a good map because many of the trail's best offerings are just off the main path. If you don't take the short spur routes to reach them, you'll miss out on some spectacular scenery. Note: The view of Yosemite Falls from the Pohono Trail in front of Sentinel Dome is the best in all of Yosemite. For the best overall vista along the trail, it's a toss-up between Glacier Point, Taft Point, and Dewey Point.

PANORAMA TRAIL

Distance: 8.5 miles (13.7 km) one-way
Duration: 4-5 hours
Elevation Change: 3,900 feet (1,200 m)
Effort: Moderate to strenuous
Trailhead: Glacier Point (see map p. 126)
Directions: From Highway 41, turn east on Glacier Point Road and drive 15.7 miles (25.2 km) to Glacier Point. Park and walk toward the main viewing area across from the café and gift shop. Look for the Panorama Trail sign about 150 feet (45 m) southeast of the café, on your right.

The Panorama Trail follows a spectacular route from Glacier Point to Yosemite Valley, heading downhill most of the way, but you must have a shuttle car waiting at the end or it's one heck of a long climb back up. A great option is to take the Yosemite Valley Lodge tour bus (209/372-1240) for one leg of the trip.

The aptly named Panorama Trail begins at **Glacier Point,** elevation 7,214 feet (2,199 m). You switchback downhill, accompanied by ever-changing perspectives on Half Dome, Basket Dome, North Dome, Liberty Cap, and, in the distance, Vernal and Nevada Falls. You will gape a lot. After passing **Illilouette Fall** and ascending a bit for the first time on the trip, continue eastward to the Panorama Trail's end near the top of **Nevada Fall.** Turn right to reach the top of the fall and have a rest at the overlook; then continue downhill on the **Mist Trail** on the north side of the river. After a view-filled descent along the north side of Nevada Fall, you'll cross the river in 1.4 miles (2.3 km) and walk alongside lovely Emerald Pool on your way to the top of **Vernal Fall.** Enjoy the show here and then tromp down the granite staircase on the busy trail back to **Happy Isles.**

Note that the route has a 3,200-foot (975-m) elevation loss over its course, but there is also a 760-foot (232-m) climb after you cross Illilouette Creek that is exposed to the sun and often quite warm. Also be forewarned that while the starting miles of the trip are quite tranquil, the final 2 miles (3.2 km) near Vernal Fall can feature a parade of people.

ILLILOUETTE FALL

Distance: 4 miles (6.4 km) round-trip
Duration: 2 hours
Elevation Change: 1,200 feet (365 m)
Effort: Easy to moderate
Trailhead: Glacier Point (see map p. 126)
Directions: From Highway 41, turn east on Glacier Point Road and drive 15.7 miles (25.2 km) to Glacier Point. Park and walk toward the main viewing area across from the café and gift shop. Look for the Panorama Trail sign about 150 feet (45 m) southeast of the café, on your right.

Panorama Trail and Illilouette Fall

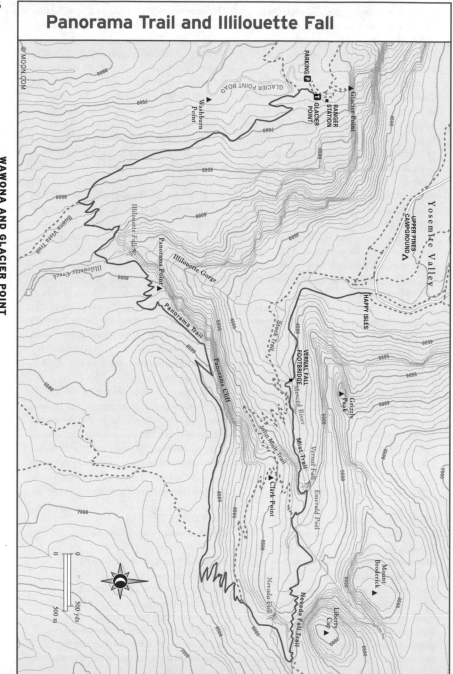

PARKING

GLACIER POINT ROAD

Glacier Point

RANGER
STATION

GLACIER
POINT

Washburn
Point

Buena Vista Trail

Illilouette Falls

Panorama Point

Illilouette Creek

Illilouette Gorge

Panorama Trail

Panorama Cliff

Yosemite Valley

UPPER PINES
CAMPGROUND

HAPPY ISLES

Stock Trail

VERNAL FALL
FOOTBRIDGE

Merced River

Grizzly
Peak

John Muir Trail

Mist Trail

Vernal Fall

Clark Point

Emerald Pool

Mount
Broderick

Nevada Fall

Nevada Fall Trail

Liberty
Cap

0   500 yds.

0   500 m

Those who can't afford the time or make the car shuttle arrangements necessary to hike the entire Panorama Trail should at least take this incredible out-and-back trip on the top portion of the route. **Glacier Point** is your starting point, and the bridge above Illilouette Fall becomes your destination, but what happens in between is sheer magic. Some say that hiking the Panorama Trail is like staring at a life-size Yosemite postcard, or perhaps simply being *in* the postcard. As you walk, you feel as if you've become one with the magnificent panorama of Half Dome, Basket Dome, North Dome, Liberty Cap, and far-off Vernal and Nevada Falls. The trail is downhill all the way to **Illilouette Fall** in 2 miles (3.2 km), which means you have a 1,200-foot (365-m) elevation gain on the return trip. The path is extremely well graded, so even children can make the climb. After viewing the waterfall from a trailside overlook, walk another 0.25 mile (0.4 km) and stand on the bridge that is perched just above the 370-foot (115-m) drop. For obvious reasons, don't think about swimming here.

Wawona

These three hikes are listed in order of their occurrence from the South entrance station north to Wawona.

MARIPOSA GROVE

Distance: 2-6.4 miles (3.2-10.3 km) round-trip
Duration: 1-3 hours
Elevation Change: 400-1,200 feet (120-365 m)
Effort: Easy to moderate
Trailhead: Mariposa Grove (see map p. 128)
Directions: Take the free shuttle bus from the Mariposa Grove parking lot near the South entrance to the Mariposa Grove shuttle stop.

The Mariposa Grove is the largest and most impressive of the three groves of **giant sequoias** in Yosemite National Park. The star tree in the Mariposa Grove is the **Grizzly Giant,** with a circumference of more than 100 feet (30 m). At approximately 2,700 years old, it's one of the oldest known giant sequoias. If you want to see only the most famous trees in the grove, including the Grizzly Giant, take the well-signed 2-mile (3.2-km) hike through the lower grove and turn around at the signs pointing to the upper grove. If you hike the entire lower and upper groves, you'll cover 6.4 trail miles.

WAWONA MEADOW LOOP

Distance: 3.2 miles (5.2 km) round-trip
Duration: 1.5 hours
Elevation Change: None
Effort: Easy
Trailhead: Wawona Meadow
Directions: From the park's South entrance station on Highway 41, drive north for 2 miles (3.2 km) to the trailhead just south of the golf course and across the road from the Big Trees Lodge.

Sometimes you just want to take a stroll in the park, and the Wawona Meadow Loop is exactly that. Many hikers ignore this trail because of its proximity to the Big Trees Lodge Golf Course, but they are missing out on an easy, pleasant meander. In early summer on this level trail (a former stage road), you can see a variety of wildflowers and enjoy the good company of butterflies as you take a lazy stroll. From the signed trailhead across the road from the **Big Trees Lodge,** hike to your left on the dirt road, following the split-rail fence. At the end of the meadow the old road crosses the stream and loops back to the starting point on the north side of the **golf course.** If you wish, you can even bring your dog or ride your bike on this trail. If you're staying at the Big Trees Lodge, you can hike from there, crossing the Wawona Road on your way out and back.

CHILNUALNA FALLS

Distance: 8.2 miles (13.2 km) round-trip
Duration: 4-5 hours
Elevation Change: 2,400 feet (730 m)
Effort: Strenuous
Trailhead: Chilnualna Falls (see map p. 129)
Directions: From the South entrance station, drive 5 miles (8 km) north on Highway 41 to Wawona. Turn east on Chilnualna Falls Road and drive 1.7 miles (2.7 km) to the parking lot on the right side of the road.

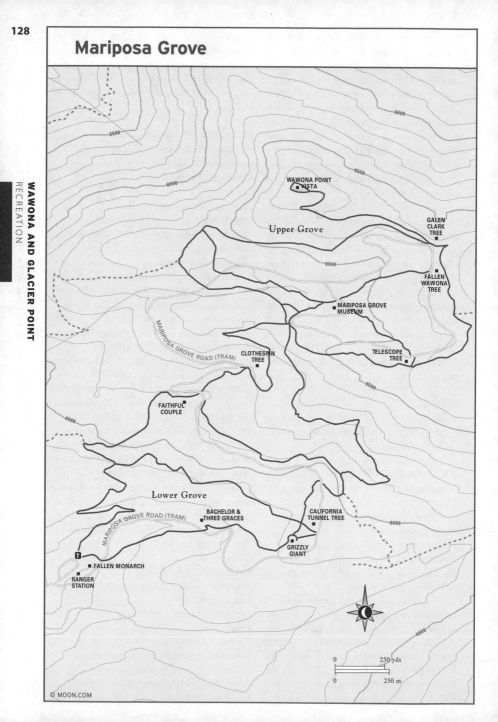

Mariposa Grove

WAWONA POINT
VISTA

Upper Grove

GALEN
CLARK
TREE

FALLEN
WAWONA
TREE

MARIPOSA GROVE
MUSEUM

MARIPOSA GROVE ROAD (TRAM)

CLOTHESPIN
TREE

TELESCOPE
TREE

FAITHFUL
COUPLE

Lower Grove

MARIPOSA GROVE ROAD (TRAM)

BACHELOR &
THREE GRACES

CALIFORNIA
TUNNEL TREE

GRIZZLY
GIANT

FALLEN MONARCH

RANGER
STATION

0   250 yds

0   250 m

© MOON.COM

Chilnualna Falls

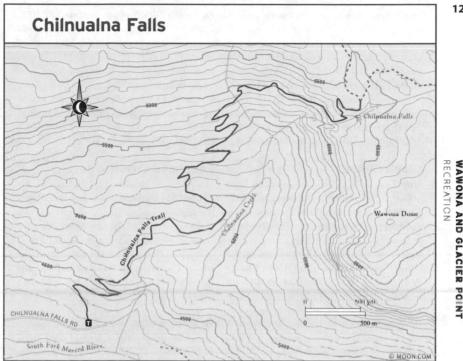

Walk back to Chilnualna Falls Road and pick up the single-track trail across the pavement.

Are you ready to climb? It's good to be mentally prepared for this hike, which includes a steady, moderately graded, 4-mile-long (6.4-km) ascent, gaining 2,400 feet (730 m) to reach the top of Chilnualna Falls. Pick a nice cool day because this trail is in the lower-elevation part of Yosemite. Your nose will continually pick up the intoxicating smell of bear clover, which joins manzanita and oaks in comprising the majority of the vegetation along the route. Halfway up you get a great view of **Wawona Dome** (elevation 6,897 ft/2,102 m) from a granite overlook. This is a great place to take a break and stretch your hamstrings. Shortly thereafter you glimpse a section of **Chilnualna Falls** high up on a cliff wall, still far ahead. The trail leads above the brink of the fall's lower drop to a series of higher cascades. Keep hiking until you reach the **uppermost cascade,** which consists of five pool-and-drop tiers just 300 feet (90 m) off the granite-lined trail. You'll want to spread out a picnic here before you begin the long descent back to the trailhead.

BACKPACKING

Some of the best, and least crowded, backpacking opportunities in Yosemite are found in the southern portion of the park. You must have a permit to spend the night in Yosemite's wilderness, so your best bet for information about backpacking trips is the Wawona or Yosemite Valley **wilderness permit office** (209/372-0740). Backpackers must also take precautions against bears. Hanging food from a tree is ineffective in Yosemite (the bears have long since smartened up to that routine), so use hard plastic bear canisters to store your food for overnight trips.

Many excellent trips (Clover Meadow, Upper Chiquito, and Granite Creek) start in Sierra National Forest lands just outside the park boundary and then head into the remote southern region of Yosemite—a land completely unreachable by car or day hiking. The most popular of these paths is the **Chiquito Pass Trail,** which leads to the Chain Lakes, Buena Vista Crest, and the Clark Range.

If you'd rather have someone else plan and guide a backpacking trip for you, contact the **Southern Yosemite Mountain Guides** (800/231-4575, www.symg.com) in Bass Lake.

Glacier Point

From Glacier Point Road, backpackers head to Ostrander Lake, or beyond it to Hart Lake. The **McGurk Meadow Trail** leads day hikers and backpackers to the meadow and beyond to Dewey Point (4.1 mi/6.6 km); backpackers can set up camp near Bridalveil Creek on the Valley's south rim. Longer trips from Glacier Point Road's **Mono Meadow Trailhead** include Merced Pass (12.1 mi/19.5 km) and around the Buena Vista Crest, or to the Ottoway Lakes (16 mi/26 km), through the peaks of the Clark Range, and then north to Washburn Lake and Merced Lake.

A very popular trail for both day hikers and backpackers is the **Panorama Trail** from Glacier Point. While day hikers follow this trail to drop down to the Valley, backpackers can use it as a route to Half Dome or the Merced Lake High Sierra Camp.

Wawona

From Wawona, backpackers can head up above Chilnualna Falls to **Buena Vista Peak** (14.4 mi/23.2 km). A popular 40-mile (64-km), five-day loop visits a series of high mountain lakes: Crescent, Johnson, Royal Arch, Buena Vista, and Chilnualna.

BIKING

Bicycles are available for rent in Yosemite Valley, or you can bring your own. More mountain biking adventures are possible in the lands of Sierra National Forest, just south of Yosemite National Park. For more information about biking near Fish Camp, Oakhurst, and Bass Lake, contact

the **North Fork Ranger Station** (559/877-2218). A good source of biking information is **Yosemite Bicycle and Sport** (40680 Hwy. 41, Oakhurst, 559/641-2453, www.yosemitebicycle.com, 11am-6pm Mon.-Fri., 10am-6pm Sat.), behind the McDonald's in Oakhurst. The shop offers ride guides, morning and weekend group rides, mountain biking shuttles, and trail maps for those who want to set out on their own.

Four-Mile Fire Road

One option for mountain bikers is to ride the **Four-Mile Fire Road** that begins across from the Big Trees Lodge. This old dirt road is one of the few "trails" in the park where bikes are allowed, although it is much more of a road than a trail. (It's a section of an old stagecoach route.) The scenery is pleasant, and the gentle grade will give you a chance to spin your wheels.

Glacier Point Road

The challenge of riding **Glacier Point Road** calls to many a road cyclist each summer. Despite the fact that the road has a narrow-to-nonexistent shoulder and plenty of tourist traffic, cyclists pedal this road almost every summer day. If you leave your car at Chinquapin junction and ride out and back to Glacier Point, you'll have a 32-mile (52-km) round-trip with a 2,300-foot (700-m) elevation gain. The toughest part of the trip is the initial 2-mile (3.2-km) climb on the return trip from Glacier Point. Fortunately, you can fuel up with water and snacks at the Glacier Point snack stand (summer only) before you ride out. If possible, plan this ride for a weekday, and the earlier in the day the better: The fewer cars you see on this narrow, steep road, the more you'll be able to enjoy the world-class scenery.

FISHING

Near Wawona and Glacier Point Road, most fishing takes place in streams and rivers (Apr.-Nov.). The **South Fork Merced River** runs through Wawona and is popular with anglers.

Various holes can be accessed a short distance off Highway 41, near both the Wawona Campground and the village of Wawona.

On Glacier Point Road, **Bridalveil Creek** (near the campground of the same name) offers a chance at catching brook trout, and more rarely, brown and rainbow trout. **Illilouette Creek**, accessible by a downhill hike from Glacier Point on the Panorama Trail, is populated by rainbow trout. (Head upstream from the waterfall and bridge.) The most easily reached lake is **Ostrander Lake**, accessible via a long hike (6.1 mi/9.8 km) from Bridalveil Creek Campground off Glacier Point Road. The lake is a popular backpacking destination and a dependable producer of brook trout. Rainbows are also sometimes taken. Ostrander has not been stocked for many years, so the fish there are a self-sustaining population.

Big Creek

About 2 miles (3.2 km) south of Wawona in Fish Camp lies **Big Creek**, a popular angling stream in early spring. Most people park by the Highway 41 bridge in Fish Camp and fish downstream using flies and spinners. If you stay off the neighboring private property, you can work your way down a 2-mile (3.2-km) stretch of the creek. If you are camping at Summerdale Campground, you have easy access to Big Creek (you can't park in the campground unless you are camping there).

Bass Lake

No discussion of fishing would be complete without **Bass Lake.** The 1,000-acre (400-hectare) lake is just outside of Oakhurst, 14 miles (22.5 km) from Yosemite's South entrance. It is well loved by anglers, even though they must share its lovely blue waters with water-skiers, Jet Skis, and boats of every variety. Fishing is quite good but, contrary to its name, not necessarily for bass. Instead, trout fishing is popular in winter and spring, when the Department of Fish and Wildlife drops in heavy plants of rainbows. In summer, people catch a little bit of everything: catfish, bluegill, bass, crappie, and trout. The lake level usually drops substantially by late summer, which hinders the lake's fishing as well as its scenic value.

GOLF

Across the street from the Big Trees Lodge is a real oddity for a national park—the nine-hole, par-35 **Big Trees Lodge Golf Course** (209/375-6572, open daily spring-fall), complete with a pro shop and putting green! The historic golf course was built in 1917, and when it opened it was the first regulation course in the Sierra Nevada. Today it is one of the few organic golf courses in the United States; no pesticides are applied to the course, and only reclaimed gray water is used for watering the greens. Weekend greens fees are $25.50 for 9 holes, $41.50 for 18 holes (weekdays are a few bucks less). Electric cart rentals are $19.50 for nine holes; club rentals are $17.50.

SWIMMING

The **South Fork Merced River** in and around Wawona is rife with swimming holes and sandy beaches. Many swimmers jump in the river just upstream from the Pioneer Yosemite History Center and its covered bridge, but an even better choice is the big, boulder-lined pool near Wawona's **Swinging Bridge.** Getting there requires a walk of about a mile up the dirt road/path from the Chilnualna Falls parking lot.

If you are willing to take a long hike, **Ostrander Lake** usually warms up enough for swimming by mid- to late summer. Hike to it from Bridalveil Creek Campground (6.1 mi/9.8 km) or the Ostrander Lake Trailhead (6.2 mi/10 km) on Glacier Point Road. If you'd prefer to get your feet wet somewhere that's a little easier to reach, the historic Big Trees Lodge has a swimming pool, but it's for guests only.

HORSEBACK RIDING

There's no better way to get into the spirit of the Old West than to climb on a horse and

ride off into the sunset. **Big Trees Stable** (209/375-6502, 7am-5pm daily summer only) offers horse and mule rides, although you'll have to leave earlier in the day, not at sunset. Two-hour and four-hour rides depart daily ($61-83); the shorter ride travels the historic wagon road over Chowchilla Mountain and around the Wawona Meadow and golf course into Wawona. The four-hour ride follows the Alder Creek Trail, offering expansive mountain views. An all-day ride to Alder Creek Falls can also be arranged ($123), as well as multiday pack trips into the wilderness. Reservations are strongly recommended. Saddlebags are provided for longer rides so you can store a picnic lunch, water, camera, and a jacket. Children must be at least 7 years old and 44 inches (112 cm) tall. Helmets are required for all riders and are available free of charge. The maximum a rider may weigh is 225 pounds (102 kg). The stables are in Wawona, next door to the Pioneer Yosemite History Center.

Just 2 miles (3.2 km) outside of the park in Fish Camp is **Yosemite Trails Pack Station** (7910 Jackson Rd., Fish Camp, 559/683-7611, www.yosemitetrails.com). One hour guided horseback rides ($50 per person) depart several times a day for a loop alongside Big Creek and through the Sierra National Forest lands near the stables. Two-hour trips ($90 per person) heading for scenic Vista Pass leave twice a day. A five-hour trip (noon Wed. and Sat., $160 per person) heads to the Mariposa Grove of Giant Sequoias. All riders spend an hour walking around the grove. Then the group mounts their horses and heads back to the stable. In winter, the pack station offers sleigh rides ($35 adults, $22 children 4-12) when the snow permits. Yosemite Trails is on Jackson Road, 1.3 miles (2.1 km) east of Highway 41 in Fish Camp.

1: summit of Sentinel Dome **2:** Chilnualna Falls
3: the Swinging Bridge near Wawona

WINTER SPORTS

Snowshoeing and Cross-Country Skiing

When **Mariposa Grove Road** is closed in winter, cross-country skiers and snowshoers can glide or tromp up the road to the giant sequoias, which are gloriously crowned in snow. This is one of the loveliest winter sights in all of Yosemite. Beginners will want to keep to the road and the trails in the lower grove; more advanced snowshoers and skiers can head to the upper grove.

Downhill Skiing and Snowboarding

Yosemite Ski & Snowboard Area (209/372-8430 or 209/372-8444 for ski conditions, www.travelyosemite.com,, $55 all-day adult lift ticket, $48 half day, 9am-4pm daily Dec.-Mar.) offers skiing, snowboarding, and snow tubing, a low-tech version of sledding in which snow lovers slide down the slope on inner tubes. Lesson packages and equipment rentals are available—just wear your warmest clothes, carry chains in your car (or better yet, ride the free shuttle bus from Oakhurst or Yosemite Valley), and show up at the ski resort. Sadly, the snowy season in Yosemite is too brief, the resort typically opens in late December and closes on the last day of March.

First opened in 1935, Yosemite Ski & Snowboard Area (previously known as Badger Pass) is California's oldest ski resort. In the 1930s, downhill skiing was a relatively new sport in the United States, so Badger Pass hired a series of European ski instructors to teach the Swiss sport of skiing to clumsy Americans. Yosemite's Badger Pass was the proud owner of the West's first mechanical uphill lift, aptly called the Upski.

In 1948, Nic Fiore, a Canadian, was hired to teach skiing in Yosemite. By the late 1950s he was director of the ski school, and in the following years he made many important changes, such as adding T-bars and chairlifts. He died in 2009 at the age of 88, but he remains a legendary figure at the ski resort. Fiore taught so many people how to ski that he is credited as being largely responsible for popularizing the sport of downhill skiing in the United States.

Today, Yosemite Ski & Snowboard Area has five lifts that service 85 acres (34 hectares) of ski slopes. The resort emphasizes family-oriented skiing and snowboarding. With only 10 total runs that are mostly rated as beginner and intermediate, black-diamond lovers won't find much to hold their interest. But for adult beginners and families, the resort is a great place to spend the day in the snow, and prices are substantially less than what you'll find at the ski resorts around Lake Tahoe. And even when the ski conditions aren't that great, you can still take the youngsters to the snow-tubing hill (11:30am-4pm daily, $17 per person for two hours).

In the winter months during non-holiday periods, Yosemite Valley Lodge, Half Dome Village, and the Big Trees Lodge offer **stay-and-ski packages** (888/413-8869, www. travelyosemite.com) with reduced lodging rates and lift tickets included in the package price. Free shuttles travel daily from various points in Yosemite Valley to Badger Pass, so you don't have to worry about driving your car in the snow. On weekends, shuttle buses (www.travelyosemite.com, $20 per person) travel to Yosemite Ski & Snowboard Area from Tenaya Lodge in Fish Camp and Miller Mountain Sports in Oakdale.

Cross-Country Skiing

Cross-country skiers can start their adventures at **Yosemite Ski & Snowboard Area,** and unless they are renting equipment, their fun is free of charge. Both groomed and ungroomed cross-country trails depart from the parking lot at the ski resort, including 25 miles (40 km) of machine-groomed track and 90 miles (145 km) of marked trails. One of the most popular routes simply follows snow-covered **Glacier Point Road** (the road is groomed with traditional cross-country skiing tracks and also a skating lane). Three miles (4.8 km) of gliding brings you to Bridalveil Campground, where the Ghost Forest Loop leads through a stand of dead lodgepole pines. You can ski farther by following Bridalveil Creek Trail off the Ghost Forest Loop.

Ski rentals and cross-country skiing lessons are available at **Yosemite Cross Country Ski Center** (209/372-8444, 8:30am-4pm daily, lesson packages $46-65 per person) for beginners and intermediates as well as for those who wish to learn telemarking or cross-country skiing or skating skills.

In late February, Yosemite Ski & Snowboard Area holds an annual **Nordic Holiday Race.** The two-day event includes an 18K (11-mile) classic or striding event with prizes for best costumes, a downhill telemark race through marked gates, and a 38K (23-mile) cross-country skating race to Glacier Point and back. A $50 registration fee allows admission to all three races and an evening awards party.

Snowshoeing

While cross-country skiing requires some skills, snowshoeing doesn't. The busiest of Glacier Point's snowshoe routes is to **Dewey Point** via the Meadow Ski Trail (7 miles round-trip, 4 hours). Although skiers use this route as well, the vast majority of visitors are snowshoers, many of whom are trying out their functional snow footwear for the first time. The well-marked route is mostly level, with one good climb on the way out to Dewey Point. You can return the way you came or loop back on the Ridge Ski Trail. If the weather is nice, hang out at Dewey Point for a while to enjoy its spectacular view of El Capitan, Half Dome, Mount Hoffman, Mount Conness, and the Clark Range. (Bring a rubber mat or something to sit on, and plenty of snacks and drinks.)

Snowshoe tours (9am-3pm Wed. and Sat., $60 including snowshoe rental, $50 without, children must be 12 or older) to Dewey Point are offered in winter. Groups are limited to 10 people. For reservations, call the Yosemite Ski & Snowboard Area Nordic

1: Ostrander Ski Hut **2:** outcrop at Dewey Point

Center (209/372-8444) or the Yosemite Valley Lodge Tour Desk (209/372-1240).

Much easier **guided snowshoe walks** (1pm-4pm Sat.-Sun., $21 adults, $11 children, including snowshoe rental) depart from Yosemite Ski & Snowboard Area for a mellow climb up to the summit and an overlook of the Clark Range. During full-moon nights in winter, naturalists lead **full-moon snowshoe walks** (209/372-1240, $19.50 including snowshoe rentals, $7.50 if you bring your own) from the ski lodge. Group size is limited and reservations are required.

Glacier Point Ski Hut

In summer, the **Glacier Point Ski Hut** (209/372-8444, www.travelyosemite.com, Nov.-May) operates as a snack stand and gift shop. In winter, staff at the Yosemite Cross Country Ski School remove the store shelves and cash registers, install 20 bunk beds, and lead guided ski trips with an overnight stay at the hut. The trip is suitable even for beginners because the 10.5-mile (16.9-km) route from Yosemite Ski & Snowboard Area is on well-groomed track that follows Glacier Point Road all the way. With one guide in front of your group and one in back, everybody skis at their own pace and nobody gets left behind. Most people make it to Glacier Point in 4-5 hours.

The ski school issues skiers their own lightweight liners to stuff inside the hut's sleeping bags. Skiers carry only the liners and some water and snacks for the trip; the guides take care of the rest, including all meals and wine. The ski hut is equipped with indoor lavatory facilities, a dining room, and several cozy sofas surrounding a big woodstove. Except for the dormitory-style sleeping arrangements, it's surprisingly luxurious.

The minimum number of people per night is 6; the maximum is 20. On weeknights, you (and your guides, of course) might have the place to yourselves. On weekends, you're likely to share the place with company, unless you managed to convince 19 friends to go with you. Reservations are required. For a **guided one-night ski trip,** the fee is $350

per person, including all meals. For a **guided two-night ski trip,** the fee is $550 per person, including meals.

More advanced skiers can ski on their own, without a guide, and enjoy the same overnight stay at the hut, complete with a delicious hot dinner, wine, and breakfast the next morning. The fee for a **self-guided trip** is $138 per person, per night, including meals.

Ostrander Ski Hut

You have to work pretty hard to earn your stay at the **Ostrander Ski Hut** (209/379-2317 or 209/379-5161, www.yosemiteconservancy. org, mid-Dec.-early Apr. depending on snow conditions, $40-60 per person). The trip to Ostrander is only for those who are strong and skilled enough to ski or snowshoe 10 miles (16.1 km) each way from the Yosemite Ski & Snowboard Area on mostly ungroomed snow. For those who make the journey, the reward is a warm night in a two-story stone cabin built in 1941 on the edge of Ostrander Lake. The elevation is 8,500 feet (2,590 m), so snow is fairly dependable from mid-December to early April. This is a way of experiencing Yosemite that few people will ever know.

The hut sleeps 25 people and has bunks, mattresses, a woodstove, solar lights, a kitchen with gas stove for cooking, and assorted cooking and eating utensils. For drinking water, walk 100 feet (30 m) down to Ostrander Lake, fill up a bucket, and then bring it back to filter.

You're on your own for your trek to Ostrander Ski Hut, so you must possess some winter backcountry skills. Skiers should be at least intermediate level and in good physical shape. You have to haul a fair amount of equipment: sleeping bag, sleeping pad, headlamp, water filter, water bottle, snow emergency gear, food, and so on. Even with all these prerequisites, reservations can be tough to come by. The hut is particularly popular with telemark skiers, as the slopes provide wonderful opportunities for this type of skiing. Making it even more attractive, the nightly fee is very low.

The Ostrander Ski Hut is operated by

the nonprofit **Yosemite Conservancy** (reservation office 209/379-5161, www.yosemiteconservancy.org); discounts are offered for Yosemite Conservancy donors. The Yosemite Conservancy begins accepting reservations via a lottery system in October and early November. A lottery form is online; if you can't get the dates you want, try phoning the reservation office after December 1 to see if there are cancellations. Your chances are much better midweek than on weekends.

Entertainment and Shopping

Pianist/singer Tom Bopp plays live music in the **Big Trees Lodge Lounge** (5:30pm-9:30pm Tues.-Sat. spring-fall, occasional weekends in winter, free). Bopp plays and sings vintage camping songs and music that spans Yosemite's history from 1874 to 1954, with a variety of styles ranging from cowboy tunes to sentimental love songs. Sitting and listening is free; cocktails will cost you a few bucks. For more information on Bopp's schedule and music, visit www.yosemitemusic.com.

RANGER PROGRAMS

Guided walks are held daily in summer; a list of ranger-led hikes in the Wawona and Glacier Point area is posted at the Information Station at the Big Trees Lodge and at the Wawona Campground (or phone 209/372-1153 for an updated schedule). In the **Mariposa Grove,** 1.5-hour interpretive hikes leave from the grove parking lot twice a day at 10am and 2pm in the summer (10am on autumn weekends). These easy walks stay within the lower grove and are appropriate for hikers of all abilities. About once each week in summer, rangers lead longer hikes from Wawona to destinations such as **Chilnualna Falls.** At **Glacier Point,** rangers lead hikes to Taft Point, Sentinel Dome, and Illilouette Fall several days each week.

Evening Programs

Sunset ranger programs (8pm) are held several nights each week in summer at the **Glacier Point** railing or amphitheater. Stargazing programs are held on clear Saturday nights. A telescope is set up for viewing the heavens.

Scheduled events are posted at Glacier Point, or visit www.travelyosemite.com.

The **Glacier Point Starry Night Skies Over Yosemite Tour** (Sun.-Thurs. June-Sept., $64 adults, $55 children ages 5-12) departs Yosemite Valley Lodge at 7pm on summer evenings, arriving at Glacier Point just before dark. Tours last about four hours and a one-hour astronomy program takes place after dark. Stargazing tours may be canceled due to cloudy skies; ticketholders should call (209/372-4386 or 209/372-8323) the day of the tour to confirm. (Refunds are given if the tour is canceled.) If you're staying in the Wawona area, you can drive your own car to Glacier Point and pay $10 per person to participate in the one-hour stargazing program.

HORSE-DRAWN STAGECOACH RIDES

In Wawona, docents occasionally dress in period costumes and take visitors on tours inside Yosemite's historic buildings. On the south side of the Pioneer Yosemite History Center's covered bridge, **horse-drawn stagecoach rides** (daily in summer, $4 adults, $3 children 3-12) depart every 15-20 minutes from the stables. The 10-minute ride loops around Wawona and gives visitors a taste of what early-days transportation in Yosemite was like.

SHOPPING

The **Wawona Store & Pioneer Gift Shop** (8am-8pm daily summer, shorter winter hours) is a surprisingly well-stocked grocery store where you'll find all the necessary picnic and camping supplies, plus memory cards and batteries for your camera. Another small grocery store is about a mile east on Chilnualna Falls Road, in the residential area of Wawona.

The **Big Trees Lodge Golf Shop & Snack Stand** (209/375-6572, 8am-6pm daily summer) has golf equipment and rentals, clothing, and photo supplies. A snack stand allows hungry golfers the chance to fuel up before hitting the greens. The shop is near the main hotel building.

After driving all the way out to Glacier Point, you may be happy to find the **Glacier Point Snack Stand and Gift Shop** (10am-5pm daily in summer only). The shop is housed in a handsome log cabin and has souvenir-type trinkets plus a good selection of guidebooks on Yosemite. Fast food and drinks are available at the snack stand in the same building.

Food

Aside from the grocery store, there are only three places to find food in the southern area of the park, and two are open in summer only (Glacier Point Snack Stand and Big Trees Lodge Golf Shop). If you strike out here, your best bet is to head south on Highway 41 to the town of Fish Camp (45 minutes from Glacier Point and 10 minutes south of Wawona).

INSIDE THE PARK
Glacier Point

A hot dog never tastes so good as when you are standing on Glacier Point looking out at Half Dome and all its granite neighbors. Yup, this is one tasty hot dog. The sandwiches and baked potatoes hit the spot, too. But the biggest draw here, especially on warm summer days, is the wide selection of ice cream treats at **Glacier Point Snack Stand** (10am-5pm daily summer only, $8).

Wawona

You don't have to stay at the Big Trees Lodge to eat here—everybody is welcome. The ★ **Big Trees Lodge Dining Room** (209/375-6556 or 888/413-8869, www.travelyosemite.com, 7am-10am, 11am-1:30pm, and 5pm-9pm daily in summer, winter hours vary, $18-34) is popular and the food is delicious. Typical dinner entrées include roast duck, prime rib, and freshly caught trout. As at so many places in and around Yosemite (although it's

a mystery why), French onion soup is a popular item. The restaurant doesn't take reservations unless you have a party of six people or more. Waiting around for a table is not so bad, however; the hotel lounge is always hopping with live piano music and guests making merry. You don't have to dress up for dinner, although some people do.

In the summer months, a **barbecue** (5pm-7pm Sat.) is held outside on the lawn, complete with heaping portions of corn on the cob, hamburgers, steak, potato salad, and lots more good old American food. If you ever wanted to try square dancing, this is the time and the place. A live band plays and a caller shouts out instructions.

Snacks and sandwiches are available for the hungry golfer (or anybody else) who wanders into **Big Trees Golf Shop & Snack Stand** (209/375-6572, 8am-5pm daily in summer only), located in the Annex area of the Big Trees Lodge complex. While ordering your lunch, you can rent a set of clubs or ask the pro for advice on your swing.

SOUTH OF THE PARK: HIGHWAY 41
Fish Camp
TENAYA LODGE

The resort at **Tenaya Lodge** (1122 Hwy. 41, Fish Camp, 888/514-2167 or 559/692-8985, www.tenayalodge.com) has three full-service

Dining South of the Park: Highway 41

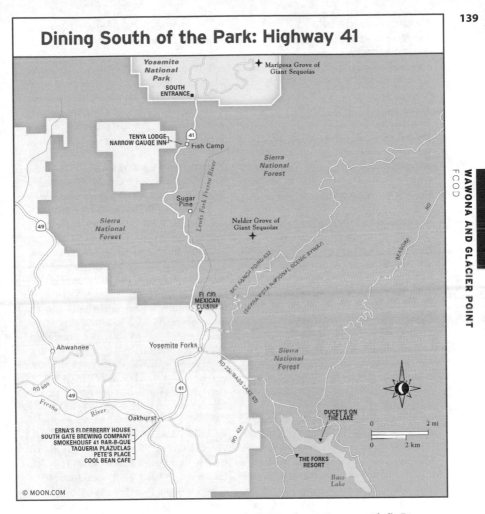

© MOON.COM

restaurants available: Embers, Sierra Restaurant, and Jackalope's Bar and Grill, plus a pizzeria and deli. **Embers** (6pm-close daily in summer, $25-50) is an elegant affair with a menu that changes biweekly, but a few of its signatures are an exotic fruit gazpacho, buffalo short ribs, and "blue-flaming coffee." **Sierra Restaurant** (breakfast 6:30am-11am, dinner 5:30pm-10pm daily, $14-30) is also on the upscale side, but with summertime outdoor seating and a cozy limestone fireplace inside, this isn't the kind of place in which you have to dress up. There's a children's menu for the kiddies (crayons are provided). Dinners range from casual burgers and salads to fancier entrées like stuffed quail and cedar plank salmon. **Jackalope's Bar and Grill** (11am-11pm daily, $20-34), is even more laid-back. Soups, salads, burgers, and pasta dishes are well prepared. Other food options include the **Parkside Deli** for a morning bagel and cappuccino or to pick up to-go lunches, and **Timberloft Pizzeria** (5pm-10pm daily, $16-25), next door to the main lodge at the Tenaya Lodge Cottages.

NARROW GAUGE INN

The **Narrow Gauge Inn** (48571 Hwy. 41, Fish Camp, 559/683-7720 or 559/683-6446, www.narrowgaugeinn.com, 7:30am-9:30am and 5pm-9pm daily Apr.-Oct., $17-43) serves lodge-style dinners in a dark and woodsy dining room. The restaurant looks a bit like a historical hunting lodge, complete with trophy animal heads on the walls. A couple of stone fireplaces, antiques, white linens, and oil lamps complete the decor. The menu emphasizes meat, with a few unusual choices like pan-seared duck and beef carpaccio. For traditionalists, there are plenty of standards, like filet mignon and Chilean sea bass. All dinners include soup or salad, potatoes, and vegetables, so come prepared to fill your belly. Adjacent to the dining room is the **Buffalo Bar,** decorated with an authentic birchbark canoe and Yosemite memorabilia.

Oakhurst and Vicinity
EL CID MEXICAN CUISINE

El Cid Mexican Cuisine (41939 Hwy. 41, Oakhurst, 559/683-6668, www.elcidmexicancuisine.com, 10:30am-9pm Sun.-Thurs., 10:30am-10pm Fri.-Sat., $9-22) is an old favorite in the Oakhurst restaurant scene. Take your pick from nearly 100 combinations and dinner plates—chili verde, chili Colorado, sautéed seafood, tacos, enchiladas, burritos, and more. Just reading the menu will take up a good portion of your evening. The outdoor deck is the place to be on warm summer evenings, and El Cid's margaritas are coveted throughout the southern Yosemite region. If you're more in the mood for drinking coffee, breakfast is served all day.

SOUTH GATE BREWING COMPANY

This microbrewery serves up great beer and more, like a bacon and cheddar burger that will satisfy your protein needs after a long day of hiking. **South Gate Brewing Company** (40233 Enterprise Dr., Oakhurst, 559/692-2739, www.southgatebrewco.com, 11am-9pm daily, $9-16) prides itself on its house brews (Sawtooth IPA, Glacier Point Ale, Deadwood Porter, Gold Diggin' Blonde Ale), but plenty of non-beer-drinkers frequent this place for its pizza and grass-fed beef burgers. This is an ultracasual place—patrons order at the counter, then find a seat—and it can be packed and noisy during the dinner hour, but nobody seems to mind. For dessert, order the root beer float made with house-made root beer.

TAQUERIA PLAZUELAS

For those who understand the culinary joys of truly authentic Mexican food, a stop at **Taqueria Plazuelas** (39993 Hwy. 41, Oakhurst, 559/658-7771, 11am-8:30pm Mon.-Sat., $5-12) is a must. The exterior of this restaurant leaves a lot to be desired; it's a classic hole-in-the-wall (or hole-in-the-strip mall, in this case). Even once you go inside, don't expect much in terms of ambience. You'll order at the counter from a fairly limited menu and a server will bring your food to you. You won't be able to get a margarita, but that's a fair trade-off for fresh homemade tortillas, carne asada with mole sauce, sopes, gorditas, chiles rellenos, and burritos filled with a variety of meats and beans. Everything is made from scratch, so be patient.

PETE'S PLACE

For fast service at breakfast or lunch, it's hard to beat **Pete's Place** (40093 Hwy. 41, Oakhurst, 559/683-0772, 7am-3pm Mon.-Tues., 7am-8pm Wed.-Sun., $8-15), where the food is a mix of American and Greek. No matter what you order, this is mountain food in mountain-sized portions (a two-fisted breakfast burrito or heaping piles of fried zucchini sticks or onion rings alongside a big hamburger), and it's served with a Greek accent: About half of the menu consists of falafel, Greek salad, gyros, *tzatziki,* and the like. If you've just finished up a backpacking trip, order the BLT with avocado and your stomach will thank you. The closest thing to "healthy" on this menu is the ostrich burger. If you're in a really big rush, order at the drive-through.

THE COOL BEAN CAFE

Nothing hits the spot before a long day of hiking better than a double shot of espresso. Forego Starbucks and stop in at **The Cool Bean Cafe** (40120 Hwy. 41, Oakhurst, 559/683-7575, www.thecoolbeancafe.com, 6:30am-6pm Mon.-Sat, $6-9) and you'll be stronger, faster, and a whole lot more cheerful on your drive into Yosemite. If you're not in a big hurry, order a muffin, quiche, smoothie, or breakfast sandwich and hang out on the flower-filled patio while planning the day's activities, or use the free wireless Internet to check your email.

ERNA'S ELDERBERRY HOUSE

If you think there is no such thing as a gourmet dining experience in Oakhurst, think again. ★ **Erna's Elderberry House** (48688 Victoria Ln., Oakhurst, 559/683-6800, www.elderberryhouse.com, 5:30pm-9pm daily, $42-112) is the restaurant connected to the fabulous Château du Sureau, and it shares the same elegant country-estate atmosphere. Divided into three lavishly furnished dining areas, the restaurant serves courses such as poached salmon, braised Sonoma duck, roast beef tenderloin, a salad of local greens, and dessert. A 700-bottle wine list is available for perusing. Sunday **brunch** (11am-1pm, $68 per person) is also a culinary treat. The food is wonderful and the restaurant's decor is a feast for the eyes, with antique French furnishings and walls adorned with tapestries and original oil paintings.

SMOKEHOUSE 41 BAR-B-QUE

Fans of real pit-smoked barbecue will find their happy place at **Smokehouse 41 Bar-B-Que** (40713 Hwy. 41, 559/642-2271, www.smokehouse41.com, 11am-9pm Tues.-Sun., $8-26). Order your food at the counter and then grab a seat and wait for the servers to bring you heaping plates of rib racks, pulled pork, tri-tip, chicken legs, and the like. All of the meats are smoked on California oak wood for up to 14 hours. Even if you aren't a meat-lover, you'll be super happy with a big order of jalapeno macaroni and cheese or cheesy potato casserole.

Bass Lake

DUCEY'S ON THE LAKE

Ducey's (39255 Marina Dr., Pines Village, Bass Lake, 559/642-3131, www.basslake.com, 7am-11am and 4pm-9pm daily, $25-35) is the "fancy" restaurant at Bass Lake, offering classic American dining with a winning lake view. You won't find any entrées for less than 20 bucks. Rib eye, pork chop, filet mignon, rack of lamb, duck, shrimp scampi, and prime rib are served in large portions, steak house style, along with soup or salad and seasonal vegetables. Order a couple of appetizers ($12)—crab cakes, artichoke hearts, or oysters Rockefeller—and you probably won't need dinner. Breakfast may be the best meal at Ducey's, for both its value and its flavor. A full array of omelets, plus French toast, eggs Benedict, and quiche are served. For a more casual meal, take a seat at the upstairs **Ducey's Bar and Grill** (11am-9pm Sun.-Thurs., 11am-10pm Fri.-Sat., $10-15), which serves proletarian fare like burgers, sandwiches, and salads.

THE FORKS RESORT

There's nothing fancy about the café at **The Forks Resort** (39150 Road 222, Bass Lake, 559/642-3737, www.theforksresort.com, 7am-8pm daily in summer, $7-13), and maybe that's why it's so likable. You can come inside in your fishing or hiking clothes and sit down to a hearty stack of pancakes, a double cheeseburger, or a club sandwich. "The home of the world-famous Forks Burger" is right out of the 1950s. Your meal isn't going to break the bank, so go ahead and add on a milk shake or a root beer float.

Accommodations

The historic Big Trees Lodge is in the southern part of the park, near the Mariposa Grove of Giant Sequoias and about an hour south of Yosemite Valley. Two additional lodgings are on private land holdings within the national park: The Redwoods at Wawona (cabins) and Yosemite West (cabins, rental houses, and bed-and-breakfasts). Because these are not on the park's central reservation system, they're generally easier to reserve.

INSIDE THE PARK

Big Trees Lodge
(FORMERLY WAWONA HOTEL)

The white-and-green Victorian main building of the ★ **Big Trees Lodge** (8308 Wawona Rd., 888/413-8869, www.travelyosemite.com, $145-295, closed Thanksgiving to Christmas, closed Jan.-Mar.), makes an elegant impression. It has a Southern appeal with a wide veranda out front and porch chairs scattered about its green lawns. Considered one of California's oldest mountain hotels (one of its cottages was built in 1876; the main hotel was added three years later), the lodge is a great place to stay if you enjoy historic buildings and don't need the amenities of the Ritz. The hotel has a vintage quality, and it's not just due to the preponderance of brass doorknobs, crown molding, Victorian wallpaper, and steam radiators. The building itself is a National Historic Landmark. The room furnishings include wicker chairs, brass beds, and some antique furniture—even a few clawfoot tubs.

The 104 rooms are on the small side but comfortable. Those in the main building are not quite as nice as those in various buildings around the grounds. The **rooms with private baths** cost about $50 more per night; the remaining **rooms without baths** share communal bath and shower facilities, which are surprisingly comfortable and private. Bathrobes are provided in rooms without baths for late-night trips to the restroom. Rooms at the hotel are often sold as rate packages, with "extras" included, such as breakfast in the dining room, a guidebook to hiking trails, or a history-oriented tour.

The **Big Trees Lodge Dining Room** is dependably good. The restaurant is not particularly formal, but it has the same grand, vintage feel as the rest of the hotel, with high ceilings and big windows overlooking a green lawn. That lawn plays host to an old-fashioned Western barbecue every Saturday evening in summer, complete with lots of sticky sauce, baked beans, and a little bit of square dancing.

Most other standard hotel services are found at the Big Trees Lodge, including a swimming pool and tennis court. A piano player entertains in the main lobby every evening. This is fortunate because the dining room doesn't take reservations unless your party is larger than eight, so most small groups end up waiting for a table.

A major advantage to staying in the Wawona area is the peace and quiet. You're far from the hustle and bustle of the Valley, which is an hour's drive away. Yet the hotel is very convenient to the many trailheads and the spectacular vista point on Glacier Point Road, a half hour away. The Mariposa Grove of Giant Sequoias and the trailhead for Chilnualna Falls are minutes away, the Pioneer Yosemite History Center is nearby, and a nine-hole golf course is just across the road.

The Redwoods

The Redwoods Vacation Home Rentals (877/753-8566 or 888/225-6666, www.redwoodsinyosemite.com, $249-980 summer, $163-520 winter) is a collection of private inholdings within the national park, where anyone can own (or rent) a home. Many of the houses are truly "cabins" (meaning they're on the rustic side) and sit densely clustered on small lots.

The Redwoods arranges its 130 vacation rentals into **four categories.** "Bronze" rentals are the smallest and have the fewest amenities (no fireplace or satellite TV). "Platinum" cabins are the priciest; they may have as many as six bedrooms, plus frills like a hot tub, pool table, or a gas grill. In between are the "Gold" and "Silver" cabins. Every home is privately owned and reflects the owner's personal tastes and requirements.

Fees depend on the size and category of the rental. For about $250 per night in summer, two people can rent a small, simply furnished cabin complete with linens, cookware, dishes, a barbecue grill, and firewood. Larger houses can accommodate a whole family or large group. There is a three-night minimum stay in summer and on holidays, and a two-night minimum stay in the off-season.

Note that a stay here puts you about an hour's drive from Yosemite Valley and two hours from Tuolumne Meadows. However, many devoted fans of The Redwoods find there is plenty to do within a short drive or walk of their cabin—hiking to Chilnualna Falls, visiting the sequoias in the Mariposa Grove, or swimming and fishing in the South Fork Merced River, which runs alongside many of The Redwoods' cabins.

Yosemite West

Yosemite National Park is packed with people every day all summer long, but over at **Yosemite West** (Hwy. 41 and Glacier Point Rd., $375-750 per night for 4 people) you can hear a pin drop on your cabin's deck. A 40-year-old subdivision that consists of a collection of private homes, Yosemite West is on a hillside right across from Chinquapin junction; it's only about a 30-minute drive from either Yosemite Valley or Glacier Point. The neighborhood is a private inholding within the federal park boundary. Some year-round residents live here, but more than 140 homes in the neighborhood serve as vacation rentals or bed-and-breakfasts.

The rental homes at Yosemite West are on the upscale, modern side. They vary in size

from 2-6 bedrooms, and most come with extras like a hot tub, barbecue, pool table, or home entertainment center. Many have fireplaces, and free firewood is provided. The homes' lot sizes are fairly large, so you probably won't hear or see much of your neighbors. This place is for those who want peace and quiet.

Although many park travelers book a stay at Yosemite West in the summer, it's also an ideal choice for a winter trip because it's the closest lodging to the downhill runs at Yosemite Ski & Snowboard Area, a 20-minute drive away.

Several companies, as well as private individuals, rent homes or bed-and-breakfast-style rooms in Yosemite West. For B&B fans, the best of the lot is **Yosemite West High Sierra Bed-and-Breakfast** (7460 Henness Ridge Rd., 209/372-4808, www.yosemitehighsierra. com, $270-340 including breakfast). Those who would prefer a "home" of their own (including a kitchen) should contact one of several Yosemite West vacation rental companies: **Yosemite West Reservations** (559/642-2211, www.yosemitewestreservations.com), **Yosemite's Scenic Wonders** (888/967-3648, www.scenicwonders.com), or **Yosemite's Four Seasons Vacation Rentals** (800/299-0396, www.yosemitelodging.com). Prices vary widely according to the size and amenities of each rental; condos and apartments are generally much cheaper than stand-alone houses.

SOUTH OF THE PARK: HIGHWAY 41

Visitors approaching Yosemite from Los Angeles, the Central Coast, and Southern California often use the Highway 41 approach to the park's South entrance through Fresno and Oakhurst. **Oakhurst** is the last "big town" before Yosemite's South entrance and the most developed of any of the towns near Yosemite's borders.

Bass Lake is a popular fishing and water-skiing destination near Oakhurst and offers its own lodging possibilities. Both Oakhurst and Bass Lake lodgings are convenient for

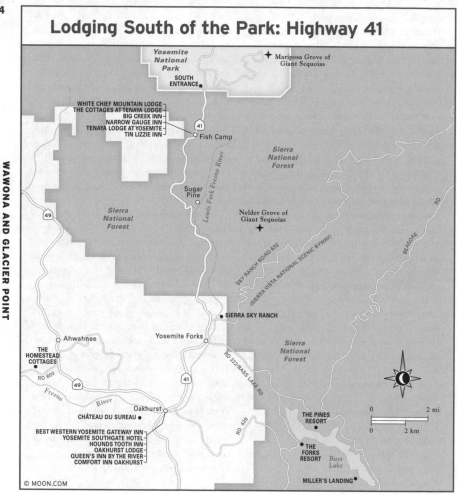

Lodging South of the Park: Highway 41

Yosemite National Park

✛ Mariposa Grove of Giant Sequoias

SOUTH ENTRANCE

WHITE CHIEF MOUNTAIN LODGE
THE COTTAGES AT TENAYA LODGE
BIG CREEK INN
NARROW GAUGE INN
TENAYA LODGE AT YOSEMITE
TIN LIZZIE INN

41

Fish Camp

Sierra National Forest

Lewis Fork Fresno River

Sugar Pine

49

Sierra National Forest

Nelder Grove of Giant Sequoias ✛

SKY RANCH RD/RD 632
(SIERRA VISTA NATIONAL SCENIC BYWAY)

BEASORE RD

● SIERRA SKY RANCH

● Ahwahnee

Yosemite Forks

THE HOMESTEAD COTTAGES
●

RD 600

49

Fresno

River

41

Sierra National Forest

RD 222/BASS LAKE RD

Oakhurst

CHÂTEAU DU SUREAU ●

BEST WESTERN YOSEMITE GATEWAY INN
YOSEMITE SOUTHGATE HOTEL
HOUNDS TOOTH INN
OAKHURST LODGE
QUEEN'S INN BY THE RIVER
COMFORT INN OAKHURST

RD 426

THE PINES RESORT ●

● THE FORKS RESORT

Bass Lake

MILLER'S LANDING ●

0   2 mi
0   2 km

© MOON.COM

---

visitors who want to spend most of their Yosemite vacation in the southern part of the park. If you plan to spend a lot of time in Yosemite Valley, understand that it will take you about 90 minutes to drive there from Bass Lake.

North of Oakhurst is the tiny hamlet of **Fish Camp,** an old logging town that today consists of only a couple of small stores and a few private homes.

Fish Camp

At Fish Camp, you are only **2-3 miles from**

Yosemite's South entrance and right next door to the Yosemite Mountain Sugar Pine Railroad, a destination especially popular with families. On its outskirts are two large resorts and multiple smaller lodgings, including several bed-and-breakfasts.

WHITE CHIEF MOUNTAIN LODGE
This budget lodging option in Fish Camp is just 2 miles (3.2 km) from Yosemite's South entrance. Situated 900 ft/275 m off the main highway, **White Chief Mountain Lodge** (7776 White Chief Mountain

Rd., Fish Camp, 559/683-5444, www. whitechiefmountainlodge.com, $149-179) goes unnoticed by the vast majority of visitors. Back when fur coats were in fashion, it was a chinchilla ranch; now it's just a rustic motel that's perfect for people who don't want much more than a place to lay their heads. The owners of White Chief keep their business simple: They rent out 20 no-nonsense rooms and six cabins with all the basics but no frills. There's also a **restaurant** (breakfast and dinner daily, hours vary seasonally).

BIG CREEK INN

On the upscale side for a bed-and-breakfast, the **Big Creek Inn** (1221 Hwy. 41, Fish Camp, 559/641-2828, www.yosemiteinn.com, $299-309 in summer, lower winter rates) is a place that caters to adult guests who can appreciate some of the finer elements of a quality inn: a modern, beautifully appointed dining room, spa services available in the privacy of your own room, and a sitting room with a state-of-the-art robotic telescope for gazing at the galaxies. Three rooms are available in the inn's sprawling, 5,000-square-foot (465-sq-m) building. Rooms have king or queen beds, fireplaces, flat-screen televisions, Blu-ray players, and private balconies. Add to this the sight and sound of tumbling Big Creek and you have a very special bed-and-breakfast experience, just 2 miles (3.2 km) from Yosemite's South entrance.

NARROW GAUGE INN

The **Narrow Gauge Inn** (48571 Hwy. 41, Fish Camp, 559/683-7720 or 888/644-9050, www. narrowgaugeinn.com, $174-379 in summer, lower winter rates) rents 27 rooms situated on a steep hillside lined with incense-cedars, oaks, and pines. Located just 4 miles (6.4 km) from the southern entrance to Yosemite, the inn gets its name from the neighboring Yosemite Mountain Sugar Pine Railroad, which offers scenic train rides aboard a restored late-1800s steam locomotive. All of the Narrow Gauge Inn's rooms have balconies or decks (some private and some shared) with views of the forest and surrounding mountains. The rooms are small with older furnishings, but the lovely grounds are a huge selling point—flowers seem to bloom from every crevice. The larger Mission Suite includes two bathrooms (one with a claw-foot tub) and goes for $350-375 in summer. Two major highlights for kids are the antique fire engine housed on the property and the small outdoor swimming pool. Cat lovers will enjoy visiting with Knuckles, a sweet kitty who naps in the inn's office. A **restaurant** (559/683-6466, 5pm-9pm daily) is on the property; reservations are suggested.

TENAYA LODGE AT YOSEMITE

Since it opened in 1990, **Tenaya Lodge** (1122 Hwy. 41, Fish Camp, 559/683-6555 or 888/514-2167, www.tenayalodge.com, $309-479 in summer, lower winter rates) has won the AAA Four Diamond award each year. The lodge is managed by Aramark's Yosemite Hospitality, which also manages all the lodgings within Yosemite. The guest rooms look and feel like those of a modern mountain lodge, with earth-toned, Native American patterns on the furnishings and local art on the walls. Plenty of in-room luxuries are offered, including a mini-fridge honor bar and an in-room safe for your diamond tiara.

The huge, 250-room lodge seems a bit out of place in the small town of Fish Camp, but it has created a world unto itself. The resort is spread out over 35 acres (14 hectares) and comes complete with multiple restaurants, including the classy **Embers** and the kid-friendly **Timberloft Pizzeria,** plus indoor and outdoor pools, a fitness center, and a 10,000-square-foot (930-sq-m) spa, Ascent. The spa offers massages of all kinds, plus body wraps and facials.

Because this is a corporate, full-scale resort, organized activities are plentiful. If you want someone to plan your entire visit to Yosemite and the surrounding region, that service is available. Families will find a variety of programs for kids, including gold panning, fishing, biking, and hiking.

THE COTTAGES AT TENAYA LODGE

Set on 7 pine-covered acres (2.8 hectares), the **Tenaya Lodge Cottages** (1110 Hwy. 41, Fish Camp, 888/514-2167, www.tenayalodge. com, $435-575 in summer, lower winter rates) are a short walk from the main Tenaya Lodge property and enjoy a prime location right off Highway 41. If the main Tenaya Lodge seems a bit too citified for your taste, these cute yellow-and-green cottages may be just right.

The 53 duplex- and triplex-style cottages, plus one stand-alone unit, are cheerfully decorated; all come with convenient amenities like refrigerators, microwaves, and coffeemakers. Ceiling fans, wicker chairs, and plaid quilts are a recurring theme. Each unit has a gas fireplace and patio or balcony, plus one king or two queen beds. A swimming pool, hot tub, and racquetball court are on the property, as is the **Timberloft Pizzeria.** A short footpath leads to the restaurants at Tenaya Lodge's main buildings.

TIN LIZZIE INN

Victoriana fans rave about the **Tin Lizzie Inn** (7730 Laurel Way, Fish Camp, 559/641-7731, www.tinlizzieinn.com, $325-475). This tiny bed-and-breakfast offers three lodging options in a fabulous woodsy area of Fish Camp, plus an unusual amenity: All guests receive a tour of Fish Camp in a Model T Ford. The inn's luxurious rooms include the Lizzie Suite with a king bed, gas fireplace, claw-foot tub, flat-screen TV, and private balcony; and the two-story Tin Lizzie Cottage, with a queen bed upstairs, Murphy bed downstairs, flat-screen TV, and an outdoor patio. If your party is more than two people, you might opt for the Carriage House, a two-bedroom vacation home with a gourmet kitchen, adjacent to the main inn. Although the Tin Lizzie Inn's look is pure Victorian—stained-glass windows, intricate wood moldings, pull-chain toilets—the building itself is a modern replica, built in 2006.

Oakhurst

A stay in Oakhurst puts you **15 miles (24 km) from the South entrance** to Yosemite, and about 45 miles (72 km) from Yosemite Valley. This town of about 13,000 inhabitants has several bed-and-breakfasts, inns, motels, and even a spectacular château. You can buy pretty much anything in Oakhurst, from hardware to hiking boots to a fancy dinner.

SIERRA SKY RANCH

Almost 140 years old, **Sierra Sky Ranch** (50552 Road 632, Oakhurst, 559/683-8040, www.sierraskyranch.com, $145-250, children under 12 stay free) is an unusual lodging where you can experience a touch of the Old West. The ranch was built in 1875 and renovated in 1946; its 27 rooms are clean, comfortable, and loaded with historical charm. If you want to teach your kids about the way California used to be, bring them here for vacation. The ranch is set on 14 acres (5.7 hectares) of foothill country, with Lewis Creek flowing right past the property. The steak dinners at the **Branding Iron** (559/658-2644 or 559/683-8040) steak house have satisfied legions of travelers. There's also a swimming pool. The entire facility is sometimes rented for weddings and corporate retreats. The ranch is 5 miles (8 km) north of Oakhurst off Highway 41; it is a 10-mile (16.1-km) drive north to Yosemite's South entrance.

HOUNDS TOOTH INN

Though the **Hounds Tooth Inn** (42071 Hwy. 41, Oakhurst, 559/642-6600 or 888/642-6610, www.houndstoothinn.com, $135-249 guest rooms, $210-279 cottage) is a hop, skip, and a jump away from busy Highway 41, it does an excellent job of concealing its roadside location. Set below the highway and out of its sight line, the inn's 3-acre (1.2-hectare) grounds are beautifully landscaped with walkways, trees, and foliage. Twelve guest rooms are decorated in nouveau Victorian style and come with a variety of amenities, including spas and fireplaces; each has its own outside entrance. A separate 850-square-foot (80-sq-m) cottage features a large suite with a king-size bed, spa, fireplace, and a (small) kitchenette, plus its own private patio with a garden and mini waterfall. (The cottage is frequently used for honeymoons but can also house a small family.) A complimentary breakfast buffet and afternoon juice, coffee, and tea are served each day in the common area.

QUEEN'S INN BY THE RIVER
Okay, so the river is more like a creek, but the **Queen's Inn by the River** (41139 Hwy. 41, Oakhurst, 559/683-4354, www.queensinn.com, $136-236) is a great moderately priced overnight spot. Eight rooms feature flatscreen TVs, contemporary furnishings, and a private deck or patio; most have gas fireplaces, and a few have whirlpool tubs. The adjacent **Wine & Beer Garden** (4pm-10pm Wed -Sat) makes a fun diversion, especially when there is a live band playing. The motel owners also run the award-winning **Idle Hour Winery** (559/760-9090, 11am-5pm daily) next door. A pleasant walking path runs alongside the creek; Adirondack chairs are strategically placed so you can read a book or watch the resident wildlife. If you prefer to avoid the frilliness of most B&Bs or the vanilla flavor of most chain motels, you'll be happy here.

OAKHURST LODGE
A dependable and affordable bet, the **Oakhurst Lodge** (40302 Hwy. 41, Oakhurst, 559/683-4417 or 800/655-6343, www.theoakhurstlodge.com, $189-249 in summer, lower winter rates) has 33 rooms with all the touches you'd expect from a modest chain motel (queen beds, cable TV, HBO, free Internet service, in-room coffee, swimming pool, guest laundry), except this isn't a chain. The rooms won't win any prizes for interior decorating, but the rates are modest and the owners actually care that you have a good experience on your vacation.

COMFORT INN OAKHURST
If you want the convenience and amenities of a decent-sized town, Oakhurst's **Comfort Inn** (40489 Hwy. 41, Oakhurst, 559/683-8282 or 888/742-4371, www.comfortinn.com,

$169-299 in summer, lower winter rates) fits the bill. Its 117 rooms have phones, refrigerators, and cable TV with HBO. A complimentary breakfast buffet is served each morning in the guest lobby. At the end of the day, splash around in the outdoor pool or sit back and relax in the spa.

BEST WESTERN YOSEMITE GATEWAY INN
The nicest chain motel in Oakhurst is the **Best Western** (40530 Hwy. 41, Oakhurst, 559/683-2378 or 888/256-8042, www.yosemitegatewayinn.com, $260-325 in summer, $129-199 in winter). This particular BW has a little more kitsch, including a 25-foot (8-m) Statue of Liberty flanked by the American and California flags and a big waterwheel out front. But guests enjoy the indoor and outdoor swimming pools, the lush landscaping on the motel grounds, the stonewalled lobby with its high vaulted ceiling, and the hand-painted murals of Vernal Fall, Half Dome, and other Yosemite icons. An on-site **restaurant** (6am-10am, 11am-3:30pm, and 5pm-9pm daily) offers all the charm of your average Denny's. Still, the 133 guest rooms are pleasant enough and you can count on certain amenities: air-conditioning, direct-dial phones, cable TV, HBO, free wireless Internet, a small exercise room, and some noise from guests in adjoining rooms (get an upstairs room to minimize the noise). Some two-room suites are available for groups of up to six people.

YOSEMITE SOUTHGATE HOTEL/ YOSEMITE SIERRA INN
A dependable bet in Oakhurst is the **Yosemite Southgate Hotel** (40644 Hwy. 41, Oakhurst, 559/683-3555 or 888/265-7733, www.yosemitesouthgate.com, $149-249). The 81 guest rooms have been remodeled and refreshed in recent years and come with a generous amount of "freebies": a substantial continental breakfast, cable TV, mini-fridges, microwaves, coffeemakers, free wireless Internet, and coin-operated washers and

dryers. An outdoor swimming pool is welcome on hot summer days. If you strike out here, try the neighboring **Yosemite Sierra Inn** (40662 Hwy. 41, Oakhurst, 559/642-2525 or 877/642-2525, www.yosemitesierrainn. com, $149-259), which has similar amenities.

CHÂTEAU DU SUREAU

★ **Château du Sureau** (48688 Victoria Ln., Oakhurst, 559/683-6860, www.chateausureau. com, $385-585 including breakfast) has been praised by just about every major travel magazine. Dreamed up by Erna Kubin-Clanin, an Austrian woman with amazing talent and a perfectionist streak, the château is an elegant, castlelike inn. Imagine a classic French château and you have an idea: featherbeds, goosedown comforters, Oriental carpets, trompe l'oeil frescoes, Parisian balconies, Italian linens, a grand piano, and a wealth of antiques. No expense has been spared in decorating this 9,000-square-foot (835-sq-m) manse.

The Château du Sureau has 10 guest rooms, each with a fireplace and private bath. A separate 2,000-square-foot (185-sq-m), two-bedroom villa ($2,950) comes stocked with china and crystal, a 24-hour personal butler, a supply of your favorite vintage wines, and the use of a complimentary, fully insured Jeep Cherokee for the duration of your stay.

An overnight at Château du Sureau is a spendy proposition, to say the least. Is it worth the money? Since it opened in 1991, the Château has earned the Mobil Five Star and AAA Five Diamond awards. It's definitely worth it.

Don't miss the 3-foot-tall (1-m) chess pieces arranged on a giant game board in the manicured garden. Play a little bocce ball or make a wish on one of the stone fountains while you're outside. For about $200, you can get one heck of a massage at the on-site Spa du Sureau. All this and you're only 16 miles (26 km) from the southern entrance to Yosemite.

If you have the dough to spend a few nights here, eat at the adjacent restaurant, **Erna's Elderberry House,** which is also run by Kubin-Clanin. It is as equally divine and expensive as the Château.

Bass Lake

Bass Lake is 5 miles (8 km) east of Oakhurst via Bass Lake Road and **18 miles (29 km) from Yosemite's South entrance** via Highway 41, about a 45-minute drive. A stay at Bass Lake fits the bill for anybody who likes boating or fishing. With several campgrounds, restaurants, and resorts, plus numerous places to rent boats or buy fishing equipment, the lakeshore is more like a vacation town than a peaceful mountain retreat.

MILLER'S LANDING

At the southern edge of the lake, **Miller's Landing** (37976 Road 222, Wishon, 559/642-3633, www.millerslanding.com, $250-350 in summer) offers refreshingly easy access to Bass Lake's commercial services, yet is far removed from the hubbub of the Pines Village area. The 12 cabins at Miller's Landing run the gamut from basic to elaborate. The most deluxe cabins sleep eight, with two bedrooms, two baths, satellite TV, and a full-size kitchen. A picnic table and fire ring are right outside your door. The resort is self-contained—it has a restaurant and its own marina with boat rentals (patio boats, ski boats, WaveRunners, fishing boats, kayaks, and canoes).

THE FORKS RESORT

Set right on the lakeshore, **The Forks Resort** (39150 Road 222, Bass Lake, 559/642-3737, www.theforksresort.com, $175-305) is one of the old-style resorts on Bass Lake; it's been owned and operated by the same family for three generations. The resort's 13 one-, two-, and three-bedroom cabins make the perfect base camp for a combined Yosemite/Bass Lake vacation. Only a handful offer lake views, but all are right across the road from the water's edge. Each cabin has a fully equipped kitchen, plus a porch with a barbecue grill so you can cook up all the fish you catch. The largest cabins can accommodate up to eight people.

The resort has a general store, its own dock with boat rentals (patio boats, motorboats, rowboats, and canoes), and a café. This is a family-oriented place, which is reinforced by a "no party" policy. That keeps the ambience quiet and peaceful even though this is a very busy and popular resort.

THE PINES RESORT

Right in the center of busy Pines Village on the shores of Bass Lake, **The Pines Resort** (54432 Road 432, Bass Lake, 559/642-3121 or 800/350-7463, www.basslake.com, $249-399) offers visitors 84 two-story chalets, most with kitchens, fireplaces, and/or private decks. The chalets are modern in style; they were built in 1978 and renovated in 1997. This is more like staying in a town house or a condo than in a mountain cabin, but it's convenient if you want to be near Bass Lake. Another lodging choice (in a separate building by Ducey's Restaurant) is The Pines' 20 romantic lakefront suites, each with a king bed, fireplace, and deck, as well as a lovely lake view. Get a room on the 2nd floor for more privacy; the 1st-floor rooms all share a common deck. Two luxury honeymoon suites, Bridalveil and Rudi's Retreat, run $440 per night in summer. The Pines has tennis and basketball courts, a swimming pool, hot tub, a children's playground, and boat rentals. A restaurant and bar are on the premises.

Ahwahnee

The town of Ahwahnee is **21 miles (34 km) from Yosemite's South entrance,** near the junction of Highways 49 and 41.

THE HOMESTEAD COTTAGES

The tiny hamlet of Ahwahnee is a much quieter place to stay than busy Oakhurst, only a few miles away. And one of the most peaceful places to stay in Ahwahnee is **The Homestead** (41110 Road 600, Ahwahnee, 559/683-0495 or 800/483-0495, www.homesteadcottages.com, $179-269), an oak-dotted resort on 160 acres (65 hectares).

The Homestead's five one-bedroom cottages plus one much larger "ranch house" ($379-410) are modern in style and beautifully appointed. Their interiors are lined with Saltillo tiles, warm pine wood, and simple but tasteful furnishings. Each cottage, including an above-the-barn stargazing loft, has a fully equipped kitchen and a fireplace for cool nights. The units also have air-conditioning, a real bonus in the summer at this 2,000-foot (600-m) elevation. The drive to Yosemite's South gate will take just under an hour.

Camping

Campground choices are not plentiful in the southern part of the park. If you don't have a reservation at Wawona Campground, you can take a chance at getting a site at first-come, first-served Bridalveil Creek. If it's late in the day in the summer, you are probably out of luck and would do better heading south, out of the park, to find a campsite. The kiosk at the park's South entrance can provide updates on which park campgrounds are full, so check before making the 24-mile (39-km) drive up to Bridalveil Creek.

INSIDE THE PARK
Reservations

Reservations for in-park campgrounds are available (and highly recommended) at **Recreation.gov** (877/444-6777 or 518/885-3639 from outside the U.S. and Canada, www.recreation.gov) and can be made up to five months in advance. Reservations are available in blocks of one month at a time, up to five months in advance, on the 15th of each month starting at 7am (Pacific Standard Time). Both the telephone and the online reservation systems are open 7am-7pm Pacific Standard Time November to February, until 9pm March through October.

Campers without reservations can try the **first-come, first-served** sites at Bridalveil Creek on Glacier Point Road.

Glacier Point

There's only one campground up on Glacier Point Road, and ★ **Bridalveil Creek** (110 sites, first come, first served, July-Sept., $18) is it. If you want to camp close to Glacier Point's great day-hiking trails or be able to enjoy sunsets from the world-famous overlooks at Glacier Point or Sentinel Dome without facing a long drive afterward, this camp is where you want to be. The trick is to get here early to secure a site; **no reservations are accepted.** The camp typically fills early, especially on weekends. Many would-be campers who get turned away in Yosemite Valley wind up here looking for a site.

The 110 sites can accommodate tents or RVs up to 35 feet (10.7 m). Because the elevation is 7,200 feet (2,200 m), the camp is open only from about July 1 to early September. Although many of the sites are quite densely packed, there are a few winners on the outside of the loops. If you score one of these outer, private sites, you're in heaven. Bridalveil Creek runs right through the camp, and the meadows alongside it produce wonderful wildflowers in July.

A trail to Ostrander Lake leaves right from the campground; the 13-mile (20.9-km) round-trip is a wonderful, though long, day hike. Swimming in the lake is popular on warm summer days. Yosemite Valley is a 45-minute drive. If you want to visit Tuolumne Meadows, you're about two hours away.

Of all the camps in Yosemite, this is the one where you want to be the most self-contained—in other words, bring everything you need. If you forgot the hamburger patties, it's a long drive to the nearest store. There is a snack shop (9am-5pm) at Glacier Point in the summer months, but it has a very limited menu.

The camp has drinking water, flush toilets, picnic tables, and fire grills. Two **group sites** for groups of 13-30 people ($50) and three horse camps ($30) are also available. Reservations are required for the group sites (877/444-6777 or 518/885-3639 from outside the U.S. and Canada, www.recreation.gov).

The camp is 8 miles (12.9 km) east of Highway 41 on Glacier Point Road, or 24.5 miles (39.5 km) from the park's South entrance.

Summerdale Campground

Wawona

Some visitors like **Wawona Campground** (93 sites, open year-round, reservations required Apr.-Sept., $26) because of its setting on the South Fork Merced River. Others regard this 93-site campground with disdain because it is in an open flat right alongside Highway 41, with little shade or privacy. Whether you see the glass half full or half empty depends on how lucky you are. If fortune is smiling on you, you'll obtain one of the sites that are right on the river. If you're unlucky, you'll get one of the sites farther from the river, in full view of the road.

The camp offers drinking water, flush toilets, picnic tables, and fire grills. Sites accommodate tents or RVs up to 35 feet (10.7 m), and RVers are particularly fond of this campground; it has easy access and there is a dump station nearby in Wawona. A **group site** accommodates 13-30 people (reservations required, $50), and two horse camps (877/444-6777, $30) are also available. From mid-October to mid-April, about 20 sites (A Loop, $18) are first come, first served.

Wawona Campground is 1 mile (1.6 km) north of Wawona off Highway 41, 7 miles (11.3 km) north of the park's southern entrance.

SOUTH OF THE PARK: HIGHWAY 41

Several Forest Service campgrounds in **Sierra National Forest** (North Fork Ranger Station, 559/877-2218, www.fs.usda.gov/sierra) provide great options for campers driving into the park from Fresno and Los Angeles. Some camps require a drive of up to 12 miles (19.3 km) from the main highway, but your reward for this effort is a peaceful campsite in a beautiful setting. If you are planning to center your vacation in Yosemite Valley, you will face a drive of 90 minutes one-way. However, if you're planning your trip around Wawona, the Mariposa Grove, and Glacier Point Road, you'll be conveniently situated.

Fish Camp

SUMMERDALE

★ **Summerdale Campground** (26 sites, 559/642-3212 or 877/444-6777, www.recreation.gov, May-Sept., $30-32) might as well be in Yosemite—it's that close to the park border. Located within a mile of the park's southern entrance, it is just as popular as the campgrounds within the park. Sites are reservable on the Forest Service reservation system, and you'll definitely need a reservation in the summer months (except midweek). The 29-site camp is on Big Creek at 5,000 feet (1,500 m) elevation. Many campers spend summer afternoons cooling off in the stream's deep, clear swimming holes. Fishing is good, too, but it gets better the farther you go from camp. Although the camp is just below the busy highway and road noise can sometimes be noticeable, nobody who scores a spot here ever complains. The camp has drinking water, picnic tables, fire grills, and vault toilets.

The camp is 1 mile (1.6 km) north of Fish Camp on the west side of Highway 41.

SUMMIT

If you have a high-clearance vehicle and don't mind a 5-mile (8-km) drive on a dirt road, an overnight at **Summit Campground** (6 sites, first come, first served, June Oct., $22) puts you inside the Yosemite gates, which means you won't have to wait in line at the entrance station in the morning. For the price of a long, bumpy drive and being largely self-reliant, you are staying within Yosemite's gates for free. Fire rings are provided, but not grills. The camp has no toilets, so bring a trowel to bury your waste. This is more like backpacking than car camping—bring your own water and a camp stove, and pack out your own trash.

The campground is reached by following the dirt road across Highway 41 from the Big Trees Lodge, then driving past the golf course. The road leads out of the national park and into neighboring Sierra National Forest; after 4.5 miles (7.2 km) from Highway 41, turn left on Road 5S09A to reach the camp. The elevation is 5,800 feet (1,770 m).

Camping South of the Park: Highway 41

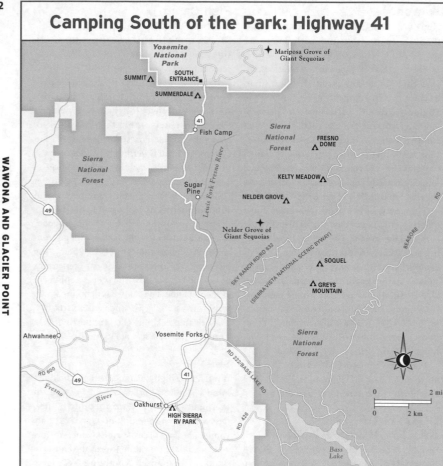

Mariposa Grove of Giant Sequoias

Yosemite National Park

SUMMIT

SOUTH ENTRANCE

SUMMERDALE

41

Fish Camp

Sierra National Forest

FRESNO DOME

Lewis Fork Fresno River

Sierra National Forest

KELTY MEADOW

Sugar Pine

NELDER GROVE

49

Nelder Grove of Giant Sequoias

SKY RANCH RD/RD 632

(SIERRA VISTA NATIONAL SCENIC BYWAY)

SOQUEL

GREYS MOUNTAIN

BEASORE RD

Ahwahnee

Yosemite Forks

Sierra National Forest

RD 222/BASS LAKE RD

RD 600

49

Fresno River

Oakhurst

HIGH SIERRA RV PARK

RD 426

Bass Lake

0   2 mi

0   2 km

© MOON.COM

Oakhurst

HIGH SIERRA RV PARK

The **High Sierra RV Park** (40389 Hwy. 41, Oakhurst, 559/683-7662, www.highsierrarv. com, $23-28 tents, $41-54 RVs) isn't in the High Sierra, but it's only 16 miles (26 km) to Yosemite's southern entrance and 8 miles (13 km) from Bass Lake. A small stream runs through the property, although it goes dry by mid-July. All the usual amenities of a well-equipped RV park are offered: restrooms, showers, laundry, phone hookups, picnic tables, a snack and gift shop, and an RV dump.

Most of the tent and RV sites (full hookups available) are packed together like sardines. Campers in tents probably won't love this place, but RVers will be very happy.

The camp is in downtown Oakhurst, about a block from the highway at an elevation of 3,000 feet (900 m).

Sierra National Forest

NELDER GROVE

If you're a fan of giant sequoias, you've come to the right campground. At **Nelder Grove Campground** (7 sites, first come, first served, free), you can put up your tent right next to one of several giant sequoia stumps left from an old logging operation and then take a hike through the nearby Nelder Grove of sequoias (where fortunately the trees stand intact) on the Shadow of the Giants Trail. The camp is pleasant, shaded, peaceful, and, best of all, free. Its seven sites have picnic tables, fire grills, and vault toilets. Bring your own drinking water, or plan to filter or boil water from nearby California Creek.

To reach the camp, drive 6 miles (9.7 km) east on Sky Ranch Road (Road 632, which becomes Road 6S10), off Highway 41 5 miles (8 km) north of Oakhurst. Turn left at the sign for Nelder Grove; follow the signs for 2 miles (3.2 km) to the camp.

SOQUEL

Soquel Campground (9 sites, 877/444-6777, www.recreation.gov, May-Nov., $24-26) is one of the few reservable campgrounds in this somewhat remote region of Sierra National Forest south of Yosemite. Set at a pleasant 5,400 feet (1,650 m) in elevation, the 11 sites have most of the basics: picnic tables, fire grills, and vault toilets. You must bring your own drinking water.

To reach the camp, drive 7 miles (11.3 km) east on Sky Ranch Road (Road 632, which becomes Road 6S10) off Highway 41 5 miles (8 km) north of Oakhurst. Turn right on Road 6S40 and drive 1 mile (1.6 km) to the camp.

GREYS MOUNTAIN

It's a 9-mile (14.5-km) drive from Highway 41 to **Greys Mountain Campground** (26 sites, first come, first served, $26-52), some of it on a rough dirt road, but the reward for this trek is one of 26 campsites near a wonderful swimming hole on Willow Creek. The campground is lined with firs and incense-cedars. It has picnic tables, fire grills, and vault toilets, but no water, so bring your own.

To reach the camp, drive 7 miles (11.3 km) east on Sky Ranch Road (Road 632,

which becomes Road 6S10), off Highway 41 5 miles (8 km) north of Oakhurst. Turn right on Road 6S40, which is signed for Soquel Campground, and then drive 2 miles (3.2 km) to Greys Mountain Campground.

KELTY MEADOW

If you're traveling with your horse, there's room for both of you at **Kelty Meadow Campground** (7 sites, 877/444-6777 or 518/885-3639 from outside the U.S. and Canada, www.recreation.gov, May-Sept., $25-52). Reserve one of seven sites and you'll wind up with the double-wide kind, big enough for you and your horse trailer. Kelty Creek flows right past the campground, which is a great bonus for anglers (and everyone else, because you'll need to filter or boil water from this creek, there's no water in the campground).

To reach the camp, drive 10 miles (16.1 km) east on Sky Ranch Road (Road 632, which becomes Road 6S10), off Highway 41 5 miles (8 km) north of Oakhurst.

FRESNO DOME

Lovely **Fresno Dome Campground** (15 sites, first come, first served, $26-48) comes with a bonus: It's only 2.5 miles (4 km) from the trailhead for the easy, scenic hike to the top of Fresno Dome. The 15 sites have picnic tables, fire grills, and vault toilets. You must bring your own drinking water. It will take a while to drive from this camp back to the highway and up to Yosemite, but the surrounding area is so pretty you probably won't mind.

To reach the camp, drive 11 miles (17.7 km) east on Sky Ranch Road (Road 632, which becomes Road 6S10), off Highway 41 5 miles (8 km) north of Oakhurst. Take the left fork signed for Fresno Dome Campground and drive 1.5 miles (2.4 km) to the camp. If you don't like the choices at Fresno Dome Campground, you can always continue another mile to Little Sandy Campground, which offers similar amenities.

Tioga Pass and Tuolumne Meadows

At 8,600 feet (2,600 m) in elevation, this pristine meadow extends for more than 2 miles (3.2 km) along the Tuolumne River, making it the largest subalpine meadow in the entire Sierra Nevada. From its tranquil edges, trails lead in all directions—to the alpine lakes set below the spires of Cathedral and Unicorn Peaks, to a series of roaring waterfalls on the Tuolumne River, and to the summits of lofty granite domes with commanding vistas of the high country. The Tuolumne Meadows region is the centerpiece of a huge High Sierra playground for hikers and backpackers and a welcoming place for less ambitious visitors who simply want to sit at a picnic table and wallow in the scenic beauty.

The regions on either side of the meadow, following the 39-mile

Highlights

Look for ★ to find recommended sights, activities, dining, and lodging.

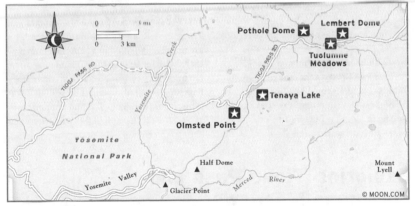

★ **Olmsted Point:** In a park rife with impressive overlooks, Olmsted Point may be the most impressive of them all. Seen from here are Clouds Rest, Tenaya Canyon, and an unusual side view of Half Dome, as well as high-country peaks and passes (page 160).

★ **Tenaya Lake:** This deep-blue granite tarn is right alongside Tioga Pass Road, enticing many drive-by sightseers to slam on the brakes and go for an impromptu swim in its frigid waters or picnic along its sandy shores (page 160).

★ **Pothole Dome:** Even non-hikers will enjoy the short walk to the top of this low granite dome

on the western edge of Tuolumne Meadows (page 160).

★ **Tuolumne Meadows:** The largest subalpine meadow in the Sierra Nevada, this grassy expanse inspires awe in even the most jaded travelers. Numerous trails lead from its edges, but many visitors are happy just to stop and stare (page 162).

★ **Lembert Dome:** Take a 2.8-mile (4.5-km) round-trip hike around to the sloping back side of Lembert Dome and then climb to the top for a thrilling view of the high country. Or simply hang out at the base to watch the rock climbers strut their stuff (page 173).

Where Can I Find...?

- **Banks and ATMs:** There are no banking services on Tioga Pass Road. If you drive east to Lee Vining at U.S. 395, you'll find ATMs at the **Tioga Gas Mart** and the **Mono Market.**

- **Gas:** at **Crane Flat** (Big Oak Flat Rd., 209/379-2742, 8am-8pm daily) you can pay at the pump 24 hours a day with a credit card. If you are farther east when the needle registers "E"—say somewhere near Tuolumne Meadows—it might be smarter to drive downhill and out of the park rather than backtracking to Crane Flat. Your first chance for gas will be the **Tioga Gas Mart** (760/647-1088), 11 miles (17.7 km) east of Tioga Pass, but it's downhill all the way.

- **Showers:** Try **Mono Vista RV Park** (760/647-6401, 9am-6pm daily, $3 for 5 minutes) at the north end of Lee Vining on U.S. 395. Call ahead to confirm hours.

(63-km) length of Tioga Pass Road from Crane Flat to Tioga Pass, offer more wonders. Two giant sequoia groves—the Merced and Tuolumne Groves—wait to be explored, as do meadows filled with wildflowers at Crane Flat and White Wolf. The drive-to vista at Olmsted Point provides an unusual view of Half Dome and a peek into the funneled granite walls of Tenaya Canyon. Just beyond the overlook, Tenaya Lake sparkles in the sunshine, dazzling visitors with its beauty.

Tioga Pass Road reaches the park's eastern boundary at 9,945-foot (3,030-m) Tioga Pass, the highest-elevation highway pass through the Sierra Nevada. But the fun doesn't end there—the drive through its reaches and down to U.S. 395 is one of the most thrilling stretches of road in the West. Most of the 3,000-foot (900-m) descent takes place without the aid of guard rails, so it's critical to keep your eyes on the road and not on the spectacular mountain scenery.

PLANNING YOUR TIME

Tioga Pass Road and Tuolumne Meadows are usually blanketed in a thick layer of snow **late October to late May.** That leaves **June through September** for a visit, when Tioga Pass Road is usually open. At these high elevations, it's rare to have daytime temperatures above 80°F (27°C), and nights will often drop close to freezing.

Exploring Tioga Pass and Tuolumne Meadows

VISITORS CENTER

The second largest of the park's visitors centers is located on the west end of Tuolumne Meadows, on the south side of Tioga Pass Road. Open from Tioga Pass Road's opening date until late September, the **Tuolumne Meadows Visitor Center** (209/372-0263, 8am-5pm daily summer only) is housed in a historic building that often has a cozy fire burning in the fireplace. Exhibits focus on the area's geology, wildflowers, wildlife, and ecology. A few displays interpret humans' relation to the Yosemite high country, including John Muir's perspective on the value of Yosemite as a national park. Books and maps are for sale.

Previous: hiker in Tuolumne Meadows; a lake near the Vogelsang Loop; Lower Sunrise Lake.

For visitors driving into the park through the Big Oak Flat entrance on Highway 120, the small **Big Oak Flat Information Station** (8am-5pm daily year-round) is 100 feet (30 m) south of the entrance kiosk, on the west side of the road. A few books and maps are for sale, and wilderness permits are available.

ENTRANCE STATIONS

The **Big Oak Flat** entrance station on Highway 120 offers western access to Tioga Road and Tuolumne Meadows. To the east is the **Tioga Pass** entrance station (June-Sept.), which offers seasonal access through the park and from the Eastern Sierra.

SHUTTLES AND TOURS

During the summer months, a **free shuttle bus** (7am-7pm daily June-Sept.) runs along Tioga Pass Road, stopping at all major trailheads between Olmsted Point and Tioga Pass. The first shuttle of the day leaves Tuolumne Meadows Lodge at 7am; shuttles arrive at each stop at approximately 30-minute intervals. Check at the Tuolumne Meadows Visitor Center, White Wolf, or Tuolumne Meadows Lodge for a detailed schedule, or phone 209/372-1240.

Driving Tour

Tioga Pass Road is a 39-mile (63-km) scenic drive through red fir and lodgepole pine forest, past meadows, lakes, and granite domes and spires. Now a part of California State Highway 120, the road has an interesting history: It was built in 1882-1883 as a mining

road to service the silver mines in the Tioga Pass area. It was realigned and modernized in 1961.

YOSEMITE VALLEY TO TIOGA PASS

If you are driving to Tioga Pass from Yosemite Valley, plan on about **two hours** from the time you leave the Valley until the time you reach the Tioga Pass entrance station. It will take about 30 minutes to get to **Crane Flat** and the start of Tioga Pass Road, which is 20 miles (32 km) north of the main lodgings and campgrounds in Yosemite Valley via Big Oak Flat Road. At Crane Flat you'll find a gas station and small store for supplies.

From this 6,000-foot (1,800-m) elevation, Tioga Pass Road slowly climbs its way east through dense forests to the **White Wolf** turnoff at 14 miles (22.5 km). (A restaurant, small store, and restrooms are available at White Wolf.) In another dozen miles you reach the pullout for the spectacular vista at **Olmsted Point; Tenaya Lake** is 2 miles (3.2 km) beyond. You have now left the thick stands of trees behind and entered a granite wonderland.

At world-famous **Tuolumne Meadows,** 6 miles (9.7 km) beyond Tenaya Lake, you have another chance for snacks and supplies (as well as plenty of chances to admire the scenery); then it's on to 9,945-foot (3,030-m) **Tioga Pass.** This is the highest mountain pass you can drive through in California. Here the road exits Yosemite National Park and drops down to Mono Lake, the Eastern Sierra, and U.S. 395.

Tioga Pass and Tuolumne Meadows

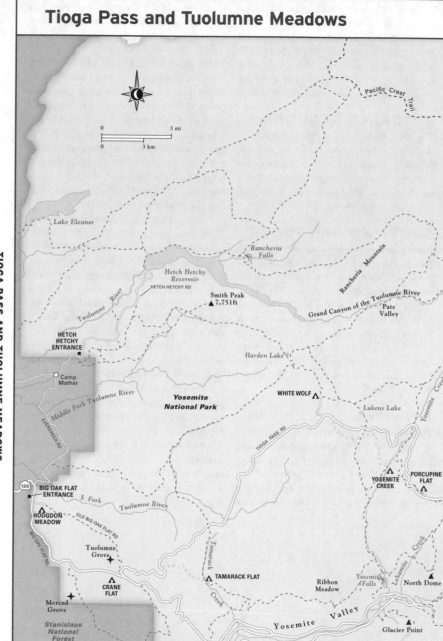

N

0   3 mi

0   3 km

Pacific Crest Trail

Lake Eleanor

Rancheria Falls

Hetch Hetchy Reservoir

HETCH HETCHY RD

Tuolumne River

Smith Peak
▲ 7,751ft

Rancheria Mountain

Grand Canyon of the Tuolumne River

Pate Valley

HETCH HETCHY ENTRANCE

Harden Lake

Camp Mather

Middle Fork Tuolumne River

Yosemite National Park

WHITE WOLF ▲

Lukens Lake

EVERGREEN RD

Yosemite Creek

TIOGA PASS RD

BIG OAK FLAT ENTRANCE

120

S Fork

Tuolumne River

HODGDON MEADOW

OLD BIG OAK FLAT RD

YOSEMITE CREEK ▲

PORCUPINE FLAT ▲

BIG OAK FLAT RD

Tuolumne Grove

Tamarack Creek

TAMARACK FLAT ▲

Ribbon Meadow

Lehamite Creek

Yosemite Falls

North Dome ▲

CRANE FLAT ▲

Merced Grove

Stanislaus National Forest

Yosemite Valley

Glacier Point ▲

© MOON.COM

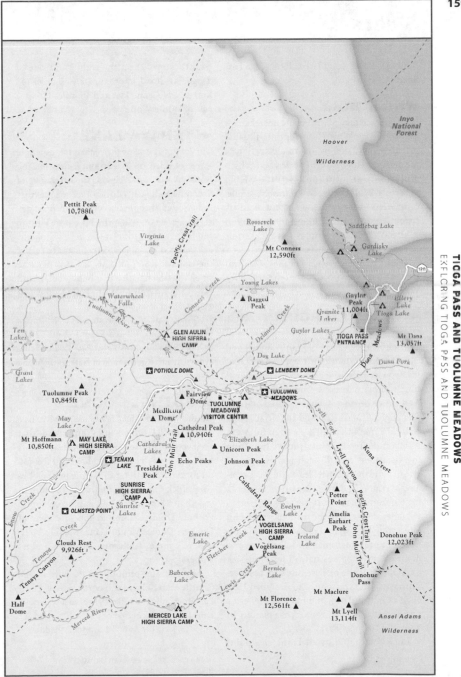

Sights

Sights are listed west to east along Tioga Pass Road.

WHITE WOLF

Likely named for a Sierra coyote mistaken for a wolf, **White Wolf** (July-Sept.) is situated at 8,000 feet (2,400 m) on an old section of the original Tioga Road. The drive-in **White Wolf Campground** (no reservations) and the **White Wolf Lodge** (www.travelyosemite.com), a tent-cabin resort, are here, as is an excellent **restaurant.** The meadows around White Wolf usually display beautiful wildflowers in June and July.

From Crane Flat, drive 14 miles (22.5 km) east on Tioga Pass Road to the left turnoff for White Wolf.

★ OLMSTED POINT

Olmsted Point offers a wide-open vista of Yosemite Valley's array of granite domes and cliffs, but from a much different vantage point than you have anywhere else in the park. First-time visitors may have trouble picking out Half Dome because it looks so different from this angle. Clouds Rest and the skyscraping walls of Tenaya Canyon are also in full view. A 0.25-mile (0.4-km) interpretive trail from this vista point leads through a series of glacial erratics and gives a brief lesson in park geology. Marmots and pikas are often seen poking out from the rocks. If you walk or drive to the far eastern end of the turnout, you get an interesting look at Tenaya Lake and the multitude of granite domes and peaks beyond it. Olmsted Point was named for Frederick Law Olmsted, one of Yosemite's first preservationists (and the man who designed New York's Central Park), and his son, Frederick Law Olmsted Jr., who worked as a planner in Yosemite National Park.

Look for the Olmsted Point viewpoint (shuttle stop 12) on the right-hand side of Tioga Pass Road, approximately 30 miles (48 km) east of Crane Flat and 16 miles (26 km) east of White Wolf.

★ TENAYA LAKE

The last of the Ahwahneechee tribespeople were rounded up at **Tenaya Lake,** ending Native Americans' reign as the caretakers of Yosemite Valley. It's difficult to imagine that sad piece of history on a beautiful August day at Tenaya Lake, when the lakeshore's white sands are lined with picnickers and sunbathers. Plenty of people swim in Tenaya Lake, but the water is icy cold. This is a fine place to sit on the beach with a pair of binoculars and watch the rock climbers on Polly Dome, just across Tioga Pass Road.

Tenaya Lake (shuttle stop 9) is 2.5 miles (4 km) east of Olmsted Point (32 mi/52 km east of Crane Flat) on Tioga Pass Road. Picnic areas with fire grills are on both ends of the lake.

★ POTHOLE DOME

On the western edge of Tuolumne Meadows lies **Pothole Dome,** a low granite dome that even young children can hike. An easy, short **trail** parallels the road for about 100 feet (30 m) to a stand of trees; the dome lies just beyond. Pick any route you like to the top. In less than 15 minutes, you can be on top of Pothole Dome, gazing at the fine view of Lembert Dome, Mount Dana, Mount Gibbs, and, of course, Tuolumne Meadows and its namesake river.

The parking pullout for Pothole Dome (shuttle stop 8) is on the north side of Tioga Pass Road, about 5 miles (8 km) east of Tenaya Lake (37 mi/60 km east of Crane Flat) and 2.2 miles (3.5 km) west of Tuolumne Meadows.

1: Tenaya Lake 2: view from Olmsted Point
3: Lembert Dome 4: Soda Springs

★ TUOLUMNE MEADOWS

Situated at 8,600 feet (2,600 m) above sea level, **Tuolumne Meadows** is the largest subalpine meadow in the Sierra Nevada, extending for more than 2 miles (3.2 km). The meandering Tuolumne River cuts a swath through its grassy expanse. Perhaps more impressive than the wide meadow itself are the majestic granite domes and peaks that surround it. Although the meadow is so beautiful that it is tempting to wander into it, be sure to stay on designated paths. High-elevation meadows are extremely fragile and can be damaged by foot traffic.

Tuolumne Meadows (shuttle stop 6) is 39 miles (63 km) east of Crane Flat on Tioga Pass Road, about an hour's drive. Parking and restrooms are available at the visitors center (9am-6pm daily summer) across from the meadow.

LEMBERT DOME

This glacially polished rock is an example of a roche moutonnée, a dome that has one gently sloping side and one side that drops in a steep escarpment. **Lembert Dome** was named for Jean Baptiste Lembert, a homesteader who lived in Tuolumne Meadows in the mid-1880s. Lembert was something of a hermit who made his living by herding sheep and collecting insects to sell to museums. Rock climbers ply their trade on the highway side of Lembert Dome, but hikers can head around to the back side and walk right up to the summit.

Lembert Dome (shuttle stop 4) is 1.5 miles (2.4 km) east of the visitors center; a parking lot, picnic area, and restrooms are on the left. Access the summit trail at the Dog Lake parking lot (shuttle stop 2), 1 mile (1.6 km) east on Tioga Pass Road.

SODA SPRINGS

Visitors who want a close-up look at Tuolumne Meadows should take the short walk to **Soda Springs,** on the north side of the meadow. Either trail will give you a good look at the wildflowers, grasses, and sedges of the meadow, plus a glimpse into the area's history. Soda Springs is a permanent spring that produces a true carbonated water. The Sierra Club built **Parsons Memorial Lodge** here in 1915, after purchasing this beautiful stretch of meadow so that it could never be developed (eventually the Sierra Club donated the land to the National Park Service). You'll visit the site where John Muir and Robert Underwood Johnson discussed the idea of creating Yosemite National Park.

The **trailhead** for Soda Springs and Parsons Lodge is at the Lembert Dome parking lot (shuttle stop 4). Walk north along the gravel road and watch for a gate signed Glen Aulin and Soda Springs. Plan one hour for the walk, then catch the shuttle from the visitors center back to the parking lot.

Recreation

DAY HIKES

To truly visit Yosemite's high country, you have to travel on foot. The following hikes in the Tioga Pass Road and Tuolumne Meadows area are listed in the order that their trailheads appear on Highway 120, traveling from west to east (Big Oak Flat entrance station to Tioga Pass).

Merced Grove

Distance: 3 miles (4.8 km) round-trip

Duration: 1.5 hours
Elevation Change: 350 feet (105 m)
Effort: Easy
Trailhead: Merced Grove
Directions: From the Big Oak Flat entrance station on Highway 120, drive southeast 4.3 miles (6.9 km) to the trailhead on your right. Or, from Crane Flat, drive west 3.7 miles (6 km) on Big Oak Flat Road to the trailhead on your left.

The Merced Grove was "discovered" in 1833 by a group of explorers headed by Joseph Walker

Tioga Pass and Tuolumne Meadows Hikes

Trail	Effort	Distance	Duration
Lukens Lake	Easy	1.5 mi/2.4 km rt	1 hr
Pothole Dome	Easy	1.6 mi/2.6 km rt	1 hr
Tenaya Lake	Easy	2 mi/3.2 km rt	1 hr
Tuolumne Grove	Easy	2.5 mi/4 km rt	1.5 hr
Merced Grove	Easy	3 mi/4.8 km rt	1.5 hr
Harden Lake	Easy	5.6 mi/9 km rt	3 hr
Lyell Canyon	Easy	6 mi/9.7 km rt	3 hr
May Lake and Mount Hoffmann	Easy/strenuous	2.4-6 mi/3.9-9.7 km rt	1-4 hr
Elizabeth Lake	Moderate	4.8 mi/7.7 km rt	4-5 hr
Lembert Dome	Moderate	2.8 mi/4.5 km rt	2-3 hr
Dog Lake	Moderate	3.4 mi/5.5 rt	2 hr
Middle and Upper Gaylor Lakes	Moderate	4 mi/6.4 km rt	2 hr
Sunrise Lakes	Moderate	7.5 mi/12.1 km rt	4 hr
Lower Gaylor Lake	Moderate	8 mi/12.9 km rt	4 hr
Mono Pass and Spillway Lake	Moderate	8.4-11.6 mi/13.5-18.7 km rt	5-6 hr
Glen Aulin and Tuolumne Falls	Moderate	9.2 mi/14.8 km rt	4-5 hr
North Dome	Moderate/strenuous	9 mi/14.5 km rt	4-5 hr
Cathedral Lakes	Strenuous	7.4 mi/11.9 km rt	4-6 hr
Clouds Rest	Strenuous	14 mi/22.5 km rt	7-8 hr
Mount Dana	Very strenuous	6 mi/9.7 km rt	4-6 hr

who were looking for the best route through the Sierra Nevada. Most likely, local indigenous tribes had long known about the location of the big trees. Of the three **giant sequoia groves** in Yosemite—Merced, Tuolumne, and Mariposa—the Merced Grove is the smallest and least visited. Yet surprisingly, it offers the most pleasant hiking. Generally the trail sees foot traffic only from people who enter Yosemite at the Big Oak Flat entrance and drive by this trailhead on their way to Yosemite Valley. The trail is a closed-off dirt road that is level and straight for the first 0.5 mile (0.8 km). **Bear left** at the only junction and head downhill through a lovely mixed forest of white firs,

incense-cedars, ponderosa pines, and sugar pines. Azaleas bloom in early summer beneath the conifers' branches. You will reach the first sequoias, a group of six, at about **1.5 miles (2.4 km).** More big trees lie in the next **300 feet (90 m).** Only 20 sequoias are found in this grove, but because they grow very close together, they make a dramatic impression. The two largest sequoias are directly across the road from a handsome **old log cabin** that was built as a retreat for the park superintendent but now sits empty and boarded up. Sit on its front steps and have a picnic while you admire the giant trees. Retrace your steps from the cabin, hiking gently uphill for your return.

Tuolumne Grove

Distance: 2.5 miles (4 km) round-trip
Duration: 1.5 hours
Elevation Change: 550 feet (170 m)
Effort: Easy
Trailhead: Tuolumne Grove
Directions: From the Big Oak Flat entrance station on Highway 120, drive southeast 7.7 miles (12.4 km) to Crane Flat, and then turn left to stay on Highway 120. Drive 0.5 mile (0.8 km) to the Tuolumne Grove parking lot on the left.

Up until 1993 you could drive right in to the **Tuolumne Grove of Giant Sequoias**, but now the road is closed and visitors have to hike in. The grove is on the old Big Oak Flat Road, a paved, 6-mile (9.7-km) historical road and trail that is open to bikers and hikers (although bikes are a rarity). This is a popular destination, so **arrive early in the morning** to have the best chance at solitude. Leave your car at the parking lot near Crane Flat and hike downhill into the big trees. It's **1 mile (1.6 km)** to the first sequoias; there are only about 25 giants in this small grove.

The Tuolumne Grove's claim to fame is that it has one of the two remaining **walk-through trees** in Yosemite; this one is called the **Dead Giant.** It's a tall stump that was tunneled in 1878 so that wagons, and later automobiles, could drive through. Go ahead, walk through it. No visitor can resist.

At a small picnic area, a **0.5-mile (0.8-km) trail** loops around the forest. Make sure you save some energy for the trip back uphill to the parking lot; the moderate grade ascends 550 feet (170 m). The old paved road continues downhill beyond the grove all the way to Hodgdon Meadow Campground. Some people hike the entire 6-mile (9.7-km) distance and have someone pick them up at Hodgdon Meadow.

Harden Lake

Distance: 5.6 miles (9 km) round-trip
Duration: 3 hours
Elevation Change: 500 feet (150 m)
Effort: Easy
Trailhead: White Wolf (see map p. 165)
Directions: From the Big Oak Flat entrance station on Highway 120, drive southeast 7.7 miles (12.4 km) to Crane Flat, and then turn left to stay on Highway 120. Drive 14 miles (22.5 km) to the left turnoff for White Wolf. Turn left and drive 1 mile (1.6 km) to the lodge and trailhead.

Harden Lake itself isn't a scene-stealer—by late summer, it's not much more than a large pond, framed by a few stands of aspen trees on its northeast shore. But many people come

The giant sequoias of the Merced Grove are slim in numbers, but huge in girth.

Harden Lake and Lukens Lake

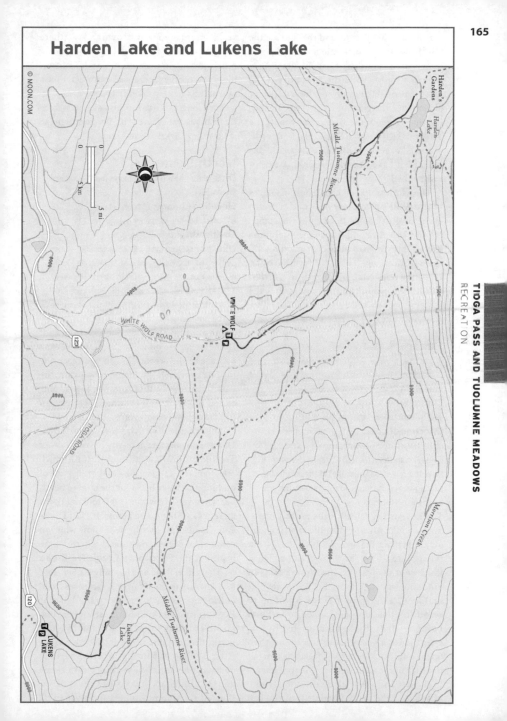

© MOON.COM

here for another reason, and that's to see the **wildflowers** that bloom in a region known informally as Harden's Gardens, about 0.25 mile (0.4 km) beyond the lake. **July** is the most dependable month for the wildflower bloom. Plus there are other rewards, including fine views of the Grand Canyon of the Tuolumne River just 0.5 mile (0.8 km) north of the lake. Also, because of the small size of Harden Lake, it is dependably warm for **swimming** by midsummer.

The hike is simple enough. The trail follows **White Wolf's gravel service road** (a stretch of the original Tioga Road) past the campground entrance and across the Tuolumne River. This old road once continued for 1.5 miles (2.4 km), but it has been replaced by an appealing trail that leads directly to **Harden Lake.** If you haven't yet gotten your fill of the flower show, proceed a short distance farther and feast your eyes on **Harden's Gardens.**

Lukens Lake

Distance: 1.5 miles (2.4 km) round-trip

Duration: 1 hour

Elevation Change: 300 feet (90 m)

Effort: Easy

Trailhead: Lukens Lake (see map p. 165)

Directions: From the Big Oak Flat entrance station on Highway 120, drive southeast 7.7 miles (12.4 km) to Crane Flat, and then turn left to stay on Highway 120. Drive 16.2 miles (26.1 km) to the Lukens Lake Trailhead parking area on the south side of the road. The trail begins across the road.

The Lukens Lake Trail is the perfect introductory lake hike for **families;** a six-year-old could make the trip easily. A bonus is that the trailhead is on the western end of Tioga Road, so it's quickly reached from points in Yosemite Valley. The trail is 0.75 mile (1.2 km) long, leading from **Tioga Road** up to a **saddle,** then dropping down to **Lukens Lake.** It winds through a dense red fir forest, filled with mammoth trees, and then opens out to a wide, flower-filled clearing at the edge of the shallow lake. The trail curves to the left and skirts along the south shore of Lukens Lake. In mid- to late July, you can

see a spectacular **wildflower** show (there are thousands of pink shooting stars, among other flowers) in the meadow. **Swimming** is highly recommended; by midsummer, this is one of the warmest lakes in the park.

For a longer trail to Lukens Lake, start from the trailhead at White Wolf Lodge and make a 4.6-mile (7.4-km) round-trip.

North Dome

Distance: 9 miles (14.5 km) round-trip

Duration: 4-5 hours

Elevation Change: 1,500 feet (455 m)

Effort: Moderate to strenuous

Trailhead: Porcupine Creek

Directions: From the Big Oak Flat entrance station on Highway 120, drive southeast 7.7 miles (12.4 km) to Crane Flat, and then turn left to stay on Highway 120. Drive 24.5 miles (39.4 km) to the Porcupine Creek Trailhead on the right, 1 mile (1.6 km) past Porcupine Flat Campground.

There are those who say that climbing Half Dome is a bit of a disappointment, and not just because of the crowds. When you reach the top and check out the commanding view, the panorama of granite is not quite as awesome as you might expect, and that's because you can't see Half Dome—you're standing on it.

That's a dilemma that's easy to fix. If Half Dome is an absolute necessity in your view of Yosemite, climb North Dome instead, which offers a heart-stopping view of that big piece of granite. The route is not for the faint of heart, but when you are way up high looking down at Tenaya Canyon and across at Half Dome and Clouds Rest—well, you'll know why you came. The preferred route to North Dome begins at the **Porcupine Creek Trailhead** on Tioga Pass Road and has only a 1,500-foot (455-m) gain to the summit. A dirt access road quickly brings you to a proper trail, signed as **Porcupine Creek.** Continue straight at two possible junctions near the **2.5-mile (4-km)** mark, heading due south for North Dome. After **3 miles (4.8 km),** your views begin to open up, providing fine vistas of North Dome and Half Dome and increasing your anticipation. At the trail junction at **4.5 miles (7.2** km), take the left spur for the final hike to North Dome's summit. Surprise—it's a downhill grade to reach it. The view from the top is sublime. Half Dome, just across the canyon, appears close enough to touch. Clouds Rest is a dramatic sight to the northeast. To the southwest, you can see cars crawling along the Yosemite Valley floor.

On your return trip, consider taking the **spur trail** 2 miles (3.2 km) from North Dome, at an obvious saddle. The spur leads a steep 0.25 mile (0.4 km) to **Indian Rock,** the only natural arch on land in Yosemite. It's great fun to climb around on.

May Lake and Mount Hoffmann

Distance: 2.4-6 miles (3.9-9.7 km) round-trip

Duration: 1 hour to May Lake; 4 hours to Mt. Hoffmann

Elevation Change: 500 feet (150 m) to May Lake; 2,000 feet (600 m) to Mt. Hoffmann

Effort: Easy to May Lake, strenuous to Mt. Hoffmann

Shuttle Stop: 11

Trailhead: Snow Flat (see map p. 168)

Directions: From the Big Oak Flat entrance station on Highway 120, drive southeast 7.7 miles (12.4 km) to Crane Flat, and then turn left to stay on Highway 120. Drive 26.6 miles (42.8 km) to the May Lake Road turnoff on the left (near road marker T-21). Turn left and drive 2 miles (3.2 km) to the trailhead.

Here's a hike that you can take the kids on—well, the first part, anyway. It's an easy 1.2 miles (1.9 km) to May Lake, tucked in below 10,850-foot (3,307-m) Mount Hoffmann. The trail to the lake has a total elevation gain of only 500 feet (120 m), and better yet, it's downhill all the way home. Attaining the summit of Mount Hoffmann, on the other hand, requires a challenging ascent and is best left to more seasoned hikers. (Leave the kids at home if continuing to the top of Mount Hoffmann.) The trail to both destinations begins at the **Snow Flat Trailhead** (2 mi/3.2 km off Tioga Pass Road), after which it passes through a lodgepole pine forest, climbs up a granite-lined slope, and then drops down to **May Lake's southern shore.** (The **May**

Lake High Sierra Camp is located here.) May Lake is bitterly cold for swimming, but few can resist its sparkling waters. Wandering along the scenic, granite-ringed shoreline is a pleasant way to spend the afternoon.

To turn this easy walk into a butt-kicker, follow the obvious use trail to the west, which leads around to the north side of May Lake. From the northwest shore, a fairly distinct use trail leads to **Mount Hoffmann's summit.** This is not an official park trail, and it requires scrambling skills and sure footing, especially as you near the top. It also requires good lungs and legs: You have to gain another 1,500 feet (455 m) in about 2 miles (3.2 km). So why do it? The view from Mount Hoffmann's ridgeline is first-class, with Half Dome, Clouds Rest, Tenaya Lake, and May Lake all in sight. Mount Hoffmann is the exact geographical center of Yosemite National Park. The peak has two main summits; the one with the weather station on top is the higher one. Explore the entire ridgeline, and visit both summits if you have the time; the view is surprisingly different.

Clouds Rest

Distance: 14 miles (22.5 km) round-trip

Duration: 7-8 hours

Elevation Change: 2,300 feet (700 m)

Effort: Strenuous

Shuttle Stop: 10

Trailhead: Sunrise Lakes

Directions: From the Big Oak Flat entrance station on Highway 120, drive southeast 7.7 miles (12.4 km) to Crane Flat, and then turn left to stay on Highway 120. Drive 30.3 miles (48.8 km) to the Sunrise Lakes Trailhead on the right, just west of Tenaya Lake.

Hiking to Clouds Rest is a trip that's as epic as climbing Half Dome, but with far fewer people elbowing you along the way and no permit system to bother with. With a 2,300-foot (700-m) climb and 14 miles (22.5 km) to cover, it's not for those who are out of shape. The trail ascends steadily for the first **4 miles (6.4 km),** descends steeply for **0.5 mile (0.8 km),** and then climbs again more moderately. Keep the faith—the first 2.5 miles (4 km) from the

May Lake and Mount Hoffmann

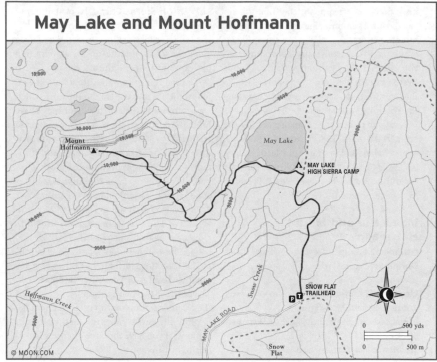

© MOON.COM

trailhead are the toughest. The **final summit ascent** is a little dicey because of the terrifying drop-offs; watch your footing on the granite slabs, and you'll be fine. Overall, the route is much safer than climbing Half Dome because the final ascent is far more gradual and there are no cables to maneuver. The view from the top of Clouds Rest—of Tenaya Canyon, Half Dome, Yosemite Valley, Tenaya Lake, the Clark Range, and various peaks and ridges—will knock your socks off.

If this long hike has made you hot and sweaty, you can stop at the **Sunrise Lakes** for a swim on the way back—the first lake is only 0.25 mile (0.4 km) from the Clouds Rest/ Sunrise Trail junction.

Sunrise Lakes

Distance: 7.5 miles (12.1 km) round-trip
Duration: 4 hours
Elevation Change: 1,000 feet (300 m)
Effort: Moderate

Shuttle Stop: 10
Trailhead: Sunrise Lakes
Directions: From the Big Oak Flat entrance station on Highway 120, drive southeast 7.7 miles (12.4 km) to Crane Flat, and then turn left to stay on Highway 120. Drive 30.3 miles (48.8 km) to the Sunrise Lakes Trailhead on the right, just west of Tenaya Lake.

With all the people hiking to Clouds Rest, combined with all the people hiking to the Sunrise Lakes, the Sunrise trailhead can look like a mall parking lot on a Saturday. But don't be scared off—the hike to Sunrise Lakes is a great day hike or easy backpacking trip, especially during the week or off-season, with only a 1,000-foot (300-m) elevation gain and a ton of stellar scenery—including great views of Clouds Rest at your back as you hike the final stretch to the lakes. Follow the trail as it climbs steeply above the edge of Tenaya Canyon. At **2.5 miles (4 km),** turn left at the sign for the **Sunrise High Sierra Camp.** In about 10 minutes of easy walking,

Lower Sunrise Lake shows up on the right, and the other lakes are just beyond it, on the left. **Upper Sunrise Lake** is the largest and by far the most popular; lots of folks like to swim and picnic there on warm summer days. Backpackers can pick a site here or continue onward for 2 more miles (3.2 km) to the backpackers' camp or the High Sierra Camp, depending on where they've made their plans.

Tenaya Lake

Distance: 2 miles (3.2 km) round-trip
Duration: 1 hour
Elevation Change: None
Effort: Easy
Shuttle Stop: 9
Trailhead: Tenaya Lake
Directions: From the Big Oak Flat entrance station on Highway 120, drive southeast 7.7 miles (12.4 km) to Crane Flat, and then turn left to stay on Highway 120. Drive 31.7 miles (51 km) to the eastern Tenaya Lake picnic area (another Tenaya Lake picnic area lies 0.5 mi/0.8 km west). The trail leads from the parking lot.

Lots of people drive east down Tioga Pass Road in a big rush to get to Tuolumne Meadows, but when they see giant Tenaya Lake right along the road, they stop short in their tire tracks. Luckily the 150-acre (60-hectare), sapphire-blue lake has a **parking lot** and **picnic area** at its east end, where you can leave your car and take a stroll down to the lake's edge. Although most people stop at the white-sand beach and picnic tables to watch the rock climbers on nearby Polly Dome, you can leave the crowds behind by strolling to the south side of the beach. Look for the **trail** there; it leads along the back side of Tenaya Lake, far from the road on the north side. When you get to the lake's west end, where the trail continues but the water views end, just turn around and walk back. It's a perfect, easy hike alongside one of the most beautiful lakes in Yosemite.

Pothole Dome

Distance: 1.6 miles (2.6 km) round-trip
Duration: 1 hour
Elevation Change: 300 feet (90 m)
Effort: Easy
Shuttle Stop: 8
Trailhead: West end of Tuolumne Meadows (see map p. 174)
Directions: From the Big Oak Flat entrance station on Highway 120, drive southeast 7.7 miles (12.4 km) to Crane Flat, and then turn left to stay on Highway 120. Drive 36 miles (58 km) to the Pothole Dome Trailhead on the left, on the west end of Tuolumne Meadows. Park your car in the pullout on the north side of the road.

On the far western edge of Tuolumne Meadows lies a low granite dome that can make even non-hikers feel like true mountaineers. The **parking pullout** is on the north side of Tioga Pass Road, 2.2 miles (3.5 km) west of Tuolumne Meadows Campground. An easy, short **trail** parallels the road for about 300 feet (90 m) to a stand of trees; the dome lies just beyond. **Leave the trail** and pick any route up the smooth granite rock to the top. In about 15 minutes from the time you get out of your car, you can be on top of Pothole Dome, gazing at the fine view of Lembert Dome, Mount Dana, Mount Gibbs, and, of course, Tuolumne Meadows and its namesake river. To explore more of this beautiful area, hike back down the dome and continue on the **trail** alongside the meadow that leads north to the **Tuolumne River.** Here the river drops in a series of photogenic cascades. It is possible to loop back to your trailhead by following the river upstream into Tuolumne Meadows and then heading south to your car, completing a round-trip of about 2.5 miles (4 km).

Cathedral Lakes

Distance: 7.4 miles (11.9 km) round-trip
Duration: 4-6 hours
Elevation Change: 1,000 feet (300 m)
Effort: Strenuous
Shuttle Stop: 7
Trailhead: Cathedral Lakes (see map p. 170)
Directions: From the Big Oak Flat entrance station on Highway 120, drive southeast 7.7 miles (12.4 km) to Crane Flat, and then turn left to stay on Highway 120. Drive 37.4 miles (60.2 km) to the Cathedral Lakes Trailhead on the right, by Tuolumne Meadows. Park

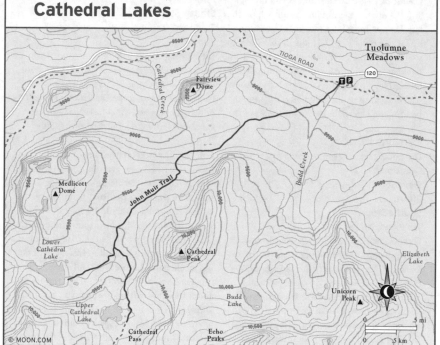

Cathedral Lakes

your car in the pullouts on either side of the road; there is no formal parking lot.

The two Cathedral Lakes make for a tremendously popular, easy backpacking destination in Yosemite, but it's such a short hike to reach them that they also make a great day trip. Located on a 0.5-mile (0.8-km) spur off the John Muir Trail, the lakes are within a classic glacial cirque, tucked below 10,840-foot (3,304-m) Cathedral Peak. It's as scenic a spot as you'll find anywhere in Yosemite. From the trail's start at Tioga Pass Road, hike 3.2 miles (5.2 km) on the **John Muir Trail,** with a 1,000-foot (300-meter) elevation gain. Much of the trail is shaded by lodgepole pines, but when the path breaks out of the trees, views of surrounding peaks (especially distinctive Cathedral Peak, which looks remarkably different from every angle) keep you oohing and aahing the whole way. At **3.2 miles (5.2 km),** turn right on the **Cathedral Lake spur** to reach the lower, larger lake in **0.5 mile (0.8 km).** You'll follow the lake's inlet stream through a gorgeous meadow to the water's edge. Many hikers stop here and go no farther, but it's a pity not to see **Upper Cathedral Lake** as well. To reach the upper lake, retrace your steps to the John Muir Trail and continue another **0.5 mile (0.8 km).** Fishing is often better in the upper lake, and the scenery is even more sublime. **Campsites** are found close to the lakes, but you will need to secure your wilderness permit far in advance in order to spend the night.

Elizabeth Lake

Distance: 4.8 miles (7.7 km) round-trip
Duration: 4-5 hours
Elevation Change: 1,000 feet (300 m)
Effort: Moderate
Shuttle Stop: 5
Trailhead: Tuolumne Meadows Campground (see map p. 174)
Directions: From the Big Oak Flat entrance station

on Highway 120, drive southeast 7.7 miles (12.4 km) to Crane Flat, and then turn left to stay on Highway 120. Drive 39 miles (63 km) to Tuolumne Meadows Campground. Turn right and follow the signs through the main camp to the group camp. The trail begins across from the group camp restrooms near group site B49.

Starting at the trailhead elevation of 8,600 feet (2,600 m), you have a mere 1,000-foot (300-m) elevation gain over 2.4 miles (3.9 km) to get to lovely Elizabeth Lake, set in a basin at the foot of distinctive Unicorn Peak. It's a day hike that is attainable for almost anybody, and you can bet that every camper at Tuolumne Meadows Campground makes the trip at some point.

For non-campers, the trailhead is a bit tricky to find—it's tucked into the **B loop** of Tuolumne Meadows Campground, across from the group camp restrooms. Once you locate it, be prepared to climb steeply for **1 mile (1.6 km)** and then breathe easier when the trail levels out. Fortunately the route is mostly shaded by a dense grove of lodgepole pines.

Upon reaching the lakeshore, you'll see that **Elizabeth Lake** is a gorgeous body of alpine water. Some visitors swim or fish here, others try to climb Unicorn Peak (10,900 ft/3,300 m), but most are happy to sit near the lake's edge and admire the views of the sculpted peak and its neighbors in the Cathedral Range.

Lower Gaylor Lake

Distance: 8 miles (12.9 km) round-trip
Duration: 4 hours
Elevation Change: 800 feet (245 m)
Effort: Moderate
Shuttle Stop: 1
Trailhead: Tuolumne Lodge/John Muir Trail (see map p. 177)
Directions: From the Big Oak Flat entrance station on Highway 120, drive southeast 7.7 miles (12.4 km) to Crane Flat, and then turn left to stay on Highway 120. Drive 39.5 miles (63.6 km) to the Tuolumne Lodge and Wilderness Permits turnoff on the right. Turn right and drive 0.5 mile (0.8 km). Park in the lot on the left signed for Dog Lake and John Muir Trail. The trail begins across

the road from the parking lot. Additional parking is available in the Wilderness Permits parking lot.

This mellow, pretty hike starts on the **John Muir Trail** near Tuolumne Lodge and then heads east along the south side of the **Dana Fork of the Tuolumne River**. After **2 miles (3.2 km)**, the trail crosses the river and Tioga Pass Road and heads uphill through a dense lodgepole pine forest to **Lower Gaylor Lake**, elevation 10,049 feet (320 m). The shallow lake is a deep turquoise color and surrounded by a grassy alpine meadow. From its edge, you gain wide vistas of the peaks in the Tuolumne Meadows area. This is classic high-country beauty at its finest.

Note that if you wish to get to the Middle and Upper Gaylor Lakes from the lower lake, you have to go cross-country—an easy trip if you have a good map of the area with you. An even easier way is to drive to the Tioga Pass Trailhead and follow the trail for the Middle and Upper Gaylor Lakes hike. Elevation at this trailhead is 9,250 feet (2,820 m); the total gain is about 800 feet (245 m) to Lower Gaylor Lake, a gentle climb the whole way.

Lyell Canyon

Distance: 6 miles (9.7 km) round-trip
Duration: 3 hours
Elevation Change: 200 feet (60 m)
Effort: Easy
Shuttle Stop: 2
Trailhead: Tuolumne Lodge/John Muir Trail
Directions: From the Big Oak Flat entrance station on Highway 120, drive southeast 7.7 miles (12.4 km) to Crane Flat, and then turn left to stay on Highway 120. Drive 39.5 miles (63.6 km) to the Tuolumne Lodge and Wilderness Permits turnoff on the right. Turn right and drive 0.4 mile (0.6 km) toward Tuolumne Lodge. Park in the lot on the left signed for Dog Lake and John Muir Trail. The trail begins across the road from the parking lot. Additional parking is available in the Wilderness Permits parking lot.

This hike is one of the easiest in the Yosemite high country, and because it starts out beautiful and stays that way, you can hike it as long or as little as you like. To reach the Lyell Fork, cross the Dana Fork on a **footbridge**

less than **0.5 mile (0.8 km)** from the parking lot. After another **0.5 mile (0.8 km),** cross the Lyell Fork on a **second footbridge** and head left along the river's south side. A **third bridge** takes you across Rafferty Creek and into Lyell Canyon. If you like looking at gorgeous meadows and a meandering river, this is your hike. Small trout are plentiful. A bonus is that **backpacking** sites are 3-4 miles out on the trail, so if you get a wilderness permit, you can linger in paradise for a few days.

The total trail length is 8 miles (12.9 km) one-way, paralleling the Lyell Fork of the Tuolumne River on the Pacific Crest Trail/John Muir Trail, but most people just head out for 2-3 miles (3-5 km), carrying their fishing rods, and turn back.

Glen Aulin and Tuolumne Falls

Distance: 9.2 miles (14.8 km) round-trip
Duration: 4-5 hours
Elevation Change: 400 feet (120 m)
Effort: Moderate
Shuttle Stop: 4
Trailhead: Glen Aulin/Soda Springs
Directions: From the Big Oak Flat entrance station on Highway 120, drive southeast 7.7 miles (12.4 km) to Crane Flat, and then turn left to stay on Highway 120. Drive 39 miles (63 km) to the Lembert Dome/Soda Springs/Dog Lake/Glen Aulin Trailhead on the left. Begin the hike on the western edge of the parking lot at a gated dirt road signed "Soda Springs .5".

Tuolumne Falls is one of the prettiest waterfalls in Yosemite, and reaching it requires only a 4.5-mile (7.2-km) one-way walk with a 400-foot (120-m) elevation loss on the way in. The climb back out is nothing to worry about, with most of the ascent in the first mile as you head up and over the various cascades of Tuolumne Falls on granite stairsteps.

Every step of this hike is lovely. Start by following the **dirt road** from the Lembert Dome parking lot toward **Soda Springs.** When you near Parsons Memorial Lodge, veer right on the signed trail to **Glen Aulin.** You'll walk through forest and then move closer to the Tuolumne River and gain inspiring views of Cathedral and Unicorn Peaks and Fairview Dome. From here on out you're never far from the river's edge.

After **3 miles (4.8 km)** you'll cross the Tuolumne River on a **footbridge,** and in another **0.25 mile (0.4 km)** you see the first stunning drop of Tuolumne Falls, a 100-foot (30-m) churning freefall. The trail keeps descending past more cascades to the base of the falls, where a **footbridge** leads back across the river to **Glen Aulin High Sierra Camp.** The final cataract of Tuolumne Falls, just before Glen Aulin, is known as **White Cascade.** Pick a spot around the edge of its large pool and have a seat to enjoy the show.

★ Lembert Dome

Distance: 2.8 miles (4.5 km) round-trip
Duration: 2-3 hours
Elevation Change: 850 feet (260 m)
Effort: Moderate
Shuttle Stop: 2
Trailhead: Lembert Dome/Dog Lake (see map p. 174)
Directions: From the Big Oak Flat entrance station on Highway 120, drive southeast 7.7 miles (12.4 km) to Crane Flat, and then turn left to stay on Highway 120. Drive 39 miles (63 km) to the Lembert Dome/Soda Springs/Dog Lake/Glen Aulin Trailhead on the left. The trail begins near the restrooms.

Lembert Dome is a roche moutonnée, which is a French geological term that means it looks something like a sheep. You may not see the resemblance, but you will feel like a mountain goat when you climb to the dome's lofty summit at 9,450 feet (2,880 m). From the parking area at Lembert Dome's base, you may see rock climbers practicing their craft on the steep side of the dome, but the hikers' trail curves around to the more gently sloped back side. You can walk right up the granite—no ropes necessary. The **Dog Lake and Lembert Dome Trail** winds steeply uphill for **0.75 mile (1.2 km)** to the dome's north side; turn left and pick any route along the granite that looks manageable. When you reach the top of the dome, you'll discover that the view of

---

1: Cathedral Lake 2: Gaylor Lake 3: Dog Lake

Tuolumne Meadows Hikes

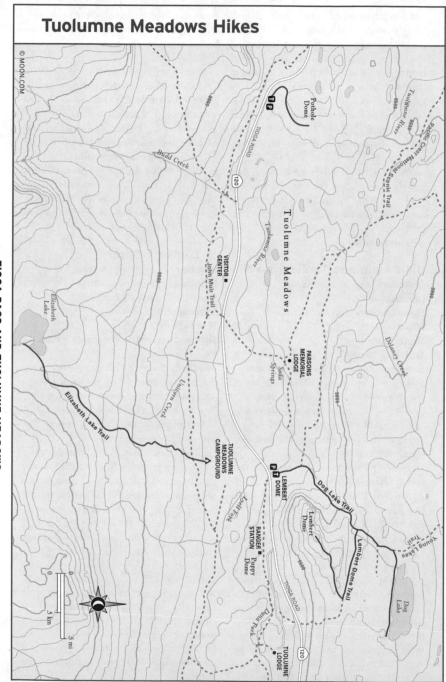

© MOON.COM

Tuolumne Meadows and surrounding peaks and domes is well worth the effort.

Dog Lake

Distance: 3.4 miles (5.5 km) round-trip
Duration: 2 hours
Elevation Change: 650 feet (200 m)
Effort: Moderate
Shuttle Stop: 2
Trailhead: Lembert Dome/Dog Lake (see map p. 174)
Directions: From the Big Oak Flat entrance station on Highway 120, drive southeast 7.7 miles (12.4 km) to Crane Flat, and then turn left to stay on Highway 120. Drive 39 miles (63 km) to the Lembert Dome/Soda Springs/Dog Lake/Glen Aulin Trailhead on the left. The trail begins near the restrooms.

Dog Lake is an easy-to-reach destination from Tuolumne Meadows and a perfect place for a family to spend an afternoon in the high country. The hike begins near the base of **Lembert Dome** and then heads through a gorgeous meadow that offers views of snowy Cathedral and Unicorn Peaks. The trail traverses a granite slab but then **splits off** from the path to Lembert Dome and starts to climb quite steeply through a lodgepole pine and fir forest.

When you reach an intersection with the **Young Lakes Trail,** you're only **0.25 mile (0.4 km)** from Dog Lake. The lake is a delight, although its grassy shoreline is often plagued with mosquitoes (don't forget the bug spray). At 9,170 feet (2,795 m) elevation, the deep-blue lake is wide and shallow. The colorful peaks to the east are Mount Dana and Mount Gibbs. You can hike around Dog Lake's perimeter, take a swim in late summer, or just sit at the peaceful shoreline and relax.

Mono Pass and Spillway Lake

Distance: 8.4-11.6 miles (13.5-18.7 km) round-trip
Duration: 5-6 hours
Elevation Change: 900 feet (275 m)
Effort: Moderate
Shuttle Stop: 1
Trailhead: Mono Pass
Directions: From the Big Oak Flat entrance station on Highway 120, drive southeast 7.7 miles (12.4 km) to

Crane Flat, and then turn left to stay on Highway 120. Drive 44.5 miles (71.6 km) to the Mono Pass Trailhead on the right near road marker T-37 (1.3 mi/2.1 km west of the Tioga Pass entrance station).

Thanks to an elevation gain of only 900 feet (275 m) spread out over 4.2 miles (6.8 km), you'll hardly even notice you're climbing on the route to Mono Pass. That's if you're acclimated, of course, because you start out at 9,700 feet (3,000 m), where the air is mighty thin.

The **Mono Pass Trail** begins in a mix of lodgepole pines and grassy meadows and then crosses the **Dana Fork of the Tuolumne River,** which is an easy boulder-hop by midsummer. (Earlier in the season you may need to find a log to cross.) The trail soon meets up with **Parker Pass Creek** and parallels it for most of the trip. As you proceed, you'll gain great views of Mount Gibbs, Mount Dana, and the Kuna Crest. At a trail junction at **2 miles (3.2 km),** bear left and start to climb more noticeably. When you reach the Mono Pass sign at **3.8 miles (6.1 km),** take the **right spur trail** (unsigned). It leads 0.3 mile (0.5 km) to a cluster of four 19th-century **mining cabins** that have been beautifully restored. It's fascinating to explore the small cabins and surrounding mine ruins and consider the hard life of those who lived and worked here. Then, heading back to the main trail, continue another **0.5 mile (0.8 km)** beyond the sign marking Mono Pass for the best views of the trip. From a granite promontory above a water-filled tarn, you can see far down Bloody Canyon to Mono Lake and the surrounding desert.

Another option on the Mono Pass Trail is to take the right fork at 2 miles (3.2 km) and head for **Spillway Lake,** a wide, shallow lake only 1.6 miles (2.6 km) from this junction. You'll have more solitude along this pathway and a pleasant walk alongside Parker Pass Creek and its adjoining meadow. Backpackers rarely travel to this lake, so day hikers are likely to enjoy some solitude here. The views of the Kuna Crest and the high alpine meadow surrounding the upper reaches of Parker Pass Creek will take your breath away.

Middle and Upper Gaylor Lakes

Distance: 4 miles (6.4 km) round-trip
Duration: 2 hours
Elevation Change: 1,100 feet (335 m)
Effort: Moderate
Shuttle Stop: 1
Trailhead: Gaylor Lakes/Tioga Pass entrance station (see map p. 177)
Directions: From the Big Oak Flat entrance station on Highway 120, drive southeast 7.7 miles (12.4 km) to Crane Flat, and then turn left to stay on Highway 120. Drive 46 miles (74 km) to the Gaylor Lakes parking lot just west of the Tioga Pass entrance station on the north side of the road.

Middle and Upper Gaylor Lakes are deservedly popular destinations because of the short distance required to reach them and their great opportunities for trout fishing. And of course, there is the draw of the spectacular high-alpine scenery. Starting near **Tioga Pass** (at nearly 10,000 ft/3,000 m), the trail climbs a steep ridge and then drops down to the middle lake. Although it's only **1 mile (1.6 km)** of ascent, it's a high-elevation butt-kicker that causes many to beg for mercy.

From **Middle Gaylor Lake,** follow the creek gently uphill to the east for **1 mile (1.6 km)** to reach smaller **Upper Gaylor Lake.** Be sure to take the trail around its north side and uphill for a few hundred yards to the site of the **Great Sierra Mine** and the remains of an **old stone cabin.** The Great Sierra Mine turned out to be not so great—no silver ore was ever refined, and the mine was eventually abandoned. The hauntingly beautiful glacial scenery is what remains. Total elevation gain on the hike to Upper Gaylor Lake is about 1,100 feet (335 m), and it's worth every step.

If you want to see more of this sublime lake basin, the twin **Granite Lakes** lie about 0.75 mile (1.2 km) northwest of Middle Gaylor Lake. Although there is no formal trail, it's an easy cross-country ramble to the lakes, which are tucked below a massive granite cirque.

Mount Dana

Distance: 6 miles (9.7 km) round-trip
Duration: 4-6 hours
Elevation Change: 3,100 feet (950 m)
Effort: Very strenuous
Trailhead: Tioga Pass entrance station
Directions: From the Big Oak Flat entrance station on Highway 120, drive southeast 7.7 miles (12.4 km) to Crane Flat, and then turn left to stay on Highway 120. Drive 46 miles (74 km) to the Gaylor Lakes parking lot just west of the Tioga Pass entrance station on the north side of the road.

Mount Dana is a grueling hike. Yet many hikers make the trip every summer, perhaps as some sort of rite of passage to affirm that the long winter has truly ended in the high country. The path to the 13,053-foot (3,979-m) summit requires a 3,100-foot (950-m) elevation gain condensed into a mere 3 miles (4.8 km). To make matters more difficult, there is no maintained trail, only a series of informal "use" trails created by generations of hardy Yosemite hikers who have traveled the route.

To join their ranks, leave your car at the **Gaylor Lakes Trailhead** by the Tioga Pass entrance station, then cross the road and hike southeast on the unsigned but obvious **trail** that begins just a few feet from the park entrance kiosk. The path starts with a pleasant ramble through **Dana Meadows** and then enters a dense lodgepole pine forest. Soon the grade becomes more intense, but this first stretch of climbing is highlighted by a spectacular wildflower show that usually peaks in late July. Lupine, larkspur, Indian paintbrush, senecio—they're all here, in all their glory. The climbing gets tougher on the **second mile** of the hike, but stick with it and soon you'll have climbed above 11,000 feet (3,350 m), and also above the tree line.

The path keeps ascending to the 11,600-foot (3,535-m) mark, where a giant trail **cairn** marks a large, rock-covered plateau. This is a good place to rest and do a check on your physical and mental state. Although the summit may look close from here, you still have a long, hard way to go. Two fairly obvious **paths**

Gaylor Lakes

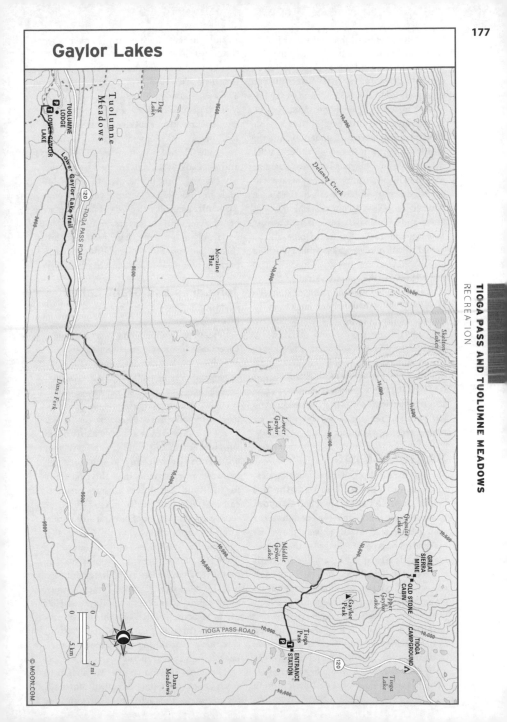

© MOON.COM

head uphill from this point; if you're feeling comfortable with the altitude, pick either one and continue onward, zigzagging your way up the shale-covered slope. In the **final mile** you must gain 1,500 feet (455 m), and to say it is slow going would be a major understatement. There's no shade, but there is often a fierce wind, plenty of loose rock underfoot, and the breathtakingly thin air of high altitude. With what may seem like your last breath, you finally reach the summit, where you are witness to one of the finest views in the Sierra. Your field of vision encompasses Mono Lake, Ellery and Saddlebag Lakes, Glacier Canyon, Tuolumne Meadows, Lembert Dome, and an untold wealth of high peaks. Bring a map and identify all you can survey, or forget the map and just take in the majesty of it all.

A few tips for making the ascent safely: First, wait until **mid-July** or later to make the trip, as Mount Dana can be snow-covered long into the summer. Second, get an **early start** in the morning so you have no chance of encountering afternoon thunderstorms. Third, carry (and drink) as much **water** as you can. Fourth, wear good sunglasses and **sun protection** at this high elevation. And last, pace yourself to give your body a chance to adjust to the 13,000-foot (4,000-m) altitude.

BACKPACKING

Some of the most popular backpacking destinations on Tioga Pass Road are **Cathedral Lakes, Sunrise Lakes,** and **Lyell Canyon.** Because these areas are close enough to the road to be reachable by day hikers, they don't make ideal backpacking trips for those seeking solitude. Too many hikers line the trails and crowd the lakeshores, and during the day, you won't have any solitude at your camp. Nonetheless, because these trails are relatively short and easy and because they lead to beautiful destinations, they are still favored by backpackers. Permits to camp along these trails are extremely difficult to come by, especially on weekends. It would be wise to save a trip to these high-profile destinations for a

weekday in September or early October, when the crowds have thinned.

The following are four somewhat lower-profile backpacking trails that lead from Tioga Pass Road or Tuolumne Meadows. On these trails you'll have a greater chance of a true backpacking experience, far from the madding crowd. Remember, though, this is Yosemite: These destinations are still popular, and you can't go without seeing other people.

Also note that if you plan to spend the night in Yosemite's wilderness, you must have a **permit.** You will also need to take adequate bear precautions; visitors are required by federal regulations to store all their food properly throughout Yosemite National Park. For backpackers, that means carrying a bear canister.

Ten Lakes and Grant Lakes

Distance: 12.8 miles (20.6 km) round-trip

Effort: Strenuous

Trailhead: Ten Lakes Trailhead

Directions: From the Big Oak Flat entrance station on Highway 120, drive southeast 7.7 miles (12.4 km) to Crane Flat, and then turn left to stay on Highway 120. Drive 19.4 miles (31.2 km) to the Yosemite Creek and Ten Lakes Trailhead parking area on the south side of the road. The trail begins on the north side of the road.

The Ten Lakes area is a spectacularly beautiful wilderness destination, so reserve your **wilderness permit** early. Also, be prepared to do some serious climbing—this isn't a trail for the timid. But the rewards are great because after a half day of hiking you'll be setting up camp at one of nearly a dozen sparkling, rockbound lakes.

From the Ten Lakes Trailhead (elevation 7,500 ft/2,300 m) the path ascends steadily for the first 4 miles (6.4 km). There's only one brutally steep stretch, which comes between miles 4 and 5 after a stroll around Half Moon Meadow. A series of tight switchbacks pulls you through a nasty 800-foot (240-m) elevation gain to the top of a ridge and the Ten Lakes/Grant Lakes junction.

There you make a choice. Turn right to reach Grant Lakes and head mostly downhill for a mile. Or to reach Ten Lakes, continue straight, soon heading steeply downhill for 1.4 miles (2.3 km). The Grant Lakes offer a little more solitude while the two larger of the Ten Lakes have the best **campsites,** with many trees along their shorelines offering protection from the wind.

Whether you go to Ten Lakes or Grant Lakes, don't miss taking a side trip to the rocky overlook above the Ten Lakes basin. It's only 0.5 mile (0.8 km) from the Ten Lakes/Grant Lakes junction; continue straight for Ten Lakes, then take the unsigned fork to the left and head for the highest point. Four of the 10 lakes are visible from this promontory, as is a section of the Grand Canyon of the Tuolumne.

Waterwheel Falls

Distance: 16-20 miles (26-45 km)
Effort: Moderate
Shuttle Stop: 4
Trailhead: Lembert Dome
Directions: From the Big Oak Flat entrance station on Highway 120, drive southeast 7.7 miles (12.4 km) to Crane Flat, and then turn left to stay on Highway 120. Drive 39 miles (63 km) to the Lembert Dome/Soda Springs/Dog Lake/Glen Aulin Trailhead on the left. Begin hiking on the western edge of the parking lot at a gated dirt road signed "Soda Springs .5".

This hike could be called the Epic Waterfall Trip. If you hike the entire route, you'll see so many waterfalls and so much water along the way that you'll have enough memories to get you through a 10-year drought.

You must arrange for a **wilderness permit** in advance or reserve a stay at the **Glen Aulin High Sierra Camp.** You can continue your trip beyond Waterwheel Falls; many backpackers make this a one-way trip with a shuttle vehicle waiting for them at White Wolf, 28 miles (45 km) away. Beyond Waterwheel Falls you'll have a lot less company.

The trail follows the Tuolumne River to **Tuolumne Falls** and Glen Aulin Camp, alternating between stretches of stunning flower- and aspen-lined meadows and stark granite slabs. Waterwheel Falls is only 3 miles (4.8 km) from the camp, and two other major cascades, **California Falls** and **LeConte Falls,** are found along the way. Waterwheel is Yosemite's most unusual-looking waterfall. Its churning water dips into deep holes in the granite riverbed and then shoots out with such velocity that it doubles back on itself. When the river level is high, the resemblance to a waterwheel is obvious.

Backpackers who continue onward will keep following the path of the Tuolumne River. The second night of the trip is usually spent at **Pate Valley.** Then with a fresh head of steam you climb up a long series of switchbacks and eventually make your way to Harden Lake and then White Wolf. You may be able to get a shuttle bus here instead of leaving a car; check with the wilderness office about the current status of the bus system on Tioga Road.

Vogelsang Loop

Distance: 19 miles (31 km) round-trip
Effort: Strenuous
Shuttle Stop: 1
Trailhead: Tuolumne Lodge
Directions: From the Big Oak Flat entrance station on Highway 120, drive southeast 7.7 miles (12.4 km) to Crane Flat, and then turn left to stay on Highway 120. Drive 39.5 miles (63.6 km) to the Tuolumne Lodge and Wilderness Permits turnoff on the right. Turn right and drive 0.4 mile (0.6 km) toward Tuolumne Lodge. Park in the lot on the left signed for Dog Lake and John Muir Trail. The trail begins across the road from the parking lot. Additional parking is available in the Wilderness Permits parking lot.

Although this loop is popular with hikers staying at the **Vogelsang High Sierra Camp,** backpackers who plan early can get a **wilderness permit** for their own self-designed trip. The traditional route is to head out on the western side of the loop along Rafferty Creek, then take a short spur and spend the night at Vogelsang Lake, which is without question the most visually dramatic spot on this trip. The lake is flanked by Fletcher Peak, a steep and rugged wall of glacier-carved granite. Few trees can grow in this sparse, high-alpine environment.

The next day you rejoin the loop and continue eastward to **Evelyn Lake,** another favorite camping spot. When it's time to return, hike down to Lyell Fork, a 2,000-foot (600-m) descent that takes a few hours. You then meet up with the John Muir Trail and follow it north through lush, green Lyell Canyon, back to the trailhead at Tuolumne Meadows.

Young Lakes Loop

Distance: 12.5 miles (20.1 km) round-trip

Effort: Moderate

Shuttle Stop: 4

Trailhead: Lembert Dome/Soda Springs/Dog Lake/Glen Aulin Trailhead

Directions: From the Big Oak Flat entrance station on Highway 120, drive southeast 7.7 miles (12.4 km) to Crane Flat, and then turn left to stay on Highway 120. Drive 39 miles (63 km) to the Lembert Dome/Soda Springs/Dog Lake/Glen Aulin Trailhead on the left. Begin hiking on the western edge of the parking lot at a gated dirt road signed "Soda Springs .5".

Starting from the Lembert Dome parking lot, the Young Lakes Loop is a classic Yosemite trip that works equally well as a short backpacking trip or a long day hike. The destination is a series of lakes set in a deep and wide glacial cirque at 9,900 feet (3,000 m). Because the mileage is short, this is a great trip for a weekend getaway.

The trip starts with a walk down the wide dirt road that leads to Soda Springs. Pick up the trail near Parsons Lodge that leads to Glen Aulin and follow it through lodgepole pines for 1.8 miles (2.9 km) until you see the right turnoff for Young Lakes. Follow the **Young Lakes Trail** for 3 more miles (4.8 km), climbing steadily. At 5 miles (8 km) out you'll see the return leg of your loop leading off to the right (signed for Dog Lake).

Continue straight for another 1.5 miles (2.4 km) to **Lower Young Lake,** where you have a stunning view of Mount Conness and **Ragged Peak.** Two more lakes are accessible within 1 mile (1.6 km) to the east. You'll

probably want to make **camp** at the lower lakes, but don't miss a hike to the third (uppermost) lake, which is the most visually stunning of them all.

When you're ready to head home, retrace your steps to the junction and take the eastern (left) fork, returning via Dog Lake and Lembert Dome. Be forewarned: If you loop back this way, it won't be an all-downhill cruise, but the scenery makes the additional climbing worthwhile.

BIKING

Biking is not permitted on Yosemite's trails, but is allowed on the park's paved roads.

Big Oak Flat Road

A 6-mile (9.7-km) section of the old **Big Oak Flat Road** passes through the giant sequoias at Tuolumne Grove, and bikes are permitted because the road/trail is paved, not dirt. You don't want to ride this old road in the summer, however, because too many hikers are using the route, especially in the first mile to the big trees. During a quiet autumn day, this one-way downhill route is very pleasant. The trail's terminus is at Hodgdon Meadow Campground, where a friend could pick you up. Ambitious cyclists can make a loop out of the trip by riding back to the Tuolumne Grove parking lot on Highway 120 (a 15-mi/24-km round-trip). Those who just want a little exercise could start at Hodgdon Meadow, ride uphill to the Tuolumne Grove, and then turn around and ride back whenever the crowds get too thick.

Tioga Pass

Almost every day of summer you will see cyclists on road and mountain bikes tackling **Tioga Pass** itself. This 9,945-foot (3,030-m) pass is not for the faint of heart. The 13-mile (20.9-km) downhill route from Tioga Pass to Lee Vining along Highway 120 is far more

---

1: fly-fishing in Yosemite 2: Tuolumne Meadows in winter 3: Ragged Peak 4: summer program at Parsons Memorial Lodge

terrifying than the uphill stretch is difficult. It can be very hard to control your bike on the steep descent, especially if the wind is blowing through the pass. This fact, combined with the number of cars driving on the route, makes this a very daring ride, one for experienced cyclists only.

FISHING

Tioga Road is well known for its easy access to alpine lakes. At one time, most of these lakes were regularly planted with trout. The National Park Service stopped all fish planting of park lakes in 1991 (stream stocking had been ended long before), and most of the fish population has since died out. If a lake did not have the proper conditions to allow the planted fish to reproduce, then the last planted fish would live out their life spans and that would be the end of the story. Some of the region's most famous bodies of water, like Tenaya Lake, are completely barren (although you often see an unknowing angler dropping a line in its blue waters).

Some Yosemite lakes do have the right conditions for reproduction, however. The **Ten Lakes,** a popular backpacking trip or long day hike off Tioga Road, have self-sustaining populations of brook and rainbow trout. The three **Young Lakes,** another favorite backpacking destination, contain fair numbers of brook trout. **May Lake,** the site of a busy High Sierra Camp and an easy 1-mile (1.6-km) hike from the trailhead parking area, has a small population of brook trout. **Upper Cathedral Lake, Elizabeth Lake,** and the **Sunrise Lakes** are all easily reached day-hiking destinations that support fair numbers of brook trout. The creeks near these lakes also are laden with fish; in fact, you might have better luck in the creeks.

More stream-fishing opportunities exist in the **South Fork Tuolumne River,** which runs parallel to Tioga Road. There are plenty of places to pull off the road and try your luck at catching the small brook trout that reside there. At the Yosemite Creek Campground or nearby Yosemite Creek Picnic Area, you can try for rainbow, brown, and brook trout in the creek (rainbows are most plentiful). An informal use trail leads out of camp both upstream and downstream. On the east side of Tuolumne Meadows, many anglers try their luck in both the Dana Fork and the Lyell Fork of the Tuolumne River.

ROCK CLIMBING

The same climbing school that offers classes in the Valley, **Yosemite Mountaineering School,** offers rock-climbing lessons on the granite domes and spires near Tuolumne Meadows. The school conducts seminars and classes for beginning, intermediate, and advanced climbers in the Tioga Pass Road area (209/372-8344, www.travelyosemite.com). Classes meet daily at 8:30am (June-Sept.), and equipment rentals are available; rates for regularly scheduled classes are $145-170 per day. Private guided climbs are available for up to three people and start at $169 per day.

The preponderance of granite domes in the stretch of highway from Tenaya Lake to the Tuolumne Meadows area makes this region a playground for rock climbers. Two of the best places for watching climbers in action are at **Polly Dome,** directly across the highway from Tenaya Lake, and at **Lembert Dome,** on the east end of Tuolumne Meadows. Two other popular domes for rock climbing in this area are **Fairview Dome** and **Medlicott Dome,** both just off Highway 120 near Tenaya Lake.

WINTER SPORTS

The **Crane Flat Gas Station** (Crane Flat off Hwy. 120, 7am-10pm daily in summer, 9am-5pm daily in winter) sells winter ski trail maps and sleds and rents snowshoes.

Cross-Country Skiing

Tioga Pass Road may be closed in the winter, but it's still a prime destination for cross-country skiers. The road is plowed up to Crane Flat, usually about 300 feet (90 m) past the parking area for the Tuolumne Grove of Giant Sequoias. The gentle grade of Tioga

Pass Road in these first few miles makes great skiing for beginners to intermediates. Highly experienced cross-country skiers head to the **Tuolumne Meadows** region on their skis (since the road is not plowed). Some skiers follow trails from Yosemite Valley to Tuolumne Meadows; others head in from U.S. 395. With a **wilderness permit**, skiers can camp and ski in and around Tuolumne Meadows for up to two weeks.

Crane Flat (Hwy. 120 at Big Oak Flat Rd.) is the starting point for several cross-country skiing loops, as well as the popular trek up the snow-covered road to the Crane Flat Fire Lookout Tower (3 mi/4.8 km round-trip).

Snowshoeing

The trails to the **Merced Grove** (3 mi/4.8 km round-trip) and **Tuolumne Grove** (2.5 mi/4 km round-trip) are most often used by snowshoers and sometimes even people wearing regular snow boots, so the snow is usually too chopped up for skiing. Snowshoers will thoroughly enjoy the short treks to the two sequoia groves—it's a special treat to see the big trees crowned with a mantle of snow.

Guided snowshoe tours (8:30am-3pm Sat., $60) to Tuolumne Grove are offered in winter; rates include snowshoe rental and transportation from Yosemite Valley (a shuttle bus departs from Yosemite Valley Lodge). Groups are limited to seven people. For reservations, call the Yosemite Ski & Snowboard Area Nordic Center (209/372-8444) or the Yosemite Valley Lodge Tour Desk (209/372-1240).

A more casual three-hour snowshoe tour ($18.50 per person with snowshoe rental, $5 per person without) skirts the trails around Crane Flat, but you'll have to drive there. Tour dates and times vary; check the Yosemite Valley Lodge Tour Desk (209/372-1240).

Snow Play

Crane Flat Campground (Crane Flat off Hwy. 120) is the site of the park's only official "snow play" area. The camp access road is plowed up to a point where there's a parking area and restrooms. This is a good place to bring the kids to make snowballs or tool around on sleds.

Entertainment and Shopping

RANGER WALKS

Check the free Yosemite newspaper for a schedule of ranger walks, or inquire at the Tuolumne Meadows Visitor Center (Tioga Pass Rd., 9am-6pm daily summer).

Rangers lead walks to the **Tuolumne Grove of Giant Sequoias** daily in the summer and on weekends in the fall. In **Tuolumne Meadows,** rangers lead walks to the top of Lembert Dome and Pothole Dome and to Lukens Lake, the Gaylor Lakes Basin, Mono Pass, and along the Tuolumne River.

EVENING PROGRAMS

Crane Flat and Tuolumne Meadows Campgrounds have one-hour evening **campfire programs** designed for families, usually starting at 8pm. Program topics vary but often include singing and storytelling. **Stargazing programs** are held later in the evening (9pm) on clear nights at Tuolumne Meadows Campground. Bring something to sit on, and dress warmly.

PARSONS MEMORIAL LODGE

Parsons Memorial Lodge (shuttle stop 6, Tuolumne Meadows, Sat.-Sun. mid-July to mid-Aug., free) hosts interpretive and arts programs in summer. The afternoon programs feature writers, naturalists, and musicians. In mid-August, the lodge plays host to an annual summer poetry festival. It's a

30-minute walk from the Tuolumne Meadows Visitor Center to the lodge.

SHOPPING

Most gas station stores don't offer much besides a dozen different kinds of chips, but the **Crane Flat Gas Station** (Crane Flat off Hwy. 120, 7am-10pm daily summer, 9am-5pm daily winter) has enough groceries for campers to be able to cook dinner and breakfast, plus a selection of guidebooks and aisles full of junk food. This store is a good bet for most anything you might need, and that's fortunate because it's the only place around for many miles. Gas is available 24 hours daily with a credit card.

If you're staying at White Wolf or Yosemite Creek Campground and you run out of, say, chocolate bars or insect repellent, you may be able to resupply at the **White Wolf Lodge Store** (Tioga Pass Rd., 8am-8pm daily summer only). But be forewarned, this is a *really* small store (basically a closet with a walk-up window on the side of the White Wolf dining room). If you want anything more than a candy bar or other basics, you'll have to drive to Crane Flat or Tuolumne Meadows.

There isn't much they haven't crammed into the canvas tent that makes up the **Tuolumne Meadows Store** (8am-8pm daily summer only). Groceries, camping gear, clothing items, souvenirs, guidebooks—you name it, it's probably there. A **post office** (9am-5pm Mon.-Fri., 9am-1pm Sat. summer only) and the **Tuolumne Meadows Grill** (8am-6pm daily summer) are next door. The grill serves remarkably good order-at-the-counter food, although you may have to wait in line during peak times. The grill's veggie chili, hamburgers, and hearty breakfasts have won legions of fans. Ice cream cones are big sellers on warm afternoons.

If you strike out everywhere else in Yosemite's high country, you can drive a few miles out of the park to **Tioga Pass Resort** (2 miles/3.2 km east of Tioga Pass, no phone, 7am-9pm daily summer only) or the **Tioga Gas Mart** (11 mi/17.7 km east of Tioga Pass, 6am-9pm daily summer only, 760/647-1088). The resort has basic items like firewood, snacks, and drinks, plus a small restaurant; the gas mart has a spacious, well-stocked store and large deli/café.

Food

There's nothing quite like high mountain air to work up an appetite. Fortunately, there are a couple good places on Tioga Road to replenish those calories lost to hiking and recreation.

INSIDE THE PARK
White Wolf Lodge
★ **White Wolf Lodge**'s restaurant (Tioga Pass Rd., 209/372-8416, 7:30am-9:30am and 6pm-8pm daily in summer only, $22-29) is open to lodge guests and nonguests alike. Dinners might include New York steak, fish of the day, chicken, a vegetarian entrée, and hamburgers. The wine list is more extensive than you'd expect in the high country, and the setting can't be beat, whether you eat inside in the small and cozy dining room or outside on the deck. **Dinner reservations are advised.** A takeout lunch is available noon-2pm. Breakfast ($9-13) consists of made-to-order omelets, blueberry pancakes, and fried potatoes. White Wolf Lodge has been in operation since 1927, so they know how to do things right.

Tuolumne Meadows Grill

When Tioga Road closes for the winter, seasoned Yosemite visitors dream of the day that Tuolumne Meadows will be free of snow and they can once again eat buckwheat pancakes from the ★ **Tuolumne Meadows Grill** (Tioga Pass Rd., shuttle stop 5, 209/372-8426,

8am-5pm daily in summer, $7-10). This place really knows how to fill up a hiker's empty stomach. The breakfasts are highly acclaimed, particularly the biscuit sandwiches filled with egg, bacon or sausage, and cheese, and the aforementioned buckwheat pancakes. For lunch, the restaurant serves hamburgers, veggie burgers, chicken sandwiches, and surprisingly good salads. The made-fresh-daily vegetarian chili is legendary. Soft-serve ice cream cones are popular on warm summer days. The grill is on Tioga Pass Road across from Tuolumne Meadows, right next to Tuolumne Meadows Store. You can't miss it—and shouldn't.

Tuolumne Meadows Lodge

A part of the Yosemite High Sierra Camp Loop, **Tuolumne Meadows Lodge Dining Room** (Tioga Pass Rd., shuttle stop 1, 209/372-0413, 7am-9am and 5:30pm-8pm daily in summer, breakfast $9-13, dinner $15-27) has a big white tent situated right on the Tuolumne River that serves as its dining room. The cheerful canvas space (with curtains lining the tent windows) is open to everyone, not just guests at the lodge, but you will need **dinner reservations** because it's a deservedly popular spot. Typical entrées include trout, chicken, steak, hamburgers, and a

vegetarian dish. This is communal-style dining, in which you're sure to get to know your neighbors at the table. Breakfast offerings include hotcakes, French toast, and eggs and toast. Takeout lunches are available, but you must place an order the night before.

OUTSIDE THE PARK
Tioga Pass Resort Café

The historic **Tioga Pass Resort Café** (Hwy. 120, 2 mi/3.2 km east of Tioga Pass, 209/372-4471, www.tiogapassresort.com, 7am-9pm daily May-Sept., lunch $9-12, dinner $18-22) has been serving travelers since 1914, except for a brief hiatus in 2017-2018 when heavy snows crushed the roof. From Tioga Pass Road's opening date each summer (usually in June) until mid-September, the small café serves three meals daily of hearty, delicious, and well-prepared food. Breakfast is just what you want to eat in the mountains—big fluffy pancakes, oatmeal, and huge omelets. For lunch, choose from hot sandwiches including Tioga burgers and tuna melts. Dinner specials vary nightly: chicken potpie, ravioli with artichoke sauce, and beef stew. For dessert, the resort's fresh fruit pies are legendary. There are only a handful of tables and counter seats, so you may have to wait a while—but it's worth it.

Accommodations

Two rustic camp-style lodgings—White Wolf Lodge and Tuolumne Lodge—are located in Yosemite's high country on Tioga Pass Road, but these are open only June-September. Another option exists just 2 miles (3.2 km) east of the park entrance at Tioga Pass.

IN THE PARK
Reservations

Reservations are made through **Aramark's Yosemite Hospitality** (888/413-8869, www.travelyosemite.com). The reservations phone line is open 7am-8pm Monday-Friday and

7am-7pm Saturday-Sunday (hours may be shorter in the winter months), or you can reserve 24 hours a day on the web. It is wise to make reservations far in advance for the busy summer season. Cancellations happen frequently, so if you strike out, keep calling back.

White Wolf Lodge

The first time you glimpse the cabins at ★ **White Wolf Lodge** (Tioga Pass Rd., 888/413-8869, www.travelyosemite.com, mid-June-early Sept., $137-156), you sense the realization of your Yosemite lodging dreams. Set at the sweet high-country elevation of 8,000 feet (2,400 m), the white wooden cabins are trimmed in hunter green, with Adirondack chairs lined up on the porches to face a wildflower-filled meadow. If you think that high-country lodgings don't get much better than this, you're exactly right.

Except you might be wrong, too. The trick is that not every White Wolf cabin is one of those quaint *Sunset* magazine-style units. Only four units fit that bill. Right behind them are 24 typical Yosemite tent cabins—large, off-white tents on raised wooden platforms, almost bare inside except for a wood-burning stove, candles for lighting (there is no electricity), and a couple of beds with linens.

The four **wooden cabins** ($156) have their own bathrooms, propane heat, daily maid service, a desk, a chair, a dresser, two double beds, and electricity (generated only during certain hours of the day). These cabins, in addition to the main lodge, underwent a major renovation in 2016, intended to fix site drainage and plumbing and electrical problems, among a host of other issues associated with their advanced age (they were built in the 1930s).

The tent cabins are more plentiful and easier to reserve, but they're also bare-bones.

You'll walk to a communal bathroom for toilets and showers, but at least you have a (canvas) roof over your head to keep out the mosquitos. Regardless of which type of cabin you reserve, everything about a stay at White Wolf is easy. An excellent **restaurant** on the premises serves breakfast and dinner and makes box lunches to go. A small store sells snacks, drinks, and a few minimal supplies. A couple of hiking trails begin at your doorstep, and a multitude of trails on Tioga Road are just a few miles away. Yosemite Valley is a one-hour drive.

So how do you get one of those white-and-green cabins? Plan on reserving at least a year in advance.

Tuolumne Meadows Lodge

Tuolumne Meadows Lodge (shuttle stop 1, 888/413-8869, www.travelyosemite.com, mid-June-mid-Sept., $137-157) has the same upsides as the nearby tent cabin resort at White Wolf, namely a chance to stay in convenient lodging right in the midst of Yosemite's best day hiking, fishing, and scenery-seeking country, with easy access to hearty meals and necessary supplies.

It also has the same downsides as White Wolf: The tent cabins are a bit dreary—canvas

cabins at White Wolf Lodge

tents on raised wooden platforms with nothing but beds, candles, and a wood-burning stove. And they are packed in so tightly that you can hear your neighbors talking, coughing, and snoring at night. The complex at Tuolumne Lodge includes a whopping 69 tent cabins—it's a small tent-cabin city. Each one can accommodate four people, although two people are more comfortable.

Of course, few who stay here ever complain. The upsides simply far outweigh the downsides. Guests come to be within 1 mile (1.6 km) of Tuolumne Meadows and not for any other reason. The cabins are 1 mile (1.6 km) down an access road that begins directly across from Lembert Dome and the Soda Springs trailhead and within a stone's throw of the John Muir Trail and Pacific Crest Trail. Tioga Pass itself, and all the hiking and fishing options on its east side, is only 6 miles (9.7 km) away. Trail choices are virtually unlimited.

After exploring the high country all day, sit down to a hearty dinner at the **Tuolumne Meadows Lodge Dining Room** alongside the Tuolumne River. The prices are reasonable, especially considering the spectacular setting.

OUTSIDE THE PARK

Visitors to Tuolumne and Tioga Pass often use the Highway 120 western approach through the town of Groveland, 25 miles (40 km) from the Big Oak Flat entrance (about 45 minutes). **Groveland** (page 98) can provide a convenient place to stay if you are visiting Tioga Pass Road, Tuolumne Meadows, or the Hetch Hetchy area of Yosemite. It's about 70 miles (113 km) total (100 minutes) from Groveland to Tuolumne Meadows.

Visitors coming from Tahoe, Nevada, or points east commonly use the Highway 120/Tioga Pass approach to Yosemite from

U.S. 395. **Lee Vining** (page 231) is the last "town" before the climb to the pass and the national park entrance. An overnight stay in Lee Vining puts you 13 miles (20.9 km) from the Tioga Pass entrance to Yosemite (20-30 minutes). It's a much longer drive to Yosemite Valley (figure on two hours), but with fabulous scenery all the way.

The closest non-park lodging lies 2 miles (3.2 km) east of the park's Tioga Pass entrance.

Tioga Pass Resort

★ **Tioga Pass Resort** (Hwy. 120, 2 mi/3.2 km east of Tioga Pass, no phone, reservations online only at www.tiogapassresort.com, $170-270) is in an ideal spot for exploring the Tioga Pass area and Tuolumne Meadows. After a two-year closure due to heavy snow damage in 2017-2018, the resort is renovated and back open for business in the summer months. "TPR," as it's called, is heavily booked for two big reasons: It's perfectly situated next to Yosemite's high country, and it has a loyal clientele of folks who come back year after year.

The resort is on Tioga Road, just 2 miles (3.2 km) from Yosemite's eastern entrance, at the mighty elevation of 9,600 feet (2,600 m). In summer, the resort's store and café are popular stops for visitors driving in and out of the park, but only a lucky few get to stay in the cabins. The 10 one- and two-bedroom rustic log cabins are painted gingerbread brown with yellow-and-green trim. They are set quite close to the road and resort parking lot, but fortunately a stream runs alongside, keeping unwanted noise to a minimum. Four motel rooms are also available. You can cook in your cabin if you wish, but it's hard to justify when **Tioga Pass Resort Café** makes such great food. Lodging reservations are online only; the resort has a satellite telephone, but it's for outgoing calls only.

Camping

For people who simply can't stand to plan ahead, the best bet for last-minute camping in Yosemite is on Tioga Road. Not in Tuolumne Meadows, mind you—that particular campground is nearly as popular, and hard to reserve, as the camps in Yosemite Valley. But at several other camps just off Tioga Road/Highway 120, you'll be able to drive right in and find a decent campsite on most days of the summer. That's because sites at several camps (Tamarack Flat, White Wolf, Yosemite Creek, Porcupine Flat) are not reservable; they operate on a first-come, first-served basis when they are open, which is generally only late June to late September but varies from year to year according to weather conditions.

Don't be too relaxed about finding a site, however. If it's a Saturday, you'd be well advised to start your search early in the day, certainly no later than noon. If it's a holiday weekend, start looking on Friday. The concessions you make to stay in these nonreservable campgrounds are relatively small: They don't have flush toilets, and some don't have running water. (The camps that do have these luxuries cost more than the camps without them, so you save money by roughing it.)

For camps without running water, it's wise to bring along the biggest bottles of water you can buy. You'll need them for drinking, cooking, washing up, and brushing your teeth. Or be prepared to filter or boil water from nearby creeks or streams; never drink water from natural sources without first filtering, boiling, or treating it.

Bear precautions are in effect at all high-country campgrounds. Use the bear box in your campsite to store any item that has a scent, or even looks like food, and you will be rewarded by having a car with all its windows and doors intact.

IN THE PARK

Reservations

Reservations are accepted (and highly recommended) at **Recreation.gov** (877/444-6777 or 518/885-3639 from outside the U.S. and Canada, www.recreation.gov) and can be made up to five months in advance. Reservations are available in blocks of one month at a time, on the 15th of each month starting at 7am (Pacific Standard Time). Both the telephone and the online reservation systems are open 7am-7pm (PST) November-February and 7am-9pm March-October.

Campers without reservations can try the **first-come, first-served** sites (summer only) at Tamarack Flat, Porcupine Flat, Yosemite Creek, White Wolf, or Tuolumne Meadows.

Hodgdon Meadow

Hodgdon Meadow (105 sites, 877/444-6777 or 518/885-3639 from outside the U.S. and Canada, www.recreation.gov, year-round, $26) is the first campground you reach after entering the park on Highway 120; it's 0.25 mile (0.4 km) down a side road 100 feet (30 m) past the Big Oak Flat entrance station. The biggest advantage to staying here is that you've made it past the entrance station and you're in the park. Don't expect peace and quiet, as the sites are packed in tightly. On most summer nights, newcomers drive around the camp hoping to find an open space. They don't find one, but they keep driving in circles anyway, shining their headlights into your tent. After September, however, this can be a very pleasant campground.

Reservations are required mid-April to mid-October; the rest of the year sites are first come, first served ($18). RVs up to 35 feet (10.7 m) long are permitted. There are four reservable **group sites** for 13-30 people (Apr.-Oct., $50). (If you are traveling with a large group in separate cars, each car still has to pay

High Sierra Camps

Among people who love to hike but hate to carry a heavy backpack, the **Yosemite High Sierra Camps** (888/413-8869 or www.travelyosemite.com, mid-June to mid-Sept., $160 per adult per night, $80 per child age 7-12) are legendary. With nothing on your back but a light day pack with water, snacks, a change of clothes, sheets, and a towel, you can hike through the high country for nearly a week. Along the way, you eat first-rate meals, enjoy hot showers, and sleep on a comfortable cot in a tent cabin each night. The five "camps" are spaced 5.7-10 miles (9.2-16.1 km) apart along a loop trail that begins at Tuolumne Meadows:

- **Glen Aulin** at 7,800 feet (2,400 m) is 5 miles (8 km) from the Lembert Dome Trailhead. No showers.

- **May Lake** at 9,300 feet (2,850 m) is 1 mile (1.6 km) from the May Lake Trailhead.

- **Sunrise Camp** at 9,400 feet (2,900 m) is 5 miles (8 km) from the Sunrise Trailhead.

- **Vogelsang Camp** at 10,300 feet (3,100 m) is 7 miles (11.3 km) from the Tuolumne Meadows Trailhead. Vogelsang is the smallest and most intimate. No showers.

- **Merced Lake Camp** at 7,200 feet (2,200 m) is 15 miles (24 km) from Tuolumne Meadows or 13 miles (20.9 km) from Yosemite Valley. Merced Lake Camp is the largest with a 60-person occupancy; the others fit 30-40 quests at a time.

The arrangement is basically the same at all five camps, although each has a different number of tent cabins. Overnight accommodations are "dormitory-style," which means that each tent contains four to six cots; there are a few two-person and eight-person tents. The camp staff tries to keep families and large groups together, but if you are traveling with fewer than four people in your party, you'll probably share a tent with strangers. Breakfast and dinner are included and are served in a main dining tent; box lunches ($18 adult, $8 child) can be purchased to go. The camps are very social: Meals are served family-style, and the tent cabins are spaced within a few feet of each other, so you'll probably get to know your neighbors.

RESERVATIONS

Reservations are taken on a lottery basis each October, and only a lucky few win the lottery. To obtain a spot, submit an **online application** (www.travelyosemite.com) for the following summer during the autumn lottery. Lottery winners are notified in January. Any spaces not filled during the lottery are available for online reservations starting in early March. When summer comes, any remaining open dates (or last-minute cancellations) are listed online (www.travelyosemite.com), so even last-minute planners have a fair chance. Check online availability often to find a spot, and/or call the concessionaire at 888/413-8869.

GUIDED TRIPS

High Sierra Camp wannabes can sign up for organized five- and seven-day trips led by park naturalists; these cost more but include guide service for your trip. **Guided hikes** ($709 per adult for 5 days) and **horseback trips** ($1,317 per adult for 4 days) of varying lengths are available. For information on guided trips, phone 209/372-8344.

TIOGA PASS AND TUOLUMNE MEADOWS
CAMPING

the park entrance fee.) The camp has drinking water, flush toilets, picnic tables, and fire grills. The elevation is 4,900 feet (1,500 m), which means pleasantly warm summer nights. The main attractions on Tioga Road and in Yosemite Valley are about 45 minutes away.

Crane Flat

Crane Flat (166 sites, 877/444-6777 or 518/885-3639 from outside the U.S. and Canada, www.recreation.gov, July-mid-Oct., $26) is the second campground you reach after entering the park on Highway 120 at the Big Oak Flat entrance station. Crane Flat's location is ideal for visiting both Yosemite Valley and the trailheads along Tioga Pass, plus it is only a few minutes from easy hiking in two giant sequoia groves: Tuolumne and Merced. Families usually enjoy this campground; the evening ranger programs are excellent and your kids will get to mingle with plenty of other young campers.

The 166 sites are spread out over five loops, and there is plenty of room for RVs up to 35 feet (10.7 m) long. Among a host of not-so-desirable sites a few winners can be found, namely the even-numbered sites from 214 to 228 and from 502 to 522, which have the most space and the fewest neighbors. **Reservations are required for all sites.** The camp has drinking water, flush toilets, picnic tables, and fire grills. The elevation is 6,200 feet (1,900 m), which is why it's open only in the summer, and even then there's usually a chill in the air in the evenings and mornings.

Crane Flat is 10 miles (16.1 km) east of the Big Oak Flat entrance station on the south side of Highway 120, just west of the Crane Flat junction and gas station. Yosemite Valley and Tioga Pass are each about 30 minutes away.

Tamarack Flat

Tamarack Flat (52 sites, first come, first served, late June-mid-Oct., $12) is the first campground you'll find that **doesn't take reservations.** The camp's access road is part of the old Big Oak Flat Road, 3 miles (4.8 km) off Highway 120 on a rough paved road that gets rougher as you go. Because there isn't any visible "authority" at this camp, some campers get a little rowdy here. Don't expect that your neighbors will follow the "quiet time at 10pm" rule. You might get lucky and have respectful, quiet neighbors; then again, you might not.

This is primarily a **tent-only campground** with sites located on a series of one-way spurs; RVs and trailers are not recommended. Many of the sites are quite private due to the large amount of space around them and the number of big boulders and lodgepole

pines. The camp has vault toilets, picnic tables, and fire grills. Bring your own drinking water, or plan on filtering it from Tamarack Creek. The camp's elevation is 6,300 feet (1,900 m); that makes this one of the warmer camps at night on Tioga Pass Road.

The signed access road to Tamarack Flat is 3.7 miles (6 km) east of Crane Flat on Highway 120. Turn right and drive 2.9 miles (4.7 km) along the paved, narrow road to the camp. You are less than an hour's drive from Yosemite Valley and about 40 minutes from Tuolumne Meadows.

White Wolf

★ **White Wolf** (74 sites, first come, first served, late June-mid-Sept., $18) is a favorite of many who come to Yosemite year after year. **Reservations are not accepted** and you have a decent chance at a site on most nights (except Saturday and possibly Friday). Besides its location, White Wolf is popular because it has all the advantages of a fully developed car campground, including flush toilets. An even greater luxury is **White Wolf Lodge** (about 300 ft/90 m from the camp), where you can enjoy delicious homemade meals if you don't feel like blackening another hot dog. The lodge also has a small store that sells drinks and snacks.

The camp has a pleasant setting at 8,000 feet (2,400 m) elevation amid a forest of lodgepole pine. Some sites are tucked in among rocky boulders and others are on the outside of the loop among the trees, so you can achieve a modicum of privacy. However, the sites are packed in too densely for this small area. Small RVs (less than 27 feet/8 m) can fit in here. The camp has drinking water, flush toilets, picnic tables, and fire grills. Trails to Harden Lake and Lukens Lake lead right from the camp and/or the lodge, and many other trails are close by.

From Crane Flat, drive 14 miles (22.5 km) east on Highway 120. Turn left at the White Wolf sign and drive 1 mile (1.6 km) to the campground. The camp access road is smoothly paved, so it's easy to cruise in and look for a spot. If you strike out, just head for one of the other camps on Tioga Pass Road.

Yosemite Creek

Yosemite Creek (75 sites, first come, first served, late June-early Sept. weather permitting, $12) is a good option for people who prefer a more primitive camping experience. The camp is a whopping 4.7 miles (7.6 km) off Highway 120 and the access road takes a tedious 20 minutes to drive. The long drive gives the camp a remote feel and discourages people from cruising in just to look around. (If you'll have to drive in and out of camp several times a day, this pothole-ridden road will make you crazy.) Yosemite Creek tends to attract campers who want to do their own thing and enjoy the wilderness.

This is a **tent-only campground**; RVs and trailers are not permitted. The camp has vault toilets, picnic tables, and fire grills, but no drinking water (pack bottled water or boil or filter it from Yosemite Creek). The elevation is 7,700 feet (2,350 m), so it is often quite chilly at night.

The camp is 14.3 miles (23 km) east of Crane Flat on Highway 120 (0.25 mi/0.4 km past the turnoff for White Wolf Camp). Turn right at the Yosemite Creek Campground sign and drive 4.7 miles (7.6 km) to the campground. The trailheads on Tioga Road are within an hour's drive.

Porcupine Flat

The easternmost of the camps on Tioga Road, **Porcupine Flat** (52 sites, first come, first served, July-mid-Oct., $12) is generally more popular with tent campers than RV campers; its road is mostly dirt and many sites aren't large enough for even small RVs. Set at 8,100 feet (2,450 m), the camp is a stone's throw off Highway 120, with 52 sites for tents or small RVs up to 24 feet (7.3 m) long. If you head for some of the sites on the far north end, you can get away from most of the road noise. Sites become larger and more private the farther back into the campground you go. The camp has vault toilets, picnic tables, and fire grills. Bring your own drinking water.

Porcupine Flat is 23.7 miles (38.1 km) east of Crane Flat on the north side of Highway 120. The camp has an ideal location close to Tuolumne Meadows and Tioga Pass. All of the trailheads of Yosemite's high country are close by, as are the many attractions east of Tioga Pass just outside of the park boundary.

a campsite at Tioga Lake

Tuolumne Meadows

Tuolumne Meadows (shuttle stop 5, 304 sites, 877/444-6777 or 518/885-3639 from outside the U.S. and Canada, www.recreation. gov, late June-late Sept., $26) is Yosemite's largest camp. The camper density level is high, to say the least. Everybody wants to camp here for three reasons: location, location, location. You are right across the road from Tuolumne Meadows. Many trailheads are within walking distance of the camp, as is the Tuolumne River. A decent grocery store and the **Tuolumne Meadows Grill** are right next door, so if you forget to bring food, it's no problem.

Elevation is 8,600 feet (2,600 m) at Tuolumne Meadows, bringing with it the fresh, cool air of the high country. **Half of the sites can be reserved in advance;** the others are first come, first served. This system results in a line of hopeful campers every morning outside the Tuolumne Meadows Reservations Office (209/372-4025), praying that they'll score a site. If they get there early Monday-Friday, they have a decent chance. Weekends are much tougher.

Considering its massive size, the camp has many sites that have a lot going for them. A dense forest of lodgepole pine lends some sites a modicum of seclusion. One of the camp's loops has a number of riverside sites. Others have an A-plus view of Lembert Dome. Nonetheless, it is an unalterable law of nature that 304 separate groups of campers can never be quiet at the same time. Camping here can feel like camping in the city. If you need to get some solid sleep so that you can wake up the next morning and climb Cathedral Peak, pack earplugs for sure.

The camp has drinking water, flush toilets, picnic tables, and fire grills. Sites will accommodate tents or RVs up to 35 feet (10.7 m). Seven **group sites** are available for 13-30 people ($50). Four **horse camps** are also available ($30). The **backpackers' campsites** ($6) are designated for those beginning or ending a wilderness trip. Campers who wish to stay in these sites may do so for only one night before or after their backpacking trip, and they must have their wilderness permit in hand. The sites are walk-in only, and only backpacking equipment may be brought in.

The camp is 39 miles (63 km) east of Crane Flat on the south side of Highway 120, just past the Tuolumne Meadows Grill and Store.

OUTSIDE THE PARK

Forest Service campgrounds in **Inyo National Forest** (Mono Basin Scenic Area Visitor Center, 760/647-3044, www.fs.usda. gov/inyo) are within a few miles of the Tioga Pass entrance to Yosemite. Most are first come, first served; **no reservations are taken.** Whereas the National Park Service usually shuts down the park's four campgrounds on Tioga Road by mid-September, the Forest Service camps stay open through the month of October. Since Tioga Road is usually open until November 1, visitors get an entire extra month to camp and play in Yosemite's high country.

Tioga Lake

The sight of granite-lined Tioga Lake is a real stunner for drivers coming through Tioga Pass. The high mountain lake and the small **Tioga Lake Campground** (13 sites, www. fs.usda.gov, first come, first served, $22) are plainly obvious from Highway 120. Highway or no highway, this is some world-class scenery. The campground is at 9,700 feet (3,000 m) elevation, and none of the sites have much, if any, protection from the wind that frequently whips off the surface of the lake. Of the campsites, sites 13 and 14 are the most coveted because they are situated right on scenic Tioga Lake's edge. Avoid site 3, set just below a curve in Highway 120 (if someone throws something out the window as they drive by, you'll get hit on the head). Tioga Lake is regularly stocked with rainbow trout by the Department of Fish and Wildlife; it provides a good place to fish from shore or from a float tube.

The camp has drinking water, picnic tables, fire grills, and vault toilets. It's on Highway

120, 1.2 miles (1.9 km) east of the Tioga Pass entrance station and 11 miles (17.7 km) west of U.S. 395.

Junction

Junction Campground (13 sites, www. fs.usda.gov, first come, first served, $17-19) is a stone's throw from Tioga Pass Resort near the junction of Saddlebag Lake Road and Highway 120. For proximity to Yosemite—and Saddlebag Lake, Tioga Lake, Ellery Lake, and Lee Vining Canyon—it doesn't get much better than this. The small camp is first come, first served, and because of its location it is filled almost all summer long. Sites 12 and 13 are the best choices, but anything from number 6 on up is pretty good. The camp has picnic tables, fire grills, and vault toilets. Bring your own water, and dress warmly—the elevation is 9,600 feet (2,600 m). One advantage to staying here is that you can walk over to Tioga Pass Resort for meals if you don't feel like cooking. A trail to the historic mining settlement of Bennettville leads right from camp.

Junction is 150 feet (45 m) north on Saddlebag Lake Road off Highway 120, 2.5 miles (4 km) east of the Tioga Pass entrance station and 10 miles (16.1 km) west of U.S. 395.

Ellery Lake

★ **Ellery Lake** (12 sites, www.fs.usda.gov, first come, first served, $22-24) is a gorgeous blue, granite-lined gem of a lake just 3 miles (4.8 km) west of the Yosemite border, at an elevation of 9,600 feet (2,600 m). Surrounded by jagged granite peaks, it provides excellent fishing and bird-watching opportunities. The camp is first come, first served, but unless you happen to pull in just as someone else is leaving, it's nearly impossible to get a site here until after mid-September, when the summer vacation crowds disperse; its sites are filled up almost all the time. The best sites are set off from the main cluster of sites by a 300-foot (90-m) access road, which places them in a spot not easily seen from the highway. Lucky campers who snare these sites are insulated from the road noise. The camp has drinking

water, picnic tables, fire grills, and vault toilets. Campers with small RVs will like that the parking slips are paved.

This campground is on Highway 120, 3 miles (4.8 km) east of the Tioga Pass entrance station and 9.5 miles (15.3 km) west of U.S. 395.

Sawmill Walk-In

★ **Sawmill Walk-In** (12 sites, www.fs.usda. gov, first come, first served, $17) is the most beautiful campground in or near Yosemite. This is a **walk-in camp,** which means you park your car in a central parking lot and then walk about 300-600 feet (90-185 m) to your campsite. You can't see the cars from the campground, so once you are at your site, the setting feels like a backpacking experience. The sites are spaced remarkably far apart (as much as 150 feet/45 m), so camping here is more private than traditional car camping. And every campsite has a drop-dead gorgeous view of the High Sierra countryside—mountain peaks, a subalpine meadow with a stream running through it, scattered stands of conifer trees, and all the high alpine beauty that comes with this 9,600-foot (2,900-m) elevation. If there is camping in heaven, this is what it looks like. The camp has picnic tables, fire grills, and vault toilets. Bring your own water.

Sawmill is 1.5 miles (2.4 km) north on Saddlebag Lake Road off Highway 120, 2.5 miles (4 km) east of the Tioga Pass entrance station and 10 miles (16.1 km) west of U.S. 395.

Saddlebag Lake

Saddlebag Lake (www.fs.usda.gov, first come, first served, June-Oct., $22) is the highest lake you can drive to in California—it's at 10,087 feet (3,075 m) elevation—and it sits in a stark landscape high above the tree line. This is a favorite spot of both hikers and anglers and a major entrance point for the Hoover Wilderness leading into the spectacular 20 Lakes Basin. Plus, it's only slightly more than 5 miles (8 km) outside Yosemite's eastern border, sealing its fate as a well-known and popular destination all summer long. The lake has two separate campgrounds—one called Saddlebag Lake for individuals and families (20 sites) and one called **Trailhead** (877/444-6777 or 518/885-3639 from outside the U.S. and Canada, www.recreation.gov, $94) for large groups of up to 25 people. The two camps are spaced far enough apart so that if there is a Boy Scout troop at Trailhead, you won't feel like you're a part of their campout. Both camps are less than a 300-foot (90-m) walk from the lakeshore. Sites 16 and 18 of the main camp, perched high above Saddlebag Lake, have an unobstructed water view to die for. The campground has drinking water, picnic tables, fire grills, and vault toilets.

Saddlebag is 2.8 miles (4.5 km) north on Saddlebag Lake Road off Highway 120, 2.5 miles (4 km) east of the Tioga Pass entrance station and 10 miles (16.1 km) west of U.S. 395.

Hetch Hetchy

Most everybody in California has visited

Yosemite Valley at one time or another, but substantially fewer people have visited Hetch Hetchy Valley, Yosemite's "twin" in the northern section of the park. Hetch Hetchy Valley was flooded in 1923 to create a water supply for San Francisco. It was the tragic end of a long fight by naturalist John Muir, who tried in vain to save Hetch Hetchy from the big-city politicians. Muir described Hetch Hetchy Valley as Yosemite Valley's "wonderfully exact counterpart." Although smaller in size, Hetch Hetchy was shaped by the same geological forces that created Yosemite's glacially carved valley.

When people see pictures of what Hetch Hetchy looked like before it was dammed and flooded, they are struck by how much it resembles

Highlights

Look for ★ to find recommended sights, activities, dining, and lodging.

★ **O'Shaughnessy Dam:** A remarkable feat of engineering, the 312-foot-high (95-m) dam that forms Hetch Hetchy Reservoir took almost seven years to build. See the dam in spring when its overflow valves are spraying thousands of gallons of water into the free-flowing stretch of the Tuolumne River (page 199).

★ **Tueeulala and Wapama Falls Hike:** In spring and early summer, these two spectacular waterfalls drop more than 1,000 feet (300 m) to the lakeshore at Hetch Hetchy. To see them up close, take a 4.8-mile (7.7-km) round-trip hike along the reservoir's northern edge and enjoy a fabulous wildflower display along the way (page 202).

★ **Carlon Falls:** A favorite swimming hole for more than 100 years, the pools below Carlon Falls make a fine destination for a short hike on a hot summer day. Plenty of people never make it as far as the falls; they just pick an inviting spot along the river (page 203).

★ **Horseback Riding:** Ride off into the sunset on a trusty steed from Mather Saddle and Pack Station, enjoying end-of-the-day views of the Grand Canyon of the Tuolumne River. Or start the day right with a two-hour Breakfast Ride, featuring a meal cooked over an open fire (page 209).

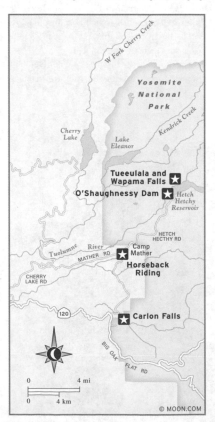

Where Can I Find...?

When driving to Hetch Hetchy, you'll need to be completely **self-reliant.** Once you drive past Camp Mather and Evergreen Lodge, no supplies are available for the final 9 miles (14.5 km) to Hetch Hetchy.

· **Banks and ATMs:** The nearest ATM is at the Yosemite Lakes store on Highway 120.

· **Gas:** The nearest gas pumps are at the **Yosemite Lakes Store** (31191 Hardin Flat Rd., 209/962-0110), 6 miles (9.7 km) east of the Big Oak Flat entrance station just off Highway 120, or 8 miles (12.9 km) inside the park at **Crane Flat** (Big Oak Flat Rd. and Hwy. 120).

· **Supplies: Evergreen Lodge** (33160 Evergreen Rd., 209/379-2606, www.evergreenlodge. com) has a small store and restaurant. **Camp Mather** (35250 Mather Rd., 209/379-2284) has a small camping-supply store with a few grocery items.

today's Yosemite Valley. Photos show the stark, pristine granite of Kolana Rock and Hetch Hetchy Dome jutting upward from the valley floor, waterfalls dropping hundreds of feet from hanging valleys like rivers falling from the sky, and lush, flower-filled meadows lining the edge of the meandering Tuolumne River. You can't help but wonder, what on earth were those politicians thinking?

But here's the reality of the situation: Despite humans' best efforts to destroy it, Hetch Hetchy remains beautiful. Without question, the valley has lost an irreplaceable amount of its original splendor. But when you hike along the shoreline of 306-foot-deep (93-m) Hetch Hetchy Reservoir and observe the higher sections of granite and waterfalls that tower imposingly above the waterline, you get the sense that Nature has ceased crying over Hetch Hetchy. Instead, she has done what she does best—heal, beautify, and make the most of what is here now. Wildflowers blossom in the understory of massive ponderosa pines and incense-cedars. Birds and other wildlife make their homes along the edges of the deep-blue reservoir. Hetch Hetchy's waterfalls still flow with exuberance, and its granite towers still stand guard over the valley.

PLANNING YOUR TIME

Hetch Hetchy is best visited in **spring,** when its waterfalls are flowing at their fullest and temperatures are still mild and cool. **April** and **May** are the prime months here, not only for waterfall watching but also for wildflower viewing. Summer can be quite hot, with temperatures frequently reaching 90-100°F (32-38°C). The valley's waterfalls run dry by midsummer. **Autumn** is another good time to visit Hetch Hetchy, when temperatures drop to a more comfortable level and the region's deciduous trees put on a lovely fall color show. Snowfall will sometimes, but not often, close the road to Hetch Hetchy in the winter.

Of the five park entrance stations, Hetch Hetchy sees the fewest number of cars passing through day after day. Casual day-trip visitors can make the winding, 18-mile (29-km) drive to Hetch Hetchy from Big Oak Flat, walk along the top of **O'Shaughnessy Dam,** read the series of interpretive signs that explain the reservoir's history, and get a good look at the area's cliffs and waterfalls. Those who are in the mood for a short, level hike can walk the path to the base of impressive **Wapama Fall.** Longer day hikes or backpacking trips can be made to the far end of the reservoir and **Rancheria Falls,** or to many other worthwhile destinations in this remote region of Yosemite.

HETCH HETCHY

Previous: view of Hetch Hetchy; freshly caught trout cooking on a canister stove; rock-lined trail.

Hetch Hetchy

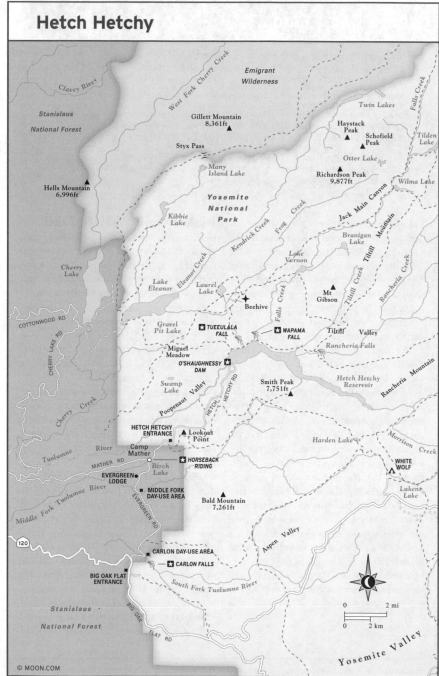

Clavey River

Emigrant
Wilderness

Stanislaus

National Forest

West Fork Cherry Creek

Gillett Mountain
8,361ft

Styx Pass

Twin Lakes

Haystack
Peak

Schofield
Peak

Tilden
Lake

Otter Lake

Richardson Peak
9,877ft

Wilma Lake

Many
Island Lake

Hells Mountain
6,996ft

Yosemite
National
Park

Kibbie
Lake

Kendrick Creek

Frog Creek

Jack Main Canyon

Tiltill Mountain

Cherry
Lake

Lake
Vernon

Branigan
Lake

Rancheria Creek

Laurel
Lake

Lake
Eleanor

Eleanor Creek

Falls Creek

Mt
Gibson

Tiltill Creek

COTTONWOOD RD

Beehive

Gravel
Pit Lake

★ TUEEULALA
FALL

★ WAPAMA
FALL

Tiltill   Valley

Rancheria Falls

CHERRY LAKE RD

Miguel
Meadow

O'SHAUGHNESSY
DAM ★

Smith Peak
7,751ft

Hetch Hetchy
Reservoir

Rancheria Mountain

Swamp
Lake

Poopenaut   Valley

HETCH HETCHY RD

Cherry   Creek

HETCH HETCHY
ENTRANCE

Lookout
Point

Camp
Mather

Harden Lake

Morrison Creek

Tuolumne   River

MATHER RD

Birch
Lake

★ HORSEBACK
RIDING

WHITE
WOLF △

EVERGREEN
LODGE

■ MIDDLE FORK
DAY-USE AREA

Lukens
Lake

Middle Fork Tuolumne River

EVERGREEN RD

Bald Mountain
7,261ft

120

CARLON DAY-USE AREA

Aspen   Valley

★ CARLON FALLS

BIG OAK FLAT
ENTRANCE

South Fork Tuolumne River

Stanislaus

National Forest

BIG OAK FLAT RD

Yosemite Valley

0   2 mi

0   2 km

© MOON.COM

Exploring Hetch Hetchy

There are no visitors centers in this region of Yosemite, but the ranger at the **Mather Ranger Station** (Hetch Hetchy Rd., 209/379-1922) will happily answer any questions.

ENTRANCE STATION

The small **Hetch Hetchy entrance** station lies 9 miles (14.5 km) north of Highway 120 via Evergreen Road and Hetch Hetchy Road. These two roads are sometimes closed in winter. Because the roads are narrow and winding, vehicles longer than 25 feet (7.6 m) or wider than 8 feet (2.4 m) are prohibited at all times. It's best to prepare for a trip to Hetch Hetchy by having everything you might need or want already in your car. Opportunities for food and supplies are limited once you leave Highway 120. Also, note that unlike other roads in the park, the **Hetch Hetchy Road is not open 24 hours a day.** You can drive the road from 7am to 9pm daily from May through Labor Day (reduced hours the rest of the year, depending on daylight hours).

DRIVING TOUR

Hetch Hetchy Reservoir is a 40-mile (64-km) drive from Yosemite Valley via Highway 120 and the Evergreen and Hetch Hetchy Roads.

Plan on about 75 minutes to make the drive in good weather. Starting from the Big Oak Flat entrance to Yosemite, head west on Highway 120 for 1 mile (1.6 km) and then turn right on **Evergreen Road** (road may be closed in winter). Seven miles down this road is the **Evergreen Lodge,** a cabin resort with a good restaurant and store. A half mile farther is **Camp Mather,** a camp run by the city of San Francisco. Bear right on **Hetch Hetchy Road** (road open 7am-9pm daily May-Labor Day, may be closed in winter) at Camp Mather, and in 1.5 miles (2.4 km) you will pass through the **Hetch Hetchy entrance station** to Yosemite. Get any information you might need here; this is probably your last chance to see a park ranger.

Hetch Hetchy Road continues for another 7.5 winding miles (12 km) to **O'Shaughnessy Dam.** This road was the route of the Hetch Hetchy Railroad, which carried men, machinery, and materials to the dam's construction site. At several points in the road you will gain some long distance peeks at the reservoir and its waterfalls. Park at the dam and take a closer look at what humans, and Mother Nature, have created in Hetch Hetchy Valley.

Sights

★ O'SHAUGHNESSY DAM

Built by the City of San Francisco between 1914 and 1923 to provide power and water for its citizens, **O'Shaughnessy Dam** was a product of its time. Although the dam's construction was adamantly opposed by John Muir, the Sierra Club, the Pacific Gas and Electric Company, and the cities of Turlock and Modesto—all for their own reasons—the dam came into existence because of a piece of Congressional legislation called the Raker Act, signed into law by President Woodrow Wilson. (Although some progressives claimed this was a noble victory because it would mandate the breakup of Pacific Gas and Electric Company's San Francisco energy monopoly by creating a municipal, public power source, this never came to fruition.) The prevailing political mood at the time, particularly at the federal level, could not allow the preservation of a national park to be more important than the twin themes of progress and development. And so the massive dam was built, Hetch Hetchy Valley was flooded, and the world will never again see the twin to Yosemite Valley in its pristine state.

Whatever else we may think or say about it, the dam is a remarkable feat of engineering. It took almost 7 years to build, and another 14 years before the aqueduct lines were completed over the 155-mile (250-km) course to San Francisco, which required building 37 miles (60 km) of tunnels. The system operates entirely by gravity. The original cost of construction was more than $12 million—a fortune at the time. When the reservoir's water finally flowed to San Francisco, the cost had risen to $100 million. But the building didn't stop. In 1938, the original dam was modified, which raised its height by 85 feet (26 m). Currently, the dam can hold back approximately 117 billion gallons (445 million cubic meters) of water. The reservoir is 8 miles (13 km) long and 306 feet (93 m) deep at its deepest point.

O'Shaughnessy Dam is 7.5 miles (12 km) north of the entrance station on Hetch Hetchy Road. After parking at the dam, be sure to walk across its massive, 600-foot-long (185-m) concrete surface.

TUEEULALA AND WAPAMA FALLS

In the spring and early summer months, two waterfalls are visible from O'Shaughnessy Dam: **Tueeulala and Wapama Falls.** Both falls drop about 1,000 feet (300 m) before they hit the waterline of Hetch Hetchy Reservoir, which means they were nearly 1,800 feet (550 m) high before the great man-made flood. By July, wispy Tueeulala Fall usually runs dry, but Wapama keeps a fair flow going into August. In spring, Wapama Fall sometimes runs with such force that the National Park Service is forced to close the trail below it. A 4.8-mile (7.7-km) round-trip **hike** leads from the dam to the falls.

O'Shaughnessy Dam at Hetch Hetchy

Hetch Hetchy Hikes

Trail	Effort	Distance	Duration
Lookout Point	Easy	2.8 mi/4.5 km rt	1.5 hr
Lake Eleanor	Easy	3 mi/4.8 km rt	1.5 hr
Carlon Falls	Easy	4 mi/6.4 km rt	2 hr
Tueeulala and Wapama Falls	Easy	4.8 mi/7.7 km rt	2.5-3 hr
Preston Falls	Moderate	8.8 mi/14.2 km rt	4 hr
Smith Peak	Very strenuous	13 mi/20.9 km rt	6 hr

Recreation

DAY HIKES

Lookout Point

Distance: 2.8 miles (4.5 km) round trip
Duration: 1.5 hours
Elevation Change: 600 feet (185 m)
Effort: Easy
Trailhead: Mather Ranger Station (see map p. 201)
Directions: From Groveland, drive east on Highway 120 for 22.5 miles (36.2 km) to the Evergreen Road turnoff signed for Hetch Hetchy Reservoir. Drive north on Evergreen Road for 7.4 miles (11.9 km) and turn right onto Hetch Hetchy Road. Drive 1.5 miles (2.4 km) to the entrance kiosk near the Mather Ranger Station; the trail begins 300 feet (90 m) past the entrance kiosk, just beyond the ranger station on the right.

Check your calendar. Is it springtime? Are most of the high-country trails in Yosemite National Park still snowed in? Then it's time to take the easy jaunt to Lookout Point, where you can admire Hetch Hetchy Reservoir and its waterfalls from an unusual perspective and count the plentiful wildflowers along the trail as you walk. The Lookout Point Trail begins near the Mather Ranger Station on Hetch Hetchy Road. Begin hiking at the trail sign for **Cottonwood** and **Smith Meadows.** Turn left at the first **junction;** then follow the trail as it roughly parallels Hetch Hetchy Road for **0.5 mile (0.8 km).** The trail turns away from the road with a brief uphill stretch and then

enters a level, forested area that was severely burned in the wildfires of 1996. This is where the flowers bloom profusely in springtime.

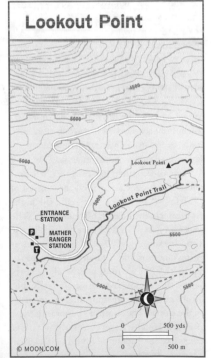

Lookout Point

Look for a trail junction at **1 mile (1.6 km)** out, and bear left for Lookout Point, **0.3 mile (0.5 km)** away. The path gets rather faint in places, but **rock cairns** mark the way. Just head for the highest point you see atop a granite knob dotted with a few pines. You'll know you're at Lookout Point when you can see the west end of Hetch Hetchy Reservoir (including its immense dam) and Wapama and Tueeulala Falls. If you visit much later than May or June, you may see only Wapama, the most robust of Hetch Hetchy's waterfalls; Tueeulala dries up early in the year. Although the vista is not perfect from Lookout Point—it would be better if it were 500 feet (150 m) higher or if there weren't so many trees—this is still a fine spot to spread out a picnic. You probably won't have any company, either.

Smith Peak

Distance: 13 miles (20.9 km) round-trip
Duration: 6 hours
Elevation Change: 3,700 feet (1,130 m)
Effort: Very strenuous
Trailhead: Smith Peak
Directions: From Groveland, drive east on Highway 120 for 22.5 miles (36.2 km) to the Evergreen Road turnoff, signed for Hetch Hetchy Reservoir (1 mi/1.6 km west of the Big Oak Flat entrance to Yosemite). Drive north on Evergreen Road for 7.4 miles (11.9 km) and turn right onto Hetch Hetchy Road. Drive 1.5 miles (2.4 km) to the entrance kiosk by the Mather Ranger Station; then continue 6 miles (9.7 km) to the Smith Peak trailhead on the right side of the road.

A steep and challenging 13-mile (20.9-km) round-trip hike will earn you the summit of 7,751-foot (2,363-m) Smith Peak, the highest pinnacle in the Hetch Hetchy area. The peak and part of its trail were hit hard by the **Rim Fire** of August 2013, so this is an interesting place for hikers to view the process of regrowth after a fire. It will be many years before this region recovers completely, but shrubs and young trees are already greening up the slopes. The summit's panoramic view of Hetch Hetchy Reservoir and the Grand Canyon of the Tuolumne River is still as awesome as it ever was.

Smith Peak can be accessed from several trailheads, but the shortest trip—still a prodigious 13 miles (20.9 km)—begins at the **Smith Peak Trailhead** on Hetch Hetchy Road. From the road, the trail climbs alongside Cottonwood Creek to **Cottonwood Meadow** and then **Smith Meadow** beyond (both can be very wet and boggy until mid-June). Beyond Smith Meadow you'll see the most intense fire devastation; the final 1.5 miles (2.4 km) to the **summit** were completely torched. The peak is covered with pock-marked granite boulders, and its wide summit vista of Hetch Hetchy Reservoir, 4,000 feet (1,200 m) below, as well as the Cathedral and Clark Ranges to the north and east, offers a fine reward for the climb.

★ Tueeulala and Wapama Falls

Distance: 4.8 miles (7.7 km) round-trip
Duration: 2.5-3 hours
Elevation Change: 350 feet (105 m)
Effort: Easy
Trailhead: O'Shaughnessy Dam (see map p. 203)
Directions: From Groveland, drive east on Highway 120 for 22.5 miles (36.2 km) to the Evergreen Road turnoff, signed for Hetch Hetchy Reservoir (1 mi/1.6 km west of the Big Oak Flat entrance to Yosemite). Drive north on Evergreen Road for 7.4 miles (11.9 km) and turn right onto Hetch Hetchy Road. Drive 9 miles (14.5 km) to the dam and trailhead.

The trail to this spectacular early-season waterfall starts by crossing the giant **O'Shaughnessy Dam,** where you may pause to curse the San Francisco politicians who believed that flooding Hetch Hetchy Valley was a good idea. If this is your first trip to this part of Yosemite, be sure to stop at the dam and read the interpretive plaques that explain the building of Hetch Hetchy Reservoir and its service to San Francisco. After passing through a lighted, 500-foot-long (150-m) tunnel, the trail opens out to a mixed forest along the edge of the deep-blue lake. Wildflower displays are often excellent in late spring. In **1.5 miles (2.4 km)** you reach **Tueeulala Fall,** a delicate wisp of a freefall

Tueeulala and Wapama Falls

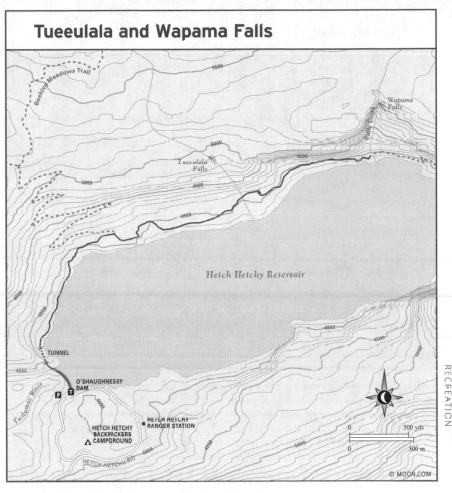

© MOON.COM

that only runs during peak snowmelt and is often dry by late May. Less than a mile farther you reach powerful **Wapama Fall** on Falls Creek, a Bridalveil-like plume of white water that makes a dramatic plunge into the reservoir. Depending on how early in the year you visit, you may get soaking wet standing on the sturdy steel bridges that cross over Wapama Fall's coursing flow. In early spring, Wapama Fall sometimes flows so furiously that the park rangers have to close this trail.

★ Carlon Falls

Distance: 4 miles (6.4 km) round-trip

Duration: 2 hours

Elevation Change: 350 feet (105 m)

Effort: Easy

Trailhead: Carlon Day Use Area (see map p. 204)

Directions: From Groveland, drive east on Highway 120 for 22.5 miles (36.2 km) to the Evergreen Road turnoff, signed for Hetch Hetchy Reservoir (1 mi/1.6 km west of the Big Oak Flat entrance to Yosemite). Drive north on Evergreen Road for 1 mile (1.6 km) to the far side of the bridge, just past Carlon Day Use Area. Park in the pullout on the right. Begin hiking on the closed-off road, heading upstream.

Carlon Falls is not located in Hetch Hetchy Valley; its trailhead is found on the road to

Carlon Falls

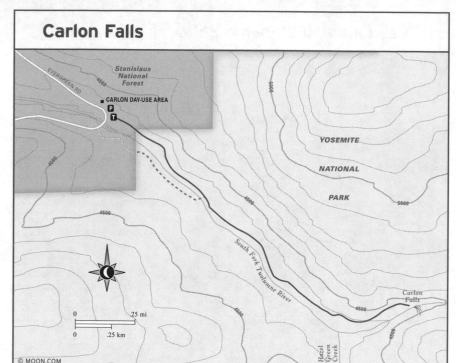

Stanislaus National Forest

EVERGREEN RD

CARLON DAY-USE AREA

YOSEMITE

NATIONAL

PARK

South Fork Tuolumne River

Carlon Falls

Hazel Green Creek

0   .25 mi

0   .25 km

© MOON.COM

Hetch Hetchy (Evergreen Rd.). This means it gets missed not just by the large number of Yosemite visitors who never see Hetch Hetchy, but also by visitors who are heading so intently to Hetch Hetchy that they ignore everything along the way. This waterfall on the South Fork Tuolumne River shouldn't be passed by. It has two big factors going for it: It's accessible by an easy, nearly level, pleasant hike; and it's a river waterfall, so it has a dependable amount of flow even in autumn, when Hetch Hetchy's and Yosemite's waterfalls have all but gone dry.

Follow the obvious **trail on the north side** of the river from Carlon Day Use Area (the trail on the south side is an unmaintained anglers' route). Although you begin your hike in Stanislaus National Forest, you will soon walk into Yosemite National Park. The trail passes through an impressive old-growth pine and fir forest, highlighted by wildflowers in the spring and colorful oak and dogwood leaves in the autumn. After **2 miles (3.2 km)** of riverside meandering, you'll reach 30-foot (9-m) **Carlon Falls,** a lacy cascade that drops over a granite ledge in the river. The rocks below it make a fine picnic spot. The waterfall's namesakes are Dan and Donna Carlon, who operated the popular Carl Inn from 1916 to 1930 near what is now Carlon Day Use Area.

Lake Eleanor

Distance: 3 miles (4.8 km) round-trip
Duration: 1.5 hours
Elevation Change: 100 feet (30 m)
Effort: Easy
Trailhead: Cherry Lake
Directions: From Groveland, drive east on Highway 120 for 14 miles (22.5 km) toward Yosemite National Park. Turn left on Cherry Lake Road and drive 24 miles (39 km) to Cherry Lake's dam, then across it. On the far side of the dam, bear right and drive 0.4 mile (0.6 km); then turn right on the dirt road that is signed for

Lake Eleanor. Follow this road (open May 1-Sept. 15) for 4 miles (6.4 km) to its end at the gated national park boundary, 0.25 mile (0.4 km) south of the lake. The road is usually closed beyond Cherry Lake's dam.

Lake Eleanor is a second, less famous reservoir in the Hetch Hetchy region of Yosemite. Originally a naturally shallow glacial lake, Lake Eleanor was "improved" by the City of San Francisco by damming Eleanor Creek in 1928, five years before O'Shaughnessy Dam at Hetch Hetchy was completed. The dam raised the lake's water level 40 feet (12 m). Today it is the second-largest lake in Yosemite after Hetch Hetchy. Its waters are used by San Francisco not as a drinking water supply, but rather to generate power.

Set at an elevation of 4,657 feet (1,419 m), Lake Eleanor is popular with hikers who tote along a fishing rod while traversing the trail around the 3-mile-long (4.8-km) lake's edge. The access road to Lake Eleanor ends at a **gate** 0.25 mile (0.4 km) before the lake, so you start your hike there and then take a mellow walk along the lake's **south shore.** Much of Lake Eleanor's western side is dotted with picturesque islands. A backcountry **ranger station** is on the southwest shore; it is usually staffed in the summer months.

It takes more than an hour's drive from Highway 120 to access Lake Eleanor, so people who come here to hike or fish often plan on spending the night. A **first-come, first-served campground** is at nearby Cherry Lake.

Preston Falls

Distance: 8.8 miles (14.2 km) round-trip
Duration: 4 hours
Elevation Change: 750 feet (230 m)
Effort: Moderate
Trailhead: Early Intake/Kirkwood Powerhouse
Directions: From Groveland, drive east on Highway 120 for 14 miles (22.5 km) toward Yosemite. Turn left on Cherry Lake Road and drive 8.5 miles (13.7 km) to Early Intake, where you cross a bridge over the Tuolumne River. Turn right on the far side of the bridge and drive 0.8 mile (1.3 km) to the trailhead parking area at the end of the road, just beyond Kirkwood Powerhouse.

The Preston Flat trailhead is off Cherry Lake Road in Stanislaus National Forest, outside Yosemite's border. The path travels 4.4 miles (7.1 km) up the north side of the Tuolumne River Canyon on a gently undulating grade. Shortly before the trail's end is a rock chimney and a few other remains of an old cabin that was built here by a homesteader named Preston. A few hundred yards farther is a vista of **Preston Falls,** a cascade formed where the Tuolumne River drops 15 feet (4.5 m) over a granite ledge into a wide, clear pool. The cataract is just 0.5 mile (0.8 km) downstream of Yosemite's boundary line. If you want to stay overnight, you can: Several good campsites are found along the trail, which sticks closely to the river for most of its length.

BACKPACKING

The **Preston Flat Trail** is in Stanislaus National Forest, just outside of Yosemite. The trail heads to a stretch of river just west of Poopenaut Valley and offers good fishing and swimming opportunities, as well as many camping spots. The 4-mile (6.4 km) hike to **Kibbie Lake** is a popular weekend backpacking trip. The Kibbie Ridge Trail leads through lodgepole pine forest to the granite-bound lake at 6,800 feet (2,070 m) elevation. The lake is fairly shallow and supports a good population of rainbow trout. This is a very short, rewarding backpacking trip that is suitable for most beginners.

Although the last few miles to the summit were severely burned in the 2013 Rim Fire, the trail to **Smith Peak** remains open to backpackers and day hikers. The trail can be accessed from several points; for ease of parking, most backpackers begin by the Mather Ranger Station (the trail begins 300 feet/90 meters past the entrance kiosk, just beyond the ranger station on the right). Follow the Lookout Point Trail for 1.2 miles (1.9 km); then cut off on the trail to Smith Meadow. You'll pass Base Line Camp Road and then climb up along Cottonwood Creek to Cottonwood Meadow, soon followed by Smith

The Battle for Hetch Hetchy

Although **John Muir** is widely known for his role in creating the formalized boundaries of Yosemite National Park—a protected area much larger than its original borders, which included only Yosemite Valley and the Mariposa Grove of Giant Sequoias—one of Muir's greatest battles took place over the damming of Hetch Hetchy Valley to create a water supply for San Francisco. Muir's defeat in this battle reportedly broke his heart and spirit.

Muir first visited Hetch Hetchy Valley in 1871, and two years later he wrote of its wonders in the *Boston Weekly Transcript* and *Overland Monthly*. "It is a Yosemite Valley in depth and width, and is over 20 miles in length, abounding in falls and cascades, and glacial rock forms," wrote Muir. "The view from my first standpoint is one of the grandest I have ever beheld."

Despite the fact that in landscape and natural features Hetch Hetchy was nearly a twin to Yosemite Valley, and more importantly, a designated area of a federally sanctioned park, the City of San Francisco proposed damming the valley to create a public water supply. The request was twice denied by Secretary of the Interior Ethan Hitchcock, first in 1903 and later in 1905. Muir was aghast at the idea of a dam, and beginning in 1901, he led the newly formed Sierra Club and a consortium of other organizations in a campaign to protect Hetch Hetchy. It was one of the first efforts at what today is known as "grassroots lobbying," in which individual citizens were urged to write letters and contact their elected officials to express their opinions on an issue.

Muir wrote in the January 1908 *Sierra Club Bulletin*, "Dam Hetch Hetchy! As well dam for water-tanks the people's cathedrals and churches, for no holier temple has ever been consecrated by the heart of man."

But with Congress's passage of the Raker Act in 1913, Muir's battle was lost. Within a decade, Hetch Hetchy Valley was filled with water. To add insult to injury, much of the lumber used to build the dam—more than 6 million board feet—was cut from trees within the national park.

For the future of the conservation movement, the contest over Hetch Hetchy was not a complete defeat. The loss of the beautiful valley ("a grand landscape garden, one of nature's rarest and precious mountain mansions," as Muir described it) awakened many Americans to the idea that our national parks should be sacrosanct—that once they have been established, their natural resources should not be tampered with. Since that time, conservationists have followed Muir's example and stopped dams from being built in Grand Canyon National Park and Dinosaur National Monument.

Meadow. A trail comes in on the right beyond Smith Meadow; this is another popular route to Smith Peak leading from White Wolf Lodge and Campground off Tioga Road. Campsites are found near this junction of trails. Get a good night's rest before bagging Smith Peak the next morning. You've hiked 6 miles (9.7 km) thus far; it's only 2 more miles (3.2 km) to the summit. The 7,751-foot (2,363-m) peak is covered with pockmarked granite boulders and offers a panoramic view of Hetch Hetchy Reservoir and the Grand Canyon of the Tuolumne River.

Rancheria Falls

There's no better time than spring to hike along the northern edge of Hetch Hetchy Reservoir (elevation 3,796 ft/1,157 m) and admire the three stunning waterfalls—Tueeulala, Wapama, and Rancheria—along the way. An easy overnight backpacking trip leads to the eastern edge of the reservoir and **Rancheria Falls** (6.5 mi/10.5 km). Beware that the bears in this area are some of the boldest in all of Yosemite; bear canisters are required.

O'Shaughnessy Dam is the trailhead for Rancheria Falls. The trail to the Rancheria Falls backpackers' camp is mostly level, with a total elevation gain of only 1,300 feet (400 m) spread out over 6.5 miles (10.5 km). This makes it manageable even for most beginners. Fishing in the reservoir is fair to middling in spring and fall. And remember: Swimming is not allowed in this public water supply.

More adventurous backpackers will continue past Rancheria to **Tiltill Valley,** 3 miles (4.8 km) farther. **Vernon Lake** lies a half-day's hike beyond (another 6.5 mi/10.2 km). The granite-backed lake is popular with those who tote along fishing gear in the hope of inviting a few rainbow trout to dinner. Good campsites can be found on Falls Creek (permits required) and also near the lake. Take this trip in the early season, however, because the route through Tiltill Valley is notoriously hot and dry in summer. You can easily turn this into a 27-mile (43-km) loop by heading back via Beehive Meadow and Laurel Lake and then hiking south to Hetch Hetchy.

Beehive Trail to Laurel Lake

The same destinations can be reached via a shorter route (that's preferred by many). Take the **Beehive Trail** northward from the edge of Hetch Hetchy Reservoir, 1 mile (1.6 km) from the trailhead at O'Shaughnessy Dam. The trail follows an old road through a series of switchbacks, climbing 1,200 feet (365 m) over 2 miles (3.2 km) to the canyon rim. The trail then departs from the road and meanders on a much easier grade through pine and incense-cedar forest. Beautiful **Laurel Lake** is 8 miles (12.9 km) from O'Shaughnessy Dam. The lake is surrounded by aspen groves, firs, and lodgepole pines, and its waters are a fair bet for rainbow trout fishing. Spend your weekend here or set out for even more scenic Vernon Lake the next day (4 mi/6.4 km distant). Loop back via Tiltill Valley or retrace your steps.

Poopenaut Valley Trail

A short but steep Hetch Hetchy backpacking trail is the **Poopenaut Valley Trail,** which provides fast access to a beautiful stretch of the Tuolumne River. It's a merciless downhill jaunt of 1.3 miles (2.1 km) and 1,200 feet (365 m) of elevation loss to a flat river stretch west of O'Shaughnessy Dam. If you like being close to a fast and free river, you'll love the camping spots here. Fishing and swimming are excellent, but be wary of rattlesnakes, especially in

spring. Because the trail's so short, you might expect it to be crawling with day hikers, but they are noticeably absent except on occasional weekends. Nobody enjoys the return trip uphill, which, although brief, is the worst grade in all of Yosemite. Start early in the morning and make sure you've eaten everything in your pack. The trailhead is at a minuscule parking lot off Hetch Hetchy Road, 3.9 miles (6.3 km) from the Mather Ranger Station.

BIKING

Road bikers looking for a challenging ride can pedal from Evergreen Lodge or Camp Mather to Hetch Hetchy Reservoir on **Hetch Hetchy Road** (18 mi/29 km round-trip). The route is easy enough on the way in, but the climb back out offers one heck of a workout. Even though plenty of cars utilize this road, they don't cause much of a hazard to cyclists because the narrow, winding thoroughfare forces them to keep their speed down.

For an easier ride on smooth pavement, from Evergreen Lodge pedal 0.5 mile (0.8 km) north on Evergreen Road to Camp Mather. Go left on **Forest Service Road 1S02,** signed for Cherry Lake. The narrow, paved road follows a nearly level contour high above the Tuolumne River Canyon, offering wide views and colorful wildflower displays. At 7 miles (11.3 km) the road intersects with Cherry Lake Road. Retrace your tire tracks here, or turn left and continue 8 miles (12.9 km) to the waterfall and swimming hole at Rainbow Pool.

FISHING

The Tuolumne River is a well-loved trout stream, and some of its best fishing prospects are found in the northwest stretch of Yosemite in and around the Hetch Hetchy region. For good angling only a short drive from Highway 120, head for the **Middle Fork of the Tuolumne River,** which is well stocked with pan-sized rainbow trout. A popular access point is the Middle Fork Day Use Area off Evergreen Road, 1 mile (1.6 km) west of the Big Oak Flat entrance and on the road to

Hetch Hetchy. If you seek more of a challenge, the main branch of the Tuolumne River is a favorite of more seasoned anglers, who ply its waters for trophy-sized native trout.

Many park visitors don't realize that fishing is permitted in **Hetch Hetchy Reservoir.** The lake has brook trout, rainbow trout, and some large brown trout, but because anglers are permitted to fish from shore only, prospects are not great. The warm summer weather makes the fish go deep, and because anglers cannot launch boats into the lake, they have little chance of getting close to the fish. People usually fish while standing on the shoreline using spinners; no live bait is allowed. When they do catch trout, the fish are large. Fishing is best in spring and fall.

Those looking for more of a sure thing head for the west side of **O'Shaughnessy Dam** and the free-flowing stretch of the Tuolumne River. Hiking the short Poopenaut Valley Trail is one way to get to the river, but it's too steep for all but the most ambitious anglers. Many prefer the mellower Preston Flat Trail off Cherry Lake Road.

If you're willing to take a backpacking trip from Hetch Hetchy, you will find plentiful fish in **Laurel Lake** and **Lake Vernon.** Both lakes have self-sustaining populations of rainbow trout, although both lakes are fished heavily. The stretch of **Falls Creek** near Lake Vernon is popular with fly fishers.

Cherry Lake is just outside of the Yosemite National Park boundary in Stanislaus National Forest, so in addition to excellent fishing for rainbow, brook, and brown trout, it features several amenities: a boat launch, a designated swim area, and a Forest Service-operated campground. The lake is stocked regularly.

★ HORSEBACK RIDING

The closest place to rent horses near Hetch Hetchy is at **Mather Saddle and Pack Station** (Camp Mather, 35250 Mather Rd.,

1: Hetch Hetchy **2:** Native American grinding holes along the trail to Smith Peak **3:** Laurel Lake **4:** bridge at Wapama Falls

209/379-2350, www.potagoldadventures.com). One- and two-hour rides are available June-August. A popular choice is the two-hour Breakfast Ride ($93 per person, 8am start); horses and riders travel about an hour over a scenic mountain pass and then drop into a grassy meadow where a big scrambled eggs-and-bacon breakfast is waiting. Another good choice is the two-hour Sunset Ride ($100 per person), in which riders and horses travel along the rim of the Grand Canyon of the Tuolumne River at sunset. The younger set will enjoy the one-hour evening wagon ride, which includes a stop at a roaring campfire to roast s'mores ($22.50).

RAFTING

Just a few miles west of Hetch Hetchy Reservoir lies the **Tuolumne River Canyon,** a spectacular area known to rafters as a whitewater jewel. Several commercial outfitters run trips down the canyon in the summer months. Access to this designated Wild and Scenic stretch of river—known to its biggest fans simply as "the T"—is a few miles off Highway 120 between Groveland and the Big Oak Flat entrance. The rafting put-in point is just north of Buck Meadows; the take-out is at Wards Ferry just east of Don Pedro Reservoir. Rafters usually meet at **La Casa Loma River Store** (Ferretti Rd. off Highway 120), 8 miles (12.9 km) east of Groveland.

Water flow on this 18-mile (29-km) section of the Tuolumne is dependent on releases from Hetch Hetchy, and only two trips are allowed per day, so you won't share this white water with a bunch of other boats. When the river flow is high, it creates an advanced and exciting run in a remote canyon filled with birds, big trout, and other wildlife. Class IV rapids are the rule, not the exception. Clavey Falls, a series of three staircase drops at mile 5.0, creates the biggest drama, but expect nonstop whoops and hollers on this paddle. Leave your cell phone at home; you're in remote wilderness here. You can kiss your digital life good-bye for a day or two.

Several local outfitters offer one-, two-, and

three-day trips on the T April-September. The most luxurious are OARS "Wine on the River" or "Craft Beer Tasting" trips, running on select dates between May and September. After rafting all day, you'll paddle up to camp and enjoy a gourmet riverside dinner served on linen tablecloths. Beverage pairings are carefully selected by a brewmaster or wine expert who accompanies you on the trip. For more information on rafting the T, contact **OARS Inc.** (800/346-6277, www.oars.com), **Zephyr Whitewater** (800/431-3636, www. zrafting.com), **ARTA River Trips** (209/962-7873 or 800/323-2782, www.arta.org), or **All-Outdoors California Whitewater Rafting** (925/932-8993, www.aorafting.com). Typical cost for a one-day trip is $189-249 per person; two-day trips are $329-499 per person; three-day trips are $499-649 per person.

Graduates of the T might want to try a trip on the Upper T, better known as Cherry Creek—an even more thrilling white-water stretch. Contact the outfitters listed above for information on Cherry Creek trips.

Food and Accommodations

There are no accommodations or developed campgrounds in the Hetch Hetchy region of Yosemite. The town of **Groveland**, on Highway 120 about 45 minutes (25 mi/40 km) west of the Big Oak Flat entrance, provides the nearest lodging, camping, and food.

The Hetch Hetchy **backpackers' campsites** (no reservations) are designated for those beginning or ending a wilderness trip. Campers who wish to stay in these sites may do so for only one night before or after their backpacking trip, and they must have their **wilderness permit** in hand. The sites are walk-in only, and only backpacking equipment may be brought in.

Evergreen Lodge

Nine miles (14.5 km) from the Big Oak Flat entrance and about halfway up the road to Hetch Hetchy, ★ **Evergreen Lodge** (33160 Evergreen Rd., Groveland, 209/379-2606 or 800/935-6343, www.evergreenlodge.com, $210-475) is a convenient place to stay for visiting either Yosemite's high country or Hetch Hetchy's spectacular water-filled valley. You can spend a comfortable night in your cabin and then get up early and head to the trailhead at Hetch Hetchy's impressive dam, or drive into the main part of the park and cruise over to Tuolumne Meadows and Tioga Pass. Yosemite Valley is about an hour away.

The lodge's original 16 one- and two-bedroom **cabins,** which date back to the 1920s, sit side by side with 72 brand-new cabins, mostly duplexes. All of the cabins have custom-designed "woodsy" interiors, plus modern features like satellite radio. Those looking for a lower-priced overnight option can stay in one of 16 **"custom campsites"** ($110-145 in summer), which come furnished with tents, mattresses, sleeping bags, and pillows; all you need to bring is your toothbrush. Additionally, large groups can rent the **John Muir House** ($725-1,300 in summer), a 2,500-square-foot (230-sq-m) vacation house.

The lodge can accommodate about 300 people at any one time, and on most summer nights, the resort is completely booked. There are tons of organized activities—nature hikes, full-moon hikes, guided bike rides—most requiring an additional fee. The 2,000-square-foot (185-sq-m) saline swimming pool is a big hit with kids, and an in-ground hot tub can accommodate up to 14 people. With everything going on here, this is an ideal place for families and groups to stay.

The **Evergreen Lodge Restaurant** (7am-10pm daily in summer, shorter hours in winter, $14-28) is worth a stop whether you're staying here or not. The menu changes often, but frequent highlights include wild boar tenderloin, grilled flatiron steak, elk tenderloin, and wild Alaskan salmon. An outdoor dining patio adds more summertime seating options.

Note that Evergreen has a sister resort, Rush Creek Lodge, just a few miles away on Highway 120 (see the *Yosemite Valley* chapter).

Dimond O

Much of the national forest surrounding **Dimond O** (36 sites, 34660 Evergreen Rd., Groveland, 209/379-2258 or 877/444-6777, www.recreation.gov, Apr.-Oct., $26) was badly burned in the Rim Fire of August 2013, but the camp and its immediate surroundings were spared. This medium-sized campground, a short and easy drive off Highway 120, is meticulously managed by a concessionaire for the U.S. Forest Service. It's just far enough off the highway that it is peaceful and quiet amid the incense-cedars and ponderosa pines, but it's still only about 15 minutes from Yosemite's Big Oak Flat entrance. Dimond O makes a convenient choice if you plan to visit Hetch Hetchy (10.5 mi/16.9 km away) or if you want to fish in the Middle Fork of the Tuolumne River. A day-use area for the river is only 0.5 mile (0.8 km) from the camp.

Dimond O's sites are reservable May-September; sites are first come, first served in October and April. The camp has drinking water, picnic tables, fire grills, and vault toilets; small trailers and RVs are fine here. The 4,400-foot (1,300-m) elevation makes for pleasant temperatures, even on the hottest days. And if you feel warm, you can walk a short trail from camp right down to the river.

Dimond O is 5.6 miles (9 km) north of Highway 120 on Evergreen Road. The Evergreen Road turnoff is 25 miles (40 km) east of Groveland or 1 mile (1.6 km) west of the Big Oak Flat entrance.

Camp Mather

A summer camp owned and operated by the city of San Francisco, **Camp Mather** (35250 Mather Rd., Groveland, 209/379-2284, www.campmather.com or www.sfrecpark.org, $8-15 day-use fee, mid-June-mid-Sept.) is just 1.5 miles (2.4 km) south of the Hetch Hetchy entrance to Yosemite. If you're a resident of San Francisco (or a very lucky nonresident), you may be able to win the reservation lottery and reserve a week's stay. Residents get top priority in the lottery ($100 fee), which opens in early January and ends in early February each year. The family-friendly camp consists of 100 rustic **cabins** ($457-1,222 per week) that sleep up to six people and 20 **tent sites** ($247-333 per week). Bathhouses provide water and laundry services. A meal plan purchase ($20-38 per day) is also required.

The Eastern Sierra

Less visited but as spectacular as the high country of Yosemite is the land that lies just east of Tioga Pass along the corridor of U.S. 395. Known in generic terms as the Eastern Sierra, this region includes two major mountain resorts, Mammoth Lakes and June Lake, plus a host of unusual features and destinations, including Bodie State Historic Park, a gold rush-era ghost town, and Mono Lake, a 700,000-year-old saline lake.

The Eastern Sierra also includes another unit of the national park system—Devils Postpile National Monument—plus a wealth of natural resources well suited to outdoor recreationists: mountain slopes for skiers and snowboarders, miles of trails for hikers and equestrians, crystal-clear streams and rivers for anglers, and alpine lakes backed

Highlights

Look for ★ to find recommended sights, activities, dining, and lodging.

★ **Mono Lake:** This saline lake, as large as a small sea, is one of the oldest in North America, having been formed approximately 700,000 years ago. To see it up close, take a hike on the Mark Twain Scenic Tufa Trail or go for a guided canoe tour with the Mono Lake Committee (page 217).

★ **Bodie State Historic Park:** The largest unrestored ghost town in the American West, the 1870s gold rush settlement of Bodie is remarkably well preserved. Take a walk around the old buildings and follow your imagination back in time (page 217).

★ **Bennettville:** Don't miss the easy hike to this site of a 19th-century silver-mining settlement at 10,000 feet (3,000 m) in elevation. A couple of buildings and mine ruins remain from its 1870s heyday (page 219).

★ **Mammoth Lakes Basin:** Five scenic high-alpine lakes here are accessible by car. Dozens more are within easy hiking distance. Hikers, campers, and anglers will be in their element (page 245).

★ **Devils Postpile:** The undisputed highlight of this scenic park along the banks of the San Joaquin River is its namesake, the Devils Postpile, a fascinating collection of columnar basalt "posts" remaining from an ancient lava flow (page 246).

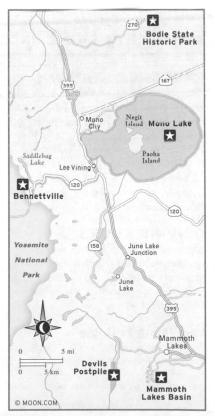

by granite cliffs for photographers and scenery lovers.

Much of this land was once a part of Yosemite National Park. In 1890, when the region surrounding Yosemite Valley was designated by Congress as national parkland, the boundary lines included a large area southeast of today's Yosemite—a wide swath of the Minarets and Ritter Range and the land that is now Devils Postpile National Monument. But pressure from mining and timber interests was so strong that in 1905 land comprising more than 500 square miles (1,300 sq km) on the east side of the Sierra Nevada was removed from federal protection. The miners may have gotten their way, but it didn't work out to their advantage: Despite a massive effort at prospecting for gold and silver in the Eastern Sierra, hardly any was ever found.

PLANNING YOUR TIME

Most of the Eastern Sierra is blanketed in a thick layer of snow **November to May.** However, because winter recreation is so popular in this area, most roads stay plowed and open year-round, except for portions of the June Lake Loop and Highway 120 from Lee Vining into Yosemite. From **Memorial Day until Labor Day,** count on mild days and cool nights at the mostly high elevations of the Eastern Sierra. It is rare for summer daytime temperatures to exceed 85°F (29°C), but nights will often drop down close to freezing. September and October daytime and nighttime temperatures can be considerably cooler, and frost is common on fall evenings.

Exploring the Eastern Sierra

ENTRANCE STATIONS

Yosemite visitors who exit the park from the eastern **Tioga Pass** entrance station make a precipitous descent over the 13 miles (20.9 km) from the entrance station at 9,945 feet (3,030 m) in elevation to the valley floor at U.S. 395 at 6,800 feet (2,070 m). Waiting at the bottom of this spine-tingling drive is the small town of Lee Vining, the gateway to the Eastern Sierra.

DRIVING TOURS

A driving tour of the Eastern Sierra is best split into two parts taking place over two days, with one tour leading north to Bodie State Historic Park and another leading south to Mammoth Lakes.

Lee Vining to Bodie

Pick up snacks and drinks in Lee Vining and then drive 2 miles (3.2 km) north on U.S. 395

to the **Mono Basin Scenic Area Visitor Center** turnoff on the right. Here you can obtain all kinds of information about the region and enjoy a wide vista of Mono Lake from the visitors center's high vantage point.

After a visit, return to U.S. 395 and head north. If you are fortunate enough to be traveling during September or October, turn west at Lundy Lake Road 7 miles (11.3 km) north of Lee Vining and drive through groves of bright yellow quaking aspens to large, narrow **Lundy Lake.** Or continue north on U.S. 395 for 11 more miles (17.7 km), driving over Conway Summit to the right turnoff for **Bodie State Historic Park,** a still-standing ghost town. Turn east here and drive 13 slow miles (20.9 km) to Bodie; the last few miles are gravel. A visit to Bodie can easily take the rest of the day. There are no services or accommodations near Bodie, so plan to return to Lee Vining to spend the night.

Previous: aspen groves on the June Lake Loop; Rainbow Falls at Devils Postpile; Parker Lake.

The Eastern Sierra

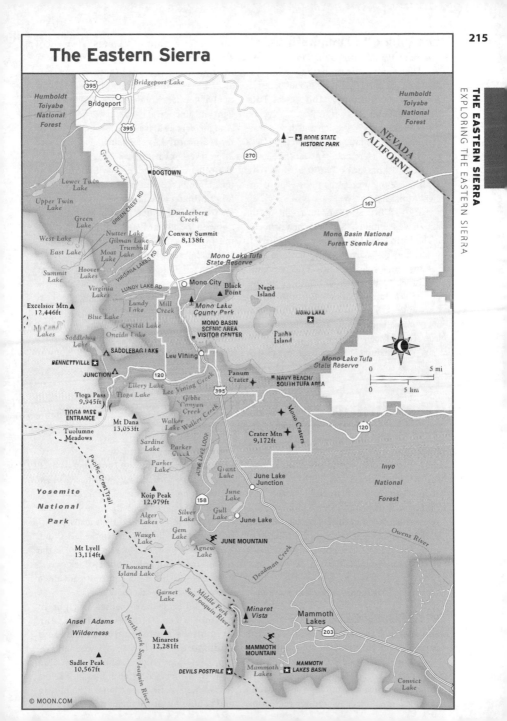

© MOON.COM

Lee Vining to Mammoth Lakes

From Lee Vining at the junction of U.S. 395 and Highway 120, drive south for 5 miles (8 km) on U.S. 395/Highway 120 and turn left (east) for the turnoff to **Mono Lake Tufa State Reserve** (Hwy. 120 East). Drive 4.6 miles (7.4 km); then turn left and drive 1 mile (1.6 km) to the Mono Lake Tufa State Reserve parking area. Here you can walk the level, 1-mile (1.6 km) **Mark Twain Scenic Tufa Trail** to see the tufa spires at the edge of ancient Mono Lake.

Backtrack to U.S. 395 and turn right (north) and drive 0.5 mile (0.8 km) to the north end of the **June Lake Loop** (Hwy. 158). Turn left (west) here and drive the length of the loop, passing four lovely lakes—Grant, Silver, Gull, and June—all of which are set under the imposing granite cliffs of 10,909-foot (3,325-m) Carson Peak. Supplies are available at resorts and stores along the loop and in the main village area of June Lake.

Where the June Lake Loop returns to U.S. 395, head south for 15 miles (24 km) to the turnoff for **Mammoth Lakes** (Hwy. 203). Turn right here and head into the town of Mammoth Lakes, where supplies are available. Then continue beyond the town (for a total of 4 mi/6.4 km from U.S. 395) to a stoplight and junction at Lake Mary Road. Here, go straight on Lake Mary Road for a scenic tour of the **Mammoth Lakes Basin** and its five sparkling lakes, or turn right to stay on Highway 203/Minaret Road for a 5-mile (8-km) drive to the Mammoth Mountain Ski Area. Just beyond it lies Minaret Overlook and the shuttle stop for **Devils Postpile National Monument.** Between the hours of 7am and 7pm, all visitors must ride a shuttle bus into Devils Postpile. If you choose to board a bus into the monument, you'll be granted many options for short hikes and sightseeing. If you don't have the few hours necessary for Devils Postpile, make a quick stop at **Minaret Overlook** and take in a memorable vista of the sawtooth peaks of the Minaret Range. Sunset watching at this drive-up overlook is a deservedly popular activity in Mammoth Lakes.

Lee Vining and Vicinity

People visit the small town of Lee Vining for one of two reasons: to go to Yosemite National Park or to visit Mono Lake. With a population of less than 8,000 year-round residents, Lee Vining subsists primarily on its tourist business, which is strengthened by the fact that U.S. 395 runs right through the middle of town. Lee Vining is composed of a handful of motels, restaurants, gas stations, and stores—everything the traveler might need for visiting its two neighboring world-class attractions.

VISITORS CENTERS

The **Mono Basin Scenic Area Visitor Center** (760/647-3044, 8am-5pm daily Apr.-Nov.) is on the east side of U.S. 395, 1 mile (1.6 km) north of Lee Vining. This large, modern building, perched on a hill high above Mono Lake, is a great place to stop for recreation and local history information. It also boasts an amazing view of Mono Lake from its back deck. Be sure to watch the informative video about Mono Lake entitled *Of Ice and Fire*, which plays every hour in the auditorium. A 1.3-mile-long (2.1-km) trail leads downhill from the visitors center to the lakeshore. North of the visitors center on U.S. 395 is the turnoff for **Mono Lake County Park** (www.monolake.org), where an easy trail leads along a boardwalk to the lakeshore.

A smaller visitors center is right in downtown Lee Vining. The **Mono Lake Committee's Information Center and Bookstore** (760/647-6595, www.monolake.org, 8am-9pm daily in summer, 9am-5pm daily in winter) stocks an impressive selection of hard-to-find books about the human and natural history of the Eastern Sierra and offers plentiful information about Mono Lake's unique features and history.

SIGHTS
★ Mono Lake

You may have heard of **Mono Lake** (www. monolake.org), but until you've seen it, it's hard to imagine. You'll catch your first glimpse as you drive east out of Tioga Pass from Yosemite—an enormous 60,000-acre (24,300 hectare) lake, as wide as a small sea and containing two massive islands. Framed by snowcapped mountains on one side and sagebrush plains on the other, Mono Lake is remarkably photogenic. Almost every evening of summer, photographers line up along the lake's edges in the hope of capturing the perfect sunset image. This saline body of water is one of the oldest lakes in North America. No trip to the Eastern Sierra is complete without a walk to the edge of this mighty, ancient lake.

SOUTH TUFA AREA

The best introduction to Mono Lake is gained by visiting **Mono Lake Tufa State Natural Reserve** (760/647-6331, www.parks.ca.gov, adults $3). From Lee Vining, drive 5 miles (8 km) south on U.S. 395, then turn east on Highway 120 and drive 4.6 miles (7.4 km) to the left turnoff for the reserve. The **Mark Twain Scenic Tufa Trail** (0.5 mi/0.8 km) leads to the edge of the lake, passing its namesake tufa formations along the way. Naturalists from the Mono Lake Committee lead **free guided walks** (10am, 1pm, and 6pm daily in summer) along this trail, but you are also welcome to walk this path on your own. Interpretive signs explain the natural history of the lake and what humans have done to alter it.

The trail is named for American author Mark Twain, who visited the lake in 1863 and wrote extensively about it in his book *Roughing It*. Twain was fascinated by the coral-like structures found near the edges of the lake, called tufa. These off-white mineral formations are created when underwater springs release water containing calcium into the lake bottom, where it combines with the lake's saline water. This process forms calcium carbonate, the chemical expression for tufa.

As you walk the trail, you'll see some high-and-dry inland tufa formations before reaching the lakeshore. The path continues along the edge of the lake, passing miniature islands of tufa. If you touch the tufa, you'll find it feels surprisingly hard, almost like concrete, although it appears brittle to the eye. The tufa formations grow upright, swelling into odd vertical shapes up to 6 feet (1.8 m) high as springwater pushes upward inside them. The tufas only stop growing when exposed to air, which in effect ruins the chemistry experiment. Although tufas are found at various points along Mono Lake's 16,000 acres (6,500 hectares) of lakeshore, the best examples are seen here at the South Tufa Area.

CANOEING AND KAYAKING

Guided canoe tours (760/647-6595, www. monolake.org, $30 per person) on Mono Lake are offered by the Mono Lake Committee on most weekends in summer. Trips leave at 8am, 9:30am, and 11am on weekends and usually last about one hour. Canoes, life jackets, and paddles are provided; no experience is necessary.

Longer, more extensive guided tours are available from **Caldera Kayaks** (Navy Beach, 760/934-1691, www.calderakayak.com, Apr.-Aug., $120 per person for 2 people, $85 per person for 3 or more people). April 1 to August 1, Caldera's paddle trips stick close to Mono Lake's shoreline; after August 1, they lead trips to Paoha Island when weather permits. If you would rather paddle without a guide, you can rent equipment from **Mono Basin Kayak Rentals** (760/937-1934, www. monobasinkayakrental.com, $40-45 per hour, $90 per day), just north of Lee Vining at the Tioga Lodge (54411 U.S. 395).

★ Bodie State Historic Park

One of the most popular tourist attractions in the Eastern Sierra is located way out in the middle of nowhere. **Bodie State Historic**

Saving Mono Lake

canoe tour on Mono Lake

Looking like a small sea surrounded by a vast tract of desert, Mono Lake is three times as salty as the ocean and 80 times as alkaline. Located near the town of Lee Vining, just east of the Sierra's crest at Yosemite National Park, this majestic body of water covers about 60 square miles (155 sq km), its wide expanse filling the landscape to just west of the Nevada state border. Visited by travelers from all over the world, it is one of California's most popular tourist attractions. Photographers, both amateur and professional, are particularly attracted to the lake's unusual scenery and spectacular sunsets.

Among its many charms, Mono Lake is one of the oldest lakes in America, at more than 700,000 years. The lake has no natural outlet, only inlet streams that continually feed it. As a result, over the course of the lake's long life, salts and minerals have washed into its waters from its feeder streams and never left. Freshwater constantly evaporates from the big lake, leaving the salts and minerals behind and creating the tufa formations that line its shoreline and lakebed. If you swim in Mono Lake, you will be nearly buoyant.

The most apparent wildlife at Mono Lake is the birds—many thousands of them. The lake is a major stopover for migratory species passing over the desert lands to the east, and it's also a huge breeding area for California gulls. In fact, 85 percent of the gulls that live on the California coast are born here at Mono Lake. For the birds, Mono Lake's biggest attraction is its population of tiny brine shrimp. From April to November, thick masses of brine shrimp cluster near the lake surface.

Two standout features of Mono Lake are its huge, bald islands, **Paoha** and **Negit.** These islands have figured prominently in the lake's preservation. Starting in 1941, four streams that fed Mono Lake were diverted into the California Aqueduct to provide water for Los Angeles. The lake started to shrink rapidly, losing an average of 18 inches (46 cm) per year. As the water level dropped, a land bridge formed that reached to the islands. Coyotes and other predators could access Paoha and Negit, where gulls and other birds were nesting, and they devastated the bird populations. This led to a long conservation battle that continues to this day. After much legal wrangling, current law states that California's Water Resources Board must regulate the level of Mono Lake so that its natural resources are protected. Since this regulation, the lake level has risen substantially, and it will continue to rise over the coming decades. Today, Mono Lake is viewed as one of California's great environmental victories.

Park (Hwy. 270, Bridgeport, 760/647-6445, www.parks.ca.gov, 9am-6pm daily Apr.-Oct., 9am-4pm daily Nov.-Apr., access Nov.-Feb. may require snow transportation, $8 adult, $5 children 6-16, children under 6 free), the largest unrestored ghost town in the American West, sprawls across a windswept valley in the hills north of Mono Lake. The state-run park is a genuine 1870s gold-mining town, devoid of the scourge of tourist shops and high-priced entrance fees that travelers find at many other California ghost towns.

The town's history is similar to that of many other gold rush towns throughout the Sierra Nevada, except that everything that happened here took place on a larger, more exaggerated scale. Gold was discovered in Bodie in 1859. The town experienced its heyday in the 1870s, when it boasted more than 30 operating mines, 65 saloons and dance halls, three breweries, and a population of more than 10,000 people. Partly because of its remote location far from law-abiding civilization (the area around Bodie was then, and still is now, an extremely desolate region southeast of Bridgeport), the town developed a reputation for having more drinking, gambling, and shooting than any other mining town. Robberies, stage holdups, and street fights took place in the course of a normal week. Killings occurred frequently; death was too often the answer to any disagreement.

Like most mining towns, Bodie eventually suffered a complete decline, and all its residents moved elsewhere. Oddly, they seemed to have departed in a hurry. The townspeople left the store shelves stocked and the school with writing on the blackboard.

With some minimal help from California State Parks, Bodie's buildings have withstood the test of time. The town is maintained in a state of "arrested decay," which means the powers that be don't fix up the structures, but they don't let them fall down, either. Visitors can walk around the streets of town, peek in the windows of buildings, and imagine what life was like in another era. The **Bodie State Park Foundation** (760/647-6564, www.

bodiefoundation.org) offers several **guided tours** in spring and summer, including daily history talks and stamp mill tours (50 minutes, May-Sept., $6 per person). There is a **museum** and **visitors center** (daily mid-May to mid-Oct., hours vary), but there is no food, gas, or services of any kind along the road to Bodie; stock your car with everything you need before making the long drive.

To get to Bodie from Lee Vining, drive 18 miles (29 km) north on U.S. 395 and turn east on Highway 270. It's 13 miles (20.9 km) to the ghost town (the last few miles are gravel).

Autumn Color Scenic Drives

If you are fortunate enough to visit the Eastern Sierra during mid-late September or early October, you are in for a visual treat. Mountain canyons and lakeshores are transformed by blazing shows of autumn color, thanks to the quaking aspens and cottonwoods. The best fall color viewing is generally found in **Lee Vining Canyon,** along Highway 120 from U.S. 395 west to Tioga Pass (road closed in winter); in **Lundy Canyon,** 7 miles (11.3 km) north of Lee Vining on U.S. 395 (turn left onto Lundy Lake Rd.); and along the **June Lake Loop** (Hwy. 158 at U.S. 395). Don't forget your camera.

RECREATION
Hiking
An amazing wealth of hiking trails is found in the region just east of Yosemite's Tioga Pass entrance station. With few exceptions, these trails feature scenic beauty that rivals anything you'll find in Yosemite, but they are usually much less crowded than park trails. The following are some of the best trail choices (listed in order of their proximity to the Tioga Pass entrance station). For more information on any hikes in the area, contact the Mono Basin Scenic Area Visitor Center (760/647-3044).

★ BENNETTVILLE
Distance: 2.6 miles (4.2 km) round-trip
Duration: 1 hour

Lee Vining Hikes

Trail	Effort	Distance	Duration
Bennettville	Easy	2.6 mi/4.2 km rt	1 hr
Slate Creek Trail to Green Treble Lake	Easy	4.5 mi/7.2 km rt	2 hr
Gardisky Lake	Moderate	2 mi/3.2 km rt	1.5 hr
Lundy Canyon	Moderate	4.4-10 mi/7.1-16.1 km rt	2-5 hr
Gibbs Lake	Moderate	5.4 mi/8.7 km rt	2.5 hr
Virginia Lakes Trail	Moderate	6.2-10.2 mi/10-16.4 km rt	3-5 hr
Lake Canyon and May Lundy Mine	Moderate	7 mi/11.3 km rt	3.5 hr
Saddlebag Lake and 20 Lakes Basin	Moderate	8.4 mi/13.5 km rt	4 hr
Green Creek Trail to Green Lake	Moderate/strenuous	4.6 mi/7.4 km rt	3 hr

Elevation Change: 500 feet (150 m)

Effort: Easy

Trailhead: Junction Campground

Directions: From the Tioga Pass entrance to Yosemite, drive east on Highway 120 for 2 miles (3.2 km) to the left turnoff for Saddlebag Lake. Turn left and then left again immediately to enter Junction Campground. The trail begins at the campground entrance.

This first-class high-country hike is suitable for even the most novice hikers and is sure to spark your imagination. The remote high-country region of Bennettville was the site of a 19th-century silver-mining community. Although the town thrived only from 1882 to 1884, it was the primary reason for the construction of the Tioga Pass Road from the west. The original road, called the Great Sierra Wagon Road, was built by the Great Sierra Consolidated Silver Company in anticipation of the riches it would make from the mines at Bennettville and nearby. Ultimately, no valuable minerals were ever extracted, and the company went broke in record time. A mostly level trail leads to the two buildings that remain from Bennettville's heyday: the assay office and a **barn/bunkhouse.** An open mine tunnel lined with railcar tracks can also be seen, as can some rusting mining equipment. Much of the machinery and supplies for this mine were hauled here from the May Lundy Mine over Dore Pass. Men and animals carried several tons of equipment on their backs and on sleds, sometimes through driving snowstorms in the middle of winter at this 10,000-foot (300-m) elevation.

You can extend this hike by following the trail alongside **Mine Creek** 0.5 mile (0.8 km) uphill from the mine buildings to small Shell Lake, which is followed by three more shallow lakes in the next mile or so: Mine, Fantail, and finally Spuller. More mine sites can be seen along the way. The high-country landscape here is a mix of open meadows, delicate high-alpine wildflowers, and wind-sculpted whitebark pines. The scenery is as photogenic as you'll find anywhere, and you'll want to return to this area again and again.

GARDISKY LAKE

Distance: 2 miles (3.2 km) round-trip

Duration: 1.5 hours

Elevation Change: 800 feet (245 m)
Effort: Moderate
Trailhead: Gardisky Lake
Directions: From the Tioga Pass entrance to Yosemite, drive east on Highway 120 for 2 miles (3.2 km) to the left turnoff for Saddlebag Lake. Turn left and drive 1.3 miles (2.1 km) north on Saddlebag Lake Road; the parking area is on the left side of the road and the trail is on the right.

A short but fairly difficult trail leads to lovely Gardisky Lake. The **1-mile** (1.6 km) trail goes straight up, gaining 800 feet (245 m) in too little distance, with not nearly enough switchbacks. To make matters more difficult, the trailhead is at 10,000 feet (3,000 m), which means you will want to be acclimated to the high elevation before you pant your way up this kind of grade. The trip offers many rewards, though, such as fewer people than at nearby Saddlebag Lake and a stellar high-alpine setting.

Once you gain the ridgetop, you have a nearly level **0.25-mile** (0.4-km) stroll through a fragile alpine meadow to reach **Gardisky Lake,** a shallow body of water. It's not the lake itself that is the highlight of this trail; it's the beauty and delicacy of the total landscape at this high elevation. That 11,500-foot (3,500-m) mountain you see as you climb (ahead and to your right) is Tioga Peak; some hikers choose to ascend to its summit from Gardisky Lake. White Mountain and Mount Conness, both over 12,000 feet (3,600 m), are also prominent.

SADDLEBAG LAKE AND 20 LAKES BASIN

Distance: 8.4 miles (13.5 km) round-trip
Duration: 4 hours
Elevation Change: 800 feet (245 m)
Effort: Moderate
Trailhead: Saddlebag Lake
Directions: From the Tioga Pass entrance to Yosemite, drive east on Highway 120 for 2 miles (3.2 km) to the left turnoff for Saddlebag Lake. Turn left and drive 2.7 miles (4.3 km) north on Saddlebag Lake Road to the trailhead parking area.

Starting from the (now closed) resort buildings at the south end of Saddlebag Lake (10,087 ft/3,075 m elevation), you can design a wonderfully scenic hiking trip into the 20 Lakes Basin of any length that suits your time and energy. To get started, follow the **trail** on either the lake's east or west side. The east side trail is more scenic; the west side trail is shorter. If you just want to make a **short 3.6-mile (5.8-km) loop,** hike out on one trail and back on the other, but be sure to take the short **left spur** at Saddlebag's northwest edge to **Greenstone Lake,** which is backed by photogenic North Peak.

If you want to hike farther, you can continue past Greenstone Lake to **Wasco Lake** and then on to deep, stark **Steelhead Lake** (3 mi/4.8 km out if you start on the west side trail). Several more lakes lie beyond, including Shamrock, Helen, and Odell. If you hike the entire loop and visit all six lakes that lie immediately beyond Saddlebag, you'll have an 8.4-mile (13.5-km) day. No matter how far you go, you'll be awed by the incredible high-country scenery—a blend of blue sky, granite, water, and hardy whitebark pines.

SLATE CREEK TRAIL TO GREEN TREBLE LAKE

Distance: 4.5 miles (7.2 km) round-trip
Duration: 2 hours
Elevation Change: 500 feet (150 m)
Effort: Easy
Trailhead: Sawmill Campground
Directions: From the Tioga Pass entrance to Yosemite, drive east on Highway 120 for 2 miles (3.2 km) to the left turnoff for Saddlebag Lake. Turn left and drive 1.5 miles (2.4 km) north on Saddlebag Lake Road to Sawmill Campground's parking area on the left.

One of the most beautiful and serene campgrounds in the High Sierra, **Sawmill Campground** is accessed by a 0.25-mile (0.4-km) walk from its parking area. The trail continues through and past the campground's widely spaced sites into **Hall Research Natural Area,** a specially protected region of Inyo National Forest that is open to day hikers only (no backpacking). The trail leads 1 mile (1.6 km) to **Timberline Station,** an old research station built in 1929. From here you can ford Slate Creek and hike another 1 mile (1.6 km) to Green Treble Lake at the headwaters of Slate Creek. Where two forks of the creek join, about **0.5 mile** (0.8 km) beyond Timberline Station, follow the south fork (left) another **0.5 mile** (0.8 km) to **Green Treble Lake.** This is a remarkably level hike at 10,000-plus feet (3,000-plus m) in elevation—pristine high country that is only accessible a few months each year.

GIBBS LAKE

Distance: 5.4 miles (8.7 km) round-trip
Duration: 2.5 hours
Elevation Change: 1,500 feet (455 m)
Effort: Moderate
Trailhead: Upper Horse Meadow
Directions: From Lee Vining, drive 1.3 miles (2.1 km) south on U.S. 395 and turn west on an unsigned road, which is Forest Road 1N16. Drive 3.4 miles (5.5 km), past Upper Horse Meadow, to the trailhead at the end of the road. A high-clearance vehicle is recommended.

The **2.7-mile** (4.3-km) hike (one-way) from Upper Horse Meadow to Gibbs Lake is a great day hike that sees surprisingly few people. Because the trailhead isn't located at a lake or some other attractive setting, nobody gets here by accident. The trail starts at Upper Horse Meadow (elevation 8,000 ft/2,400 m) and climbs up Gibbs Canyon to Gibbs Lake, which sits at 9,530 feet (2,900 m). That's about a 1,500-foot (455-m) climb, and unfortunately the first stretch goes **straight uphill** on an old dirt road with nary a switchback. Once you get through that grunt of an ascent, the rest of the route is on a much mellower grade as it travels alongside **Gibbs Creek.** The trail ends at **Gibbs Lake,** a lovely glacial cirque that is backed by bare granite and fronted by conifers.

Are you feeling ambitious? Study the lake's back wall for a few minutes, and it will soon become obvious that there is another, higher lake in this drainage. If you are sure-footed and have plenty of energy, you can pick out your route and go take a look at that lake. Although Gibbs Lake is pretty, the higher

Kidney Lake (10,388 ft/3,166 m) is a stunner. It will take you about 40 minutes of challenging cross-country scrambling to get from Gibbs to Kidney; you'll gain almost 900 feet (275 m) in less than a mile. Just pick your route carefully and go slowly. Kidney Lake is indeed kidney-shaped, and is flanked by the Dana Plateau on one side and Mount Gibbs (12,773 ft/3,893 m) on the other.

LAKE CANYON AND MAY LUNDY MINE

Distance: 7 miles (11.3 km) round-trip
Duration: 3.5 hours
Elevation Change: 1,000 feet (300 m)
Effort: Moderate
Trailhead: Lundy Lake's dam
Directions: From Lee Vining, drive north on U.S. 395 for 7 miles (11.3 km) to Lundy Lake Road. Turn west on Lundy Lake Road and drive 5 miles (8 km) to Lundy Lake's dam. Turn left and drive 0.25 mile (0.4 km) to a locked gate and trailhead.

The Lundy Lake area is blessed with two first-rate day-hiking trails that lead into two separate and distinct canyons: Lundy Canyon and Lake Canyon. Both paths offer so many rewards that when you drive up to Lundy Lake, it's hard to decide which one to take. History buffs and fishing-minded hikers would do well to take this trip from Lundy's dam into Lake Canyon, where they can see the remains of the May Lundy Mine. The mine was worked continuously for two decades starting in 1878, producing a total of about $2 million in gold. As a result, the surrounding community of Lundy grew to support 500 people, despite severe winters and deadly avalanches. Besides mining, a primary activity here was the operation of three sawmills along Lundy Creek, used to supply timber to the nearby bustling gold rush town of Bodie.

The hike to the May Lundy Mine is a fairly **steep 3.5 miles** (5.6 km) one-way, climbing above Lundy Lake on the old mine road that

---

1: the visitors center at Mono Lake 2: tufa towers at Mono Lake 3: Gardisky Lake 4: old mining cabin in Bennettville

was built in 1881. You can see the trail plain as day from the trailhead on the east side of Lundy Lake. The road/trail passes **Blue Lake** and **Crystal Lake,** where mining relics can be found. (Crystal Lake is 0.3 mi/0.5 km off the trail via a left fork.) Continue on the main trail, and you'll see the **mine remains**—old railcar tracks, tailings, and a closed-off mine shaft. Just beyond is **Oneida Lake,** whose waters were used to run the stamp mill for the mine. Even without the fascinating traces of history, this is an extraordinarily beautiful place. You'll want to linger for a while at sparkling Oneida Lake; both the scenery and the fishing are quite rewarding.

LUNDY CANYON

Distance: 4.4-10 miles (7.1-16.1 km) round-trip
Duration: 2-5 hours
Elevation Change: 400-1,500 feet (120-455 m)
Effort: Moderate
Trailhead: Lundy Lake
Directions: From Lee Vining, drive north on U.S. 395 for 7 miles (11.3 km) to Lundy Lake Road. Turn west on Lundy Lake Road and drive 5 miles (8 km) to Lundy Lake. Continue past the lake for 2 more unpaved miles (3.2 km) to the end of the road and the trailhead.

The Lundy Canyon Trail is the back door into the **20 Lakes Basin,** a well-traveled area of the Hoover Wilderness that is most commonly accessed from Saddlebag Lake off Highway 120. The trailhead lies about 2 miles (3.2 km) past Lundy Lake, a long, narrow pool set at 7,800 feet (2,400 m). From here, the trail rises alongside Mill Creek, passing several beaver ponds, a dilapidated trapper's cabin, and two small but boisterous waterfalls (Lower and Upper Lundy Falls, also called **Mill Creek Falls**).

Most visitors hike to the first or second falls, enjoying the gorgeous Eastern Sierra scenery with a relatively mellow walk, and then hike back out. Those who continue farther find that the trail, which climbed gently but steadily for the first **2.2 miles (3.5 km),** suddenly reaches what appears to be the back of the canyon. But look straight up the canyon wall to your left—that's where a narrow "goat trail" continues uphill to the 20 Lakes Basin. This unmaintained route leads **0.8 mile** (1.3 km) upward through a frighteningly steep wall of shale. The Forest Service has long since stopped maintaining this trail, which is hit by avalanches almost every winter. But still, every summer some hikers insist on climbing it. Do so at your own risk—it's sketchy at best and perilous at worst.

Note that one of the best times to visit

Oneida Lake lies beyond the mine ruins at the end of the Lake Canyon Trail.

here is in **October,** when Lundy Canyon's stands of quaking aspen turn bright gold and seem to dance in the breeze. This is one of the best places to admire fall colors in the Eastern Sierra. **July** is another first-rate time to visit; the canyon's wildflower displays are remarkable.

VIRGINIA LAKES TRAIL

Distance: 6.2 10.2 miles (10-16.4 km) round-trip
Duration: 3-5 hours
Elevation Change: 1,400 feet (425 m)
Effort: Moderate
Trailhead: Big Virginia Lake
Directions: From Lee Vining, drive 12 miles (19.3 km) north on U.S. 395 to Conway Summit. Turn west on Virginia Lakes Road and drive 6.5 miles (10.5 km) to the trailhead at the Big Virginia Lake day-use area.

By following the Virginia Lakes Trail, you can easily hike to a series of high-alpine lakes—eight are found within a 2-mile (3.2-km) radius. The trailhead is at 9,500 feet (2,900 m), and from there you hike west past **Blue Lake** to **Cooney Lake** and on to **Frog Lakes** (a very easy **1.4 mi/2.3 km**). You then start climbing in earnest, continuing almost **1.8 more miles (2 km)** to 11,110 foot (3,385-m) **Summit Pass** (sometimes called Burro Pass). The landscape is windswept, barren, and beautiful—a mix of rock, occasional whitebark pines, and high-alpine wildflowers. Many hikers take a look at the scene from the pass and then retreat to one of the aforementioned lakes to spend the afternoon, resulting in a **6.2-mile (10-km) day.**

If you continue beyond the pass, you curve downhill through dozens of switchbacks for **1.4 miles** (2.3 km) and then climb gently **0.5 mile** (0.8 km) west to **Summit Lake** at 10,203 feet (3,110 m) in elevation, on the northeast boundary of Yosemite National Park. Summit Lake is set between Camiaca Peak (11,739 ft/3,578 m) to the north and Excelsior Mountain (12,446 ft/3,794 m) to the south. This is the logical place for backpackers to make **camp** and for day-trippers to turn around for a **10.2-mile (16.4-km) day** (with an elevation change of 2,400 ft/730 m).

GREEN CREEK TRAIL TO GREEN LAKE

Distance: 4.6 miles (7.4 km) round-trip
Duration: 3 hours
Elevation Change: 1,045 feet (320 m)
Effort: Moderate to strenuous
Trailhead: Green Creek
Directions: From Bridgeport, drive south on U.S. 395 for 4.5 miles (7.2 km) to Green Creek Road (dirt). Turn west and drive 8.2 miles (13.2 km) to the signed trailhead parking area shortly before Green Creek Campground.

It's only 4.6 miles (7.4 km) round-trip to **Green Lake,** just one of three beautiful lakes—Green, East, and West—situated right around 9,000 feet (2,750 m) in elevation in the spectacular Hoover Wilderness. They offer fair trout fishing and are accessible via the Green Creek Trail (sometimes called the Green Lake Trail). The Green Creek Trail climbs, of course—not so much that you'll be worn out when you reach Green Lake, but rather just enough to provide you with expansive valley views most of the way. The path closely parallels the tumbling cascades of the west fork of Green Creek, and the July wildflower show is outstanding here. (The autumn aspen show is also noteworthy.) The main trail reaches the lakeshore 600 feet (185 m) past the West Lake turnoff.

East Lake can be reached by heading left off the main trail and gaining another 500 feet (150 m) in elevation over 2 miles (3.2 km) for an 8.6-mile (13.8-km) round-trip (with an elevation gain of 1,460 ft/445 m). Or, you can take a 1.5-mile (2.4-km) spur off the main trail for a much steeper (but well worth it) jaunt to stark, rockbound West Lake. The turnoff for **West Lake** is on the right at 2.2 miles (3.5 km); it's 4.2 miles (6.8 km) from the Green Lakes Trailhead to West Lake with 2,050 feet (625 m) of elevation gain. The trail makes a memorably steep 1,000-foot (300-m) ascent over 1.5 miles (2.4 km), climbing high above Green Lake. After the easy grade of the first 2 miles (3.2 km) of trail, this last stretch can really take you by surprise. For solitude lovers, West Lake is your best bet—but all three lakes are sparkling, rockbound gems, so you can't go wrong here no matter which one you choose to visit.

Some people make a short backpacking trip out of this hike and see all three lakes. If you do, note that Green Lake is the only one of the three that is just below 9,000 feet (2,750 m) in elevation, which means it is the only one where campfires are permitted. (You must use the established campfire rings.) At the other, higher lakes, only backpacking stoves are allowed. The fishing is generally better at East and West Lakes than at Green Lake, although it's nothing to write home about—the high mountain scenery, on the other hand, will knock your socks off.

Biking

Just east of the Tioga Pass entrance to Yosemite lies a U.S. Forest Service-sanctioned trail built just for fat-tire lovers. The **Moraines and Meadows Loop** (11.4 mi/18.4 km round-trip) starts by Highway 120, but the route quickly enters a world of alpine meadows and glacial moraines. The trail provides wide looks at giant-sized Mono Lake and the neighboring Mono Craters, and adds a visit to Upper and Lower Horse Meadows. A predominant feature is also visible: the Los

Angeles Aqueduct. To reach the trailhead from U.S. 395 in Lee Vining, drive west on Highway 120 for 3 miles (4.8 km); then turn left at the Lee Vining Ranger Station and park at the signed trailhead.

Several other trails in this region of Inyo National Forest are also open to mountain bikers. The best source of information is the **Mono Basin Scenic Area Visitor Center** (1 mi/1.6 km north of Lee Vining on U.S. 395, 760/647-3044, www.fs.usda.gov, 8am-5pm daily Apr.-Nov.).

Fishing

Some of the best fishing in California is found in the lakes and streams of the Eastern Sierra.

ALONG HIGHWAY 120

Saddlebag Lake is the highest California lake you can drive to, at elevation 10,087 feet (3,075 m). Many anglers fish from the lakeshore for golden, brook, or rainbow trout. There are no services here—Saddlebag Lake Resort has been closed for several years, although its buildings still stand. Saddlebag Lake is 2 miles (3.2 km) east of the Tioga Pass entrance or 13 miles (20.9 km) west of Lee Vining on Highway 120. From Highway 120, turn north

fishing in the Eastern Sierra

Trout of the Eastern Sierra

Trout fishing in the Eastern Sierra is some of the best to be found in California. Regularly stocked streams and lakes tucked into mountain canyons on the west side of U.S. 395 provide dependably good fishing. East of U.S. 395, fly fishers can test dry-fly and nymphing skills for wild trout on classic spring creek sections of the Owens River and Hot Creek.

When fishing in the lakes and streams of the Eastern Sierra, expect to catch one of five trout species. The most common is the colorful **rainbow trout,** distinguished by its signature pink or rose stripe on its side and black spots on its olive-colored back. Despite these fairly distinctive markings, this species can fool anglers by taking on a wide variety of shapes, colors, and sizes, which vary according to the conditions found in the water in which it lives.

The second most common trout species, and the most common in high-alpine lakes, is the **brook trout.** These trout are not native to California and were first planted here in the 1870s. The "brookie" is considered by many the best-tasting trout, and it is generally quite easy to catch. The fish are dark gray or olive, with many large yellowish spots and a few small red spots. Their bellies are white except during spawning, when the males develop a bright reddish orange color on their undersides. Brook trout are the smallest of the five Eastern Sierra trout; adults are typically only 9-11 inches (23-28 cm), whereas other trout species grow to 14 inches (36 cm) and larger.

The **brown trout** is also not native to California, although it has been planted here since the late 1800s. The species comes from Europe and is common in Germany and Scotland. True to their name, brown trout are brown on top with olive-colored sides, usually dotted with large dark brown spots and small red spots. The brown trout can tolerate higher water temperatures than other trout.

Two other species of trout are caught in the Eastern Sierra, although more rarely than the others. The **golden trout** is a close cousin to the rainbow trout and is even more colorful. With a bright golden-yellow color on its sides and lower parts, its identity is unmistakable. It has gray-and-red patches along its lateral line and a bright red belly. The golden trout is California's official state fish, although its numbers have dwindled significantly throughout the state. It is native only in Kern County in the southern portion of the Sierra Nevada. Golden trout often breed with rainbow trout, creating a hybrid species.

The **cutthroat trout,** with its olive and rust-colored body painted with black spots and a distinctive slash of red on both sides of its throat, is found only in limited areas of the Eastern Sierra: June Lake, the Upper Owens River, Crowley Lake (south of Mammoth Lakes), Topaz Lake, and the Walker River (north of Bridgeport).

Remember to always check with local fish and tackle stores or marinas for updates on fishing regulations. What is legal at one spot in the Eastern Sierra may not be legal at another.

on Saddlebag Lake Road and drive 2.5 miles (4 km) north to the lake.

Tioga and **Ellery Lakes** are both within 4 miles (6.4 km) east of the Tioga Pass entrance station along Highway 120, and are popular with shore fishers and anglers using float tubes. Both brook and rainbow trout are caught at the two lakes.

Lee Vining Creek parallels Highway 120 in the stretch from Tioga Pass to U.S. 395. An access road runs between U.S. 395 and the stream, allowing entrance to a series of campgrounds. The creek is an excellent place for both fly fishing and bait fishing. The town

of Lee Vining has shops with bait, tackle, and plenty of fishing advice.

ALONG U.S. 395

From Lee Vining, drive 6 miles (9.7 km) north on U.S. 395 and turn left onto Lundy Lake Road to reach cobalt-blue Lundy Lake, where brown and rainbow trout are regularly planted by the Department of Fish and Wildlife. **Lundy Lake Resort** (626/309-0415) rents boats with or without motors, and plenty of anglers fish from shore, too. Mill Creek, the stream that feeds Lundy Lake, is also stocked.

Anglers who hike into Lundy Canyon can catch brook and rainbow trout.

Twelve miles (19.3 km) north of Lee Vining on U.S. 395, turn left for Virginia Lakes Road and three more lakes: **Little Virginia, Big Virginia,** and **Trumbull Lakes.** All three are planted weekly with rainbow trout, and trophy fish are stocked on a monthly basis. **Virginia Lakes Resort** (Virginia Lakes Rd., 760/647-6484, www.virginialakesresort.com, June-Sept.), at Little Virginia Lake, offers services. The three lakes, plus seven others in the surrounding basin, also contain populations of eastern brook and German brown trout.

Horseback Riding

The **Virginia Lakes Pack Outfit** (Virginia Lakes Rd., 760/937-0326, www.virginialakes.com), 12 miles (19.3 km) north of Lee Vining and 6 miles (9.7 km) west of U.S. 395, specializes in multiday pack trips into the Hoover Wilderness. They also offer fly-fishing trips and 2.5-hour rides ($95 per person), four-hour rides ($105 per person), and all-day rides that include lunch ($150 per person).

Winter Sports

Mammoth Mountain in Mammoth Lakes may be a world-famous skiing and snowboarding hot spot, but the Lee Vining and Tioga Pass area has its own claim to fame in the winter sports category. It's not the type of sport that appeals to those who ride the gondola wearing the latest ski fashions, but the skiing just outside of **Tioga Pass** is world-class. There are no lift lines, lift tickets, or even lifts; the slopes around Tioga Pass are a telemark (free heel) skier's paradise. Most years, both deep powder and spring corn snow are in plentiful supply, but they come with a price: Just getting to Tioga Pass requires a hefty hike (or shuffle, if you are wearing skis) of about 6 miles (9.7 km) from the point where Tioga Pass Road is gated. If everything goes well, you'll make it a few miles farther to Tuolumne Meadows, where you can stay overnight in the **ski hut** (no reservations; it's first come, first served).

FOOD
Lee Vining and Vicinity
TIOGA GAS MART AND WHOA NELLIE DELI

It's not often that people plan on going to a gas station for dinner, but in Lee Vining hundreds of people do just that every day. The ★ **Tioga Gas Mart** (junction of Hwy. 120 and U.S. 395, Lee Vining, 760/647-1088, www.whoanelliedeli.com, 6am-9pm daily in summer, closed in winter, $15-22) isn't any ordinary gas station—it's the home of the **Whoa Nellie Deli,** which makes truly outstanding fast food for breakfast, lunch, and dinner. Are you hungry? Imagine portions big enough for a pack of rock climbers. Are you craving fast food with real flavor? Try the lobster taquitos on a bed of black beans with tomatillo pineapple salsa ($16). Want a big meal? Order buffalo meatloaf with port wine au jus ($19). If you're driving, stay far away from the easy-to-slurp mango margaritas. The deli also makes sandwiches, veggie burgers, hamburgers, hot dogs, and pizza, by the slice or whole. Breakfast includes cowboy steak and eggs, omelets, and Tioga egg sandwiches ($8-15). For the caffeine-addicted, espresso drinks are available. On weekend nights, this place often turns into a big party scene, complete with a live band.

EPIC CAFÉ

A relative newcomer in Lee Vining, **Epic Café** (349 Lee Vining Ave., Lee Vining, 760/965-6282, www.epiccafesierra.com, 7am-9pm Mon.-Sat., $7-10) opened in 2016 on the grounds of Lakeview Lodge. Chef Linda Dore, who has run a catering business in the Eastern Sierra for 15 years, serves up three meals a day in a charming garden setting. The breakfast menu includes frittatas, waffles, and bagels with gravlax. Lunch consists of paninis and variety of salads (Caesar, kale, spinach, and more); dinner entrées vary daily. The café serves wine and beer, too, and you can eat outdoors among the flowers or indoors in the colorful café.

Dining East of the Park: U.S. 395

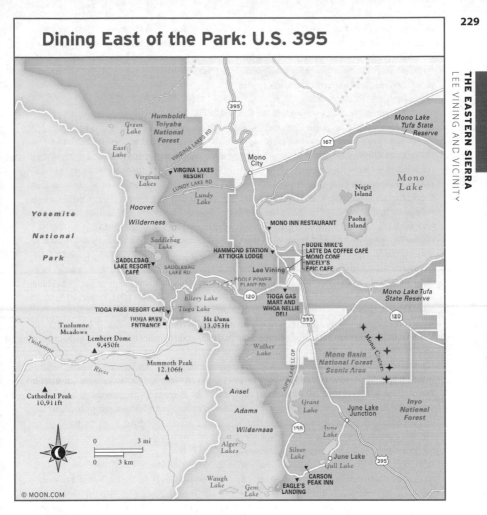

© MOON.COM

NICELY'S

Lee Vining's version of a Denny's, **Nicely's** (51343 U.S. 395, Lee Vining, 760/647-6477, 7am-9pm daily in summer, 7am-9pm Thurs.-Mon. in winter, $9-20) serves conventional American food for breakfast, lunch, and dinner. The food goes along with the Mayberry-style decor, which looks like it hasn't been updated since the 1950s. No matter, though; if you are hungry, you'll be happy to partake in the huge meals at this family restaurant where even the menu is large. Breakfast is highlighted by pancakes that are almost a foot in diameter. Lunch includes salads and hot sandwiches, including classics like the patty melt, chili size, or French dip. Dinners include seafood, steaks, fried chicken, and pasta dishes. The homemade pies and milk shakes are always a hit. A children's menu is available.

BODIE MIKE'S

Always a happening place on warm summer evenings, **Bodie Mike's** (51357 U.S. 395, Lee Vining, 760/647-6432, 11:30am-10pm daily in summer, $16-26) is the place to go when you are craving a big slab of ribs (beef or pork) or half a barbecued chicken. Barbecue sandwiches are a great choice for lunch ($10). The beer-battered onion ring appetizer is a big hit, but after you eat it you probably won't have room for dinner. A children's menu allows the little ones to eat for about $5.

Diners can sit indoors or outside on the deck overlooking Lee Vining's main drag, and drinkers can hang out at the bar. Besides the relaxed atmosphere and the finger-licking food, a big hit with customers is the roll of dental floss on a fishing reel available for the taking at the cash register. (It's a big relief to remove those last bits of grilled meat from your molars.) Another highlight is the framed display showing 24 different types of barbed wire and their respective names. Choose your favorite, and then go home and fence in those dang wanderin' cattle.

LATTE DA COFFEE CAFÉ

A cheerful little espresso café at the age-old El Mono Motel serves as the center of community life in Lee Vining. The offerings at **Latte Da Coffee Café** (51 U.S. 395, Lee Vining, 760/647-6310, www.elmonomotel.com, 7am-8pm daily in summer) include espresso drinks and exotic teas, plus a few tasty baked goods (huge cookies and an unforgettable pumpkin spice cake). Buy a book at the neighboring Mono Lake visitors center and sit at one of this café's handful of tables, or grab a spot out on the porch to listen in on the local gossip. In summer, the motel's sunflower-filled gardens and flitting goldfinches and hummingbirds will entice you to hang out all day. If you make a purchase, you can get the code for the wireless Internet and email Tioga Pass photos to all your jealous friends.

MONO CONE

They might as well call this place "Mondo Cone." The portions, and the menu itself, are as big as the neighboring saline lake. **Mono Cone** (U.S. 395, Lee Vining, 760/647-6606, 11am-6pm summer only, $6-8, cash only) serves an amazing array of burgers (blue cheese, bacon, guacamole, Ortega chili, you

name it), fries, and ice cream. The list of possible milk shake options alone will leave you shaking your head. Indoor and outdoor seating is available.

HAMMOND STATION AT TIOGA LODGE

Hammond Station Restaurant (U.S. 395, 2 mi/3.2 km north of Lee Vining, 760/647-6423, www.tiogalodgeatmonolake.com, 7:30am-10:30am and 5:30pm-9:30pm daily, $11-25) is located at Tioga Lodge in a 100-year-old building that was moved here from the town of Bodie. The wood-plank floor under the dining tables looks antique, but in fact the owners had to remove the original floor due to rot and old age. They photographed it first, though, and had a nearby mill make identical boards out of the same type of lumber. These boards were then carefully installed to create an exact duplicate.

Tioga Lodge's owners put the same kind of painstaking effort into their restaurant's food. Breakfast entrées include pancakes, tofu or egg scrambles, and omelets stuffed with a variety of fillings. Dinner is more eclectic; it could be shepherd's pie, spaghetti and meatballs, or an Asian lettuce wrap. In summer, seating is available outside on the patio.

MONO INN

The views of Mono Lake from the historic **Mono Inn** (55260 U.S. 395, 5 mi/8 km north of Lee Vining, 760/647-6581, www.monoinn. com, 5pm-9pm daily, $20-38) will blow you away, but the food is even more surprising. The menu offers interesting choices like a roasted beet salad, braised bison, and spiced pork tenderloin. More traditional eaters can stick to the New York steak or grilled salmon. Reservations are a good idea, especially on weekends. On warm evenings, be sure to ask for a seat on the outside patio, although indoor diners are also treated to a mesmerizing lake view through the restaurant's big windows. The old wooden cottage has some interesting history: It was once the site of a destination resort on Mono Lake and its islands, where guests would water-ski, fish, and hike. Since 1996, the inn has been owned by descendants of Ansel Adams, the great photographer.

Virginia Lakes
VIRGINIA LAKES RESORT

You might not think of eating at **Virginia Lakes Resort** (at the end of Virginia Lakes Rd., 6 mi/9.7 km west of U.S. 395 and 12 mi/19.3 km north of Lee Vining, 760/647-6484, www.virginialakesresort.com, 8am-6:30pm daily in summer, $7-9, cash only) unless you happen to be staying there, but it's worth the 25-minute drive from Lee Vining to bite into their Ortega chili Spanish omelet or "freedom" toast made with sheepherder bread. For lunch, try the Fisherman Special (grilled cheese on sheepherder bread, $8) or the Campground Favorite (hamburger and fries, $8). The food is good, but even better is the view of Virginia Lake from the deck (not from the café itself) and the friendly demeanor of everybody who works here. The restaurant accepts cash only.

ACCOMMODATIONS

An overnight stay in Lee Vining puts you 13 miles (20.9 km) from the Tioga Pass entrance to Yosemite, and those miles cover one of the most spectacular drives in the West—climbing up through the granite walls of Lee Vining Canyon to 9,945-foot (3,030-m) Tioga Pass. To the north of Lee Vining is a lonely corridor of U.S. 395 heading north toward Bridgeport. A few lodgings are found along (or a few miles off) this route, all of them in spectacular mountain scenery.

Lee Vining and Vicinity
LAKE VIEW LODGE

The lake referred to in this motel's name is spectacular Mono Lake, one of the oldest lakes in North America and without question the most surreal looking. Unfortunately, you can't see it from most of the rooms at the misnamed **Lake View Lodge** (30 U.S. 395, Lee Vining, 760/647-6543 or 800/990-6614, www.lakeviewlodgeyosemite.com, $134-184 in summer,

from $69 in the winter). A few rooms are on the lake side of the highway, with a fair-to-decent perspective on the water, but the vast majority are not. No matter—the lodge provides its own lovely scenery with its park-like grounds, beautiful gardens lined with rock pathways, and an embarrassment of flowers in July and August. It also has clean, comfortable, no-nonsense rooms, plus an on-site coffeehouse, the Garden House. In the summer months, the lodge owners operate neighboring **Lake View Cottages** ($169-309), plus a tent campground and RV park. The cottages have 1-3 bedrooms, a full kitchen, and a dining area.

YOSEMITE GATEWAY MOTEL

Sure, the small rooms are on the rustic side at the **Yosemite Gateway Motel** (51340 U.S. 395, Lee Vining, 760/647-6467, www.yosemitegatewaymotel.com, $179-249 in summer, from $59 in winter), but each one has a framed vista of Mono Lake—some even have a fairly expansive view, not a tiny, peek-a-boo view that makes you long for more. This is a good thing, because aside from the lake view the rooms are unremarkable. Furnishings are of the thrift-store variety, and aside from coffeemakers and cable TV, there are no "amenities" to speak of. The trucks on the highway roar past early in the morning, so don't expect to sleep very late. Still, all of downtown Lee Vining is a few footsteps away.

EL MONO MOTEL

The unofficial motto at the 1920s-era **El Mono Motel** (51 U.S. 395, Lee Vining, 760/647-6310, www.elmonomotel.com, $76-136, open summer and fall only) is "We do funky very well." With room rates this low, you might expect shabby furnishings, but the rooms are cheerful and decidedly not boring. Warmed by steam heat from an antique boiler, each room is colorfully painted. The original glass is still in many of the windows. Porches and patios are lined with willow chairs. Sunflowers grow and songbirds gather in the motel's gorgeous garden; the owner has

Lodging East of the Park: U.S. 395

VIRGINIA CREEK
SETTLEMENT

395

Humboldt
Toiyabe
National
Forest

Green
Lake

East
Lake

167

Mono Lake
Tufa State
Reserve

Mono
City

VIRGINIA LAKES RD

Virginia
Lakes

VIRGINIA LAKES RESORT

LUNDY LAKE RD

Negit
Island

Mono
Lake

Hoover

Lundy
Lake

Wilderness

Paoha
Island

Yosemite

National

Saddlebag
Lake

TIOGA LODGE

EL MONO MOTEL
MURPHEY'S MOTEL
YOSEMITE GATEWAY MOTEL
LAKE VIEW LODGE

Park

SADDLEBAG
LAKE RD

Lee Vining

POOLE POWER
PLANT RD

Mono Lake Tufa
State Reserve

Ellery
Lake

120

395

120

TIOGA PASS RESORT

Tioga Lake

Tuolumne

TIOGA PASS
ENTRANCE

Mono Craters

Tuolumne
Meadow

Lembert Dome
9,450ft

Mt Dana
13,053ft

Walker
Lake

JUNE LAKE LOOP

Mono Basin
National Forest
Scenic Area

River

Mammoth Peak
12,106ft

Ansel

Grant
Lake

June Lake
Junction

Inyo

Cathedral Peak
10,911ft

Adams

National

Wilderness

158

June
Lake

BIG ROCK
RESORT

Forest

0   3 mi

0   3 km

Alger
Lakes

Silver
Lake

June Lake
Gull Lake

395

SILVER LAKE
RESORT

© MOON.COM

Waugh
Lake

Gem
Lake

DOUBLE
EAGLE
RESORT

FOUR SEASONS
REVERSE CREEK LODGE

FERN CREEK LODGE

created an oasis of color and beauty surrounding the building. Rooms are available with private or shared baths. A bonus is that the owner operates **Latte Da Coffee Café** in the motel's "lobby," so you can wander out in your slippers in the morning to get a cappuccino, then drink it while watching the hummingbirds in the back garden. Because of its low rates and abundance of charm, this place fills up fast in summer, so reserve early.

MURPHEY'S MOTEL

A good base camp for exploring Lee Vining and the surrounding area is **Murphey's Motel** (51493 U.S. 395, Lee Vining, 760/647-6316 or 800/334-6316, www.murpheysyosemite.com, $85-170 in summer, from $58 in winter), a family-run motel where the rates are reasonable and the air-conditioning works. The motel caters to ice climbers in the winter months; in the summer it welcomes the usual cabal of Yosemite tourists and U.S. 395 travelers. The AAA-approved rooms are clean and pleasant if not especially noteworthy, and they include in-room coffee, phones, and cable TV. Everything in Lee Vining is within walking distance, which means you can pick from a handful of restaurants, burger joints, and coffee shops. Spectacular Mono Lake is only a stone's throw away.

TIOGA LODGE

This historic lodge is right smack on U.S. 395. Although you might think the road noise would deter from the lodge's desirability, the effect is greatly mitigated because its roadside setting allows open vistas of Mono Lake. The cabins at **Tioga Lodge** (54411 U.S. 395, 2 mi/3.2 km north of Lee Vining, 760/647-6423 or 619/320-8868, www.tiogalodgeatmonolake.com, $139-189, summer only) have a clear view of that spectacular saltwater oddity, with its coral-like tufa spires and strange volcanic islands.

Although the lodge opened in 2000, a few of its buildings were transported here in the 1880s from the nearby gold-mining town of Bodie, now a state historic park. They sit side by side with newer one- and two-bedroom cabins that are furnished with late-1800s antiques and pine log furniture. No two accommodations are alike; each has its own personality that reflects the Mono Basin area's history. A favorite is the Joseph Walker Mountain Man Room, with its handmade pine log bed and a wall-mounted elk head and rifle. The lodge has its own **restaurant,** which serves surprisingly gourmet food for breakfast and dinner.

Tioga Lodge is just 2 miles (3.2 km) north of the Mono Basin Scenic Area Visitors Center, where you can learn everything about the 700,000-year-old body of water.

Virginia Lakes
VIRGINIA LAKES RESORT

"Watch your step; sea level is 9,770 feet down," notes the sign above the door at **Virginia Lakes Resort** (Virginia Lakes Rd., 6 mi/9.7 km west of U.S. 395 and 12 mi/19.3 km north of Lee Vining, 760/647-6484, www.virginialakesresort.com, $117-367 per night with 3-night minimum, June-Sept.). The resort is on Little Virginia Lake, which is right next to Big Virginia Lake and within a half mile of Trumbull Lake. Behind the lakes rise a few magnificent Sierra summits: Dunderberg Peak, Mount Olsen, Virginia Peak, and Black Mountain.

This is a classic mountain lodge resort, at the end of a 6-mile (9.7-km) drive from the main highway. Although plenty of people go fishing while they are here, this isn't a fish camp. Virginia Lakes Resort caters to a somewhat upscale crowd; the place is clean, attractive, and appealing with tidy cabins and newer furnishings.

Nine of the 19 cabins have lake views; the other 10 are on Virginia Creek. For the best experience, make sure you request a cabin with a kitchen, a fireplace, and a deck overlooking the lake. Not surprisingly, the resort is wildly popular, so its cabins are usually rented only by the week June 15-Labor Day ($675-2,200 per week, depending on the number of people and size of cabin). In addition to cabins, the resort has a store, a **café** (breakfast and lunch only), and rowboat rentals. Bring plenty of cash or travelers checks with you; credit cards are not accepted.

VIRGINIA CREEK SETTLEMENT

If you want to visit the ghost town at Bodie, there's no better place to stay than **Virginia Creek Settlement** (U.S. 395, 20 mi/32 km north of Lee Vining, 760/932-7780, www.virginiacreeksettlement.net, $59 tent cabins, $134-185 motel rooms, $174-189 housekeeping cabins). This is especially true if you have kids (or kids at heart) with you. Not only is Virginia Creek Settlement the closest lodging to Bodie State Historic Park, but it's also designed to get you in the Old West spirit.

The place looks like a movie set. Its six "Camptown" cabins are actually large converted sheds with Western-style false fronts, cleverly crafted to look like the buildings of an Old West town. Each represents a different "enterprise," with signs declaring Cooper's Freight and Mercantile Company, Assay and

Land Office, and Anthony Agony MD. Three covered wagons, also for rent, complete the scene. For something more conventional, the resort has motel rooms and tent sites, but why spoil the ghost town mood?

The **cabins** and **covered wagons** ($42) consist of one single room with double beds and electric lights—that's it. Bring your own linens or sleeping bags. A communal restroom and coin-operated showers are a few feet away. Much more luxurious **housekeeping cabins** ($110-145) come with TVs, private baths, and kitchenettes. Meals are available at the resort's **dining room;** the menu is a mix of Italian and American, including pizza and wine.

The resort is a 45-minute drive from the Tioga Pass entrance of Yosemite, but if you want to see both Bodie and Yosemite in one trip, this place makes a good base camp.

CAMPING

Several Forest Service campgrounds in **Inyo National Forest** (Mono Basin Scenic Area Visitor Center, 760/647-3044, www.fs.usda.gov/inyo) are within a few miles of the Tioga Pass entrance to Yosemite. Most are first come, first served; no reservations are taken. Tioga Road is usually open until November 1; the Forest Service and Mono County camps stay open through the month of October.

Lee Vining and Vicinity
MORAINE, BOULDER, AND ASPEN GROVE

★ **Moraine, Boulder,** and **Aspen Grove Campgrounds** (www.fs.usda.gov, first come, first served, $14) are located side by side along Poole Power Plant Road, just off Highway 120 in Lee Vining Canyon. When you take the turnoff, a sign points you left to Moraine and right to Boulder and Aspen Grove Campgrounds. Take your pick of these three camps at 7,500 feet (2,300 m) in elevation; they're all good, they cost the same, and all three usually have a couple of sites open, even on summer weekends.

Each camp has several fantasy-level sites

located right on Lee Vining Creek, offering complete privacy thanks to abundant aspens and willows and boasting great views of nearby granite peaks and the sight and sound of Lee Vining Creek flowing right by your tent. (The creek is a fine spot to try your luck fishing.) Other sites are quite primitive, with little more than a makeshift fire ring on the edge of a dirt parking lot. But at least you have found a peaceful place to sleep, and you're only a couple minutes from Yosemite.

Moraine (an overflow site) and Boulder are the closest to the turnoff, which is useful if it's late at night and you just want to land a spot and get to sleep. Aspen Grove (May-Oct.) is a 1.5-mile (2.4-km) drive down Poole Power Plant Road; it may be the prettiest of the camps, but it's a close call. It does have the advantage of a drinking-water faucet located at the entrance to the camp; the other two camps have no water, so you must bring your own. The camps have picnic tables, fire rings, and vault toilets; bring your own grill to set on top of the fire for cooking.

The camps are on Poole Power Plant Road off Highway 120, 9 miles (14.5 km) east of the Tioga Pass entrance station and 3.5 miles (5.6 km) west of U.S. 395.

BIG BEND CAMPGROUND

Big Bend Campground (www.fs.usda.gov, first come, first served, $22) is exactly the same as, and simultaneously completely different from, its neighboring campgrounds in Lee Vining Canyon. The camp is nestled in the heart of Tioga Pass, its granite walls towering thousands of feet overhead. The 17 sites are tucked into an aspen and Jeffrey pine forest along beautiful Lee Vining Creek. But while the other nearby camps are more primitive, Big Bend is deluxe, and that is either a minus or a plus depending on your point of view. On the one hand, RVs have a much easier time of it here because the sites are paved and comparatively easy to pull in and out of. The vault toilets are spick-and-span and are even lit up at night. But the sites are too close together (site number 17 is a favorite; it's the

Camping East of the Park: U.S. 395

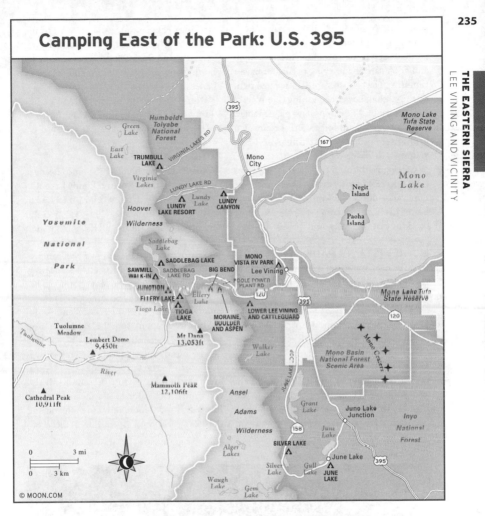

© MOON.COM

only one that doesn't have any direct neighbors). Still, the scenery is lovely, the creek fishing is excellent, and Yosemite is close at hand. The camp has drinking water, picnic tables, fire grills, and vault toilets.

Big Bend is located on Poole Power Plant Road off Highway 120, 9 miles (14.5 km) east of the Tioga Pass entrance station and 3.5 miles (5.6 km) west of U.S. 395. Drive 2.5 miles (4 km) west on Poole Power Plant Road to the camp.

LOWER LEE VINING AND CATTLEGUARD

Lower Lee Vining and **Cattleguard** (www. fs.usda.gov, first come, first served, $14) are separate from the other three camps on Poole Power Plant Road in Lee Vining Canyon. Each has its own entrance from Highway 120, 0.25 mile (0.4 km) apart. The camps have much in common with their cousins up the road but have fewer sites. In Cattleguard Camp, sites 1 and 2 are away from the creek and out in the open in the sagebrush plains, offering a stunning view of Tioga Pass but little or no protection from the wind. A couple of huge Jeffrey pines provide a little shade. These sites are good bets if you are pulling in late at night and don't care about trying to cook or have a campfire. The best sites are 8-10, located right on the stream; Lower Lee Vining Camp's best sites are 11-13. The camps have picnic tables, fire rings, and vault toilets. Bring your own grill to set on the rock fire ring. Also bring your own drinking water.

Cattleguard Camp (13 sites) is 9.5 miles (15.3 km) east of the Tioga Pass entrance station and 3 miles (4.8 km) west of U.S. 395. Lower Lee Vining Camp (51 sites) is 0.3 mile (0.5 km) east of Cattleguard.

MONO VISTA RV PARK

If you've been hiking for days and desperately need a shower, you'll kiss the ground at **Mono Vista RV Park** (U.S. 395, 760/647-6401, www. monovistarvpark.net, $28 for tents, $35-42 for RVs). This private, clean, and pleasant campground has full hookups for RVs, grassy tent sites, and—the best part—hot **showers** ($3 for five minutes). Buy your shower tokens at the office. A laundry and dump station are also available. The camp is right beside the highway and close to town, so although it isn't optimal for scenery, it's very convenient.

The Tioga Pass entrance station is a 14-mile (22.5-km) drive. The camp has picnic tables, fire grills, and flush toilets. Reserve a site by phoning ahead, or just pull in and take your chances.

Mono Vista is on the north end of Lee Vining on U.S. 395, 1 mile (1.6 km) north of the Highway 120 junction.

LUNDY LAKE RESORT

"Resort" may be a bit of a misnomer, because rustic **Lundy Lake Resort** (Lundy Lake Rd., 5 mi/8 km west of U.S. 395 and 7 mi/11.3 km north of Lee Vining, 626/309-0415, $35-45) consists of 21 tent sites, 5 full RV hookup sites, and a general store with tackle, bait, and groceries. But that's just the way plenty of campers like it. At elevation 7,800 feet (2,400 m), Lundy Lake is 1 mile (1.6 km) in length and has 100 surface acres (40 hectares). Motorboats are for rent and the trout fishing is excellent. A hiking trail leads uphill from the lake's dam to an old mining site, and another trail leads into nearby Lundy Canyon. The scenery is classic Eastern Sierra: tall pines, quaking aspens, and breathtaking granite mountains. If you can time it right, don't miss the astonishing July wildflower bloom in Lundy Canyon and the colorful autumn aspen show in October.

Aspen Grove Campground in Lee Vining Canyon

From Lee Vining, drive 7 miles (11.3 km) north on U.S. 395 and turn left onto Lundy Lake Road. Drive 5 miles (8 km) west to the west end of Lundy Lake.

LUNDY CANYON CAMPGROUND

The Mono County Department of Public Works operates **Lundy Canyon Campground** (760/932-5440, www.monocounty.org, first come, first served, $16, cash only), a favorite among people who like fishing and peace and quiet. The 37-site camp is set in a dense grove of aspens. Camping here in late September or October can seem like paradise when the trees are decorated in their autumnal colors. Choose between sites right along the stream and others in a mixed aspen and Jeffrey pine forest. (Although they look terribly tempting, the first 10 "sites" in Lundy Camp are day-use only; keep driving back into the canyon until you reach the 37 overnight sites.) Lundy Lake is a couple of miles west of the campground, up Lundy Lake Road. The camp is equipped with picnic tables, fire rings (some sites have grills, some only rock rings), and vault toilets. Bring your own drinking water.

Lundy Canyon is 2.7 miles (4.3 km) west on Lundy Lake Road, which is 7 miles (11.3 km) north of Lee Vining on U.S. 395. Because of this location north of town, the vast majority of Yosemite visitors miss the camp and you can almost always find a spot here.

Virginia Lakes
TRUMBULL LAKE CAMPGROUND

This may be too far for most Yosemite visitors to go to find a campground, but considering what it has to offer, maybe not. The efficiently managed and well-run **Trumbull Lake Campground** (34 sites, 877/444-6777 or 760/932-7092, www.recreation.gov, June-Oct., $23) sits a short distance from the two Virginia Lakes and is ideal for anglers. It's also ideal for those who like high mountain scenery—the camp is set at 9,500 feet (2,900 m), in a fairly dense lodgepole pine forest. A nearby trailhead leads into the Hoover Wilderness. A big selling point is that sites are **reservable in advance** from July through the first week in September.

The camp has drinking water, picnic tables, fire grills, and vault toilets. It's a 20-minute drive from Lee Vining for groceries and supplies. If you're lucky, the little store at neighboring Virginia Lakes Resort (late May-mid-Oct.) might have what you need, and the resort's small café gives you an option for breakfast or lunch.

Trumbull Lake is 5.9 miles (9.5 km) west of U.S. 395 on Virginia Lakes Road, 12 miles (19.3 km) north of Lee Vining. It will take about 45 minutes to make the 29-mile (47-km) drive to Yosemite's Tioga Pass entrance. For more information, contact the **Bridgeport Ranger Station of Humboldt-Toiyabe National Forest** (760/932-7070, www.fs.usda.gov).

June Lake

An angler's paradise consisting of a chain of four drive-up lakes, the community of June Lake is a full-service resort along Highway 158, just off U.S. 395. Home of world-class trout fishing and myriad opportunities for hiking, biking, camping, and boating, June Lake is a popular vacation destination for visitors who may or may not choose to make the 40-minute trek to the Tioga Pass entrance to Yosemite. After all, there is plenty right here in June Lake to fill one's vacation days.

VISITORS CENTERS

The small town of June Lake doesn't have its own visitors center, but the local chamber of commerce operates two **websites** with information about the area: www.junelakeloop.org and www.junelakeloop.com. The nearest

June Lake Hikes

Trail	Effort	Distance	Duration
Parker Lake Trail	Easy/moderate	3.8 mi/6.1 km rt	2 hr
Yost Lake	Moderate	9.4 mi/15.1 km rt	4.5 hr
Rush Creek Trail	Moderate/strenuous	4.6-14 mi/7.4-22.5 km rt	2-7 hr
Bloody Canyon Trail	Strenuous	8.2 mi/13.2 km rt	4 hr

visitors centers are in **Lee Vining.** A number of the cabin resorts stationed along the June Lake Loop (Hwy. 158) are also excellent sources of information. The best bets for local knowledge, especially outdoor recreation information, are the **Double Eagle Resort** (760/648-7004) and **Silver Lake Resort** (760/648-7525).

RECREATION
Hiking

Several excellent day-hiking trails can be accessed from points on, or near, the June Lake Loop.

BLOODY CANYON TRAIL
Distance: 8.2 miles (13.2 km) round-trip
Duration: 4 hours
Elevation Change: 1,800 feet (550 m)
Effort: Strenuous
Trailhead: Walker Lake
Directions: From Lee Vining, drive 5 miles (8 km) south on U.S. 395 to the north end of the June Lake Loop (Hwy. 158). Turn right and drive 1.3 miles (2.1 km) on Highway 158; then turn right on a dirt road signed for Parker and Walker Lakes. Drive 0.5 mile (0.8 km) to a junction, turn right, and then drive 0.3 mile (0.5 km) and turn right again, following the signs for Walker Lake. Drive 0.5 mile (0.8 km) and turn left on Forest Road 1S23; then drive 2.7 miles (4.3 km) to the Walker Lake Trailhead.

Lower Sardine Lake is a jewel cradled in a high glacial cirque, the kind of lake that makes the Ansel Adams Wilderness one of the most treasured places in the world. Beyond the first easy mile, this hike is tough and steep. Much

of the trail is a historic Native American trading route, used by the Indians of the Mono Basin to visit the Indians of the Yosemite high country. This was the route used by Chief Tenaya and his tribe in their flight from the U.S. Army in 1852.

The first mile (1.6 km) to **Walker Lake** is an easy downhill cruise, dropping 600 feet (185 m) in elevation. The lake is a popular destination for anglers and has a small private resort on its eastern shore. From the aspen-lined western edge of the lake, you head up **Bloody Canyon,** climbing nearly 2,000 feet (600 m) in about 3 miles (4.8 km). The hike parallels Walker Creek, requiring two stream crossings on the way up to **Lower Sardine Lake.** For anyone who is either out of shape or not acclimated to the altitude, the climb can be rough going. As you near Lower Sardine Lake, the sight of a beautiful **waterfall** (the lake's outlet stream) will help to spur you on. When you reach the lake at elevation 9,888 feet (3,014 m), you'll find that it is surrounded by rocky cliffs on three sides and provides great views of the Mono Basin to the east. Backpackers can continue hiking up and over Mono Pass and into Yosemite National Park's remote backcountry.

PARKER LAKE TRAIL
Distance: 3.8 miles (6.1 km) round-trip
Duration: 2 hours
Elevation Change: 500 feet (150 m)
Effort: Easy to moderate
Trailhead: Parker Lake
Directions: From Lee Vining, drive 5 miles (8 km) south on U.S. 395 to the north end of the June Lake

Loop (Hwy. 158). Turn right and drive 1.3 miles (2.1 km) on Highway 158; then turn right on a dirt road signed for Parker and Walker Lakes. Drive 2.4 miles (3.9 km) to the Parker Lake Trailhead at the end of the road.

This mellow trek is suitable for **families** and anyone seeking an easy walk to a beautiful lake. Although the nearby June Lake Loop gets a lot of vacation traffic, this trailhead is obscure enough that most visitors pass it by. And get this: The **1.9-mile-long (3.1-km) trail** has an elevation gain of only a little more than 300 feet (90 m). Beginning at an elevation of 8,000 feet (2,400 m) above Parker Creek, the trail follows the creek upstream on a fairly mellow grade before arriving at **Parker Lake**, at 8,318 feet (2,535 m). As you ascend, the landscape transitions from sagebrush plains into a mixed forest alongside Parker Creek, complete with quaking aspens and mammoth-sized Jeffrey pines. Look behind you once in a while, and you'll catch great views of Mono Lake. In short order, you will emerge from the forest onto the lake's shore. Parker Lake is a deep-blue beauty backed by 12,861-foot (3,920-m) Parker Peak—a great place to have a picnic or just sit and enjoy the scenery.

RUSH CREEK TRAIL

Distance: 1.6–14 miles (7.1–22.5 km) round-trip
Duration: 2-7 hours
Elevation Change: 1,300 feet (400 m) to Agnew Lake; 2,200 feet (670 m) to Waugh Lake
Effort: Moderate to strenuous
Trailhead: Rush Creek
Directions: From Lee Vining, drive about 11 miles (17.7 km) south on U.S. 395 to June Lake Junction. Turn right on Highway 158/June Lake Road and drive 7.2 miles (11.6 km) to the Rush Creek Trailhead, between Silver Lake Resort and the pack station.

The most well-known trail in the June Lake area is the Rush Creek Trail. Although it is most **heavily used** by backpackers and horse packers, day hikers can follow it upstream along Rush Creek to a series of alpine lakes. The trailhead lies near the pack station at **Silver Lake** (elevation 7,215 ft/2,200 m). After departing Silver Lake, follow the trail as it climbs above the June Lake Loop and soon

starts to parallel **Lower Rush Creek.** You'll cross over an old tramway system that was used for the hydroelectric projects found in this watershed. Near the dam at **Agnew Lake** is a trail **junction,** 2.2 miles (3.5 km) from the start. The left fork heads up to Agnew Pass, but continue straight and in one more mile (1.6 km) you arrive at beautiful **Gem Lake** (9,058 ft/2,761 m), followed by **Waugh Lake** (9,442 ft/2,878 m) at the 7-mile (11.3-km) point.

YOST LAKE

Distance: 9.4 miles (15.1 km) round-trip
Duration: 4.5 hours
Elevation Change: 1,200 feet (365 m)
Effort: Moderate
Trailhead: Yost Meadows
Directions: From Lee Vining, drive about 11 miles (17.7 km) south on U.S. 395 to June Lake Junction. Go right on Highway 158/June Lake Road and drive 2 miles (3.2 km) to the town of June Lake. The trailhead is on the west (left) side of the road, across the road from the fire station.

Yost Lake is a small glacial lake hidden at 9,000 feet (2,750 m) on the slopes of June Mountain. Many people visit the June Lake area for years without even knowing Yost exists. But it is up here, tucked away and accessible only to those willing to hike. From the trailhead (7,800 ft/2,400 m) at June Lake, the **Yost Meadows Trail** rises very steeply in the first mile (1.6 km), climbing 800 feet (245 m)—a real butt-kicker. That discourages many from going farther—after all, it is **4.7 miles (7.6 km) to the lake.** But after that first grunt of a climb, the trail gets much easier, contouring across the mountain slopes. It rises gradually to the headwaters of Yost Creek and then drops into the small basin that guards the lake.

A shorter option is to begin at the Yost Creek/Fern Lake trailhead, making it a much shorter **4.8-mile (7.7-km) round-trip.** It is just as pretty, but it has a more difficult grade and can be slippery for those not wearing heavy, firm-gripping hiking boots. The trailhead is 3 miles (4.8 km) west of the town of June Lake, on the west (left) side of June Lake Road.

Biking

The **Panorama Mountain Trail** (10.7 mi/17.2 km), a mountain bike route sanctioned by the Forest Service, consists of three consecutive loops on jeep roads and graded dirt roads that lead through sagebrush and Jeffrey pines. Small brown Forest Service signs guide you along the route, as do a few prominent landmarks: U.S. 395, which is visible every time you climb a bit; the Mono Craters, a chain of barren-looking volcanic vents poking up from the surrounding sagebrush plains; and the Aeolian Buttes, where the most recent volcanic activity in this area occurred, perhaps only 600 years ago. The third of the three loops circles the buttes and will take you up high enough to get surprising views of Mono Lake and its neighboring craters to the northeast, plus the snowcapped, granite mountains of the Eastern Sierra to the west. It's startling to see this juxtaposition of glacier-carved mountains and volcanic vents and tablelands—all in one glance. The trailhead for this ride is found off U.S. 395, 450 feet (137 m) north of June Lake Junction. Turn east on Forest Service Road 1S35 and drive 300 feet (90 m) to the signed trailhead.

For road bikers, pedaling the **June Lake Loop** (28.8 mi/46.3 km) is an obvious choice. Of course, the "Loop" is not really a loop at all, but more like a horseshoe shape on Highway 158 that is made into a loop by connecting with U.S. 395. While this may be fine for car drivers, it's not ideal for cyclists, who do better by riding out and back on Highway 158, rather than completing the loop on the busy U.S. highway.

Start on Northshore Drive at the southern turnoff for the June Lakes Loop. Along Highway 158, you'll be treated to some of the finest scenery in the Eastern Sierra—imposing granite peaks, the dancing leaves of aspen groves, and four sparkling, bright blue lakes.

Because the route has many places to stop for supplies or breaks, this ride is well within the abilities of most cyclists. Traffic is heavier on summer weekends, lighter the rest of the time.

On the north end of the "Loop," a good turnaround point is the Mono Craters Viewpoint; it's 1.2 miles (1.9 km) from the road's end at U.S. 395. At the viewing point, you get a good look at the barren, pumice-covered volcanic cones known as the Mono Craters, which were created by a series of volcanic eruptions as recently as 600 years ago.

Fishing

The four drive-to lakes along the **June Lake Loop** (Hwy. 158)—Gull, June, Silver, and Grant—are planted with rainbow, brook, and brown trout. Boats can be rented at the various resorts and marinas along the lakeshores. Anglers on foot often head for **Rush Creek,** particularly the section between Silver Lake and Gull Lake.

If you'd like to learn how to fly fish, or just brush up on your skills, the **Double Eagle Resort** (760/648-7004, www.doubleeagle. com) at June Lake offers lessons daily in summer. Full guide service is available, and the resort has a fly-fishing shop. There's even a fly-fishing pond just for kids.

Horseback Riding

Frontier Pack Train (June Lake, 888/437-6853 or 760/648-7701, www.frontierpacktrain. com, summer only, $40-120 per person), next to Silver Lake, leads one-hour to all-day trail rides following the Rush Creek Trail alongside the gurgling waters of Rush Creek. Trips can be as short as one hour or as long as several days. If you'd like to live the life of a cowboy or cowgirl for a few days, you can join in the horse drives each spring and fall, when the pack station's 100 horses and mules are transferred from their summer home in June Lake to their winter pastures in Round Valley, and then back again.

1: Sardine Lake, along Bloody Canyon Trail
2: Parker Lake

Winter Sports

The **June Mountain Ski Area** (3819 Hwy. 158, June Lake, 888/586-3686, www.junemountain.com, Dec.-Apr.) is a longtime favorite resort for families and casual skiers. June Mountain receives an average 250 inches (635 cm) of snow each year, and with 1,400 skiable acres (550 hectares) the mountain is small compared to its gigantic neighbor, Mammoth Mountain. But that doesn't seem to bother the legions of devoted fans. June's longest run is 2 miles (3.2 km) with a 2,600-foot (790-m) drop. A total of 35 named trails are available.

Those who prefer a non-vertical and completely free-of-charge winter adventure can strap on a pair of snowshoes or cross-country skis and glide along the 10-mile (16.1-km), unplowed section of the **June Lake Loop** (Hwy. 158), which is closed to cars in winter.

FOOD

June Lake Brewing Company

At the **June Lake Brewing Company** (131 S. Crawford Ave., 858/668-6340, www.junelakebrewing.com, 11am-8pm Sun.-Thurs., 11am-9pm Fri.-Sat., $10-15), everybody feels right at home. Dogs are seated with their owners at the outside tables or even right at the bar, kids are playing foosball, ski buddies are hanging out at the wooden tables, and everybody is having a good time in the rustic, industrial-garage-style space. The focus is on beer at this spot run by San Diego natives who migrated to June Lake, but the food is great, too, thanks to the Ohana's 395 food truck, which is permanently parked out front. The food is loosely Hawaiian—poke bowls, Honolulu noodles, kalua pork, ahi tuna tacos and burritos—and it's all good. Try the beer flight (four sample-sized glasses) and pick your favorite.

Carson Peak Inn

Diners in June Lake have been heading to the **Carson Peak Inn** (Hwy. 158, June Lake, 760/648-7575, 5pm-10pm daily, $31-51) for as long as anybody under 55 can remember.

The inn first opened its doors in 1966, and the owners haven't missed a beat since then. Huge portions come standard at this cozy, old-fashioned dinner house. All the standards are done well here: prime rib, filet mignon, king crab legs, lobster tail, trout, and scallops. A few oddball items are found on the menu, like chicken livers. All dinners come with soup and salad (not soup *or* salad), a baked potato, and garlic bread. You'll have to roll yourself out of here when it's all over. The Carson Peak Inn prides itself on being open 365 days a year, no matter what the weather. Thanksgiving and Christmas dinners are a big event.

Eagle's Landing

The finest dining establishment in June Lake is the Double Eagle Resort's restaurant, **Eagle's Landing** (Hwy. 158, June Lake, 760/648-7004, 7:30am-9pm daily, breakfast $11-15, dinner $18-32). You don't need to stay at the resort to eat here; just stop in. Sit indoors and gaze out the floor-to-ceiling windows at Carson Peak and Reversed Creek, or sit outdoors on the deck and enjoy the warm Sierra sun. Breakfast includes a lobster frittata, steak and eggs, and three types of eggs Benedict (turkey, crab, or ham). Dinner entrées include salmon, lamb shank, and rainbow trout.

ACCOMMODATIONS

Fifteen miles (24 km) south of Lee Vining lies the popular winter and summer resort town of June Lake. This area includes four large drive-to lakes set off a looping highway and provides lodging options at classic mountain cabin resorts, as well as spectacular fishing and hiking. If you're willing to drive 45 minutes to reach the Tioga Pass entrance to Yosemite, June Lake could be an ideal spot to make a base camp for your Yosemite vacation. Yosemite Valley would be too far for a day trip (2.5 hours each way), but much of Yosemite's spectacular high country is within an hour's drive.

Fern Creek Lodge

All of the cabin resorts in June Lake are clean, serviceable, and well situated for recreation enthusiasts. But some simply have more character than others, and **Fern Creek Lodge** (4628 Hwy. 158, June Lake, 760/648-7722 or 800/621-9146, www.ferncreeklodge.com, year-round, $125-400 depending on size of cabin) falls in that category. Maybe it's because the lodge has been around since 1927, or maybe it's because each of its nine cabins is completely different in style and appearance, but there's just something about this resort that makes it cozy and appealing.

The cutest cabin is the Old Schoolhouse, a tiny little house for two people only; it's at the back of the property, farthest from the road. Dutch Lady and Heart Tree are the largest cabins; they're both two-story units with four bedrooms, two bathrooms, and a sun deck around the front.

A barbecue area and fish-cleaning facilities are available. All cabins have fully equipped kitchens, but if you don't feel like cooking, several restaurants are nearby.

Big Rock Resort

The eight cabins at **Big Rock Resort** (120 Big Rock Rd., June Lake, 760/648-7717, www.bigrockresort.net, $215-295, lower rates in Sept., Oct., and May, excluding holidays) are perched alongside big, blue June Lake, giving summer visitors easy access to excellent trout fishing, sailing, and boating. The resort provides motorboat and paddleboat rentals, or cabin guests can bring their own boat and launch it for free.

The cabins have one, two, or three bedrooms, plus fully equipped kitchens with everything you need for your June Lake/Yosemite vacation. Some of the cabins are duplexes, so make sure you request a single unit if you don't want to share walls.

Four Seasons

If looking out your cabin's floor-to-ceiling windows at 10,909-foot (3,325-m) Carson Peak appeals to you, stay at the **Four Seasons** (Hwy. 158, 5 mi/8 km west of U.S. 395, June Lake, 760/648-7476, www.junelakeaccommodations.com, $189-329, 3-night minimum stay usually required). The resort's A-frame chalets are just off the main highway at the base of Carson Peak. The five chalets are packed in like sardines (they're almost touching each other), and from the front they don't look like much. But once you're inside, you remember why you came here: The view of Carson Peak's snow-covered granite is truly stunning.

Each chalet is identical: 900 square feet (85 sq m) in size, with an enclosed master bedroom plus a loft bedroom that overlooks the living room. The living room has giant windows with the view. For an even better view, sit outside on your chalet's sundeck. The chalets have outdoor gas barbecues (in summer); if you prefer to cook indoors, the kitchens have everything you might need (except an oven; stovetops only).

Reverse Creek Lodge

"Our family welcomes yours" is the motto at **Reverse Creek Lodge** (Hwy. 158, 4.5 mi/7.2 km west of U.S. 395, June Lake, 760/648-7535 or 800/762-6440, www.reversecreeklodge.com, $135-225). The Reverse Creek family is David and Denise Naaden and their 12 children, whom they call their "cleaning crew." The family has been operating the lodge and its cabins and A-frame chalets for more than 20 years.

The property's rustic cabins are set in the pines along Reversed Creek, but the modern A-frame chalets are the more popular rentals. Down the street about 300 feet (90 m) from the rest of the resort, the chalets are perched above Reversed Creek in a cluster of pines. Some have a fair view of Carson Peak, a mammoth granite landmark in June Lake. The chalets are packed together tightly, each one only a few feet from the next.

Like the cabins, the A-frames have fully stocked kitchens, cable TV, gas fireplaces, gas barbecues, and all the other amenities of home. For big groups, the resort has a "private residence cabin" ($310-380) with four bedrooms and two full baths.

Silver Lake Resort

Most people agree that 110-acre (45-hectare) Silver Lake is the prettiest of the four lakes on the June Lake Loop, which is a major reason that **Silver Lake Resort** (Hwy. 158, 7.5 mi/12.1 km west of U.S. 395, June Lake, 760/648-7525, www.silverlakeresort.net, $145-340 June-Oct., weather permitting) is so popular. The full-service resort was established in 1916, which makes it the oldest resort in the Eastern Sierra.

The 17 cabins are set amid a grove of aspen trees, giving the illusion of seclusion even though they are grouped close together. Rustic, yet clean and well cared for, many have been redone on the inside, with new curtains and bedding. All have fully equipped kitchens. The cabins are only a stone's throw from the lake; a few have lake views. Most resort guests take advantage of fishing on Silver Lake; motorboats and canoes are for rent by the hour or the day. The resort has a general store, a café, and an RV park.

Double Eagle Resort

Double Eagle Resort (5587 Hwy. 158, June Lake, 760/648-7004, www.doubleeagle.com, rooms $249, cabins $329-399) opened in 1999 and quickly established itself as one of the best lodging destinations in the Eastern Sierra. If you like the idea of an upscale version of a mountain lodge and cabin resort, Double Eagle does it well.

Double Eagle's 14 cabins are two-bedroom models with fully equipped kitchens and fireplaces, tastefully decorated and large enough to fit 4-6 people. All the extra amenities are provided: microwave, barbecue, TV/DVD player, phones, and the like—so it's not surprising that they will cost you dearly. If you don't need all that space, "luxury rooms" are available for less. These have either a king bed or two queen beds, a 32-inch (81-cm) television with DVD player, whirlpool tub, and balcony or deck. Rooms are equipped with a fully stocked minibar and coffee service. Breakfast is included in the rate.

The resort includes the Creekside Spa and Fitness Center, which has a 60-foot (18-m) indoor pool and hot tub, and an on-site full-service salon. Delicious meals can be had at the resort's **Eagle's Landing Restaurant.** So when you've finally finished your pedicure, aromatherapy massage, tai chi class, and gourmet lunch, what's next? Head outside and try out the resort's trophy trout pond, which is stocked with trout up to 18 pounds (8 kg). There's even a fly-fishing pond just for kids. Full guide service is available, as is a fly-fishing shop.

CAMPING

Forest Service campgrounds in June Lake (www.fs.usda.gov/inyo, reservations at 877/444-6777, www.recreation.gov) are nearly as popular as those in Yosemite, so it's wise to reserve in advance. The most coveted camp is 28-site **June Lake Campground** ($23), set in a quaking aspen forest on June Lake's shoreline. Some sites are within 10 steps of the water, and campers have easy access to the lake's marina and boat rentals. Another popular choice is 63-site **Silver Lake Campground** ($23), which has flush toilets, drinking water, and trailhead access into the Ansel Adams Wilderness. The beautiful waters of Silver Lake are just a short walk away.

Mammoth Lakes

Famous for its ski resort at Mammoth Mountain, the town of Mammoth Lakes is a year-round vacation destination. Spring, summer, and fall activities include hiking, lake and stream fishing, mountain biking, and horseback riding. Winter activities have expanded from the obvious (skiing and snowboarding) to the more esoteric: dogsledding, bobsledding, and sleigh rides. The town even boasts a small outlet mall and a number of day spas and salons. In and around Mammoth Lakes, there truly is an activity for everyone.

VISITORS CENTERS

The **Mammoth Lakes Welcome Center** (760/924-5500, www.fs.usda.gov, 8am-5pm daily) is on the north side of Highway 203 as you enter Mammoth Lakes from U.S. 395 (across from McDonald's). The staff can provide you with information on lodging, restaurants, camping, and recreational activities. A small bookstore sells maps and guidebooks.

SIGHTS
★ **Mammoth Lakes Basin**
The scenic, lake-filled basin just east of the town of Mammoth Lakes is what gives this region its name. The five drive-to lakes in Mammoth Lakes Basin—**Mary, Twin, George, Mamie,** and **Horseshoe**—offer a wealth of opportunities for anglers, and the surrounding land is laced with hiking trails and campgrounds. It takes only 20 minutes to drive around the five lakes, but it's unlikely you'll want to spend so little time here. Bring a picnic lunch and stay a while. If you are interested in gold rush history, take the short walk to see the preserved buildings and equipment from the **Mammoth Consolidated Gold Mine;** the trailhead to the mine is at Coldwater Creek Campground.

To reach the Mammoth Lakes Basin, head east on Lake Mary Road from its junction with Highway 203/Minaret Road. To reach the trailhead at Coldwater Creek, continue straight on Lake Mary Road and drive 3.5 miles (5.6 km) to a fork just before Lake Mary; turn left and drive 0.6 mile (1 km) to the Coldwater Campground turnoff on the left. Turn left and drive 0.5 mile (0.8 km) to the trailhead.

Mammoth Mountain
SCENIC GONDOLA RIDE
In summer, visitors can take the **Scenic Gondola Ride** (9am-4:30pm daily mid-June-late Sept., www.mammothmountain.com, $29 adults, $24 teens and seniors, $10 children 12 and under) to the top of Mammoth Mountain. The view-filled trip takes about 15 minutes each way. While many hikers and bikers use the gondola to access Mammoth Mountain's highest trails, the ride is also a fun adventure for sightseers. If your dog likes mountain scenery, he or she can join you on the gondola ride (leashes required). The best ticket deal is the "Lookout Lunch" ($34 adults, $29 teens and seniors, $12 children 12 and under), where you can ride the gondola and have lunch at the resort's Eleven 53 Café.

ELEVEN 53 INTERPRETIVE CENTER
Situated at Mammoth Mountain's summit at 11,053 feet (3,369 m), the **Eleven 53 Interpretive Center** (9am-4:30pm daily mid-June-late Sept., www.mammothmountain.com) has exhibits on volcanic history, geology, weather patterns, and more. It features an outstanding view of the Minaret Range, Mono Lake, and 400 miles (645 km) of the Sierra Nevada's highest peaks. Free naturalist-led walks around the summit are offered in summer (11am and 1pm Thurs.-Sat.). While you're at the top of the mountain, you can have lunch with a view at the on-site Eleven 53 Café.

Mammoth Lakes Hikes

Trail	Effort	Distance	Duration
Barrett and TJ Lakes	Easy	1 mi/1.6 km rt	30-40 min
Emerald Lake and Sky Meadows	Easy to moderate	4 mi/6.4 km rt	2 hr
Crystal Lake and Mammoth Crest	Easy to moderate	3.8-7.8 mi/6.1-12.6 km rt	2-4 hr
Devils Postpile and Rainbow Falls	Easy to moderate	5 mi/8 km rt	2.5 hr
Red Cones Loop	Moderate	6.7 mi/10.8 km rt	3.5 hr
Shadow Lake	Moderate	7.6 mi/12.2 km rt	4 hr
Duck Pass Trail to Duck Lake	Moderate	10 mi/16.1 km rt	5 hr

Inyo Craters

The **Inyo Craters** (www.fs.usda.gov) are part of a chain of craters and other volcanic formations that reaches from Mammoth to Mono Lake. Evidence of Mammoth's fiery past, the craters are the remains of a volcanic explosion of steam that happened only 600 years ago. At that time the mountain was a smoldering volcano. Melted snow found its way inside, and when the cold water hit hot magma, an explosion occurred that created the craters. The walk to the craters is a 0.25-mile (0.4-km) uphill trek through a lovely open forest of red fir and Jeffrey pine. In each of the two Inyo Craters lies a tiny pond that fills with the collected drops of melting snow each spring and then dries up during summer.

To reach the trailhead for the Inyo Craters, turn right (north) on Highway 203/Minaret Road at its junction with Lake Mary Road in downtown Mammoth Lakes. Drive 1 mile (1.6 km), and at the sign for Mammoth Lakes Scenic Loop, turn right and drive 2.7 miles (4.3 km). Turn left at the sign for Inyo Craters (the road turns to dirt) and drive 1.3 more miles (2.1 km) to the Inyo Craters parking lot.

★ Devils Postpile

Devils Postpile National Monument (760/934-2289, www.nps.gov/depo, June-Oct.)

features two geologic marvels: the Devils Postpile itself—an amazing collection of columnar basalt "posts" remaining from an ancient lava flow—and 101-foot (31-m) **Rainbow Falls,** one of the Sierra's most beautiful waterfalls. Seeing the Postpile requires a 0.3-mile (0.5-km) walk from the ranger station at the monument. Visitors can turn back at the Postpile or continue onward to Rainbow Falls for a total 5-mile (8-km) round-trip, or you can divide the trip into two shorter walks by starting at two different trailheads; a shorter trail to Rainbow Falls begins near Reds Meadow Pack Station at the end of Devils Postpile Road.

Most visitors will ride a **shuttle bus** (7am-7pm mid-June-Labor Day, $8 adults, $4 children 3-15) into the monument. When the shuttle bus is not operating, there is a standard $10 amenity fee. If you are disabled (with handicap placard or car plates), a camper with reservations in Devils Postpile, a guest at Reds Meadow Resort, or traveling with a cartop boat, there is no fee. Once you're in the park, you can ride free shuttle buses from one trailhead to another.

To reach Devils Postpile from the town of Mammoth Lakes, drive 4 miles (6.4 km) west on Highway 203 and then turn right on Minaret Road (still Hwy. 203). Drive 4 miles

(6.4 km) to the Forest Service Adventure Center located in the Mammoth Mountain Ski Area Gondola Building (adjacent to the Mammoth Mountain Inn). You can buy access passes and pick up the shuttle bus here.

RECREATION

Hiking

Just minutes from downtown Mammoth Lakes are dozens of hiking trails leading to alpine lakes and flower-filled meadows. The number of short, rewarding day hikes in the Mammoth Lakes Basin alone is remarkable.

BARRETT AND TJ LAKES

Distance: 1 mile (1.6 km) round-trip
Duration: 30-40 minutes
Elevation Change: 500 feet (150 m)
Effort: Easy
Trailhead: Lake George
Directions: From the Mammoth Lakes junction on U.S. 395, turn west on Highway 203 and drive 4 miles (6.4 km) through the town of Mammoth Lakes to the junction of Minaret Road/Highway 203 and Lake Mary Road. Continue straight on Lake Mary Road and drive 4 miles (6.4 km) to a junction for Lake George. Turn left here, drive 0.4 mile (0.6 km), and then turn right and drive 0.3 mile (0.5 km) to Lake George. The trailhead is near the campground.

Campers at Lake George, and those who want a short and easy day hike, will be pleased to find that this "no-sweat" trail provides access to hidden Barrett and TJ Lakes. The trail starts on the northeast shore of **Lake George,** which in itself is a gorgeous spot, and follows the lakeshore for about 300 feet (90 m). It then climbs alongside a small stream to little **Barrett Lake.** The tiny lake is framed by Red Mountain in the background. Since this was so easy, you might as well continue another 0.25 mile (0.4 km) to **TJ Lake,** the more scenic of the two lakes. The distinctive granite fin of Crystal Crag (10,377 ft/3,163 m) towers above TJ Lake's basin, adding drama to the scene. In addition to the pretty but popular lakes, this trail shows off some lovely mountain meadows, gilded with colorful

penstemon, shooting stars, and paintbrush in midsummer.

CRYSTAL LAKE AND MAMMOTH CREST

Distance: 3.8-7.8 miles (6.1-12.6 km) round-trip
Duration: 2-4 hours
Elevation Change: 700-1,400 feet (215-425 m)
Effort: Easy to moderate
Trailhead: Lake George
Directions: From the Mammoth Lakes junction on U.S. 395, turn west on Highway 203 and drive 4 miles (6.4 km) through the town of Mammoth Lakes to the junction of Minaret Road/Highway 203 and Lake Mary Road. Continue straight on Lake Mary Road and drive 4 miles (6.4 km) to a junction for Lake George. Turn left, drive 0.4 mile (0.6 km), and then turn right and drive 0.3 mile (0.5 km) to Lake George. The trailhead is on the right, near some cabins.

If you think Lake George is gorgeous, wait until you see Crystal Lake, southwest of Lake George in a bowl scoured by glaciers and tucked into a hollow below 10,377-foot (3,163-m) Crystal Crag. The trail to reach it has a 700-foot (215-m) elevation gain and is pleasantly shaded by a hardy hemlock, pine, and fir forest. The path begins near the cabins at **Woods Lodge** but rises quickly above them. Many hikers huff and puff as they climb this ridge, but the view of the Mammoth Lakes Basin makes it all worthwhile. You gain a bird's-eye look at the basin's four major lakes: George, Mary, Mamie, and Twin. At a junction at **1 mile (1.6 km),** go left and descend to **Crystal Lake.** The lake is a true jewel, highlighted by permanent snowfields that line its granite backdrop. You aren't likely to find much solitude here because the lake is so easy to reach, but the scenery more than makes up for it.

To turn this into a longer hike, take the other trail at the fork and head 2 miles (3.2 km) farther to **Mammoth Crest,** at 10,400 feet (3,200 m) elevation. The trail gains another 700 feet (215 m) as it leaves the forest and enters a stark, volcanic landscape peppered with whitebark pines. The expansive view from the high point on the crest includes the Mammoth Lakes Basin, the San Joaquin River, the Minaret Range, and Mammoth Mountain. If this hike hasn't taken your breath away, the vista will.

EMERALD LAKE AND SKY MEADOWS

Distance: 4 miles (6.4 km) round-trip
Duration: 2 hours
Elevation Change: 500 feet (150 m)
Effort: Easy to moderate
Trailhead: Coldwater Campground
Directions: From the Mammoth Lakes junction on U.S. 395, turn west on Highway 203 and drive 4 miles (6.4 km) through the town of Mammoth Lakes to the junction of Minaret Road/Highway 203 and Lake Mary Road. Continue straight on Lake Mary Road and drive 3.5 miles (5.6 km) to a fork just before Lake Mary; turn left and drive 0.6 mile (1 km) to the Coldwater Campground turnoff on the left. Turn left and drive 0.5 mile (0.8 km) through the camp to the trailhead at the first parking lot.

This is one of the Eastern Sierra's premier wildflower trails, and it's easy enough for children to hike. The trail starts just south of **Lake Mary,** at the end of the Coldwater Campground road. The hike is short and direct, climbing straight to **Emerald Lake** on an easy grade. Picnickers are often found seated among the rocks at the water's edge, although by midsummer the tiny lake dwindles to something that more closely resembles a pond. No matter, the lake is not the star of the show here; the flowers are. The trail skirts the east shore of Emerald Lake and continues along its inlet stream. Three brief climbs lead you past Gentian Meadow to the southeast edge of **Sky Meadows,** which is filled with wildflowers throughout the summer. Beyond the meadows, permanent snowfields decorate the granite cliffs of Mammoth Crest. Among the wide variety of flower species to be seen and admired, one standout is the tall orange tiger lily, a flower showy enough to be in a florist's shop.

DUCK PASS TRAIL TO DUCK LAKE

Distance: 10 miles (16.1 km) round-trip
Duration: 5 hours
Elevation Change: 1,900 feet (580 m)
Effort: Moderate
Trailhead: Coldwater Campground
Directions: From the Mammoth Lakes junction on U.S. 395, turn west on Highway 203 and drive 4 miles (6.4 km) through the town of Mammoth Lakes to the junction of Minaret Road/Highway 203 and Lake Mary Road. Continue straight on Lake Mary Road and drive 3.5 miles (5.6 km) to a fork just before Lake Mary; turn left and drive 0.6 mile (1 km) to the Coldwater Campground turnoff on the left. Turn left and drive 0.8 mile (1.3 km) through the camp to the Duck Pass trailhead at the farthest parking lot.

The Duck Pass Trail offers myriad options for day hikers and backpackers. You can stop at one of the lakes found along the way—**Arrowhead Lake** (1.3 mi/2.1 km), **Skelton Lake** (2 mi/3.2 km), or **Barney Lake** (3 mi/4.8 km)—or head out for 5 miles (8 km) to **Duck Lake,** elevation 10,450 feet (3,185 m). If you head all the way to Duck Lake, you'll climb 1,600 feet (500 m) to the top of **Duck Pass.** Just beyond the pass, the trail drops 300 feet (90 m) to reach Duck Lake, one of the largest natural lakes in the Eastern Sierra. Most of the climbing is in the stretch from Barney Lake to the pass as the trail switchbacks up a talus-covered slope. Day hikers can make their way from Duck Lake on a faint path to Pika Lake, visible in the distance about 0.5 mile (0.8 km) away.

RED CONES LOOP

Distance: 6.7 miles (10.8 km) round-trip
Duration: 3.5 hours
Elevation Change: 800 feet (245 m)
Effort: Moderate
Trailhead: Horseshoe Lake
Directions: From the Mammoth Lakes junction on U.S. 395, turn west on Highway 203 and drive 4 miles (6.4 km) through the town of Mammoth Lakes to the junction of Minaret Road/Highway 203 and Lake Mary Road. Continue straight on Lake Mary Road and drive 4.8 miles (7.7 km) to the road's end at Horseshoe Lake. The trailhead is on the northwest side of the lake, signed for Mammoth Pass.

Horseshoe Lake, elevation 8,900 feet (2,700 m), lies at the end of Lake Mary Road and has an excellent trailhead that makes

The Volcanic Marvels of Devils Postpile

Few U.S. national parks are designated with monikers as colorful, or as intriguing, as **Devils Postpile National Monument.** First-time visitors all want to know: What the heck is the Devils Postpile? In brief, the Postpile is a formation of towering volcanic rock posts, or columns, made from lava that was forced upward from the earth's core. At the base of the upright 30-foot (9-m) columns is a huge pile of rubble—the crumbled remains of those that have collapsed.

The top of the Devils Postpile looks like hexagon-shaped tiles

The Devils Postpile is proof positive that the Mammoth Lakes area is volcano country. Less than 100,000 years ago, lava filled the San Joaquin River valley more than 400 feet (120 m) deep. As the lava began to cool from the airflow on top, it also cooled simultaneously from the hard granite bedrock below. This caused the lava to harden and crack into tall, narrow pieces, forming nearly perfect columns or posts. Although there are other lava columns found throughout the world (the closest example is at Columns of the Giants on Highway 108 in Sonora Pass, north of Yosemite), the Devils Postpile is considered the globe's finest example. The columns here are more regular in size and shape and more distinctively hexagonal than anywhere else.

You will notice, however, that although many of the lava columns are almost perfectly straight, others curve like tall candles that have been left out in the sun. This curvature was caused by the varying rates at which the massive lava flow cooled. If you take either of the side trails to the top of the Postpile, you can stand on the columns and marvel at the fact that so many are nearly the same height. Under your feet, the tops of the columns look like honeycomb or tiles that have been laid side by side.

A trip to Devils Postpile National Monument is not complete without a visit to **Rainbow Falls** on the San Joaquin River. The falls can be accessed by a 1-mile (1.6-km) trail from Reds Meadow Pack Station, or by taking a longer trail from the Devils Postpile Ranger Station and passing the Devils Postpile along the way. Rainbow Falls, besides being an extraordinarily beautiful river waterfall, is another geologic wonder. The fall drops over volcanic rock of a different type than the basalt of Devils Postpile. The waterfall's cliff is rhyodacite, which forms an extremely hard horizontal layer at the waterfall's lip. This keeps the San Joaquin River from eroding the waterfall and eventually beveling it off. Rainbow Falls can expect to hold on to its impressive height of 101 feet (31 m) for a long, long time.

True to its name, Rainbow Falls does have a rainbow that dances through the mist near its base. The rainbow is best seen at midday, when direct light rays are passing through the water droplets that plummet over the falls.

for a great day hike. Don't be put off by the dead trees and the barren look of Horseshoe Lake's shoreline. A small area near the lake has been affected by carbon dioxide gas venting up through the soil—the result of localized seismic activity—but you leave this strange ghost forest quickly. Set out from the **northwest** side of the lake, ascend the slope, and take the left fork for **McLeod Lake.** In just under 2 miles (3.2 km) you'll reach the start of the loop. Go right to reach **Crater Meadow,** a beautiful little spot set just below Red Cones (a series of small cinder cones), and then circle around to **Upper Crater Meadow.** Either meadow makes a fine destination.

DEVILS POSTPILE AND RAINBOW FALLS

Distance: 5 miles (8 km) round-trip
Duration: 2.5 hours
Elevation Change: 500 feet (150 m)
Effort: Easy to moderate
Trailhead: Devils Postpile Ranger Station
Directions: From the Mammoth Lakes junction on U.S. 395, turn west on Highway 203 and drive 4 miles (6.4 km) through the town of Mammoth Lakes to Minaret Road (still Highway 203). Turn right and drive 4 miles (6.4 km) to the Forest Service Adventure Center, in the Mammoth Mountain Ski Area Gondola Building (adjacent to the Mammoth Mountain Inn). Buy an access pass and pick up the shuttle bus here. Disembark at the Devils Postpile Ranger Station.

The first time you lay eyes on 101-foot (31-m) Rainbow Falls, this tall, wide, and forceful waterfall comes as an awesome surprise. Most first-time visitors see it before or after a trip to the Devils Postpile, a fascinating collection of volcanic rock columns and rubble left from a lava flow that occurred nearly 100,000 years ago.

Start at the **ranger station** and hike to the Devils Postpile lava columns in only **0.5 mile (0.8 km).** Stop and gape at this geologic wonder, and perhaps take the short but steep side trip to the top of the columns; then continue downhill to **Rainbow Falls** at **2.5 miles (4 km).** In order to see the rainbow that gives the waterfall its name, you must show up in late morning or at midday. The rainbow is the result of a prism effect from sun rays refracting through the falling water. Two **overlook areas** across from the waterfall's brink give you an excellent view, but you can hike down a series of **stairsteps** to the waterfall's base for an even better vantage point.

SHADOW LAKE

Distance: 7.6 miles (12.2 km) round-trip
Duration: 4 hours
Elevation Change: 1,900 feet (580 m)
Effort: Moderate
Trailhead: Agnew Meadows
Directions: From the Mammoth Lakes junction on U.S. 395, turn west on Highway 203 and drive 4 miles (6.4 km) through the town of Mammoth Lakes to Minaret Road (still Highway 203). Turn right and continue 4 miles (6.4 km) to the Forest Service Adventure Center, which is in the Mammoth Mountain Ski Area Gondola Building (adjacent to the Mammoth Mountain Inn). Buy an access pass and pick up the shuttle bus here. Disembark at Agnew Meadows.

Those seeking a longer trek in Devils Postpile National Monument should make the trip to Shadow Lake from the trailhead at **Agnew Meadows.** The 7.6-mile (12.2 km) round-trip starts out quite mellow as it wanders through the wildflowers at Agnew Meadows, after which it follows the **River Trail** along the Middle Fork of the San Joaquin River. Just beyond shallow Olaine Lake at 2 miles (3.2 km) lies a **junction;** here you go left for Shadow Lake. Cross a **bridge** and prepare to climb. A long series of steep, shadeless switchbacks ensues as you ascend alongside a narrow creek gorge. Fortunately, the view looking down the San Joaquin River canyon becomes ever more grand as you rise upward. At last you reach the **waterfall** on the lake's outlet stream and climb the final stretch to **Shadow Lake** (elevation 8,737 ft/2,663 m). Its backdrop is like something you've seen on postcards of the Sierra, with the Minarets, Mount Ritter, and Mount Banner towering above the lake. Pick a spot along the lakeshore and drink in the view.

Biking

A great event for road cyclists is the **Mammoth Fall Century & Gran Fondo** (Mammoth Lakes, www.fallcentury.org, Sept., $70-120), a 102-mile (164-km) ride that takes place on a course just east of Tioga Pass, roughly from Bishop to Mono Lake. Short courses of 30 or 45 miles (48 or 72 km) are also offered.

MAMMOTH LAKES

Mammoth Lakes is a mecca for mountain biking. Beginning mountain bikers can ride the **Shady Rest Loop** (5 mi/8 km) at Shady

---

1: TJ Lake 2: Emerald Lake

Rest Park (Sawmill Cutoff Rd.), near the entrance to the town of Mammoth Lakes, or put together a combined dirt and paved loop from Mammoth Creek Park (Old Mammoth Rd.) by starting out on its paved bike trail. More advanced riders can ride the **Knolls Loop** (10 mi/16.1 km), which branches off the Shady Rest Loop.

MAMMOTH LAKES BASIN

If you prefer to do more cruising and less hard climbing on your road bike, take an easy spin around the Mammoth Lakes Basin. For a nearly level 12-mile (19.3-km) loop around the five lakes, start at **Twin Lakes,** on the north end of Twin Lakes Road. Ride south along Lake Mary Road, which circles the lake and continues past Lake George and Lake Mamie to end at Horseshoe Lake.

MAMMOTH MOUNTAIN

The best-known mountain-biking trails are found at **Mammoth Mountain Bike Park** (760/934-0706 or 800/626-6684, www.mammothmountain.com, trail and gondola passes $59 adults, $33 children 12 and under), the summertime persona of Mammoth Mountain Ski Area. The park is famous for its occasional pro races, when all the big-name mountain bikers show up. Most of the time, though, it's just regular vacationers cruising around the more than 100 miles (160 km) of single-track trails, which run the full spectrum from easy to extremely difficult. You can take the gondola to the 11,053-foot (3,369-m) summit of Mammoth Mountain and then race all the way back downhill, navigating a 3,000-foot (900-m) descent. Bike rentals are available from the Adventure Center ($45-99 adults, $25-35 children 12 and under).

Mountain bikers seeking challenging single-track should try the **Mountain View Trail** (5.5 mi/8.9 km), which runs from the Earthquake Fault access road off Highway 203 (Minaret Rd.) to Minaret Vista near the Mammoth Mountain Ski Area. You can retrace your tire treads for the route home, or loop back on the paved Minaret Road.

INYO CRATERS

If you'd rather ride farther from the crowds, check out the wealth of trails on Inyo National Forest lands. The **Inyo Craters Loop** (10 mi/16.1 km) is a popular mountain-biking loop on mostly dirt and gravel roads, suitable for strong beginners and intermediates. The loop begins about 0.25 mile (0.4 km) before the parking lot for Inyo Craters and heads west.

DEVILS POSTPILE

Road bikers seeking a challenge should try out the demanding ride from Mammoth Mountain Ski Area to Reds Meadow at **Devils Postpile National Monument** (20 mi/32 km round-trip, 760/934-2289, www. nps.gov/depo, June-Oct.). The road into the monument is quite narrow and has a 1,500-foot (455-m) elevation change (down on the way in, up on the way back, with 1,000 ft/300 m of change concentrated in a 2.5-mi/4 km stretch). Incredibly scenic throughout its entire length, the trip offers a major bonus for cyclists: In summer, a mandatory shuttle bus system operates during daylight hours, so the amount of traffic on the Devils Postpile road is severely restricted. This makes cycling here surprisingly safe, considering the popularity of this park.

Fishing

Of the five lakes in the Mammoth Lakes Basin, four are anglers' happy hunting grounds: Mary, Twin, George, and Mamie. (Horseshoe Lake, the fifth of the lot, is considered barren.) Each lake is regularly planted with catchable rainbow trout. Occasional brown trout and brook trout are also caught. You can rent boats and fishing rods at Lake Mary at the **Pokonobe Lodge Store** (760/934-2437, www.pokonoberesort.com) or at **Twin Lakes Store** (760/934-7295).

A good source for Mammoth Lakes fly-fishing information, as well as lessons and rentals, is **The Trout Fly** (760/934-2517, www.thetroutfly.com), at the junction of Main Street and Old Mammoth Road. Experienced fly fishers flock to **Hot Creek,** a few miles southeast of Mammoth Lakes on the east side of U.S. 395. Hot Creek originates as an underground creek, formed from a combination of 11 different springs. It bubbles forth from a fissure in volcanic rock; then it runs down a narrow gorge, creating excellent habitat for wildlife, including wild rainbow and brown trout. How big are the fish? The standard trout is at least 12 inches (30 cm), and fish in excess of 20 inches (50 cm) are not unusual. This is a remarkable, world-class fishing stream.

Just a few miles south of Mammoth Lakes is **Convict Lake** (Convict Lake Rd. off U.S. 395), a large drive-up lake with a cabin resort and campground near its edges. This big lake is filled with planted rainbow trout, but it has developed a reputation for hoarding some big brown trout. **Convict Lake Resort** (760/934-3800 or 800/992-2260, www.convictlake.com) rents motorboats, pontoon boats, rowboats, and canoes, and sells bait and tackle.

Horseback Riding

Mammoth Lakes Pack Outfit (Mary Lake Rd., 888/475-8747 or 760/934-2434, www. mammothpack.com, June-Sept.) is located in Mammoth Lakes Basin. Two-hour guided horseback rides ($80 per person) are scheduled daily, and they also offer four- to six-day horseback vacations and customized wilderness pack trips. You can even join in the spring and fall horse drives, when the pack outfit's horses and mules are moved between their winter pasture near Independence and their summer home in Mammoth Lakes Basin, and then back again.

Reds Meadow Resort and Pack Station (Minaret Summit Rd., 760/934-2345, www. redsmeadow.com), on the border of Devils Postpile National Monument, offers two-hour ($68 per person), half-day ($95 per person), and full-day ($150 per person) horseback rides. It also runs a dizzying array of multiday trips into the wilderness.

Convict Lake Pack Station (2000 Convict Lake Rd., 760/934-3800 or 800/992-2260, www.convictlake.com, 9am and noon Tues.-Sun. May-Sept., $67 per person) at Convict Lake, south of Mammoth Lakes, leads guided horseback rides along the lakeshore and longer rides into the John Muir Wilderness.

Rock Climbing

The Eastern Sierra, especially the region between Mammoth Lakes and Bishop, 30 miles (48 km) south, has no shortage of rocks to climb. The **Sierra Mountain Center** (200 S. Main St., Bishop, 760/873-8526, www.sierramountaincenter.com) is a large guide service that can set you up on a rock-climbing or mountaineering adventure. In Mammoth Lakes, **California Alpine Guides** (877/686-2546, www.californiaalpineguides.com, 10am-4pm Mon.-Fri.) offers two- and four-day rock-climbing courses. Beginner, intermediate, and advanced courses are available, as well as guided climbs to Matterhorn Peak and "The Incredible Hulk," two well-known climbing sites west of Bridgeport in the Sawtooth Range. If you need local climbing beta or supplies, **Mammoth Mountaineering Supply** (3189 Main St., Mammoth Lakes, 760/934-4191, www. mammothgear.com) and **Kittredge Sports** (3218 Main St., Mammoth Lakes, 760/934-7566, www.kittredgesports.com, 7am-7pm Sun.-Thurs., 7am-8pm Fri.-Sat.) are good sources for climbing equipment and local knowledge.

Winter Sports

Mammoth Mountain Ski Area (1 Minaret Rd., Mammoth Lakes, 800/626-6684, www. mammothmountain.com, Nov.-June weather permitting) is considered one of the finest ski resorts in California. The resort has a lot to brag about: 3,500 skiable acres (1,400 hectares), 3,100 vertical feet (945 m), 29 lifts, 10 express quads, an average 400 inches (10 m) of snow, and 300 days of sunshine per year. The 11,053-foot (3,369-m) summit of Mammoth Mountain is easily accessible via a glass-paneled gondola; a passel of chairlifts ($100-120) are always in motion up and down the slopes.

Tamarack Lodge (163 Twin Lakes Rd., 760/934-2442, www.tamaracklodge.com) is a cross-country ski resort on Twin Lakes in the Mammoth Lakes Basin. In the lands surrounding this historic lodge, more than 19 miles (31 km) of groomed track are open to cross-country skiers and snowshoers. The resort has cabins for rent in the winter and offers equipment rentals and instructions. Clinics, races, and nature tours are offered on the weekends.

DJ's Snowmobile Adventures (29500 U.S. 395, 760/935-4480 or 800/709-4501, www.snowmobilemammoth.com, 8am-7pm daily Dec.-Apr. weather permitting) offers snowmobile rides through the Inyo National Forest. Both guided and self-guided tours are available; trip options include a 1.5-hour self-guided tour ($103) and a two-hour guided tour ($142-182 per hour). All tours depart from Smokey Bear Flat on U.S. 395. This is a great option for families with children six and older.

ENTERTAINMENT AND EVENTS

Mammoth Lakes is a town that likes to party. The town hosts a series of **festivals** (www.mammothmountain.com) throughout August, usually multiday events featuring live concerts, beer and wine tasting, food from some of Mammoth's fine restaurants, and local and regional artists. The **Mammoth Festival of Beers and Bluesapalooza** (www.mammothbluesbrewsfest.com, Aug.) is a celebration of microbrews and blues. The five-day **Mammoth Jazz** (www.mammothjazz.org, July) features dozens of jazz bands playing to more than 25,000 spectators.

FOOD

Mammoth Lakes is large enough to offer a good range of dining choices. Most restaurants cater to hikers and skiers, so the ambience and food tend to be on the casual side, although there a few fine-dining options.

Good Life Café

Going out to breakfast is something of a Mammoth tradition, and many visitors' first choice is **Good Life Café** (126 Old Mammoth Rd., 760/934-1734, www.mammothgoodlifecafe.com, 6:30am-9pm daily, $8-18). This laid-back spot in the back corner of a strip mall serves an array of egg dishes, including three kinds of eggs Benedict (turkey, crab, and traditional), plus pancakes and French toast. If you sleep in too late, come for lunch or dinner and you can choose from burgers, salads, burritos, quesadillas, and even a New York steak or grilled salmon.

The Lakefront at Tamarack Lodge

For dinnertime alpine ambience, it's tough to beat **The Lakefront at Tamarack Lodge** (off Lake Mary Rd., Lakes Basin, 760/934-2442, www.tamaracklodge.com, 11:30am-2pm and 5:30pm-9pm daily in summer, 11:30am-2pm and 5:30pm-9pm Thurs.-Mon. in winter, $24-45), just a few steps from the shores of Twin Lakes. Chef Bobby Brown serves up elk loin, duck breast, steaks, and seafood in a cozy knotty pine-paneled cabin. There are only 10 tables, so reserve in advance and ask for a table with a view of Twin Lakes. At lunchtime, snag a seat on the outside deck.

Mammoth Brewery

In 2015, the **Mammoth Brewery** (18 Lake Mary Rd., 760/934-7141, www.mammothbrewingco.com, 10am-9:30pm Sun.-Thurs., 10am-10:30pm Fri.-Sat., $10-18) opened its new tasting room and beer garden in downtown Mammoth, and ever since then, its outdoor picnic tables have been the busiest spots in town all summer long. In winter, the food-and-drink action moves indoors, with separate seating areas spread out across three floors. Grab a seat and gulp down a Golden Trout Pilsner or a 395 IPA, and if you're hungry, order an Irish Caesar salad (a yummy recipe made with kale, not romaine), gooey nachos, or a to-die-for burger. The West Coast's highest-altitude brewery has been making award-winning beer in Mammoth since 1995, but this central and spacious location has elevated them even higher. You gotta love their bottle cap logo—a smiling bear face.

Gomez's

If you're in the mood for Mexican food, or if you're just in the mood to sip a margarita on an outdoor patio, **Gomez's** (The Village Plaza, 100 Canyon Blvd., 760/924-2693, www.gomezs.com, noon-9pm daily, $9-18) is a winning bet. Their claim to fame is having the largest selection of tequila (500 bottles) at the highest elevation (8,054 ft/2,455 m) in the world. With a prime location next to the gondola in Mammoth Village, this spot is always hopping in the winter months, but tends to have a mellower vibe in the summer, when all the action is outside on the deck. The menu features lots of burritos, nachos, chiles rellenos, and enchiladas, but with a Latin fusion twist. Happy hour (3pm-6pm) is a great deal, with two-for-one tacos and reduced-price beer and margaritas.

Toomey's

Travelers who have eaten at the Whoa Nellie Deli at the Tioga Gas Mart in Lee Vining will recognize the menu here. Matt Toomey, the talented chef who turned a small-town gas station into a go-to spot for foodies, now operates a successful location in downtown Mammoth Village. **Toomey's** (6085 Minaret Rd., 760/924-4408, www.toomeyscatering.com, 7am-9pm daily, $9-18) features the same food that made the gas station world-famous (lobster taquitos, pan-seared ahi, seafood jambalaya, Angus beef sliders), plus a few surprises, like the coconut mascarpone pancakes for breakfast. Baseball fans will enjoy the collection of memorabilia on the restaurant's walls.

ACCOMMODATIONS

Mammoth Lakes offers an interesting assortment of lodging options, from rustic lakeside cabin resorts in the Lakes Basin to budget chain motels (Motel 6, Quality Inn, Travelodge, Shilo Inn) in the downtown area.

Westin Monache Resort

Feel like you'd rather pamper yourself than get dirty and sweaty in the great outdoors? Even non-nature-geeks will be happy at the luxurious **Westin Monache Resort** (50 Hillside Dr., Mammoth Lakes, 760/934-0400, www.westinmammoth.com, $220-520). Let your spouse hike and bike on Mammoth's trails, while you shop at Mammoth Village or lounge by the heated pool and its two massive Jacuzzis. Each of 210 suites has a kitchen or kitchenette, but the tasty food at the resort's **Whitebark** restaurant will deter you from cooking. Canine guests are welcome; Fifi will love her fluffy dog bed.

Best Western Plus High Sierra Hotel

For a reasonably priced stay that's a few notches above many of Mammoth's two-star hotels, book a room at the **Best Western Plus High Sierra Hotel** (3228 Main St., Mammoth Lakes, 760/924-1234 or 800/568-8520, www.bestwestern.com, $189-269). The hotel has an indoor pool and hot tub, plus a small café where a complimentary breakfast buffet is served. Standard rooms feature king or queen beds; suites have kitchenettes or Jacuzzi tubs. The rooms aren't anything special, but the price is right, the service is dependable, and the location is smack in the middle of downtown Mammoth.

Mammoth Creek Inn

Built in 1972 by a German plumber and his wife and then run by a Scottish family for nearly 30 years, the **Mammoth Creek Inn** (663 Old Mammoth Rd., Mammoth Lakes, 760/934-6162, www.themammothcreek.com, $145-225) has gone through many name changes, renovations, and managers over the years. Its present incarnation offers 26 rooms in a quiet, pleasant retreat just a short distance from downtown Mammoth. Some rooms have kitchens, some do not, but all have been remodeled to look chic and modern, with flat-screen televisions, tasteful furniture, and a few luxuries like down comforters and plush bathrobes. A few loft suites ($229-379) can accommodate up to six people. The inn's main lobby and second-floor study offer cozy places to curl up by the fireplace (or wood stove) with a good book. A billiard room and indoor spa with Jacuzzi, dry sauna, steam room, and fitness center offer options for days when the weather isn't perfect. Pets are welcome in most rooms for a modest fee.

CAMPING

Inyo National Forest Service (www. fs.usda.gov/inyo) campgrounds in Mammoth Lakes are nearly as popular as campgrounds in Yosemite. The most favored camps are those just outside of town in the Mammoth Lakes Basin, home to five beautiful bodies of water. A paved bike trail runs through the basin, connecting the lakes and the campgrounds, and hiking trails abound. The most popular choices include **Twin Lakes Campground** (94 sites, May-Oct.), where each site is within a few steps of the water. A camp store and café are here, as are boat and kayak rentals. More intimate lakeside camping is found at **Lake George Campground** (15 sites, first come, first served, summer only) and **Lake Mary Campground** (48 sites, June-Sept.).

Reserve in advance (877/444-6777, www. recreation.gov, $21-24) for spots at Twin Lakes and Lake Mary, especially in the peak summer months. Drinking water, flush toilets, and bear boxes are provided at the campgrounds.

Sequoia and Kings Canyon

Just south of Yosemite lie two less-visited but

equally spectacular national parks, famous for giant sequoias, soaring mountains, deep canyons, and roaring rivers. Established in 1890, Sequoia was California's first national park and the United States' second (Yellowstone was the first). Kings Canyon was awarded national park status in 1940; today it consists of more than 400,000 acres (162,000 hectares), most of which is backcountry wilderness.

Managed as a single unit by the National Park Service, these two adjacent parks abound with superlatives. Within their borders are Mount Whitney (the highest point in the contiguous United States at 14,494 ft/4,418 m) and several other summits topping out above 14,000 feet (4,200 m); the powerful Kings, Kern, and Kaweah Rivers; and the Kings

Highlights

Look for ★ to find recommended sights, activities, dining, and lodging.

★ **Kings Canyon Scenic Byway:** The drive from Grant Grove to Road's End at Cedar Grove is a 31-mile (50-km) stretch of eye candy following the free-flowing Kings River (page 265).

★ **General Grant Tree:** It's an easy walk to the nation's Christmas tree, the second-largest tree on earth by volume (page 266).

★ **Buena Vista Peak:** It's a mere 1-mile (1.6-km) walk to this spectacular 360-degree vista (page 272).

★ **Roaring River Falls:** A short walk leads to a rocky gorge that rushes with snowmelt in spring (page 276).

★ **Zumwalt Meadow Loop:** This 1.8-mile (2.9-km) loop covers one of the quieter stretches of the Kings River—and nearly everything that's great about Kings Canyon (page 277).

★ **General Sherman Tree:** This mind-boggling giant sequoia—the largest tree on earth by volume—is a must-see (page 282).

★ **Giant Forest Museum:** Check out the exhibits in this historic building to learn about the amazing lives of giant sequoias and their long reign on earth. Then see the giants in person on the Big Trees Trail (page 283).

★ **Moro Rock:** A heart-pumping climb up 390 stairsteps takes you to the top of this 6,725-foot (2,050-m) granite dome (page 284).

★ **Tokopah Falls:** This gentle hike along the Marble Fork Kaweah River leads to views of Tokopah Falls as it crashes over granite slabs and then fans out along the valley floor (page 287).

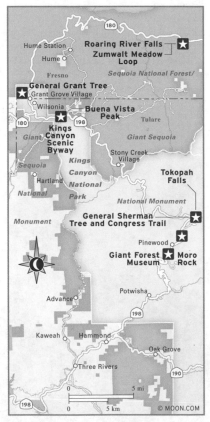

★ **Congress Trail:** Escape the crowds on this beautiful loop past some of the world's most spectacular trees (page 289).

River Canyon, which at a depth of 8,000 feet (2,400 m) is deeper than the Grand Canyon. Travelers who make the long drive on the Kings Canyon Scenic Byway eventually find themselves at Road's End, where civilization ends and the wilderness begins. To continue through the Sierra, your only choice is to walk.

Of all their spectacular sights, the parks are most revered for their giant sequoias. Although sequoias were once widespread across North America, their range has since been reduced to only this narrow band on the western slope of the Sierra Nevada. Of the 75 remaining sequoia groves, more than 50 are found in Kings Canyon and Sequoia National Parks and neighboring Giant Sequoia National Monument. No nature experience is quite as humbling as hiking through a grove of these titans or gazing up in awe at the General Sherman Tree, the world's largest tree by volume.

PLANNING YOUR TIME

Sequoia and Kings Canyon National Parks are open **year-round,** although the **Kings Canyon Scenic Byway closes in winter.** Temperatures throughout the park are affected by elevation; Cedar Grove at 4,500 feet (1,370 m) and the Foothills region at 2,100 feet (640 m) can be very hot in summer (90-105°F/32-41°C), while Giant Forest, Grant Grove, and Mineral King are usually 15-25 degrees cooler. Rain is quite rare during the summer months, but thunderstorms occur occasionally, most often in **July and August.** Winter daytime temperatures average 30-55°F (−1-13°C), and nights often drop below freezing. Snow may fall in the parks any time between **late October and late April** and park roads may close; tire chains can be required on park roads at any time. You must carry chains in your vehicle at all times in the winter season.

Exploring Sequoia and Kings Canyon

VISITORS CENTERS

In addition to the Sequoia and Kings Canyon National Park visitors centers, the **Giant Sequoia National Monument Visitors Center** (35860 Kings Canyon Rd., Sequoia National Forest, 559/784-1500, www.fs.usda. gov/sequoia, 8am-4:30pm Mon.-Fri.) is located 19 miles (31 km) west of Kings Canyon's Big Stump entrance.

Grant Grove

Kings Canyon Visitor Center (559/565-4307, 9am-4pm daily year-round) is 3 miles (4.8 km) east of the park's Big Stump entrance on Highway 180 in Grant Grove Village. Exhibits focus on the area's wildlife and natural history, and a 15-minute film about the parks is shown at regular intervals. Books and maps are available and backpackers' wilderness permits are also issued.

The **Giant Sequoia National Monument Visitors Center** (35860 Kings Canyon Rd., Dunlap, 559/338-2251, 8am-4:30pm Mon.-Fri. year-round) offers visitor information for the national parks, Giant Sequoia National Monument, and Sequoia National Forest, plus books and maps. This Forest Service-run office is outside the national park boundaries, 19 miles (31 km) west of the Big Stump entrance on Highway 180.

Cedar Grove

The small **Cedar Grove Visitor Center** (559/565-3793, 9am-5pm daily May-early Sept.) is near Sentinel Campground at the end of Kings Canyon Scenic Byway. It's a 30-mile

---

Previous: Grant Grove; Mitchell Peak, near High Sierra Camp; Weaver Lake.

Sequoia and Kings Canyon

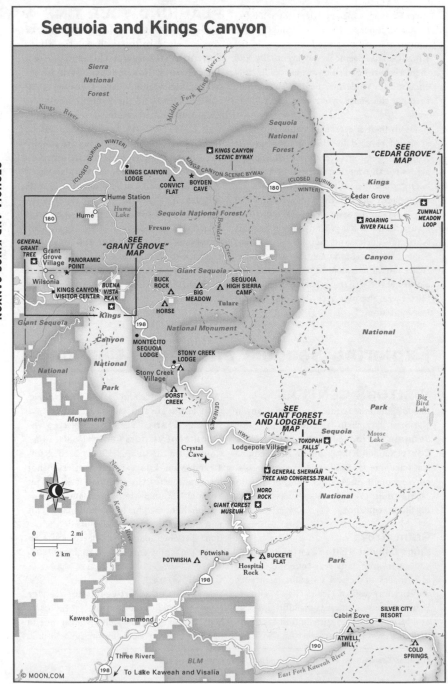

Sierra

National

Forest

Kings River

Middle Fork Kings River

Sequoia

National

Forest

SEE "CEDAR GROVE" MAP

KINGS CANYON SCENIC BYWAY

KINGS CANYON LODGE

KINGS CANYON SCENIC BYWAY

CONVICT FLAT

BOYDEN CAVE

180 (CLOSED DURING WINTER)

Kings

Cedar Grove

ZUMWALT MEADOW LOOP

ROARING RIVER FALLS

(CLOSED DURING WINTER)

Hume Station

Hume Lake

Sequoia National Forest

180

Hume

Fresno

Boulder Creek

Canyon

GENERAL GRANT TREE

Grant Grove Village

PANORAMIC POINT

SEE "GRANT GROVE" MAP

Giant Sequoia

Wilsonia

KINGS CANYON VISITOR CENTER

BUENA VISTA PEAK

BUCK ROCK

BIG MEADOW

SEQUOIA HIGH SIERRA CAMP

HORSE

Tulare

Kings

198

National Monument

National

Giant Sequoia

Canyon

MONTECITO SEQUOIA LODGE

STONY CREEK LODGE

National

Park

National

Stony Creek Village

Monument

DORST CREEK

GENERALS HWY

SEE "GIANT FOREST AND LODGEPOLE" MAP

Sequoia

Park

Big Bird Lake

Crystal Cave

Lodgepole Village

TOKOPAH FALLS

Moose Lake

GENERAL SHERMAN TREE AND CONGRESS TRAIL

MORO ROCK

GIANT FOREST MUSEUM

National

0   2 mi

0   2 km

North Fork Kaweah River

Potwisha

POTWISHA

BUCKEYE FLAT

Hospital Rock

Park

198

SILVER CITY RESORT

Kaweah

Hammond

Cabin Cove

ATWELL MILL

COLD SPRINGS

190

Three Rivers

BLM

198   To Lake Kaweah and Visalia

East Fork Kaweah River

© MOON.COM

Where Can I Find...?

- **Gas:** Gas is available at **Hume Lake Christian Camp** (559/305-7770, year-round), 11 miles (17.7 km) north of Grant Grove via Highway 180, and at **Stony Creek Lodge** (559/565-3909, May-mid-Sept.), a few miles north of Wuksachi Lodge on the Generals Highway. There is **no gas available at Stony Creek Lodge in winter.** Fill up outside the parks in Three Rivers (Hwy. 198, 5 mi/8 km from Ash Mountain/Foothills entrance) or Squaw Valley or Clingan's Junction (Hwy. 180, 20 mi/32 km from Big Stump entrance).

- **Internet service: Wuksachi Lodge, John Muir Lodge, Grant Grove Restaurant, Stony Creek Lodge,** and **Montecito Sequoia Lodge** all have fairly reliable wireless Internet service.

- **Phone service:** Cell coverage is very weak in Sequoia and Kings Canyon, but pay telephones are located at various points in the park.

(48-km) drive east of the Grant Grove area; the road is closed in winter.

Giant Forest and Lodgepole

In Sequoia National Park, the **Lodgepole Visitor Center** (559/565-4436, 7am-5pm daily late May-Oct.) is midway along Generals Highway, 21 miles (34 km) north of the Ash Mountain/Foothills entrance. The film *Bears of the Sierra* is shown several times a day. Books, maps, and bear canisters are available, and wilderness permits and Crystal Cave tour tickets are issued here. A park shuttle stops here daily in summer.

South of Lodgepole on the Generals Highway (and 2 mi/3.2 km south of the General Sherman Tree), the **Giant Forest Museum** (559/565-4480, 9am-6pm daily year-round, shorter hours in winter) has exhibits on the ecology of giant sequoias. Books, maps, and trail information are available. Crystal Cave tour tickets are sold here when the Lodgepole Visitor Center closes in winter. A park shuttle stops here daily in summer.

Foothills

One mile north of the Ash Mountain entrance to Sequoia National Park is the **Foothills Visitor Center** (559/565-4212, 8am-4:30pm daily year-round), just north of the town of Three Rivers on Highway 198. Exhibits focus on the ecology of the low-elevation Sierra foothills. Books, maps, and bear canisters are available, and wilderness permits and Crystal Cave tour tickets are issued here.

Mineral King

The very small **Mineral King Ranger Station** (559/565-3768, 8am-4pm daily late May-late Sept.) is along Mineral King Road, 24 miles (39 km) east of Highway 198. RVs, buses, and trailers are not allowed along this road. Books, maps, and bear canisters are available and an attendant is on hand to answer questions and issue wilderness permits.

ENTRANCE STATIONS

The vehicle entrance fee is $35 for Sequoia and Kings Canyon National Parks and the surrounding lands of Giant Sequoia National Monument; the pass is good for a seven-day stay (motorcycles pay only $30). You must show your receipt any time you pass through one of the parks' entrance stations.

There are two main park entrances: the **Big Stump** entrance on Highway 180 enters Kings Canyon National Park from the north. The **Ash Mountain/Foothills** entrance on Highway 198 enters Sequoia National Park in the south. A third park entrance is at Lookout Point along Mineral King Road, which provides summer access to Mineral King only. Driving times in Sequoia and Kings Canyon can be highly deceptive—curvy mountain roads mean 30 miles (48 km) can easily take an hour, and construction delays are common. Always fill up your gas tank before entering the parks.

No roads cross the Sierra from west to east. The only way to reach the eastern side of the Sierra Nevada is a weeklong backpacking trip. For an update on winter road conditions, contact Caltrans (800/427-7623) or the National Park Service (559/565-3341).

Big Stump Entrance

From Fresno, **Highway 180** winds uphill for 55 miles (89 km) to the Big Stump entrance to Kings Canyon. Shortly past the entrance is a fork in the road; a left turn brings you to **Grant Grove** in about 3 miles (4.8 km). This entrance makes a good choice for visitors with only a short amount of time to spend in the park; it's also the only access for the **Kings Canyon Scenic Byway** and **Cedar Grove** (a one-hour drive).

A right turn at the fork leads south along the **Generals Highway** toward the **Giant Forest** and **Lodgepole** areas in Sequoia National Park. Plan on one hour for the 25-mile (40-km) drive.

Ash Mountain Entrance

From Visalia, **Highway 198** heads east for 36 miles (58 km) to the small town of Three Rivers. From Three Rivers, the road becomes Generals Highway and leads north for 6 miles (9.7 km) to the Ash Mountain entrance and the **Foothills** region of Sequoia National Park. The Foothills Visitor Center is 1 mile (1.6 km) past the entrance.

It's a 16-mile (26-km) drive north along Generals Highway from the Ash Mountain entrance to the **Giant Forest** area and the General Sherman Tree. Plan on about 45 minutes for this drive, which navigates 130 curves and 12 switchbacks on its way to the Giant Forest. **Lodgepole** is another 15 minutes' drive north; it takes a full hour to reach Grant Grove and Highway 180.

Lookout Point Entrance

From Three Rivers on **Highway 198,** a very curvy, winding drive leads 11 miles (17.7 km) north to the Lookout Point entrance to **Mineral King** (the entrance is usually not staffed). The region's hiking trails, campgrounds, and cabins are another 14 miles (22.5 km) east along **Mineral King Road.** The 25-mile (40-km) road navigates 698 curves, and it takes about 75 minutes to drive. It's typically open May to October only and does not connect to any other roads in the park.

From Yosemite

Plan on **3.5 hours** if driving to Sequoia and Kings Canyon from Yosemite. Start from Yosemite's South entrance near Wawona and drive south on Highway 41 for 65 miles (105 km) to Fresno. Turn east on Highway 180 and drive 60 miles (97 km) to the Big Stump entrance for Kings Canyon National Park. From the entrance station, plan on another 10 minutes of driving to reach Grant Grove or another 60 minutes to reach Giant Forest.

SHUTTLES

Sequoia National Park operates a shuttle bus system (559/565-3341, www.nps.gov/seki). Shuttles run 8am-6pm daily from late May through September 1 and during the Thanksgiving and Christmas holidays (10am-4:30pm daily). Four free in-park routes are offered, as well as a shuttle from Visalia that costs $15 per person round-trip; no additional entrance fee is charged.

- **Giant Forest** (Route 1/Green): This frequently traveled route shuttles between the Giant Forest Museum and the Lodgepole Visitor Center, stopping at the lower trailhead for the General Sherman Tree. Shuttles arrive every 15 minutes for the 30-minute trip.

- **Moro Rock/Crescent Meadow** (Route 2/Gray): The second most frequent route runs along Crescent Meadow Road (3 mi/4.8 km) from the Giant Forest Museum to Crescent Meadow, stopping at the Moro Rock trailhead only on the outbound trip. Shuttles arrive every 10 minutes for the 15-minute trip.

Crescent Meadow Road is closed to private vehicles weekends and holidays (8am-7pm), so riding the shuttle is the only way to visit Moro Rock or Crescent Meadow. (If you arrive before 9am or after 6pm, or if you have a valid disabled parking permit or overnight wilderness permit, you may drive your own car.) All shuttle buses are wheelchair accessible.

- **Lodgepole/Wuksachi/Dorst** (Route 3/ Purple): The northernmost shuttle travels between Lodgepole Visitor Center, Wuksachi Lodge, and Dorst Creek Campground (beginning in June). From Lodgepole, it is possible to connect to the Giant Forest shuttle and continue farther south. Shuttles arrive every 20 minutes.

- **Wolverton/General Sherman** (Route 4/Orange): The very short Wolverton-to-General Sherman shuttle travels from the upper General Sherman Tree trailhead at Wolverton to the lower General Sherman Tree trailhead on the Generals Highway. This allows for an all-downhill walk to the Sherman Tree. Shuttles arrive every 15 minutes starting at 9am.

- **Giant Forest/Foothills/Visalia:** (Blue) During the summer months, you can ride the **Sequoia Shuttle** (877/287-4453,

www.sequoiashuttle.com, reservations required, $15 round-trip, no park entrance fee) from Visalia or Three Rivers into the park. The Sequoia Shuttle stops at the Giant Forest Museum, where you can transfer to the free in-park shuttle. Buses leave the Visalia Transit Center hourly (6am-10am); the return trip leaves Giant Forest hourly (2:30pm-6:30pm). It's a two-hour ride each way.

TOURS

Sequoia Sightseeing Tours (559/561-4189, www.sequoiatours.com) is a private company that offers three shuttle van tours into Sequoia and Kings Canyon. Part of the appeal is that groups are small, typically fewer than 10 people. The **Sequoia Half Day Tour** (10am-1:30pm, $79 adults, $59 children 12 and under) departs from Wuksachi Lodge and visits the General Sherman Tree, Tunnel Log, Moro Rock, and Crescent Meadow. The **Sequoia Full Day Tour** (8:30am-4:30pm, $149 adults, $99 children 12 and under) departs from Three Rivers and visits all of the highlights of the Giant Forest area and then heads to Wuksachi Lodge for lunch before returning to Three Rivers. The **Kings Canyon Full Day Tour** (mid-May-mid-Oct. only, $139 adults, $89 children 12 and under) departs

A free shuttle bus travels around Giant Forest in the summer months.

The Best of Sequoia & Kings Canyon

- **Best Backpacking Trip:** Rae Lakes Loop (page 280)

- **Best Cheap Thrill:** Moro Rock in Giant Forest (page 284)

- **Best Giant Sequoia Grove:** House and Senate Groves on the Congress Trail in Giant Forest (page 289)

- **Best Meal:** Lunch or dinner at Wuksachi Lodge (page 292)

- **Best Riverside Walk:** Zumwalt Meadow Loop, near Road's End (page 277)

- **Best Swimming Hole:** Middle Fork Kaweah River, near Buckeye Flat Campground (page 297)

- **Best Tent Camping:** Stony Creek Campground (page 296)

- **Best Wheelchair-Accessible Trail:** Big Trees Trail in Giant Forest (page 284)

- **Best Winter Adventure:** Pear Lake Ski Hut (page 292)

- **Most Luxurious Wilderness Experience:** Sequoia High Sierra Camp (page 294)

- **Most Secluded Giant Sequoia Grove:** Redwood Mountain Grove (page 270)

- **Most White-Knuckle Drive:** Mineral King Road (page 299)

from either Wuksachi Lodge or John Muir Lodge and travels through Grant Grove to Cedar Grove.

Driving Tours

Within the parks are two exceptional driving tours: the **Kings Canyon Scenic Byway,** which leads from Grant Grove to Road's End in Cedar Grove; and the **Generals Highway,** which traverses a 50-mile (81-km) stretch from Grant Grove to the Foothills Visitor Center. Allow a full day for each drive to have plenty of time to enjoy the scenery and take a few excursions on foot.

GENERALS HIGHWAY

The scenic 50-mile (81-km) Generals Highway was built in 1935 to connect the General Grant Tree in Kings Canyon to the General Sherman Tree in Sequoia National Park. Start your tour at the Big Stump entrance on Highway 180 in Kings Canyon and allow a full day for the drive.

From the Big Stump entrance, turn right at the junction and onto the Generals Highway. Drive 4 miles (6.4 km) south to **Redwood Mountain Overlook** and stop to look southward over the 3,400-acre (1,400-hectare) **Redwood Mountain Grove,** the world's largest remaining stand of sequoias. More than 15,000 sequoias larger than a foot in diameter thrive in this grove. Continue driving south for 2 miles (3.2 km) to the **Quail Flat junction.** A right turn accesses the trailhead for hikes into the Redwood Mountain Grove; a left turn leads to Hume Lake.

Continue south on the Generals Highway for 1 mile (1.6 km) to the 7,100-foot (2,200-m) **Kings Canyon Overlook,** with views of the Middle and South Forks of the Kings River. Across the highway is the trailhead for the hike to **Buena Vista Peak** (1 mi/1.6 km).

The drive continues southeast, reaching **Stony Creek Lodge** in 7 miles (11.3 km), where groceries and gas are available. From here, the Generals Highway climbs to 7,335-foot (2,236-m) Little Baldy Saddle (a 2-mile/3.2-km trail leads to Little Baldy's summit), and then drops down to the left turnoff for **Wuksachi Lodge,** a great place for a meal or an overnight stay.

One mile (1.6 km) south is **Lodgepole Village,** with its well-stocked grocery store, visitors center, deli and pizza parlor, campground, showers, laundry, and trailheads for a number of hikes. Continuing southward, the highway enters **Giant Forest.** To see the chart-topping **General Sherman Tree,** the largest tree on earth by volume, turn left at the sign for Wolverton/General Sherman Parking and then follow the 0.5 mile (0.8-km) trail downhill to the tree. During the summer months, leave your car and ride the free **shuttle bus** to other highlights in the Giant Forest area, including **Moro Rock, Crescent Meadow,** and the **Giant Forest Museum.** If the bus isn't running, you can drive yourself (the 3-mi/4.8-km-long Crescent Meadow Road is a left turn off the Generals Highway just past the Giant Forest Museum). More than 40 miles (64 km) of trails travel through the Giant Forest; pick any one and take a walk among nature's majestic sentinels. The 1-mile (1.6-km) **Big Trees Trail,** which starts at the Trail Center shelter by the museum, is a great introduction.

Past the Crescent Meadow turnoff, the Generals Highway begins to lose elevation. At Commissary Cove, a side road descends 6.5 miles (10.5 km) to **Crystal Cave** (get cave tour tickets in advance at the Lodgepole or Foothills Visitor Centers). After this fork, the main highway descends a series of steep switchbacks, dropping into the deep canyon of the Middle Fork Kaweah River. In less than 10 miles (16.1 km), the road loses more than 3,000 feet (900 m) in elevation, and the air temperature rises substantially. Pause at the turnout at **Amphitheater Point** to look back uphill at precipitous **Moro Rock,** which seems to cling to the mountainside, and then stop at **Hospital Rock** to see the Native American pictographs and *morteros* (rock holes) once used for grinding seeds.

After passing two campgrounds, **Buckeye** and **Potwisha,** the Generals Highway finally winds downward to pass underneath **Tunnel Rock** before it reaches the **Foothills Visitor Center.**

★ KINGS CANYON SCENIC BYWAY

There's an undeniable allure about a place called **Road's End.** That enticing moniker designates the eastern terminus of Highway 180, the **Kings Canyon Scenic Byway.** The road's snaking, winding pavement reaches an end 6 miles (9.7 km) past Cedar Grove Village, and that's where the wilderness begins. If you want to continue farther into Kings Canyon,

Kings River

you have to walk. At one time, engineers talked of building a highway from here across to U.S. 395 and the Eastern Sierra, but wilderness prevailed and the plan was dropped in 1965.

The drive to reach Road's End is half the fun: From Grant Grove, the Kings Canyon Scenic Byway zigzags east for 31 miles (50 km), skirting the banks of the roaring **Kings River.** You'll need to stop often for photo ops, especially in the early season when snowmelt turns the river into a tumbling sea of white water. Pullouts along the highway provide overlooks into **Kings Canyon,** one of the deepest canyons in the world—a stunning 8,200 feet (2,500 m) from top to bottom. Be sure to pause at **Junction View** to look down at the confluence of the Middle and South Forks of the Kings River. It's not hard to envision the relentless force of the Kings River chiseling away at the canyon walls over eons. Continuing east, you'll see evidence of the 2015 Rough Fire, which burned for nearly

five weeks and destroyed most of the buildings at the historic Kings Canyon Lodge (but the lodge's 1928 gravity-flow gas pumps were saved and are as photogenic as ever).

Stop at **Boyden Cavern,** tucked into tall gray marble cliffs, for a 45-minute guided tour of its speleothems. In spring and early summer, nearby **Grizzly Falls** is worth a gander; the 80-foot (24-m) waterfall swells with snowmelt as it tumbles off a granite cliff.

Once you arrive at **Cedar Grove Village,** you won't be overwhelmed by choices for dining and lodging. "Village" is a bit of an exaggeration. A handful of campgrounds, one small lodge, a ranger station, and a burger-flipping café put the period on civilization, but hiking trails abound.

Note that the Kings Canyon Scenic Byway is **closed in the winter months.** It opens by the end of April each year; autumn closing dates vary depending on weather. Most services in Cedar Grove (food, camping, and lodging) are not open until mid- to late May.

Grant Grove

Many visitors get their first glimpse of Sequoia and Kings Canyon at **Grant Grove Village.** In 1890, the Grant Grove area was known as General Grant National Park; in 1940, it was absorbed into the much larger Kings Canyon National Park. Today, Grant Grove's large visitor services area includes a lodge and cabins, a restaurant, grocery store, post office, and several nearby campgrounds. The **Kings Canyon Visitor Center** (559/565-4307, 8am-4:30pm daily year-round) is also here. This is a great place to stop for maps, guidebooks, and advice from rangers.

After arriving via the Big Stump entrance on Highway 180, continue north for 3 miles (4.8 km) through the park. (Ignore the junction's south turnoff to Generals Highway and Sequoia National Park.) The village complex will be on the right across from the park campgrounds.

SIGHTS
★ General Grant Tree

The main attraction in Grant Grove is the **General Grant Tree** and its surrounding sequoias. The General Grant Tree is also known as "the nation's Christmas tree," so dubbed by President Calvin Coolidge. Every year since 1926, the park has held a Yuletide celebration around the tree's base. The General Grant Tree is the world's second-largest tree at 268 feet (82 m) tall and 107.5 feet (32.8 m) in circumference. Measured at its base, the Grant Tree is 40 feet (12.2 m) wide, a diameter that tops that of the park's General Sherman Tree.

A paved, 0.6-mile (1-km) trail loops around the tree and visits neighboring giants, including the **Fallen Monarch,** a downed sequoia that was hollowed out by fire. (Because of its immense girth, it was once used as a stable for the U.S. Cavalry's horses.) Also found on the

Grant Grove

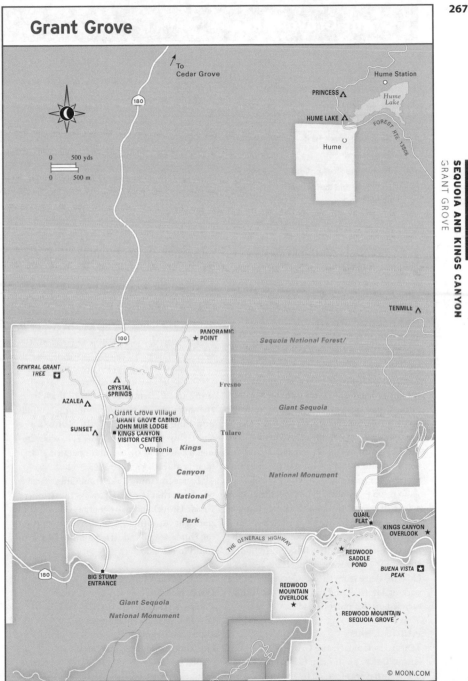

To
Cedar Grove

Hume Station

PRINCESS

Hume
Lake

HUME LAKE

Hume

FOREST RTE 13S08

180

0   500 yds
0   500 m

TENMILE

PANORAMIC
★ POINT

Sequoia National Forest/

180

GENERAL GRANT
TREE

CRYSTAL
SPRINGS

Fresno

AZALEA

Giant Sequoia

Grant Grove Village
GRANT GROVE CABINS/
JOHN MUIR LODGE
■ KINGS CANYON
VISITOR CENTER
Wilsonia   Kings

SUNSET

Tulare

Canyon

National Monument

National

Park

QUAIL
FLAT

KINGS CANYON
OVERLOOK ★

THE GENERALS HIGHWAY

★ REDWOOD
SADDLE
POND

BUENA VISTA
PEAK

180

BIG STUMP
ENTRANCE

REDWOOD
MOUNTAIN
OVERLOOK
★

Giant Sequoia

National Monument

REDWOOD MOUNTAIN
SEQUOIA GROVE

© MOON.COM

Grant Grove Hikes

Trail	Effort	Distance	Duration
Big Stump Trail	Easy	1 mi/1.6 km rt	30 min
Buena Vista Peak	Easy	2 mi/3.2 km rt	1 hr
Boole Tree Loop	Easy	2.4 mi/3.9 km rt	1 hr
Big Baldy	Moderate	4.2 mi/6.8 km rt	2.5 hr
Redwood Creek Trail	Moderate	4.4 mi/7.1 km rt	2 hr
Sunset Trail	Moderate	5 mi/8 km rt	2.5 hr
Park Ridge Fire Lookout	Moderate	5.2 mi/8.4 km rt	3 hr
Hart Tree and Redwood Creek Loop	Moderate	7.3 mi/11.8 km rt	3 hr

trail is the Gamlin Cabin, which was built by sheepherder Israel Gamlin in 1872. It later became the first ranger station in General Grant National Park, now known as Kings Canyon.

Panoramic Point

The Grant Grove area is more than just sequoia central. To get better acquainted with the Kings Canyon landscape, head for Panoramic Point, where vistas span nearly the entire length of Kings Canyon National Park. From the parking lot at Panoramic Point, a 0.5-mile (0.8-km) loop trail leads to Panoramic Point, elevation 7,520 feet (2,290 m). The point overlooks a maze of canyons and sawtooth Sierra peaks; it's especially impressive at sunrise.

To reach Panoramic Point from the visitors center, drive east through the Kings Canyon Visitor Center parking lot. Turn left around Bradley Meadow, then make a right at the junction just before the John Muir Lodge, signed for Panoramic Point. It's a 2.3-mile (3.7-km) drive from the visitors center to the parking lot. (RVs and trailers are not recommended on this narrow road.)

Hume Lake

Ten miles from Grant Grove Village lies Hume Lake, an 85-acre (34-hectare) body of water that was formed by the world's first concrete-reinforced multiple-arch dam. Built in 1908 by the Hume-Bennett Lumber Company, the dam and its lake supplied water to a flume that floated lumber from logged sequoia trees 67 miles (108 km) to the town of Sanger. The flume was the longest ever built, and was used first by the lumber company and later by thrill-seeking tourists who would ride down the flume in specially designed boats.

Today the lake has lovely beaches for swimming and a 2.5-mile (4-km) trail that circles the shoreline, plus a number of campgrounds and summer camps for kids. Hume Lake Christian Camp (559/305-7770, www.humelake.org) has owned and operated a large facility at the lake since 1945.

To reach Hume Lake from Grant Grove, head northeast on Highway 180 (toward Cedar Grove) and drive 9 miles (14.5 km) to the right turnoff for Hume Lake. Turn right on Hume Road and drive 3 miles (4.8 km) south to the lake.

RECREATION

Day Hikes

PARK RIDGE FIRE LOOKOUT

Distance: 5.2 miles (8.4 km) round-trip
Duration: 3 hours
Elevation Change: 300 feet (90 m)
Effort: Moderate
Trailhead: Panoramic Point near Grant Grove Village

Directions: From Grant Grove Village, turn north on the road by the visitors center and drive past the Grant Grove cabins. Go left around the meadow; just before the John Muir Lodge, turn right onto the road signed for Panoramic Point (RVs and trailers are not recommended). It's 2.3 miles (3.7 km) from the visitors center to Panoramic Point.

Start your trip by taking the 0.25-mile (0.4-km) walk from the parking area to Panoramic Point, which delivers what its name promises. An interpretive display names the many peaks and valleys you can see, including the prominent pointy summit that is Mount Goddard (13,560 feet/4,135 m). From Panoramic Point, follow the Park Ridge Trail, which leads to the right along the ridge. Your views continue as you contour along the ridgeline, now looking toward the west and the San Joaquin Valley as you head gently uphill. The trail intersects a dirt road; follow it for about 150 feet (45 m), then bear left onto the trail again. You'll intersect this dirt road once more about 300 feet (90 m) before the lookout tower. Follow the road to Park Ridge Fire Lookout (elevation 7,540 ft/2,300 m) and check out the nifty outdoor shower at its base. This lookout station was established in 1916, but the structure you see here was built in 1964. The tower is operated by volunteers during the fire season (typically May-Oct.). If someone is working inside, he or she may give you permission to come up and take a look around.

For your return trip, walk down the trail back to Panoramic Point or take the shorter fire road, which also leads back to the parking lot. Views are much better along the trail.

BOOLE TREE LOOP

Distance: 2.4 miles (3.9 km) round-trip
Duration: 1 hour
Elevation Change: 500 feet (150 m)
Effort: Easy
Trailhead: Boole Tree
Directions: From Grant Grove Village, drive 4.2 miles (6.8 km) north on Highway 180 to the left turnoff for Forest Road 13S55, signed for Boole Tree, Converse Basin, and Stump Meadow. Drive 2.6 miles (4.2 km) on

an unpaved road and park in the wide parking pullout. The drive to the Boole Tree trailhead is worth the trip in itself: You pass through a beautiful, ghostly meadow filled with giant sequoia stumps, a sight so otherworldly that it may stay ingrained in your memory. The Boole Tree hike is a loop; take the right side first to make the ascent more gradual. You climb 500 feet (150 m) to the top of a ridge and then descend the other side, reaching the Boole Tree in 1 mile (1.6 km). (It's just off the main loop, accessible via a short, obvious spur.) At 269 feet (82 m) tall and with a diameter of 35 feet (10.7 m), the Boole Tree is the largest tree in any of the national forests, and it's one of the largest trees in the world. Named for the foreman of the Converse Mill, Frank Boole, this behemoth is one of a very few giant sequoias left standing in the Converse Basin grove. The rest were clear-cut in the late 1800s. In the remaining leg of the loop, you'll be rewarded with a stellar panorama of Spanish Mountain and the Kings River Canyon.

SUNSET TRAIL

Distance: 5 miles (8 km) round-trip
Duration: 2.5 hours
Elevation Change: 1,300 feet (400 m)
Effort: Moderate
Trailhead: Sunset Campground
Directions: Park near the visitors center at Grant Grove Village. Cross the road (Hwy. 180) and follow the paved trail toward Sunset Campground's amphitheater. Continue left through the camp to site 118 and the trailhead.

The Sunset Trail leaves Sunset Campground (elevation 6,590 ft/2,010 m) and heads gently downhill for 2.25 miles (3.7 km) to Ella Falls, a pretty 40-foot (12-m) cascade on Sequoia Creek. At 1.5 miles (2.4 km) after the falls, you reach a junction with the South Boundary Trail where you can take a short side trip to the left to Viola Falls; it isn't much of a waterfall but it is a memorably scenic spot on granite-sculpted Sequoia Creek. Most people just mosey down the trail, enjoying the big pines and firs and the flowering western azaleas. If you like, you can follow the trail for its entire 2.5-mile (4-km) length to **Sequoia Lake**. Although the lake is privately owned, hikers are allowed to walk along its edge—but the return trip is all uphill with a 1,300-foot (400-m) elevation gain, so save some water and energy.

BIG STUMP TRAIL

Distance: 1 mile (1.6 km) round-trip
Duration: 30 minutes
Elevation Change: 200 feet (60 m)
Effort: Easy
Trailhead: Big Stump Picnic Area
Directions: From the Big Stump entrance station on Highway 180, drive 0.5 mile (0.8 km) to the Big Stump Picnic Area and the trailhead.

The Big Stump Trail is a pleasant nature walk that provides an excellent history lesson as well. The short loop circles a meadow filled with stumps of mind-boggling size. Most of the big trees were cut for timber in the 1880s. Besides the stumps, other evidence of logging activities remains, including piles of sawdust that were created more than a century ago (sequoia wood decays very slowly). A few mature sequoias still thrive along the route, their cinnamon-colored bark stark against the rest of the forest. Highlights include the **Burnt Monarch**, a shell of a giant sequoia that has been ravaged by fire but still stands. The **Mark Twain Stump** belonged to a 26-foot-wide (8-m) tree that took two men 13 days to cut down in 1891. Be sure to pick up an interpretive brochure at the trailhead.

REDWOOD CREEK TRAIL

Distance: 4.4 miles (7.1 km) round-trip
Duration: 2 hours
Elevation Change: 700 feet (215 m)
Effort: Moderate
Trailhead: Redwood Saddle Road
Directions: From Grant Grove, drive 5 miles (8 km) south on the Generals Highway to Redwood Saddle and the Hume Lake turnoff. Turn right on narrow, unpaved Redwood Saddle Road and drive 1.8 miles (2.9 km) on the dirt road to the trailhead parking area.

The Redwood Mountain Grove is one of the few places on earth where hikers can see more than 2,000 giant sequoias in one relatively small area. A few loop trips are possible in the grove, but one of the loveliest and simplest routes is an out-and-back walk alongside Redwood Creek. The beauty begins even before you start walking. On the last mile of the drive to the trailhead, the dirt access road winds through giant sequoias that are so close, you can reach out your car window and touch them. Take the trail signed for the **Hart Tree** and head downhill. At a junction reached at 0.3 mile (0.5 km), follow **Redwood Creek Trail** to the right. Because of the life-giving presence of Redwood Creek, these sequoias grow amid a dense background of dogwoods, firs, ceanothus, and mountain misery. Although the standing sequoias are impressive, some of the fallen ones are even more astounding. Only when these trees are lying prone can you get some perspective on their immense size. Be sure to hike the full 2.2 miles (3.5 km) to the **stream crossing** of Redwood Creek. Some of the best tree specimens are found there, near the junction with the **Sugar Bowl Loop Trail.** The return trip is all uphill, gaining 700 feet (215 m), but it's easier than you'd expect.

HART TREE AND REDWOOD CREEK LOOP

Distance: 7.3 miles (11.8 km) round-trip
Duration: 3 hours
Elevation Change: 1,100 feet (335 m)
Effort: Moderate
Trailhead: Redwood Saddle Road
Directions: From Grant Grove, drive 5 miles (8 km) south on the Generals Highway to Redwood Saddle and the Hume Lake turnoff. Turn right on narrow, unpaved Redwood Saddle Road and drive 1.8 miles (2.9 km) on the dirt road to the trailhead parking area.

For a more extensive exploration of the magnificent Redwood Mountain Grove, hike this 7.3-mile (11.8-km) loop that visits many of the grove's highlights. Start on the trail signed for the **Hart Tree** and head downhill. In just over

1: Buena Vista Peak **2:** Grant Grove

0.3 mile (0.5 km), you reach a **junction** where you should head left, leaving the Redwood Creek Trail for your return. Cross **Barton Creek** at 0.6 mile (1 km) and shortly you'll come across the **Redwood Log Cabin,** a hollowed-out fallen sequoia with a stone fireplace inside. The makeshift "cabin" was used as a homestead as late as the 1930s. The trail ascends the hillside and then reaches an exposed granite knob at 2 miles (3.2 km), where you can enjoy a view of Big Baldy to the southeast.

On your descent from this viewpoint you'll pass by lovely **Hart Meadow** and many fine sequoia specimens. Walk through the passageway in the **Tunnel Log** and cross a creek at 3.2 miles (5.2 km). In another 0.25 mile (0.4 km), take the short spur trail to see the **Hart Tree,** one of the 25 largest sequoias in the world at 278 feet (85 m) tall and with a ground circumference of 75 feet (23 m). The tree was named after Michael Hart, the man who discovered it in the 1880s. About a mile farther is the spur trail to the **Fallen Goliath,** a massive downed tree. In summer 2014, this huge log caught fire from an illegal campfire that burned out of control. Despite the efforts of firefighters, the Fallen Goliath burned from the inside out for more than a month. It's still intact, though—giant sequoias are remarkably fire-resistant. After crossing **Redwood Creek,** turn right and head back uphill to the parking lot in 1.6 miles (2.6 km).

★ BUENA VISTA PEAK

Distance: 2 miles round-trip
Duration: 1 hour
Elevation Change: 420 feet (128 m)
Effort: Easy
Trailhead: Kings Canyon Overlook/Buena Vista Peak
Directions: From Grant Grove Village, drive 7 miles (11.3 km) south on the Generals Highway to the Buena Vista trailhead on the right, just across the road and slightly past the large pullout for the Kings Canyon Overlook.

Near the drive-up Kings Canyon Overlook lies a trail that delivers expansive 360-degree views, plus a chance at a private picnic spot. Buena Vista Peak is not a summit but a rocky dome, and at 7,603 feet (2,317 m) it is one of the highest points west of Generals Highway. It offers far-reaching views of what looks like a million conifers at your feet (those are the giant sequoias of the Redwood Mountain Grove) and the hazy foothills to the west, but the best vistas—of the snowcapped peaks of the John Muir and Monarch Wildernesses—are to the east. An easy **30-minute walk** leads south and then winds up the gentler "back side" of the dome, passing through pine and fir forest and dense swaths of manzanita. Don't miss the **giant boulder sculptures** in the trail's first 0.25 mile (0.4 km); these rounded monoliths were formed underground, then exposed by erosion. Once on the nearly level top of **Buena Vista Peak,** you can wander around the spacious granite summit, enjoying different perspectives on the vista. Big Baldy is clearly visible to the south, about 500 feet (150 m) higher than the summit you're standing on. Look to the east to pick out Buck Rock Fire Lookout Tower, which seems to pop out from nowhere on a conifer-covered ridge, and the jagged ridge of the Great Western Divide, an awe-inspiring panorama of peaks. Stay and enjoy the scene. The hike back to your car is all downhill.

BIG BALDY

Distance: 4.2 miles (6.8 km) round-trip
Duration: 2.5 hours
Elevation Change: 650 feet (200 m)
Effort: Moderate
Trailhead: General Grant Tree
Directions: From Grant Grove Village, drive 8.5 miles (13.7 km) south on the Generals Highway to the Big Baldy Trailhead; the trailhead is on the right, shortly before the junction for Big Meadows.

The trip to Big Baldy comes with expansive views—you'll see Redwood Canyon, Redwood Mountain, Buena Vista Peak, Little Baldy, Buck Rock, and the Great Western Divide—and a little workout. The trail climbs 650 feet (200 m), but the gain is nicely spread out over 2 miles (3.2 km). The trail alternates between dense firs and pines and open granite slabs as it winds along the rim of Redwood Canyon.

The trail's initial vistas are to the west, but they keep changing and getting more interesting all the way to Big Baldy's 8,209-foot (2,502-m) **summit,** where the scene opens up to 360 degrees. Here you get your first panoramic views of the High Sierra peaks and the Great Western Divide to the east. A bonus: The first mile of trail faces to the west, making this a great spot for watching the sunset. The Big Baldy Trail is also ideal for snowshoeing in the winter.

Horseback Riding

Grant Grove Stables (559/335-9292, www. nps.gov/seki) offers one- and two-hour guided horseback rides. A one-hour ride ($40) loops around the North Grove and Dead Giant area near the General Grant Tree. Most people prefer the two-hour ride ($75), which follows a more interesting path through the giant sequoias and down to Sequoia Lake. Either ride is suitable for people who have never ridden; the horses are led at a very sedate pace—no galloping or trotting. The stables are near the General Grant Tree and reservations are recommended. Children must be at least seven years old; helmets are provided but not required. Credit cards are not accepted.

Winter Sports

Winter is one of the best seasons to visit Sequoia and Kings Canyon. There is nothing quite as delightful as the sight of giant sequoias crowned in fresh snow, their cinnamon-colored trunks and deep-green needles dusted in white. Bring your sleds, cross-country skis, snowshoes, and warm clothes and get ready to see the quieter face of these national parks. Cross-country skis, snowshoes, and snow gear can be rented at the **Grant Grove Gift Shop** (Grant Grove Village, 9am-5:30pm daily Dec.-Apr.). Any snow-covered park trails are fair game for snowshoeing and cross-country skiing. In the Grant Grove area, your best bets are in **General Grant Grove** itself and along the trail to **Park Ridge Lookout.** If there's not enough snow there, head south toward Little

Baldy Saddle, where the elevation is higher. If you'd rather not fiddle with any snow gear, simply drive to the **Big Stump** snow-play area (near the entrance station) and build a snowman with the kids.

The Kings Canyon Scenic Byway to Cedar Grove is closed during the winter months, but all other park roads are open. (Though park roads are plowed, you must carry tire chains in your car October-May, even if you have a four-wheel-drive vehicle.)

FOOD

The aptly named **Grant Grove Restaurant** (866/807-3598, breakfast 7am-10am, lunch 11:30am-3:30pm, dinner 5pm-9pm daily year-round, www.visitsequoia.com) has been feeding Kings Canyon and Sequoia visitors since it first opened in the 1950s. But times have changed. In 2014, Grant Grove Restaurant and its nearby lodgings were acquired by Delaware North Companies (DNC), the same company that runs Wuksachi Lodge in Sequoia National Park. DNC tore down the aging building and constructed a much larger and more stylish restaurant that opened in 2017. The new dining space has big windows overlooking Bradley Meadow, vaulted ceilings, a fireplace, an outdoor dining patio, and a large courtyard with picnic tables. In summer, a walk-up window allows visitors to quickly purchase to-go items like coffee and ice cream.

The **Grant Grove Market** (8am-9pm daily in summer, 9am-6pm daily in winter), in Grant Grove Village, is mere steps from the restaurant, with a surprisingly large selection of food and drinks.

ACCOMMODATIONS

Grant Grove has the largest variety of lodging options in the parks, including tent cabins, stand-alone cabins, duplex cabins, and rooms at the John Muir Lodge.

Grant Grove Cabins

The 15 historic **Grant Grove Cabins** (559/335-5500 or 877/436-9615, www.

visitsequoia.com, $70-129) look and feel like throwbacks to the 1920s. The most coveted cabin is Number 9, also known as the Honeymoon Cabin; built in 1910, it's the oldest structure in Grant Grove Village. In summer, Grant Grove's tent cabins (May-Nov.) are budget-conscious choices starting at $78. Rustic and bare-bones, the tent cabins are furnished with two double beds and a picnic table (no heat or electricity). Some cabins come with private baths and some are without. For guests staying in cabins without baths, public showers and toilets are a few steps away.

John Muir Lodge

For a modern hotel-style stay, the two-story, 34-room **John Muir Lodge** (559/335-5500 or 877/436-9615, www.visitsequoia.com, $200-250 in summer, $150 in winter) provides a comfortable year-round option. The lodge was built in 2000 and remodeled in 2014, when the concessionaire added extra insulation to the walls to improve soundproofing. Standard rooms feature two queen beds, while deluxe rooms include one king bed and one sofa bed. The lodge's "great room" has cozy chairs and tables for reading by the stone fireplace. The Grant Grove Restaurant is within easy walking distance.

CAMPING

Sunset, Azalea, and Crystal Springs

Three popular campgrounds (www.nps. gov/seki) lie within 2 miles (3.2 km) of each other, the General Grant Tree, and Grant Grove Village. **Sunset** (mid-May to mid-Sept., $22) is the largest campground, with 127 sites for tents or RVs up to 30 feet (9 m). It's the first campground you'll come to after entering the park through the Big Stump entrance and is directly across the park road from Grant Grove Village. ★ **Azalea** (year-round, $18) lies just north of Sunset, along the turnoff to the General Grant Tree. Its 110 sites are scattered among several forested loops; some sites are tent-only. Azalea is usually the first camp in this area that is open in early summer and has many large, shaded sites. In May and June, lucky visitors get to see the camp's namesake azaleas in bloom. It's a five-minute walk to the market and restaurant at Grant Grove, and a separate trail leads from camp to the giant sequoias at the Grant Grove. **Crystal Springs** (mid-May to mid-Sept., $18) lies across the park road from Azalea and has 36 campsites for tents and RVs and 14 group sites ($40) that can accommodate 7-15 people.

The wooden Grant Grove Cabins are a throwback to the 1940s.

All the camps are at about 6,800 feet (2,100 m) in elevation, where summer days are warm but the nights are cool. Drinking water and flush toilets are available, and a restaurant, store, and hot showers (summer only) are across the road in Grant Grove Village, 0.5 mile (0.8 km) away. All sites are first come, first served; reservations are not accepted.

Princess

If you can't find space at the three Grant Grove campgrounds, the nearest option is **Princess Campground** (877/444-6777, 559/335-2232, www.recreation.gov, mid-May to mid-Sept., $27-54), outside the park boundaries about 8 miles (13 km) northeast along Kings Canyon Scenic Byway. The 64-site camp is set in a beautiful meadow bordered by giant sequoias and is just 4 miles (6.4 km) from Hume Lake. The camp has drinking water and vault toilets and reservations are accepted.

Hume Lake

Privately managed **Hume Lake Campground** (877/444-6777, www.recreation.gov, mid-May to mid-Sept., $25-54) is on the shore of 85-acre (34-hectare) Hume Lake, which is also home to a number of summer camps for kids. (Expect to hear a lot of campfire songs in the evenings.) The camp has 64 sites with drinking water and flush toilets. A store, café, laundry, and bike and canoe and kayak rentals are available nearby.

Reservations are accepted up to six months in advance.

Landslide, Tenmile, and Convict Flat

Three first-come, first-served Forest Service campgrounds are in Giant Sequoia National Monument near the Hume Lake area; because none of them take reservations, they usually have last-minute sites available. **Landslide** ($18, late May-Oct.), at 5,800 feet (1,770 m), has nine sites (six are tent-only) with vault toilets and drinking water. From Grant Grove, drive 9 miles (14.5 km) north on Highway 180. Turn right on Hume Road and drive 3 miles (4.8 km) south to Hume Lake, then continue on Forest Road 13S09/Tenmile Road and drive 3 miles (4.8 km) to Landslide campground.

Tenmile (Tenmile Rd., $23, year-round) has 11 sites at an elevation of 5,800 feet (1,770 m). The campground has vault toilets but no drinking water. From Grant Grove, drive 9 miles (14.5 km) north on Highway 180. Turn right on Hume Road and drive 3 miles (4.8 km) south to Hume Lake, then continue on Forest Road 13S09/Tenmile Road and drive 5.5 miles (8.9 km) to Tenmile campground.

Convict Flat (Hwy. 180, Apr.-Oct., free) lies 19 miles (31 km) northeast of Grant Grove at only 3,000 feet (900 m). There are five sites with vault toilets, but there's no drinking water.

Cedar Grove

From the Big Stump entrance station on Highway 180, set aside at least an hour for driving the 35 winding miles (56 km) northeast along Kings Canyon Scenic Byway. At the bottom of this scenic descent lies Cedar Grove Village, where a lodge and campgrounds are located. The road is typically open April-October but closes in winter. Food and lodging in Cedar Grove is not available until late May, but you can sightsee and hike any time the road is open.

SIGHTS

Knapp's Cabin

During the 1920s, wealthy Santa Barbara businessman George Owen Knapp, the first president of Union Carbide Corporation, enjoyed taking luxurious trout-fishing trips in Kings Canyon. This one-room cabin, now the oldest building in Cedar Grove, was used as a storage shed for his rather extravagant gear. Knapp, who believed in living in fine style, is also well known for building Knapp's Castle, a lavish sandstone mansion (now mere ruins, but in a spectacular spot) in the mountains above Santa Barbara. Knapp's Cabin is an interesting structure, but the canyon views from the grounds surrounding it are the real draw.

A short walk to the cabin begins at a signed pullout 2 miles (3.2 km) east of the Cedar Grove Village turnoff.

Muir Rock

One of the best activities at Cedar Grove is just sitting by the Kings River and watching the water roll by. There may be no better place to do that than at Muir Rock, also known as Muir's Pulpit. This large, sloping granite slab at the edge of the South Fork was a spot favored by John Muir in the early 20th century. Legend has it that he would stand on the rock and give enthusiastic preservation talks to groups of Sierra Club members. Generations of visitors have jumped off this rock into the frigid river water—it's about an 8-foot (2.4-m) drop)—but make sure you wait until late summer when the current is calmer. Just downriver is a sandy beach where you can lay out a towel and watch the action.

The rock is accessible via a 300-foot (90-m) trail from the parking lot at Road's End.

★ Roaring River Falls

It's an easy stroll to Roaring River Falls, a pretty waterfall that drops through a narrow gorge into the South Fork Kings River. What's extraordinary about the waterfall is not the cascade itself, but the giant rocky pool into which it falls—it's at least 50 feet (15 m) wide. This is the only waterfall in Sequoia and Kings Canyon that is at least partially accessible via wheelchair (one section may be too steep for some wheelchair users).

The trailhead parking area is 3 miles (4.8 km) east of the Cedar Grove Village turnoff. At the spot where the paved trail ends, the waterfall is perfectly framed by two big conifers. Hikers can continue heading downstream on the River Trail to Zumwalt Meadow in 1.6 miles (2.6 km) or Road's End in 2.7 miles (4.3 km).

RECREATION

Day Hikes

HOTEL CREEK TRAIL TO CEDAR GROVE OVERLOOK

Distance: 5 miles (8 km) round-trip
Duration: 2.5 hours
Elevation Change: 1,200 feet (365 m)
Effort: Strenuous
Trailhead: Cedar Grove Village
Directions: In Cedar Grove Village, turn left (north) at the sign for the visitors center and Cedar Grove Lodge. Continue past the market on the main road, heading north for 0.25 mile (0.4 km). The Hotel Creek Trailhead is on the left at the junction with the pack station road. The destination of this hike is a stunning overlook of Kings Canyon, but the canyon

Cedar Grove

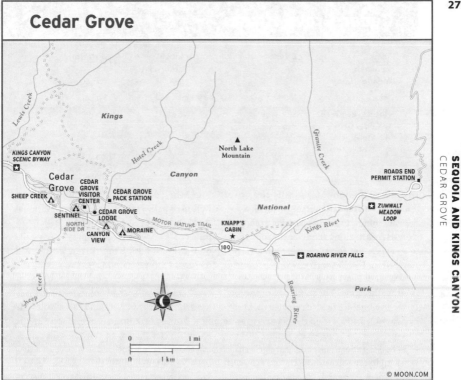

vistas come at you nonstop for most of the walk. Even if you don't go all the way to the overlook, you'll still get an eyeful. The **Hotel Creek Trail** consists of dozens of switchbacks over sunny, exposed slopes, climbing 1,200 feet (365 m) over 2 miles (3.2 km) to a trail junction with the **Overlook Trail.** Turn left to head to the **overlook,** which peers down on Cedar Grove and the length of Kings Canyon. The best views are of Monarch Divide's high peaks to the north. This is a great place to break out the picnic supplies. For a 5-mile (8-km) round-trip, retrace your steps back to Cedar Grove.

If you want to walk farther, you can continue from the overlook junction for another 1.5 miles (2.4 km) and turn left, hiking downhill on the **Lewis Creek Trail** and making a 7-mile (11.3-km) loop. This stretch of the Lewis Creek Trail is lined with sweet-smelling ceanothus. Unfortunately, the final 1.2 miles (1.9 km) of this loop parallel a park road, but the trail overlooks the South Fork Kings River, and it's not uncommon to spot wildlife here.

★ ZUMWALT MEADOW LOOP

Distance: 1.8 miles (2.9 km) round-trip
Duration: 1 hour
Elevation Change: 150 feet (45 m)
Effort: Easy
Trailhead: Zumwalt Meadow
Directions: From Cedar Grove, drive 5 miles (8 km) east on the Kings Canyon Byway to the Zumwalt Meadow Trailhead.

A scenic 1.8-mile (2.9-km) loop alongside the South Fork Kings River, the Zumwalt Meadow Loop is a delight for hikers of all abilities. Many people bring their fishing rods to try their luck in the river, but for most, the scenery is better than the fishing. At the edge of

Cedar Grove Hikes

Trail	Effort	Distance	Duration
Zumwalt Meadow Loop	Easy	1.8/2.9 km mi rt	1 hr
Mist Falls	Moderate	9.2 mi/14.8 km rt	5 hr
Hotel Creek Trail to Cedar Grove Overlook	Strenuous	5 mi/8 km rt	2.5 hr

fern-filled Zumwalt Meadow lie clear river pools and a fragrant forest of incense-cedars and pines. From the parking area, walk **downstream** along the river (to your right) to a suspension **footbridge.** Cross it, then turn left and walk **upstream.** The loop begins at an obvious **fork,** and you can hike it in either direction. The south side of the loop traverses a boulder field of jumbled rocks that have tumbled down from the massive granite cliff of the Grand Sentinel, elevation 8,504 feet (2,592 m). The north side cuts through a thick, waist-high fern forest and follows a **wooden walkway** over a marsh. The trail offers many views of one of Kings Canyon's most obvious landmarks: 8,717-foot (2,657-m) North Dome, an imposing chunk of granite that was carved by glacial action. The towering walls of North Dome and the Grand Sentinel rise 3,500 feet (1,100 m) from the valley floor. The meadow is named for Daniel Zumwalt, a lawyer who once owned this beautiful spot and encouraged Congress to designate Kings Canyon as a national park.

MIST FALLS

Distance: 9.2 miles (14.8 km) round-trip
Duration: 5 hours
Elevation Change: 650 feet (200 m)
Effort: Moderate
Trailhead: Road's End, Cedar Grove
Directions: From Cedar Grove, drive 6 miles (9.7 km) east on the Kings Canyon Scenic Byway to Road's End. The trailhead is next to the wilderness permit station.

The Mist Falls Trail is probably the most well-used pathway in Kings Canyon National Park, and with good reason. It's a stellar 4.6-mile (7.4-km) walk to an impressive cascade on the South Fork Kings River, with only a 650-foot (200-m) gain in elevation along the way. Many backpackers use this trail to access Paradise Valley and points beyond, while most day hikers turn around at Mist Falls. The first **2 miles (3.2 km)** are a level walk up the Kings River Valley, with canyon walls towering above you on both sides. You're in a dry, open forest much of the time. At 2 miles (3.2 km), go left at a trail **junction.** You'll start to climb over granite (almost all of this hike's elevation gain happens in the second half). The farther you go, the more expansive the views become; make sure you keep turning around so you can take in the whole panorama. At **4 miles (6.4 km),** the trail gains elevation and the river gets more boisterous, with crashing pools and rocky granite slides. In 0.25 mile (0.4 km) you reach **Mist Falls,** which fans out over a 45-foot-wide (14-m) granite ledge and crashes into a boulder-lined pool. It creates a tremendous spray and mist in early summer, and mellows out as the season goes on. Take a look at the falls, then walk back down the trail 0.2 mile (0.3 km) to the obvious, immense slab of granite you just passed. This is a favorite spot to have lunch with a wide-open view of 10,007-foot (3,050-m) Avalanche Peak. Look carefully and you can pick out the stone face

1: Mist Falls **2:** Zumwalt Meadow **3:** Muir Rock

of The Sphinx, so named by John Muir for its resemblance to the Egyptian monument.

Backpacking

Cedar Grove marks the end of the paved road into Kings Canyon, and it's a prime jumping-off spot for backpackers who want to explore the spectacular backcountry between the western and eastern Sierra. From the aptly named Road's End, numerous backpacking options are available. Wilderness permits are required for overnight travel and each trail is subject to daily entry quotas.

Wilderness permits are available from the **Road's End Permit Station** (559/565-3766, www.nps.gov/seki, 7am-3:45pm daily May-Sept., $15). Daily trailhead quotas are in effect from late May to late September. Reservations are available for three-quarters of each quota; reserve in advance for the most popular trips. The remaining quota spots are available on a first-come, first-served basis (after 1pm the day before departure, or on the day of departure). Even with a reservation, backpackers must pick up a permit at the wilderness permit station on the afternoon before a trip (after 1pm), or no later than 9am on the morning of departure. Outside of the quota period (Sept.-May), self-issue permits are available outside the permit station, but the road into Cedar Grove is closed in winter.

Reservations are accepted starting on March 1 up to two weeks prior to your trip. A permit application is available online (www.nps.gov/seki); completed forms must be mailed (Wilderness Permit Reservations, 47050 Generals Hwy. #60, Three Rivers, CA 93271) or emailed (seki_wilderness_reservations@nps.gov) as a PDF attachment.

RAE LAKES LOOP

The most popular backpacking trip is the **Rae Lakes Loop** (41 mi/66 km round-trip), which climbs from 5,035 feet (1,535 m) at the Road's End trailhead to nearly 12,000 feet (3,700 m) at spectacular, boulder-strewn Glen Pass (which may be impassable until mid-July). The loop can be hiked in either direction, following either the Mist Falls/Paradise Valley Trail or the Bubbs Creek Trail from Road's End, but most hikers choose the former. This is considered one of the most scenic backpacking trips in the Sierra, with one photo opportunity after another, including beautiful Dollar Lake, Arrowhead Lake, Fin Dome, suspension bridges, and numerous stream crossings (go late in summer if you want to avoid cold waist-high water). The Rae Lakes themselves are so popular that there is a two-night stay limit per lake.

LEWIS CREEK TRAIL

A less "glamorous" hike that attracts far fewer people than Rae Lakes, the **Lewis Creek Trail** (9.7 mi/15.6 km one-way) climbs 3,200 feet (975 m) over the course of 5.5 miles (8.9 km) to pristine **Frypan Meadow** at 7,800 feet (2,400 m) elevation. After many, many switchbacks, the trail crosses lovely Comb Creek at 3.2 miles (5.2 km), then Lewis Creek 1 mile (1.6 km) farther. In early summer, verdant Frypan Meadow is littered with wildflowers, a glorious vision after this strenuous ascent.

COPPER CREEK TRAIL

For a longer three-day trip, follow the **Copper Creek Trail** (21 mi/34 km round-trip) to gorgeous **Granite Lake.** The trailhead is at 5,000 feet (1,500 m) and Granite Lake is at 9,972 feet (3,039 m), so if you're up for a backpacking trip with a 5,000-foot (1,500-m) elevation gain over 10 miles (16.1 km), the Granite Lake Basin is your ticket to happiness. This trail is considered one of the most strenuous in the Cedar Grove area; the route is often hot and dry as it switchbacks up manzanita-covered slopes. Your first night's **camp** is at Lower Tent Meadow, 4 miles (6.4 km) in at 7,800 feet (2,400 m). After that, your luck improves. With Mount Hutchings looming over your left shoulder, the second day's 6 miles (9.7 km) will go easier, bringing you to rocky, jewel-like Granite Lake in only a few hours.

Horseback Riding

Cedar Grove Pack Station (559/565-3464

Visiting Mount Whitney

At 14,505 feet (4,421 m), Mount Whitney is the highest peak in the contiguous United States. The peak is named for Harvard geology professor Josiah Dwight Whitney, who served as the first director of the California Geological Survey. In the 1860s, he sent a team of five men, including explorer William Brewer, to map the southern Sierra Nevada. Brewer named the peak Mount Whitney to honor his supervisor.

Mount Whitney is one of the most popular peaks to climb in the entire Sierra Nevada. Despite the length and difficulty of the trail to its summit, it has become so well traveled that trailhead quotas are in place not only for backpackers, but even for day hikers. Although the peak is within the borders of Sequoia National Park, the vast majority of people access it from outside the park, on the eastern side of the Sierra, by hiking from the Whitney Portal trailhead near Lone Pine off U.S. 395. That's because from any trailhead in Sequoia (the western approach) the summit is a minimum of 56 miles (90 km) away, about a week's worth of hiking for most backpackers. From the east side, however, it's a mere 11 miles (17.7 km), and most hikers choose to accomplish this as a very long day hike of 22 miles (35 km) round-trip.

Mount Whitney

Making the eastern approach as a day hike requires ascending and descending more than a vertical mile along the way (6,131 ft/1,869 m in all). For most hikers, that means a predawn start and a grueling march. If you're in great physical condition, it's manageable, but unfortunately many people who attempt it are not, and they wind up suffering from dehydration, hypoglycemia, and even altitude sickness, never making it to the top. Even when starting from the east side, it's much easier to divide the trip into two or even three days. Inyo National Forest (760/873-2483, www.fs.usda.gov/inyo) administers a lottery every February to allocate wilderness permits for both day hikes and overnight hikes starting from Whitney Portal. If you don't enter the February lottery for the following summer, you won't have much chance of getting a permit later in the year unless you wait until very late in the autumn, and by then the days are growing very short.

To make your trip the best it can be, get a permit for a weekday in September or early October, when the crowds will have thinned considerably. The month of August sees the highest trail usage. Spend a couple of days at high elevation before you set out on the Mount Whitney Trail, and come prepared with sunglasses, sunscreen, good boots, and warm clothes for the summit. And there's one additional element to plan for: With tens of thousands of people visiting this fragile alpine environment every year, human waste and toilet paper must be packed out. "Pack-out kits" are available at the Eastern Sierra Interagency Visitor Center in Lone Pine or along the High Sierra Trail near the Crabtree Ranger Station.

If you strike out on a permit for the eastern approach, you can always take a week and hike in from the west side in Sequoia National Park. Permits (559/565-3341, www.nps.gov/seki) for the western approach are easy to come by. Several routes are possible, but the most popular is the High Sierra Trail from Crescent Meadow. If you start here and exit via the Mount Whitney Trail at Whitney Portal, you will have traveled 80 miles (129 km) across the Sierra Nevada and witnessed some of the most spectacular high-country scenery imaginable. It's the trip of a lifetime. The only hurdle is that you need to have car transportation arranged at Whitney Portal. The drive from there to Crescent Meadow, where you'll start your hike, is about 300 miles (485 km). It takes about six hours of driving (from Lone Pine, you need to drive south to Mojave, cross Walker Pass to Bakersfield, and then head north to Sequoia), but it's the only option unless you feel like turning around and retracing your steps.

in summer, 559/337-2413 in winter, www.nps.gov/seki) provides one-hour ($40) and two-hour ($70) guided horseback rides along the Kings River. They also offer multiday pack trips: visitors ride "horse pack" into the backcountry, to destinations such as the Monarch Divide and the Rae Lakes Loop, and camp overnight. The pack station is just outside Cedar Grove Village. Reservations are recommended and helmets are provided (but not required).

FOOD AND ACCOMMODATIONS

Cedar Grove Lodge

When heading out the Kings Canyon Scenic Byway to Cedar Grove, there's only one dependable choice for a roof over your head. At the **Cedar Grove Lodge** (877/436-9650, www.visitsequoia.com, late May-mid-Oct., $120-165), patios and balconies overlook the Kings River and all rooms feature two queen beds, air-conditioning, and telephones (cell phones won't work here). The lodge's small **Cedar Grove Snack Bar** (7:30am-8pm daily late May to mid-Oct., $8-10) has a grill for flipping pancakes and French toast for breakfast, and burgers and steaks for dinner.

There's not a huge range of choices, but who's going to complain about a tri-tip sandwich, a half rack of ribs, or a Caesar wrap way out here at Road's End? If you prefer to cook your own meals, you'll find limited groceries at the **Cedar Grove Lodge Gift Shop and Market** (next to the snack bar). Otherwise, bring a well-stocked cooler.

CAMPING

Cedar Grove has four campgrounds (www.nps.gov/seki) with sites near the Kings River: ★ **Sheep Creek** (111 sites, May-mid-Oct., $18), **Sentinel** (82 sites, May-Sept., $18), **Moraine** (120 sites, May-Sept., $18), and **Canyon View** (May-mid-Oct., $35-50), which has 16 group sites for 7-19 people. The camps are relatively similar in terms of scenery and amenities (picnic tables, fire grills, flush toilets); Sheep Creek is the top choice for its proximity to the South Fork Kings River, plus the tall pines that provide welcome shade. All sites are first come, first served; no reservations are accepted. If you show up in the late morning hours (10am-11am) when campers are vacating their sites, you'll have the pick of the litter. The Cedar Grove Ranger Station is a short walk away.

Giant Forest and Lodgepole

Giant Forest and Lodgepole are at the midway point of the Generals Highway in Sequoia National Park. These areas contain a high concentration of visitor services, giant sequoias, and hiking trails.

SIGHTS

TOP EXPERIENCE

★ General Sherman Tree

It's difficult to adequately express your feelings when you see the **General Sherman,** the world's largest living tree. Other trees are taller or wider, but none has the combined weight and width of this leviathan. The giant sequoia is 275 feet (84 m) tall—taller than a 27-story building—and is still growing. At its base, the circumference is 102.6 feet (31.3 m). Every year it adds enough wood to make another 60-foot-tall (18-m) tree. One branch of the General Sherman is so big—almost 7 feet (2.1 m) in diameter—that it's larger than most trees east of the Mississippi. Even at approximately 2,200 years old, it's not the world's oldest tree; some other, smaller sequoias are 1,000 years older.

The General Sherman Tree attracts a crowd, which is why the park runs **shuttle buses** to two separate stops, one above and

Giant Forest and Lodgepole

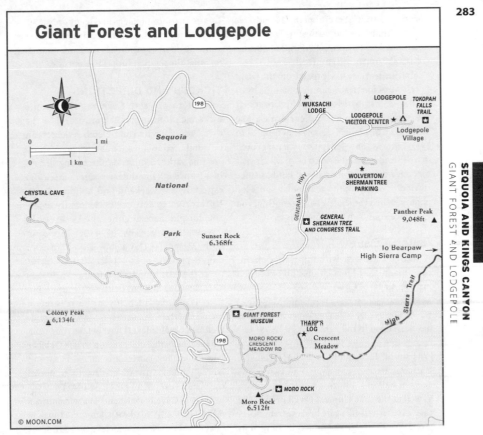

© MOON.COM

one below this amazing tree. Many visitors get off at the upper stop and walk 0.5 mile (0.8 km) downhill to the lower stop, passing the General Sherman along the way. That's fine for a quick trip, but there's much more to do here. Get an even bigger dose of sequoia awesomeness by hiking the adjacent **Congress Trail,** a 2.1-mile (3.4-km) paved loop that travels through dozens of sequoias.

To reach the General Sherman from Lodgepole, drive 1 mile (1.6 km) south on Generals Highway to the General Sherman Tree parking lot off Wolverton Road. Follow the trail downhill to the General Sherman Tree or take the free shuttle bus.

★ Giant Forest Museum

Giant Forest has the most impressive collection of giant sequoias in Sequoia and Kings Canyon National Parks. Among its 8,000 giant sequoias are the General Sherman and a host of less famous but equally impressive trees. Naturalist John Muir named this grove "Giant Forest" in 1875 because its trees are so colossal in size they startle the imagination. Walk among them to fully appreciate their cathedral-like majesty.

Start your exploration at the **Giant Forest Museum** (559/565-4480, 9am-6pm daily in summer, shorter hours in winter), housed in a renovated 1928 building designed by architect Gilbert Stanley Underwood. (Underwood was famous for designing Yosemite's Ahwahnee Hotel.) Originally a market, the building now serves as a museum, visitors center, and bookstore, and as the trailhead for many Giant

Forest-area trails. Several paths are suitable for wheelchairs, including the **Big Trees Trail** (less than 1 mile) and the 0.5-mile (0.8-km) **General Sherman Tree Trail.**

Shuttles traverse a side road from the Giant Forest Museum in the summer months, providing access to **Moro Rock, Crescent Meadow,** and two big-tree curiosities: The **Tunnel Log,** a fallen sequoia that toppled in 1937 and was tunneled out so that cars could drive through; and the **Auto Log,** which visitors once could drive on top of but has since started to decay. Both are popular spots for photos. When the shuttle isn't operating, you can drive your own car along this road.

Crystal Cave

A marble karst cave with impressive chambers, magnificent formations, and polished marble, **Crystal Cave** (559/565-4251, www. sequoiaparksconservancy.org, mid-May-Nov.) was discovered by park employees in 1918 and has been open to the public for 70 years. The cave is one of more than 200 limestone caverns found in Sequoia and Kings Canyon National Parks. (Fun fact: The two parks contain half of California's mile-long caves, as well as the state's longest cave.) Behind the cave's spiderweb-like gate lies a secret underground world—a glittering 3-mile-long (4.8-km) maze of marble decorated with beautiful speleothems. Paved pathways and solar-powered electric lights accommodate the 50,000 people that enter its recesses each year.

Crystal Cave is open for a variety of guided tours. The standard **Family Tour** (50 minutes, $16 adults, $8 children 5-12, $5 children under 5), while a great choice for the mildly curious and families with young children, doesn't rate high on the adventure scale. For more excitement, sign up for the **Wild Cave Tour** (559/565-4251, Sat. June-Aug., ages 16 and up, $135 pp), a four- to six-hour belly-crawling trek through total darkness. Headlamps and knee and elbow pads are provided, and participants should be prepared to get dirty as they stoop-walk, crawl, and climb through off-trail passageways. There's also a **Junior**

Caver Tour for preteens and teens only ($30, ages 10-15 years). Don't forget a jacket: It's about 50 degrees inside Crystal Cave no matter what the temperature is like outside.

TICKETS AND DIRECTIONS

A visit to Crystal Cave requires some **advance planning;** tickets are not sold at the cave. From March to mid-October, tickets can be purchased in advance at www.recreation. gov (the park recommends purchasing 30 days in advance during the busy summer season, especially for weekend and holiday visits). Unreserved tickets are occasionally available for purchase at either the **Lodgepole** (Generals Hwy., 559/565-4436, 7am-5pm daily Memorial Day-Labor Day, 8am-5pm daily Sept.-Oct.) or **Foothills Visitor Center** (near the Ash Mountain entrance, 559/565-4212, 8:30am-4:30pm daily year-round), but there is no guarantee. If your heart is set on seeing Crystal Cave between March and mid-October, obtain tickets well before your visit. During the parks' quiet season in late October and November, tickets are not sold at www. recreation.gov; instead, go directly to one of the visitors centers to purchase tickets.

Crystal Cave is at the end of a winding 6.5 miles (10.5 km) road off Generals Highway near Giant Forest (no vehicles over 22 ft/6.7 m long permitted). Driving to the cave from either visitors center takes about 1.5 hours, plus additional time to hike the steep 0.5-mile (0.8-km) trail to the cave entrance.

TOP EXPERIENCE

★ Moro Rock

At least once in your life, you gotta do it, even if you don't buy the T-shirt afterward: climb **Moro Rock.** The 6,725-foot (2,050-m) precipice—a bald granite dome that protrudes from a forested ridge—is accessed via a series of ramps and staircases. To reach the top, you climb 390 stairs, holding tight to railings that line the rock-blasted trail. The trip is only 0.25 mile (0.4 km) one-way, but even the hardiest hikers will be huffing and puffing. Catch your

Giant Forest and Lodgepole Hikes

Trail	Effort	Distance	Duration
Crescent Meadow and Tharp's Log	Easy	1.6/2.6 km mi rt	1 hr
Congress Trail	Easy	2.1 mi/3.4 km rt	1.5 hr
Tokopah Falls	Easy	3.6 mi/5.8 km rt	2 hr
Muir Grove	Easy	4 mi/6.4 km rt	2 hr
Little Baldy	Moderate	3.4 mi/5.5 km rt	2 hr
Heather Lake and the Watchtower	Strenuous	9.2 mi/14.8 km rt	5 hr
Alta Peak	Strenuous	13 mi/20.9 km rt	8 hr

breath by stopping to admire the view of the Kaweah River gorge far below, or the zigzagging switchbacks of the Generals Highway as it heads south toward Three Rivers.

Once you've gained Moro Rock's flat summit, lean on the iron railing and take in the panorama of the Great Western Divide, a sawtooth skyline of alpine cirques and glacier carved peaks that is sure to inspire. This chain of mountains runs north-south through the center of Sequoia National Park, dividing the watersheds of the Kaweah River to the west and the Kern River to the east. A good map will help you name the myriad peaks and passes; some obvious landmarks are Castle Rocks, Triple Divide Peak, and Mount Stewart. To the west, you can see all the way to the Coast Range, 100 miles (160 km) away; in closer focus is the Middle Fork of the Kaweah River, 4,000 feet (1,200 m) below.

For the best visibility, hike Moro Rock early in the day. The sky is clearest early in summer mornings and on the cooler days of fall and spring. But no matter how good the visibility, there's one summit you can't see—Mount Whitney, the highest peak in the contiguous United States. It's almost due east from Moro Rock and only about 60 miles (97 km) away, but because the peaks of the Great Western Divide reach altitudes of 12,000 feet (3,600 m) or higher, you can't see over the tops of them.

Moro Rock lies 2 miles (3.2 km) south of the Giant Forest Museum off Generals Highway. Crescent Meadow Road, the access road east to Moro Rock, is closed to private cars during peak times in summer. From the Giant Forest Museum, park your car in the lot across the road and ride the free shuttle bus to Moro Rock; the bus leaves every 15 minutes.

RECREATION
Day Hikes
LITTLE BALDY

Distance: 3.4 miles (5.5 km) round-trip
Duration: 2 hours
Elevation Change: 750 feet (230 m)
Effort: Moderate
Trailhead: Little Baldy Saddle
Directions: From the Big Stump entrance on Highway 180, drive 1.5 miles (2.4 km) and turn right on the Generals Highway, heading south for Sequoia National Park. Drive approximately 18 miles (29 km) to the Little Baldy Trailhead on the left, 1 mile (1.6 km) past the turnoff for Dorst Creek Campground (look for the sign for Little Baldy Saddle).

Along this stretch of the Generals Highway, there are so many peak trails that offer far-reaching views that it's hard to choose where to start. If it's a warm summer day, start at the trailhead for Little Baldy, where the higher elevation (7,335 ft/2,236 m) and mostly shaded trail will keep you relatively cool. A climb of only 750 feet (230 m) to Little Baldy's summit provides eye-popping drama for remarkably

Giant Sequoia National Monument

Most visitors don't realize when they've crossed the boundary line between Sequoia and Kings Canyon National Parks and Giant Sequoia National Monument; signs along the road are fairly nondescript. **Giant Sequoia National Monument** (Hume Lake Ranger District, Sequoia National Forest, 559/338-2251, www.fs.usda.gov/sequoia or www.gsnma.org) is a section of Sequoia National Forest. Many tourists miss the distinction because the park and forest lands are patched together like a mosaic, with boundaries that aren't clearly marked. Here's what matters: The rules are a bit more relaxed in the monument. Your dog can hike with you on monument trails, but not on national park trails. Roadside or "informal" camping outside of established campgrounds is permitted within monument lands (unless posted otherwise), but not in national parks. In general, you'll find more visitor services on national monument lands—gas stations, lodgings, restaurants, and the like—than on the national park lands. The Giant Sequoia National Monument **visitors center** (35860 Kings Canyon Rd., 8am-4:30pm Mon.-Fri.) is 19 miles (31 km) west of Kings Canyon's Big Stump entrance.

Two areas of Giant Sequoia National Monument—the lands northeast of Grant Grove and the Big Meadows/Jennie Lakes area—offer some fascinating highlights.

KINGS CANYON SCENIC BYWAY

East of Grant Grove, Highway 180 becomes the **Kings Canyon Scenic Byway.** You'll pass the **Converse Basin,** once reputed to be the largest sequoia grove in the Sierra. Walk the 2-mile (3.2-km) **Boole Tree Loop** through the grove's sad remains—a maze of immense stumps amid a second-growth mixed forest and the solitary **Boole Tree,** which was named for the lumber foreman who cut down all the other sequoias in this grove. Nearby is the wheelchair-accessible **Chicago Stump Trail.** A 20-foot (6-m) stump is all that remains of a sequoia named the General Noble, which was sawed into sections, transported to Chicago, and reassembled and exhibited at the 1893 World's Columbian Exposition. Continuing east toward Kings Canyon, you'll see the devastation from the 2015 Rough Fire, which burned for nearly five weeks. Most of the build-

little effort. Some claim that this peak's view of the Silliman Crest, the Great Western Divide, Castle Rocks, Moro Rock, the Kaweah River Canyon, and the San Joaquin foothills is the best panorama in the park. To decide for yourself, set out from the **trailhead,** climbing through tree-shaded **switchbacks,** heading first north, then south. Check out the unusual view of Big Baldy off to your left (far across the highway) as you climb. After **1.2 miles (1.9 km),** the trail exits this lovely fern- and wildflower-filled forest and the views start to open up. Hike along Little Baldy's **ridgeline,** passing several worthy viewpoints, and then descend slightly before making the final steep ascent to the **summit.** Once on top of Little Baldy (elevation 8,044 ft/2,452 m), you'll want to stay a while. Amid a banquet of massive peaks, a standout is red-colored Mount Silliman at 11,188 feet (3,410 m) in elevation.

It is one of Sequoia's more popular peaks to climb even though there is no maintained trail.

Be sure to pick a clear day for this hike. In summer, your best bet is to hike the trail early in the morning, before the Central Valley haze rises to the mountains.

MUIR GROVE

Distance: 4 miles (6.4 km) round-trip

Duration: 2 hours

Elevation Change: 500 feet (150 m)

Effort: Easy

Trailhead: Dorst Creek Campground

Directions: From the Big Stump entrance on Highway 180, drive 1.5 miles (2.4 km) and turn right on the Generals Highway, heading south for Sequoia National Park. Drive approximately 17 miles (27 km) to the turnoff for Dorst Creek Campground. Turn right and drive through the campground to ings at the historic Kings Canyon Lodge were destroyed, so there are no services available. Stop at **Boyden Cavern** (10am-5pm daily May-Sept., 11am-4pm daily Apr. and Oct., $13.50 adults, $8.50 children 4-12, www. caverntours.com), decorated with a collection of natural speleothems—crystalline cave features. A 15-minute guided walking tour through the cavern's main passageway shows off its highlights. A bonus is the five-minute walk to the cavern's entrance, which provides breathtaking views of the Kings River, 150 feet (45 m) below.

BIG MEADOWS AND JENNIE LAKES VIA GENERALS HIGHWAY

South from Grant Grove along the Generals Highway, the road passes through national monument lands between Big Meadows Road and Stony Creek Village. Big Meadows Road leads to **Buck Rock Fire Lookout** (www. buckrock.org), a fire tower that was built in 1916 in a most precarious-looking spot—on top of a bald granite outcrop at 8,502 feet (2,591 m). A steel stairway of 172 steps leads to the summit, where an on-duty volunteer may invite you inside the tower for a visit. Also in this vicinity are several Forest Service **campgrounds** (Big Meadow, Buck Rock, and Horse Camp), the luxurious Sequoia High Sierra Camp, and hiking trails that lead into the 10,500-acre (4,250-hectare) **Jennie Lakes Wilderness.** One of the most popular hikes is the 7-mile (11.3-km) round-trip to **Weaver Lake** from the Big Meadows Trailhead.

Kings Canyon Scenic Byway

the amphitheater parking lot. The trail begins at a footbridge between the amphitheater parking lot and the group campground.

Few people hike this trail unless they are staying at Dorst Creek Campground, so you have a lot better chance of seeing giant sequoias in solitude in the Muir Grove than at many places in the park. After crossing a wooden **footbridge,** the trail enters a mixed forest of red fir, white fir, sugar pines, and incense-cedars. In early summer, you can count the many varieties of wildflowers along the trail as it crosses tiny streams. The path heads west and curves around a deeply carved canyon at **1 mile (1.6 km).** Just off the trail to your right is a **bare granite slab** with an inspiring westward view. It's easy to pick out the prominent dome of Big Baldy. The trail undulates, never climbing or dropping much, making this an easy and pleasant stroll. At 1.9

miles (3.1 km), you reach the **Muir Grove,** an almost pure stand of more than 1,000 mature sequoias. The first one you come to on your left is a doozy. The grove is made even more enchanting by the thick undergrowth of blue and purple lupine blooming among the trees in early summer.

★ TOKOPAH FALLS

Distance: 3.6 miles (5.8 km) round-trip
Duration: 2 hours
Elevation Change: 500 feet (150 m)
Effort: Easy
Trailhead: Lodgepole Campground
Directions: From the Big Stump entrance on Highway 180, drive 1.5 miles (2.4 km) and turn right on the Generals Highway, heading south for Sequoia National Park. Drive approximately 25 miles (40 km) to the Lodgepole turnoff. Turn left and continue 0.75 mile (1.2 km) to the Log Bridge area of Lodgepole

Campground. Park in the large lot just before the bridge, then cross the bridge to access the trailhead. The best waterfall day hike in Sequoia and Kings Canyon National Parks leads to 1,200-foot-high (365-m) Tokopah Falls. It's also a perfect family hike, easy on the feet and even easier on the eyes, following closely along the banks of the Marble Fork of the Kaweah River. The trail begins by the three huge campgrounds in the **Lodgepole Village** complex, so it sees a lot of foot traffic; your best bet is to start early in the morning. The scenery is spectacular for the entire distance, from the up-close looks at the waterway, wildflowers, and fir forest dotted by granite boulders to the more distant views of the **Watchtower,** a 1,600-foot (500-m) glacially carved cliff on the south side of **Tokopah Valley.** Then there's the valley itself, with Tokopah Falls pouring down the smooth back curve of its U shape. Wildlife sightings are a near guarantee: black bears are common, especially near the campgrounds, and there are more yellow-bellied marmots on the Tokopah Falls Trail than almost anywhere else in the two parks. The cute little blond critters are often sunning themselves on rocks. They may whistle at you as you walk by.

HEATHER LAKE AND THE WATCHTOWER

Distance: 9.2 miles (14.8 km) round-trip
Duration: 5 hours
Elevation Change: 2,200 feet (670 m)
Effort: Strenuous
Trailhead: Wolverton
Directions: From the Big Stump entrance on Highway 180, drive 1.5 miles (2.4 km) and turn right on the Generals Highway, heading south for Sequoia National Park. Drive approximately 27 miles (43 km), past Lodgepole Village, to the Wolverton turnoff on the east side of the road. Turn left and drive to the trailhead.

The Wolverton trailhead, at 7,200 feet (2,200 m) elevation, gives hikers a boost for this trip into the high country. While backpackers tend to favor this trail for its multiple lakes and moderate grade, day hikers will find plenty to like here, too. A great 9.2-mile (14.8-km) round-trip follows the first section of the **Lakes Trail,** which begins in a red fir forest and then ascends to the top of the 1,600-foot (500-m) **Watchtower,** a big chunk of granite that offers vistas of Tokopah Valley and beyond. The route to the Watchtower is a ledge trail, blasted into hard granite, that creeps along the high rim of Tokopah Valley. Your view is 1,600 feet (500 m) straight down. (You can even see tiny people walking on the path to Tokopah Falls.) Just 0.75 mile (1.2 km) after the Watchtower, you're at **Heather Lake** (day use only, no campsites), which has a steep granite backdrop and a few rocky ledges to sit on. If there are too many people here, it's only another mile on a nearly level trail to even prettier **Emerald Lake.**

If you're hiking in spring or early summer, call the park (559/565-3341) to make sure the Watchtower Trail is open. Otherwise you'll have to take the alternative Hump Trail, which is steeper and nowhere near as scenic.

ALTA PEAK

Distance: 13 miles (20.9 km) round-trip
Duration: 8 hours
Elevation Change: 4,000 feet (1,200 m)
Effort: Strenuous
Trailhead: Wolverton
Directions: From the Big Stump entrance on Highway 180, drive 1.5 miles (2.4 km) and turn right on the Generals Highway, heading south for Sequoia National Park. Drive approximately 27 miles (43 km), past Lodgepole Village, to the Wolverton turnoff on the east side of the road. Turn left and drive to the trailhead.

If you like heights, here's your trail: a thigh-burning 4,000-foot (1,200-m) climb to the top of 11,204-foot (3,415-m) Alta Peak. Alta and Mount Whitney are the only major summits in Sequoia National Park that have established trails, but both of them are still butt-kickers to reach. The trail to Alta Peak and Alta Meadow starts from the Wolverton parking area, then heads south (right) to **Panther Gap,** at 1.8 miles (2.9 km). After climbing through the forest to Panther Gap (8,450 feet elevation/2,575 m), you get your first set of eye-popping views of the Middle Fork Kaweah River and the Great Western Divide. Continue on the **Alta Trail** to **Mehrten Meadow** at 3.9 miles (6.3 km), a popular camping spot. At the next junction, you can go left for Alta Peak or right to Alta Meadow. If you're exhausted, just walk to **Alta Meadow** on a level 1-mile (1.6-km) trail and enjoy its flower-filled grasses and exquisite mountain views. **Alta Peak** is 2 miles (3.2 km) away via the left fork, with an additional 2,000-foot (600-m) climb. Those 2 miles (3.2 km) are considered one of the toughest stretches of trail in Sequoia National Park due to the brutal grade and the thin air at this 10,000-plus-foot (3,000-plus-meter) elevation. But the rewards are great: The summit offers a complete panorama of the Great Western Divide's countless crags, plus a dizzying 6,000-foot (1,800-m) drop to the Kaweah River canyon. Even Mount Whitney and the Coast Range are visible on a clear day.

★ **CONGRESS TRAIL**

Distance: 2.1 miles (3.4 km) round-trip
Duration: 1.5 hours
Elevation Change: 200 feet (60 m)
Effort: Easy
Trailhead: General Sherman parking area near Wolverton
Directions: From the Big Stump entrance on Highway 180, drive 1.5 miles (2.4 km) east and turn right on the Generals Highway, heading south for Sequoia National Park. Drive approximately 27 miles (43 km), past Lodgepole Village, to the Wolverton/Sherman Tree parking turnoff on the east side of the road. Turn left, then make a right at the sign for the General Sherman Tree parking area. (If riding the free Giant Forest shuttle bus, disembark at either the upper or lower parking lot for the General Sherman Tree. The lower trailhead gets you to the Congress Trail quicker.)

The Congress Trail is a much-traveled route through the Giant Forest's prize grove of sequoias. The paved loop starts at the **General Sherman Tree** and meanders through dozens of sequoias with diameters the size of most living rooms. Make sure to pick up an interpretive brochure at the trailhead or at the Lodgepole Visitor Center. After you leave the General Sherman Tree and head north on the Congress Trail, the crowds lessen substantially. Soon you'll pass by many huge trees with placards displaying their monikers. The **House and Senate Groves,** two massive sequoia clusters near the trail's end, are the most impressive, but another standout is the **Washington Tree,** which was long considered the world's second-largest tree. It used to be just 20 feet (6 m) shorter than the General Sherman, but after a lightning-caused fire burned its upper reaches in the late 1990s, it no longer makes the top 30. Named or unnamed, every giant sequoia on this trail is worth stopping to gape at—and the farther you walk, the more solitude you get.

CRESCENT MEADOW AND THARP'S LOG

Distance: 1.6 miles (2.6 km) round-trip
Duration: 1 hour
Elevation Change: 100 feet (300 m)
Effort: Easy
Trailhead: Crescent Meadow
Directions: From the Big Stump entrance to Kings Canyon National Park, drive 1.5 miles (2.4 km) and turn right on the Generals Highway, heading south for Sequoia National Park. Drive approximately 30 miles (48 km), past Lodgepole and Wolverton, to the Giant Forest Museum on the left. Park across the road in the large day-use lot and board the free shuttle bus to the Crescent Meadow parking lot. If the shuttle is not running, turn onto Crescent Meadow Road and drive 3.5 miles (5.6 km) to the Crescent Meadow parking area.

Beautiful Crescent Meadow is more than 1.5 miles (2.4 km) long and is surrounded by giant sequoias—John Muir called it "the gem of the Sierras." Follow the pavement for 600 feet (185 m) from the parking lot's east side, and just like that, you're at the southern edge of beautiful Crescent Meadow. Take the right fork and head for **Log Meadow** and **Tharp's Log.** Log Meadow is as large and beautiful as Crescent Meadow, and a short walk around its circumference will lead you to Tharp's Log, the summer abode of rancher Hale Tharp. The

first white man to enter Giant Forest, Tharp grazed cattle and horses here, and built his home inside a hollowed, fire-scarred sequoia log. He lived in it for nearly 30 summers from 1861 to 1890. Muir visited Tharp here and called his log "a noble den." You can still see the front door, window shutters, and chimney that Tharp built into the log, plus his simple dining room table inside. (Tharp died at his ranch in Three Rivers at the ripe old age of 84.) From Tharp's Log, continue your loop back to Crescent Meadow and walk around its west side, which returns you to the north edge of the parking lot.

Backpacking

The Giant Forest area is a great starting point for backpackers because the trailhead elevations are high and the terrain tends toward shady forest. **Wilderness permits** (559/565-3766 www.nps.gov/seki, $15 permit fee) are required for overnight travel. Permits are available on a first-come, first-served basis at the wilderness permit station at the **Lodgepole Visitor Center** (559/565-4436, 7am-6pm daily late May-Oct.). Each trail is subject to daily entry quotas from late May to late September. Reserve your spot in advance for the most popular trips. Approximately one-third of each daily quota is available on a first-come, first-served basis starting at 1pm the day before departure, or on the day of departure at the permit station closest to the trailhead. Reservations are available for the other two-thirds of each quota; reserve in advance by mail or email. Even with a reservation, you must pick up your permit at the wilderness permit station on the afternoon before your trip (after 1pm), or no later than 9am on the morning of your departure.

HIGH SIERRA TRAIL

One of the most popular backpacking routes is the **High Sierra Trail** (70 mi/113 km one-way), which travels from Crescent Meadow all the way to Mount Whitney—though you don't have to hike that far to have a great trip. A popular destination along the trail is **Hamilton Lake** (30 mi/48 km round-trip); the trail is extremely gradual for the first 11.4 miles (18.4 km) all the way to Bearpaw Meadow. The route ascends gently through a giant sequoia grove from Crescent Meadow to Eagle View, and then continues on a very mellow grade along the north rim of the Middle Fork Kaweah River Canyon. It's views, views, views all the way. After a good night's sleep at Bearpaw, continue another 4 miles (6.4 km) to Upper and Lower Hamilton Lakes, set at 8,300 feet (2,530 m) in a glacially carved basin at the foot of the peaks of the Great Western Divide.

TWIN LAKES

A great multiday backpack trip is possible from Lodgepole Campground to **Twin Lakes** (13 mi/20.9 km round-trip) or Ranger Lakes. The two Twin Lakes are only 6.8 miles (10.9 km) from the trailhead with a 2,700-foot (800-m) elevation gain, making this a relatively easy (and fairly heavily traveled) backpacking route. The terrain is an interesting mix of dense conifer forests, glacial moraine, and open meadows. From the trailhead, the trail climbs past Wolverton's Rock to Cahoon Meadow at 3 miles (4.8 km). Continue to Cahoon Gap at 4.2 miles (6.8 km), cross over Clover Creek at 5 miles (8 km) (campsites are found along the creek), bear right at the J. O. Pass Trail junction at 5.5 miles (8.9 km), and reach the Twin Lakes at 6.8 miles (10.9 km). The trail deposits you at the larger Twin Lake; the smaller one is reached via a short spur. Both are shallow and have forested banks. To leave the crowds behind, hike over rocky Silliman Pass (at 10,100 ft/3,078 m) to the less-visited **Ranger Lakes** (19 mi/31 km round-trip), 3 miles (4.8 km) farther.

THE LAKES TRAIL

A popular weekend backpacking trail is **The Lakes Trail** (13.4 mi/21.6 km round-trip) from the Wolverton trailhead to Pear

1: Giant Forest Museum **2:** the climb to the top of Moro Rock **3:** summit of Little Baldy **4:** the House Grove of giant sequoias, near the far end of the Congress Trail

Lake. Although plenty of day hikers follow this path for the first 4.6 miles (7.4 km) to **Heather Lake,** beyond that point the crowds thin. Part of the route can be hiked via a choice of two trails, with the preferred route—less steep and more scenic—traveling up and over the **Watchtower,** a 1,600-foot-tall (500-m) granite cliff that offers incredible vistas of the Tokopah Valley. The trail begins in red fir forest, then enters polished granite country and culminates in a rocky basin with three gemlike lakes—Heather, Emerald, and Pear—as well as many sparkling creeks. The total climb to Pear Lake is a mere 2,300 feet (700 m), spread out over 6.7 miles (10.8 km). Backpackers may camp only at Emerald and Pear Lakes. Overnight reservations are not available for this trail; permits are issued on a first-come, first-served basis.

Winter Sports

With a little preparation, winter can be a great time to travel to Sequoia and Kings Canyon. Cross-country skis, snowshoes, and snow-play gear can be rented from December to April at Wuksachi Lodge and Montecito Sequoia Lodge. If you want to keep your snow activities simple, drive to the **Wolverton snow-play area** (off Generals Hwy., north of Giant Forest) and go sledding.

Your best chance at finding good snow is in areas where the elevations are highest. The trails to **Little Baldy** and **Big Baldy** are great options for snowshoers and cross-country skiers, and the Giant Forest area often has solid snow coverage. The most popular winter trail is the **Congress Trail** (2.1 mi/3.4 km round-trip), with a side trip to see the General Sherman. The **Tokopah Falls Trail** from Lodgepole Village also makes a perfect snowshoeing trail. On many winter weekends, the park offers free snowshoe walks with rangers (check the park newspaper for a schedule).

Montecito Sequoia Lodge (63410 Generals Hwy., 559/565-3388, www.ms-lodge.com, $25 day-use fee), 9 miles (14.5 km) south of Grant Grove, offers the most

developed facilities for snow play, with 19-31 miles (30-50 km) of groomed cross-country ski trails. Snowshoe trails are groomed and marked, and sledding, snowboarding, and snow-tubing hills are available. The lodge offers cross-country ski lessons for beginners and intermediates. Day-use passes include lunch as well as trail use. Equipment rentals are available.

Experienced cross-country skiers and snowshoers can reserve an overnight stay at **Pear Lake Ski Hut** (559/565-4251, www.sequoiaparksconservancy.org, mid-Dec.-late Apr., $40 per person per night), a steep 6 miles (9.7 km) from the Wolverton trailhead. The historic stone-and-wood structure is less than 0.5 mile (0.8 km) from Pear Lake, at 9,200 feet (2,800 m) in elevation where the snow is deep and dependable. Heated by a pellet stove, the hut sleeps 10 people in bunks. Propane cooking stoves are provided, but you must bring your own fuel, as well as food, clothing, and sleeping gear. This is a great winter adventure for those who come well prepared. The ski-in is rated as intermediate to advanced, with 2,000 feet (600 m) of elevation gain. Advance reservations are required; registration forms are available online for the lottery held in early November.

FOOD AND ACCOMMODATIONS

The grocery store at **Lodgepole Market Center** (8am-9pm daily Apr.-Oct.) is surprisingly well stocked. In the same complex is the **Watchtower Deli** (11am-6pm daily Apr.-Oct.), where you can get hot pizza slices or fresh sandwiches to take on the trail.

Wuksachi Lodge

The best place to stay in the Giant Forest and Lodgepole area is ★ **Wuksachi Lodge** (64740 Wuksachi Way, 888/252-5757, 559-625-7700, www.visitsequoia.com, $225-365 in summer, $120-250 in winter), a complex of three buildings with a total of 102 guest rooms. Rooms are configured with one or two queen beds (or one king bed) and have

Guided Hikes

Park rangers offer free walks and talks in the Foothills, Giant Forest, Lodgepole, Grant Grove, Mineral King, and Cedar Grove areas. The park newspaper lists current offerings, or you can ask for a schedule at the visitors centers.

John Muir Lodge and Wuksachi Lodge offer free hikes and activities led by knowledgeable guides from the **Sequoia Parks Conservancy** (559/565-4251, www.sequoiaparksconservancy.org). These include wildlife walks, nighttime flashlight hikes, family birding walks, wilderness skills classes, and stargazing programs. Check at the lodges' front desks for a list of current offerings. Most free activities are held on Wednesday, Friday, Saturday, and Sunday in summer.

The naturalists at the **Sequoia Parks Conservancy** are the only authorized in-park guide service in Sequoia and Kings Canyon. You can hire a guide specifically for the dates you want for your family or small group ($375 full-day, $275 half-day for groups of 1-6 people). They will personalize an itinerary for you depending on what you want to see and do. They also guide longer **wilderness trips** (3-9 days, $300-600 per person) to various backcountry destinations: White Chief Mine in Mineral King, the Dusy Basin, the LeConte Basin, Rae Lakes, Alta Peak, and more. Taking part in one of these trips is a great way to see the backcountry and gain valuable wilderness skills.

refrigerators, coffeemakers, televisions, ski racks, and telephones (cell service is unreliable). "Superior" rooms are designed for families, with lots of extra floor space plus a pullout sofa bed in addition to a king or queen bed. It's not inexpensive, but Wuksachi is by far the nicest "drive-up" place to stay in the parks. There are lots of perks included in your stay, such as free guided walks and talks that start at the lodge. And if you need a boxed lunch ($13 adults, $9 kids) to take on a hike during the day, just leave an order form on your doorknob the night before and the lodge will have it ready in the morning.

Wuksachi Lodge's casually elegant 90-seat restaurant, **The Peaks** (559/565-4070, 7am-10:30am, 10:30am-3pm, and 5pm-9:30pm daily year-round, $10-45) is housed in a separate structure about 300 feet (90 m) from the guest rooms. A huge dining room features soaring ceilings and massive windows overlooking the forest. Lunch and dinner menus include plenty of choices for salad fans, steak lovers, and gluten-free gourmands alike, with an emphasis on organic, local, and sustainable ingredients. Vegetarian and vegan options include grilled tofu, vegan corn chowder, and a vegan Mediterranean wrap. Breakfast is served buffet-style. Reservations are required for dinner, especially in summer. A small cocktail bar serves drinks.

Montecito Sequoia Lodge

Montecito Sequoia Lodge (63410 Generals Hwy., 559/565-3388 or 800/227-9900, www. mslodge.com, $170-340 for two people, includes meals), in Giant Sequoia National Monument, is a High Sierra version of Club Med with an emphasis on organized activities for children. Guests stay in private cottages, motel-style rooms, or cabins with shared baths; room rates include three meals daily. In summer, most of the rooms are rented out by the week, but in winter, reservations are much easier to come by. Because the lodge is at 7,400 feet (2,300 m), it's a great place for snow sports, with miles of groomed trails for cross-country skiing and snowshoeing. The lodge is open year-round, and winter rates can be as low as $79 per person, including meals.

Stony Creek Lodge

Stony Creek Lodge (off Generals Hwy., 559/565-3388 or 877/828-1440, www.sequoia-kingscanyon.com, mid-May-early Oct., $120-219), in Giant Sequoia National Monument, is more bare-bones and contains only 12 rooms. It's one of the lowest-priced lodging options in the parks, so if you just want a pillow on which to lay your head at night, this place works just fine. It has a small café that usually serves pizza, as well as a grocery store and a gas station. The lodge is 15 miles (24 km) north of Giant Forest off Generals Highway.

Sequoia High Sierra Camp

For a memorable splurge, book a couple of nights at ★ **Sequoia High Sierra Camp** (866/654-2877, www.sequoiahighsierra-camp.com, June-Sept., $255 adults (includes all meals), $155 children ages 3-11, two-night minimum) in Giant Sequoia National Monument. The "camp" provides luxury in the wilderness with its 30 tent cabins that probably don't fit your notion of camping—tents are equipped with comfortable beds (one king or two twins) and colorful rugs. The tents are spaced comfortably far apart, so you won't hear every word spoken (or sneeze or snore emitted) in your neighbor's tent. Some tents are perched fairly high on the camp's hill, so you may have a steep walk to the dining room. The camp's alfresco **restaurant** serves three meals daily (meals are included in the room rate), and the food is superb, even if you measure it by city standards, not wilderness standards. Fresh raspberries and blueberries at

breakfast? Omelets made right before your eyes? Jumbo shrimp appetizers? A wide selection of French wines? Yup, this is what you'll be treated to, along with hot showers and flush toilets at the communal bathhouse. On chilly evenings after dinner, guests gather around the lodge's fireplace for conversations and s'mores. During your stay, be sure to take the steep hike to **Mitchell Peak** for inspiring views, or the longer hike to Seville Lake for swimming and fishing. The resort's wilderness experience is enhanced by its hikers-only access (even though it's a very short hike). Guests' cars are left 0.75 mile (1.2 km) away.

CAMPING

Campers can choose between two very large, family-oriented campgrounds—Lodgepole and Dorst Creek—plus five campgrounds in nearby Sequoia National Forest. Reservations are accepted up to six months in advance.

Lodgepole

Lodgepole (877/444-6777, www.recreation.gov, mid-Apr.-mid-Oct., $22) is a huge 214-site camp with all the amenities, including a grocery store, a deli and pizza counter, shower and laundry facilities, and a visitors center. Campers don't have to rough it here; bags of

Sequoia High Sierra Camp

Bearpaw High Sierra Camp

the dining hall at Bearpaw High Sierra Camp

It's nearly impossible to secure a spot, but if you plan way in advance and work the reservation system with the same rigor you'd use to score Rolling Stones tickets, you might earn a stay at Bearpaw High Sierra Camp. An oak-shaded cluster of six tent cabins perched on the edge of a granite gorge, the camp is accessible only by an 11.5-mile (18.5-km) hike on the **High Sierra Trail** starting from Crescent Meadow. Bearpaw has been welcoming guests since 1934 to its spectacular 7,000-foot (2,400-m) granite slab that overlooks the Great Western Divide. Its simple tents, comfy beds, delicious home-cooked meals, hot showers, and flush toilet (one toilet for the whole camp to share) provide surprising luxury in the midst of wilderness. For a few extra bucks, guests can even enjoy a glass of wine with dinner. Each cabin has two twin beds; if there are three in your party, one person can bring a pad and sleep on the cabin's wooden floor. At most there will be only 18 guests in camp, but 12 is more typical. A stay here is an intimate experience and you're sure to make friends with your neighbors.

The 11.5-mile (18.5-km) hike is long and often hot, but it has only 1,000 feet (300 m) of elevation change as it follows the north rim of the Middle Fork Kaweah River Canyon. It's views, views, views all the way, and since your food and bedding are provided at camp, you don't need to carry much on your back besides a change of clothes, some snacks, and water. After a big dinner and a good night's sleep at Bearpaw, most guests take an 8-mile (12.9-km) round-trip day hike to Upper and Lower Hamilton Lakes, set in a glacially carved basin at the base of the peaks of the Great Western Divide. If you're staying an extra day, you might try the 8-mile (12.9-km) round-trip hike to Tamarack Lake. Or you might just sit outside in a chair to enjoy the fantastic view of the Great Western Divide. This chain of mountains runs north-south through the center of Sequoia National Park, dividing the watersheds of the Kaweah River to the west and the Kern River to the east.

RESERVATIONS

The camp is open from mid-June to mid-September. To reserve a spot, phone the reservations line (866/807-3598) starting at 7am on January 2 of each year. Full payment is required when you reserve. If you don't have success obtaining a booking on January 2, go to www.visitsequoia.com to see if any summer dates are available. Rates are $175 per adult based on double occupancy, which includes breakfast and dinner each day. (Boxed lunches are available for purchase at the camp.) For questions about the camp (not for reservations), call the Bearpaw's general manager at 559/565-4070.

potato chips and six-packs of beer are just a short walk away. Sites are set near the Marble Fork Kaweah River, and trails lead from the camp to Tokopah Falls and Twin Lakes. The Giant Forest is only 5 miles (8 km) away, and a shuttle runs from Lodgepole Village to the big trees in summer.

Dorst Creek

Dorst Creek (877/444-6777, www.recreation.gov, mid-May-early Sept., $22) is a family-friendly camp named for the park's first superintendent, Army captain Joseph Dorst. The camp has 218 sites amid multiple loops that cut through a forest of red and white firs along Dorst Creek. Hot showers and food are available a few miles away at Stony Creek Village or Lodgepole. A 2-mile (3.2-km) trail to the Muir Grove of giant sequoias starts from camp. In the peak summer months, a free shuttle runs from the camp to Giant Forest. Dorst Creek is off Generals Highway, 9 miles (14.5 km) north of Lodgepole Village and about 18 miles (29 km) south of the Big Stump entrance.

Stony Creek

For campers seeking a more intimate experience, ★ **Stony Creek Campground** (877/444-6777, www.recreation.gov, mid-May to mid-Sept., $27), in Sequoia National Forest, has only 48 sites on a peaceful spot on the banks of Stony Creek. Conveniences like showers, laundry, and groceries are right next door at Stony Creek Lodge. Neighboring **Upper Stony Creek Campground** is even smaller at 24 sites (mid-May to mid-Sept., $23), but it has vault toilets.

Big Meadows

If you want to get away from the main park roads and crowds, drive down Big Meadow Road to these campgrounds in Sequoia National Forest: **Buck Rock Camp** (5 sites), **Horse Camp** (5 sites), or **Big Meadow Camp** (43 sites), all of which stay open until the season's first snowfall. Big Meadows is the only camp that charges a fee ($23); reserve its sites in advance at 877/444-6777 or www.recreation.gov. Vault toilets are provided, but only Big Meadow has bear boxes. All three campgrounds are 4 miles (6.4 km) east on Big Meadow Road off Generals Highway. The Big Meadows Trailhead is right next door for easy access to the Jennie Lakes Wilderness.

Foothills

The Foothills area lies in the southern region of Sequoia National Park. The Ash Mountain entrance provides access to this lower-elevation landscape via Highway 198. The nearest gateway town is **Three Rivers.**

SIGHTS

Two of the most photographed sights in Sequoia National Park lie within 2 miles (3.2 km) of the Foothills Visitor Center. Just past the entrance station stands a huge, hand-carved **wooden sign** that depicts the face on the old Indian head nickel. The sign was made by a Civilian Conservation Corps employee in the 1930s. About 1.5 miles (2.4 km) north of the sign is famous **Tunnel Rock,** a large granite boulder that was tunneled by the Civilian Conservation Corps in 1938 so that cars could drive through.

Hospital Rock

A large quartzite rock just off the Generals Highway, **Hospital Rock** was once home to hundreds of Potwisha Native Americans, a subgroup of the western Mono Indians. Archaeological evidence suggests that the Indians used this site as far back as 1350, most likely only in the cooler winter months. Walk across the street from the picnic area to see the ancient pictographs painted on a large rock wall. Also visible are more than a dozen bedrock mortars (holes in the rock), which were utilized by Native American women to grind acorns into flour. A very short trail built by the Civilian Conservation Corps leads to a cascade on the Middle Fork Kaweah River.

Settler Hale Tharp named this site Hospital Rock because of two separate incidents: In 1860, he and his brother-in-law John Swanson were exploring Giant Forest when Swanson injured his leg. Swanson was transported to this site and treated by local Indians. Then, in 1873, James Everton suffered a shotgun wound and he too was carried to this site for treatment.

Eleven Range Overlook

The **Eleven Range Overlook** (south of Giant Forest along the Generals Highway) offers a jaw-dropping vista overlooking the Kaweah Canyon toward the San Joaquin Valley. This is one of the most popular roadside spots in the parks for sunset photographs. (Odd as it sounds, the smog and haze from the Fresno and Visalia area adds to the drama.)

RECREATION
Day Hiking
MARBLE FALLS

Distance: 7.4 miles (11.9 km) round-trip
Duration: 4 hours
Elevation Change: 2,000 feet (600 m)
Effort: Moderate
Trailhead: Potwisha Campground
Directions: From the Ash Mountain entrance, drive 3.8 miles (6.1 km) northeast on the Generals Highway to the left turnoff for Potwisha Campground. Park in the trailhead parking area; the trail begins across from site number 15.

Check your calendar: If it's **late winter** or **spring,** don't miss this hike. March and April are particularly good months to visit because of high flows in the Marble Fork Kaweah River and the blooming wildflowers in the grasslands and chaparral that line the trail. From its rather banal start as a **gravel road** at Potwisha Campground's upper end, this trail keeps getting better as it follows the twists and turns of the river. There are **no trail junctions** to worry about; at 3.7 miles (6 km), the path simply dead-ends near the lower cascades of **Marble Falls.** Although much of the waterfall is tucked out of sight in a narrow, rocky river gorge, what is visible is a wide, billowing cascade of white water that swoops and scatters over white granite. Be very careful on the slippery granite near the river's edges; the current and the cold water are even more dangerous than they look. Aside from the waterfalls and the wildflowers, the other highlights on this trail are the colorful outcroppings of marble, particularly in the last mile as you near the falls.

Remember to time your visit carefully. In summer, these foothills can bake like an oven. If you make the trip from late May to September, get an early-morning start.

PARADISE CREEK

Distance: 2 miles (3.2 km) round-trip
Duration: 45 minutes
Elevation Change: 350 feet (105 m)
Effort: Easy
Trailhead: Buckeye Flat Campground
Directions: From the Ash Mountain entrance, drive 6.3 miles (10.1 km) northeast on the Generals Highway to the right turnoff for Buckeye Flat Campground, across from Hospital Rock. Turn right and drive 0.6 mile (1 km) to the campground. Park in any of the dirt pullouts outside the camp entrance; no day-use parking is allowed in the camp. You can also park at Hospital Rock and walk to the campground. The trailhead is near campsite 28.

From Buckeye Flat Campground, Paradise Creek Trail meanders through oaks and buckeyes and crosses a long, picturesque **footbridge** over the Middle Fork Kaweah River. An inviting Olympic-sized pool is on the right side of the bridge, and campers often go **swimming** here on summer afternoons. Save the pool for after your walk; for now, take the signed **Paradise Creek Trail,** at the far side of the bridge. You'll briefly visit the creek and then leave it, climbing into oak and grassland terrain. You'll enjoy long-distance views of Moro Rock and Hanging Rock, but most of the beauty is right at your feet in the springtime flowers that grow in the grasses and in the leafy blue oaks that shade them. The maintained trail ends when it reaches Paradise Creek again, although a faint route continues along its banks.

FOOD

You'll need some serious calories before a long day in the parks. For a hearty sandwich, head to **Sierra Subs and Salads** (41717 Sierra Dr., Three Rivers, 559/561-4810, www.sierra-subsandsalads.com, 10:30am-6pm Tues.-Sat., 10:30am-3pm Sun., $7-12), which is a gigantic step above any of America's popular chain sandwich shops. Sit at outdoor picnic tables or in the air-conditioned dining room and chow down on a huge variety of sandwiches, wraps, paninis, and salads, all made with fresh ingredients. Vegetarians, vegans, and gluten-free eaters will find lots of choices here.

One of the best places for breakfast or dinner in Three Rivers is a food truck. The **Ol' Buckaroo** (41695 Sierra Dr., Three Rivers, 559/465-5088, www.theolbuckaroo.com, 5:30pm-9pm Mon. and Thurs., 5:30pm-10pm Fri., 9:30am-1:30pm and 5:30pm-10pm Sat., 9:30am-1:30pm and 5:30pm-9pm Sun., $7-15) serves a very short selection from its walk-up window, but everything on the menu is tasty. Weekend breakfasts include lemon ricotta pancakes or fried chicken and waffles. For dinner, choose from grass-fed hamburgers, fried chicken, sliders, or grilled cheese, plus a few salads and veggies served à la carte. Don't miss the sweet potato fries. Seating is at picnic tables set near the river.

ACCOMMODATIONS

There are no accommodations in the southern Foothills region of Sequoia National Park. (The closest in-park lodging is at Wuksachi Lodge north of Giant Forest, an hour's drive on extremely curvy mountain roads.) If you are driving from Los Angeles or Fresno and arriving in the evening, your best bet is to spend the night in **Three Rivers,** just 7 miles (11.3 km) west of the Foothills entrance. The small town doesn't have a ton of choices for services, but there is just enough for travelers who need a good night's sleep, a shower, gas in their car, and maybe some groceries for their cooler.

For an overnight stay at a dependable chain motel, book a room at the **Lazy J Ranch/America's Best Value Inn** (39625 Sierra Dr./Hwy. 198, Three Rivers, 559/561-4449, www.redlioninn.com, $109-169), where all 18 rooms are ground level, you can park right outside your door, and a free continental breakfast is served each morning. On hot summer days, the outdoor pool is a bonus.

Also in the chain category, but larger and newer, is the 103-room **Comfort Inn and Suites** (40820 Sierra Dr./Hwy. 198, Three Rivers, 559/561-9000, www.choicehotels.com, $139-279), which was remodeled in 2006. There's a big difference between the lowest- and highest-priced rooms here—the former are very basic, while the latter (26 suites and 20 "deluxe" rooms) have amenities like in-room whirlpool tubs, fireplaces, and refrigerators and microwaves. An outdoor pool and whirlpool tub are available to all, and a bare-bones continental breakfast is served each morning.

For home-style charm, stay at **The River Jewel Suites** (43325 Sierra Dr./Hwy. 198, Three Rivers, 559/799-8201, www.theriverjewel.com, $250). Larry and Diana Jules rent three suites in their home, and each one sits within steps of the lovely Kaweah River. Each suite has a kitchenette; two suites overlook the river and one overlooks the mountains. Their riverfront backyard is a lovely, serene spot.

CAMPING

Thanks to the Foothills region's low elevation, the 42 sites at **Potwisha Campground** (877/444-6777, www.recreation.gov, $22) are open for camping year-round, although it can be very hot in summer. The Kaweah River runs nearby. Nearby **Buckeye Flat Campground** (877/444-6777, www.recreation.gov, May-Sept., $22) has 28 sites for tents only. Reservations are accepted up to six months in advance.

Off South Fork Road, tiny **South Fork**

Campground (first come, first served, www. nps.gov/seki, year-round, $12) has 10 sites for tents only, but you must bring your own water.

Mineral King

The least-visited area of the parks, the 7,800-foot-elevation (2,400-m) Mineral King Valley is a glacier-carved bowl surrounded by massive peaks and crowned by the distinct pointed pinnacle known as Sawtooth Peak. Mineral King is a mecca for hikers, who can choose from a wide variety of day hiking and backpacking trails, many of which lead to high-elevation alpine lakes.

Many first-time visitors are surprised to find a large cluster of private cabins in Silver City, 6 miles (9.7 km) from the road's end; another collection of cabins is sprinkled among the trailheads in Mineral King Valley. The area has had a fascinating and somewhat controversial history, beginning with the mining boom that took place here in 1872, when silver was discovered. To service the mines, the Mineral King Road was built the next year, but the silver boom was quickly followed by bust. Still, Mineral King remained popular with residents of Fresno and Visalia, who built summer homes here to escape the Central Valley's heat.

In the 1960s, cartoonist, filmmaker, and entrepreneur Walt Disney envisioned Mineral King Valley as the potential site of a world-class ski resort. Preservationists fought the plan, but it was Mother Nature that dealt the final blow to Disney's dream: In the winter of 1969, a massive avalanche wiped out several buildings on Disney's property, including the Mineral King store and post office.

Mineral King Road is open from Memorial Day weekend through October (depending on the weather, it may be open longer). From Highway 198 in Three Rivers, drive 2.5 miles (4 km) east to Mineral King Road. From there, reaching Mineral King requires a circuitous 25-mile (40-km) drive (RVs and

trailers are discouraged) that takes a very slow 75 minutes.

One more note about driving your car into Mineral King: You may have heard the rumors, and they are strange but true. **Yellow-bellied marmots,** those cute, chubby members of the squirrel family that are common throughout the Sierra Nevada, are something of a menace in Mineral King. No one is sure why, but in Mineral King (and nowhere else in the Sierra) they like to chew on the plastic wiring and rubber radiator hoses of vehicles. A good number of visitors—especially backpackers who leave their cars for extended periods—have found their vehicles disabled by hungry marmots. This seems to occur most often in late spring and early summer; rangers say that by mid July, the marmots' food cravings change and they lose interest in cars. Some visitors wrap their cars in tarps, but marmots chew right through them. Cabin owners in Mineral King protect their cars by wrapping the undersides in chicken wire. During May and June, you might want to take precautions—or take your chances.

SIGHTS
Historic Cabins
The Mineral King area includes several historic cabin communities, including **Silver City** and **Cabin Cove,** both of which were added to the National Register of Historic Places in 2003. Most of the cabins date to the late 19th and early 20th centuries; none have electricity, although most are now equipped with propane stoves and lights. Although the majority of the cabins are privately owned and not open to visitors, the Mineral King Preservation Society (www.mineralking.org or www.mineralking.us) keeps the

Honeymoon Cabin, also called the Point Cabin, open to the public on summer days. Located next to the White Chief/Eagle Lake Trailhead in Mineral King Valley, the cabin was built in 1914 and completely restored in 1989. Sitting on land that is still owned by the Walt Disney Company, it is the only cabin remaining from the resort hotel that was owned and operated by Arthur Crowley in the early 1900s.

Black Wolf Falls

An obvious landmark in Mineral King Valley, **Black Wolf Falls** tumbles down a canyon wall near the Sawtooth trailhead. The waterfall's name is an alteration of its original moniker, Black Wall Falls. It was named for the Black Wall copper mine that was located at the waterfall's base. In the 1870s, when miners believed that Mineral King was rich in more than just scenery, they mined the base of Monarch Creek with a modicum of success. Today you can walk right up to the falls and, when its flow is low, peek into the mine tunnel on the cataract's right (south) side. A well-used but unsigned trail travels 0.25 mile (0.4 km) from the Mineral King Road alongside Monarch Creek to the waterfall. On summer Saturdays, park rangers often lead guided interpretive hikes here; check with the Mineral King Ranger Station for a schedule.

RECREATION
Day Hikes
COLD SPRINGS NATURE TRAIL

Distance: 2 miles (3.2 km) round-trip
Duration: 1 hour
Elevation Change: 100 feet (300 m)
Effort: Easy
Trailhead: Cold Springs Campground
Directions: From Three Rivers, drive 2.5 miles (4 km) east on Highway 198 and turn right on Mineral King Road. Drive 23.5 miles (37.8 km) to Cold Springs Campground on the right. The trail begins near campsite 6. If you aren't camping, park by the Mineral King Ranger Station and walk into the campground.

You may not expect much from a campground nature trail, but Cold Springs Nature Trail is guaranteed to exceed your expectations. Not only is it lined with wildflowers and informative signposts that teach you to identify junipers, red and white firs, cottonwoods, and aspens, but the views of the Sawtooth Ridge are glorious. The loop is **less than 0.5 mile (0.8 km),** but from the far end of it, the trail continues along the **East Fork Kaweah River,** heading another mile into Mineral King Valley. Walk to the loop's far end, and then continue at least **another 0.25 mile (0.4 km)** along the trail. It just gets prettier as it goes. You're in for a real treat if you take this walk right before sunset, when the mountain peaks surrounding the valley turn every imaginable shade of pink, orange, and coral, reflecting the sun setting in the west. The vistas are so beautiful that they can practically make you weep.

MONARCH LAKES

Distance: 8.4 miles (13.5 km) round-trip
Duration: 5 hours
Elevation Change: 2,500 feet (760 m)
Effort: Strenuous
Trailhead: Sawtooth
Directions: From Three Rivers, drive 2.5 miles (4 km) east on Highway 198 and turn right on Mineral King Road. Drive 24.5 miles (39.4 km) to Mineral King Valley and the Sawtooth parking area, about 0.5 mile (0.8 km) before the road ends.

The Monarch Lakes Trail leads from the Sawtooth trailhead at 8,000 feet (2,400 m) elevation and climbs 2,500 feet (760 m) to the rocky, gemlike Monarch Lakes. While the first half of the hike is memorably steep, the second half is much mellower, and the scenery along the entire trail is remarkable. Walk 0.25 mile (0.4 km) from the **trailhead** and take the right fork for **Monarch** and **Crystal Lakes.** After a brutal 1-mile (1.6-km) ascent, you'll reach **Groundhog Meadow,** named for the yellow-bellied marmots that inhabit the area. Beyond the meadow, the trail starts switchbacking in and out of red fir forest, making a gut-thumping climb to the **Crystal Lake trail junction.** The trail forks sharply right for Crystal Lake, but you should head left for

Mineral King Hikes

Trail	Effort	Distance	Duration
Cold Springs Nature Trail	Easy	2 mi/3.2 km rt	1 hr
Mosquito Lakes	Moderate	7.2 mi/11.6 km rt	4 hr
White Chief Mine	Moderate	6 mi/9.7 km rt	3 hr
Eagle Lake	Strenuous	6.8 mi/10.9 km rt	4 hr
Monarch Lakes	Strenuous	8.4 mi/13.5 km rt	5 hr

one more mile, enjoying the easiest grade of the trip. The path is chiseled out of colorful rock cliffs; a few stalwart western junipers grow in this austere landscape of rusty red shale, white marble, and gray granite. Snow is often found near the lake even in late summer, and the vista is dramatic, with Sawtooth Peak dominating the skyline.

From **Lower Monarch Lake**, the main trail continues northward to Sawtooth Pass, but a use trail leads southeast for 0.5 mile (0.8 km) to **Upper Monarch Lake**. It's worth the climb if only to look back down on the lower lake from above. The upper lake lies at the base of barren, pointy Monarch Peak, and it has an immense rock dam built by Southern California Edison. When the water level is high, it's a dramatic sight. When the water level is low, it just looks sad.

EAGLE LAKE

Distance: 6.8 miles (10.9 km) round-trip
Duration: 4 hours
Elevation Change: 2,200 feet (670 m)
Effort: Strenuous
Trailhead: Eagle/Mosquito
Directions: From Three Rivers, drive 2.5 miles (4 km) east on Highway 198 and turn right on Mineral King Road. Drive 25 miles (40 km) to the end of the road and the Eagle/Mosquito Trailhead (schedule more than an hour to drive this road).

Eagle Lake has always been the glamour destination in Mineral King, the trail to hike if you can hike only one trail in the area. Why? The blue-green lake is drop-dead gorgeous; that's why, and the trail to reach it is steep and challenging yet still manageable for most hikers, with a 2,200-foot (670-m) elevation gain spread out over 3.4 miles (5.5 km). The Eagle Lake Trail follows the same route as the **Mosquito Lakes Trail** until the 2-mile (3.2 km) point, near the **Eagle Sink Holes**. These geological oddities are small craters where Eagle Creek suddenly disappears underground. At the trail junction by the sinkholes, go left for **Eagle Lake**. Enjoy the brief level stretch here, because you'll soon gain another 1,000 feet (300 m) over 1.4 miles (2.3 km). Much of the climb travels over an exposed boulder field that gets baked by the sun on warm days, although well-graded switchbacks make it easier. Soon you arrive at Eagle Lake's **dam** at 10,000 feet (3,000 m). The big lake is surrounded by glacially carved rock and has a few rocky islands. Brook trout swim in its clear waters. The trail continues along the lake's west side to many good picnicking spots and photo opportunities.

MOSQUITO LAKES

Distance: 7.2 miles (11.6 km) round-trip
Duration: 4 hours
Elevation Change: 1,500 feet (455 m) to Mosquito Lake No. 1
Effort: Moderate
Trailhead: Eagle/Mosquito
Directions: From Three Rivers, drive 2.5 miles (4 km) east on Highway 198 and turn right on Mineral King Road. Drive 25 miles (40 km) to the end of the road and the Eagle/Mosquito Trailhead (schedule more than an

hour to drive this road).

The Eagle/Mosquito Trailhead is at 7,830 feet (2,390 m), and the four Mosquito Lakes lie between 9,000 and 10,000 feet (2,700 and 3,000 m), so if you want to reach a handful of alpine lakes without too much suffering, this is your best choice in Mineral King. Just minutes from your car, you cross a **footbridge** over Spring Creek's cascade, called **Tufa Falls** because of the calcium carbonate in Spring Creek's water. The **junction** for Eagle Lake, the Mosquito Lakes, and the White Chief Trail is reached at 1 mile (1.6 km) out. Take the **right fork,** climbing steadily. At **2 miles (3.2 km),** you reach the Mosquito Lakes junction; go right. Climb up **Miner's Ridge,** topping out at 9,300 feet (2,850 m), and then drop down the other side. The final descent covers 0.5 mile (0.8 km); you reach **Mosquito Lake** number one at 9,040 feet (2,755 m) and 3.6 miles (5.8 km). This is the easiest lake to reach in Mineral King, with a mostly shaded trail and a mere 1,500-foot (455-m) gain (plus a 250-ft/75-m gain on the way out). But this first lake is small and shallow, and may only whet your appetite for something more dramatic. If so, follow **Mosquito Creek** uphill (there is no maintained trail, but stay on the obvious path on the stream's west side). The climb from lake number one to **lake number two** is steep—a 600-foot (180-m) elevation gain in 0.5 mile (0.8 km)—but it's worth it. Lake number two is a blue, deep, granite-bound beauty. Intrepid hikers should go all the way to **lake number five,** a total of 5 miles (8 km) from the trailhead.

WHITE CHIEF MINE

Distance: 6 miles (9.7 km) round-trip
Duration: 3 hours
Elevation Change: 1,500 feet (455 m)
Effort: Moderate
Trailhead: Eagle/Mosquito
Directions: From Three Rivers, drive 2.5 miles (4 km) east on Highway 198 and turn right on Mineral King Road. Drive 25 miles (40 km) to the end of the road and the Eagle/Mosquito Trailhead (plan more than an hour to drive this road).

The trail to White Chief Bowl is a scenic route with much to offer, including an exploration of the White Chief Mine tunnel. The **first mile** (1.6 km) follows the same route as the hike to Eagle and Mosquito Lakes, but you'll leave everyone behind when you continue straight at the junction while they bear right for the lakes. The **White Chief Trail** continues with a hefty grade—this **second mile** (1.6 km) is the toughest of the trip—until it tops out at the edge of a high-alpine meadow where some of Mineral King's colorful, pointed peaks pop into view. These rocky summits are composed of rusty red shale, white marble, gray granite, and black metamorphic slate. Just after you cross a seasonal stream (often a dry ravine by late summer), look for the ruins of **Crabtree Cabin** to the right of the trail. A few scraps of metal and logs are what is left of the oldest remaining structure in Mineral King, an 1870s cabin built by the discoverer of the White Chief Mine. Next comes **White Chief Meadows,** surrounded by high granite walls and filled with dozens of downed trees, evidence of harsh winter avalanches. Foxtail pines, one of the rarer species of Sierra conifers, grow in this area.

Beyond the meadow, the trail ascends slightly until it nears a **waterfall** on White Chief Creek. Shortly before the falls, the trail crosses the creek and heads uphill. In mid- to late summer, this area hosts an explosion of tiny alpine wildflowers. Look for the opening to **White Chief Mine** in a band of white marble just above the trail. Scramble uphill a short distance to reach it; if you feel adventurous, walk inside the horizontal passageway. The tunnel dead-ends in about 150 feet (45 m). (Don't linger; no mine tunnel is ever safe from cave-ins.)

Beyond the mine, the trail continues for another mile (1.6 km) to **Upper White Chief Bowl,** passing dozens of limestone caverns along the way. Although tempting, these

1: Monarch Lake **2:** the Honeymoon Cabin at Mineral King **3:** Eagle Lake **4:** cabin at Silver City Mountain Resort

caverns should only be explored by those who are experienced and properly equipped.

BACKPACKING

Many of the day-hiking trails (Monarch Lakes, Mosquito Lakes, Eagle Lake, White Chief Mine) are also popular with backpackers, especially weekenders looking for relatively short hikes to reach their destination (at Mosquito Lakes, you have to hike to lakes 2-5 to camp; the first lake is a day-hiking destination only). **Wilderness permits** are required for overnight travel, and each trail is subject to daily entry quotas. Permits are available on a first-come, first-served basis at **Mineral King Ranger Station** (559/565-3766, www.nps.gov/seki, 8am-4pm daily summer only, $15 permit fee). Trailhead quotas are in effect from late May to late September; reserve your spot in advance for the most popular trips. Approximately one-third of each quota is available on a first-come, first-served basis starting at 1pm the day before departure, or on the day of departure at the permit station closest to the trailhead. Reservations are available for the other two-thirds of each quota; reserve in advance by mail or email. Even with a reservation, you must pick up your permit at the wilderness permit station on the afternoon before your trip (after 1pm), or no later than 9am on the morning of your departure.

Franklin Pass and Farewell Gap

For a two- or three-day trip, hike 5.4 miles (8.7 km) on the **Franklin Pass Trail** to Lower Franklin Lake, set below Tulare and Florence Peaks. The first 2 miles (3.2 km) are nearly level as the route winds along the bottom of Mineral King's canyon, following **Farewell Gap Trail** alongside the East Fork Kaweah River. The trail leaves the valley floor and starts to climb moderately, reaching Franklin Creek's cascades at 1.7 miles (2.7 km). After crossing Franklin Creek, continue south along Farewell Canyon, negotiating some switchbacks as the views get better and better. One mile (1.6 km) farther, **Franklin Lakes Trail** forks left off Farewell Gap Trail and starts climbing in earnest up the Franklin Creek Valley. At nearly 10,000 feet (3,000 m), the trail crosses Franklin Creek again, after which it parallels the creek for another mile (1.6 km) to the lower and largest Franklin Lake. It's a dramatic sight, surrounded by steep, snow-covered slopes and a few pines and junipers.

It's possible to remain on the Farewell Gap Trail (at the fork) and cross over 10,600-foot (3,230-m) **Farewell Gap,** which will take you out of the national park and into the lands of Golden Trout Wilderness and destinations such as the Bullfrog Lakes and Little Kern River.

Sawtooth Trail

On the opposite end of Mineral King Valley, backpackers can continue from **Monarch Lakes** for 1.3 miles (2.1 km) up and over 11,630-foot (3,545-m) **Sawtooth Pass** (an oxygen-sucking 1,200-ft/365-m ascent), which provides access to loop options that include **Little Five** or **Big Five Lakes.** Sawtooth Pass offers one of the most inspiring views in the southern Sierra.

FOOD AND ACCOMMODATIONS

There's only one place in Mineral King to get a bed, a meal, and a roof over your head—fortunately, it's a wonderful place. ★ **Silver City Mountain Resort** (559/561-3223, www.silvercityresort.com, late May-late Oct.) has 16 cabins and chalets ranging in size from the diminutive and adorable historic cabins ($170-200, no bath) to family cabins ($245, restrooms but no showers) to newer and fully equipped chalets ($360-495) that can accommodate 4-8 people. Almost all of the cabins have kitchens. The resort is off the grid, so generators churn out electricity for 10 hours every day; after 10pm, guests must rely on propane lanterns for light. There's no cell service, but the resort has Wi-Fi that works when the generators are running. Restrooms and showers for those staying in cabins without such facilities are a few steps away.

The **Silver City Restaurant** (8am-8pm Thurs.-Mon., 8am-7pm Tues.-Wed., $8-12) serves food that's simple but delicious—salads, burgers, and quesadillas for lunch and dinner, plus huge breakfasts of eggs, pancakes, and French toast. The bakery is famous for its homemade pies; at least a half dozen varieties are available every day. On Tuesday and Wednesday, the café operates on a shoestring and serves a very limited menu, sometimes only coffee and pie. The adjacent Silver City Store carries a very limited supply of groceries and edibles (9am-5pm Tues.-Wed., 8am-8pm Thurs.-Mon.). The store does not sell ice, so bring your own—and a cooler to keep it frozen.

CAMPING

Tent campers will be happy in Mineral King—RVs can't negotiate the road into the valley, so you won't hear generators running in the

middle of the night. All sites are first come, first served; no reservations are accepted. Vault toilets are provided at the campgrounds, and water is available seasonally.

Closest to Mineral King Valley, 40-site **Cold Springs Campground** (www.nps.gov/seki, late May-mid-Oct., $12) offers proximity to alpine lakes, giant sequoia groves, and awe-inspiring views of the jagged Sawtooth Ridge. Tent sites are set on the river or in the quaking aspens; some sites are walk-in. Showers are available at Silver City Mountain Resort, 2 miles (3.2 km) from camp.

When Cold Springs fills up, the next-best choice is 21-site **Atwell Mill Campground** (www.nps.gov/seki, late May-mid-Oct., $12), located among giant sequoia stumps at the site of an old logging camp. The camp is a bit farther from the trailheads of Mineral King Valley, but closer to the store, showers, and great meals at Silver City Mountain Resort.

Background

The Landscape

GEOLOGY

The tale of Yosemite began about 400 million years ago when the land that is now the Sierra Nevada lay quietly beneath an ancient sea. This landmass was made up of thick layers of sediment that were piled thousands of feet deep. As the number of layers continued to build, pressure caused the bottom layers to be folded, twisted, and compressed into rock forms. Eventually these massive rocks were thrust upward above the sea's surface by movements of the Pacific and North American continental plates. In the process, a mountain range was formed—what

would eventually become the **Sierra Nevada,** the longest and highest single mountain range in the contiguous United States.

As the mountains rose, molten rock welled up from deep within the earth and cooled slowly beneath the layers of rock and sediment, forming the substance we know as granite. Over eons, erosion gradually wore away almost all the overlying sediment and exposed the granite underneath. Most of the rock we see today in Yosemite is granite, although some of the original sedimentary rock can still be viewed in the western foothills of the Sierra Nevada. (Easy to distinguish from other types of rock, **granite** bears a salt-and-pepper appearance, created by a random distribution of light- and dark-colored minerals.)

Next, around 20 million years ago, the entire block of the mountain range was uplifted and tilted to the west, creating the long, gentle slope of the foothills to the west and the steep escarpment of the Sierra's east side. Fast-flowing water and snowmelt worked to cut deep river channels into the gentle western slope. The major structure of the Sierra was now formed and only required a few finishing touches.

Those final touches came about 2 million years ago, when the planet cooled, the ice age descended, and the entire mountain range was engulfed in snow and ice. **Glaciers** went to work on the exposed granite, moving slowly down established river valleys and carving Yosemite's landmark shapes and forms. Softer, weaker rock was chiseled away and ground into rubble by the fierce power of the glaciers' grinding ice and rock. Valleys were rounded out from a sharp V shape to a gentler U shape. Lake basins were formed at the bases of towering peaks. Only the sturdiest chunks of granite withstood the glaciers' onslaught—monoliths like **El Capitan,** at 3,593 feet (1,095 m) the tallest unbroken cliff in the world. What we see is only the tip of the iceberg—El Cap's solid granite sinks 7-10 miles (11-16 km) into the earth.

It is uncertain how many times glacial ice moved through Yosemite, advancing and then retreating, although there is evidence in other areas of the Sierra Nevada that at least 3 major glaciations occurred, perhaps as many as 10. The last passage of glaciers in Yosemite, called the Tioga glacial period, ended only about 10,000 years ago.

Another process was also taking place as the softer rock was being eroded and carried away. With the top layers of rock removed, the bottom layers were under much less weight and pressure and so began to expand. As they expanded, their surfaces cracked, and the top layers of rock peeled off in sheets, like layers from an onion.

Slowly, through this process known as **exfoliation,** irregularities in the rock were removed and all that remained were smooth, rounded surfaces. This is one reason for the number of bald **granite domes** we see in Yosemite today, such as Half Dome, Sentinel Dome, and North Dome. A good example of granite in the midst of the exfoliation process is the Royal Arches in the Valley, on the canyon wall behind the Majestic Yosemite Hotel.

The Sierra Nevada's geologic upheaval isn't over. On a broad scale, the mountains are still rising, although only by about one foot every thousand years. On a more noticeable scale, weathering and erosion continue to shape the face of Yosemite. A few small glaciers still exist within the park borders (the Lyell Glacier is the most famous) and are still grinding away. At the same time, another geologic agent is always at work, continually changing the face of Yosemite: gravity. Landslides and rockfalls are common occurrences in the park, particularly in Yosemite Valley with its sheer vertical walls, many of which are severely fractured both on the surface and underneath.

The most famous **rockslide** in Yosemite Valley's recent history occurred in the Happy

---

Previous: golden mantle squirrel.

Geology Definitions

- **Arête:** A narrow, jagged ridge, usually between two cirques.

- **Cirque:** A bowl-shaped basin in which a glacier was formed. Water expands as it freezes, eventually digging out rock to form a large basin. These basins often contain lakes; May Lake off Tioga Pass Road is a classic glacial cirque lake.

- **Erratics:** Large boulders that were left behind by retreating glaciers. As the glaciers melted, big rocks that were carried along in their midst were dropped in place like pebbles. Two easy places to see glacial erratics are at Olmsted Point and in the stretch of Tioga Pass Road near Tenaya Lake.

- **Exfoliation:** The process by which concentric sheets of granite fracture and "peel off" from the surface of a rock formation. The rock layers, which can be more than 100 feet (30 m) thick, crack and then strip off, as if the rock is shedding an outer shell.

- **Glacier:** A mass of rock and ice formed by the freezing and refreezing of snow crystals. The mass moves forward, or flows, pushed by the force of gravity at the snail-like pace of a few inches per day.

- **Hanging valley:** While a large glacier was busily scouring the main channel of Yosemite Valley, smaller streams of ice were at work in the Valley's feeder streams and tributaries. These smaller glacial extensions could not cut as deeply as the large Valley glacier, and so when the ice retreated, tributary valleys were left "hanging" above the low Valley floor. Bridalveil Creek flows through a hanging valley to create spectacular 620-foot (189-m) Bridalveil Fall.

- **Roche moutonnée:** A granite dome that has a smooth, gentle slope on one side and a steep, vertical slope on the other side. Lembert Dome and Pothole Dome, on the east and west ends of Tuolumne Meadows, respectively, are prime examples of roches moutonnées (a French term that roughly means "sheeplike rock"). You can walk right up one side of a roche moutonnée, but the other side is the playground of elite rock climbers.

- **Talus:** A pile of rough, angular rock fragments deposited at the base of a cliff or steep slope. Talus fields can be seen all over Yosemite and are easily viewed along Northside Drive in Yosemite Valley in the vicinity of the Three Brothers.

- **Terminal moraine:** A mix of rubble, rock, and sand pushed ahead of the advancing glaciers and then left in place when the glaciers melted, usually forming a ridge.

Isles region on July 10, 1996, when an 80,000-ton (73,000-tonne) slab of granite broke off the southeast side of Glacier Point and fell 1,000 feet (300 m). The impact created 160 mph (255 kph) winds and devastated 10 acres (4 hectares) of forest. When it was all over, nearly everything in the Valley was covered by 2 inches (5 cm) of dust. This massive slide made the evening news all over the country, yet smaller rockslides are a common occurrence in the Valley. The largest historical rockfall in Yosemite occurred in March 1987, when an estimated 1.5 million tons (1.4 million tonnes) of debris landed at the base of the Three Brothers, closing Northside Drive for several months. Almost every year Northside Drive is closed for at least a short period of time due to falling rocks near the Three Brothers.

Although the glacial theory is now the accepted story of Yosemite's geologic past, it wasn't always so. Naturalist **John Muir** first put forth the glacial theory around 1870, after spending years studying Yosemite's rocks and landscape up close. The famous geologist **Josiah Whitney,** the director of the California Geological Survey, thought Muir's theory was ludicrous; he called Muir an "ignoramus." Whitney argued that Yosemite Valley was formed by a single, great cataclysmic event, which caused the bottom to drop out of its mighty rocks, forming the Valley floor. According to Whitney, that same event would have created Half Dome by shearing a much larger dome in half.

One of Whitney's assistants, Clarence King, disagreed with his superior and discovered glacial scars and other evidence of glaciation in the park. Later Muir came upon small glaciers still in existence in remote areas of Yosemite, adding strength to his and King's glacial theory.

As many as a dozen other theories as to Yosemite Valley's origin persisted until 1930, when **François E. Matthes** settled the matter by synthesizing many of them but in essence siding with John Muir. Matthes was a cartographer and geologist with the U.S. Geological Survey who wrote the definitive *Geologic History of the Yosemite Valley*. Geologists continue to study Yosemite and the Sierra Nevada today. Certainly all its ancient secrets have not yet been revealed.

CLIMATE

Yosemite National Park encompasses a wide swath of the slope of the Sierra Nevada, with elevations that range from 4,000 feet (1,220 m) in Yosemite Valley and Hetch Hetchy Valley to 13,000 feet (4,000 m) in the high country. Given that range, the weather variations within

the park are dramatic. Summertime temperatures can reach 100°F (37.8°C) in Yosemite Valley or Hetch Hetchy, but it can snow any month of the year in the high country.

Generally, the climate is quite mild year-round in the Valley, with daytime temperatures 80-90°F (27-37°C) in summer and nighttime temperatures ranging 50-60°F (10-20°C). Spring and fall are somewhat cooler. Winter days average 30-55°F (-1-13°C), and nights will often drop below freezing. Snow falls in Yosemite Valley a few times each winter, but it usually does not last more than a week or two. Accumulations above 1-2 feet (30-60 cm) are rare. Rain is fairly common in winter but quite rare between May and October.

In the high country at Glacier Point or even higher along Tioga Pass Road—snow as deep as 10 feet (3 m) closes the roads most years from late October until early June. Summer in Tuolumne Meadows and on top of Glacier Point is usually dry and cool, with temperatures rarely reaching higher than 75°F (24°C). Nighttime temperatures often drop to 40-49°F (4-9°C) and by September can approach freezing. Afternoon thundershowers are common throughout Yosemite's high country July through September, when the Central Valley's temperatures are consistently high.

Plants

The wide range of elevation and climate in Yosemite produces an incredible variety of flora, from chaparral plants that only survive in hot, dry areas to subalpine plants that grow only at 12,000 feet (3,650 m) during the few short weeks of summer. The park contains 37 kinds of native trees, from the grand giant sequoia to the delicate dogwood, and 1,400 species of flowering plants. The vegetation changes with elevation and occurs in broad bands called life zones. Four main life zones are found in the park. They are most easily

understood by considering the places where park visitors would encounter them and what major species are indicative of each zone.

LOWER MONTANE LIFE ZONE

In Yosemite Valley and Hetch Hetchy Valley lies the lower montane life zone. Elevations range 3,500-6,000 feet (1,100-1,800 m). These two valleys are filled with dense mixed forests of ponderosa pine, sugar pine, Douglas-fir, incense-cedar, white fir, and giant sequoia.

Mixed in with the conifers are leaf trees such as black oak, big-leaf maple, dogwood, and cottonwood. These deciduous trees create a fine color show in the Valley in autumn. Visitors from the East Coast won't find that it competes with fall in Vermont, but for California, this is a good autumn display.

The conifers of this region can be identified by a few easy-to-remember characteristics. The **ponderosa pine** is recognized by its clearly delineated, jigsaw puzzle-like bark and long needles (4-10 in/10-25 cm). The **sugar pine** is the tallest and largest of more than 100 species of pine trees in the world—old trees frequently reach 7 feet (2 m) in diameter and 200 feet (60 m) tall. This venerable pine has unmistakable cones, befitting a tree this size: They are 10-18 inches (25-46 cm) in length, the longest cones of any conifer. The cones hang down like Christmas ornaments off the tips of the sugar pine's long branches. While they are still green, they weigh up to 5 pounds (2.3 kg). One of the best places to see sugar pines and their giant cones is between the Big Oak Flat entrance station and the Crane Flat area, off Highway 120.

The **Douglas-fir** is also easily spotted by its cones, which hang downward while those of true firs sit upright, and its needles, which grow out in all directions from its branches. The tree is actually not a fir at all, which is why its name must be correctly spelled with a hyphen—indicating that "fir" is not the species but simply a moniker. The tree is not a pine, either, or any other commonly known tree, but rather a species unto itself. Because of its fast-growing nature, the Douglas-fir has the unhappy distinction of being the most important lumber tree in the United States. In Yosemite, of course, Douglas-firs are protected from logging.

The **incense-cedar** can be identified by its lacy foliage and unusual needles, which are completely flat at the ends, as if they have been ironed. Its bark is shaggy in appearance, and the tree emits a slight spicy odor (some people think its scent is reminiscent of pencils). Like Douglas-fir, the incense-cedar's name is hyphenated because it is not a true cedar.

The sturdy **white fir** has a white-gray trunk, and the tree commonly reaches a width of 5 feet (1.5 m). It has needles that grow in flat sprays that are distinctly two-dimensional. White firs are easily spotted in Yosemite's three sequoia groves, where their seeds germinate in the thick duff that covers the ground beneath the giant sequoias. Most people recognize white firs because the young

Most people know the dogwood by its "flowers," which are actually bracts.

ones look like little Christmas trees; indeed, this is a commonly marketed Christmas tree in California. Older trees easily attain heights of 150 feet (45 m).

The last of the conifers in the lower montane life zone is the **giant sequoia,** which is well known not just for its gargantuan height and girth, which combine to make this tree the largest living thing on earth, but also for its distinctive cinnamon-colored bark. Three native groves of these amazing tree giants exist in Yosemite—Mariposa, Merced, and Tuolumne—and a few planted sequoias live in Yosemite Valley, near the Majestic Yosemite Hotel and at the Yosemite Cemetery.

Among the deciduous trees of the lower montane life zone, the **black oak** was the most prevalent species in the Valley prior to the 1850s. The activities of white settlers in the last 150 years, particularly efforts designed to reduce flooding and a long-standing policy of fire suppression, have caused the Valley's stands of black oaks to dwindle to about 10 percent of their historical numbers. In their place, a greater number of conifers have taken over. Through replanting efforts, the National Park Service is working diligently to restore black oaks to Yosemite Valley. Seedlings and young trees are fenced off to prevent trampling by humans and browsing by animals. The black oaks are an important food source for deer and squirrels, as they once were for the Native Americans who lived in the Valley. Grinding rocks, or *morteros,* upon which American Indian women ground acorns into meal, can be found throughout Yosemite.

One of the showiest tree species of the lower montane life zone is the **western dogwood.** If you visit Yosemite Valley in May, you will be delighted by the sprays of white blossoms on this small, delicate tree that grows under the canopy of large conifers. The dogwood's 5-inch-wide (13-cm) blooms are not truly flowers, but rather petal-like bracts that surround the true flowers—a dense, yellow cluster in the middle of the bracts. One of the most beautiful evening sights in Yosemite Valley is that of flowering dogwoods lit up by the full moon. The tree also develops attractive red berries in the fall, a favorite food of robins.

In the understory of this wide variety of deciduous trees and conifers lives a low-growing shrub that, despite its small size, garners its share of attention in the lower montane life zone. It's a plant with three common names: **mountain misery,** bear clover, or kit-kit-dizze. Visitors may not know it by any of its names, but they will certainly recognize its scent; the fern-like shrub emits a strong, sweet, evocative odor. Once you smell mountain misery, you will always associate its scent with the lower Sierra Nevada. Many visitors encounter the plant for the first time as they drive into the park on Highway 41 from Oakhurst. Both sides of the road are carpeted with mountain misery for several miles south and north of the park's South entrance station. The scent follows you past Wawona, up to the entrance to Glacier Point Road, and down to the Valley at Bridalveil Fall.

Other chaparral plants common in the lower montane life zone include several species of manzanitas, currants, yerba santa, ceanothus, deerbrush, and buckbrush.

UPPER MONTANE LIFE ZONE

On Glacier Point and along the west end of Tioga Pass Road lies the upper montane life zone, at 6,000-8,500 feet (1,830-2,590 m) in elevation. Tuolumne Meadows is just on the edge of this life zone, at an elevation of 8,600 feet (2,620 m). It straddles the border of the upper montane life zone and the next higher life zone, the subalpine.

At these elevations, massive red firs and lodgepole pines predominate. The deeply shaded forests in this zone also contain western white pine, Jeffrey pine, and western juniper. Wet mountain meadows are common, and within them bloom a variety of wildflowers in early summer: pink shooting stars, red-and-yellow western columbine, bright yellow coneflowers, red or orange paintbrush, and false hellebore (corn lilies), among others.

Western white pines are gray-barked

pines with blue-green needles in bundles of five. The tree has 9-inch-long (23-cm) cones that are often slightly curved. Visitors can see many large examples of the tree in the stretch of road between Porcupine Flat Campground and Tioga Pass. Western white pines rarely exceed 100 feet (30 m) in height, but their long limbs curve gracefully upward.

Red firs are easy to identify because of their reddish-brown bark. They can grow up to 6 feet (1.8 m) in diameter and are often seen in pure groves made up of only their own kind. The area of Tioga Pass Road near the Lukens Lake Trailhead shows off some remarkably large red firs. Depressions at the bases of the biggest trees are sometimes used by bears as winter dens (the same is also true for white firs).

Red firs played a large role in the early popularization of Yosemite Valley as a tourist attraction; the wood and bark of these trees was lit on fire and pushed off the top of Glacier Point to create a nightly spectacle in Yosemite Valley known as Firefall. The sight of the tumbling, burning embers dropping 1,000 feet (300 m) to the Valley floor was an event witnessed by millions of eager visitors between 1900 and 1968. Eventually the National Park Service discontinued the show, rightly deciding that it was an inappropriate activity for a national park. The crowds that gathered for Firefall each evening damaged meadows, trampled plants, and created traffic jams in the Valley. Cascading embers burned off fragile lichen growth on the cliffs of Glacier Point. And the red fir bark was growing scarce and needed to be gathered at increasingly greater distances from Yosemite Valley.

Lodgepole pines are the only two-needled pines in the Sierra. They earned their name because Native Americans used their dependably straight trunks as poles for their teepees and lodges. On Tioga Road, especially near Tuolumne Meadows, lodgepole pines do not grow very tall—most are in the 20- to 40-foot (6- to 12-m) range. Throughout history the tree has been mistakenly called a tamarack, which is actually a deciduous conifer

that does not live anywhere in the Sierra. The lodgepole pine's mistaken identity is the reason for place-names such as Tamarack Lakes and Tamarack Flat that we find in Yosemite and beyond.

Currently, lodgepole pines along and near Tioga Pass Road are suffering from an attack by the needleminer moth, an insect whose larvae obtain food and shelter by hollowing out the lodgepole pine's needles. This ultimately kills the tree, and large stands of pines in the Yosemite high country are dead or dying from this insect's activities. However, because the attack of the needleminer moth is a natural occurrence that happens every 100 years or so in a lodgepole pine forest, the National Park Service is allowing Mother Nature to run her course. In the long term, the moth may actually be good for the lodgepole pine forest because it takes out some of the older trees and allows younger, healthier stands to grow in their place.

The Jeffrey pine is a favorite of many Sierra tree lovers because of the unique scent of its bark, which smells quite sweet, like vanilla or butterscotch. Hungry hikers sometimes liken the smell of the Jeffrey pine to a breakfast of pancakes and maple syrup. The side of the pine that is warmed by sunlight generally emits the strongest scent. Sometimes the odor is so strong it wafts to you from several feet away; other times you must put your nose right up to the tree's bark crevices to smell it.

Like the ponderosa pine, the Jeffrey has jigsaw-puzzle bark (it's especially pronounced on older, wider trees). The two species are sometimes confused, but if you know at what elevation the tree sits, you can usually identify it correctly. Jeffrey pines are rarely seen below 6,000 feet (1,800 m), and ponderosa pines are rarely seen above that elevation. The Jeffrey pine is a rugged tree often seen growing on high granite domes and slopes, seemingly without the aid of soil. A very famous and much-photographed Jeffrey once lived on top of the bald summit of Sentinel Dome in Yosemite, but it finally died of old age in 1979. Other Jeffrey pines still eke out a wind-sculpted living on the dome's bald surface.

Another unique feature of the Jeffrey pine is that its cones are not prickly to the touch because their spines point downward, not outward. This feature has earned the tree the nickname "gentleman Jeffrey." The ponderosa pine's cones, by way of contrast, can be remembered as "prickly ponderosa."

Western juniper (also called Sierra juniper) is another distinctive Sierra tree, and an easy one to identify because of its bluish-green, scale-like needles and its spiraling trunk, which makes it appear as if the tree twisted in circles as it grew. The roots of this hardy tree will tunnel through crevices in granite, making it seem as if the western juniper is growing right out of rock. Western junipers in Yosemite and elsewhere in the Sierra can live as long as 2,000 years. As the juniper ages, its trunk becomes stripped of bark and bleached to a light blond. The juniper produces an abundance of blue "berries" in the summer months, which are well loved by birds. These are actually not berries at all, but the juniper's cones.

Aside from the big conifers, one small plant common in the upper montane life zone is worth a special mention. It is the **snow plant**, a thick, red, asparagus-like plant that has no green leaves. This is one of the first flora to make an appearance as the snow melts; early-season hikers will often see it protruding from the forest floor amid piles of melting snow. A member of the heath family, snow plant is so tough and determined to sprout that it can sometimes push up through asphalt.

SUBALPINE LIFE ZONE

Still higher, between Tuolumne Meadows and 9,945-foot (3,030-m) Tioga Pass, only two hardy trees survive: whitebark pine and mountain hemlock, both of which are usually low-growing. Elevations in this subalpine life zone range 8,500-10,500 feet (2,600-3,200 m). The **whitebark pine** often looks more like a shrub with multiple small trunks than

a single tree; at its tallest it grows to about 35 feet (11 m). Its cones are purple and 2 inches (5 cm) long, with seeds that are highly coveted by Clark's nutcrackers, chickarees, and chipmunks.

The **mountain hemlock** is easily identified by its uppermost branches, which droop downward or sideways, as if they are taking a bow. Naturalist John Muir was a great fan of the mountain hemlock and wrote a lengthy ode to it in his first book, *The Mountains of California*. The hemlock has greenish-blue foliage that is distinct when viewed close up; its needles are dense and completely cover the stems they grow on, like a coat of fur. The tree can be viewed from Tioga Pass Road in the high region between Tenaya Lake and Tioga Pass.

The dominant plants that grow in the high meadows of the subalpine life zone are **sedges**, not the grasses found in lower-elevation meadows. Wildflowers at these elevations include many of the same species of the upper montane life zone, although the higher the elevation, the more likely the plants will be of a smaller, more compact variety.

ALPINE LIFE ZONE

Finally, at 10,500 feet (3,200 m) and above lies the region that only hikers in Yosemite will see: the alpine life zone that is found above the timberline, where trees are rare to nonexistent. Plants that grow here are typically very small, mainly because of harsh winds. The growing season is very short, making these alpine environments extremely fragile and easily disturbed by human presence. Cushions or mats of colorful flowers like penstemon and phlox brighten the generally stark landscape of gray, rocky slopes. Some of the loveliest of these mat-like plants are the mountain heaths or heathers. John Muir wrote lovingly of the white, bell-shaped flowers of cassiope, which he described as "the most beautiful and best loved of the heathworts…ringing her thousands of sweet-toned bells." Cassiope can be seen today along high lakeshores and on Cathedral Peak.

Animals

Many visitors travel to American national parks in the hopes of seeing wildlife. In this regard, Yosemite often delivers, although you never know which of the park's 76 mammal species, 247 bird species, and 29 reptile and amphibian species will make an appearance at any given time. Although it's unlikely you'll get to see any of Yosemite's 15 species of bats, most park visitors will make the acquaintance of at least one of the park's 17 species of mosquitoes (although this is generally not a welcome meeting). Fortunately, only 3 of those 17 mosquito types feast on the flesh of humans, and those pesky critters are generally limited to the early summer season—typically in the three weeks following snowmelt at any given location. The general rule is that if the wildflowers are blooming in an area, the mosquitoes will be there, too. Once the flowers die back, the mosquitoes largely disappear.

The following is a brief guide to some of Yosemite's most commonly seen, or most notable, animal denizens.

LARGE MAMMALS
Black Bear
The only kind of bear that lives in Yosemite, or anywhere in California, is the black bear. Although the fearsome grizzly bear once roamed the state and is immortalized on the California flag, grizzlies have been extinct in Yosemite since 1895 and in the rest of California since 1924. Black bears have a somewhat misleading name, as they are commonly brown, blond, or cinnamon-colored—rarely pure black. Often they have a white patch on their chest. The smallest of all North American bears, they typically weigh up to 400 pounds (180 kg); one captured Yosemite bear weighed a whopping 690 pounds (315 kg). They can run up to 30 miles (48 km) per hour and are powerful swimmers and climbers. Despite the adult bear's enormous size, bear cubs weigh only a half pound (0.2 kg) at birth.

Black bears will eat just about anything, but their staple foods are berries, fruits, plants, insects, honeycomb, the inner layer of tree bark, fish, and small mammals. Contrary to popular belief, black bears do not hibernate. A pregnant female will "den up" in winter and usually give birth while she is sleeping, but this is not true hibernation. Male black bears are often seen roaming for food in winter.

Mule Deer
Frequently seen in Yosemite Valley and crossing roads elsewhere in the park, the mule deer is one of our largest American deer and can weigh up to 450 pounds (200 kg). The deer gets its name from its ears, which are large and rounded. Mule deer in the Sierra have a white patch on their rumps and a black-tipped tail. The antlers on the bucks, which develop in summer, are usually an elegant matched set of four points on each side.

Sierra Bighorn Sheep
The last of the native bighorn sheep vanished from Yosemite's high country in 1914. The mighty bighorn was reintroduced in the Yosemite region in 1986. Members of this small relocated herd are sometimes seen just east of Tioga Pass. The herd's numbers have dropped from approximately 90 bighorns in the early 1990s to approximately 50 in 2017, most likely due to predation from mountain lions. Throughout the entire Sierra Nevada, the bighorn sheep population numbers about 400. The sturdy sheep, with their signature thick, backward-curved horns, are listed by the state of California and by the federal government as an endangered species. The Sierra bighorn prefers elevations above 10,000 feet (3,000 m) and can travel up and down steep, rocky slopes with amazing speed and grace; John Muir called them "the greatest of all

Saving the Lives of Bears

There's only one important fact to remember about California's bears: They love snacks. The average black bear must eat 20,000 calories a day to sustain its body weight. Because its natural diet is made up of berries, fruits, plants, fish, and insects, the high-calorie food of human beings seems very appealing to a bear. A box full of candy bars is a lot easier to swallow than 1,500 acorns.

Campers have trained bears to crave the taste of corn chips, hot dogs, and soda pop. As a result, bears have become less wild, more aggressive, and largely unafraid of humans. Some bears will break into cars and buildings in the hope of finding food, and they teach their young the same bad habits. Ultimately, in the conflict between bears and people, bears lose. Once a bear has developed a taste for human food, there is no turning back. Transporting the bear to another area is ineffective, so bears that develop a reputation as "problem bears" are put to death.

Any time you see a bear, it's most likely looking for food. It's essential to keep human food packed away in bearproof storage containers when camping or staying in more rustic lodgings, like tent cabins, which bears can easily break into. The brown metal **bearproof boxes** should be closed and latched at all times.

Storing food or any item with a scent that a bear might mistake for food (soap, cosmetics, perfume, insect repellent, sunscreen, empty bottles of soda) in your car is asking for trouble. Bears are remarkably strong, and they can use their claws and muscles to "peel back" car windows and doors. If a bear breaks into your car, you won't be able to drive it home. Plan on a long discussion with your insurance agent, plus a ticket from the rangers for improper food storage. You may also be responsible for ending a bear's life. Of the roughly 500 bears that live in Yosemite, a few are put to death every year because they have become accustomed to human food and are considered dangerous as a result.

Backpackers should always use plastic **bear canisters** to store their food for overnight trips. Hanging food from a tree is ineffective and illegal in Yosemite. You can borrow, rent, or buy a bear canister in the park (at Half Dome Village Mountain Shop, Yosemite Valley Wilderness Center, Tuolumne Meadows Store, Wawona Store, Crane Flat Store, and the Hetch Hetchy entrance station). Canisters can be rented for $5 per trip; they can be returned at various locations in the park. In Sequoia and Kings Canyon, bear-proof food canisters are available for rental ($5 for three nights; $2 each additional night) at the following visitors centers or ranger stations: Foothills, Lodgepole, Grant Grove, Cedar Grove, and Mineral King.

When you are hiking, bears will most likely hear you coming and avoid you. Black bears very rarely harm human beings, but you should never approach or feed a bear, or get between a bear and its cubs or its food. If provoked, a bear could cause serious injury. If a bear approaches while you are eating, yell at it to scare it away, and pick up all your food and walk away with it. Bears respect possession and will not take food away from you. If a bear approaches your campsite, yell, throw small rocks or pine cones, and generally be as obnoxious as possible. A bear that is afraid of humans is a bear that will stay wild and stay alive.

Humans are also a menace to bears because we often drive too fast on mountain roads. From 2010 to 2017, an average of 14 bears were killed on park roads each year, although the actual number is probably higher (bears hit by cars often lumber off into the forest, injured, and die a day or two later). Red "bear markers" have been placed alongside roads in spots where bears have been recently hit to remind drivers to slow down.

To report improper food storage, trash problems, or other bear-related trouble, call the **Bear Management Team** at 209/372-0322. Your call can be made anonymously, and it may save the life of a bear.

Sierra mountaineers." The males use their horns in the autumn to butt heads and establish the chain of command, and a contest between two males can last for more than a day.

Mountain Lion

The most reclusive of all of Yosemite's creatures, the mountain lion is the largest cat in North America and is best distinguished from afar by its 2- to 3-foot-long (60- to 90-cm) tail. The adult cat's body minus its tail is often 6 feet (1.8 m) long; a male cat typically weighs 250 pounds (115 kg). The mountain lion is tawny except for its underside, which is white. It usually lives where deer, its main food source, are plentiful. Mountain lion sightings in Yosemite were extremely rare until 1994, when an abnormally high number were reported. There have been no mountain lion attacks on visitors in Yosemite, although a few attacks have occurred elsewhere in California. Although you probably won't see a lion, you may be lucky enough to find its tracks. The large, catlike footprints are easy to distinguish; they are four-toed prints that do not show claws.

Coyote

Many Yosemite visitors report seeing a wolf or a fox near one of the park roads, but usually what they have seen is a coyote. (Wolves do not live in the Sierra; foxes are quite small and rarely seen during the day.) The coyote is a doglike animal with a grayish-brown coat; its back slopes downward toward its tail. An average-size coyote weighs about 30 pounds (14 kg) and stands about 2 feet (60 cm) tall. Coyotes can run as fast as 40 miles (64 km) per hour and make a series of "yip" cries, often followed by a howl. Across California, the coyote has acclimated well to the presence of humans and is generally unafraid of them.

SMALL MAMMALS
Bobcat

A stocky feline about twice the size of a house cat, the bobcat is easily recognized by its short "bobbed" tail, only 4 inches (10 cm) long. Bobcats are mostly nocturnal but are sometimes seen hunting during the day. Their coats are gray brown in winter and reddish brown in summer, marked with black spots and bars. The bobcat's ears have short tufts above them.

Raccoon

This black-masked invader is sometimes seen scavenging in park campgrounds, particularly in the evenings. The raccoon has distinctive

Sierra bighorn sheep are magnificent creatures that are rarely seen.

rings around its tail and a large, gray-brown body that can weigh as much as 40 pounds (18 kg). Despite its girth, the raccoon is a good swimmer and climber and can run as fast as 15 mph (24 kph). Its fingerlike toes are useful for washing its food, as well as for prying open campers' coolers and food stores.

Porcupine

Only the rare and fortunate Yosemite visitor gets to see the elusive porcupine, a mammal famous for its body covering of thousands of quills—sharp, hollow spines. The porcupine's quills lie flat when the animal is relaxed, but they stand straight up when it is threatened. Porcupines spend most of their time high in trees, where they eat twigs and bark, but are sometimes seen crossing meadows or forests in search of a new feeding tree. Porcupine tracks face forward and inward; the animal walks pigeon-toed.

Yellow-Bellied Marmot

This largest and most curious member of the squirrel family is frequently seen in Yosemite's high country, particularly in rocky areas like Olmsted Point or on the borders of Tuolumne Meadows. About 7 inches (18 cm) tall and as long as 2 feet (60 cm), the bold marmot has no enemies and is frequently seen sunning itself on high boulders. The marmot's coat is buff to brown and its belly characteristically yellow. If you see two or more marmots together, they are often wrestling or chasing each other. You may hear them make a high-pitched whistling sound.

Pika

A frequently seen resident in alpine environments higher than 8,000 feet (2,400 m), the pika is a small relative of the rabbit that busily collects green grasses, then stacks them in the sun and dries them for winter food and insulation. The creature does not hibernate, so it needs to keep a full stock of dried grasses for its winter nourishment. The diminutive pika is most often seen on talus-lined slopes or rocky hillsides; it is easily recognized by its small, rounded ears and absence of a tail.

Chipmunks

Not one but eight kinds of chipmunks are found in Yosemite. Most common are the lodgepole chipmunk, alpine chipmunk, yellow-pine chipmunk, Allen's chipmunk, and Merriam's chipmunk. All chipmunks are colored in various shades of brown and have a distinctive stripe on their body and face. The yellow-pine is the most boldly striped. Generally, chipmunks at higher elevations hibernate and those at lower elevations do not. Like their cousins the squirrels, chipmunks eat nuts, seeds, and fungi.

Squirrels

The number and variety of squirrels and their close relations in Yosemite can be quite daunting to the amateur naturalist trying to identify them. One of the easiest to spot species is the golden-mantled ground squirrel, a common sight at elevations above 6,000 feet (1,800 m). Frequently mistaken for large chipmunks, these cute squirrels can be correctly identified by the fact that they lack the chipmunk's facial stripe. Otherwise, they look much the same, with one white stripe on each side of their brown bodies, bordered by a heavy black stripe. The golden-mantled ground squirrel must fatten itself up all summer to prepare for winter hibernation.

The western gray squirrel is the common gray-coated squirrel we see throughout California, with a long bushy tail and white belly. Western gray squirrels are great tree climbers and are mostly seen below 6,000 feet (1,800 m). In contrast, the Douglas squirrel (also called a chickaree) is much smaller than the western gray, and colored a mix of brown and gray. This constantly chattering and highly active squirrel is a key player in the giant sequoia forest, where it cuts thousands of seed-bearing cones per hour from the high branches of a sequoia. The cones drop to the ground, the chickaree scrambles down the tree and gnaws on their meat, and the sequoia seeds fall to the earth to regenerate.

Two additional types of ground squirrels are also seen in Yosemite, and both types hibernate in winter. The Belding ground squirrel is a high-country dweller that is brown or gray with a reddish tail; it is often spotted in meadows standing upright on its back legs. The California ground squirrel is seen at lower elevations and is best identified by a silver, V-shaped pattern on the shoulders of its brown-spotted coat.

BIRDS
Steller's Jay

Nobody visits Yosemite without seeing the Steller's jay, a bold and raucous bird that makes its presence known. The western cousin of the East Coast's blue jay, the Steller's jay has a distinctive black topknot of feathers that point backward, affording it a regal look. The jay's body is about 10 inches (25 cm) in length and a deep, pure blue. When on the ground, the Steller's jay hops—it does not walk. If you are eating a sandwich when one is near, keep a vigilant guard; the jay has no qualms about stealing food.

Clark's Nutcracker

Similar in size and behavior to the Steller's jay (noisy, cantankerous, and often seen scouting campgrounds and picnic areas for food), the Clark's nutcracker is light gray with white and black patches on its tail and wings. A group of them are often seen and heard among the upper branches of whitebark pine trees, where they quarrel with each other as they collect pine nuts. The bird stores nuts and seeds for the winter in massive granaries, usually located on south-facing slopes. One pair can cache as many as 30,000 nuts and seeds in the fall. In the spring, the birds recall the placement of every single one and retrieve them to feed their young.

Raven

Frequently mistaken for the smaller crow, the common raven is a remarkably intelligent bird often seen scrounging for leftovers near campgrounds and picnic areas. Ravens are about 2 feet (60 cm) long, with glossy black feathers and a curved beak and a strange call that sounds something like a croaking noise. In the spring, the male raven performs a spectacular aerial dance for its mate—swooping, diving, and performing barrel rolls while it cries out loudly. The raven figures prominently in the legends of the Native Americans of Yosemite Valley.

Woodpecker

Plentiful in Yosemite, woodpeckers are frequently seen and heard amid the Valley's tall trees. With some variation, they are all black and white with a dash of flaming red on their heads (although in some species only the males bear the red patch). Most common is the acorn woodpecker, which lives in colonies of up to two dozen birds and caches acorns in tree trunks, posts, or other wood structures (sometimes even in the roofs of buildings). A well-stocked granary may hold as many as 10,000 acorns, lined up in neat rows of individually drilled holes. Called *el carpintero* by the Spanish, the acorn woodpecker prevents marauding squirrels from stealing its stash by pushing the acorns into the holes, pointed end first. The wide end of the acorn sits flush with the surface of the tree trunk, giving squirrels nothing to get their paws on.

The downy woodpecker, the smallest woodpecker in North America at about 6 inches (15 cm) long, is also seen in the Valley, usually in streamside forests. In contrast, the white-headed woodpecker is seen mostly in pine forests, where it eats pine nuts and insects. White-headed woodpeckers do not drill like most woodpeckers; instead they look for food by pulling bark off trees with their beaks. The white-headed woodpecker is all black except for its white head. The male has a small red head patch.

The pileated woodpecker is the largest woodpecker in North America at 16-19 inches (41-48 cm) in length. Its loud, slow drilling can be heard from a mile away under the right conditions (smaller woodpeckers drill with a faster cadence). The pileated woodpecker, with its black body, white underwings, and bright red crest, is sometimes spotted in the Mariposa Grove of Giant Sequoias.

Peregrine Falcon

Having been almost completely wiped out by the pesticide DDT in the 1950s and 1960s, the peregrine falcon is making a comeback in Yosemite and elsewhere, although it is still listed as an endangered species. This remarkable raptor can fly faster than 200 mph (320 kph). The adult is blue gray with a whitish breast; its legs and underparts are striped gray. The peregrine falcon nests on the ledges of near-vertical cliffs; several popular rock-climbing sites in Yosemite Valley are closed seasonally to protect nesting sites. When a peregrine falcon hunts, it will circle high until it spots a smaller bird flying below, then plummet downward at breakneck speed and attack it in flight. The female falcon is noticeably larger than the male.

Blue Grouse

This chicken-like bird is curious and virtually unafraid of humans. Frequently seen around Glacier Point and May Lake, often in groups of six or more, the blue grouse pecks at the ground for conifer needles, buds, and seeds. The grouse is not blue but rather brownish gray. Young grouse are able to walk and feed themselves immediately after they hatch out of their eggs. You may hear but not see the blue grouse while hiking in the high country; the male attracts the female with a strange hooting sound that is amplified by inflating the air sacs on both sides of his neck. The effect sounds something like a hollow drumbeat echoing through the forest.

American Dipper

One of John Muir's favorite birds, the dipper (also called the water ouzel) is an unusual songbird often seen amid the spray of waterfalls—even those as powerful as Yosemite Falls and Bridalveil Fall. Although it is colored a nondescript gray, the dipper lives an extraordinary life, diving underwater to feed on insects and larvae. The bird has a third eyelid that closes over its eyes to protect it from spray, a flap of skin that closes over its nostrils to keep out water, and an extra-large oil gland that waterproofs its plumage. It often builds its nest behind a waterfall, then flies back and forth through the torrent to feed its young. When searching for food in a stream, it can walk underwater.

A baby woodpecker pokes its head out of its home.

California Gull

Many a first-time Yosemite visitor has wondered why gulls—a species associated with the seashore—are frequently seen in the high country of Yosemite, especially around Tioga Lake, Ellery Lake, and Tenaya Lake. The reason is the proximity of Mono Lake, a few miles from the eastern border of the park. The saline lake is the second-largest breeding colony in the world for California gulls. Approximately 85 percent of the gulls seen at the California coast were born at Mono Lake.

Great Gray Owl

An endangered species in California, the great gray owl is thriving in Yosemite probably better than anywhere else in the state, although here they are at the southernmost end of their habitat range. The great gray owl is the largest species of North American owl, reaching more than 2 feet (60 cm) tall. It hunts for voles and mice in the daytime as well as at night, usually in meadows surrounded by forest. The great gray owl has a memorable face, with dozens of concentric rings around its small, yellow eyes. An estimated 40 great gray owls live within the park's borders; one of the best places to see one is near Crane Flat at dusk.

FISH
Rainbow Trout

Of the five trout species found today in Yosemite—brown, brook, rainbow, cutthroat, and golden—only the rainbow trout is native. The rest were introduced through fish-planting programs in the late 19th and early 20th centuries. Although lakes and streams in the park are no longer stocked with fish, an estimated 50 park lakes have self-sustaining populations of nonnative trout. The colorful rainbow trout, with its signature pink stripe on its side and black spots on its back, was a favored food of Native Americans in Yosemite Valley.

History

NATIVE AMERICANS

It is believed that Native Americans first came to live in Yosemite Valley about 4,000 years ago. Of the original tribes, the only one we know much about is the most recent, the **Ahwahneechee,** a sector of the Southern Sierra Miwok tribe.

The last Ahwahneechee tribe to live in Yosemite, led by **Chief Tenaya,** moved in to the Valley after the area had been vacant for some years. Stories are told of a fatal disease that swept through the Valley, probably around the beginning of the 1800s, killing most of its inhabitants and forcing the rest to abandon the area. These tales align with the fact that around that same time, Native American tribes throughout California were afflicted with the diseases that accompanied the Spanish missions.

Chief Tenaya, a Yosemite Miwok Indian by descent, was raised in the Mono Lake area with the Paiute tribes. He had heard stories from his people about the glorious Valley, and when he reached adulthood, he traveled to see it. Finding it free of disease, he and about 200 other Indians resettled the Valley. They called it Ahwahnee and themselves the Ahwahneechee.

The Ahwahneechee were skilled hunters who snared birds, netted and speared trout, and hunted deer, bear, and squirrels with bow and arrow. They gathered acorns from the black oaks and ground them into meal, dug plant bulbs in the spring, and set the Valley's grasses on fire each fall to encourage better seed production the following year. They were also skilled craftspeople, making colorful baskets from willow, redbud, ferns, and strips of bark, and practical tools like knives and scrapers from antlers and bones. They traded with other bands of Indians, particularly the Mono-area Paiute Indians, for salt, pine nuts, and insect protein.

The Ahwahneechee invented stories about their Valley as a way of understanding its prominent features, such as El Capitan and Yosemite Falls. Even Half Dome had a story: An Indian woman named Tis-sa-ack and her husband, Nangas, decided to travel to the beautiful Valley they had heard so much about. Along the way, they quarreled, and Tis-sa-ack ran off from her husband. When she got to Mirror Lake, she was so tired and thirsty that she knelt down and drank all its water. Her husband caught up with her at the lake's edge, and when he saw that it was dry and there was nothing left for him, he struck her.

The gods became so angry at these two for disturbing the peace of the Valley that they decided to transform them into granite cliffs that face each other from opposite sides of the Valley, so they could never again be together. Nangas was changed into Washington Column and Tis-sa-ack became Half Dome. The dark streaks on the dome's face are said to be Tis-sa-ack's tears.

As far as anyone knows, the Ahwahneechee lived for many years without any contact with Caucasians. The Valley's sheer walls made it an impenetrable fortress. Although a few explorers, including members of the **Joseph Walker** party, had seen the Valley from its high north rim as early as 1833, none had found a way to enter it. Even other Miwok tribes avoided the Valley; many had heard rumors of the "black sickness" that had swept through it in the past, and they also knew it was carefully guarded by the Indians who lived there. Yosemite Valley was the exclusive territory of the Ahwahneechee tribe.

THE MARIPOSA BATTALION

When the cry for gold rang out across California in the mid-1800s, the Ahwahneechee's future was suddenly and irrevocably altered. Unbeknownst to them, they were on the verge of losing their exclusive domain over Yosemite. **Gold seekers** swarmed over the entire Sierra Nevada, and it was only

a matter of time before they entered Yosemite Valley. The various mountain and foothill Indian tribes looked upon these fortune-hunting invaders with distrust, and while some chose to ignore their presence, others raided their outposts and settlements, preyed upon their horses and cattle, and stole their food. Trouble was brewing, and before long the miners and settlers demanded that the U.S. government place the estimated 10,000 Native Americans living in California on reservations, where they could be no trouble.

In response to what was termed the "Indian War," federal commissioners were appointed and sent to the Sierra Nevada to convince the local tribes to sign treaties, cede their lands, and settle on established reservations. Some tribes agreed, but many others resisted. The settlers believed that stronger action needed to be taken, especially in places like the outskirts of Yosemite, where skirmishes with Indians were becoming commonplace.

By January 1851, the state-sanctioned **Mariposa Battalion** was formed. This band of volunteer soldiers planned to enter Yosemite Valley and round up the Indians who lived there. The leader of the battalion was **James Savage,** a miner who ran a trading outpost farther down the Merced River canyon. He knew several Miwok Indian languages and had employed Indians in his business operations. Savage had a personal interest in catching the Yosemite Indians, as two of his outposts had been attacked and some of his men were killed by Indians.

Soon after starting out on their mission, Savage and the Mariposa Battalion met up with the leader of the Ahwahneechee tribe, Chief Tenaya, somewhere in the vicinity of Wawona. Tenaya at first refused to move his tribe out of the Valley, but when Savage told him that if he didn't agree, all of Tenaya's people would be killed, the chief relented. Still, three days went by without any sign of the Ahwahneechee making their way out of the Valley, so the battalion decided to push on through the winter snow and remove Indians by force.

Yosemite's Place-Names

Many of Yosemite's place-names were given by the men of the Mariposa Battalion, who entered Yosemite Valley in 1851 to round up the Ahwahneechee Indians and deport them to a reservation. Dr. Lafayette Bunnell, who traveled with the battalion, questioned the captured Ahwahneechee about their names for the Valley's natural features. Some of their words he found too difficult to pronounce, so he substituted a Spanish or English word with roughly the same meaning. Other names were invented in a more random fashion. Here are the sources of a few of Yosemite's place-names:

- **Bridalveil Fall:** The Ahwahneechee called it Pohono, meaning "evil wind." The name Bridalveil was given by the editor of the Mariposa newspaper in the 1850s because of the fall's white, cascading appearance.

- **El Capitan:** The Ahwahneechee named this granite monolith for the chief of the first tribe of Yosemite Indians, Too-tok-ah-noo-lah. Bunnell substituted the Spanish word for chief, or *el capitán*.

- **Hetch Hetchy:** The Miwok Indians named this valley Hatchatchie for a type of grass with edible seeds that grew here.

- **Illilouette:** Although it sounds French, Illilouette was a rough translation of the Indian name Too-lool-a-we-ack, which meant a good place for hunting.

- **Royal Arches:** This impressive granite cliff, found behind the Majestic Yosemite Hotel, was named by one of the men in the Mariposa Battalion in honor of his Masonic membership.

- **Tenaya Lake:** Named for Chief Tenaya, the last chief of the Ahwahneechee Indians. When told that the lake had been named for him, Chief Tenaya replied that the lake already had a name: Pywiack, or "lake of shining rocks." The name Pywiack now refers to a granite dome near Tenaya Lake.

- **Tuolumne:** The name of the river and famous subalpine meadow is the Miwok word for squirrel. Spend a few minutes in Tuolumne Meadows and you are sure to see numerous Belding ground squirrels, also known as "picket pins" for the way they stand upright on their hind legs.

- **Vernal Fall:** This waterfall reminded Bunnell of springtime. He called the cataract "an eternal April."

- **Wawona:** The Indian word for "big tree," *wawona* is an imitation of the hoot of an owl, the guardian spirit of the sequoias.

- **Yosemite:** From the Indian word *uzumate*, which meant grizzly bear. The Indian peoples that lived in the Valley were called Yosemites by Caucasians and by other Indian tribes because they lived in a place where grizzly bears were common and they were reportedly skilled at killing the bears. The Mariposa Battalion named the Valley after the "Yosemite Indians" whom, ironically, they'd been sent there to evict. In a further twist, the Indians didn't call themselves Yosemites; they called themselves Ahwahneechee, and they called the Valley "Ahwahnee" or "place of a gaping mouth."

The Mariposa Battalion made it to the Valley's high southern rim in late March 1851. Although some 72 Ahwahneechee, mostly women and children, were discovered along the way and surrendered easily, more than 100 tribespeople were believed to be hiding in the Valley. Although the men of the battalion had only rousting Indians on their minds, they were taking a journey of major historical significance, being the first white men ever to set foot in Yosemite Valley. At least one member of the party stopped along the rim trail, awestruck at his first vision of the Valley. This was **Lafayette**

Bunnell, the battalion doctor, who kept a detailed account of the entire journey. His book, *Discovery of the Yosemite*, lives on as one of the only accounts of Yosemite Valley in its Edenic early days.

Upon their descent to the Valley floor, the Mariposa Battalion found no Indians. Presumably, the Ahwahneechee had seen them coming and fled to the high country. The battalion did find the Ahwahneechee's shelters, tools, clothing, and other belongings. The soldiers set fire to the dwellings, caches of acorns, and other food stores, figuring that if the Indians returned, they would be starved out. Soon after the battalion left the Valley, Chief Tenaya and most of the 72 captured Indians escaped.

Because the first Mariposa Battalion did not succeed at rounding up the Ahwahneechee, a second expedition was organized in May 1851. This band of militiamen, led by Captain John Boling, was more effective: Five Yosemite Indians were captured, including three of Tenaya's sons. They were held hostage until Chief Tenaya could be brought to the battalion's camp in the Valley. One of Tenaya's sons was killed as he tried to escape.

Forcing Tenaya to serve as guide, Captain Boling then pursued the remainder of the Yosemite Indians into the high country. His soldiers surprised the Ahwahneechee on the shore of Tenaya Lake, where they had made camp. The Indians, who were exhausted and hungry, surrendered. But they asked their captors two haunting questions: "Where can we go that the Americans will not follow us? Where can we make our homes that you will not find us?" The answer, sadly, was the Fresno reservation.

THE END OF THE AHWAHNEECHEE

Tenaya and his people did not fare well in the hot Central Valley. They were unaccustomed to the government food they were given and did not get along with other relocated tribes. The U.S. government never ratified the treaty

necessary to close the land deal with the Indians, so in less than a year, after Tenaya promised to create no more trouble, he was allowed to leave the reservation and return to Yosemite. He was soon joined by other Ahwahneechee.

But the tribe's troubles were not over. In May 1852, two prospectors were killed near Bridalveil Fall by a group of Indians. This time the U.S. Army pursued the Ahwahneechee into the high country; five of them were killed along the way in Bloody Canyon. Tenaya and the few remaining members of his band fled to live among the Paiute Indians near Mono Lake.

Still there would be no peace. Accounts vary as to how exactly it occurred, but a common story is that in the summer of 1853, members of the two tribes were engaged in a gambling game. It became competitive, and at some point a fight broke out. Chief Tenaya and several members of his tribe were killed.

Tenaya's death signaled the end for the Ahwahneechee. The last remaining members of his tribe dispersed, some joining the Paiutes and others joining Miwok tribes along the Tuolumne River. Although a few Ahwahneechee descendants continued to live in Yosemite Valley over the next several decades, their numbers were few and their culture was forever altered by the arrival of the white people.

YOSEMITE'S FIRST TOURISTS

Although the first Mariposa Battalion did not succeed in rousting the Indians, its members did arouse public interest with their descriptions of this wondrous valley with its high granite walls and amazing waterfalls. Tourists began flowing into Yosemite Valley as early as 1855, following old Indian trails on horseback.

One of the earliest visitors was James M. Hutchings, publisher of the much-read *California Magazine*. Hutchings became so enamored with the Valley that he soon moved there to open a hotel near the base of

Galen Clark: Yosemite's First Guardian

After the Yosemite Grant became federal law, Yosemite Valley and the Mariposa Grove of Giant Sequoias came under the management of a board of California commissioners. They hired home-steader Galen Clark, who ran the stagecoach stop at Wawona, as the first guardian of Yosemite Valley and the Mariposa Grove.

Among men whose names will forever be associated with Yosemite National Park, Clark stands out. He had come to California in 1854 to search for gold, but a lung ailment sent him to the mountains, where he expected to live out his final days. Apparently the fresh air was good for him, because he survived another 50 years, until just four days before his 96th birthday.

Clark set up a stagecoach station and inn at Wawona in 1857 and acted as a guide to visitors to Yosemite Valley and the Mariposa Grove. He was known as "Mr. Yosemite" and was well respected for his knowledge and love of the park. As official park guardian, he performed largely the same tasks that he had been doing as a volunteer who simply loved the area. He worked to relocate homesteaders, improved facilities for travelers, and most of all, did whatever was necessary to protect the giant sequoias and Yosemite Valley. John Muir called him "one of the most sincere tree-lovers I ever knew."

Clark selected his own grave site in the **Yosemite Valley Cemetery,** where he is now buried. His grave lies beneath five giant sequoia trees that he planted himself, with seeds trans-ported from the Mariposa Grove.

Sentinel Rock. His magazine published fa-vorable stories about the area, and more and more visitors came. Fortunately, among them were some early-day conservationists—men like **Frederick Law Olmsted,** the man who designed New York's Central Park. Olmsted and others recognized the precious nature of the resources in Yosemite Valley and the nearby Mariposa Grove of Giant Sequoias, another major attraction. They appealed to the U.S. Congress to protect these places from exploitation.

CREATION OF A NATIONAL PARK

In 1864, Senator John Conness introduced a bill to the U.S. Congress that would re-quire the state of California to protect Yosemite Valley and the Mariposa Grove of Giant Sequoias and preserve them un-disturbed. Despite the fact that the Civil War was in progress and the government's attention was on more pressing matters, President Abraham Lincoln signed the bill into law on June 30, 1864. This act, called the **Yosemite Grant,** had much greater signifi-cance than just protecting portions of what

is now Yosemite. It was also the first appli-cation of a new concept, that of the U.S. gov-ernment preserving and protecting a wild place as a "park," for public use and recre-ation. Although the law actually created a California state park, not a national park, this single legislative act ultimately paved the way for our great chain of national parks.

While visitation of the new park was reaching an all-time high, so was use of land surrounding the protected Valley and Mariposa Grove. The High Sierra region that is now part of Yosemite National Park was seen as a free resource to be exploited. Cattle and sheep ranchers used the fragile high-country meadows to graze their stock in the summer. Hundreds of sawmills were built on the west side of the Sierra Nevada, as loggers moved in to fell giant sequoias and other big conifers. Silver and gold mines sprung up in even the most remote areas, requiring lum-ber and fuel for their operations.

Another early conservationist came to the aid of Yosemite: a young Scotsman by the name of **John Muir,** who made his first trip to Yosemite in 1868 and then kept coming back for another 40 years. Muir was greatly concerned with the destructive activities taking place in the region surrounding the land protected by the Yosemite Grant. He wrote articles about it for *Century* magazine, an influential publication edited by **Robert Underwood Johnson,** who was also interested in preserving Yosemite. With prompting by Muir, Johnson, and other far-thinking Yosemite advocates, Congress was pushed to further action. On October 1, 1890, it passed a law that created Yosemite National Park and preserved the areas surrounding Yosemite Valley and the Mariposa Grove. President Benjamin Harrison put his signature on the law.

To protect this newly created federal park, the **U.S. Army Cavalry** arrived in the high country and worked to stop all grazing activities, remove illegal homesteaders, fight forest fires, and chase out poachers. In 1906, the state of California ceded its control of the Valley and the Mariposa Grove to the federal government. Those regions, too, now fell under the cloak of the national park. In 1916 the cavalry was relieved of its duties when the national parks were placed under civilian management through the Department of the Interior, and the **National Park Service** was born.

THE POPULARIZATION OF YOSEMITE

By 1874, a half dozen toll roads had been built into Yosemite Valley. With visitors now able to travel via stagecoach instead of horseback, more and more tourists came to see the famous Valley. Still, travel was far from easy. From Wawona, the trip into Yosemite Valley via a rocky dirt road took about eight hours. It was dusty and sometimes treacherous: Stagecoach holdups were not uncommon, and the horses were skittish on the narrow, steep roads. Once they made it to the Valley, travelers were surprised to find none of the fancy accommodations they were accustomed to in other places—only rustic cabins and tents.

In short order, Yosemite Valley went from being an exotic destination only visited by the very wealthy or adventurous to a place where tourists of every ilk had access. In 1886, the California state legislature made all privately owned toll roads and trails free and open to the public. **Camp Curry** (now Half Dome Village) opened in Yosemite Valley in 1889. In 1907, the Yosemite Valley Railroad was completed all the way to El Portal, where riders transferred to a stagecoach for the final passage up the Merced River canyon. This mountain railroad remained in operation until 1945 but was little used after 1926, when Highway 140, the "All-Year Highway," was completed.

Although the first two automobiles— a Stanley Steamer and a Locomobile—had entered Yosemite Valley in 1900, it wasn't until 1913 that the first park entrance fee was paid. Automobiles were banned from Yosemite after 1906, when Yosemite Valley became a part of the national park. The policy at that time was that autos were not allowed in any federal park, but in 1913, the new Secretary of the Interior relented, recognizing that automobiles were the way of the future. By 1917, enough people were traveling to Yosemite by car that the National Park Service saw the need to build paved roads. By 1920, two thirds of all Yosemite visitors were arriving by car. From then until World War II, Yosemite saw its years of greatest development, from roadways to sewer and garbage systems to luxury hotels.

A side note: The first vehicle entrance fee was $5, good for seven days. This same fee remained in effect from 1913, when it was a sizable sum, to the tail end of the 20th century, when it was equal to the price of a sandwich. The only three fee hikes in the history of the park occurred in 1997, when it was raised from $5 to $20, and in 2016, when it was raised to $30, and then again in 2018, when it was raised to $35.

John Muir: Father of the National Parks

Naturalist, conservationist, geologist, botanist, mountaineer, prolific writer, mechanical genius, wilderness advocate, founder and first president of the Sierra Club—John Muir was all these things and more. To a greater degree than anyone else, Muir's name is forever linked to Yosemite National Park. His dedicated involvement with the creation and protection of Yosemite, as well as several other national parks including Grand Canyon, Sequoia and Kings Canyon, and Mount Rainier, has led him to be called "the father of our national park system."

What kind of person would fight so passionately to preserve and protect the lands of Yosemite? Born in Scotland in 1838, John Muir was raised by a ruthlessly strict, religious extremist father, first in Scotland and then later in the wilds of Wisconsin, where the Muir family homesteaded. Muir, along with his seven brothers and sisters, worked 17 hours a day on their 80-acre (32-hectare) farm. As a teenager he was facile with machines and began to experiment with various mechanical inventions while simultaneously developing a keen interest in botany and geology.

John Muir in 1907

When Muir reached college age, he attended the University of Wisconsin, then sought employment in factories in Canada and Indiana. While working at a sawmill, an accident left Muir temporarily blind. He was forced to spend long weeks in a dark room to recover his eyesight. During this trial, Muir made a decision to leave the mechanical world behind and devote the rest of his life to studying "the inventions of God."

When Muir's health returned, he set off on a 1,000-mile (1,600-km) walk from Indiana to the Gulf of Mexico. From there, he planned to head to South America to search for the headwaters of the Amazon River. But a long and painful bout with malaria and typhoid in Florida convinced him to stay out of the tropics. He decided to travel to California instead "to see its Yosemite and Big Trees and wonderful flora in general."

Muir arrived in San Francisco in April 1868 and then made his way to Yosemite Valley. He spent a few weeks there, was suitably awed by its wonders, and then headed down out of the mountains to the San Joaquin Valley to find work. He toiled as a shepherd for a year, and in the summer of 1869 he drove a flock of sheep from the San Joaquin Valley to the Tuolumne Meadows area of Yosemite. This adventure, detailed in his famous book *My First Summer in the Sierra,* was perhaps the most significant of Muir's life. It was during this season that Muir embarked on his long and profound love affair with Yosemite.

Muir died at the age of 76 on Christmas Eve 1914 in a Los Angeles hospital. He had been visiting his daughter Helen and her family when a winter cold developed into pneumonia. Six of his books were published during his lifetime; five more were published after his death. Muir's name is immortalized on an Alaskan glacier (one of several he discovered), on a variety of California landmarks from mountain peaks to public schools, in a species of wildflower, and in an ancient redwood forest that is now a national monument.

Muir's home in Martinez, California, which he shared from 1890 to his death with his wife, Louie Strentzel Muir, and two daughters, Wanda and Helen, is preserved as the **John Muir National Historic Site** (925/228-8860, www.nps.gov/jomu).

Essentials

Getting There

Yosemite National Park is on the western slope

of the Sierra Nevada, approximately 180 miles (290 km) east of San Francisco and 400 miles (645 km) north of Los Angeles. Driving time from San Francisco is approximately four hours. A large chunk of the drive is on two-lane highways where you can't drive faster than 45 mph. Driving time from Los Angeles is about seven hours. Most of that time is spent on major freeways where you can drive 65 mph or faster. The vast majority of Yosemite visitors enter the park in a private automobile or RV, either their own or one they have rented. Taking public transportation

to the park is possible, although it requires some careful planning. Once in the park, you will probably want to have a car anyway, unless you plan to spend your time in Yosemite Valley, where free shuttle buses make cars unnecessary.

AIR

The closest airport to Yosemite and Sequoia and Kings Canyon is the small **Fresno-Yosemite Airport** (FAT, 5175 E. Clinton Ave., Fresno, 559/621-4500 or 800/244-2359, www.flyfresno.com), a two-hour drive from Yosemite's South entrance and 55 miles (89 km) west of Kings Canyon via Highway 180.

Yosemite-bound travelers can also fly into **San Francisco International Airport** (SFO, 650/821-8211 or 800/435-9736, www.flysfo.com), which is served by all major international and domestic airlines. The San Francisco Bay Area's two other major airports—**Oakland International** (OAK, 1 Airport Dr., Oakland, 510/563-3300, www.oaklandairport.com) and **Mineta San Jose International** (SJC, 1701 Airport Blvd., San Jose, 408/392-3600, www.flysanjose.com)—are also good bets for Yosemite travelers. Flights into Oakland or San Jose are often less expensive than flights into SFO. It is a four-hour drive from SFO to either the Arch Rock entrance on Highway 140 or the Big Oak Flat entrance on Highway 120; Oakland and San Jose are both about a half hour closer. Yosemite visitors should also look into flights into **Sacramento International Airport** (SMF, 6900 Airport Blvd., Sacramento, 916/929-5411, www.sacairports.org), which is a three-hour drive from the Big Oak Flat entrance on Highway 120, or a four-hour drive from the Arch Rock entrance on Highway 140.

In the summer months only, Yosemite visitors can fly into **Reno-Tahoe International Airport** (RNO, 2001 E. Plumb Ln., www.renoairport.com) in Nevada, and then make a three-hour drive to Yosemite's Tioga Pass entrance on Highway 120 off U.S. 395. Tioga Pass is usually open from mid-June through late October each year, depending on snow.

Yosemite visitors can also fly into the **Mammoth Yosemite Airport** (MMH, 1200 Airport Rd., Mammoth Lakes, www.visitmammoth.com), which is only a one-hour drive from Yosemite's Tioga Pass entrance. United Airlines (www.united.com) offers year-round flights from Los Angeles International Airport (LAX) to Mammoth Lakes, and in the winter from Denver and San Francisco. Also in winter only, JetSuiteX, which is owned by JetBlue, flies from Burbank and Orange County to Mammoth Lakes.

Smaller airports are located at Merced and Modesto, California, but they do not offer commercial passenger service.

TRAIN AND BUS

The nearest **Amtrak** (Amtrak, 800/872-7245, www.amtrak.com) station is in Merced, California, more than an hour's drive from the park. Visitors riding Amtrak will need to board a bus or rent a car to continue to Yosemite, but Amtrak makes it relatively easy with a prearranged train/bus package.

One tour company offers a prearranged one-day round-trip train tour to Yosemite from San Francisco. The **Yosemite Tour Train shuttle** (www.yosemitetourshuttle.com, $169 per adult) leaves the Ferry Building in San Francisco at 7am and takes passengers to the Amtrak train station in Emeryville. Passengers ride the train from Emeryville to Merced, and then another shuttle carries them the rest of the way to the park. Visitors spend about five hours in Yosemite Valley before returning to San Francisco around 10pm.

Bus transportation is available year-round from the Amtrak station in Merced on **VIA Trailways** (209/384-1315 or 800/842-5463, www.viatrailways.com). Travel time is 2.5 hours one-way. Reservations for VIA bus

Previous: filtering water.

service to Yosemite should be made 24 hours in advance.

FROM FRESNO

Airport

The single terminal at **Fresno-Yosemite International Airport** (FAT, 5175 E. Clinton Ave., Fresno, 559/621-4500 or 800/244-2359, www.flyfresno.com) is served by AeroMexico, Alaska/Horizon, Allegiant, American/ American Eagle, Delta/Skywest, Frontier, United/United Express, and Volaris. Because Fresno-Yosemite isn't a "major" airport, flying here usually requires making a connection through larger airports in other cities.

There is no entertainment at the diminutive Fresno airport, but free wireless Internet is available. You can get a coffee at Starbucks, have a meal or a drink at the lone bar and grill, get a haircut at the airport barbershop, or buy a souvenir or a newspaper in the polo gift shop. Otherwise, be sure you have a good book to keep you company while you wait for your plane.

Car Rentals

Several major car rental companies are located at Fresno-Yosemite Airport: **Avis** (559/454-5030 or 800/331-1212, www.avis.com), **Budget** (559/253-4100 or 800/527-0700, www.budget.com), **Dollar** (800/800-4000, www.dollar.com), **Enterprise** (559/253-2700 or 800/434-2226, www.enterprise.com), **Hertz** (559/251-5055 or 800/654-3131, www.hertz.com), and **National/Alamo** (559/251-5577, 800/328-4567, or 800/327-9633, www.nationalcar.com).

RV Rentals

RV rentals in Fresno cost about the same as elsewhere in California, which is basically the same nightly price as a stay in a good hotel. And just like at hotels, your price will vary widely whether you are traveling during the high season (summer) or low season (Oct.-Apr.). For an RV that can sleep up to five people (about 32 ft/10 m long), expect to pay about $250 per night in the low season, and as much as $450 per night in the high season (May-Sept.). On a night-by-night basis, you can save a little money by renting an RV for a week. Seven nights' rental will run about $1,400 during the low season, $2,600 during the high season. But don't forget to tack on the mileage fee. Most companies allow 60-100 free miles per day, and then charge a flat rate for extra mileage (typically about 30-35 cents per mile).

Also, plan to spend a small fortune on gasoline—most RVs get 6-10 miles to the gallon (2.5-4 km per liter). The smallest rigs may get a whopping 14 miles per gallon (6 km per liter).

To rent an RV in Fresno, contact **A Class RV** (2557 W. Cambridge Ave., Fresno, 559/264-1920, www.aclassrv.com), or contact **Cruise America** at **Clovis Truck Rental** (707 Jefferson Ave., Clovis, 559/299-9603, www.cruiseamerica.com), in nearby Clovis.

Accommodations

Because Fresno-Yosemite Airport is only a two-hour drive from Yosemite, it's unlikely you'll spend much time in Fresno. It's not that the region doesn't have its charms (hey, it's the number-one farm county in the nation); it's just that it pales when compared to Yosemite. But if your flight gets in late and you need a place to stay, three good overnight choices are located near the airport, all of which offer free shuttle service to Fresno-Yosemite and room rates of less than $150.

- **Best Western Plus Fresno Airport** (1551 N. Peach Ave., 559/251-5200, www.bwfresnoairporthotel.com)

- **Quality Inn Fresno** (5113 E. McKinley Ave., 559/375-7720, www.choicehotels.com)

- **Airport Piccadilly Inn** (5115 E. McKinley Ave., 888/611-8163, www.piccadillyairport.com)

Suggested Driving Routes

Of the five entrance stations to Yosemite, visitors coming from the south (Fresno, Los Angeles, Oakhurst) generally use the **South** entrance on Highway 41. The Mariposa Grove of Giant Sequoias is found within 2 miles (3.2 km) of the South entrance. This is also the easiest access point for Glacier Point and Yosemite Ski & Snowboard Area. Yosemite Valley is a one-hour drive from the South entrance, so figure on a total of three hours from Fresno to Yosemite Valley.

From Fresno, simply take Highway 41 north for 65 miles (105 km). Plan to drive two hours on this winding highway to reach Yosemite. The road is usually open year-round, although chains may be required during snowy periods in the winter months.

FROM SAN FRANCISCO
Air

One of the world's 30 busiest airports, **San Francisco International Airport** (SFO, 650/821-8211 or 800/435-9736, www.flysfo.com) has three main terminals plus an international terminal, which are shared by most major international and domestic carriers. The airport is not located in San Francisco proper, but rather 15 miles (24 km) south of the city near the town of Millbrae in San Mateo County. SFO's hallowed halls are filled with just about every imaginable kind of gift shop and ethnic food restaurant, as well as an excellent series of rotating art exhibits as intriguing as anything you'll find at a major city museum. SFO is not a bad place to kill a few hours.

The San Francisco Bay Area has two other major airports: **Oakland International** (OAK, 1 Airport Dr., Oakland, 510/563-3300, www.oaklandairport.com) and **Mineta San Jose International** (SJC, 1701 Airport Blvd., San Jose, 408/392-3600, www.flysanjose.com). At both airports "international" means primarily Mexico. Travelers coming from cities within the United States, especially the western states, should check fares and flight times into San Jose and Oakland as well as San Francisco. Most Bay Area locals prefer the ease of travel at the smaller Oakland and San Jose airports over mammoth SFO (and the commute to Yosemite is 30-60 minutes

shorter!). Visitors arriving from other countries will most likely fly into SFO.

Car Rentals

All the major companies have rental counters at San Francisco International Airport, although none are in the terminals. Instead, SFO has an off-airport **Rental Car Center** that houses all the car companies' rental counters. Travelers get to the Rental Car Center from any of the airport terminals by taking an automated light rail system, the **AirTrain Blue Line.** AirTrain operates 24 hours a day.

You can have your pick of the car rental companies at SFO: **Alamo** (www.alamo.com), **Avis** (www.avis.com), **Budget** (www.budget.com), **Dollar** (www.dollar.com), **Enterprise** (www.enterprise.com), **Fox** (www.foxrentacar.com), **Hertz** (www.hertz.com), **National** (www.nationalcar.com), and **Thrifty** (www.thrifty.com).

You might be able to save a little money by renting cars from an off-airport car rental company, such as **ACE** (877/822-3872, www.acerentacar.com) or **Payless** (800/729-5377, www.paylesscar.com). These companies are served by free shuttle service from the SFO Rental Car Center.

RV Rentals

RV rentals in San Francisco cost about the same nightly price as a stay in a good hotel. And just like at hotels, prices vary widely depending on whether you are traveling during the high season (summer) or low season (Oct.-Apr.). For an RV that can sleep up to five people (about 32 ft/10 m long), expect to pay about $200 per night in the low season, and as much as $400 per night in the high season (May-Sept.). On a night-by-night basis, you can save a little money by renting an RV for a week. Seven nights' rental will run about $1,300 during the low season, $2,400 during the high season.

To rent an RV, head to **El Monte RV** (111 Mason St., San Francisco, 888/337-2214, www.elmonterv.com), 14 miles (22.5 km) north of SFO in downtown San Francisco.

The RV center isn't actually located there, but customers are shuttled from this location to the RV rental center in Dublin (East Bay). Smaller Bay Area RV rental companies include **Lost Campers** (2955 3rd St., San Francisco, 415/386-2693, www. lostcampersusa.com), **Escape Campervans** (427 Beach St., San Francisco, 877/270-8267, www.escapecampervans.com), and **Adventure Touring RV Rentals** (420 San Leandro Blvd., San Leandro, 877/778-9569, www.adventuretouring.com).

Accommodations

San Francisco International Airport is approximately 190 miles (305 km) from Yosemite, so depending on your flight time, you may need to spend a night somewhere near the airport. A word of caution: Unless you possess an endless amount of patience, don't even think of driving out of the Bay Area toward Yosemite between the hours of 3pm and 7pm on weekdays. (On summer Fridays, that window is even larger—say 1pm-7pm). Traffic heading eastward at rush hour from San Francisco and its environs is hellish at best. If your plane lands at 4pm and you set out for Yosemite immediately after picking up your rental car, your 4.5-hour drive to the park could easily extend to 7 hours. It might be better to wait until the morning, when most of the traffic heads in the opposite direction.

You'd be hard-pressed to find any motels or hotels near San Francisco in the "budget" category. The following seven establishments, all within a few miles of SFO and with free shuttle service to and from the airport, will rent you a room with all the standard amenities for $100-200.

- **Holiday Inn Express Airport** (373 S. Airport Blvd., South San Francisco, 650/589-0600, www.ihg.com)

- **The Dylan at SFO** (110 S. El Camino Real, Millbrae, 650/697-7373 or 800/697-7370, www.dylansfo.com)

- **Best Western Plus Airport Grosvenor Hotel** (380 S. Airport Blvd., South

San Francisco, 650/873-3200, www. grosvenorsfo.com)

- **Holiday Inn San Francisco Airport** (275 S. Airport Blvd., South San Francisco, 650/873-3550, www.hisfo.com)

- **La Quinta Inn San Francisco Airport North** (20 S. Airport Blvd., South San Francisco, 650/583-2223, www.laquintasanfranciscoairportnorth.com)

- **Hyatt Regency San Francisco Airport** (1333 Bayshore Hwy., Burlingame, 650/347-1234, www.hyatt.com)

Suggested Driving Routes

Visitors coming from the west (San Francisco, Oakland, Sacramento) generally access Yosemite by using the Big Oak Flat entrance on Highway 120 or the Arch Rock entrance on Highway 140. The Arch Rock/Highway 140 entrance boasts the best winter access to the park because it rarely receives any snowfall. The Big Oak Flat/Highway 120 entrance is the closest western access to Tuolumne Meadows, Tioga Pass, and Hetch Hetchy, and it also provides fairly easy year-round access to Yosemite Valley (the road to the Valley is always plowed immediately after snowfall).

To reach the **Arch Rock entrance** from San Francisco, take I-80 east across the San Francisco/Oakland Bay Bridge, and then head south and east on I-580. Stay on I-580 for 55 miles (89 km), passing through Livermore, and then take I-5 south. Drive 30 miles (48 km) and turn east on Highway 140. Drive 40 miles (64 km) east to Merced, then continue east on Highway 140 for another 35 miles (56 km) to **Mariposa** (last chance for supplies), and then another 30 miles (48 km) to the Arch Rock entrance. The entire drive will take about 4.5 hours, unless you run into traffic in the San Francisco Bay Area. Avoid driving during commute hours if at all possible.

To reach the **Big Oak Flat entrance** from San Francisco, take I-80 east across the San Francisco/Oakland Bay Bridge, and then head east on I-580. Stay on I-580 for 45 miles (72 km), passing through Livermore, and then continue east on I-205. In 15 miles (24 km), connect to Highway 120 East in Manteca. Stay on Highway 120 heading east for the remaining 85 miles (137 km) to the Big Oak Flat entrance. Total driving time is about four hours if you are not stopped by traffic. If your destination is Yosemite Valley, you have another 45 minutes of driving after the Big Oak Flat entrance.

If you want to visit **Hetch Hetchy,** the access road to this region of the park begins 1 mile (1.6 km) from the Big Oak Flat entrance station, so you should use Highway 120 as your driving route.

FROM RENO
Air
Reno-Tahoe International Airport (RNO, 2001 E. Plumb Ln., Reno, www.renoairport. com) in Nevada is a good choice for summer visitors who want to see the high country of Yosemite along Tioga Pass Road and perhaps also visit Lake Tahoe, Las Vegas, Death Valley, or other destinations in and around the state of Nevada or the east side of California's Sierra Nevada. Tioga Pass Road (Highway 120), where it enters Yosemite at Tioga Pass at elevation 9,945 feet (3,030 m), is usually open from mid-June to late October each year, but if you are planning your trip far in advance, be cautious about choosing dates on either end of that window. Being able to drive through Tioga Pass cannot be guaranteed in June or October.

Reno's medium-size airport has two main terminals that serve Alaska, Allegiant, American, Delta, Horizon, Southwest, and United. Scattered among the gates are the usual cabal of airport shops: a Peet's Coffee, Pizza Hut, Taco Bell, McDonald's, a golf shop, and several gift shops and newsstands. And because this airport is in Nevada, where gambling is legal, you can try your luck at the slot machines throughout both terminals. If you'd rather fill your time with an activity less likely to empty your wallet, take advantage of the airport's free wireless Internet service.

Car Rentals
Several major car rental companies are located at Reno-Tahoe International Airport: **Advantage** (www.advantage.com), **Alamo** (www.alamo.com), **Avis** (www.avis.com), **Budget** (www.budget.com), **Dollar** (www. dollar.com), **Enterprise** (www.enterprise. com), **Hertz** (www.hertz.com), **National** (www.nationalcar.com), and **Thrifty** (www. thrifty.com).

Accommodations
Reno calls itself "the biggest little city in the world," for reasons that are altogether unclear to most visitors. Despite its best efforts to publicize and promote its gambling casinos and nightlife, Reno has always been the poor cousin to much more glamorous Las Vegas in southern Nevada. Nonetheless, the town has a great location vis-à-vis the Eastern Sierra and Lake Tahoe, which serves to keep its hotels and motels in business. Although the city's revitalized riverfront area is charming, it's unlikely you'll want to spend much time in Reno except perhaps to pull the lever on a few one-armed bandits. If you need a place to stay near the airport, here are four good choices in the under-$150 category. Each is less than 3 miles (4.8 km) from Reno-Tahoe International Airport:

• **Best Western Airport Plaza** (1981 Terminal Way, 775/348-6370, www. bestwestern.com)

• **La Quinta Inn Reno Airport** (4001 Market St., 775/348-6100, www. laquintareno.com)

• **Hyatt Place Reno-Tahoe Airport** (1790 E. Plumb Ln., 775/826-2500, www.hyatt. com)

• **Comfort Inn and Suites Airport** (1250 E. Plumb Ln., 775/682-4444, www. comfortinn.com)

Suggested Driving Routes
Visitors heading to Yosemite from the east (Reno, Mammoth Lakes, Death Valley, Bishop) generally use the **Tioga Pass**

entrance on Highway 120. Note that this road is only open in the summer months; it is usually closed November through early June. The Tioga Pass entrance delivers you to Yosemite's high country, only a few miles from famous Tuolumne Meadows. If you're heading straight for Yosemite Valley, it is nearly a two-hour drive from Tioga Pass, through some of the loveliest scenery you can imagine. This is a drive worth doing.

To access Tioga Pass from Reno, Nevada, take U.S. 395 south for 135 miles (217 km), through Bridgeport, California, to **Lee Vining**. This small town is your last chance for supplies. On the south side of Lee Vining, turn west on Highway 120 and drive 13 miles (20.9 km) to the Tioga Pass entrance.

One note: When crossing into California by automobile, all visitors are subject to agricultural inspections run by the California Department of Food and Agriculture (CDFA). The inspection may be as simple as an officer stopping your car momentarily to ask you where you have been traveling and if you are carrying any fruits, vegetables, or plants from other states. As a general rule, most out-of-state produce and plants should be kept out of California, unless they have been properly inspected by the CDFA. For more information on current regulations, visit the CDFA website at www.cdfa.ca.gov.

FROM SACRAMENTO
Air
Relatively small and pleasantly uncongested, **Sacramento International Airport** (SMF, 6900 Airport Blvd., Sacramento, 916/929-5411, www.sacairports.org) is served by these airlines: Alaska/Horizon, American, Delta, Frontier, Jet Blue, Southwest, and United/United Express. Travelers arriving from other U.S. cities will often find that airfare is less expensive to Sacramento than it is to San Francisco Bay Area airports. The usual array of airport restaurants and shops can be found here: a Starbucks, Cinnabon, Burger King, Quizno's, La Salsa, several bookstores and souvenir shops, and the like. The airport also has free wireless Internet available throughout all public areas.

Car Rentals
Several major car rental companies are located at Sacramento International Airport: **Alamo** (www.alamo.com), **Avis** (www.avis.com), **Budget** (www.budget.com), **Dollar** (www.dollar.com), **Enterprise** (www.enterprise.com), **Hertz** (www.hertz.com), and **National** (www.nationalcar.com). You might save a little money by renting from **Royal Rental Cars** (916/442-1362, www.advancerents.com) or **Payless Car Rental** (916/441-4488, www.paylesscar.com), both of which are a few miles from the airport.

RV Rentals
RV rentals in Sacramento cost about the same as a night in a good hotel. Prices vary widely whether you are traveling during the high season (summer) or low season (Oct.-Apr.). For an RV that can sleep up to five people (about 32 ft/10 m long), expect to pay about $200 per night in the low season, and as much as $400 per night in the high season (May- Sept.). On a night-by-night basis, you can save a little money by renting an RV for a week. Seven nights' rental will run about $1,300 during the low season, $2,400 during the high season. But don't forget to tack on the mileage fee. Most companies allow 60-100 free miles per day, and then charge a flat rate for extra mileage (typically about 30-35 cents per mile). Also, plan to spend a small fortune on gasoline—most RVs get 6-10 miles to the gallon (2.5-4 km per liter). The smallest rigs may get a whopping 14 miles per gallon (6 km per liter).

Sacramento RV rental companies include **El Monte RV** (4100 Florin Perkins Rd., Sacramento, 916/929-9001, www.elmonterv.com), **Advantage Caravans** (1064 El Camino Ave., Sacramento, 916/832-8824, www.advantagervrentals.com), and **Happy Daze RVs** (1199 El Camino Ave., Sacramento, 916/921-2222, www.happydazerv.com).

Accommodations

If your flight gets in late and you need a place to stay, more than a dozen hotels are near the airport. Those listed here have free shuttle service to and from the airport. Room rates are generally under $150. The Hilton Garden Inn is 9 miles (14.5 km) from the airport, and all rooms have microwaves and small refrigerators. There is a restaurant on-site. The Governors Inn is midway between the airport and downtown Sacramento; the hotel is conveniently located near the shops of Old Sacramento and the city's downtown plaza.

- **Holiday Inn Express Sacramento Airport Natomas** (2981 Advantage Way, 877/859-5095, www.ihg.com)

- **Hampton Inn & Suites Sacramento Airport Natomas** (3021 Advantage Way, 855/271-3622, www.hamptoninn.hilton. com)

- **Homewood Suites by Hilton** (3001 Advantage Way, 855/277-4942, http:// homewoodsuites3.hilton.com)

- **Hilton Garden Inn** (2540 Venture Oaks Way, 916/568-5400, www. hiltongardeninnsacramento.com)

- **Governors Inn** (210 Richards Blvd., 916/448-7224 or 800/999-6689, www. governorsinnhotel.com)

- **Residence Inn Sacramento Airport/ Natomas** (2410 W. El Camino Ave., 916/649-1300, www.marriott.com)

Suggested Driving Routes

Of the five entrance stations to Yosemite, visitors coming from the north (Sacramento and Northern California) generally use the **Big Oak Flat entrance** on Highway 120, traveling through the gateway town of **Groveland.** The Big Oak Flat entrance has the most convenient access to Tuolumne Meadows and Tioga Pass Road and is a 35-minute drive from Yosemite Valley.

From Sacramento, take Highway 99 south for 58 miles (93 km) to Manteca. Take the Yosemite Boulevard/Highway 120 East exit in Manteca. Follow Highway 120 east for 85 miles (137 km) all the way to the Big Oak Flat entrance to Yosemite. The road is usually open year-round, although chains may be required during snowy periods in the winter months.

Getting Around

DRIVING

Except on crowded summer days in Yosemite Valley, driving a car around Yosemite National Park is quite easy. More than 200 miles (320 km) of roads lace the park, and parking is not usually difficult (except in Yosemite Valley in summer). If you are visiting Yosemite Valley May-September, consider leaving your car in one of the day-use parking areas and riding the free shuttle bus or taking an organized tour.

Remember always to follow bear precautions when leaving your car parked anywhere in Yosemite, especially at night. This means nothing scented should remain inside the car, including food and toiletries. Even an empty soda can or a tube of toothpaste can inspire a bear to break into your car.

When visiting Yosemite November-April, know that **tire chains** may be required on any park road at any time. You are least likely to need chains on Highway 140, the "All-Weather Highway," but it is still always possible, and winter visitors are required to carry tire chains in their cars.

TRAVELING BY RV

Recreational vehicles (RVs) are welcome in Yosemite, except for the very biggest of the rigs: **RVs over 45 feet (14 m) long are not permitted** in most areas of the park, including Yosemite Valley.

RV Camping

You've got your rig and you're ready to roll. But when you get to Yosemite, you can't find a suitable place to camp to save your life. A vacation that is supposed to be made easier by having a self-contained vehicle suddenly turns out to be a whole lot harder instead. Here are a few guidelines for camping with your RV in Yosemite:

- All Yosemite campgrounds have RV sites except for Camp 4 in the Valley, and Tamarack Flat and Yosemite Creek on Tioga Road.

- There are no RV hookups at any campground in Yosemite.

- RVs over 40 feet (12.2 m) long are not permitted in Yosemite Valley.

- RVs over 35 feet (10.7 m) long are not permitted in many other areas of the park.

- Generator use is permitted only between 7am and 7pm.

- RV dump stations are found at Upper Pines Campground, Wawona Campground, and Tuolumne Meadows Campground.

Many RVers find they have an easier time staying outside of the park in private campgrounds that are designed for big rigs. Try one of these:

- **Indian Flat RV Park** (209/379-2339, www.indianflatrvpark.com), off Highway 140 in El Portal

- **Yosemite Lakes** (209/962-0121 or 877/570-2267, www.stayatyosemite.com), 18 miles (29 km) east of Groveland off Highway 120

- **Yosemite Pines RV Resort** (209/962-7690, www.yosemitepinesrv.com), 3 miles (4.8 km) east of Groveland off Highway 120

- **Pine Mountain Lake Campground** (209/962-8615, www.pinemountainlake.com), 2.5 miles (4 km) off Highway 120 in Groveland

- **High Sierra RV and Mobile Park** (559/683-7662, www.highsierrarv.com), off Highway 41 in Oakhurst

- **Mono Vista RV Park** (760/647-6401, www.monovistarvpark.net), off U.S. 395 in Lee Vining

Certain roads in the park are **not accessible to smaller RVs** as well. The Hetch Hetchy Road is closed to all vehicles longer than 25 feet (7.6 m). The Mariposa Grove Road is closed to RVs and trailers 9am-6pm daily in summer, but you can park your rig at Wawona and ride a free shuttle bus to the grove. The access road to Yosemite Creek Campground is closed to RVs or trailers longer than 24 feet (7.3 m), and the road to Tamarack Flat Campground is not recommended for large RVs.

If you are visiting Yosemite Valley for the day in your RV, you would be well advised to enter the park early in the morning, park your rig as soon as possible, and then ride the free Valley shuttle bus to all of the Valley's sites (or join an organized tour, or rent a bike and ride, or walk around the Valley on foot).

If you are planning to camp in your RV, know in advance that there are no utility hookups in Yosemite. Park regulations permit the use of generators 7am-7pm only. Dump stations are available at three locations in the park: Upper Pines Campground, Wawona Campground, and Tuolumne Meadows Campground.

MAPS

Park maps are available at Yosemite's five entrance stations and four visitors centers, by contacting Yosemite National Park at

209/372-0200, or by downloading one from the park website (www.nps.gov/yose). A more detailed map, better suited for people who want to explore beyond the park roads, is available for a fee from **Tom Harrison Maps** (www.tomharrisonmaps.com). This company publishes a general Yosemite National Park recreation map, which shows all the major park trails, and also produces specialized maps showing greater detail of Half Dome, Yosemite Valley, Tuolumne Meadows, and the Yosemite High Country. **Trails Illustrated** (www.natgeomaps.com) also publishes a Yosemite National Park map.

SHUTTLE BUSES

Free hybrid shuttle buses run year-round in Yosemite Valley and along a stretch of Tioga Pass Road (Tuolumne Meadows area) in summer. A free shuttle bus also runs from the Wawona Store to the Mariposa Grove of Giant Sequoias in the summer months. Unlike the shuttle buses in the rest of the park, this one is mandatory (it is used to relieve traffic on the Mariposa Grove Road). In winter , a free shuttle runs from Yosemite Valley to Yosemite Ski & Snowboard Area.

For visitors staying in towns just outside the park borders, **YARTS buses** (Yosemite Area Regional Transportation System, 877/989-2787, www.yarts.com) run from some gateway towns outside the park into Yosemite Valley. YARTS buses travel on Highway 120

East, Highway 41 South, and Highway 120 West (summer only) and Highway 140 (year-round). The bus system provides an option for visitors who would rather not drive and hassle with parking in Yosemite Valley, but this is not a free service. Tickets run $2-30, depending on your departure point. Purchase your ticket directly from the bus driver. YARTS buses travel from Merced, Catheys Valley, Mariposa, Midpines, and El Portal to Yosemite Valley along Highway 140; from Mammoth Lakes, June Lake, Lee Vining, and Tuolumne Meadows to Yosemite Valley along Highway 120 East; and from Sonora and Groveland along Highway 120 West.

TOUR GUIDES AND SERVICES

If you are visiting Yosemite for the first time, or if you are a repeat visitor who would like to expand your knowledge of the park, consider hiring a local guide. These private, independent guide services take visitors on professionally guided hikes and/or driving tours; some also offer customized camping or backpacking trips. Call ahead to schedule a tour that's suited to your desires and ability level: **Yosemite Guide Service** (530/523-3998, www.yosemiteguideservice.com), **Southern Yosemite Mountain Guides** (800/231-4575, www.symg.com), **Y Explore** (209/532-7014 or 800/886-8009, www.yexplore.com).

Recreation

DAY HIKING

The following 10 essentials will help ensure that your outdoor adventures stay safe and fun.

1. Food and water. Water is more important than food, although it's unwise to get caught without at least some edible supplies for emergencies. If you don't want to carry heavy bottles of water, at least carry a purifier or filtering device so that you can obtain

water from streams, rivers, or lakes. Never, ever drink water from a natural source without purifying it. Food selections are much-debated matters of personal choice. If you don't want to carry much weight, stick with high-energy snacks like nutrition bars, nuts, dried fruit, turkey or beef jerky, and crackers. If you're hiking in a group, each of you should carry your own food and water just in case someone gets too far ahead or behind.

2. Trail map. Never count on trail signs to get you where you want to go. Signs get knocked down or disappear due to rain, wind, or visitors looking for souvenirs. Carry a map that is much more detailed than the free map provided at park entrance stations. A variety of maps are for sale at park visitors centers and stores. Try maps published by Tom Harrison Maps or National Geographic Trails Illustrated.

3. Extra clothing. Not only can the weather suddenly turn windy, cloudy, or rainy (it can even snow!), but your body's condition also changes: You'll perspire as you hike up a sunny hill and then get chilled at the top of a windy ridge or when you head into shade. Always carry a lightweight, waterproof, wind resistant jacket. Stay away from clothing made from cotton; once cotton gets wet, it stays wet. Polyester-blend fabrics dry faster; some high-tech fabrics wick moisture away from your skin. In cooler temperatures, or when heading to a mountain summit, carry gloves and a hat as well.

4. Flashlight. Mini-flashlights are available everywhere, weigh almost nothing, and can save the day. Tiny "squeeze" LED flashlights, about the size and shape of a quarter, can clip onto any key ring. Bring two or three. Make sure the batteries work before you set out on the trail.

5. Sunglasses and sunscreen. The higher the elevation, the more dangerous the sun's rays are. Put on high-SPF sunscreen 30 minutes before you go out, and then reapply every 2-3 hours. Protect your face with a wide-brimmed hat and your lips with high-SPF lip balm.

6. Insect repellent. Find one that works for you and carry it with you. Many types of insect repellent use an ingredient called DEET, which is effective but also quite toxic, especially for children. Other types of repellent are made of natural substances, such as lemon or eucalyptus oil. If you visit White Wolf's meadows in the middle of a major mosquito hatch, it may seem like nothing works to repel bugs except covering your entire body in mosquito netting.

7. First-aid kit. Supplies for blister repair, an elastic bandage, an antibiotic ointment, and an anti-inflammatory medicine such as ibuprofen can be valuable in emergencies. If you're allergic to bee stings or anything else in the outdoors, carry medication.

8. Swiss Army-style pocketknife. Carry one with several blades, a can opener, scissors, and tweezers.

9. Compass. Know how to use it. If you prefer to use GPS, that's fine, but know that GPS may not work everywhere you go.

10. Emergency supplies. Ask, "What would I need if I had to spend the night outside?"

In addition to food and water, these supplies can get you through an unplanned night in the wilderness:

- Purchase a lightweight blanket or sleeping bag made of foil-like Mylar film designed to reflect radiating body heat. These make a great emergency shelter and weigh and cost almost nothing.

- Keep matches and a candle in a waterproof container (or zippered bag), just in case you ever need to build a fire in an emergency.

- Bring a whistle. If you need help, you can blow a whistle for a lot longer than you can shout.

- A flash from a small signal mirror can be seen from far away.

BACKPACKING

Going backpacking in Hetch Hetchy or elsewhere in Yosemite? It's far too easy to head out on the trail and realize too late that you left a critical item at home. Use this handy checklist to help you pack, or tailor it to your own individual needs.

1. Permit. First and foremost, you need a **wilderness permit** (reserve in advance at 209/372-0740 or www.nps.gov/yose/planyourvisit/wildpermits.htm). If you didn't plan ahead, then show up at one of Yosemite's wilderness permit offices and see what permits are still available. You may have to be flexible about what trailhead you use as your starting point, and you may have to wait 24 hours to leave on your trip.

2. Shelter. Tent, rainfly, poles, and stakes, plus a ground tarp (a rain poncho can serve this purpose).

3. Sleeping. Sleeping bag and sleeping pad. If you are a creature of comfort, pack along a small pillow, too.

4. Food and cooking. In Yosemite, you must store your food (and any scented items) in a bear canister. This is not just a good idea—it's the law. Buy or rent one at the Hetch Hetchy entrance station or at other locations in Yosemite. To cook and eat, you'll need a camp stove and plenty of fuel, waterproof matches or a lighter, a set of lightweight pots and pans with lids, pot grips for handling hot pots, zip-locking bags, trash bags, lightweight cutlery and dishes, and a cup for drinking. Carry as much freeze-dried or lightweight food as you can (more than you think you'll need). Most important, don't forget a water bottle and filter or some type of purifier like a Steripen ultraviolet light.

5. Clothing. A good basic packing list includes underwear, socks, T-shirts, shorts or convertible pants, a long-sleeved shirt, windproof and waterproof jacket and pants, gloves, hats (both a warm hat for cold nights and mornings and a wide-brimmed hat for sun protection), sunglasses, rain poncho, hiking boots, and lightweight camp shoes or sandals such as Tevas.

6. Toiletries. You can go without a lot in the backcountry, but you don't want to go without sunscreen and sun-protecting lip balm, insect repellent, toothbrush and toothpaste, and maybe a comb or hair bands. Some backpackers bring toilet paper; if you do, remember that you must pack it out. (Minimalists use large leaves instead.) A small plastic trowel is useful for burying human waste.

7. First-aid kit. A basic kit should include an emergency space blanket made of Mylar film, tweezers, sterile gauze pads, adhesive medical tape, adhesive bandages in assorted sizes, an elastic bandage, aspirin or ibuprofen,

moleskin for blisters, antibiotic ointment, and any prescription medications you might need.

8. Other critical stuff. Two or more flashlights and extra batteries, GPS and/or compass, small signal mirror, appropriate maps, hiking poles, whistle, 50-foot (15-m) nylon cord, candles, extra matches, repair kit and/or sewing kit, safety pins, and a Swiss Army-style pocketknife.

9. Fun stuff. Camera and memory card, extra camera battery, binoculars, fishing gear and license, pen and pencil, playing cards, star chart, and nature identification guides for birds, flowers, trees, etc.

10. What to put it all in. A backpack, of course. And if the top of your backpack doesn't separate from the main pack to make a day pack, carry along a smaller day pack for taking short outings from your base camp.

WILDERNESS PERMITS

A wilderness permit is **required year-round** for any overnight stay in the backcountry areas of Yosemite. (You do not need a permit for day hikes, except for hiking to Half Dome.) Due to the number of people who wish to backpack through Yosemite's backcountry, **quotas** are in effect May through September for the number of permits granted at all wilderness trailheads. Sixty percent of the daily quota can be reserved ahead of time; the remaining 40 percent are available on a first-come, first-served basis starting at 11am on the day before your intended hike.

One more thing: If you think you can sneak off into Yosemite's backcountry without a wilderness permit and not get caught, think again. Especially in the summer months, rangers regularly patrol Yosemite's wilderness areas and check to see that backpackers are carrying permits.

Reserve a Permit

Wilderness permit request forms are available online (www.nps.gov/yose/planyourvisit/wildpermits.htm). This site offers a complete list of trail descriptions, general wilderness information, and current regulations. You can reserve a wilderness permit in advance for $5 per person plus a $5 reservation fee. Permits are available up to 24 weeks (168 days) in advance of your trip, when the wilderness reservation offices are open (usually late Nov.-Oct.).

How to Apply

After you have filled out the online wilderness permit request form, click "send" or print and mail (Wilderness Permit Reservations, P.O. Box 545, Yosemite, CA 95389) it in. Include a valid credit card number and expiration date, or a check payable to the Yosemite Conservancy. Allow two weeks to receive a response. For last-minute backpacking trips (within the next two weeks), you must call to obtain a reservation (209/372-0740, 8:30am-4:30pm Mon.-Fri. Sept.-May, 8:30am-5pm Mon.-Fri. and 9am-4pm Sat. Memorial Day-Labor Day). The line is often busy, online permit request forms are processed before phone calls.

Reserved wilderness permits must be picked up in person no earlier than 10am on the day before your reserved trip start date.

No Reservations

If you show up in Yosemite without a permit reservation, you will have very limited choices as to where you can backpack because most of the popular trailheads' quotas (in effect May-Sept.) will be filled. Without a reservation, your best bet is to appear at one of the **wilderness permit offices** (call 209/372-0740 for current hours at Big Oak Flat Information Station, Tuolumne Meadows Wilderness Center, Yosemite Valley Wilderness Center, Wawona Information Station, or Hetch Hetchy entrance station) and see what is available. Unreserved permits for the **same day** can be picked up when the wilderness permit office opens for the day; unreserved permits for the **following day** are available on a first-come, first-served basis beginning at 11am. If you can be flexible about your destination, and/or if you are willing to wait 24 hours before leaving, you should be able to plan a backpacking trip that suits you.

Backpacker Campsites

If you need to spend a night in the park before setting off on your permitted backpacking trip, a few backpackers' campsites are available at the Valley's **North Pines Campground**, at **Tuolumne Meadows Campground**, and at **Hetch Hetchy**. Campers who wish to stay in these sites may do so for only one night before or after their backpacking trip, and they must have their wilderness permit in hand. The sites are walk-in only, and only backpacking-type equipment may be brought in.

Travel Tips

FOREIGN TRAVELERS
Entering the United States and California

Generally, citizens of foreign countries who wish to visit the United States must first obtain a **visa**. To apply for a visa, applicants must prove that the purpose of their trip to the United States is for business, pleasure, or medical treatment; that they plan to remain for a limited period of time; and that they have a residence outside the United States as well as other binding ties that will guarantee their return abroad.

However, under the Visa Waiver Program, citizens of 38 foreign countries do not need a visa for travel to the United States, provided they are staying for less than 90 days. The countries are: Andorra, Australia, Austria, Belgium, Brunei, Chile, Czech Republic, Denmark, Estonia, Finland, France, Germany, Greece, Hungary, Iceland, Ireland, Italy, Japan, Latvia, Liechtenstein, Lithuania, Luxembourg, Malta, Monaco, the Netherlands, New Zealand, Norway, Portugal, San Marino, Singapore, Slovakia, Slovenia,

South Korea, Spain, Sweden, Switzerland, Taiwan, and the United Kingdom.

As part of the customs process, the United States Department of Agriculture screens all foreign visitors at their first point of arrival in the United States (usually at the airport). Foreigners must declare, in writing, all fruits, vegetables, fruit and vegetable products, meat, meat products, and dairy products that they have brought from another country. Failure to declare an apple or orange, or a leftover sandwich containing meat, can lead to a major delay in getting through customs.

Once a foreign visitor is inside the United States, he or she may travel freely from state to state. However, all visitors (foreign or not) are subject to additional agricultural inspections when entering California by automobile from bordering states. A California Department of Food and Agriculture (CDFA) officer may stop your car momentarily to ask you where you've been traveling and if you are carrying any fruits, vegetables, or plants from other states. In rare cases, vehicles are searched. Most out-of-state produce and plants should be kept out of California. For more information on current regulations, visit the CDFA website at www.cdfa.ca.gov.

Finally, there is no compulsory or government insurance plan in the United States. Foreign travelers are advised to purchase travel and health insurance in case of an emergency.

Money and Currency Exchange

Most large banks in the United States exchange major foreign currencies. Large international airports such as San Francisco have currency exchange offices in their international terminals. If you are traveling to Yosemite, you should exchange your money before you head into the small-town regions surrounding the park. The areas around Yosemite, as well as the developed areas inside the park, are not large enough to offer currency exchange.

While traveling in California, your best bet is to use credit cards for purchases and use an ATM (automated teller machine) to get cash. ATMs are found at various business establishments in the park.

Electricity

Electrical current in the United States is 110 volts. A hair dryer or electric shaver from Europe won't work here without an adapter, which is available at most travel stores.

Foreign Language Assistance

Within the United States, you may phone 888/871-4636 for free access to emergency services and travel assistance in more than 140 languages.

California Laws

You must be 21 years of age to purchase and/or drink **alcohol** in California. Drinking and driving is a serious crime in this state; the simple act of having an open container of alcohol in your car, even if it is empty, is punishable by law. If you are arrested for driving under the influence of alcohol, you must submit to a chemical test to determine blood alcohol content.

Smoking is prohibited on public transportation and in all public buildings and enclosed spaces in California. Most restaurants and bars have no-smoking policies. For the most part, you aren't allowed to light up unless you are in a private space or outside in an open area. If someone asks you to put out your cigarette, it's best to do so. Chances are, they have the law on their side. You must be 18 years of age to purchase tobacco products in California.

It is illegal to talk on a handheld **cell phone** while driving in California or Nevada. It is legal to talk on your phone if you are using a hands-free device (such as a Bluetooth system in your car, or an earpiece).

Taxes and Tipping

The California state sales tax is 7.5 percent. Local taxes may be as much as 3 percent, adding a total 10.5 percent to almost everything you buy.

If you are staying at any hotel or lodging in or near Yosemite, expect to pay between 10 and 15 percent "transient occupancy tax" on top of the regular room rate of the hotel. Each county in California sets its own rate for this tax.

At sit-down restaurants, it is customary to tip 15-20 percent on top of the bill. The tip is your payment to your food server for good service—and in the United States, most servers count on your tip as part of their day's pay.

ACCESS FOR TRAVELERS WITH DISABILITIES

People with permanent disabilities are entitled to an Access Pass, which provides free access to all federal fee areas, including all U.S. national parks and national forests. It also allows for discounted camping fees at some campgrounds. Access Passes are available at no cost from Yosemite visitors centers and entrance stations.

A free brochure on accessibility for wheelchair users and other physically challenged visitors is available by contacting the park, or by download from www.nps.gov/yose. **Wheelchair rentals** are available at the **Yosemite Medical Clinic** (9000 Ahwahnee Dr., Yosemite Valley, 209/372-4637) and at the **Yosemite Valley Lodge bike rental kiosk** (209/372-1208).

A **sign language interpreter** is available in the park in the summer months. To request in advance that the interpreter is available at a certain park event or activity, contact the rangers in any visitors center. All requests are filled on a first-come, first-served basis. Park orientation videos and slide shows in the Valley Visitor Center are captioned.

Tactile exhibits are found at the Valley Visitor Center, Happy Isles Art and Nature Center, and Mariposa Grove Museum.

Cars with disabled person placards are allowed access on the Happy Isles Loop and paved road to Mirror Lake (east of Half Dome Village). Disabled visitors who don't have a placard may obtain a temporary one from park visitors centers.

Spring through fall, disabled people who are unable to board the Mariposa Grove Tram may drive behind the tram and listen to an audio tour of the grove.

TRAVELING WITH CHILDREN

Families and national parks are a perfect match. Yosemite and other national parks are ideal places to teach kids about nature and the environment and to let them experience a world without television sets and video games. Kids invariably have fun in the outdoors, and with all the kid-friendly activities in the park, parents are never left wondering what to do with their charges. In Yosemite, kids can go for hikes, attend a campfire talk led by a park ranger, climb on rocks, help with camp chores, learn about animals that reside in the park, ride bikes, toast marshmallows, go rafting, ride horses, learn photography skills, or just hang out in a meadow and be kids. The list of possible activities for kids in Yosemite is endless—just as it is for adults.

The **Junior Ranger program,** popular at national parks across the country, is open to kids ages 7-13. Kids earn the official Junior Ranger badge by completing an activity book ($5), attending a one-hour Junior Ranger walk, and picking up a bag of litter to help keep the park clean. Junior Ranger walks are held daily during the summer. For more information, check the park's free newspaper, or ask in any visitors center. Younger kids (ages 3-6) can join in the Little Cubs program.

Wee Wild Ones is a free 45-minute interactive program for kids ages 6 and under, featuring stories, songs, games, crafts, and activities, mostly relating to the subject of Yosemite's animals. In the summer and fall, Wee Wild Ones occurs before evening programs held at the Yosemite Valley Lodge Amphitheater or the Half Dome Village Amphitheater. In winter and spring, this program is held during the day in front of

Hantavirus

In August 2012, a rash of alarming media reports told of death and serious illness among Yosemite visitors, caused not by lightning, rockfall, or drowning, but by deer mice. The culprit was an infection known as hantavirus pulmonary syndrome (HPS), a rare but serious disease caused by a virus that can be contracted through contact with the urine, droppings, or saliva of deer mice.

Ten visitors who stayed one night or more in Yosemite in June and July of 2012 contracted the disease, which causes severe flu-like symptoms. Three people died; the other seven recovered. Nine of the 10 spent at least one night in Curry Village's "signature tent cabins," which, unlike the regular canvas-walled tent cabins, were built with drywall and insulation in order to be warmer and quieter. The insulation attracted a larger-than-normal population of deer mice, who built warm, cozy nests in the insulated walls.

Deer mice are found throughout the country, and it is estimated that 12 percent of deer mice in the United States carry hantavirus. Since HPS was first identified as a disease in 1993, approximately 600 cases have been identified nationally (60 in California). About 30 people in the United States come down with hantavirus annually. The disease has no known cure; about one-third of those who contract it will die.

Since the outbreak, the National Park Service and the park's concessionaires have gone to great lengths to reduce the possibility of mice entering the Half Dome Village cabins. The 91 insulated signature tent cabins were demolished in December 2012. Only the single-walled tent cabins remain. No Half Dome Village hantavirus cases have been reported since the demolition.

The National Park Service urges visitors to avoid touching live or dead rodents or disturbing rodent burrows, dens, or nests. They also recommend that visitors keep food in tightly sealed containers (including those stored in bear boxes) so rodents can't get to it. Overnight visitors should contact housekeeping or maintenance if they see rodents or rodent signs, including droppings or urine, in their lodgings.

the great fireplace in the Majestic Yosemite Hotel. Parents are encouraged to participate with their children.

The **Yosemite Theater** has an evening program geared especially toward kids: *Ranger Ned's Big Adventure* plays three nights a week June-August. The audience goes on a humorous, interactive trek with a rookie ranger.

SENIOR TRAVELERS

If you are 62 years of age or older and a U.S. citizen or permanent resident, you can purchase a **Senior Pass** (formerly known as the "Golden Age Passport") for $80. This one-time fee provides you with a pass that is good at all U.S. national parks for the rest of your life. If you are blind or permanently disabled and a U.S. citizen or permanent resident, you can receive an **Access Pass** (previously called a "Golden Access Passport") at no cost. This, too, is good at all U.S. national parks

for life. (People who have already received passes under their former names, "Golden Age Passport" or "Golden Access Passport," don't have to trade in their old passes for the new ones.)

TRAVELING WITH PETS

Traveling with your pet to any national park in the United States is a difficult proposition. Pets are not allowed in any lodging in Yosemite, and they are not allowed on the vast majority of trails. Pets are permitted in some campgrounds and in all parking lots and picnic areas. In campgrounds, they must be in your tent, RV, or car at night, or you risk having your pet tangle with a bear or other wild animal. Pets should never be left unattended. At all times, they must be physically restrained or attached to a leash 6 feet (1.8 m) long or shorter.

Yosemite Valley has a nine-stall **dog kennel** (209/372-8348, open May-Sept.) near the horse stables where you can board your dog, but this is a terribly sad place where dogs sit glumly in cages while their owners go off for great hikes around the Valley. To put your dog in the kennel, he or she must be at least six months old and 20 pounds (9 kg) in weight and have written proof of vaccinations (rabies, distemper, parvo, and Bordetella). Dogs weighing less than 20 pounds (9 kg) may be considered for boarding if the dog owner provides a small kennel.

On top of all that, here's one more doggone rule to keep in mind: If you insist on bringing your dog to Yosemite, you are responsible for cleaning up after him or her, and you must put all "deposits" into the nearest trash receptacle.

The bottom line: Your dog will be happier somewhere else.

HEALTH AND SAFETY

The **Yosemite Medical Clinic** (9000 Ahwahnee Dr., Yosemite Valley, 209/372-4637) can handle most emergencies big and small. In fact, they handle about 9,000 of them every year. The clinic has an experienced nursing staff, emergency physicians, a nurse practitioner, and support staff on duty. Emergency care is available 24 hours a day; drop-in visits and urgent care are available daily 8am-7pm. The nearest hospitals are in Sonora, Oakhurst, Merced, and Mammoth Lakes.

By far the biggest dangers to be faced in Yosemite are those created by visitors who don't follow posted rules and regulations. If a sign states Stay Back from the Edge, obey it. Be wary of waterfalls, slick hiking trails, and cliffs and ledges with steep drop-offs. Remain on the trails to avoid getting lost or getting yourself into a hazardous situation. Always carry a good map. If you are heading out for a hike, tell someone where you are going and when you will be back. Carry a day pack with all the essentials for a day out and a few emergencies.

Drinking Water

Always carry water with you or be able to filter or purify water from natural sources like lakes, rivers, or streams. The high-elevation air in the Sierra Nevada, combined with heat and/or wind, will dehydrate you much faster than you expect. Never, ever drink water from a natural source without purifying it. The microscopic organism *Giardia lamblia*, as well as other types of bacteria, may be found in backcountry water sources and can cause a litany of gastrointestinal problems. Only purifying, sterilizing, or boiling water from natural sources will eliminate these bad bugs.

Carrying several large bottles of water is heavy and cumbersome, so if you are hiking for more than a few hours, it may be impossible to bring enough water with you. A purifier or filtering device can substantially lighten your load. A favorite of many day hikers and backpackers is the **Steripen,** a purifier that sterilizes water using ultraviolet light. Dip your wide-mouthed water bottle into a lake or stream, then turn on your Steripen, immerse it in your bottle, and stir it around. In about 90 seconds, you have water that's safe to drink.

Other options include bottle-style filters, which are almost as light as an empty plastic bottle and eliminate the need to carry both a filter and a bottle. Dip the bottle in the stream, screw on the top (which has a filter inside it), and squeeze the bottle to drink. The water is filtered on its way out of the squeeze top.

"Old-school" ceramic water filters also work well, especially if you are filtering large amounts of water. Several companies such as Katadyn and MSR make these types of ceramic filters.

Altitude Sickness

Many hikers experience shortness of breath when hiking only a few thousand feet higher than the elevation at which they live. If you live on the California coast, you may notice slightly labored breathing while hiking at an elevation as low as 4,000 feet (1,220 m)—the exact elevation of Yosemite Valley. As you go higher, it may get worse, sometimes leading to headaches and nausea. It takes a full 72 hours to acclimate to major elevation changes, although most people feel better after 24-48 hours.

The best preparation for hiking at high elevation is to sleep at that elevation, or as close to it as possible, the night before. If you are planning a strenuous hike at 7,000 feet (2,100 m) or above, spend a day or two beforehand taking easier hikes at the same elevation. Get plenty of rest and drink plenty of fluids. Lack of sleep and drinking alcohol can contribute to a susceptibility to "feeling the altitude," which for most people simply means they feel like they are constantly struggling to catch their breath as they hike, especially going uphill.

Serious altitude sickness typically occurs above 10,000 feet (3,000 m). It is generally preventable by simply allowing enough time for acclimation. Staying fully hydrated and fueled with food will also help. If you start to feel ill (nausea, vomiting, severe headache), you are experiencing altitude sickness. Some people can get by with taking aspirin and trudging onward, but if you are seriously ill, the only cure is to descend as soon as possible.

Lightning Strikes

If you see or hear a thunderstorm approaching, avoid exposed ridges and peaks. This may be disheartening advice when you're only a mile from the summit of Clouds Rest, Half Dome, or Mount Hoffmann, but follow it anyway. If you're already on a mountaintop when a thunderstorm is threatening, stay out of enclosed places such as rock caves and recesses. Confined areas can be deadly in lightning storms. Do not lean against rock slopes or trees; try to keep a few feet of air space around you. Squat low on your boot soles, or sit on your day pack, jacket, or anything that will insulate you in case lightning strikes the ground.

Resources

Suggested Reading

GEOLOGY

Glazner, Bill, and Greg Stock. *Geology Underfoot in Yosemite National Park*. Mountain Press Publishing, 2010. Carry this book in your backpack as you hike around Yosemite. More than 27 sites within the park are described for their geological significance. Written for non-geologists, this book explains the marvels of plunging waterfalls, destructive rockslides, and moving ice.

Guyton, Bill. *Glaciers of California: Modern Glaciers, Ice Age Glaciers, the Origin of Yosemite Valley, and a Glacier Tour in the Sierra Nevada*. University of California Press, 2001. A guidebook to California's glaciers, with a heavy emphasis on the glacial formation of Yosemite Valley. The author provides a primer on glaciers and glacial landforms and a glossary of technical terms, as well as a 100-mile (161-km) Sierra field trip for readers who want to see glaciers and glacial features.

Huber, N. King. *Geological Ramblings in Yosemite*. Yosemite Conservancy, 2008. A collection of essays on the complexities of Yosemite's landscape, written by a master geologist but intended for non-geologists. For the most part, this book succeeds in unraveling the mysteries of Yosemite's spectacular rock formations, explaining the contributions of volcanoes, stream patterns, erosion, rockslides, and, of course, glaciers.

Osborne, Mike. *Granite, Water, and Light: The Waterfalls of Yosemite Valley*. Heyday Books, 2009. This short-but-sweet paperback is a cross between a coffee-table photography book and a layperson's guide to the geology of Yosemite Valley's waterfalls. Osborne documents the Valley's famous falls with elegant photographs and intelligent commentary on their geologic structures.

HUMAN HISTORY

Belden, L. Burr, and Mary DeDecker. *Death Valley to Yosemite: Frontier Mining Camps and Ghost Towns*. Spotted Dog Press, 2000. For treasure seekers and history lovers, this collection of mining town stories sheds some light on the histories of long-gone but once-bustling communities such as Dogtown, Lundy, and Bennettville. Little of the book pertains to Yosemite proper, except for the story of the old Tioga Road, but the mining towns of the nearby Eastern Sierra are described in detail. It's worth a look for the old photographs alone.

Browning, Peter. *Yosemite Place Names: The Historic Background of Geographic Names in Yosemite National Park*. Great West Books, 2005 (Kindle edition, 2013). If you are wondering why that big meadow is called Tuolumne, or Hetch Hetchy's waterfalls are Tueeulala and Wapama, this is your resource—a great way to learn about Yosemite's history without actually reading a history book.

Browning, Peter, ed. *John Muir in His Own Words: A Book of Quotations*. Great West Books, 1988. The cogent sound bites of John Muir make enjoyable reading around a campfire. The editor pulls "Muirisms" from 14 of the great naturalist's books.

Bunnell, Lafayette Houghton. *Discovery of the Yosemite, and the Indian War of 1851, Which Led to That Event*. Nabu Press, 2010. The only firsthand account of European Americans' first view of Yosemite Valley in March 1851, when the Mariposa Battalion arrived to round up the Ahwahneechee Indians. Bunnell, who served as the battalion's company doctor, writes in extensive detail and with great depth of feeling for both the scenery and the people of Yosemite.

Chase, J. Smeaton. *Yosemite Trails: Camp and Pack-Train in the Yosemite Region of the Sierra Nevada*. Nabu Press, 2012. A British gentleman who moved to California in the early 20th century, the author, often described as California's first outdoors writer, explored the Golden State on horseback from 1911 to 1918. Chase's descriptions of Wawona, Hetch Hetchy, and Tuolumne Meadows are still compelling today.

Clark, Galen. *Indians of the Yosemite Valley and Vicinity: Their History, Customs, and Traditions*. Forgotten Books, 2008. In 1857, the author became one of the first white residents in Yosemite, and he lived for many years with the last generation of Yosemite's Indians. Clark's short book includes an intriguing summary of the Ahwahneechee Indians in Yosemite, with firsthand descriptions of their way of life, from clothing and hair to hunting and fishing methods.

Farabee, Charles, and Michael Ghiglieri. *Off the Wall: Death in Yosemite*. Puma Press, 2007. This grim but fascinating read chronicles the stories behind every known death in Yosemite, from drunk tourists falling over waterfalls to daring rock climbers who forgot to check their equipment before scaling Yosemite's granite walls. Even Yosemite veterans may be surprised to find out that enough people have died in the park to make this book fill more than 600 pages.

Jones, Ray, and Joe Lubow. *It Happened in Yosemite National Park: Remarkable Events that Shaped History*. Globe Pequot Press, 2010. In 29 short stories, the authors retell some of the most famous tales that have defined our vision of Yosemite National Park, including the story of the first ascent of Half Dome, the historic meeting between Teddy Roosevelt and John Muir, the famous 1970 war protest in Yosemite Valley, and the arrival of the first automobile in 1900.

La Pena, Frank, Craig Bates, and Steven Medley. *Legends of the Yosemite Miwok*. Yosemite Conservancy, 2008. This illustrated volume contains many of the stories of Yosemite that entertained and educated the local Miwok Indians for centuries. The book is intended for children but is also entertaining for adults, and it includes the artwork of Maidu Indian Harry Fonseca.

Madgic, Bob. *Shattered Air: A True Account of Catastrophe and Courage on Yosemite's Half Dome*. Burford Books, 2007. A tragic story of young lives cut short by macho bravado and poor judgment. On July 27, 1985, five hikers made a fateful choice to climb Yosemite's fabled Half Dome even as thunder and lightning rolled in, despite being well aware of the danger. Two were killed and three were badly injured by lightning strikes. The author does a good job of exploring the psyches of these sadly misguided young men and also explains the facts and myths about lightning strikes in the Sierra.

Meyerson, Harvey. *Nature's Army: When Soldiers Fought for Yosemite*. University of Kansas Press, 2001. This book documents the period from 1890 to 1916, when

Yosemite National Park was first created but the National Park Service was not yet in existence. The U.S. Army was given the task of protecting the new national park—a job well outside its normal scope. The author describes the army's admirably competent efforts at stewardship.

Muir, John. *The Mountains of California.* CreateSpace Independent Publishing Platform, 2013. More of a naturalist's guide to the Sierra than the novelistic *My First Summer in the Sierra,* this book includes Muir's detailed observations of creatures like the water ouzel (or dipper bird) and the Douglas squirrel. Even so, Muir's attempts at hard science are always mitigated by his lyrical writing style and unbridled exuberance for the natural world.

Muir, John. *My First Summer in the Sierra.* Dover Publications, 2004. For fans of Yosemite, this Muir classic, written 40 years after his "first summer," is a must-read. Muir pulled together detailed notes from his initial Yosemite explorations to create an enthusiastic and uplifting story of his love affair with the mountains. A coffee-table version of Muir's famous work with gorgeous photographs by Scot Miller was published by Houghton Mifflin Harcourt (2011).

Muir, John. *The Yosemite.* Modern Library Classics, 2003. Many of Muir's Yosemite-specific writings are compiled in this one volume, including chapters on the Big Trees (giant sequoias), South Dome (now called Half Dome), and the damming of Hetch Hetchy Valley. An especially good read for Yosemite travelers is the chapter entitled "How Best to Spend One's Yosemite Time," which includes suggested one-, two-, and three-day excursions in the park circa 1890.

Roper, Steve. *Camp 4: Recollections of a Yosemite Rock Climber.* The Mountaineers, 1998. In the 1960s, Yosemite Valley was the center of the rock-climbing universe.

Climber and author Steve Roper spent most of 10 years living in the Valley alongside some of the best rock climbers in the world. The book examines the most significant ascents of those years as well as the personalities of the climbers who achieved them. It includes more than 50 historical photographs.

Rose, Gene. *Yosemite's Tioga Country: A History and Appreciation.* Yosemite Conservancy, 2006. Lovers of Yosemite's high country will want to own a copy of this fascinating history of the Tioga Pass Road, today's Highway 120, which bisects the park from west to east. The road is rich in tales of human history, from prehistoric Native Americans to greedy gold and silver miners to today's national park visitors.

Stetson, Lee. *The Wild Muir: Twenty-Two of John Muir's Greatest Adventures.* Yosemite Conservancy, 2013. Actor Lee Stetson has portrayed conservationist John Muir in theatrical productions for more than 30 years. This compilation of his favorite Muir stories is a great book to read around the campfire.

Walklet, Keith S. *The Ahwahnee: Yosemite's Grand Hotel.* DNC Parks & Resorts at Yosemite, 2004. Everything you ever wanted to know about the conception and construction of the grand Ahwahnee Hotel (now the Majestic Yosemite Hotel), a designated National Historic Landmark, can be found in this 64-page, full-color book. Some 50 historical photographs and more than 70 contemporary color images illustrate the elegant beauty of what many consider to be the finest hotel in the national park system.

NATURAL HISTORY

Blackwell, Laird R. *Wildflowers of the Sierra Nevada and Central Valley* and *Wildflowers of the Eastern Sierra and Adjoining Mojave Desert and Great Basin.* Lone Pine Publishing, 1999 and 2002. These two indispensable wildflower guides, written by a professor at

Sierra Nevada College, detail the colorful blooms of the west and east sides of the Sierra. High-quality color photographs and descriptive text make it easy to identify flowers.

Botti, Stephen J. *An Illustrated Flora of Yosemite National Park.* Yosemite Association, 2001. This huge coffee-table book is a treasure to own, but you can't take it with you on the wildflower trail. The volume weighs in at over 8 pounds (3.5 kg) and costs more than $100. This amazingly comprehensive book took 20 years to create and is beautifully illustrated with more than 1,000 watercolor paintings of flowers.

Horn, Elizabeth L. *Sierra Nevada Wildflowers.* Mountain Press, 1998. Good photographs accompany descriptions of more than 300 species of flowering plants and shrubs. Unlike most flower identification guides, this one is organized alphabetically (not by color of flower), which could prove problematic. Still, the photographs and descriptions are useful.

Laws, John Muir. *The Laws Field Guide to the Sierra Nevada.* Heyday Books, 2007. If you purchase only one field guide for Yosemite and/or the Sierra Nevada, this should be it. The author has cataloged over 1,700 species of Sierra trees, wildflowers, ferns, fungi, lichens, fish, reptiles, amphibians, birds, mammals, insects, and other small animals. Color tabs and a unique system of keys and organization assist the reader in quickly identifying whatever is encountered along the trail.

Laws, John Muir. *Sierra Birds: A Hiker's Guide.* Heyday Books, 2004. This easy-to-use field guide assumes no prior birding knowledge on the part of the reader and is organized for quick and easy reference. Color-coded keys eliminate the frustrating necessity of having to thumb through

a hefty guide. A cross-index of bird families is also included for more advanced birders.

Paruk, Jim. *Sierra Nevada Tree Identifier.* Yosemite Conservancy, 1998. This practical guide to the Sierra's 20 conifers and 24 broadleaf trees provides useful tips on tree identification as well as an interesting natural history of each species.

Stokes, Donald, and Lillian Stokes. *The New Stokes Field Guide to Birds: Western Region.* Little, Brown, and Company, 2013. Utilizing more than 900 full-color photographs (not illustrations, as in the popular Peterson Field Guides) the Stokeses have created a non-intimidating bird guidebook respected by novice and expert birders alike. General identification information is provided for each species, as well as feeding, nesting, and other characteristic behaviors.

Wiese, Karen. *Sierra Nevada Wildflowers.* Globe Pequot, 2013. This wildflower guide is loaded with clear, easy-to-see photographs of more than 230 wildflowers specific to the Sierra Nevada. In addition to the usual descriptive information, each listing includes an explanation of the flower's genus or species name and other interesting facts.

Wilson, Lynn, Jim Nicholas, and Jeff Nicholas. *Wildflowers of Yosemite.* Sierra Press, 2005. Gorgeous photographs and helpful descriptions of 224 flower species found throughout Yosemite are included. A separate section describes what flowers can be seen in what areas of Yosemite and provides a driving tour of several park regions with flower identification stops along the way.

OUTDOOR RECREATION AND TRAVEL

Beck, Steve. *Yosemite Trout Fishing Guide.* Frank Amato Publications, 2001. An extremely detailed full-color guide to fishing in and around Yosemite, including the

Eastern Sierra. The author appears to have left no waters unfished.

Frye, Michael. *The Photographer's Guide to Yosemite.* Yosemite Conservancy, 2012. This guidebook, written by a workshop instructor at the Ansel Adams Gallery, is specifically designed to help photographers capture the most intriguing perspectives and best light on Yosemite's iconic landscape.

Giacomazzi, Sharon. *Trails and Tales of Yosemite and the Central Sierra.* Bored Feet Press, 2001. A hiking trail book with a twist—each trail has been chosen for its interesting historical context, which is described at length. Readers can learn history

while hiking the route of the old Yosemite Mountain Sugar Pine Railroad or the Old Big Flat Road or when visiting the Merced Grove of giant sequoias via the Coulterville Road. This guide covers not just Yosemite National Park but also portions of the Gold Country, Eastern Sierra, and Sierra National Forest south of Yosemite.

Roney, Bob. *The Road Guide to Yosemite.* Yosemite Conservancy, 2013. Completely revised and updated by a Yosemite park ranger, this short guidebook is keyed to roadside markers throughout the park, providing details about what drivers can see from the road. It's an excellent introduction to Yosemite for first-time visitors, especially those making a quick tour of the park.

Internet Resources

YOSEMITE NATIONAL PARK

Yosemite National Park
www.nps.gov/yose
This official National Park Service website for Yosemite provides up-to-date information on current road and weather conditions, lodging and camping options, park rules and regulations, and wilderness permits. (The same information can be obtained by phone at 209/372-0200.) A printable travel guide is available, and you may request to have maps and information about Yosemite mailed to your home. In addition to plentiful visitor data, the website also has online exhibits on Yosemite's natural history, human history, and geology, as well as information on jobs in Yosemite, current management plans for the park, and a wide range of related links.

Yosemite National Park YouTube Channel
www.youtube.com/user/yosemitenationalpark

Yosemite National Park posts all of its official videos here, including its Yosemite Nature Notes video podcast series. Topics vary from general visitor information (how to get to the park, where to hike, where to find overnight lodging) to the natural history of frogs, bears, and beavers.

Yosemite Conservancy
www.yosemiteconservancy.org
The Yosemite Conservancy was formed in 2010 to join together the Yosemite Association and the Yosemite Fund, two nonprofits dedicated to supporting the park through visitor services, sales of books and maps, and membership activities, as well as granting funds for managing wildlife, restoring habitat, creating educational exhibits, and repairing trails in the park. The Yosemite Conservancy operates visitors center bookstores throughout the park and offers a wide range of educational courses through Yosemite Outdoor Adventures. Its website provides information on educational park activities ranging

from art classes in Yosemite Valley to performances at the Yosemite Theater to backpacking trips to the Lyell Glacier. It also includes information on how to become a conservancy member, how to contribute to various work projects in the park, current Yosemite weather conditions, upcoming seminars and events, news stories, and a webcam with live shots of Yosemite Valley.

Yosemite Hikes
www.yosemitehikes.com
This website is a veritable encyclopedia of all things Yosemite. Day hiking information is the main focus, but this clever and comprehensive site also includes tour itineraries, lodging and wildflower information, and photo galleries. The hundreds of images on this site are nothing short of awesome.

Reservations
Aramark's Yosemite Hospitality
www.travelyosemite.com
The park concessionaire, Yosemite Hospitality LLC, a subsidiary of Aramark, handles all of Yosemite's in-park accommodations, tours, events, and organized activities, all of which are described on this site. You can get information and make reservations at this website (or by phone at 888/413-8869). Whether you want to stay at a hotel in Yosemite Valley, buy a ski pass, or sign up for a guided tour, everything you need is found on this website.

Camping and Half Dome Permits
National Recreation Reservation Service
www.recreation.gov
Visitors seeking to camp in or near Yosemite can make campground reservations at this site or by phoning 877/444-6777 (or 518/885-3639 from outside the United States and Canada). Reservations are available up to five months in advance at one of three reservable campgrounds in Yosemite Valley or one of four reservable campgrounds elsewhere in the park. Reservations are also available at many national forest campgrounds a few

miles outside the park borders, particularly in Sierra National Forest. This website also handles all reservations for Half Dome day hiking permits.

Lodging and Travel Information
Yosemite Area Traveler Information
www.yosemite.com
Yosemite visitors planning to stay outside the park but still within easy driving range should check out this site, which is managed by Mariposa County. Camping, dining, hiking, and other travel information is provided. Especially useful are the lodging links for the four main Yosemite entrances (via Highway 140, Highway 120, and Highway 41).

Yosemite Area Regional Transportation System
www.yarts.com
YARTS is the voluntary-use bus system that carries visitors into Yosemite Valley from various locations outside the park. The bus system began operating in 2000 and currently serves towns in Mariposa, Merced, Tuolumne, and Mono Counties (via Highway 140 and Highway 120). The bus service can be very convenient for travelers staying in lodgings in gateway towns outside the park. YARTS can also be reached by phone at 877/989-2787.

Sierra Nevada Geotourism
www.sierranevadageotourism.org
This website offers information on travel planning for the entire Sierra Nevada, including local points of interest, lodgings, restaurants, festivals, events, maps, volunteer opportunities, and more.

HIGHWAY 140
Yosemite-Mariposa Bed and Breakfast Association
www.yosemitebnbs.com
This website offers information on bed-and-breakfasts and small inns along Highway 140 and in and around the town of Mariposa, useful for travelers planning to enter the park on

Highway 140 from the Central Valley/Merced area.

HIGHWAY 120
Stay Near Yosemite Lodgings
www.staynearyosemite.com
For Yosemite travelers planning to enter the park on Highway 120 from the San Francisco Bay Area, Sacramento, or elsewhere in Northern California, this site has information on lodgings specific to the Highway 120/Groveland-area park gateway. You can check availability at nearly a dozen lodgings simultaneously.

HIGHWAY 41
Yosemite Sierra Visitors Bureau
www.yosemitethisyear.com
For Yosemite travelers planning to enter the park on Highway 41 from Fresno, Los Angeles, or elsewhere in Southern California, this site (managed by Madera County) has information on lodging, dining, and activities specific to the Highway 41/Oakhurst-area park gateway.

EASTERN SIERRA/U.S. 395
California's Eastern Sierra
www.monocounty.org
Almost anything a traveler might need to know about the Eastern Sierra can be found at this website run by the Mono County Economic Development Staff. Whether you're traveling to Bridgeport, Lee Vining, Bodie, June Lake, or Mammoth Lakes, this site features a ton of information on lodging, activities, trip planning, and more.

The Traveler's Guide to Historic U.S. 395
www.scenic395.com
If you plan to spend some or all of your vacation around Tioga Pass or in the Eastern Sierra, go to this site for information on lodging, camping, and local businesses. A downloadable U.S. 395 map, information on weather and road conditions, downloadable audio tours, and fishing and camping guides are available.

Art and Recreation
Ansel Adams Gallery
www.anseladams.com
This website leads you to the online store of the Ansel Adams Gallery in Yosemite Valley, a great source for artistic gifts (including posters, special-edition photographs, books, and reproductions) and also for information on photography workshops in Yosemite.

Bracebridge Dinner
www.bracebridgedinners.com
Yosemite's annual Bracebridge Dinner is a December event that combines theater, music, and comedy with a seven-course feast in the grand dining room at the Majestic Yosemite Hotel. Check out this site for information on Bracebridge history, a detailed menu from the previous year's feast, and information on the current year's reservable dates and rates.

Supertopo Guides
www.supertopo.com
A website dedicated to a wealth of rock climbing "beta" (or inside information) on Yosemite's big walls, the Tuolumne Meadows area, and other regions of the American West. You'll find approach and descent facts, route histories, and lots of other details about the park's popular climbs.

Yosemite Winter Club
http://yosemitewinterclub.com
A website dedicated to promoting winter sports at Yosemite, from downhill skiing at Badger Pass to ice-skating in Yosemite Valley to backcountry ski touring in Tuolumne Meadows. The Yosemite Winter Club was founded in 1928 by Donald Tresidder, president of the Curry Company (which once managed all concessions in Yosemite Valley).

Nonprofit Organizations
Yosemite Climbing Association
www.yosemiteclimbing.org
The Yosemite Climbing Association is a nonprofit organization dedicated to preserving Yosemite's rich rock-climbing history and

making it available for public viewing and interpretation. Dedicated Valley climbers have amassed several thousand artifacts that are now ready for public viewing and interpretation. Although a small fraction of this collection is currently on display at the Yosemite Museum, the climbers are hoping to establish a permanent climbing museum in Yosemite Valley.

Nature Bridge
http://naturebridge.org/yosemite
Nature Bridge, formerly known as Yosemite National Institutes, is the largest nonprofit residential environmental education partner of the National Park Service. Nature Bridge has schools and programs in Yosemite and Olympic National Parks, the Santa Monica Mountains National Recreation Area in Los Angeles, and the Marin Headlands in Golden Gate National Recreation Area (San Francisco Bay Area). The program serves more than 40,000 children and adults annually through National Park Service partnership projects, a field science school program, and scholarship opportunities.

Restore Hetch Hetchy
www.hetchhetchy.org
The website of the nonprofit organization Restore Hetch Hetchy offers updates on the quest to drain Hetch Hetchy Reservoir and restore the valley to its pristine state.

Yosemite Valley Railroad
www.yosemitevalleyrr.com
Everything you ever wanted to know about the Yosemite Valley Railroad, the 77-mile (124-km) passenger train route that provided the main access to Yosemite National Park before the All-Year Highway (Highway 140) was built in 1926.

Yosemite Valley Chapel
www.yosemitevalleychapel.org
If you'd like to attend services at Yosemite Community Church or perhaps even get married in the Yosemite Valley Chapel, this site provides information on the chapel and its services.

SEQUOIA AND KINGS CANYON

Sequoia and Kings Canyon National Parks
www.nps.gov/seki
This official National Park Service website for Sequoia and Kings Canyon provides up-to-date information on current road and weather conditions, lodging and camping options, park rules and regulations, and wilderness permits.

Sequoia Parks Conservancy
www.sequoiaparksconservancy.org
This nonprofit organization dedicated to the preservation of both parks is partnered with the National Park Service; its naturalists lead short walks and longer backpacking excursions into the parks. The group's website provides park information, maps, travel tips, and detailed descriptions of the Crystal Cave tour.

Delaware North Companies
www.visitsequoia.com
The park concessionaire, Delaware North Companies (DNC), handles many of the in-park accommodations, tours, events, and organized activities for Sequoia and Kings Canyon. Reservations for Kings Canyon accommodations are accepted online or by calling 877/436-9615. Reservations for Sequoia National Park accommodations are accepted online or by calling 866/807-3598.

Index

List of Maps

Photo Credits

Explore California's great outdoors

Plan a weekend adventure

Or go big and go abroad

#TravelWithMoon

In these books:

- Full coverage of gateway cities and towns
- Itineraries from one day to multiple weeks
- Advice on where to stay (or camp) in and around the parks

Craft a personalized journey
through the top national parks
in the U.S. and Canada with
Moon Travel Guides.